MELDING THE PIECES

The Life of Henri Glaus

<hr />

Henrietta Glaus

ISBN 978-1-0980-1670-8 (paperback)
ISBN 978-1-0980-1671-5 (hardcover)
ISBN 978-1-0980-1669-2 (digital)

Christian Faith Publishing, Inc.
832 Park Avenue
Meadville, PA 16335
www.christianfaithpublishing.com

Printed in the United States of America

The credit of cover photo - Henri resting on a bench in the park area below Hilltop Drive, on the campus of Kent State University.

The Legend of the Iron Hoop

*"We exist in time, and our stories are
forever circulating in the hoop of nature."*

The sculpture is located on the grounds of Kent State University,
in a small picturesque park behind the main library. The art piece
was created in 1981 by Brinsley Tyrrell, Emeritus Professor of Art.

Dedicated to my progeny—those living
and those yet to be born.

CONTENTS

PROLOGUE

————— ✦ ✦ ✦✦✦ ✦ —————

My Depression-era upbringing instilled in me the value of frugality. At a very early age, that behavior morphed into saving bits and pieces of my life—scraps of gift-wrapping paper, snippets of ribbons, souvenirs from school (report cards, programs, newspaper articles), and treasures from boyfriends (notes, letters, candy box tops, inexpensive jewelry, theater tickets). These items are meticulously saved in a beige scrapbook with tattered cardboard covers, pages so brittle they crumble at the touch, and writing so faded it is almost impossible to read.

Beginning in 1963, I started to keep journals that today fill the shelves of a three-and-a-half-by-four-foot bookcase. Add to that the dozens of travel/family/friend photo albums that line three eight-foot shelves in my basement recreation room office. I'm often asked, "Henri just what do you plan to do with all of this?" My flippant answer, "Open a museum."

In 2005 I read my dad's Line-A-Day diaries, ones he kept recounting his life working in a tire factory in Akron, Ohio, as well as the years he served in the army during World War I. Brief as the entries were, reading them I felt I was having a conversation with my dad. This caused me to wonder about my maternal and paternal grandparents. I knew almost nothing about their lives and I yearned to know. At the time, two grandchildren of my maternal grandfather Squair Shuart were living in the area. I interviewed them and recorded the interview on videotape. Other than that, information about the lives of my grandparents is scanty—to be found by searching through legal and genealogical records. I didn't want that for my progeny. From that time on, the desire to write about my life consumed me.

How to start? I had the raw material, but I knew from the get-go I would need help. I contacted the Kent Free Library only to learn my computer's operating system was outdated and library personnel were unable to help. Next, I contacted hospice. I recalled there was one volunteer who served as a scribe writing life stories for hospice patients. When I spoke with her, I realized she lacked the computer skills that I so desperately needed. My third attempt bore fruit. Dr. Catherine Wing in the Department of English at Kent State University put me in contact with a former graduate student.

On January 19, 2015, my doorbell rang. I opened the front door and much to my surprise, standing there was a middle-aged lady with long, flowing, white hair, stout of build, wearing a fedora with a narrow brim, sweatshirt, jeans, multicolored jacket, and tennis shoes. Her voice gentle, her smile captivating, I had met my editor, Marybeth Cieplinski.

We talked for two hours. The first hour was taken up with get-acquainted conversation related to family and interests. The second hour was given over to my needs—someone with writing, editing, and computer skills. Marybeth was well-qualified, willing to help, and we arrived at mutually agreeable terms of employment.

At the start, my writing required major editing. Marybeth and I met weekly. At first, her comments were akin to opening my veins and allowing me to bleed. I survived and I persevered. Over time my writing improved.

Marybeth is a born teacher. She patiently instructed me in computer skills, answered my myriad questions, and provided the proverbial shoulder-to-lean-on when I mistakenly vaporized hours of writing. Throughout, she assured me it was my story and her role was to aid me in making it the best it could be.

I know my stars were in alignment when I connected with this remarkably talented woman. I needed Marybeth and, by her own admission, she needed a cause and felt me to be "a worthy one."

This is not a biography but a memoir. Loosely defined, a biography is more factual than personal; a memoir is more personal than factual. Among my memorabilia papers I found a church bulletin from the Worthington Presbyterian Church, dated December 15, 1996. Dr. Hazelton's sermon that Sunday was titled "Man in the Mirror—How Events Are Told Shape Their Reality."

I have conscientiously tried to be truthful in telling about the people and the events of my life. If I have slighted some of you, or told a happening different than recalled by you, my intent was not to displease but, from my perspective, to be honest. For this is my story, and I assume full responsibility in the telling.

ONE

＋＋＋＋＋

INTRODUCTION

MY FATHER MAY HAVE SPOKEN OF HIS PARENTS, but I have no memory of them. Add to this lack of grandparent involvement, the fact that I never knew my maternal grandfather. However, I have visited his burial site and I have met family members who did know him. It is through them that I have gained a glimmer of understanding about this man. The only grandparent that I personally knew was my maternal grandmother, and she died when I was thirteen.

＋＋＋＋＋

MY MATERNAL GRANDFATHER, Squair (also spelled Squire) Merritt Shuart, was born April 10, 1842, in Sheffield Township, Ohio. He spent some of his youthful years in Girard Township, Pennsylvania. He enlisted in the Union Army on December 18, 1861, at the age of nineteen, serving as a volunteer with the 111th Regiment, Company C of Pennsylvania; he was told the government promised a new suit of clothes to all enlistees. Squair saw action in battles at Antietam, Chancellorsville, and Gettysburg. He was wounded in battle during Sherman's March to the Sea near Dallas, Georgia. Squair recovered and was able to resume his place with his regiment and was honorably discharged on December 23, 1863, wearing the promised new suit.

Squair was married to Eliza Nuttall while on leave from active duty. Upon discharge he returned to Sheffield Township and built a house on Gageville Road. It was there he and Eliza, married for thirty years, raised their five children. However, the years following Squair's return to civilian life did not bode well for the couple. Although divorce was unheard of in the nineteenth century, Squair was listed as the defendant in the divorce papers served by Eliza in 1891, with Squair filing a cross petition in 1892. The divorce was granted in 1893.

Remaining in the area of Sheffield Township, Squair purchased thirty acres of land, one mile south of Gageville Road on Maple Road. It was there he built a second house. Needing a housekeeper, he advertised widely in newspapers (*Lonely Hearts?*), and Eda Dale May, living in La Crew, Iowa, answered his ad.

It had to have been a strange meeting that took place when Squair met Eda at the Ashtabula train station that autumn afternoon in 1894. When Eda learned that Squair's intent was only to hire a housekeeper, she refused to be taken to his house unless they were joined in holy matrimony. Squair must have agreed because they were married on September 27.

Squair and Eda had been married for seven years when an astonishing thing happened. The story is told that Eda thought whatever was making her stomach so large was just a growth. She did not realize she was pregnant. When Eda and Squair lay in bed together, Squair would place his hand on his wife's stomach and hold it there for hours. No movement was ever detected. Eda's labor started when she was out riding in their horse-drawn buggy. She was in abject misery by the time she arrived at the house. There had been no preparations for the birth of the child. Rhoda Dale (known as Dale) was born on August 1, 1901. My mother was the only child of their union. In this farm community, I wonder where Eda turned for counsel, for help. I surmise it must have been from caring women in the neighborhood, the church, or other social connections.

The couple lived in the home on Maple Road until 1929. Their daughter, Dale, was in and out; during some of her childhood years, she was with family in Girard, Pennsylvania. During her high school years, she boarded in Ashtabula. Upon graduation from high school, Dale moved to Kent and attended Kent State Normal School, a teacher training institution opened in 1910. It was at the age of eighty-seven that Squair left his second wife and daughter to live with members of his first family who had settled in Farmville, Virginia. He died two years later on February 4, 1931.

--------- ++++++ ---------

ON ROUTE 45, SIX MILES NORTH OF FARMVILLE, is a small building located on several acres of land that is now a dedicated cemetery. This building, built by his son-in-law, became Squair's home. I have visited the site. Entering the building through the garage, the first sight to meet my eyes was a white marble tombstone marking the place where Squair is buried. His 1929 Model A Ford should have been in place over his grave; however, Squair had failed to specifically state this in his will. The car was sold. The only visible hint that his prized vehicle was once parked in the garage is the Ohio 1930 license plate A62-862 nailed to the wall. Apparently Squair had kept his Ohio residency.

From the garage I entered his living quarters. Hanging from a peg on the wall is his paint-splattered blue denim jacket; another peg holds a worn broad-brimmed black hat; between the two pegs a mirror is mounted beside a 1931 calendar noting the day and date of his death (Wednesday, February 4). My mother had spoken of her father's burial place; it was just as I had envisioned it. Standing there I was enveloped with a feeling of reverence for this man whom I never knew: Civil War veteran, farmer, bee-keeper, husband, father of six children. I heard many stories about Squair from my mother and my Virginia cousins. It is from these stories that I have been able to gain some glimmer of understanding: irascible, impatient, nonconformist, bullheaded, honest-to-a-fault, hardworking, frugal (often referred to as stingy), loving, kind, endearing to family. I want to believe he changed with time and, like good wine, mellowed.

I DID KNOW MY MATERNAL GRANDMOTHER. My father, mother, brother and I lived with Granma in her home on Maple Road in Sheffield Township. Eda Shuart, née May was born in LaCrew, Iowa, on June 9, 1866, one of ten children.

My memories of my Granma, sad to say, are not the fond, fuzzy memories that usually engulf many grandchildren. Incongruous as it may seem, this comely woman with a crown of beautiful white hair, a stature of dignity, was a nonentity in the family, living on the periphery of our lives. Memories that I have are bittersweet. One day I came home from school excited about doing something of interest to me. I must have been nine or ten years old. My mother admonished me for being so self-centered and directed me to go upstairs to my grandmother's bedroom and spend some time with her.

Granma spent a lot of time in her bedroom sitting in her rocking chair by the window. I recall seeing her give herself insulin shots. She was a diabetic, and the sight of Granma pinching the skin of her upper thigh, inserting the needle of the syringe, and injecting the insulin into her leg terrified me.

It was Granma who told me to always "air out the bed" before making it. To this day when I make a bed, I think of Granma and dutifully follow her instructions. Eda ate with us at the table. Selfish brat that I could be, when it came time for dessert, I resented that Mom always cut the pie in five pieces, a smaller piece for Granma who, due to her diabetic condition, was not supposed to eat excessive starches or sugars. A pie cut in four pieces would give me a larger piece. At the time, I did not realize that Mom was allowing Granma a special treat.

Social outlets were few. Granma belonged to the Daughters of Union Veterans, the Gageville Methodist Evangelical Church, Sheffield Grange, and the Sheffield Birthday Club. I remember Granma holding her purple parasol over her head to protect her face from the sun, wearing her every-day shoes while carrying her black dress shoes, walking two miles over dirt roads to the Ladies Circle meeting at the church. Upon arriving at the church, she changed to her dress shoes. When it was time to leave, she reversed the process to walk the two miles home.

As an adult I have pondered the life of my grandmother. She married a man who could be cruel; he certainly was frugal to the point of being stingy. My mother told how Granma used to take a few eggs from the basket of eggs that were to be sold in town on Saturday. On market day Eda would sell those purloined eggs separately to get a few dollars for herself.

As the years passed, Granma became weaker, and with it came incontinence. I recall one day Granma was sitting in the living room in Squair's favorite chair, a wicker rocker. She had urinated; a large puddle was visible under the chair. When this happened, it was my job to get the floor mop and wipe up the puddle. I did not mind this chore; young as I was, I sensed Granma's life was fading away.

About a year before she died, Granma's hip gave out, causing her to fall. It was a few months after this happened that she developed pneumonia. Her bed was brought down from the second floor and set up in the living room. Knowing that the end was near, my mother did not want Granma to be alone. We took turns sitting by her bedside. It was Christmas night. Mom and Dad had gone to bed. I sat with Granma, reading out loud from the Bible when she took her last breath. I was thirteen years old.

Granma's body lay in state for three days in the living room of our home. Neighbors and friends came to pay their respects. I vividly recall one floral piece that my mother had placed on a floor tripod by Granma's casket—the Broken Wheel.

Today the Broken Wheel floral arrangement is considered a classic. Picture a wagon wheel about two feet in diameter covered with flowers. One spoke and a part of the wheel rim are missing, symbolizing the absent family member. Even at the time of my Granma's funeral, few of these arrangements were used. Living in a farm community, I suspect this type of arrangement might have appeared pretentious, as well as costly. I am certain that this was my mother's statement of respect for this noble woman who had given so much to her daughter's family.

The service was held on December 29 at the Gageville church. Few were there. The only family present to mourn Granma was her nuclear family. To this day I recall the hymns that were sung: "Jesus Savior Pilot Me" and "In the Garden." The pastor took the text for his message from Paul's second letter to Timothy (4:7). "I have fought the good fight, I have finished the race, I have kept the faith."

The service was beautiful in its simplicity. It was a fitting tribute to this most noble woman who bore the vicissitudes of her life with dignity. Her body is interred in the family lot in the Gageville Cemetery, located one quarter mile from the church.

As I write about my grandmother, a mist of sadness envelopes me. She left her family, married a stranger, and knew mostly a life of toil. Her husband left when their daughter was twenty-six years old to move to Farmville, Virginia, to be with family from his first marriage. The final years of Eda's life were spent in the house on Maple Road where her daughter and family had joined her.

What were Eda's thoughts as she sat alone in her bedroom, gently rocking in her favorite chair, looking out of her east window at the maple trees, now tall, that were only sprigs brought with her from Iowa?

------- ++++++ -------

THE HEADLINE IN THE *ASHTABULA STAR BEACON* READ "Dale Shuart of Sheffield Weds Henry A. Schumann." No family members or, to my knowledge, close friends were witnesses to the ceremony. At the time of the wedding, Dale was a student at Kent State Normal School, Kent, Ohio. Henry lived in Akron and was employed by the B. F. Goodrich Company.

Henry met Dale at the dance hall in Brady Lake, near Kent. Cupid's arrow pierced the heart of this bachelor of thirty-three years. The couple was married before a justice of the peace at the courthouse in Ravenna on February 9, 1925. The bride and groom temporarily established residence in Brady Lake, living there until June when they were able to move into their new home on Lexington Street in Akron.

Henry, born on February 9, 1892, was one of eight children (four girls and four boys) born to Wilhelm Schumann and Katharina Dorothea Hoefeldt. Both Wilhelm and Katharina were born in Germany. Wilhelm immigrated to Chicago in 1879, and Katharina followed in 1881. Wilhelm and Katharina met in Chicago and were married in 1884, later moving their growing family to Hustler, Wisconsin. I have no memory of my father talking about his parents or his growing-up years in Hustler.

I don't know how old Henry was when he moved to Chicago. From Chicago, circa 1915, he moved to Akron seeking employment in the rubber factory. Henry kept a Line-A-Day diary, and with great difficulty I have been able to decipher his small, scratchy handwriting. Reading his entries, I have been able to discern that Henry enjoyed city life. He attended live theater and the movies; he took banjo lessons and played with a group of amateur musicians; he loved to dance; he enjoyed exploring the parks around Akron. There were even some innuendos of romantic escapades.

Henry lived in several boarding houses in Akron. On my eightieth birthday, my husband, Cordell Glaus, familiar with the city, drove me to the six addresses that Henry had noted in his diary. It was a thrilling day. I actually imagined my father living in this city as we drove from one address to another: four houses still stood, Interstate 76 had taken the land of another, and the final address yielded only a vacant lot.

My father worked hard, drank little, did not gamble, and saved his money. Unfortunately, his siblings seemed to always be in "hard times" and Henry was generous to a fault in loaning them money when they asked. According to Henry's financial records, little—if any—of the money was ever repaid.

Being patriotic-minded, Henry joined the army on June 4, 1917, in Akron and was honorably discharged on May 17, 1919, at Camp Sherman, Ohio. While in the service Sgt. First Class Henry A. Schumann served in the Medical Corps in France. After being discharged he returned to Akron.

Henry brought with him from France some mementoes. One was a large, red ruby ring. It was a beautiful stone. After my parents died we three siblings gathered around the kitchen table in the farmhouse on Maple Road and divvied up the few remaining possessions of my parents, each stating what they would like. I chose the ruby ring. Later I had the ring appraised for insurance purposes, and it was then I learned the stone was man-made—a replica so perfect the jeweler had to send it to a specialist for verification. Real or fake, it made no difference to me. I treasured it for it symbolized a precious connection with my father.

Dale was a child of aged parents. Squair was fifty-nine, and Eda was thirty-five. Squair had raised a family of five children with his first wife. It was never clear to me why he thought his daughter, Agnes, married and living in Girard, would serve as a good surrogate parent for my mother. From the stories my mother related to me, it was evident Squair was head of the household and that Eda obeyed. In this twenty-first century, where marriage is looked upon as a partnership, I find this concept of dominance difficult to understand. However, thinking back to the culture of the time of my grandparents and noting the embossed declaration at the top of their Marriage Certificate—"The Husband is the Head of the Wife" and "The Wife is the Crown to her Husband"—it made sense that Squair would send Dale to spend part of her elementary school years with her elder half-sister, and that Eda would make no protest.

Dale did return home for her high school years, boarding at a house in Ashtabula during the week. For a graduation gift, Squair gave his daughter a Model T Ford and then sent her off to Kent to enroll (circa 1917) in the recently established Kent State Normal School. After completing the required two-year program, Dale returned to her home on Maple Road. Once again she found herself living in a boarding house in Ashtabula during the week and teaching students at the Harbor Junior High School. Her Model T Ford provided needed transportation.

This comely red-haired young woman must have harbored many dreams. One had to be anticipated love. Dale had met Henry at a dance while at school in Kent. She was apparently smitten with the handsome tall, dark-haired man. Two of her interesting and impassioned love letters to him survive. In one letter she spoke of her desire to improve her piano skills. "I want to play evenings in a theater… I can play that jazz stuff pretty well now, but I would like to read difficult music more rapidly." Perhaps she envisioned herself living in the city, for in another letter she wrote, "I have to keep myself very busy in order to stay around this berg."

Whether it was nature or nurture, frugality was a part of Dale's character. In one of the letters to Henry, she lamented that no matter how much she cranked her Model T, she couldn't get it started. This scene took place in the school parking lot on a Friday; she planned to go home for the weekend. She summoned a mechanic; he figured out the problem and quoted Dale a cost for repairs. Dale sensed she was being taken advantage of and chose to walk the seven miles home, returning the next day with Squair. A simple mechanical problem was found and fixed with no cost to Dale, except her shoe leather.

To this day I marvel at the level of intellectual, musical, homemaking, and parenting skills that my mother achieved. During her public school years, she was sent off to live with relatives or in boarding houses. Who was her mentor that enabled her to become a loving mother? How was she able to discipline herself to become an accomplished pianist? Where did she learn the needed homemaking skills that enabled her to provide for a family under primitive living conditions?

HENRY AND DALE WERE MARRIED during a time that the economy was strong. Henry had saved his money, invested in land, and built a home for his bride. In fact, two houses were built in Akron, one to live in and the other to rent. However, all did not remain golden for Henry and Dale. In 1927 Henry's health became an issue for the young couple when he was told by his doctor that if he wanted to live he must leave the contaminated work environment of the B. F. Goodrich Rubber Plant, where he had been employed for about fourteen years. Heeding the doctor's advice, Henry and Dale left Akron. Returning to Ashtabula County and assuming yet more debt, they purchased a farm on land contract on Lilly Road, in Sheffield Township, one mile south of Dale's childhood home. My brother, Lloyd, was born there on June 22, 1928.

Three years after leaving Akron, an economic disaster, referred to as the Great Depression of the 1930s, hit the country. There was no work for Henry. Dale, although a college graduate with a bachelor of science degree and a valid teaching certificate, would not be hired by any school district. It was policy not to hire a married woman—jobs were for the men.

Finding no work and with payments due on the farm, Henry approached the owners of the property and requested permission to harvest trees from the forested area on the land and sell the lumber. The owner refused. Henry and Dale were evicted from the property for failure to meet the terms of the land contract. They returned to Akron with their young son; this was where I was born.

Now married six years, life became even more difficult for Henry and Dale. The Depression deepened. Times were hard as well for the renters occupying the second house my parents owned. They were unable to make their rental payments. The dream of Henry and Dale to own investment property to secure their financial future evaporated. The necessary dollars to make mortgage payments were unavailable. Now, not able to make payments on either of their Akron houses, they lost both. To survive, the best option left to them was for Dale to return with her family to her childhood home on Maple Road.

SQUAIR AND EDITH, HENRY AND DALE were courageous, hardworking, frugal, and honest individuals. Henry and Dale thought they had made good financial decisions. They had no way of foreseeing the financial disaster of the 1930s. Although not openly spoken, I am convinced their strong Christian faith sustained them in their deepest hours of despair. There is a family lot in the Gageville Cemetery in Sheffield Township. On that lot stands a five foot Shuart-Schumann granite monument. Inscribed under their names is the following scripture:

Thy word is a lamp unto my feet and
a light unto my path.
Psalm 119:105

My maternal grandmother and my parents rest there; years later the ashes of my oldest son were sprinkled there.

✦✦✦✦✦✦✦

Two

FARM HOUSE

T HE STOCK MARKET CRASH on Black Tuesday, October 29, 1929, ushered in the Great Depression that imposed financial hardship on millions of Americans. Henry and Dale were caught in this economic disaster. They lost the farm they were buying on land contract, and with their young son Lloyd, the couple returned to a house they owned on Lexington Street in Akron.

Being an only child, Dale's constant companion had been loneliness. She vowed that should she marry, any child she bore would have a sibling. With this in mind, Henry and Dale defied the decline in fertility rates that correlate with bleak economic "baby-bust" eras in United States history and Dale became pregnant. Henrietta Elaine was born on April 7, 1930.

Thrilled with the birth of their second child, little did Henry and Dale realize that on the previous day, April 6, the Twinkie was "born." The Continental Baking Company located in the Chicago, Illinois, area needed a cheap snack to sell to Depression consumers. The bakery manager, James Dewar, utilizing the off-season strawberry cake tins, and after many failed attempts, settled on a yellow sponge cake recipe, originally injected with banana cream filling.

(The idea for calling the cake a Twinkie came from a billboard advertising Twinkle Toe Shoes.) The Twinkie became the top-selling snack food in America—market price, two for a nickel.

✦✦✦✦✦

MEMORIES OF MY EARLY CHILDHOOD are almost nonexistent. When the family lived on Lexington Avenue in Akron, there was a ten-year-old neighborhood girl who enjoyed taking me for strolls in my buggy. Mom said she was delighted to let her do this because the gentle rocking of the buggy would put me to sleep and she would get a respite from my crying or fretting.

In 1933 or 1934, my folks took Lloyd and me with them to Chicago. Dad wanted to visit his sister who lived there and also visit the Century of Progress Exposition, commonly known as the Chicago World's Fair. I don't remember what vehicle Dad drove or any of the sights en route or the city itself. I do have a vivid memory of the stairs in the tall apartment building where my Aunt Minnie Balch lived in Clarendon Hills, a suburb of Chicago. I must have been fascinated by the several flights of stairs that we had to climb to get to my aunt's apartment. Lloyd and I found this to be a beckoning play area. We entertained ourselves by the hour running up and down, chasing one another, pausing every so often to look over the banister into the abyss below.

I do remember a lady from one of the apartments speaking harshly to Lloyd and me, telling us that we were making too much noise. I don't recall seeing the lady talk with my aunt, but soon after my aunt called us in and told us we were not to play on the stairs. A feeling of sadness overtook me. We were having so much fun.

＋＋＋＋＋＋

I HAVE NO MEMORIES of my baby/toddler years living on Lexington Avenue in Akron. My first memories are connected with the thirty-acre farm where I grew up, located on Maple Road in Sheffield Township, Ashtabula County, Ohio. The buildings I remember are the house, barn, outdoor toilet, chicken coops, equipment sheds, milk house, and my playhouse. All of the buildings were strategically arranged on a plot of ground close to the dirt road that ran in front of our house. This was my mother's home during her growing-up years. Of all the places I have lived, my most vivid memories are of the farm. The ten-room house seemed huge. I estimate the foundation to measure thirty by twenty-four feet. One might refer to the architectural style as a two-story Cape Cod or Georgian Colonial sans the ornate front door. My grandfather built the house between 1892 and 1894.

＋＋＋＋＋＋

EACH ROOM OF THE HOUSE holds special memories for me. The basement foundation was built from field stones found on the farm. Areas of the basement floor were covered in concrete; other areas were dirt. A few small windows allowed an eerie light to penetrate the darkness. There was a dank, musty smell that filled one's nostrils. I was terrified to go down the rough-hewn plank steps because I knew animals and reptiles had easy access through the spaces in the field stone wall. I was convinced a ghost lived behind the stair, waiting to grab me should I dare to enter its space.

There was an access to the basement from the outside. This was where firewood and coal would be thrown down and stockpiled to fuel the stoves in the kitchen and living room. Mother stored the summer's harvest from the gardens, and the winter slaughter of a cow and pig, in quart jars on the shelves that lined one side of the basement room. It was necessary to preserve enough food to last the family throughout the year—a hundred quarts of peaches, fifty quarts of pears. Add to that quarts and pints of beef and pork, pickles, berries, jams, and jellies. The farm was self-sustaining; only the staples of flour and sugar were purchased at the grocery store.

THE MAIN FLOOR OF THE HOUSE consisted of a large kitchen, sink room, large living room, bedroom, and a pantry. The steep stair to the second floor was located between the pantry and sink room. Three exterior doors (one off the sink room, one off the north wall of the kitchen, and one off the east wall of the living room) allowed direct entry to the house. There were no buffer areas to waylay the winter cold, the summer heat, or the multitudes of flies. No carpets were placed by the doors to encourage family members to wipe their feet, and heaven forbid anyone should take off their shoes or boots before entering the house. Dirt and dried fecal droppings from the barnyard were everywhere. Keeping the linoleum floors clean was a never-ending, if not an impossible, task.

As a child I remember singing the following rhyme:

> Mondays washing,
> Tuesdays ironing,
> Wednesdays mending,
> Thursdays churning,
> Fridays cleaning,
> Saturdays baking,
> Sundays resting.

The sink room, kitchen, and pantry functioned as the "nerve center" of the house. The kitchen was a fifteen-by-fourteen-foot room located at the front in the northeast corner. It was sparsely furnished with a round table, five chairs, a sideboard buffet, and a black cast-iron stove. The stove pipe, reaching up through the ceiling, connected into a brick chimney in the bedroom above. To take advantage of the morning light, Mom's sewing machine was placed in front of one of the two east windows.

Mounted at standing height on the wall in the southeast corner of the room was an oblong wooden box—the party-line phone. Our phone number was 3-1R1. One long ring was the signal that the call was for us. There were a total of ten families on the 3-1R line. I always felt sorry for the family that had the 3-1R10 number. They had to listen carefully for the ten short rings that would signal the call was for them. Being a party line, nosy neighbors would stealthily take the hand receiver off the hook and listen in on conversations. We always referred to these inquisitive neighbors as "rubbering." Mom impressed on my brother and me to never "rubber" and to always be careful what you said during any phone conversation!

Next to the phone, a four-foot shelf holding a mantel clock was mounted in the center of the east wall. Behind the stove, high on the south wall, was a drying rack with five three-foot-long "fingers." Beneath the drying rack was another shelf, and below the shelf a line of hooks. There were no closets in the house, so this was where coats, hats, and mittens were kept. This area was used in the winter to dry the Monday washing, and throughout the week, to dry our outdoor clothes that inevitably would get soaked from the rain or snow.

In the summer a sticky ribbon flytrap was hung from the middle of the kitchen ceiling for the purpose of catching the flies that entered the house. Poorly fitted exterior screen doors, and removable screens placed in the windows, left adequate spaces for flies to enter. When the flies became too numerous for the sticky ribbon, Mom would close all doors and windows in the kitchen, pantry, and sink room. She would then cover all exposed food, as well as the furniture, take out the hand sprayer, and proceed to fill the room with a noxious-smelling fog of fly spray. Any family member at home would immediately flee to the outdoors and wait about thirty minutes before reentering the house. Dead flies were everywhere. For the most part, I managed to avoid the clean-up job.

The heat from the stove was welcome in the winter but brutal in the summer. During summer canning season, the large oblong copper boiler was placed on top of the stove. Quarts of fruits and vegetables were processed in the boiling water bath. In the winter the quart jars were filled with beef or pork from the butchered calf and pig. Years later Mom did get a pressure cooker that shortened the processing time. Processing the meats was much more labor intensive than processing the vegetables. Dad removed the slabs of meat from the carcasses and brought them into the sink room. Mom proceeded to cut the meat in small pieces, pack it into the quart jars, fill the jars with water (some salt added for flavoring), place the rubber jar ring around the jar, screw down the lid, and only then were the meats ready to be carefully placed in the boiling water. (Other than the old hens stewed for our Sunday dinners, this was our meat supply for the year. We ate fresh meat only at butchering time.) As best I remember, this was the only means available to preserve our year-long food supply.

More brutal than the heat needed for canning in the summer (at least we could walk away from the copper boiler) was the heat needed for making the jams and jellies. Many times I was the one appointed to stand over the hot stove. It was my job to keep stirring the syrupy mixture so it would not stick to the bottom of the pan as it boiled down to the right consistency to jell. It was a great relief when Mom would take the hot pan from me and pour its contents into the sterilized jars. The final step was to carefully seal the top of the jar with hot wax before setting the delicacy aside for family consumption.

As a child one of the naughty jokes I remember is asking the question, "What are the three most important parts of a stove?" Then gleefully giving the answer, "Lifter, leg, and poker!" (For anyone not familiar with a cast-iron stove, the "lifter" was used to lift the cast-iron lids that covered the cooking holes over the fire box. The "poker" was used to stir the fire. Stoves had "legs" to stand on.) That joke was the height of risqué behavior at the time, so of course, I made sure to tell it every chance I got.

The sink room was a smaller room located off of the northwest corner of the kitchen and had access doors to the outside and to the basement. A cabinet, with countertop areas on each side of the sink, was built into one side of the room. A shelf was mounted above the sink. Between the door and the sink, mounted on the wall the same height as the shelf, was the roller towel. Mom made the towels for the roller from a two-yard length of linen, sewing the ends together, making a continuous loop of fabric that was placed over the roller. Family members would wash up at the sink and use this towel for wiping their hands and faces.

The following poetic description of the roller towel is not too far from the truth. The family used only one clean roller towel a week.

The Old Roller Towel
How dear to this heart is the old roller towel
Which fond recollection presents to my view,
The time-honored towel that creaked on the wall.
The grimy old towel…
The tacky old towel that hung on the wall.
by Bert Leston Taylor

A work table was the only other furnishing in the room. We didn't have running water. A bucket, holding a metal dipper, sat on the counter beside the sink. We all drank from the common dipper, and it was my job to keep the bucket filled with drinking water. The well was located about forty feet from the house, so the only way to get the water was to go for it. As an adult I have said many times, "Yes, we had running water in our house when I was a child. It was my job to keep the drinking bucket full, and I had to run out and get it."

The sink room was the first stop-off for the processing of all food supplies. One year, when corn was in season, Mom processed corn all day for canning. I remember her stripping each corn cob of its kernels, tightly packing the kernels into quart jars, then placing the quart jars in the boiling water of the copper boiler for processing. I vividly recall as I prepared to go to bed that night, reaching for my toothbrush in the glass on the shelf above the sink and finding a corn worm in my toothbrush! Mom got rid of the worm, washed out my toothbrush, and tried to persuade me to use it. My protestations were so loud that she gave in and allowed me to get a new toothbrush. Apparently during the processing, a corn worm had escaped from an ear of corn, crawled up the sink room wall and made its lodging in my toothbrush.

I was quite young, but I do remember one time when the drain in the sink room became plugged. Dad had to use a pick and shovel to dig through the clay soil to expose the underground drain pipe. It was back-breaking work. I have no idea how the drain got plugged, but I do recall that Dad put the fear of God in all of us that no grease, or garbage of any kind, was ever to be allowed to flow into the drain. This made a memorable imprint on my brain, because to this day I am very careful as to what goes down any drain.

On Mondays the sink room / kitchen area became a laundry. The washing machine was a welcome appliance that was stored in the only free corner in the sink room. On Sunday night Dad would place the large tin tub on a waist-high stand by the washing machine and fill it with cold water for rinsing the clothes. Next he would fill the copper boiler on the stove and bank the fire for the night. In the morning the water would be hot, and he filled the washer tub in preparation for washing the clothes. After breakfast Dad started the small gasoline engine mounted on the washer mechanism before leaving for his factory job in Ashtabula.

I dreaded washdays. Mom sorted the clothes in piles. White clothes were first; next sheets, pillowcases, and towels; followed by colored clothes; and last, the heavy overalls. It was backbreaking work to lift the wet clothes from the washtub and run them through the wringer into the rinse tub. Clothes in the rinse tub were manually lifted up and down, rinsing them as best one could, before again putting them through the wringer. The final step was watching as the clothes dropped into the clothes basket to be carried to the outdoor clothesline for drying. Each step in the wringer process required that clothes be carefully folded over any buttons to keep the buttons from being torn off as the garment went through the wringer. To me, the worst was the ear-shattering noise of the gasoline motor that ran the washer. It took several hours to do the washing, and any effort to concentrate or converse during that time was impossible. My only escape was to go outside, far from the house.

Tuesdays were devoted to ironing—that is, if the clothes were dry from Mondays' washings. Due to lack of space, drying clothes on the kitchen racks was difficult in the winter. Mom would hang some of the larger, heavier clothes (sheets, towels, overalls) on the clothesline in the front yard to freeze dry.

When I was a child there were no wrinkle-free fabrics. All dresses, blouses, and men's shirts were starched and ironed. I first remember Mom using the heavy "sad irons" that were heated on the stove. Later she got a Montgomery Ward gasoline iron (still available today) that eased the iron-ing process.

First thing after breakfast was to sprinkle all clothes that needed to be ironed and tightly roll them up so the moisture would be evenly spread throughout the garment. Mom would let me iron the flat items (mostly pillowcases), but the sheets were not ironed. Years later, with great difficulty, I learned how to iron a starched man's shirt. It was almost impossible to keep an even heat on the ironing plate—too hot and the cotton was scorched, too cool and the wrinkles remained. Fortunately, we didn't have many items that were made of fine materials like satin, linen, or rayon that required special attention to the heat of the iron. Our wardrobe consisted mostly of cottons, wools, and flannels.

Ironing day was exhausting for Mom. As a little girl I did not help, and when I got old enough to help, I was in school. It was during the summers that Mom taught me how to iron. I never liked doing it, and to this day I am barely on "speaking acquaintance" with my iron.

On Friday nights the kitchen was transformed into a processing plant for dressing chickens. Dad raised chickens and had a standing order with Naddra's Grocery Store in Ashtabula for twenty-five fryers to be delivered every Saturday morning. I was Dad's designated helper. It was my job to accompany him to the chicken coop and help catch the birds. Once the chickens were caught and restrained by tying their feet together, we proceeded to the chopping block. Dad would release one chicken at a time, place its head on the block, and as he lifted his razor-sharp ax, I would utter a prayer for the doomed bird. After lopping off the chicken's head, Dad would release the bird, and I'd watch in fascination as the headless chicken ran around until it dropped—the proverbial "chicken with its head cut off." Neither the smell of the warm blood nor the sight of the headless bodies was offensive to me. I was a country kid, and this is how it was.

Before slaughtering the chickens, Dad filled the oblong, copper boiler with water, placed it on the kitchen stove, and stoked the fire. By the time we returned from the barnyard with the headless chickens, the water was boiling. Holding each chicken by its feet, Dad dipped the bird into the boiling water, held it there for a few seconds, then lifted it out. As soon as the feathers were cool enough to the touch, he would denude the bird— methodically beginning with the legs, moving his hands over the breast area, and down its back. If pin feathers had grown on the young bird, it was my job to remove them. When assured all feathers were plucked, I moved the bird along our production line to the table in the sink room where Mom would gut it, skillfully removing the intestines and lungs, but saving the heart and liver (delicacies). Each dressed chicken was then placed in the round tin tub filled with cold water, where they stayed overnight due to a lack of refrigeration. In the morning the chickens were removed from the tub, dried with a towel, and were ready to take to market.

The noxious stench of wet chicken feathers combined with the steam that rose from the copper boiler filled our kitchen. As a family we were used to this swampy mess; however it never failed that our minister from the United Brethren Church in Ashtabula chose Friday nights to make his pastoral visits. A knock on the door caused Mom and Dad to voice in unison, "Oh no, not tonight!" and I detected a feeling of dread in their voices. The door opened, and Reverend Hall entered the kitchen, ignoring the bizarre scene and somehow managing to retain his composure. Taking the offered chair, he'd sit there amidst the stink, steam, and feathers, carrying on a conversation with my folks while they continued at their appointed tasks. I could feel the blood rush to my face turning it red with embarrassment!

On Saturday nights the kitchen was converted into a bathroom. Once again the copper boiler would be placed on the stove and filled with water. A large tin tub would be set in the middle of the kitchen floor. When the water was hot enough, Mom summoned Lloyd and me for the ritual of our Saturday-night baths. We used the same water for bathing, so Lloyd and I would alternate who got to bathe first.

Stark naked, I folded myself into the round tin tub. With knees hitting my chin and my bare bottom soaking in the comfort of the warm water, Mom scrubbed away a week's accumulation of dirt, giving special attention to the soles of my blackened feet. With my skin smarting from the scrubbing, I stood to be rinsed off. Then shivering and with teeth chattering, I stepped out of the warm water into the drafty kitchen.

It was then my brother's turn, who had been patiently standing naked waiting to get into the tub. Lloyd would quickly settle himself into the murky water for his weekly scrubbing. The second kid in the tub didn't take as long for their bath. By this time the water was getting downright cold, and speed had its reward.

Lloyd and I were young children at the time we shared bathing night in the tin tub. I don't recall when we were old enough to realize that boys and girls were sexually different, but eventually we no longer took baths together. Perhaps it was Mom and Dad who made this decision for us. I do know that this openness with nudity gave me a feeling of wholesomeness for my body, not shame. This served me well in high school for the required gang showers after physical education classes. Our home allowed for little privacy, but my parents and grandmother were very circumspect about appearing before Lloyd or me in any inappropriate way.

According to the rhyme, Sundays were for resting, but there was precious little time for resting on the farm, even on Sundays. On Sunday morning Mom would stay home with Granma, and Dad would take my brother and me to Sunday school. When we returned home Mom would have a delicious dinner of chicken and dumplings, mashed potatoes, a vegetable, and pie for dessert. The chicken we ate was not one of the fryers that were dressed on Friday night and taken to market Saturday morning. We ate one of the old hens that was no longer laying eggs. In spite of the toughness of old hens, Mom was able to stew the bird and make delicious chicken and dumplings.

After we ate, and if Dad did not have to attend to some farm animal or other need, I'd beg him to draw me a picture of a horse. Dad would get out a pencil and paper with no lines, and I'd snuggle onto his lap. He would then proceed to draw me pictures of horses. His drawings were very good. I liked them until he would make the squiggly lines beneath the horse that resembled the ground. I begged him not to add the lines, but he ignored me. Many years later, when I was in college taking a child development class, I learned that young children develop their spatial awareness at different rates. That explains why I didn't want the picture of the horse that my dad drew to be connected to the ground—leave it in space with me where I was comfortable.

Located off the southwest corner of the kitchen was the pantry. As a child I was fascinated with a cabinet called the "dumb waiter." However, the mechanism for lowering this cabinet into the cool basement needed repair and to my memory was never used for its original purpose. It was used for storing dry foodstuffs or pots and pans.

On one side of the pantry was a four-foot-long countertop Mom used for baking. There were open shelves above and below the counter surface that held baking supplies. Sugar and flour were purchased in twenty-five-pound sacks. To accommodate these staples, two floor-level tip-out bins were built next to the baking shelf. The remainder of the wall space in the pantry had built in cabinets. One cabinet had a secret compartment behind the silverware drawer. This was used for the family "safe," where legal documents and other small valuables were stored.

The only other piece of equipment in the pantry was a cream separator, placed in front of the window. I liked to watch the milk that filled the large bowl at the top of the separator as it swirled down through the tubes separating out the cream, which flowed into the pail placed below. When I became old enough, and strong enough, I helped Mom churn the cream into butter. At first a crockery butter churn with a wooden plunger was used; later Dad purchased a cylindrical wooden churn with a crank handle. That made the process of churning much easier. Much to my brother's vexation, Dad never did make me learn how to milk the cows (that provided the milk, that gave us the cream, to make the butter). I did have to help churn, though, and he didn't! Such is life between siblings.

I also helped Mom with the cooking and baking. When I thought I was old enough, I asked Mom if I could make out the week's menus. She readily agreed. I made a list of the needed items and did the required shopping. I felt so grown-up. However, I soon tired of the task, and it all reverted back to Mom.

Access to the large living room was through double doors located on the south wall of the kitchen. A heating stove was located in one corner of the living room. A pipe went up through the ceiling to the bedroom above and connected into a brick chimney. A blackboard was mounted on the wall in another corner of the room. An upright piano, library desk, and stand for a battery-powered radio filled the remaining wall spaces between the exterior door and the windows. Grandpa and Gramma Shuart's rocking chairs, a sofa and chair with wooden arms, both covered in heavy green oilcloth, were the only other pieces of furniture. There were no rugs on the linoleum-covered floor. The absence of rugs and cloth covered furniture was by design. There was an ongoing battle with ashes from the heating stove and dirt on the floor.

I loved my chalkboard. I'd spend hours with chalk and eraser in hand practicing my cursive writing, working on my arithmetic problems, or playing school. Chalk dust covered the floor, but I paid little heed to it until it got so bad Mom would make me clean up the mess.

Dad would listen to the evening news on the radio. My favorite programs were the *Lux Radio Theater* and *The Shadow*. As I recall, the *Lux Radio Theater* was an hour-long 9:00 p.m., Sunday night program. My parents slept in the small bedroom off of the living room, and I was permitted to stay up to listen to the program only if I kept the volume low. Dad had to get up at 5:00 a.m. and needed his sleep. I remember sitting next to the radio with my ear glued to the speaker box, being carried off into a fascinating world of make-believe.

The Shadow was another matter. This fifteen-minute nightly serialized drama frightened me. I would not sit in front of a window for fear of being attacked by one of the shady characters in the story. The introduction

"Who knows what evil lurks in the hearts of men? The Shadow knows!" struck fear in my heart.

Another welcome addition to the furnishings in the living room came much later in the early 1950s. My brother had just gotten out of the navy and started his own TV business. Our family was one of the first to have a TV set. It was a small black-and-white TV. I'm remembering the screen to be about the size of a large, oval dinner platter. Due to the static snow that covered the screen, it was almost impossible to make out the picture. Nevertheless, we were the envy of the neighborhood.

In the winter, the living room was my dressing room. There was no central heat in the house. At bedtime there was room enough for me to undress in the corner, behind the heating stove, and put on my flannel nightgown in preparation for making a run to my second-floor bedroom. The procedure was reversed in the morning. Dad, who rose early, would have a fire going, and the room would be warm by the time I raced down to dress for the day.

There was a small room located off of the living room in the southwest corner of the house. During my early childhood years, this was Mom's quilting room in the winter. After the harvest season, when the canning was done, Mom would set up her wooden quilting frame. Seated in front of the quilt, she spent her free time in the winter working her needle back and forth across the width of whatever quilt was secured in the frame.

As a child this room became a favorite winter play area for me. I'd crawl under the quilt frame with my dolls and play house by the hour. I'd read to my "children," have a tea party with them, be their schoolteacher, or wherever my imagination would take me. On occasion I would get careless, unknowingly lift the top of my head too close to the quilting in progress, and get my scalp pricked with my mom's needle. Years later the room was converted into a bedroom for my parents.

———— ✦✦✦✦✦ ————

THE STAIRS TO THE SECOND FLOOR, located off the kitchen between the sink room and the pantry, were steep and narrow, with walls on both sides, but no banisters. Mom and Dad were very safety-conscious, and their admonitions to us were, never place anything on the stair, and when descending, always place your foot fully on the step with your heel touching the riser. Numerous black marks on the white-painted step risers were evidence that the family paid attention. Fingerprints covered the walls. To my knowledge no one ever took a tumble on the steps. To this day, at age eighty-five, I still recall Mom's and Dad's warnings and carefully place my foot as I descend each step.

At the top of the steps there was a landing with a window above it. Mounting the stairs and turning to the right, taking one more step up, was my brother's small bedroom. As children Lloyd and I would have a lot of fun playing games together in his room. One time, Mom found us in bed together, just talking, and admonished us that it was not proper behavior for a sister and brother. With childhood innocence, we never understood why. Years later, after my brother left home, his room was converted to a bathroom.

Standing on the stair landing and turning to your left was a large hall area furnished with a huge three-drawer chest. This crudely made pine chest was handcrafted by my Grandpa Shuart. I remember it was hard work to pull out the drawers that were used to store off-season clothing and rags. The other piece of furniture in the hall area was a smaller, red chest, also made by my Grandpa Shuart. It fascinated me to rummage through this smaller chest, because this was where Mom kept the blankets and nicer bed linens, dresser scarves, and crocheted dollies. I have no idea what happened to the larger chest. After Mom and Dad died, and we three siblings divvied up the items on the farm and in the house. I asked for the red chest and kept it with me for many years. To me it became a family heirloom. Several years ago, I passed on this chest, with a written narrative of its provenance, to my granddaughter Candice Nelson Hayes who lives in Las Vegas.

Another item, seldom mentioned but very accommodating, was the chamber pot. We had no indoor plumbing. During bad weather, and particularly in the winter, this functional item was welcomed by family members when nature "called." There were times when I was caught using the pot, and my modesty was compromised. It was my assigned chore to empty the chamber pot. Fortunately, there was a lid to cover the pot's contents, and each morning I carefully carried it down the stairs, took it outside, and dumped it over a bank located next to the outhouse. This was my least favorite chore of childhood. My brother was busy at his barn chores, so someone had to do it, and I was the one. Such was life living in a house with no modern conveniences. That early experience served me well when I did a fair amount of semiprimitive camping with my family.

The window above the stair landing played a role in my emotional maturing. I recall one summer day the window was open. I was seated on the top step, hands propped under my chin and my two feet on the landing, daydreaming. Suddenly I saw my brother emerge from the house and walk toward the barn. Can't recall what had happened, but I was annoyed with him. I proceeded to yell taunts, and much to my dismay, he just kept walking, never turning or acknowledging me. This infuriated me further. However, it taught me a life lesson. Silence can be far more effective than a response.

Other emotional experiences took place that were connected to the window above the stair. This happened in combination with the lighted kerosene lamp that I would carry up the stair and with me into my bedroom. I'd observe how the eerie light of the lamp would cast a long shadow behind me. Mom had read me the story by L. Frank Baum of "The Runaway Shadows." In the story, Jack Frost had the power to freeze shadows and separate them from their owners, making the shadow a living being. I had no idea what this meant, but I do recall that I was "afraid of my own shadow." Winter, spring, summer, or fall, whenever it was dark enough that I carried the lit lamp with me, I was fearful that my shadow would deal me some dastardly happening. It never did, and as I grew older, I learned not to fear the dark.

One day, I think I was twelve years of age at the time, it was warm weather, and the stair window was open. I ascended the stair to find my dad standing at the top. As I approached him, I noted a very sad look on his face, and he had tears in his eyes. I was startled. Dad would laugh, Dad would get angry, but I had never seen Dad cry. Being of German descent, we did not show overt emotion. I saw the letter Dad held in his hand about the same time he said to me, "Sis (his pet name for me), Aunt Dorothea died." Immediately I felt a great sadness for my dad, who always spoke so fondly of this sister. This was the first time I remember feeling a deep emotional response to another's pain. I don't know what I said. I do remember standing there with him, a warm summer breeze caressing my skin. Our silence communicated our sorrow.

Creative experiences were a result of visits from Jack Frost. We did not have storm windows, and in the winter the moisture would condense and freeze on the windows in any unheated area in the house. My favorite viewing place, for Jack Frost's visits, was the window above the stair landing. I still remember the thrill of waking up in the morning to see my breath in the bedroom and, as I hurried downstairs to the warmth of the living room, observing the evidence on the stair window that Jack Frost had made his visit.

Once warmly dressed, I would return to the stairway landing and sit on the top step, first just staring, and then using my forefinger to trace the intricate designs that Jack Frost had painted. My imagination would prod me to see fairies, delicate feathers, beautiful faces, stars, intricate leaf patterns, snowflakes of multitudinous designs, and on, and on, and on, ad infinitum. When I was older, I would make paper cutout designs of flowers, people silhouettes, stars, hearts, words, and whatever else came to mind. At night, before going to bed, I'd wet the paper and stick it to the window. The next morning I'd remove the paper cutouts. The objects, or words, would be clearly defined by the frost around their edges, and I marveled at my creative ability given Jack Frost's help.

Facing east, to the front of the house, there were two large bedrooms. My mom and dad used the one to the north, and my grandma used the one to the south. A brick chimney, built in the center of the house, came up through the bedroom occupied by my parents. The stovepipe from the coal stove in the kitchen connected into the chimney. This was the only source of heat for their room in the winter. Granma's room had the advantage of the stovepipe from the living room heating stove coming up through the floor into her room and connecting through the wall to the brick chimney in my parents' bedroom. She also had the luxury of a large register built into the floor that provided a good source of rising heat from the living room. The room had a southern exposure; consequently, Granma's room remained quite comfortable in the winter. Both of their rooms were sparsely furnished. No closets, only pegs or hooks on the wall for clothing, a dresser, and a chair or two. The rooms were made cheerful by the colorful floral wallpaper that covered the walls, the beige pull-down roller shades at each window, and the white starched curtains. Granma did have a rocking chair in her room, and this was where she spent a lot of her time. After she died, when I was thirteen, my parents let me move into Granma's room.

The black trunk in my parents' room held items of both interest and fascination for me. My dad was a World War I veteran, and his uniform was kept in this trunk, along with other military memorabilia. There were also George and Martha Washington costumes, complete with wigs. Mom and Dad loved to dance. Every Halloween they would dress as George and Martha, attend a local Halloween dance and, without fail, take first prize for the best costume. There were other items of sentimental value in the trunk that I learned about years later—Dad's diaries, Mom's love letters, and pictures, to name a few. By mutual sibling agreement the trunk was an item claimed by my brother, now with my nephew.

My first bedroom, larger than my brother's but much smaller than the two front bedrooms, was located off the south wall of the hall. This was the only room without a door. A heavy curtain suspended on a rod above the opening provided me with semiprivacy. Cut into the ceiling of my room was an access opening to the attic. The sides of the opening were covered with a wood frame. There was also a wood cover that could be pulled over the opening. The only way to get into the attic was to climb the crude wooden ladder leaning against the opening.

I loved my room. It had a southern exposure—sunlight in the winter and a cool southern breeze in the summer. Like all the other bedrooms, mine was sparsely furnished: a single bed, hooks on the wall for my clothes, a small dresser, and a vanity shelf and bench. The vanity and bench were my pride and joy. Dad had fashioned the shelf and built a bench with a storage area underneath. He installed the shelf at sitting height and hung an oval mirror above it. Yellow was my favorite color, and Mom let me select the fabric as well as the wallpaper for my room. Yellow flowers almost danced off the chintz fabric used for the vanity shelf, the bench, and the cushion, as well as the wallpaper that covered the walls. Pull-down roller shades at the windows were for privacy and protection against the summer sun. I did have a small, oval rag rug on the painted floor by my bed. White starched, ruffled tie-back curtains completed my decor selections. I loved to clean my room. My final touch, when seasonal flowers were in bloom (peonies, tulips, red or yellow roses, or lilacs) would be to pick a bouquet of flowers from the garden and place them in a vase on my vanity table.

I always kept all my dolls on my bed. I can't remember the exact number, but somehow in my childish mind I felt I must place all the dolls under the covers with me when I went to bed. Crowded as I was in the single bed, this act was comforting to me. I "knew" my dolls had feelings, and I did not want for any one of them to feel neglected.

There were times I would develop an aggravating cough during the night. It was my dad who would come into my bedroom and give me a spoonful of honey to soothe my throat. The honey, along with Dad's reassuring presence, is a comforting memory of my childhood.

I had little fear of anything lurking in the attic that might harm me. (This may seem strange after expressing my fear of a ghost behind the basement stair, or fear of my shadow from the kerosene lamp as I mounted the stair to the second floor.) It was too cold to enter the attic space in the winter, but when it was warmer, I would freely climb up the wood steps of the ladder and enter this mysterious space that ran the entire length of the house. The attic was an unfinished room with small dirty windows at the north and south ends that emitted a ghostly light. The highest point in the room was at the roof peak, and anyone standing over five feet tall must stoop not to hit their head. Due to the sharp angle of the rafters connecting the peak with the exterior second-floor walls of the house, exploration in the attic for me was limited to two or three feet each side of the centerline. This was a good thing, because spiderwebs hung in abundance from the rafters. Loose boards provided walkways from one end to the other. Crude bookcases were fastened onto each end of the room.

During daylight hours I would prowl this magical space. Mom enjoyed reading, and many of her books were on the shelves. I remember only two of those books. One was *Twenty Thousand Leagues Under the Sea* by Jules Verne. I attempted to read this book, but it held no interest for me. The other book was a first reader. I still have it in my possession.

I do recall that during World War II, when sugar was rationed, Mom and Dad saved enough ration stamps to get their sugar in twenty-five-pound bags and stored it in the dry attic. However, soap in any quantity was impossible to buy. Dad and Mom solved this problem by making their own soap for family bathing and for washing clothes. I don't recall the recipe for making the soap, but I do remember that lye and lard were the principle ingredients. Lye, a very caustic chemical, was available, and Dad supplied the lard by rendering the fat of the slaughtered pig.

The soap was made on the hot coal stove in the kitchen. Lloyd and I were strictly forbidden to be anywhere close during the "cooking" process. When ready, the hot liquid soap mixture was poured into a cardboard box lined with wax paper. Once cooled, Mom would cut the soap into bars. It was then stored in the dry attic alongside the sugar. To this day, I think I would recognize the acrid, pungent smell that was emitted from this strong soap.

The item in the attic that held the greatest fascination for me was stored in a box. It was a long swath of my mother's hair. This hair was different from the hair on my mother's head. It was a deep, rich red, soft to the touch. Mother's hair lacked this luster. I don't know if Mom ever had any awareness of how often I would remove the hair from its protective box and caress it, feeling its warm richness. That swath of Mom's beautiful, youthful hair is gone. I have no idea where, now only a memory to treasure.

If Mom or Dad knew how many hours I spent in the attic, nothing was ever said. Access was so easy from my bedroom. Brushing aside the dust and the spiderwebs, it was a mystic place for quiet contemplation.

———— ·+++++· ————

OUR TEN-ROOM HOUSE was given a thorough cleaning each spring. As soon as the weather was warm enough, before spring planting, Mom would begin the process. Money was scarce, but somehow Mom managed to get enough to buy the needed supplies of paint, wallpaper cleaner, and varnish. The smoke from the kitchen coal stove and the living room heating stove had blackened the ceilings and the sidewalls of each room in the downstairs. These rooms were the first to be attacked by the cleaning squad.

The ceilings in the kitchen, sink room, and pantry were painted white. It was my dad's job to do the overhead work. With water dripping down his arm, he would scrub the soot from the ceilings. When needed, he would give them a fresh coat of white paint. When he painted, it was my job to follow around after him and wipe up the paint drips that fell on the floor. (Dad never did clean a paintbrush properly. The paint would dry at the top of the bristles, allowing any excess paint in the brush to drip.) While the ceilings were being washed, Mom would begin the task of cleaning the sooty wallpaper. I liked helping. Wallpaper cleaner was green and had a delicious smell, making it tempting to eat. (I never did.) When a new can of cleaner was opened, it was necessary to "work" the spongy substance in your hand until it became smooth and would not crumble on the wall. There is a technique to cleaning wallpaper and not leaving any streaks. Mom showed me how to carefully move the ball of cleaner in my hand over the wall so that it lifted the soot from the paper and transferred it to the ball, turning the fresh, green ball black. The walls were very sooty in the kitchen, and I was not able to cover much wall area before the ball became too black to continue using.

Fresh newspapers were used as the shelf paper in the pantry. It was my job to remove all items from the cupboards and shelves and replace the soiled newspapers with fresh ones. I loved this task because it made the shelves look so much neater and cleaner. Inlaid linoleum was too costly, so all that was ever used on our floors was linoleum that had a surface print, and that soon wore off in the heavily trafficked sink room / kitchen / pantry area. When too badly worn, the linoleum would be replaced as cheaply as possible.

Curtains were removed from the windows, repeatedly soaked in a tub of hot, sudsy water until clean, then rinsed and starched. The curtain stretchers were set up out in the yard and the clean, starched curtains attached to the stretchers. Tiny pins lined the frame of a stretcher, and this task required skill not to prick one's fingers and draw blood, staining the clean curtain, while attaching it to the frame.

There were no rugs or carpets on the linoleum floors. During spring cleaning this was a blessing in disguise, because those items needed to be dragged outside, hung over the clothesline, and beaten with a rug beater to dislodge the year's accumulation of dust and dirt. Furniture was moved so that the entire floor could be scrubbed, but there was no overstuffed furniture to clean. The wooden-framed, oilcloth-covered sofa and chair were washed down. Windows were washed inside and out. Doors, woodwork, and cupboards were washed. If the woodwork was too dull, Mom would apply a coat of gloss varnish. I never liked this because it gave the woodwork a shine that, I thought, gave it a cheap look.

The same cleaning procedure took place for the bedrooms. However, these rooms were much easier to clean as the stove soot did not make it to the second floor. All beds were completely stripped, and sheets, blankets, and coverings were washed, and then hung on the clothesline to dry in the warm spring sun.

It took at least three weeks of hard work to clean the house. However, when done, I took great pride in the clean-smelling rooms, sparkling windows, starched white curtains, clean furniture and floors. I had done my share of the hard work.

During spring cleaning, any farmwork that could be put off was delayed. However, it was not possible to delay the routine of farm life for too long. Inevitably, all family members resumed their usual tasks, and the rhythm of daily living was evident, for with it came the return of the dust and grime.

THREE

LIVING ON THE FARM

I N 1893 THE DIVORCE OF ELIZA AND SQUAIR was finalized. Eliza was awarded the farm on Gageville Road where they had raised their family. The other property, located one mile to the south on Maple Road and jointly owned by the couple, was awarded to Squair. The land was undeveloped, and it was here that Squair, at the age of fifty-two, built a house, barn and other outbuildings. The lumber for the buildings came from trees on the property. Squair felled the trees and hauled the wood to the sawmill. At the mill, the logs were cut to building specifications. The wood was aged and used as needed. Baseboards and trim for the interior of the house were custom cut. This was where I grew up.

THE FARM PROVIDED the subsistence for our family. Other than the plot of ground close to Maple Road where all buildings were located, the thirty acres were divided to accommodate pastures for the livestock, fields for crops, an orchard, and two gardens—a kitchen garden and a larger garden for raising vegetables and fruits for canning. All of our food except store-bought staples (flour, sugar, salt) was raised and processed on the farm. Preparation of the soil, planting the crops, caring for the plants, and harvesting was hard, hot, heavy, and backbreaking work. At the time that I grew up there was no mechanized equipment used on the farm. There was a team of horses—Dad, Mom, and at times, Lloyd and I—who did all the work.

A small area by the orchard was devoted to an apiary. The bees provided the family with honey, a taste treat to spread on Mom's homemade bread. My fascination with bees came about due to Mom's "bee hat" and a weird piece of equipment called a smoker. I remember the washed-out brown bee hat with the wide brim. Netting was sewn onto the brim of the hat and when placed on Mom's head fell over her face. For protection from bee stings, the netting could be tightly secured around the neck by pulling a cord that was sewn into the bottom. I played with the hat but was not allowed to mess with the smoker. Mom talked about the queen bee, the swarming, the smoker, but it meant little to me. I only remember that Mom knew when to put on her hat and cover her body as completely as she could in preparation for removing the honeycombs from the beehives. I loved to eat honey in the comb. Chewing the waxy substance released the sweet nectar, and when that was gone, I would continue chewing the beeswax like gum. Our honey had the taste of clover, as that was the predominant source of nectar for the bees.

In the fields, hay, oats, summer wheat, and corn were raised to feed the animals; potatoes were raised for the family. Dad was knowledgeable regarding soil depletion and therefore careful to rotate the crops to preserve the productive capacity of the soil. The manure pile located to the side of the barn, as well as any decaying hay and straw from the previous year's harvest, was returned to the soil and provided nutrients to fertilize the fields.

The orchard had a variety of fruit trees. There were three kinds of apple trees (Golden Delicious, Macintosh, and another red apple whose name I can't recall), a pear tree, and several plum trees. Sweet corn, tomatoes, green onions, peppers, peas, radishes, leaf lettuce, Postlethwaite Wonder green beans (named for the pastor of the small community church who shared the seeds with his parishioners), carrots, rhubarb, and strawberries were grown in the kitchen garden. During the summer there was a constant supply of fresh vegetables and fruits for the table, a welcome taste treat from the jars of canned foods we ate during the winter. The same foods were grown for canning in the larger garden, located behind the barn. In addition, delicious jams and jellies were made from red and black raspberries grown in the garden, elderberries picked in nearby fields, and quince from a quince tree near the house.

Dad loved flowers, and they grew in abundance near the house. Three lilac trees (dark purple, light purple, and white), a snowball bush, trumpet vines with orange flowers, tiger lilies, gladiolas, and tulips lined the gravel drive by the house. One side of the kitchen garden was edged with ant-laden peonies, and yellow and red rose bushes that were grown from seed-lings Dad brought with him from Wisconsin. All flowers, as well as garden plantings, were generously fertilized with manure, giving off an inoffensive barn smell that encircled the house.

Granma had brought a number of maple tree seedlings with her from Iowa. Now full grown, five of these trees lined the front lawn by the road. Four more maple trees provided shade behind our house. I remem-ber Mom and Granma setting up the tin washtubs under the trees in the spring and doing the family wash on a scrub board. In the summer a canvas hammock was strung between the trunks of two of the trees. A heavy rope tied to a large tire was suspended from a high branch on another maple tree, providing Lloyd and me with a swing. Our enjoy-ment of the trees was not limited to lying in a hammock or pumping and swinging as high as the rope allowed. Large lower branches gave us access for climbing, and this we fearlessly did, using our bare feet and toes to grip the trunk as we climbed. Hours were spent aloft sitting in the crotch of a branch, our back to the tree trunk, talking, daydreaming, or reading a book. At times we were daredevils, swinging from branch to branch. When Mom or Dad caught us doing this, we were harshly scolded, advised of the involved risks, and told to "Stop!" Miraculously neither one of us ever fell out of a tree.

The front and side lawn for the house took a half acre. Our "lawn mower" was a cow that Dad pastured in the front yard. Not sure why, with all else we had to deal with, but this became a source of embarrassment to me. I was about twelve years old when I persuaded Dad to get a push lawn mower. Somehow, I got my brother to help me, and together we regularly mowed the half-acre front yard. Using a reel push mower over the uneven ground through tough grass was hard work. We gained a great respect for the cow that we had replaced. Although tempted, we did not relent and ask to have the cow back, now contentedly chewing its cud in the pasture. To me mowing the grass was the better option as I didn't like accidently stepping in a soft cow pie and having it squish between my toes, or having the assigned task of finding and picking them up when dry. I will add that the duck droppings in the barnyard were worse—small, stinky, and every-where! The only solution to that problem was to get rid of the ducks, and that Dad would not do.

Farm animals are a part of farm life. The team of horses, Babe (spir-ited) and Major (slower, the plow horse), was used for the plowing, plant-ing, and harvesting of the crops. There were other times when the snow was deep, and the roads impassable, that Dad would need to take Major to pull a car out of a snow bank or ditch.

At most, there were four hybrid Jersey-Guernsey milk cows in the barn. After the morning milking, Dad would turn the cows out to pasture to graze for the day. Many times it was my job to fetch the cows for the evening milking. Sometimes they were at the barn gate ready to be brought in; other times they would be in the back pasture, about a quarter mile hike away.

I clearly remember one afternoon I was sent to get the cows from the back pasture. Leaving the house, running past the barn through the hay and grain fields, I came to the fenced-in lane leading to the back pasture. I attempted to climb the fence, placing one foot on the barbed wire secured at the fence post. When I lifted my other leg over the fence, the post gave way, throwing me to the ground. As I fell, my left leg was ripped open on the barbed wire. I looked down and saw a long, wide bloody gash on the front of my leg. I was by myself, about one tenth of a mile from the house. In terror, I managed to get myself up and started to limp home. Dad was in the barn and heard my cries. He came running, saw what had happened, picked me up, carried me to the well, and washed my injured leg with the cold water before taking me into the house. Dad had just finished a first aid course and had learned how to use "butterfly" adhesive bandages to bind up a wound. He didn't think it necessary to take me into town to the doctor. Once he had my leg cleaned and observed the gash, he proceeded to close it with the adhesive butterfly strips, all the time reassuring me I would be all right and my leg would heal properly. Well, the leg did heal and there was no infection, but to this day I carry a scar a quarter inch wide and six inches long—a permanent identifiable injury mark. That was the end of my fetching the cows that summer.

Before government restrictions were put in place to control milk production, Dad sold milk to a local creamery. I remember how difficult it was to clean and sterilize the twenty-gallon metal milk cans with boiling water. This was Mom's job, and I did help. The sterilized milk cans were kept in a large, oblong tub in the milk house that was filled with cold water from the well, our only method of refrigeration. After morning and evening milking, Dad would pour the warm milk from his pail into the cans in the milk house. Twice a day he would drain the water from the tub and refill it with cold water, taken from the well located right next to the milk house. Once a week on the scheduled day, in the early hours of the morning, Dad would load the half dozen filled milk cans onto the farm wagon. He'd hitch Babe and Major to the wagon and drive one mile south to the designated pickup point for the local creamery truck. If Dad were late and missed the pickup, the milk had to be dumped. It would not hold for another week.

After Dad got a full-time job at the Electro Metallurgical Company in Ashtabula, he no longer sold milk to the creamery. A cream separator was purchased and used by family members to separate the cream from the milk. The cream was made into butter, with a byproduct of buttermilk, and the skim milk was fed to the pigs. The butter and buttermilk were sold to customers on our egg route in Ashtabula.

It was a mystery to me why Dad would never let me go with him when he took one of the cows up the road to the neighbors. It was years later that I learned he took the cow to a neighboring farm to be bred by the farmer's bull. Dad did not keep a bull on the farm. Any male calf that was born, Dad would castrate and raise the steer to be butchered for our meat supply. I never observed the actual birth of a calf, the piglets, or any other animal on the farm, not even the kittens. Dad and Mom must have thought it in my best interest (possibly because I was a girl) not to be exposed to animals copulating and later giving birth. I've come to realize that I was denied valuable life lessons related to animal reproduction.

Pigs were another barn animal on our farm. Dad was known for the quality of pigs that he raised. He did not believe in pure-bred farm animals, for inbreeding weakened the genetic strain. Pigs are intelligent animals, and Dad had a special sensitivity in caring for his pigs. When a sow is about to farrow, she prepares a nest from the straw in her pen. Dad would be there keeping a close watch. My sister tells me that when Dad died, one of the sows farrowed the next day and unexpectedly killed her litter of piglets. The only explanation Mom could give for the sow's action was that the pig missed Dad's presence at the time that she farrowed.

Also in the barn was a room that housed the young chickens; fryers that were slaughtered, dressed, and sold to Naddra's Market in Ashtabula. Adjacent to the barn was a chicken coop that housed about fifty hens. These were the laying hens that supplied the eggs for our egg route in town. One of my assigned chores was the daily task of gathering the eggs from the wooden boxes built along one side of the coop for chicken nests. Eggs were collected, cleaned, and taken to town on Saturday mornings to be delivered to our customers.

As an adult I have learned how fortunate I was not to have contacted a serious eye condition, ocular histoplasmosis, from being in the chicken coops. The disease is caused by a microscopic fungus released into the air. Years ago, I was told by an ophthalmologist that I had traces of this eye disease. I never knew I had it; my body's immune system must have overcome the infection without treatment. A dear friend of mine was not so fortunate. She contacted the disease, and because of it, she is legally blind.

It was necessary to always keep a population of chickens in the chicken coops. To do this, Dad would periodically purchase one hundred White Plymouth Rock chicks from Pruden's Hatchery outside of Ashtabula. These were dual purpose chickens. When young, they were tasty fryers for eating; when older, they were good laying hens. Dad and Mom would prepare the brooder house for the new arrivals, placing clean straw on the floor, lighting the coal-fed brooder stove to provide the necessary warmth, and carefully checking to be certain the water containers and food troughs were filled.

The day the chicks were scheduled to arrive was a magical day for Lloyd and me. We would position ourselves at the window in my second-floor bedroom. This was the observation point where we could view the gravel road that we knew would be the truck's route to the farm. There was little traffic on rural roads, so as soon as we spied a trail of dust made by a vehicle, we would scamper down to the brooder house yard to be standing there when the truck drove up. Two men would get out and begin to unload the large cardboard boxes containing the chicks. The boxes were taken into the brooder house and carefully placed on the floor. It was then we first heard the peeping of the baby chicks.

It was Mom or Dad who took the lid off each box and lifted the fluffy yellow chicks out, carefully placing them on the floor. I watched, fascinated, as the chicks scurried about on their tiny legs and four-toed feet, exploring their newfound freedom. Lloyd and I were cautioned to carefully handle the tiny chicks. This I did, cupping a little furry body in my hand, stroking its soft yellow fluff with my finger.

My brother was not too interested in the chicks. His attention was given over to the boxes. By the time the chicks were all settled in, he had collected most of the one-inch-round cardboard pieces that were left hanging from the air holes in the boxes. Once the chicks were released, it was not long before they huddled *en masse* under the brooder stove cover for warmth. By then, I had tired of the chicks as well and turned my attention to the boxes. We played in the brooder house for what seemed hours, more interested in the boxes and the cardboard circles than the chicks. The boxes were large, about two feet by two feet by six inches. We would stack them, stand them on edge, and maybe even flatten them out. Then using the one-inch cardboard push-out pieces, we would stack them up, place them in rows, grab a handful to use later for barter, or anything else that came to mind in our make-believe world of play.

We had an egg route on the east side of Ashtabula. To get to the east side one crossed the East Forty-Sixth Street Bridge spanning the Ashtabula gorge. Many Jewish families lived in this area, and they made up most of the twenty customers on our egg route. This was by design. These were still Depression years, and jobs were hard to come by. It was known that Jewish families held together, supporting one another, in good times or bad. Dad knew that his best chance for getting money for his eggs was with the Jewish customers. Some Jewish families also requested live chickens. Orthodox Jews would eat only kosher meat, and this required that the animal be slaughtered by the rabbi, or shochet, according to Jewish law.

For years I tagged along with Dad or Mom on Saturday mornings. There were times my brother would take over the egg route. One time he reported to Dad that a lady on the route complained every week that one of the eggs had a blood spot in it and requested that the egg be replaced. Lloyd asked Dad's advice how to handle the situation. Dad told Lloyd to tell her to keep the raw, blood-spotted egg as evidence. After that, Lloyd never had to replace an egg.

Later when I had my driver's license, I took care of the egg route myself. I never liked doing it. Somehow I felt inferior to those "city folk." By city standards, I was shabbily dressed, the car I drove was dilapidated and old, and I lacked good communication skills—tongue-tied some might say. I'd walk up onto the porch of a house and ring the bell. When someone came to the door, I'd ask, "How many eggs today?" I'd count out the requested number of eggs into the container provided, quickly take the money, and hastily retreat to the car and on to the next customer. Years later, my oldest son found a greeting card that read, "Don't I know you? Didn't you have an egg route in Ashtabula, Ohio?" Yes, I did—much to my mortification.

We always had at least two barn cats and Teddy, our collie dog. I can't remember the names of any of our cats. I played with them on occasion and was thrilled with their litters of kittens—so tiny, eyes shut at birth, soft to the touch. Then one day the kittens would be gone, and the mother cat would be giving out the most pitiful cries. Mom told me that Dad had gotten rid of the kittens. We couldn't have the farm overrun with cats. Harsh as it might seem to some, it was another reality of farm life.

Lloyd and I both loved our dog, Teddy, but I think Lloyd loved Teddy the most. After all, I had my dolls. Teddy was an outside dog, living in the animal warmth of the barn in the winter. It was only after Teddy became old and feeble that Mom allowed him in the house. One day Teddy was not there. Later I learned that Teddy died a natural death, and Dad buried him under a large rosebush located off the southwest corner of our house. Teddy was given all the respect due to a loyal four-legged family member.

THERE WERE OTHER OUTBUILDINGS on the farm—granary, toolsheds, large garage built to house the school bus, and an outhouse. With no indoor plumbing, the "necessary" building was strategically placed a distance from the well used for our drinking water, but close enough to the house for convenience. Some farm outhouses were built of brick. When a farmer would refer to a stout woman, you'd hear him say, "She is built like a brick shithouse." It was the men who would use this despicable phrase, never the women. If Lloyd or I got caught saying it, Mom or Dad would make it clear this was a saying of disrespect and to never utter the words again. Seemed to me this was a double standard, but who was I to question?

Anyway, our outhouse was made of wood, and it had a board seat with three holes in it—two large and one small. Generally, farm families were large, and outhouses were built to accommodate family needs. Our outhouse was supplied with newspapers and an old Sears and Roebuck Catalogue. Commercial toilet paper was unheard of, so the newspaper and catalogue pages were crinkled to soften for use on sensitive butts. When the Sears and Roebuck catalogue first appeared in the outhouse, the middle tissue-paper-thin pages were quickly used up. I know I never used the outhouse when anyone else was in it. I can't speak for the other members of the family. Our small family did not require the "three-holer."

ASHTABULA WAS THE FAMILY'S SHOPPING, purchasing, selling, employment, and recreational destination. The city is located seven miles to the north of our farm. Ashtabula means "river of many fish," named by the Delaware Indians (Lenape). The city is a port on Lake Erie where coal and ore are brought down by freighters from the Mesabi Range in Minnesota, then transported by railcar to inland steel plants further south.

When I was a child, Ashtabula was a multiethnic city. Proximity to water is what brought the Finns and the Swedes to the area. Construction of the railroads brought the Italians. There were other European ethnic peoples in the city, but not as prominent as the three previously mentioned. The once prosperous city, with a thriving industrial base, has faced hard times. Today industry is almost nonexistent, and the thriving city with a population at one time about twenty-five thousand is now under twenty thousand, with 60 percent of its population on some type of government subsidy.

During my growing-up years Ashtabula was a bustling city. North Park anchored the north end of Main Street. On streets surrounding North Park were the First Baptist Church, a medical building, a pharmacy, the police station with jail, and the Ashtabula Post Office. The commercial area of Main Street was anchored on the south by South Park. St. Peter's Episcopal Church was located there, as well as private homes, and a few small businesses on the streets surrounding the park. Stores of all types lined the two-and-a-half blocks of Main Street between the two parks—Naddra's Grocery, Candyland, Carlisle's Department Store, Sugar Bowl, Montgomery Ward, Sears and Roebuck, Mabelle's, Hotel Ashtabula, Warren Hotel, Palace Theater, Roller's Shoe Store, Neisner's and Woolworth's five-and-dime stores, Penny's, as well as ladies' dress and hat shops.

There was an incident that happened in a store on Main Street that remains with me to this day. It had to do with my sensitivity to criticism and feelings of inferiority. Lloyd was old enough to drive, and I was with him one Saturday morning when we went into town to take care of the family errands. Mom had given us a shopping list and several of the items needed to be purchased in Carlisle's Department store. There was an elevator that traversed the five floors in the store with a female attendant. She stood by the control lever and stopped at whatever floor was requested by the occupants. Lloyd and I were having great fun riding the elevator from floor to floor in search of the items on our list. After we had entered and exited the elevator a few times, the operator berated us with the question, "Are you kids just riding this elevator for fun?" Well, yes, and no! We were having fun doing our shopping while riding the elevator. However, her stern voice did take the pleasure out of our adventure, and we hurriedly purchased what was needed and left the store.

WITHIN A HALF MILE OF OUR FARM lived several families with children near the age of Lloyd and me. The Fischer and Nemitz families each had five children—four boys and one girl. The Van Slyke family had five girls. The Fields family had two girls. Most of the girls in the neighborhood were either too young or too old for me. Joy Fields was the only girl near my age that I had for a playmate. Much to my brother's displeasure, I was always joining the boys. Yes, I was a tomboy!

———— ++++++ ————

THE SEASONS PROVIDED A YEARLY RHYTHM of farm activities: spring was planting, summer and fall were harvesting, and winter was for repairing, recovering, and just existing. Lloyd and I were expected to do our share. We were assigned chores appropriate to our age. However, there was always enough time for play.

The Fischer farm was contiguous to our property to the north. Their woods held a fascination for me. In the spring, as soon as the weather moderated to where the temperature was below freezing at night but above freezing during the day, I knew it was maple syrup time. The Fischer men would tap the maple trees in their woods. The sap flowed into the metal buckets and, when full, was collected and transported to the sugar bush.

The sugar bush was a tin-roof shed with a door, and openings for windows. I only remember the huge, black stove that was used to boil the sap down to a syrupy consistency—that mouthwatering, sweet, golden liquid that people pour over their pancakes. Boil the sap down more, and the result is maple sugar candy. A piece of the candy was what I hoped to get if I were fortunate enough to be at the door of the sugar bush shack at the right time. More often than not, I was disappointed. Given that the men were busy making the syrup and candy, they would ignore me and let me stand there, with mouth watering, too shy to speak.

Later in the spring, after the snow melted and the frost left the ground, I would walk through our dandelion- and thistle-infested front yard to trudge the tenth of a mile down the gravel road to enter the woods again. This time my mission was in search of wildflowers. Immediately upon entering the woods, I sensed a dank, rotting odor from the decaying leaves that covered the wet ground. At first the darkness and stillness of the woods frightened me. As soon as my eyes adjusted to the shaded light, I heard the sound of birds singing and a woodpecker at work on a tree. My uneasiness lessened as I walked a short distance into the trees. Mom had cautioned me to always be sure I could see the outline of the edge of the woods. This would keep me from wandering in too far and losing my sense of direction. As I walked along, the umbrella plants caressed my ankles—the name I gave the plant with the large, dark-green leaf shaped like an umbrella. They were everywhere. Trilliums were in abundance, and I would pick a bouquet for our kitchen table. If I were lucky, I would spy a jack-in-the-pulpit to add to my bouquet. There were not many of these flowers in the woods, and to find one was a rare prize. Today wildflowers are under the aegis of the Environmental Protection Agency—enjoy their beauty, but do not disturb!

Following the sugar bush visits of late winter, and the flower picking adventure of spring, my next planned trek down the gravel road to the Fischer woods was to pick the wild strawberries that ripened in June. There was a steep embankment on one side of the road before entering the woods. This was where the wild strawberries grew. Anyone having tasted the sweetness of the wild berry knows there is no comparison in taste to the cultivated tame strawberries grown commercially.

One year, when I was about six years old, I planted myself on the side of the hill and proceeded to pick the sweet tiny, red berries, popping one or two in my mouth to every one I dropped in the berry basket. Then it happened—I did not see the small, brown-and-yellow garter snake eating the berry that I was reaching to pick. I screamed and bolted from the hillside faster than a lightning strike, never again to return to pick wild strawberries on the hillside. One thing Mom had done, due to her fear of snakes, was to instill in me a horror of them, even the tiny garter snake so beneficial to the farmer.

When the maple trees were leafing out, the danger of frost past, Dad would spread the manure, then plow, disk, and/or harrow the ground in preparation for the spring planting. The earth for the gardens was refined the most. This made for easier planting of the seeds, bulbs, and tender young plants.

Lloyd and I were expected to help. Mom would mark the rows in the kitchen garden with stakes and string. We planted seeds for cucumbers, peas, melons, beans, corn, lettuce, turnips; placed the small onion bulbs for green onions; tenderly laid out the tomato and pepper plants in the dug trenches, fertilizing everything with manure. There probably were more things we planted, but I don't recall.

When Lloyd and I were no longer needed, we gave our attention to the rhubarb patch. While helping Mom, we noted this delicious plant was ready for eating. One of us would run into the house, grab the sugar bowl from the kitchen pantry, return to the garden, and we'd both plop ourselves down in the middle of the rhubarb patch. In turn, we'd break off a piece of rhubarb, dip it in the sugar bowl, and eat it raw. Tart, raw rhubarb, sweetened with sugar—it was a spring taste treat given us by the gods, and I can't remember ever getting a bellyache from the eating of it.

Through the spring, we did help Mom with weeding the garden. One day I was busy hoeing the corn and the beans, when out of the corner of my eye I saw my brother coming at us with something dangling from the end of the pitchfork he was carrying. It was a dead (I think) snake! Mom and I both screamed and ran. Lloyd laughed, thinking it was a good prank. He knew Mom was afraid of snakes. My brother didn't pull pranks very often, and I can't remember that Lloyd got paddled that time, but there was a time I do remember he got a good back/butt-slapping paddling.

It was a Saturday night. Pruden's Hatchery had made a delivery of baby chicks late that afternoon. Dad was out in the fields, and Mom took over looking after the chicks in the brooder house. Lloyd and I delighted in the arrival of the chicks, so we were there with Mom. It was bath night. Dad came in from the fields and filled the tin bathtub with hot water for our baths. We were summoned to the house, and Dad returned to the barn to do the evening's chores. As we left to go in to take our baths, we unwittingly locked the brooder house door with Mom still inside. Lloyd and I were in the kitchen dutifully taking our baths. I was first and finished, but Lloyd was in the tub when Mom, face red, hair more disheveled than usual, came stomping into the kitchen and started to pound on my brother's back and butt. I screamed for her to stop, not knowing what had caused this outbreak of anger, for Mom never laid a hand on us. Mom wailed that we had intentionally locked her in the hot brooder house, and after much pounding on the door, she had finally been able to break the lock and get out.

We were innocent of the accused action, but nothing I said satisfied her. Lloyd, hurting and speechless, cried and said nothing. This could have been an incident that caused my brother to feel I was favored over him, and in this incident I was, because Mom never touched me. However, this behavior of my mother was atypical. She was a sacrificing, loving, caring woman. I can only believe that she was tired to the point of exhaustion and this outburst was a release. What a night!

In the spring of my fifth birthday, Dad planted a willow tree in the side front yard. I have a picture of me on my tricycle and my brother on his bicycle by this twig of a tree.

Over the years the tap root of the tree reached out to the water supply in the well about twenty feet away, providing the needed water to grow to about thirty feet tall. Growing up, I became very attached to the tree, often referring to it as "my tree." I loved playing under the willow branches that drooped to the ground forming a magical room beneath. After I moved away, the tree was hit by lightning and half of it destroyed. It was not long after that the owners of the farm removed my willow tree. It stands there no more.

I don't know how Dad ever found the time, but one spring he built me a playhouse. It was a structure that measured about twelve feet by twelve feet, and it was built out of red boxcar doors. It had two front picture windows, a front door, and a porch. The interior was one large room with a loft on one side. I remember Mom asked me to choose some wallpaper for the interior. I chose something with yellow flowers in the design. Yellow was my favorite color when I was a child. Once Mom had the walls of the playhouse wallpapered, it had a wondrously homey feeling.

In warm weather, I spent hours and hours of solitary play there. I played school with my dolls; I would spend hours reading out loud to them, or silently to myself; I would pretend to cook in my kitchen; or do whatever else I fancied. On rare occasions, my neighborhood girlfriend, Joy Fields, would come over to play. It was double the fun when I had someone to share the joys of my playhouse with me. Playhouses were for girls, and Lloyd had no interest in playing there. Years later I learned Lloyd was very resentful that Dad built this for me. Lloyd had yet another item to place in his store of resentments that Dad favored me over him.

The clothesline in our front yard was there all year round. In the winter it had minimal use, but in the spring it was filled every Monday with clothes from the week's wash hung out to dry. Mom did follow the "rules" of the clothesline:

- Clean the clothesline before hanging any clothes (ours was a heavy rust-resistant wire).
- White clothes were hung first and like clothes hung with like clothes (organization was a worthy value).
- Hang a shirt by its tail, never the shoulders (no visible marks).

- Hang "unmentionables" inside of the folded sheet (modesty, you know).
- Hang clothes in subzero weather; they will "freeze-dry" (so do fingers).
- When taking down clothes, never leave clothes pins on the line (tacky).
- Due to clothesline space and required clothespins, always hang clothes so that two pins were not needed for each item, but one pin shared with the next clothing item (lesson in frugality).

I am in love with my clothesline. I have had a clothesline in every home where I have lived, even the condo where I ignored the rule of "no clotheslines" and used our large deck. Recently I bought a new washer and dryer, and my daughter-in-law chided me, saying, "Henri, I can't understand why you bought a new dryer, you never use it." She got no argument from me; it is just the thing to do when you are buying a new washer.

In late spring, before the hay, oats, and wheat were tall enough to hide the wild mustard that grew in the fields, it was Lloyd's and my job to walk the acreage and pull out all the yellow mustard plants that we could find. Too much of this weed would sicken the animals. Lloyd and I liked to perform this chore. Dad paid us a penny for every plant that we pulled up with the roots intact; otherwise, the invasive plant would grow back. We would wait until after a soaking rain and then walk the fields, carefully looking for the penny prize. One hundred plants with roots meant $1—big money for Lloyd and me. There were thistles in the fields, but Dad took care of those prickly weeds himself. Due to our diligence each spring in pulling out the wild mustard, and Dad destroying the thistles, the fields of hay, oats, and wheat were (almost) weed-free. However, it was a never-ending battle because the neighbor to the south, whose fields bordered on our farm, was negligent in weeding his hay and grain fields. The southern breezes and the birds managed to keep planting weed seeds in our fields.

As Lloyd and I grew older, the work required of us became more strenuous. The fields were fertilized, plowed, disked, harrowed, and planted with our team of horses, Babe and Major, pulling the equipment. At times it was necessary for either Lloyd or me to drive the team, and Dad would operate the piece of equipment. This was critical at potato planting time. I was the one who helped Mom prepare the seed potatoes for planting that had been saved from last season's harvest. The whole potato needed to be cut into pieces with each piece having an "eye." This is a brown nub on the potato that will take root once underground. Dad had a single-row potato planter with a seat. Someone had to sit on the seat of the planter and keep placing pieces of potato in a funnel-like structure that would drop the potato into the ground. Then the wedge-shaped metal piece that trailed behind the funnel covered them up. Dropping the potato into the funnel required a careful rhythm to ensure even spacing of the plants. When Lloyd was old enough, this job was assigned to him, and later to me.

It was Dad who tended the potato patch during the growing season and used a cultivator to control the weeds. However, in the fall when the potatoes were ready to be dug up, it was both Lloyd and me who followed behind the potato digger and picked up the potatoes—backbreaking work!

Each spring after I was old enough to drive (Dad was then working full time in a factory), I went to the Dorset livestock auction to bid on a calf. The calf would be fattened and, come winter, slaughtered. This provided the family with a meat supply for the year. We had no refrigeration, so the meat was cut in small pieces and canned.

Attending the livestock auction was a mortifying assignment for me. Farmers brought their livestock to the auction to be sold. The barn smells of manure and musty smell of animal heat did not bother me—I was used to it. However, I did find the auction itself to be quite intimidating. Bleachers were built around three sides of a small, circular fenced-in area. Farmers interested in bidding sat on the bleachers. Few, if any, women were ever in attendance. The livestock were brought into the arena, and the auctioneer started the bidding. Usually the calves were the last to be sold in the afternoon. I would take a seat on a bleacher in the arena. My body felt the oppressive heat in the building, and my nose crinkled from the stink of the farmers seated around me. The entire situation was most unpleasant, but I knew I had to endure. Dad had carefully instructed me as to the size of the calf, as well as the highest amount I could bid. By the time the calves were brought out, my ear had become accustomed to the rapid-fire chattering of the auctioneer. I also learned, early on, to shoot up my hand when I wanted to place a bid. Best I can remember, the years I went to the auction I was always successful in getting a calf and making the necessary arrangements for it to be trucked to our farm. I clearly recall a great feeling of relief when my calf-purchasing mission was accomplished and I left the auction grounds to drive home.

・・◆◆◆◆・・

SPRING WOULD BECOME SUMMER, and with it the harvesting of crops. Hay was the first field crop to be harvested, followed by oats or wheat. Dad did the field work related to the mowing and windrowing for drying. Haying was a family operation—Dad, Mom, Lloyd, me, and a hired hand. Dad hitched the team of horses to the wagon and, with Mom and the hired hand, drove to the hayfield where he had previously raked the windrows into mounds of hay. As Mom slowly drove the team between the rows of hay mounds, the hired hand would pitch a mound onto the wagon, where Dad carefully placed it. Placement of the hay on the wagon was critical for two reasons. First, it meant that the hay load would stay in place on the rough ride back to the barn, and second, it ensured that when setting the hayfork, it would lift a full fork load of hay off the wagon and into the hayloft.

On the north and south sides of the barn, huge doors on the second floor were opened. The hayfork, attached with rope to a track that ran the length of the peak of the barn, was lowered. On the south side, a pulley was secured to a large tree by the milk house. The rope ran through the pulley and was attached to the whiffletree on the harness of Major, our plow horse. Lloyd and I were responsible for two important jobs. The first was to lead Major out the required distance to pull the loaded hayfork into the barn; the second was to pull the rope back through the pulley in preparation for the next run.

Dad would set the fork in the hay and then yell, "Pull away." I led Major out, carefully listening for the hired man's shout from the hayloft—"Stop!" Dad tripped the hayfork, and his command of "All clear" meant I could turn Major around and head back to the starting point. Lloyd's job was to pull the rope back through the pulley. This gave Dad the rope needed to operate the hayfork, and the process was repeated until the wagon was empty. Then it was back to the hayfield for the next load. In the blistering sun and heat of summer, haying season held no equal in hard work.

One day Lloyd was too quick to grab the rope as I turned Major, and his hand was yanked into the pulley. Lloyd screamed in pain! I stopped Major. Both Mom and Dad came running and taking one look at Lloyd's injured hand. Dad immediately got the car then remained behind to tend to Major. Mom grabbed Lloyd, along with me, got behind the wheel, and drove as fast as the washboard and rough brick road would allow into Ashtabula and Doc Graves's office. Doc Graves saw Lloyd immediately. Miraculously the tendons in his hand were not injured. The hand was bandaged, and the severe rope burn healed, leaving only scars as a reminder.

A year later, when I was about ten years of age, I was in charge of the rope at the pulley. I made the same mistake injuring my left hand. This time it was I, with Lloyd in tow, when Mom frantically drove into Ashtabula. I remember her driving down Main Street, blowing the car horn all the way, until we reached the doctor's office. My injury was not as severe as my brother's, but to this day there is a slight residual evidence of my rope burn accident.

There were two fields used for growing grains. I don't remember if Dad grew both oats and wheat every season, alternating the fields, or if he grew one grain, then the other grain, alternating the years. Suffice to say that when the annual harvesttime for the wheat or the oats came around, it was hard, hot work for the farmers and their wives, but mostly fun for the children.

My earliest memories of threshing were when Dad would cut the wheat with a handheld scythe, swinging it rhythmically as he mowed a wide swath down the field of grain. Once cut, the grain would be raked into windrows, dried, and then tied into bundles. The bundles were stood tepee-style to avoid being soaked by the rain. Later the grain was brought by wagon to the barnyard, where Dad had fashioned a makeshift wooden threshing floor. Placing the grain on the wooden platform, Dad would use a flail to separate the edible grain from the inedible chaff. The final step before taking the grain to be stored in the granary was to toss it in the air, winnowing it to separate out the chaff. Like haying, this too, was hot, hard work. I remember taking water to Dad as he labored under the hot sun in the fields, or when wielding the flail in the barnyard. Early in the 1990s, while on a bicycle tour in China, I observed the Chinese using this method of threshing in one of the communes that we visited.

The excitement of the grain harvest came with the threshing machine. By the time I was about six years of age, Dad had a horse-drawn binder that cut the grain and fed it onto a conveyor belt that spewed it out in tied bundles. Mom, Lloyd, and I had the job of following the binder, collecting the grain bundles, and placing the bundles in grain tepees called shocks. This was done in preparation for threshing day.

Only farmers with large acreage could afford their own threshing machine. Part of their farm income came from contracting out the machine to farmers who had only a small amount of grain to be threshed. Threshing was weather-dependent. Grain was ripe and cut at the end of July, beginning of August. Hopefully, there was a dry spell at this time because any rain would delay the cutting of the grain. Once the grain was cut and shocked, it was necessary that it remain dry for the threshing. If it got wet, Dad had to wait for nature to dry it out again.

Farmers seemed to have a sixth sense regarding forecasting of the weather. My dad was no exception. All area farmers needed the threshing machine at the same time, and Dad knew his small farm would be allowed only one day. Aware of the time constraint and the labor intensity of threshing, once Dad knew his assigned day, he would contact neighboring farmers, and as many as could would come to help. When it was the neighbor's day to have the threshing machine at their farm, Dad would be there to help them in return.

Early in the morning of threshing day, as soon as the dew was off the fields, the road in front of our house would be filled with four to six teams of horses, driven by area farmers, pulling flat-bed wagons up our drive and into the field where the shocked grain was standing. Some of the farmers brought their wives to help Mom prepare the noon meal. Much to my delight some of the children came as well—that meant fun for me.

Just as the first load of grain was brought into the barnyard, the roar of a tractor pulling the threshing machine was heard. Once set up for operation, this mechanical wonder—with its large belt wheel, blowers, conveyor system, and pipes—would separate the edible grain from the inedible husks and straw. One large pipe deposited the grain into a sack carefully held by one of the men, while the other large pipe belched the chaff and straw onto the ground, forming a straw mountain by the end of the day.

We kids did not tarry long by the thresher; it was dangerous to get too close. If we did, one of the workers was sure to swear at us to get the hell out of the way. Off we would run, as many as ten of us, to the orchard. I remember that the Golden Delicious apples were ripe at this time of year. We kids would climb that apple tree and eat the delicious tree-ripened fruit with the juice running out of our mouths and over our chins, turning faces and hands into a sticky mess. Bellies full, we'd look for other adventures.

The hayloft in the barn held a great fascination for all. We'd climb the inside barn steps to the second floor and gambol in the hay, inhaling its sweet but otherwise-indescribable scent. We'd jump from the large exposed wooden beams, the daring kids turning summersaults on their way down. We'd play hide-and-seek, covering ourselves with mounds of hay. One of the taller boys would climb onto a third-tier loft and reach the rope dangling from the hayfork. This gave us the opportunity to sit on the hayfork's cross bar and be pulled back and forth across the length of the barn. Somehow, no arms or legs were ever broken, and no one ever smothered under the hay. It is true that a guardian angel looks after children.

After a couple of hours in the hayloft, we kids would get tired and hungry. We welcomed the musical sound of the dinner bell summoning the men for their noon meal. This meant that we would soon be eating as well. The men came in from the barnyard and the fields, their faces inflamed from the sun, shirts and overalls soaked with sweat, red handkerchiefs tied around their necks. (The handkerchiefs were used to cover their noses and mouths to keep from inhaling the chaff and dirt kicked up by the threshing.) Cold tubs of water and rough towels set out under the maple trees beckoned them to wash up. They eagerly found a place on one of the benches at the long table that had been set up under the trees and helped themselves to my mother's famous chicken and dumplings, mounds of mashed potatoes with gravy, fresh green beans, leaf lettuce flavored with vinegar and sugar, home baked white bread, fresh churned butter, cold water from the well, and milk from the milk house. Rhubarb or apple pies were in abundance. The men ate their fill before us kids were allowed at the table. Once the men had eaten, they all found a place in the shade by the trunk of a maple tree and leaned back for a half hour's nap. When the call was given to return to the barnyard and fields, the men wearily got up, slowly limping back to their assigned jobs and the hard labor of the threshing.

For the kids, the fun and games of the morning had worn us out as well. After we ate, some of the kids walked back to their farms. Those that stayed settled down in the backyard, content to play on the swing or lie in the hammock. The women were the last to eat. Tired as they were, they got up and cleared the table of the dirty dishes and the leftover food. Mom brought out two large dishpans for washing the dishes. One was filled with hot soapy water, the other with hot clear water. Several women busied themselves with the washing, rinsing, and drying of the piles of plates, cups, and silverware before attacking the stacks of cooking pots and pans. Preparing food over a hot stove, on a hot day, was exhausting for them as well. When the cleanup work was done, a few of the women who lived close walked home. Those who lived a distance away sat down under the maple trees, napping or visiting, waiting for their husbands to come in from the fields. The men worked until the job was done, knowing more work awaited them when they returned to their own farms to do the evening chores.

I know Dad and Mom gave thanks when the weather cooperated and the threshing went as planned. Should it rain, and the grain got wet, the situation had to be dealt with as best it could. I loved threshing day: the excitement, the fun playing with the neighborhood kids. Best of all—I didn't have to do any of the work!

Threshing usually took place the last week of July. Come the first week of August, it was time for the Ashtabula County Fair. This annual event took place (and still does) at the fairgrounds in Jefferson, the county seat, located about ten miles to the south of our farm.

The county fair in August was every bit as exciting for me as Christmas in December. Mom and Dad always made sure that Lloyd and I had a full day to spend at the fair. The night before we were to leave, my excitement was so great I couldn't sleep. I remember one year the morning of fair day passed so slowly that I occupied myself by taking some of my toys into the granary, sitting in a bin of newly threshed grain, and amusing myself as best I could until time to leave. Mom would be busy preparing a picnic lunch of fried chicken, potato salad, homemade apple pie, and lemonade. Sometime around the middle of the morning, Dad would summon Lloyd and me and, with Granma, off the family went to the fair.

Once we were on the fairgrounds, we split up until time for lunch. I don't recall what Lloyd did. I know Dad headed to the animal barns. I dutifully trotted along with Mom and Granma to the exhibit buildings that showcased the bounties of the harvest and the needlecraft skills of the women. Truthfully, these were of little interest to me. I wanted to get to the fairway to see what freak shows were there, maybe buy some cotton candy or an elephant ear, but most of all to ride the merry-go-round.

Mom gave Lloyd and me each one dollar to spend. Most of my money would be spent riding the painted galloping horses on the merry-go-round. I loved everything about the merry-go-round—the music, the brass ring, the painted animals. I would not ride an animal that didn't gallop. They were too tame for my imagination.

Usually Granma would tire early and find a place in the shade to rest, but Mom stayed with me while I explored the midway. We would stand and watch some of the barkers advertising the freak shows, like the one where a woman handled snakes or the one featuring humans of grotesque proportions. However, I never spent any of my precious dollar on a side-show ticket. Finally! We'd get to the end of the midway where the rides were located.

I bypassed the Ferris wheel and the rides that whirled you about because they made me sick. The merry-go-round was usually located across from the first aid building. That was where Mom, now exhausted, would find a seat next to Granma on the shaded porch. They rested there watching me as I bought one ticket after another to ride again and again. This went on until Dad and Lloyd showed up and it was time to leave.

My most vivid memory of the merry-go-round was the year I lost my ride ticket. I'd spent my dollar and begged Mom for just one more ride before we left. She dug in her purse, found a nickel, and handed it to me, telling me that was the last of her money. I skipped over to the ticket seller and got my ticket. As I hurriedly stepped onto the platform of the carousel and started to mount my favorite galloping horse, I dropped my ticket, and it fell between the boards of the platform onto the ground beneath. There was no way I could reach it. The merry-go-round slowly started. The attendant was there wanting my ticket, and when I told him what had happened, he made me get off. I tearfully ran to Mom who was waiting for me on the porch of the first aid building. There was nothing she could do. Her money was gone. I was heartbroken. Mom took my small hand, and together we walked back to our car and went home.

Another anticipated event of the summer was our trip to beautiful Lake Shore Park. These once-a-month trips during June, July, and August required a sacrifice of time and effort for Mom. By the time I was about ten, Dad had a job at the Electro Metallurgical Company plant, ten miles from our home. The plant was located on Lake Erie near Lake Shore Park. We only had one car, and Dad had to be at work by 7:00 a.m. Mom would get up early, drive Dad to work, return home, pack a picnic lunch for the four of us (Granma joined us while she was living), and retrace the route back to Lake Shore Park.

Once at the park, Lloyd and I would spend the afternoon playing hide-and-seek in the rock garden, feeding stale bread to the ducks in the pond, but best of all—swimming in the lake. With its sand beaches, the lake was a delightful swimming experience when compared to the swimming hole in the creek near our farm with its rocky bank and critters that crept and crawled. By three o'clock in the afternoon, Lloyd and I were exhausted, and Mom helped us collect our belongings. Returning to our car, she drove the short distance to the plant where Dad worked, and we would be there to greet him when the shift-end whistle blew at three thirty. A hard day's work for Dad in the plant, as well as for Mom who did all the preparation on top of the driving, but pure bliss for Lloyd and me.

During the long daylight hours of summer days, with no school, there were many hours to be filled. For the most part I entertained myself. The entire family looked forward to the daily mail delivery that came out of the Jefferson Post Office, especially Dad and Mom who were avid readers of two daily papers, the *Ashtabula Star Beacon* and *The Cleveland Plain Dealer.* (In rural areas newspapers were sent through the post office.) Mail delivery was not made in front of our house. Our mailbox, with two others, was placed at the intersection of Sheffield-Gageville and Maple Roads, one tenth of a mile to the south of our home. Mail was usually delivered around noon. With nothing else to occupy my time many days, I would walk the dusty gravel road up a slight hill and position myself on the bank under a tree behind the mailboxes to wait for the mailman. Looking a mile to the west, I would first spy the mailman's car by the trail of dust on Benetka Road. I liked greeting the mailman, who called me by name. We didn't get a lot of personal mail but the newspapers, and monthly *Saturday Evening Post*, were welcome reading at the end of a hard workday.

Another activity that would occupy me during those lazy days of summer was visiting the "stink factory" located about a mile to the south on Sheffield-Gageville Road. Dead horses were processed at this plant, obtaining collagen that is used in making glue. The farmland on which the plant was located was owned by a man named Holden and accounted for the name Holden Rendering Works. The stink of the plant explains why it was located far from any homes in the area. On days when I had nothing else to do, I would run across the fields to visit my friend, Joe, who worked there. I would still be a distance from the plant when the odor first stung my nostrils. By the time I reached my destination, my nose must have become accustomed to the stink because it no longer bothered me.

As I approached the plant, I called out a greeting to Joe, and he would appear at the door always expressing pleasure that I came for a visit. I was someone to break the monotony of his existence. Joe and I would sit together, chatting for an hour or so, and then I'd head back to my house. Thinking back, anyone who held this job might have been a social pariah—perhaps due to the stink that permeated the clothes and the skin, or the lower social status given to anyone working in such a place. Mom must have thought it safe for me to visit Joe, for she always gave her permission. In today's world, this would be unheard of with child molestations, kidnappings, and drugs so prevalent in our society.

There were several boys in the neighborhood that my brother played with from the Nemitz and Fischer families. Due to the fact that there were few girls for me to play with, I hung around a lot with my brother. Consequently, I became quite a tomboy. However, one girl I played with was Joy Fields. I liked going up to Joy's house. We'd play a game called "Andy-Andy-Eye-Over," also known as "Annie-Annie-Eye-Over." All that was needed was a softball and a building. The ball was easy to come by, and there was an ideal building about fourteen by ten by twelve feet, with a peaked roof, located close to Joy's house on the grass-free, hard-packed earth of the barnyard. Actually this is a group-tag game, but there were only two of us to play, so Joy and I made up our own rules. Somehow we decided between us who would be the "thrower," and that left the other one of us to be "it." We'd both stand on the same side of the building. Given that I was the thrower, I'd take the ball, toss it over the roof while hollering "Andy-Andy-eye-over," and we'd take off in opposite directions running around the building to be the first on the other side to catch the ball as it rolled over and off of the roof. I was taller than Joy, had longer legs, was the faster runner, and frequently caught the ball before Joy. On occasion, Joy would catch the ball before me, and when this happened, she would get to be the thrower and I was the it person. We enjoyed playing this game until either a collision, exhaustion, or poor sportsmanship ended our play for that day.

Another game Joy and I would play, and sing, was "Roll Out the Barrel." We'd place a wooden barrel on its side and then test our balancing and mobility skills by climbing atop the barrel. We'd rise to a standing position and roll the barrel with our feet until gravity and/or our clumsiness took us down.

My enjoyment of going to Joy's house ended one day when I was in the kitchen and Joy's dad, Bill, was there seated at the kitchen table. He grabbed me, sat me on his lap, and then rubbed his whiskered face against my soft skin. He laughed in glee, and the louder I protested, the harder he rubbed. He frightened me. I don't remember returning to Joy's home to play with her after that, although she occasionally came to visit and we would play together in my playhouse. I returned to being a tomboy, playing with my brother and his friends.

When I was about ten years old, I was strong enough to ride my bicycle with my brother on the seven-mile trip over washboard gravel and rough brick roads into Ashtabula to attend the Sunday matinee at Shea Theater. Riding in was fun. I would anticipate seeing the movie and our ice cream treat at Isaly's Dairy before the ride back home. I think the cost of the movie ticket was ten cents for me and fifteen cents for Lloyd. My brother was in charge of the money. One Sunday Lloyd would be given thirty-five cents to pay for our movie tickets and enough-for-two five-cent, hand-packed "skyscraper" ice cream cones. The following Sunday, Lloyd was given forty-five cents to cover the cost of our movie tickets and enough-for-two ten-cent soda treats that we would enjoy while sitting in an Isaly's store booth before starting our trek back home. With limited family funds for entertainment, the amount Mom set aside for us each week was a size-able amount. That explains why she had us alternate each week between the skyscraper cones and the ice cream sodas.

One Sunday the lady in the ticket booth questioned my age. I was under twelve and eligible for the children's rate. I know I was tall, and I wasn't skinny or fat; I was healthy-looking. The term "corn-fed," a descrip-tive phrase used by farm folk, aptly described my appearance. Lloyd tried to convince her that I was telling the truth. She indifferently responded, "Bring your birth certificate the next time you come." The next Sunday I did appear with my birth certificate, proving my age, but no apology came from the lips of this haughty ticket seller.

Riding my balloon-tire bike the seven miles into Ashtabula was tiring for my young legs. I could do it because the most difficult mile over the gravel road was at the beginning of our ride. On the return trip, the reverse was true. By the time I had pedaled six miles over rough brick roads, and started the final gravel mile, I was near exhaustion. It was then my brother would take my hand and pull me along beside him as I laboriously pedaled that last mile to our house. I still remember this brotherly act of loving kindness toward his pest of a tomboy kid sister. Over the years, I've told this story many times, the last at his private graveside service.

If possible, when the circus came to town Mom would take us into Ashtabula to see the parade down Main Street. We never went to the circus as a family; tickets for four cost too much. I do recall the year I wanted to see an actual circus performance. I begged and begged Mom to take me. But it was a Friday night, and Mom and Dad were busy preparing fryers for market in the morning. Mom suggested I walk up to the Fischer farm to find out if they were going. Maybe I could ride with them. I followed Mom's suggestion, and as I trotted up the hill toward their house, I held high hopes for seeing the circus. Mrs. Fischer answered my knock and invited me inside. Yes, they were going to the circus that evening, but she gave no indication that she would invite me to ride with them. Again, I was too shy to ask. Disappointed, I left and dejectedly shuffled my way back home. All my hopes for seeing the circus had evaporated. When I entered the kitchen, Mom asked me what had happened, and when I told her I was too shy to make the request, she just let it go.

Every Fourth of July there was a parade down Main Street. One year Montgomery Ward announced it would give prizes for the best-decorated bicycles. I was determined to enter and win! I was eight years old and had just gotten my new blue Elgin bicycle. My brother had a red bicycle. I don't remember the make. I recall my brother reluctantly decorating his bicycle. Not me! I enthusiastically proceeded to decorate my bike using the blue and white crepe paper streamers Mom had bought. I wove them in and out between the spokes, tying them in bows on the handlebars allowing plenty of length for the streamers to flow as I rode. The *piece de resistance* was the fresh red roses from our garden secured to the carrier and the handlebars.

The morning of the parade, Dad securely fastened our bikes on the fenders of the car and drove the family into Ashtabula. As he drove, the wind played havoc with our decorated bikes. When Dad finally parked the car, I hurriedly got out to see the damage and immediately started to cry. My hopes for winning a prize were destroyed by the wind. Mom tried to quiet and reassure me, all the while repairing the damage as best she could. Tears dried, I found my place in the parade and proudly rode my bicycle down Main Street. At the end of the parade route, riders were directed to assemble in an area reserved for the judging. I remember self-assuredly standing by my bike as the judges passed by.

The moment came to announce the winners. I stood there holding my breath. Third place announced—not me; second place—still not me. Was it possible? Could I be the first-place winner—or worst of all, no prize? My ears must have been deceiving me. Did I hear, "The *first-place winner* goes to Henrietta Schumann!"? As one of the judges walked toward me to hand me my prize, it was only then that I realized the first-place prize was a **BB gun**! Lloyd did not win any of the three prizes, yet he won anyway. I gave him my BB gun. Now that is true sibling generosity.

There were few organized activities available for us farm kids in the summer. One activity was the 4H Club. Mrs. Kemp lived two miles to the north and east of us, and she was the leader of the 4H Club. There were different types of activities connected with 4H—gardening, cooking, and sewing. The club Mrs. Kemp directed was for sewing. One day of each week during the summer, I would attend the 4H Club meeting held in her home. We were to make a dress. Mrs. Kemp selected and entered the best dresses from her club in the sewing exhibits at the Ashtabula County Fair. My sewing skills were poor, and my dress was never one that was selected. Was I disappointed? Not really. My interest wasn't in sewing.

Another opportunity open to me was the Sheffield Juvenile Grange. Dad and Mom were both members of the Sheffield Grange—an organization founded in 1867 for the purpose of advancing methods of agriculture, as well as to promote the social and economic needs of area farmers. Dad was the one who would attend the monthly Saturday-night meetings; Mom stayed home with Granma. I can't recall at what age I joined, but children between the ages of five and fourteen were eligible for membership in the juvenile grange. I attended meetings for several years and when older was elected to the office of juvenile grange master.

After the adult grange meeting ended, there was a square dance—a caller and a fiddler were all that were needed. Dad taught me how to square dance. He'd take me as his partner and position himself fourth couple in the square. Many times he'd say, "Sis, carefully watch the other three couples when it is their turn to dance and observe their moves. Then when it is our turn, you'll have an idea what to do."

Square dancing, where only one couple at a time dances, is known as traditional; Western square dancing involves all four couples dancing simultaneously and requires a higher level of dancing skills. For me, it was thrilling to be with my dad and dance to the simple calls of allemande left, promenade, do-sa-do, etc. One of the first square dances that I learned was "Birdie in the Cage." Years later, I square danced with my brother, but those special memories of square dancing with my dad will always remain with me.

Square dancing was a social event after each grange meeting, but another social event of the Grange that took place before the meeting was the semiannual, box-social fund-raiser. Women—old, young, even children—would elaborately decorate a box, pack it with a meal for two, and anonymously place it with other decorated boxes to be auctioned off to the highest bidder. When I was mature enough, not yet in my teens, I wanted to have a box lunch in the auction. Mom helped me decorate a shoebox, and then filled it with a mouthwatering meal for two consisting of her delicious sandwich mixture of corned beef, sweet pickles, and mayo thickly spread between layers of scrumptious homemade bread. There would also be a generous piece of homemade peach pie.

The night of the event, I placed my decorated box in the pile with the others. Then I sat back and, with excitement mounting in my chest, anxiously waited for my box to be selected by the auctioneer. All the females hoped that in the bidding process their box would be bid on enough to bring a good price. If not, it was an embarrassment. When mine came up for bid, this thought was what caused my heart to race and my pulse to quicken. Can't say I remember how much my decorated box added to the fund, but I do remember that one of the handsome tall, young men in the senior grange bid the price of my box up, and I was elated. After all the boxes were sold, the lady would seek out the gentleman whose bid won her box, and the two would sit down for their meal together. I did not know the young man who bought my box, but I do remember that my face was burning with embarrassment as I walked over and made my identity known.

———— ·+·+·+·+· ————

THE DAYS OF SUMMER PASSED, and suddenly it was September. For Lloyd and me it was back to school. One could smell fall in the air. Days were warm, but the nights were cool. September was the time of fall harvest. The winter pears were picked from the tree, brought into the house, and spread out on the floor to ripen in an unused upstairs bedroom. Only a few of the apples from our small orchard were good enough to eat or use for baking. Most of our apples were purchased from a nearby orchard. Any apples we used for cooking and eating were purchased from the owner of a local orchard. I can remember being with Dad when he stopped and we entered the apple storage building to select a bushel of apples. Dad would always choose apples that were labeled "seconds." They cost less. I'd look at the best apples and drool. They were so shiny and perfect, not like the seconds with their bumps, bruises, scabs, and other imperfections—another evidence of the frugality of my parents that informs my spending habits to this day.

In fall, late-ripening apples from the orchard were used to make apple butter. This was a family operation—collecting and washing, in preparation for tossing the apples into a large copper kettle of boiling water hung on a tripod over a woodfire that Dad built. The first cooking of the apples did not require a lot of attention, but once they were cooked, the apples were removed from the boiling water and run through a colander, with the resultant globules (applesauce) dropping into a large container. When full, the container of applesauce was poured back into the cleaned empty copper kettle hung once again on the tripod over the fire. Now full attention must be given to the constant stirring of the applesauce in the kettle. This was done using a large wooden paddle to scrape the bottom of the kettle, keeping the mixture from sticking and burning. Family members traded off on this task, as the thickening process could take more than an hour. As the mixture thickened, it became more difficult to stir, and for this reason some arms tired more quickly than others, and it was necessary to keep changing stirrers. Dad kept the fire going, and I would watch, mesmerized, as the substance started to bubble. As it bubbled, it thickened, changing from applesauce to apple butter. Periodically throughout the thickening process, Mom seasoned and tasted. When Mom determined the taste was right, the apple butter was ready for preserving. Fruit jars and lids were sterilized, and the simmering apple butter was carefully poured into the jars. A rubber ring was placed around the mouth of the jar, a zinc lid applied and screwed down tight to ensure the jar was sealed, and then stored in our basement beside the jams and jellies. I don't have Mom's recipe, but what I do remember is the delicious-tasting apple butter, a winter treat to be spread on homemade bread.

Halloween was a time for pranks. Halloween night, the boys, with me in tow, gathered at dusk to perform our escapades. Trick-or-treat was unheard of in our farm community; it was tricks with no request for treats. The worst prank I ever pulled was soaping the neighbor's windows. However, the boys were up to other shenanigans. Flipping over wooden outhouses was a favorite. Any farmer having a brick shit house was safe. But it was my brother, along with some of his buddies, who pulled off a top-notch Halloween prank. The year must have been around 1943.

Mac Van Slyke, our neighbor a half mile to the south, had bragged, "Those boys are not going to move my wagon this Halloween, I've chained it up!" Lloyd took this as the ultimate challenge. During the day, Lloyd observed that Mac had chained his wagon to a post near his house, probably so that he could hear any ruckus that might occur during the night. That evening after dark, Lloyd and his buddies, driving two cars with no lights, parked on the road near the driveway of Mac's house. Lloyd had brought with him a pair of chain cutters; it did take some effort, but he managed to cut the log chain holding the wagon to the post. Without starting the car's engine, the boys pushed Lloyd's car into position so that he was able to hook the wagon to the bumper of the car. On signal, the fellows piled into the two cars. Lloyd started his car and without lights peeled out of Mac's driveway and took off down the road, pulling the wagon. At the same time his buddy started the other car, turned on the lights, and followed Lloyd. As the tale is told and the saga unfolded, Mac heard the ruckus in his yard, ran out of his house, jumped into his car, and flew (as fast as cars would go in those days) down the road following the only car he saw ahead of him.

About a half mile down the road from Mac's home was a crossroad, and it was here that Lloyd, wagon in tow, turned to the left. His buddy turned to the right. Mac wasn't close enough to see that the car he was following was not pulling a wagon. It was just as Lloyd had it planned; in pursuit Mac followed the wrong car. It was a distance down the road before Mac realized he had been "had." Mac's wagon was returned the following day, and eventually peace was restored to the neighborhood.

Thanksgiving was a special holiday for the family. Mom had her choice recipes for the feast. Dad would kill and dress a duck, and the bird was stuffed with sage dressing. There were snowy mashed potatoes and brown gravy in abundance, alongside the homemade bread. Mashed sweet potatoes made into balls with a marshmallow center and coated with chopped pecans was another delicacy. Mom made a special cranberry salad with nuts, pineapple chunks, apple, and celery that called for lemon Jell-O. (Any recipe requiring gelatin could not be made in the summer since there was no refrigeration. Ice cream was another winter-only treat.) Apple and rhubarb pies were our dessert, and Mom's piecrusts, made with lard, were unsurpassed for their flakiness. Our best white linen tablecloth and napkins were used. There was no fancy china or silver, so the table was set with the everyday plates and eating utensils, but we paid no mind. The food was delicious, and everyone ate their fill. There were no other families or friends who shared the meal with us, just we five—Dad, Mom, Granma, Lloyd, and me.

The dinner that Mom prepared was created without conveniences. No electricity or running water, only a coal stove for cooking and baking. The sink room / pantry / kitchen layout required a lot of walking for meal preparation. I would help as best I could. When I was old enough, I particularly enjoyed setting the table. As long as Granma was able, she would help with the dishwashing. Removing the dirty dishes from the kitchen table to the sink room for washing, and then carrying them from the sink room into the pantry where they were stored, required a lot of steps. It is no wonder that many nights Mom would say, "Just let the dishes go until morning, Henrietta. Come have another cup of tea with Granma and me. I am just too tired to do one more thing tonight."

++++++

FALL SETTLED INTO WINTER, and with it came the excitement of Christmas. As soon as Lloyd and I were out of school for Christmas vacation, we would climb the ladder in my bedroom into the attic and bring down the holiday decorating boxes. Opening the boxes, we sometimes found to our dismay that the attic mice had played havoc with the paper chains and crepe paper streamers. I think these paper products must have supplied good nesting material for the mice. One look and we immediately knew what needed to be replaced: broken Christmas tree ornaments due to carelessness in packing; colored paper to make new chains; red, white, and green crepe paper for making streamers that we used to crisscross our living room ceiling that provided a canopy of color; and boxes of silver icicles. We unwrapped the Nativity set for the library table. We examined my brother's mechanical wind-up train set, and found all the pieces needed for assembling it around the trunk of our tree. When I was old enough, maybe fourteen, I made cookie dough that I cut in various shapes, baked, and decorated to make fir trees and a Hansel and Gretel house. This was placed on top of the upright piano in the living room.

While Lloyd and I were busy looking over and checking all our Christmas decorations, Mom carefully listened to our wish-list talk of what we wanted Santa to bring us for Christmas. Somehow Mom managed to save fifty dollars, divided evenly between Lloyd and me, to spend on our Christmas gifts. Mom was frugal when spending the gift money. She would not buy any wrapping paper or ribbon, instead using newspapers (funnies when available) and string to wrap our gifts. Come Christmas Eve, she would drive into Ashtabula to do her Christmas shopping. She knew that was when the merchants put everything on sale, unlike today when sales are used as a marketing strategy. Of course, she ran the risk that some of our wish-list items would be unavailable. However, for the most part, she was successful—the evidence was under the tree on Christmas morning.

It was a tradition that our Christmas tree not be cut and brought into the house before Christmas Eve day. Both Dad and Mom felt decorating the tree in advance took away from the delight of Christmas morning. On the practical side, the type of fir tree that we brought in from the woods lost its needles very quickly because the cut trunk was never placed in water. However, the tree remained up until New Year's Day. I remember Lloyd and me sweeping up and playing with piles of dried needles, loading them into his toy trucks or open rail cars that were part of the train that was set up under the tree.

The day before Christmas, Lloyd, saw in hand and with me in tow, walked across the road into the woods to find our prize. Seldom did we find a perfect tree—usually one side would be bare of branches and/or it would have a slight tilt. However, we did our best, and after spending considerable time trudging through the snow, would settle on what seemed the "best of the bunch." Once cut, we gleefully dragged our prize home. Dad mounted the tree on a homemade wooden stand, and once in the living room the tree was strategically placed so that only the better sides could be seen.

Our excitement knew no bounds as we began to decorate our tree. The fragile bulbs were hung first, then the colorful paper and popcorn chains, and last the icicles. Hanging the icicles was a tedious task. We removed bunches of foil tinsel strings from their boxes. Our small fingers would carefully separate out each individual strand, press it flat with our fingers, then carefully place it on a bough of the tree. Darkness came early in December, and Mom would light the kerosene lamps in the living room. The result was a soft golden light that illuminated the tree, revealing a multitude of shimmering dancing lengths of silver. It was then the magic of the evening descended. Lloyd and I would sprawl out on the floor, admiring the result of our day's work. Even the shadows in the room, that on any other night held dread for me, projected unusual warmth.

Like any other night, Christmas Eve was no exception, and we were made to go to bed at our usual nine-o'clock bedtime. However, we were allowed to get up anytime after midnight to return to the living room and open our Christmas gifts. Many a Christmas Eve I lay in bed watching the hand on the clock creep toward the witching hour of midnight. I know I slept some, but I was always the one who awakened first, rushed into my brother's room, and shook him awake. Together we would charge down the stairs and into the living room where a lamp had been left lit for us.

We were never disappointed. Santa had come! There were the packages wrapped in newspapers and tied with string clearly marked for Lloyd or me. As soon as Dad and Mom heard us up, they would join us in the living room. The first thing Dad did was stoke the fire in the heating stove, providing us with welcome warmth. Then our parents sat back, watching as Lloyd and I hurriedly opened each of our gifts.

Miraculously Santa had brought gifts we wanted. How did Santa know? Children mature and become adults, and with age the identity of the gift giver becomes known. It was Mom and Dad's devotion to us, their generosity in sacrifice, their love that filled this season with such beauty and joy. To this day, the magic of those childhood Christmases remains.

Once all of our gifts were opened, our parents returned to bed for a few more precious hours of sleep before they had to get up and attend to the daily routine of the farm. Lloyd and I would stay up the rest of the night, and through the next day, playing with our new toys. One year Lloyd got a steam engine that was fueled by an alcohol burner. He also got his erector set that year. Over the next days, between Christmas and the New Year, my brother spent hours building with his erector set. I remember the Ferris wheel he built. He used a belt system to connect the steam engine with the Ferris wheel. I watched in fascination as the Ferris wheel slowly turned, bringing to mind the ride at the county fair. I don't recall that he ever built me a carousel—maybe he didn't have the instructions, maybe he didn't have the needed pieces for assembly, or maybe he just wasn't interested.

Santa always brought me a doll with a complete wardrobe of clothes—years later I realized it was Mom who made the doll clothes, not Mrs. Santa Claus. I had dolls with porcelain feet, hands, and faces with eyes that opened and closed; baby dolls that wet their diapers and cried; and some dolls just made to be loved. I kept my dolls with me in my bedroom, and I took them all to bed with me each night. It became very crowded in my single bed. Unknowingly, I had attributed my dolls with human characteristics. In my childlike mind I just knew that any one of them would feel sad if left out. Given that I humanized my dolls, even to this day it puzzles me why I did not save any of them.

There was one year, I must have been about twelve, that I spied a white Persian cat in the stuffed animal kiosk on the mezzanine floor of Carlisle's Department Store in Ashtabula. The cat was costly—maybe twenty dollars. By then I was old enough to know that Mom and Dad were Mr. and Mrs. Santa Claus and funds were limited. Nevertheless, I begged Mom for the cat. To my overflowing joy, I found it there on Christmas morning under the tree. I must add there was not much else in the way of presents for me that year—the cat took most of my share of the Christmas budget. I loved that cat. It had a zipper pocket in its side, and if I had worn silk or satin pajamas, I would have stuffed them into that side pocket, but not my bulky flannel nightgown.

Before Dad married Mom, he had a Kodak camera and took many pictures. Every Christmas he got out his camera and purchased one eight-exposure roll of Kodak colored film. He cautioned us that due to the expense of the film and the developing process, it was crucial that we carefully select those eight pictures. A picture of Lloyd and me posing with our toys in front of our decorated Christmas tree, the Nativity set, the Hansel and Gretel cookie house set among the cookie fir trees were selected poses that used up some of the precious exposures. Sometimes Mom and Dad would reluctantly allow their picture to be taken. One year a picture was taken of the family seated at our kitchen table. Whatever scenes were selected, they captured the essence of our family at this holiday season. The few pictures that survived the years are priceless relics of Christmases past and evidence of the love of our parents who sacrificed so much to make the holiday special for us.

Once the corn was harvested, the stalks, with the corn ears still attached, were piled in the barn for Dad to husk during the long winter evenings. I recall one evening, after supper was over, Dad went to the barn to do the evening's chores. He didn't return to the house at the usual time, so Mom sent me to fetch him. I trudged the narrow, beaten path through the snow to the barn, and immediately upon entering, I felt the warmth emitted by the cows and horses. I observed the soft yellow glow of lantern light coming from the area behind the cows. I heard Dad before I saw him. He was sitting there among the corn stalks, methodically pulling an ear of corn off each stalk. He was wearing a hooked corn-shucking glove on his right hand. It seemed to me that in one motion he plucked the corn ear from the stalk and at the same time removed the husk, flipping the stripped ear into a nearby basket and quickly grabbing the next stalk to repeat the process. While he was doing this I heard him say, "It's Postlewaite. No, it is Posthewaite. Not right yet. It's Postlethwaite, that's it! I've got it!" Dad kept repeating this final pronunciation over and over to ensure that his brain, tongue, and lips worked together to correctly pronounce the name of the new pastor of our country church. When he saw me standing there, it was an embarrassing moment for him, but I paid no mind. I was amused. The new pastor's name was difficult for all of us to pronounce.

On rare occasions, when the gravel roads were covered with packed snow and Dad had time, Lloyd and I would be taken for a sleigh ride. Dad would hitch Babe, our spirited horse, to the one-seat sleigh and adjust the harness, making the sleigh bells jingle. Climbing into the sleigh, settling onto the middle of the cold seat, Dad would motion for Lloyd and me to climb aboard. With a sense of anticipation, we eagerly hopped up into the sleigh and snuggled as close to Dad as possible for warmth. Mom was there to cover the three of us with a warm blanket and place warmed soapstones at our feet.

With a "giddyup" from Dad, Babe started off. The sound of the jingling harness bells provided us with melodic music as Babe gained speed, and we seemed to fly over the hard-packed snow of the road. As we flew, the cold wind burned my face, but it was a small price to pay for the exhilarating experience of the ride. Mom's warm blankets and the soapstone at my feet gave, at least the lower half of my body, a comfy, cozy feeling.

In Ashtabula County, the township roads are laid out in squares; north-south roads intersect with east-west roads at one-mile intervals. Dad would take us around one of those squares, providing us a brisk, breezy four-mile ride. I can't truthfully say that I remember snowflakes gently falling on one of those rare rides. Had that been true, the adventure would have been winter-wonderland perfect.

There were other cold winter rides that had to be endured. Every Saturday Dad delivered fryers to Naddra's Grocery, made the rounds of the egg customers, and did the shopping no matter what the weather. Most times I would accompany Dad on this routine. Lloyd would have remembered the type of car the family owned at the time. I don't. What I do remember is that it was an old four-door sedan, some of the fenders held in place with bailing wire, windowpanes cracked or broken, and an open floorboard on the passenger side of the front seat. There was no defroster and no heater. Mom did the best she could to ensure I wouldn't freeze. She provided me with a warm blanket and heated a soapstone for my feet. This was better than nothing, but the cold still penetrated my body, leaving me with half-frozen feet, fingers, and a very cold nose.

Without a defroster to keep the windshield free of condensation, Dad had wired a small fan into the electrical system of the car and mounted it on the dashboard aiming it at the windshield. The cold circulating air from the fan did keep a peephole clear so Dad could see where he was driving, but the moving cold air only added to my misery.

For the better part of the winter, Dad put chains on the back wheels of the car. However, traveling over bare sections of roads en route to the city, chain links would invariably break. This provided a discordant, rhythmical clanking sound, not the soft, jingling music of sleigh bells heard on our sleigh ride. When this happened, and the noise got too jarring, Dad would stop the car, get out, and fix the broken links with hog rings that were secured in place using hog ring pliers.

Equally comparable to the cold of the weekly car rides into Ashtabula were the sled rides of childhood. The car rides were misery personified, while sled rides were thrilling experiences. Somehow the boys of the neighborhood knew when the temperature was right and would gather behind the Fischer barn with their water buckets to ice the sled riding hill. Throughout the afternoon of the appointed day, there would be a brigade of about eight boys, and me, carrying buckets of water from the nearby creek to pour over the sloping grade. Given twenty-four hours, the water-drenched path on the hill would freeze and be perfect for sled riding.

Daylight sledding was fun, but it was the times we gathered with our sleds after dark that was truly exhilarating! The boys from the Nemitz and Fischer families, along with my brother and me, would bring lighted lanterns from our homes and place them at intervals along the full length of the iced path. There could be as many as ten of us at one time. There were contests to see who could ride their wooden flyer sled the farthest—shooting down the iced track of the hill, continuing over the flatland of the pasture before finally encountering uneven ground that would bring their sled to an abrupt halt.

The boys would have solo contest rides; they had contests riding double (more dangerous); and then there was me. On rare occasions my brother would condescend to let me ride double with him. Of course, the contests were usually won by the oldest, heaviest kid in the group. The prize for winning was the status that went with it. Kissing me, the only girl, was never mentioned. Had it been, I suspect that would have ended any further contests.

Our sled riding went on into the late-night hours until someone's parent called their kid to come home. That broke up the sled-riding party, and everyone would gather up their lantern and sled to head for home. When we were fortunate, the cold weather lasted for several days, rarely weeks, before a thaw. The thrill of zooming over the iced path on my wooden flyer sled remains another precious memory of my childhood.

In rural areas winters could be brutal however. As I recall, the winter of 1941 was very severe. The storms were intense. Snowdrifts stood several feet deep. Inadequate snow-removal equipment could not keep even the main roads open. There was one week in January when Dad was not able to get home from the factory where he worked. Roads were impassable.

Dad stayed in town at the Warren Hotel in Ashtabula so he would be able to work every day while waiting out the storm.

That week schools were canceled. Mom, Lloyd, and I were together in the farmhouse, and the responsibility for caring for the livestock was ours alone. I recall the snow was so deep it was a herculean effort to shovel a path to the well for water, to the barn to care for the livestock, and to the chicken coop to care for the chickens and gather the eggs before they froze. No one used the outhouse; the chamber pot served our needs. We were marooned in an ocean of white.

To conserve the limited fuel supply of coal and wood in the basement, Mom kept only the fire in the kitchen stove burning. To conserve the kerosene supply, only one lamp was lit and placed in the center of the kitchen table. When we were not outside tending to the livestock and chickens, we huddled around the stove to keep warm. An evening treat was to pop popcorn, using the large, black cast-iron skillet. We entertained ourselves by reading and playing checkers or monopoly.

Our crank telephone, mounted on the kitchen wall, was our only communication with the outside world. Each evening Mom would anxiously await the sound of the telephone giving out one long, sharp ring, the party line signal that the call was for us. Dad made a nightly three-minute, long-distance call to check with Mom that all was safe and well with the family as well as with the livestock and chickens. Calls were always limited to three minutes. Even that short time was costly, and any additional time was charged by the minute.

After one week, the storms ceased, and the county snowplow was able to clear the main roads. Dad was able to drive the car within one tenth of a mile of the farmhouse. He walked the final distance, and it was a joyous sight to see him trudging through the deep snow, up our drive, and into the house. All was not only "white" but "right" with the world when our dad was able to join us once again.

One year Mr. Fischer, who owned the woods across the road from our house (where we purloined our Christmas tree), decided to have some of the large trees cut down. This provided me with yet another interesting experience of visiting the campsite of the two lumberjacks hired to do the job. On weekends I would trudge through the snow to visit with them. Their campsite consisted of a large canvas tent with a wooden floor. Inside were two cots, a table, and a couple of straight chairs. A woodstove used for cooking also provided some warmth to the interior. A lean-to gave shelter to the horse that was needed to pull the cut logs to a central collection site near the road.

Each visit provided me with interesting tales to tell at home. I was particularly absorbed with how the men cut down the trees. They used a long (maybe eight-foot) crosscut saw. It had a handle on each end, and as the lumberjacks worked the saw back and forth, it would make a soft, humming sound. Whenever they were close to felling a tree, they made certain I was out of the way as it crashed to the ground.

One weekend Mom sent me to invite the lumberjacks for Sunday dinner. The men readily accepted. Mom's traditional Sunday dinner was fried chicken, mashed potatoes, green beans, homemade bread, and apple or berry pie. This was washed down with either milk or hot tea. To say I remember how they thanked Mom and Dad for their hospitality would be only a figment of my imagination. However, the men must have been pleased as they trudged back to their primitive living quarters, bellies full, nostrils filled with the lingering smells from the kitchen, and thoughts of a welcoming family who shared this simple fare with them.

Then came the weekend. I again trudged through the snow to visit with my lumberjack friends. A vacant campsite greeted me. The trampled snow revealing footprints of man and horse was the only evidence that they were once there. To my child's mind, they were my friends. Why did they not tell me they would be leaving? Visiting their campsite, talking with them, watching their rhythmical skill as they used the crosscut saw to fell the trees filled many idle Saturday hours for me that winter. I returned home with a heavy heart.

An annual ritual that took place in January or February was the butchering of a pig. Dad did not have the luxury of a butchering shed with a system for heating the water used for scalding, a vat for dipping, or a heavy wooden table for holding the pig as it was cut into the desired pieces. Nor did Dad have the luxury of a block-and-tackle system especially designed for lowering and raising a pig in and out of the scalding vat. Instead, in preparation, Dad built a metal frame on the north side of the barn conveniently placed underneath the hayfork. This frame held a fifty-five-gallon metal drum filled with water, carried bucket by bucket from the well forty feet away. Beneath the drum, Dad built a wood fire to bring the water to a boil.

Dad always selected a pig that was eight to ten months old and weighed about 180 pounds for slaughter. This ensured tender pork and easier handling. Never as a young child did I watch the pig being killed. However, I do remember watching the scalding process. The hind legs of the pig were securely fastened to the hayfork, and the process for raising and lowering was the same as used in the summer to lift the hay from the wagon. In the summer, it was Lloyd or I in charge of our plow horse, Major. In the winter, Mom took over this tricky part of the operation. On commands from Dad, Mom would lead Major the few feet required to raise the pig from the ground high enough to be slowly lowered into the scalding water in the drum. The pig was left there for a very short time before Dad hollered for it to be raised. Then he would scrap the skin to remove the hair. This process for lowering and raising the pig went on until all hair was removed.

As I recall, Dad sectioned the pig into the desired cuts while it was still hanging from the hayfork. Once cut into sections for ease of handling, he would bring the meat into the sink room of the house. It was here that Mom would cut the meat into small pieces, packing it into quart mason jars for canning in a boiling water bath. This took several hours. The jars of canned pork were stored in the basement to be eaten throughout the year. We did not have a smokehouse on the farm, but I do recall that slabs of bacon were placed in brine for curing. I do not remember if a cut of pork was ever cured for ham. However, enough cuts of meat were set aside to be eaten by the family during the cold winter months. Pork chops and pork roasts were a rare treat, a welcome relief from our Sunday chicken dinners.

There was one taste treat I will always remember that came from the rendering of the pig fat. Pieces of fat were placed in our large cast-iron skillet and rendered over the hot fire of the kitchen stove. The cracklings were skimmed out of the melted fat to be eaten later. The lard was stored in an earthen crock in our basement to be used by Mom for making flaky pie crusts, in cooking, and for soap making. The black cast-iron skillet, ever present on the stove, always contained some of the lard. Dad would heat this lard to its liquid state and then soak a thick slice of homemade bread with the substance, place it on his plate, sprinkle it with sugar, and devour it tasty bite by tasty bite. I would do the same, and to this day my mouth waters as I think of placing a piece of this lard-soaked bread sprinkled with sugar in my mouth and sensing the crackle of the sugar on my tongue as I chew this tasty morsel. Yes, most unhealthy, loaded with cholesterol, but I'm still here. Thinking about it, this same type of treat can be purchased at a concession stand at county fairs and carnivals—just ask for an elephant ear.

IN 1937 MY FATHER RECEIVED AN INHERITANCE of $750 from the Hoefeldt Estate. Dad's mother was a Hoefeldt, and as a descendent he was entitled to one thirty-second of this estate. Dad bought a Farmall Tractor, and Mom got a new washing machine with a gasoline engine. These two items lightened their workload but did not lessen the hardships of living in a house with no electricity.

It was in 1935 that Congress, under the Roosevelt administration, passed the Rural Electrification Act. This act provided federal loans, administered by local electric companies, for the installation of an electrical distribution system to rural areas of the United States. A requirement of the act was that the poles, placed along the side of the road needed for stringing the wire, must be paid for by the land owner. In the latter half of the 1930s, the Fischer farm to the north of us and the van Slyke farm to the south got their electricity. Mr. Fischer paid for the electrical right of way that brought the electricity to his farm. This right of way passed in front of our house, but there was no money for my parents to pay their share of the cost.

It was not until mid 1940s that our home was wired for electricity. Dad was working at the Electro Metallurgical Company at the time, and my parents had been able to save enough money to pay their share of the right-of-way. My brother was in the navy and home on a two-week leave. He wired the house, the barn, and selected outbuildings. He must have followed the government protocol that was used for the wiring of rural homes. One light was placed in the center of the ceiling of each room in the house, operated by a single light switch; only one wall plug was installed per room. As an aside, there were limited funds for the project. Only needed electrical supplies were purchased—no fixtures. Lloyd solved this problem by soldering the light bulbs to the wire that dropped out of the hole cut in the ceiling. I don't recall how a burnt-out light bulb ever got changed.

When electricity came to the farm, it was a time for celebration. Over a span of years, as money became available, appliances were purchased. One of the first appliances was an electric washing machine that retired the washer with the ear-shattering gasoline engine. A refrigerator was soon to follow, providing a cold place for storage of perishable foods in warm weather.

A small appliance that got top priority was an electric iron. I remember the sad iron. It was a pointed triangular piece of heavy metal, weighing five to nine pounds—"sad" referring to heft—that Mom would heat on the coal stove. The sad iron was replaced by a gasoline iron using pressurized gasoline from a tank mounted on the back, lit, providing heat on the inside of the iron. Dangerous. Then came the electric iron, and all Mom had to do was plug it into the wall outlet—such luxury.

If permanent press linens and clothing items were available, my family did not have any. Mom insisted on standing at the ironing board and ironing the pillowcases, linen towels, and other small flat items from the wash basket. When Mom got an electric mangle—a heated, rotating, padded drum set in a table-high frame—ironing flat pieces became easier and faster, but best of all, convenient. She urged me to try using it. I did, but I wasn't interested. To me it was still "work."

It was the Christmas of 1948, and we decided to get Mom an electric stove. We wanted it to be a surprise. Lloyd bought the stove and planned to install it Christmas Eve. It was our turn to stay up late and play Santa Claus. After Mom and Dad retired for the night, Lloyd brought the stove into the house and set it in place. He then went to the basement to wire the fuse box for the stove. This took some pounding. I was upstairs in the kitchen, heard the ear-shattering noise, and was terrified that Mom or Dad would come out to see what was happening. After a few tense minutes passed, and not a stir from our parents, Lloyd went ahead with the final installation and checked to be sure the stove was properly installed. That being done, I tied a wide, red ribbon around the stove and placed a card on the stove top reading, "To our Mom, with love, Lloyd and Henrietta."

I could not sleep that night and was downstairs early Christmas morning to see Mom's face when she emerged from their bedroom and walked into the kitchen. The look of surprise, which gave way to utter joy, is a memory I cherish to this day. Mom claimed she never heard the pounding. If she did, she had the good sense not to explore the source of the noise.

It wasn't long before Mom became efficient at using the stove for all the cooking and baking. Much to her delight, the kitchen coal stove was relegated to providing only the heat needed in the kitchen area of the house.

Two other major conveniences for the house, also dependent upon the availability of electricity, were a furnace and indoor plumbing. The first was the installation of a coal-fired, forced-air furnace. It was the winter of 1953, and my husband, Sidney Nelson, was working for the Ziegler Furnace Company in Ashtabula. Sid had the connections to get the materials at cost; he had the know-how to do the installation. These two factors made it possible for my folks to come up with the necessary dollars. With the installation of the furnace in the basement, the coal- and wood-fired stoves in the kitchen and living room were removed. Now, the mess connected with the coal and wood as well as the daily ash clean-out were done away with—another labor saving bonus for Mom.

The second much-needed improvement in the house was the installation of indoor plumbing in 1954. No longer would running water mean "run out and get it," and the chamber pot could be removed from the bedroom. My brother was out of the service, working and living in Ashtabula. Due to Lloyd's business connections in town, and his jack-of-all-trades genius, the installation was affordable for Mom and Dad. Installing the plumbing for the sink room was not a problem, but the decision to locate the bathroom, with sink, commode, and tub, in the small second-floor bedroom just off the top of the stair required not only ingenuity but muscle—both attributes my brother had in abundance.

<hr>

I HAVE OFTEN REMARKED that our family was poor but that I didn't know we were poor. What is poor, really? I observed that other folks dressed better, had fancier homes, drove better cars, and in general had more material things. We lived in a spartanly furnished house. Most of our food came from the farm. I was never hungry. Our neighbors were friendly, giving help when asked. We owned a car that provided us with transportation. For the most part we all had good health. If not, Doc Graves in Ashtabula provided the needed medical attention. I had clothing to keep me warm in winter, and summers were not a problem. I felt secure in the love of my parents. As an adult, I have come to realize that material things are ephemeral. My parents, through their ethics and values, provided me with the means to ride out the vicissitudes of my life.

Why is it that "Vee Get Too Soon Oldt, und Too Late Schmardt?"

I was not poor; I was rich.

FOUR

MOM AND DAD

I HAVE PREVIOUSLY WRITTEN OF MY GRANMA from the myopic, self-centered perspective of childhood. As an adult I view her in a different light. This adult recognition of my Granma's character is based on stories told to me by family members, but perhaps more importantly from studying pictures of her face, for I firmly believe a person's character is revealed in their face. Her eyes shine with intelligence and integrity. The slight smile detected in the relaxing of her mouth and the soft expression on her face verify what I have come to realize: she was a kind and soft-spoken person. I never knew her to raise her hand or her voice to me. She had to have spunk and been very shrewd, for I think she needed these traits to remain married to Squair—a miser and curmudgeon (although family members who knew Squair in the final years of his life might disagree with this assessment of his character). She sacrificed her desires and needs for her daughter and her daughter's family. After my grandpa, a Civil War veteran, died, Granma received a monthly pension of forty dollars. She gave half of this to my mother, keeping the remainder to buy medicine and personal items. This provided Mom with a few dollars to spend—I suspect mostly on Lloyd and me. Granma was the unsung matriarch of our home. She never had the opportunity to be a doting grandma to her grandchildren. We all lived together, and she was confined to the periphery of our lives. Granma died at the age of seventy-seven in the same house she came to fifty years earlier as a bride from Iowa in 1894.

+✦✦✦✦+

I was blessed with two siblings. My sister, Brenda, was born when I was twelve years of age. As a child she was a pest; as adults we became, and remain, very close. My brother, Lloyd, and I were twenty-two months apart in age. As children, we were very loyal to one another and remained so until his death in 2015. He was eighty-five years old.

"Mom, I'm home," and her reply, "I'm in here, Henrietta." This was my call each night after I got off the school bus and ran up the drive and into the house. One of the warmest memories of my childhood was knowing that Mom would always be there when I came home from school.

Rhoda Dale Shuart Schumann was well educated, attending Kent Normal School, and received her bachelor's degree in education in 1929 from what became Kent State College. She was an outstanding public speaker, engaging in debates, taking active leadership roles in her church and with the Daughters of Union Veterans (DUV). At home she entertained Lloyd and me with tongue twisters. Two that come to mind are "How much wood could a woodchuck chuck..." and "Betty Botter bought some butter..." Almost daily, Mom would find time to read to us. My favorite book was *Little Black Sambo*. Mom was so good at imitating the Negro dialect that I would beg her to "talk like Little Black Sambo." Later, Jules Verne's *Twenty Thousand Leagues Under the Sea* became one of my favorite books.

When I was eight years old, Mom arranged for me to have weekly elocution lessons with Mrs. Warren who lived in Ashtabula. To this day I credit these lessons with training me in the proper techniques of breathing, voice, and gesture control that gave me confidence when speaking before an audience. I still remember parts of "Casey at the Bat" and "Little Orphant Annie," poems that I recited in speaking contests sponsored by the Woman's Christian Temperance Union. I have in my keepsake jewelry box a WCTU pin signifying that I won first place in two of these contests. However, the third contest I entered is memorable for another reason. My dad's sisters, Minnie and Sophie, were visiting from Chicago and were with Mom and Dad in the audience. I didn't win first place. I placed second and was recognized with an honorable mention—a devastating loss knowing that my two aunts, whom I seldom saw, were there.

Apparently eight was also the age to start me with piano and voice lessons. Due to her reputation as an outstanding piano and voice teacher,

Mom chose Miss Rachel Davis, daughter of the Davis Furniture Store owner in Ashtabula, for my teacher. Miss Davis lived with her father on the Davis Estate, located just outside of Ashtabula, in a large, white two-story mansion with verandas and balconies. The two acres of manicured grounds surrounding the house were landscaped with a variety of trees and shrubs. For the convenience of my family, the lessons were on Sunday mornings before church. From the time of my first lesson, I felt a gnawing feeling in my stomach as Dad drove up the drive, parked the car, and we entered the cavernous house. I am sure Dad did not share my feelings of angst; he would be ushered into the first-floor library to sit in a comfortable chair and read their Sunday paper while I took my thirty minute lesson.

Miss Davis would escort me up the wide, seemingly never-ending staircase to the music room located on the second floor. Soon after my first lesson, I am certain she realized I had minimal musical talent. My voice lessons were limited to singing only soprano parts; I could not harmonize. Piano lessons were not fun. Stern Miss Davis had no intention of making them fun. Any mistake I made, a black mark was placed on the music sheet. If I made the same mistake the following week, the black mark turned to red. Woe to me if the mistake were repeated. Then a sharp ruler struck my fingers, making me cry. When this happened, Miss Davis was always very solicitous and kind the final five minutes of my lesson, having me wipe away my tears before exiting down the stairs to meet my dad and, thankfully, leave the house.

For the four years that I took lessons, I performed in the annual spring recital for parents. It was probably out of frustration that one Sunday morning Miss Davis told me I was wasting my parents' money; they could ill afford the one dollar per lesson she charged. Perhaps it was after I repeated this comment to Mom that I was finally allowed to quit.

Not only did Mom do her best with the limited resources available to enrich the cultural part of my life (books, music, elocution), she provided me with basics in homemaking skills. From the time I was a little girl, she would let me help her with the baking and cooking. She also taught me how to embroider, crochet, and sew.

Mom had acquired exceptional sewing skills, considering that all she had to work with was a treadle Singer sewing machine. To save money, she sewed nightgowns, sheets, pillowcases, and dish towels from the plain beige-colored material of feed sack bags. Other feed sack bags came in colorful printed materials, and from these Mom made dresses and aprons.

Out of store-bought material, Mom made a set of A, B, C quilt blocks for me. On each individual block, she outlined an alphabet letter with a simple object representing that letter. My assigned task was to embroider each of the blocks. Mom's plan was to assemble the twenty-five squares into a quilt top (for some reason she had omitted the letter Z) and make a quilt for me. Mom started me on this project when I was as young as six. It was obvious I lacked enthusiasm for the task. When I was well into my seventh year, Mom told me that I would not be getting the promised new bicycle for my eighth birthday if I didn't get those blocks done! That was the motivation that made me realize Mom might be serious. I vividly remember the spring of my eighth birthday sitting on the step of the concrete porch on the north side of the house and frantically embroidering those last few blocks that must be completed before my April 7 birthday. I made the deadline! On the morning of my eighth birthday, there on the north porch, where I had spent so many hours embroidering, was a beautiful blue Elgin bicycle ready for me to ride. I'm not sure if Mom would have carried through with her threat; she was very lenient with me.

Mom was keenly sensitive to the needs, feelings, and safety of others—providing food to those less privileged, giving of herself in times of sickness, and branding our brains with her sage advice. As a child I saw few Negroes, knew none personally, but Mom would emphatically say whenever speaking about a Negro person, "Never use the word *nigger*." Another bit of her sage advice related to guns. All farmers had guns in their homes, but it was Mom who admonished my brother and me, "Never point a gun, even a play gun, at anyone."

Given that Mom was so sensitive to the needs of others, it was strange that she never hugged or kissed Lloyd or me. One time she said, "Henrietta, in this family we do love one another, but the Germans are a restrained people and do not outwardly show their affection with hugs and kisses." However, I felt my mom's love in more subtle ways. It was an emotional connection I shared with her when, as a teenager and later as an adult, we would sit at the kitchen table together drinking tea and talking by the hour. This was not true for my brother. As a grown man, he expressed to me that he felt our mother and father did not love him. Mom related to me as a daughter in a way that, tragically, she was not able to relate to her son. It was during our teatime talks that Mom expressed some of her innermost thoughts, including her pride and love for her son. I never doubted that she loved each of us equally and was not aware that my brother felt slighted because of her inability to express that love.

I look back and realize that Mom was too prone to hear only one side of a story, and that was from the side of her children. When I was in the first grade, I came home from school one day with a mark on my arm. Mom asked me how it happened, and I said, "Geraldine bit me on the playground." Mom questioned me no further. The next morning she took me to school and confronted the teacher, Miss Holtsclaw, with the fact that Geraldine had bitten me. Geraldine claimed innocence, which was true. Mom was so emphatic. Miss Holtsclaw asked no questions of me, and Geraldine was disciplined. To this day I am ashamed of myself for this lie. I had injured my own arm but was too embarrassed to tell Mom how it really happened. I was bored in class and had put my arm up to my mouth, sucking on my skin, leaving a bloodsucker mark. Had Mom been without prejudice in her accepting of the situation, or had the teacher questioned me further, I am quite certain I would have relented and told the truth, saving Geraldine from a paddling and aiding me in one small step toward maturing.

Somehow, without realizing it, Mom communicated mixed messages to me. On the one hand she would say, "Henrietta, you can be anything you want to be, there is always room on top." On the other hand I observed that, having missed out on her own potential, she conveyed to me feelings of inferiority. She was a college graduate but used incorrect grammar. I think she did this because she did not want to stand out in the community as being better than others—haughty. I recall the time there was a legal matter that needed my attention, so I made an appointment with a lawyer in Jefferson to discuss the issue. For some reason his use of words, his vocabulary, impressed me. When I returned home, I told Mom about this. Mom's comment to me was something to the effect, "You don't have opportunities to associate with professional people. We are just country folk." That remark diminished the feeling of a nascent confidence that had been slowly developing within me.

Before Mom married, she taught school. During the Depression married women were not hired by school districts. Years later, when this restriction was lifted, Mom considered returning to teaching. At the time I was in high school and excited and proud to think my mom would be a teacher. However, she made the decision not to return to the classroom, remarking that she enjoyed teaching but not the discipline of the unmanageable children.

When Dale wanted to buy a new piano for my sister, who was doing much better with her piano lessons than I had ever done, she picked peaches and grapes for two years to earn the $1,000 needed. Once Mom had the money (she refused to buy anything on credit), it was I who drove into Cleveland, accompanied by my former music teacher. Mom was depending on the musical knowledge of Miss Davis to select the best piano available for the money, and that piano was found in the Halle Brothers Department Store. The sale for the George Steck spinet piano was finalized and delivered to the farmhouse. Brenda has this piano in her home today. It was a disappointment to Mom when she learned that the salesman had sent Miss Davis a "thank-you" check of $100. No offer was made to share any of this money—dollars earned by Mom in the heat of the day working as a migrant laborer.

As a young lady just out of high school, Dale's desire was to be a nurse, not a teacher. Her father would not allow his daughter to consider a career in nursing—it wasn't proper for a woman to see men's bodies. Apparently, Dale held on to this unfulfilled desire because, when she was in her early fifties, she applied for an aide position at the Longview Hospital. During the interview Dale learned there were no jobs available for aides but was told there was an opening for a cook. Could she cook? If so, would she like to be considered for that position? Mom answered yes, she could cook, and yes, she would like to be considered for the position. She was hired.

Mom's sensitivity to the needs of others became very obvious as she related to each of the approximately fifty patients in the hospital. Dale made it a practice to walk through the wards and talk with each person, learning what their favorite foods were, especially their favorite pie. Then on a rotating basis, she would provide each with their special meal treat. Unfortunately, Mom's enjoyment of her job was cut short by illness. She was diagnosed with aplastic anemia in the winter of 1963. She took a medical leave and died in May of that year.

There were patients (some wards of the county) still living when Brenda secured a position in 1965 as supervisor of nurses at Longview Hospital. When it became known she was Dale's daughter, those who knew Mom had nothing but the highest praise for this woman who had brought a humble bit of joy into their lives.

As I write these incidents about my mother, I gain a better understanding of this woman from the objective perspective of time and maturity. Granma sacrificed her personal life in providing for the needs of her daughter's family; my mother sacrificed her personal needs in providing for her husband and children. From both of these women, that was visible

LOVE—different from the casual "I love you" that has become so much a part of today's culture.

Today I look back in wonder that my mother, born of aged parents, who was shuffled from pillar to post throughout her growing-up years, well educated, estranged from her father after her marriage, who survived a Depression, through all remained married and served as someone I have emulated in the formation of my character.

———— ++++++ ————

HENRY AUGUST SCHUMANN was born in 1890. His formal schooling was limited. He attended through the eighth grade; high school was not available to him. His education came through life experiences. As a youth he helped on the family farm in Hustler, Wisconsin. Henry's early years, leaving Hustler, shifting to Chicago, living in Akron, moving to his in-laws' home near Ashtabula, are documented in chapter one.

Memories of my father begin in 1934. The first memory I have of my dad was working for the Works Project Administration (WPA), part of President Roosevelt's New Deal of the 1930s. Dad dug ditches and at the same time worked the farm.

The next job I remember my dad getting was driving a school bus for Jefferson Schools. Lloyd and I had been attending a one-room schoolhouse, located one and a half miles to the south of our farm on Lillie Road. In the extreme cold of winter, Dad would transform the farm wagon into a covered wagon and haul all the kids on Maple Road to the school. He called it his "kid wagon." In 1937 the one-room rural schools in Ashtabula County were consolidated. It was at this time that the Jefferson School District was formed. Our farm, located ten miles from Jefferson, was on the northern periphery of the district. School bus drivers were needed. Dad applied for a contract with the district to transport children. When interviewed by the board of education, Dad related his "kid wagon" experiences, stating that he was the logical one to be granted the contract. He was hired. Dad's next hurdle was to buy a school bus. At that time school bus drivers owned their own bus and contracted with the district to haul the students. Dad applied at the bank for the required $2,000 to purchase the bus. His reputation of integrity and honesty served him well; his request for a loan from the bank was approved with no equity required.

Dad drove his school bus for a number of years while also working the farm. He was popular with all ages of kids who rode on his bus. On the last day of school before Christmas vacation, he gave each student a box of Christmas candy; on the final school day of the year, all were treated to an ice cream bar.

Industry came to Ashtabula in the early 1940s, and Henry sold his school bus after getting a job at the Electro Metallurgical Company located on Lake Erie. I often heard Mom say that Dad worked his full-time job at the Electro Met to support the farm. Cash flow from the sale of pigs, fryers, eggs, butter, and buttermilk was minimal, not enough to support the family. Dad's job at the plant was cleaning and sorting coal for the furnaces that were used in the processing of ferro-metal alloys. Henry was liked by the men with whom he worked, recognized for his leadership ability by management, and offered the position of group foreman, which he declined. Henry preferred to be just one of the guys. The compulsory retirement age for factory workers at the Electro Met was sixty-five; however, Dad passed required physical examinations that allowed him to work an additional two years. He retired when he was sixty-seven years old.

Throughout all my growing-up years I recall that at the end of each workday, Dad would pick up the *Cleveland Plain Dealer* or the *Saturday Evening Post* and read by lamplight before going to bed. The part I objected to regarding Dad's reading was his desire to repeat in detail what he had read. I spent many an hour listening to Dad's voice droning on and on about recent articles that held great interest for him but were of little interest to me.

Dad had the ability to remain composed, objective, and coolheaded in emergency situations. I was in high school when a terrifying happening the summer of 1945 could have changed the life of our family. The brooder house roof, covered with tar paper, was leaking. Dad, working on the roof, used hot tar to make the repairs. The tar was heated in a large metal container on a kerosene stove located in the shed off the sink room of the house. I was in the kitchen and needed to go outside. It was by chance that I walked through the sink room and opened the door to the attached back shed. To my horror, I saw the shed was ablaze. The tar had boiled over! I screamed for Dad. From his vantage point on the brooder house roof, Dad could see what was happening.

In my memory, the next few minutes were like a slow-motion scene in a movie. I clearly remember that Dad took his time coming down the ladder before running to the well next to the milk house. Once at the well, he took off his jacket, soaked it with water, and covered his arm as he ran the final forty feet toward the house. Once there, he reached into the fire and pulled out the metal container of tar, eliminating the fire's source. By now Mom and Lloyd were there, and the three of us formed a line from the well to the house, providing Dad with pails of water to douse the fire. Dad later rebuilt the shed, making it larger and better suited to the needs of the house. I have often thought of Dad's act of fearlessness and level headedness that saved our home.

It is a fact that Henry worked to the point of exhaustion. No matter what job Dad held, he continued to farm, working evenings and week-ends to plant and harvest the crops, all weather-dependent activities. His migraine headaches and mood swings would come at the time of planting and harvesting, the most labor-intensive days for a farmer. With his head-aches and fatigue came difficult, moody behaviors that affected the rest of the family. One of Dad's ways of coping was to resort to silence. He would go for as long as two weeks without saying a word to Granma, Mom, Lloyd, or me. During these days, a miasma of gloom descended on the family, and even family meals were eaten in silence. Henry would sleep in the barn. I knew that the mood swing had ended when I would come downstairs to breakfast one morning and Dad would be sitting at the table, talking and laughing with Mom. Apparently, the previous night he had come in from the barn, carrying his pillow with him, to sleep once again beside my mother in bed. To this day I ponder how Henry could have slept so many nights in the barn, especially after learning from Mom, in one of our tea-time talks, how much Dad enjoyed sex.

For the most part, the rearing of Lloyd and me was left to Mom. As a child I sensed that Mom and Dad did not agree on how to raise us. Dad was more of a disciplinarian, while Mom was lenient. Since Dad was always working, he abdicated the rearing of us to Mom. I had trouble following instructions when Dad gave me a chore to do. If Mom was in the area and heard what Dad said to me, it was not a problem. She would make the task clear. However, if Mom was not close enough to hear Dad's instructions, it became a challenge for me to know what I was expected to do. Mom had previously advised me that when this happened, I should listen as carefully as I could, relate to her what Dad had said, and she would help me figure out the assigned task. Apparently, Dad knew Mom's protocol with us kids regarding his instructions, for whenever Dad got me alone, he would bom-bard me with unending criticism. Saturday and Sunday morning trips into Ashtabula provided him with the opportune time for his harsh criticism of anything that came to mind. I would listen in stony silence. I had no choice.

After Dad retired with a modicum of financial security and pressures of work lessened, the headaches and mood swings were less frequent and ultimately ended. He again assumed the persona of the loving person I had read about in his Line-A-Day diary—loaning (giving) money to his siblings in need, writing sensitive, loving letters to any family member in trouble and/or experiencing serious illness. I am certain that employment in the contaminated work environment of the Akron rubber factories compromised his health and the economic devastation of the Depression destroyed his life's ambitions and dreams. These two major factors, combined with unending toil in providing for the needs of his family, changed his personality.

————————+++++++————————

I HAVE A GLIMMER OF UNDERSTANDING of my mom and my dad when, as an adult, I relate to each as individuals. When I think of them as a couple, I feel frustration and sadness. As a child I wondered if they loved one another. When I was older, and I asked Mom's advice about something, she responded, "You'll have to make your own decisions. I did. I made my bed, and I have to lie in it." This comment has caused me to wonder if Mom felt she had chosen wisely when she married my dad, a blue-collar worker with limited formal education. Apparently, while Lloyd and I were still quite young, Mom had thought of divorcing Dad, taking us with her, and starting life anew. When she asked my brother how he would like to live in town, Lloyd answered, "You mean I would not be able to go down to the creek and shoot frogs with my BB gun?" According to Mom, again in one of our teatime talks, this was a decisive factor in her decision to remain with Dad.

Other happenings caused me to question whether my mom and dad loved one another. Too many mornings in my childhood I would be awakened by my parents' loud voices, and I knew they were having another one of their dreadful verbal fights. It was obvious that neither of them knew how to stop an argument once it started. When the screaming ended, a stone wall of silence was built. As the years passed, and my folks had more money, a tractor, a few electrical appliances to ease the workload, Mom and Dad seemed to develop an inner peace and were able to control these emotional outbursts.

In my parents' final years, I became aware of their dedication and love for one another. Mom was working at the county home; I was married, a young stay-at-home mom who could always use extra dollars. Mom asked if I would clean the house once a week; she would pay me for my efforts. Dad helped with the housework as best he could, but it would relieve both of the task. I eagerly accepted. Dad was retired at the time, and when I would visit the farm for the daylong task of cleaning, he and I had the opportunity for some enjoyable, relaxed conversations. I observed that when it came time for Mom to come home, Dad always made certain the tea kettle was filled with water and boiling on the electric stove in preparation for making her a cup of tea. It would be time for me to leave, to attend to my own home-maker responsibilities, but it was pleasant to see the two of them sit down together and discuss the day's happenings over a cup of hot tea.

Henry died at home of a heart attack on August 4, 1960. He was sixty-eight years old. I was on campus at Kent State University that summer, studying in the Rockwell Hall Library, when my name was called over the loudspeaker system directing me to pick up the nearest phone. I heard my sister's voice saying, "Dad has died."

Mom lived on in the farmhouse for a time. On one of my visits, I found her sitting alone in the living room, rocking. We chatted for a bit, and it was then she said to me, "Henrietta, I am so lonesome for your dad. I miss my companion." I was dumbstruck. I honestly thought Mom would be relieved as she would no longer have to deal with the moodiness, the need to satisfy a husband's desire for sex. It was many years later when I became a widow and was living alone, after my children had moved on with their lives, that I fully comprehended the depths of my mother's loneliness.

Dale died at home of complications from aplastic anemia on May 28, 1963. She was sixty-one years old. It was a warm, sunny Tuesday afternoon. I had finished my teaching day with Buckeye Schools in Ashtabula and drove the seven miles to the farm to see my mother and visit with my sister. As I drove in the drive that afternoon, my brother-in-law Paul walked out to greet me. His first words were, "Dale's gone."

IN MATURITY I HAVE MOVED from the childhood close-up view of my mom and dad to a landscape view of their lives. My sister stated it so well when she wrote to me, "They were hardworking, honest, sincere, caring parents, and they felt a deep responsibility to any obligation they had assumed." My brother, my sister, and I are blessed with the genetic makeup of our being that we, in turn, have passed on to our children.

❖❖❖❖❖❖

FIVE

SCHOOL YEARS (1-12)

THE YEAR WAS 1935. I was five years old. I felt quite grown-up now that I could be enrolled in the first grade in the one-room schoolhouse my brother had attended for the past two years. In preparation for me to enter school, Mom took me with her to the country bookstore located in a farmhouse about two miles from our home. All I remember about the place is that it was very large, no different from most farmhouses. When we entered the front door, I was amazed to see neatly shelved books in several of the downstairs rooms.

Mom knew what books and other supplies I needed as the purchase was made, and I proudly carried my new schoolbooks out of the house, into the car, and home. My one schoolbook that survives is a LaRue first reader—not a McGuffey reader, so common in use at the time. My LaRue book is tattered, pages missing, obviously water-soaked, and there is evidence of it being nibbled on by mice. To this day, my favorite story in that book remains "The Little Tin Train"—I think I can, I think I can, I think I can...

I have no idea what the schoolhouse I attended was named. It could have been named after a farmer who donated the land, maybe after one of the tall, stately oak or maple trees that grew there, or perhaps the small creek that meandered through the property. My first- and second-grade report cards, part of my memorabilia collection, provide no clue as the only reference to name is Ashtabula County Schools.

The school was located in the center of the townships that comprised the four-square-mile area that made up the district. No child was to walk more than one mile to school. That might have been true as the crow flies, but our farm was located almost to the northern and western periphery of the district, and walking the gravel roads added another one-tenth mile. To save time and distance, we kids used to cut across the fields as we made our daily trek to and fro. In the severest of winter weather, my dad hitched up his "kid wagon" to haul us.

Our school was a wood-framed building with horizontal clapboard siding and a gabled roof that was covered with cedar shingles, a common roofing material in use at that time. There were front and back doors with a semipermanent awning mounted over the front door that provided only minimal protection from the elements. The clapboard siding of the school was painted white. There were no modern conveniences. A dug well, with a hand pump, was the only source of drinking water for the school. The two other buildings on the property were outhouses—one for the boys, the other for the girls. As I recall there were three sets of double hung windows on each side of the building that provided natural light to the schoolroom. Kerosene lamps that gave off only a dim flickering light were the sole source of artificial light used on dark days or when needed at night. Windows were opened when the weather was insufferably hot and flies flitted about, annoying students and teacher alike.

The interior of the school had a black iron heating stove that provided a minimal amount of heat in the winter. A stand in one corner of the room held a water bucket with a common dipper. Some students furnished their own drinking cups, but the other students used the common dipper when their concern about germs or a contagious disease was overcome by thirst. There was a teacher's desk at the front of the room. Rows of permanently installed student writing desks with attached seats, in gradations of size from small to large, accommodated the students in grades one through eight. All desks had an open-ink well located in the upper-right-hand corner of the desktop. There were times when some mischievous boy seated behind a girl, unfortunate enough to have long curls or braids, could not resist the temptation to dip her hair in the ink well. This action would be followed by a shriek from the girl, laughter from the class, and usually a few firm, well-placed swats administered by the teacher with the school paddle on the mischievous student's backside.

Shelves were mounted on each side of the room that held lunchboxes and any other extra supplies that didn't fit under the desktop in the storage area of a student's desk. Clothes hooks, evenly spaced under the shelves, provided a place to hang outdoor clothing. The room was very spartan, but no more so than most of the houses where the seventeen students enrolled in the school lived.

The school year was 160 days. Our first day of school was sometime after Labor Day in September, and our last day was the end of April. The school year accommodated the need for farmers to have their older children at home for the fall harvesting and spring planting of crops.

I remember my teacher, Miss Lorena Holtsclaw. During the school year, she lived with the Lillie family who had several children enrolled in the school. I didn't know it at the time, but her personal life was always being scrutinized by the community. Any misstep in her moral character would have been cause for immediate dismissal. By the 1930s, it was required that teachers have a two-year teaching certificate. Prior to that, the only requirement for anyone interested in teaching in a rural one-room school was to pass a qualifying examination. In many instances, the teacher would be only a few years older than her oldest students. It is possible Miss Holtsclaw received her teaching certificate from the recently established Kent State Normal School in Kent, Ohio.

Miss Holtsclaw, with the help of older students, would oversee that the drinking water bucket was filled each morning, inspect the lamps, and if needed, clean the glass globes and fill the lamp bowls with kerosene. In cold weather they stoked the fire in the heating stove, replenished the fuel supply, swept the schoolroom floors, and checked the outhouses for any needed maintenance. All this had to be done before it was time for someone to ring the school bell signaling the beginning of the school day.

My first day of school must have been very exciting for me, but I have no memory of it. I do remember Miss Holtsclaw. She was a tall soft-spoken lady who was kind to me. I was the only student in the first grade. I sat in the front row by the windows, where there were the smallest desks. The part I remember best about the school day was having the older children help me with my schoolwork and listening to the teacher as she instructed the upper-level classes.

According to the attendance record on my report card, it is evident I missed a lot of school that first year—thirty-eight and a half days. Thinking back, I had scarlet fever. The county nurse posted a red scarlet fever sign on our house, and the family was quarantined. My bed was placed in the living room, and when the doctor came to see me, he took my temperature by inserting a rectal thermometer—a mortifying experience that had to be endured. An aftereffect of the scarlet fever, which I dealt with into adulthood, was ear infections. This occurred every winter, and smelly puss would run from my left ear, requiring me to keep a cotton batten earplug in the ear.

My first- and second-grade report cards evidence the beautiful penmanship of my teacher. My report cards have given their whiteness over to a washed-out shade of brown but remain very legible. I averaged a B in all my subjects at the end of first grade, and by second grade, As and Bs were equally divided.

For all children, recess was the highlight of the day. I know this is where I learned the game "Andy-Andy-Eye-Over" that I played in the summers with Joy Fields. "Red Rover, Red Rover, send (player's name) on over" was a favorite game. Two captains were named and teams were selected. Each team would form a long line, lacing their arms together and firmly grasping the wrists of the person on each side. The two lines would stand about thirty feet apart and loudly chant the rhyme, calling someone over. Whoever was called would run as fast as possible into the opposite line of firmly laced arms, attempting to break through. I do remember that the older kids were reluctant to choose me to be on their team. I didn't have the strength in my hands to hang on to my partners' wrists, and I'd be a sure breakthrough spot for the competition to score points.

"Crack the Whip" was also popular. Here there is a "leader" and a "caboose." Being one of the youngest in the school, I never got to be the leader, but the kids loved to have me as a caboose. Once the line got started running, twisting, turning, it wasn't long before I would get thrown off, hitting the ground with a solid **whomp**! Obviously, the last person standing was the winner, and they would be the new leader.

Snowball fights were common in the winter. Otherwise, "Fox and Geese" was a favorite game. The first day that deep, fresh-fallen snow covered our playground, the older children would tromp out what appeared to be a large wagon wheel in the snow. The diameter of this snow wheel would be at least thirty feet, and the wheel was divided into eight sections. The hub, or center, of the wheel was the safe area in the game. Play would start with one student designated as the fox, the rest of us the geese. It didn't take long for a fox to catch me, and then I became the fox and had to tag one of the geese. Well, that seldom happened because I couldn't run the wagon wheel course fast enough to get one of the geese before it stood in the safe area of the wheel's hub. I didn't mind being the fox for long periods of time—at least I got to play.

We welcomed the fresh air, exercise, and camaraderie that took place during our recess and lunchtimes. The fights and occasional injuries were taken in stride. We were all farm kids and quite tough, taking the rough and tumble along with the fun.

The school celebrations that I remember best were the Christmas parties for students and their parents. It was like Christmas at home, only with a lot more people. A fir tree was cut, brought into the school, and decorated with paper and popcorn chains, glass bulbs, and icicles. The party was always held at night, and like at home, the light of the kerosene lamps caused the icicle strings to shimmer, and the glass tree bulbs reflected the lamp light, transforming the schoolroom into a magical, festive place. The coal heating stove seemed to give off additional warmth in the room, or perhaps it was the animal heat of many people gathered in a small space. A side table was laden with sandwiches, cookies, and cakes. I'm not sure what we had to drink, but there had to be something other than water from the classroom bucket.

The merriment inside the school would be interrupted when sleigh bells were heard, and a jolly voice rang out with a "Ho, ho, ho, Merry Christmas!" The door burst open, and jolly ole Saint Nick entered. In my imagination, I was certain Santa's sleigh and eight reindeer were parked just outside the door. Once inside, Santa dug in his pack and handed out candy to all the children—young and old alike.

It had to be either my first- or second-grade Christmas that Santa had, in addition to my candy, a present for me in his pack. He called my name and handed me the gift-wrapped box, placing it in my eagerly extended open hands. I excitedly tore off the wrapping paper. To my amazement it was a tiny four-drawer chest, measuring about eight-by-four-by-two inches and decorated with a colorful floral paper. My neighbor Evelyn Fischer, a student in the eighth grade, had given it to me. I kept that little chest on the dressing table in my bedroom and filled the small drawers with articles from treasured collections—necklaces, pins, small stones, etc. I had it for many years, but somehow in one of my many adult moves, the tiny chest was lost, never to be recovered.

The year was 1997, and we were celebrating my niece's fortieth birthday. She had invited me to join her, her husband, her brother, and his family on their trip to Europe. We were in a small German town, browsing in a curio shop, when I spied a smaller chest very similar to the one I had lost those many years ago. Seeing it, I lamented the story of the lost chest to my family. Peter, my nephew, immediately picked up the little chest, walked over to the clerk, and purchased it. He then came toward me and in a loving gesture placed it in my hands, saying this was to replace the one that had been lost. The small chest is covered with a dark-green paper embellished with pictures of roosters and flowers in a bucolic setting. Today it sits on my dresser, reminding me of the special little chest of my child-hood, and with it are added memories of demonstrated love.

By 1937 the state of Ohio had started the consolidation of one-room schoolhouse districts. The school I attended on Lillie Road was closed and became a part of the Jefferson School District in Ashtabula County. Somehow my dad managed to salvage one large, black slate chalkboard out of the school. He mounted it in one corner of our living room, and throughout my remaining elementary school years I used that slate to prac-tice my handwriting, do arithmetic problems, draw pictures, or perhaps just scribble. A pile of white chalk dust on the floor beneath the slate gave evidence of the hours I spent entertaining myself on those long winter evenings in the warmth of our living room. I didn't realize it at the time, but the closing of the one-room schoolhouse evidenced the passing of an uncomplicated era in my life.

MOM DID NOT HAVE TO AWAKEN ME for my first day of school that September of 1937. There would be no more walking to school for me. I would be rid-ing on my dad's school bus with about thirty-five other students he picked up along his ten-mile route into Jefferson. Students who boarded the bus that first day were of all ages. Some had attended Jefferson Local School District before; others of us were new and would be experiencing a school environment totally foreign to us.

My heart must have been beating rapidly as Dad pulled the bus into the school lot, stopped, opened the door, and all students exited the bus. I have no memory of how I knew where to go. Someone must have been there to give directions. I do vividly recall entering the two-story, nine-room brick school building that housed grades one through six. The large dou-ble doors at the entrance opened, and once inside I stood in a dark, dimly lit cavernous hallway illuminated by electric lights. A flight of steps went down to the basement where the toilets and the drinking fountains were located; a longer flight of steps led upward to the second floor. Somehow I managed to climb those steps and find the third grade classroom that would be my "home" for the remainder of the school year.

I later learned that all classrooms were furnished somewhat alike—stationary desks permanently fastened to the floor in six rows, with six desks per row to accommodate no more than thirty-six students. The teacher's desk, in the front of the room, faced the students' desks. Black chalkboards were mounted on two sides of the classroom. Above the chalkboards were pull-down maps. Beginning in the third grade, the Palmer method of cursive writing was taught, and these writing charts adorned the wall above the maps. At the back of the classrooms were cloak rooms with shelves for lunch boxes and hooks for the outdoor clothing. There were large double hung windows across the remaining side of the room that the teacher opened on extremely warm days. Large tables and chairs were placed at the back of the room and used to display students' projects. There was no playground equipment in the schoolyard. The uncompromising belief of the school superintendent was that children needed to socially interact, engaging in group games, during their noon and recess breaks.

Throughout all of my elementary grades, there were between thirty and thirty-five students in a classroom. Instruction was primarily by rote— reciting in unison our multiplication tables and spelling words. During reading class, we would be asked to take turns reading aloud. For me, the most fun was arithmetic instruction, when we would go to the blackboard to work our problems. Spelling bees were a favorite among the students.

Checking my elementary report cards, I find the record of my teachers' names, my attendance, and my grades. A school year required by law for city and village schools was 180 days, a twenty-day increase over the 160 days for the rural one-room schools that accommodated the needs of farm families.

Overall my yearly attendance was very good, with the exception of the third grade when I was absent for seventeen days. I must have had another childhood disease, but I don't remember which one. Academically I was a B student. In the third grade I was given a D in music, which only supported my piano teacher's comment, "Henrietta, you are wasting your parents' money taking piano lessons."

My third-grade teacher was Miss Edith Kister. Like Miss Holtsclaw, she was a tall, comely lady, soft-spoken and kind. The class was given maps of Ohio with the eighty-eight counties outlined on the map, and Miss Kister directed us to use a different color for each county. I started to cry. Miss Kister came to my desk and asked me why I was crying. I told her my crayon box only had sixteen colors in it and my folks could not afford to buy me a larger box of crayons. She gently leaned over and in a soft voice assured me the sixteen crayons would work very well. I could color some of the counties dark, some very light, just make sure I didn't use the same color for any two counties next to one another. It was in the third grade I learned that Ashtabula County was the largest county in the state and Lake County, located adjacent to the west, was the smallest county. Somehow this geographical fact fascinated me, and I felt so proud when I learned that I lived in the largest county in the state.

Another memory is related to our class play. Every elementary class was required to put on a play for the other elementary grades. The play was performed on the auditorium stage in the high school building. Our class was assigned the December play. I was an angel and wore a floor-length white dress and had a halo attached to my crop of thick, reddish-brown hair. I remember my angel wings were made from a bent wood frame covered with white tissue paper. This apparatus was secured to my shoulders and my arms so that when I moved my arms up and down, my angel wings gave the illusion that I was flying! Perhaps my latent thespian talents surfaced, for I felt so grown-up that day the class performed for the school and my parents were in the audience to see "their angel" in flight.

Sometimes it is almost frightening to me, the minutia that clutters my mind. Yet of everything that happened that year, those are the only two memories that stay with me. Why?

That first year I attended a school with other students in the same grade provided me the opportunity to actually have girlfriends. There was one girl, Esther, whom I liked very much. Her mom and dad operated the five-and-dime store in town. She lived close enough to the school to walk home for lunch, and there were times she invited me to join her. We became good friends, and over the years I would spend nights at her house. I remember we had our most fun roller-skating on the top floor of their garage building, or going to Isaly's for an ice cream cone, a soda, or the best taste treat of all—a banana split. To reciprocate, I invited Esther to come home with me on the bus to spend the night. Whenever I asked, Mom and Dad always gave their approval. The attraction at my home was playing in the hayloft of the barn, swinging on the tire rope swing, or helping me with my chores, which usually was collecting the eggs. We remained friends throughout our elementary school years. It is sad for me to admit, but as we advanced through the grades, we no longer shared common interests or talents, and by the time we entered the seventh grade, our friendship waned.

As I recall, by reputation, I had an exceptionally good teacher in my fourth grade, Miss Katherine O'Brien. That year I did very well in my academic subjects—almost all As.

In the fifth grade I was placed in Miss Betty Kopp's class. Her classroom was reminiscent of a one-room school, but instead of eight grades in one room, there were two grades, fourth and fifth. This time I was an upperclassman and occasionally was asked to help a fourth-grade student.

I recall reading in my fifth-grade geography book about the strong winds that blew over the prairie of the Great Plains. There were pictures of trees planted in rows near the farm buildings and along the edge of fields. These were called "windbreaks," and they served to lessen the force of the prevailing westerly winds that swept across the plains. I couldn't believe this to be true, that winds could be that strong. Years later when I was touring through Nebraska, I observed the open fields and felt the ferocity of the winds on the car in which I was riding. It was only then I realized the necessity for the windbreaks that provided protection to the buildings and aided in the prevention of land erosion, as well as the conservation of moisture in the soil.

One other geography fact I remember is the "siesta." The class was studying Mexico, and here I learned that due to the extreme heat, people took afternoon breaks to nap. Well, I'd experienced hot weather on the farm, and my dad used to keep working anyway. When I'd complain, Dad would say to me, "Get busy, Sis, and then you won't think about it and keep on working." In my young mind, I thought people that took a siesta were lazy. Years later, when I lived in Las Vegas and experienced the heat of the desert, I finally realized why a siesta was necessary to survival. It had nothing to do with being lazy.

My sixth-grade teacher was Miss Frances Leonard. Students in the sixth grade were at the top of the grade school totem pole. At noon and recesses, boys strutted around the playground, "making tough" with some of the younger students. The girls were more sedate and mostly hung together in their cliques or played games. Jumping rope was the favorite girls' game. All that was needed was a rope about ten or twelve feet long with a person at each end to hold the rope and swing it for the "jumper." Next to the school building was a wide area of concrete walk, an ideal place for turning the rope. Here we would jump to rhymes of "Mississippi," "I Like Coffee," "Ladybug, Ladybug," "Teddy Bear, Teddy Bear," and others too numerous to mention.

Sixth grade is the first time I recall that a boy showed any interest in me. During breaks, when I would walk about the playground with my girl-friend, I noticed one boy kept trailing me. His name was Kenneth Walker.

I'll never forget this first puppy love that amounted to nothing more than innocent playground shadowing.

It was in the sixth grade that my year-end report card averages had notations of some Cs. Obviously, something had distracted me from my studies. Maybe it was Kenny's flirtations, or maybe it was more difficult subject matter, perhaps a combination of the two.

School ended that year, and with a whoop and a holler, I boarded my dad's bus and eagerly accepted the ice cream bar that he handed out to each of the students on his route. I knew that when I returned in the fall, I would be entering the high school building, and with it a more demanding phase in my schooling would begin.

MOVING FROM THE ELEMENTARY SCHOOL to the high school building that housed grades seven through twelve was not as traumatic as leaving the rural one-room school and entering the unfamiliar environment of a "city" school. A major change for all sixth-grade students was being assigned a homeroom and changing classes every forty-five minutes, and with each change came a new teacher. Academically I did okay during my seventh and eighth grade years. Looking at my report cards, I note that my attendance was good, and I maintained a B average. There were no recess breaks in the morning or the afternoon; we now had scheduled physical education classes. The lunch break did allow time for students to walk around outside of the building or walk to the downtown area about a tenth of a mile distant.

During times of inclement weather, movies were shown in the auditorium for (I think) a nickel. That was a treat for me because living in the country, I seldom had the opportunity to go to the movies. I had no special girlfriends I hung out with, and boys gave me little attention. Many times I sat by myself in the darkened auditorium to watch the movie. Overall, I have few memories related to my first two years in the high school building.

My favorite teacher in the seventh grade was Mr. E. Charles Foster, who taught mathematics. He was a towering figure, standing well over six feet, whose impressive stature commanded respect from all his students. He made math class fun. One time, our class was studying the compass. Mr. Foster invited one of the upperclassmen to visit our room and give a demonstration on the 32 Cardinal Points of the compass. I was impressed as this older student stood by the chalkboard, pointed to the large chalk diagram of a compass, and while moving his hand in a clockwise motion around the circle, rattled off in an auctioneer's rapid-fire speech the names of those thirty-two cardinal points.

Another memory I have while a student in Mr. Foster's class was a most unfortunate one for a classmate. The class was not aware that one of the students was prone to epileptic seizures. It was during one of our class sessions that this boy suddenly fell out of his seat, onto the floor, writhing and foaming at the mouth. I was seated across from him in the next row and was terrified. Mr. Foster immediately came to the boy's aid, placing something between his teeth, and in his calm voice he assured the class the seizure would be over in a few minutes. He was right, but I for one was shaken by what I had observed.

AT THE CLOSE OF THEIR EIGHTH-GRADE YEAR, the students who had been attending the Lennox School, located a few miles south of Jefferson, were bused to Jefferson High School for the ninth grade. I was delighted to see some new faces in the freshman class. These were country kids like me, and I found I had a lot in common with them. Two of the girls that lived in Lennox became my closest friends and remained so until they died years later.

Near the end of the eighth grade, a guidance counselor had met with each student for the purpose of declaring their high school course of study. Mom made it clear that I was to take only college preparatory classes. Dutifully abiding by my parents' wishes, my classes that freshman year were English, algebra 1, general science, and Latin 1. It is the Latin 1 class that stays in my memory. I recall we had a first-year teacher. She was tall and thin, her voice was flat, and her entire demeanor imparted a pending nervous collapse. Sensing another person's vulnerability, children can be as cruel to another human being as chickens in a henhouse can be to an injured fowl. No mercy is shown as the hens peck the injured bird to its death. Sensing that our teacher did not know how to control the class, we students were unmerciful in our behavior. We laughed, cut up, and pulled pranks, and consequently little learning took place. The building principal, who had the dual role of also being the school superintendent, came into our classroom and severely reprimanded us for our disrespectful behavior. The class calmed down for a short time but soon reverted to previous antics. I know our misbehavior professionally destroyed our teacher, at least for that year. I, too, paid a price. I learned almost nothing in my Latin 1 class, and it was only with my brother's tutoring that I got through Latin 2.

In my sophomore year, I continued with classes in English and history, but my poor study habits were beginning to catch up with me. I would complete my assignments but did not have a great deal of concern for the quality of my work. I managed to get through my freshman year algebra 1 class, but I wasn't doing very well in plane geometry. Fortunately, I sat next to a boy who liked me, and he helped me get through the class.

Physical education (gym) classes were required each year from seventh through twelfth grades. Mom made my gym outfits. She made two identical white cotton one-piece top-and-short outfits. I thought they were quite stylish. During the fall and spring, classes were held outside. Archery and tennis were my favorite sports. During the winter our classes were in the gym, and calisthenics and half-court basketball were the common activities. Girls were admonished not to overexert ourselves and consequently, due to our "delicate" monthly condition, we were excused from gym class and showering. The forty-five-minute, semiweekly classes provided very limited time for actual participation. Dressing and showering took up half of the class time.

It was during my junior and senior years that teachers would say to me, "So you are Lloyd's sister." The comment was usually said by the science and math teachers and, although unspoken, inferred that I would be an outstanding student in these areas, as was my brother. In his senior year Lloyd had placed first in the state in one of the competitive science tests.

My mind did not work in the abstract arena of mathematics, and I certainly had no interest or aptitude for the sciences. Truth be told, I was made to feel quite inferior in intelligence to my brother—a feeling I did not recover from until well into adulthood. I plodded along through those last two years of high school with more end-of-year Cs than Bs. I never came close to being nominated for the National Honor Society—that was for the smart kids.

The thespian talent I had was enough that I was selected for parts in both the junior and the senior class plays, as well as a one-act play. Due to my height and mature appearance, I was always given matronly roles, playing someone's aunt, mother, or grandmother. Fortunately, during my high school years, I had formed a close friendship with a girl, Jean Roberts, who lived just on the outskirts of Jefferson. Her family would let me stay with them the night of play rehearsals.

School plays were performed in the high school auditorium. Mom and Dad were always in the audience for at least one performance of each play I was in. I know they were proud of me.

I lived ten miles from the school and that hampered me in my desire to take part in extracurricular activities. In the *1946-1947 J-HI-LIFE* publication, I am credited with chorus 1, 2, 4; band 1, 2; sophomore and senior class plays, and the one-act play. As a member of the chorus, I sang in the soprano section; I couldn't harmonize to sing with the altos. I was never selected for the chorus line of the Minstrel Show productions—I was too tall. I quit the band after my sophomore year—another indicator that I had little desire to discipline myself to use whatever musical talent I did have.

Room 14, located on the second floor of the school, was a large classroom that doubled for a study hall and the school library. This room held a special significance for me. During my freshman year, it was here that my first serious puppy love affair blossomed. Windsor (Windy) Sullivan was one of the Lennox School students. Windy stood about five feet two inches tall, with blond hair, a catching laugh, and an infectious smile. We were not in any of the same academic classes, but we were assigned the same period for study hall in room 14. We both sat in the row next to the blackboards, three seats apart. Windy first expressed his attraction for me by passing a note to my attention. This required the discreet cooperation of the girls who were seated between us. Once our friendship was established, his writings—the paper meticulously folded with actual musical notes surrounding my name—became a daily study hall ritual. I kept those notes for several years, but at the time of my first marriage, I foolishly destroyed them. How sad, for they were a treasure trove of a first love.

Our attraction was more than a room 14 study hall adventure. Windy had a driver's license; on Saturday nights he would drive the fifteen miles from Lennox to my home and take me to a movie in Ashtabula. After the movie we would enjoy a soda at the Isaly's store. When he brought me home, he would escort me to the door, and due to the six-inch difference in our heights, he would stand on the back step to give me a good-night kiss. Why he ever chose me—a tall, auburn-haired, gangly girl from the country—I'll never know. Windy and I dated during our freshman and sophomore years, and then we went the way of most puppy love affairs—without cause or reason it ended.

Another event that took place in room 14 was with my high school English teacher, Miss Doris March. This occurred in the spring of my junior year. I was now seated in a row by the windows on the opposite side of the room. Miss March approached my desk, knelt down to my seated eye level, and informed me I was the girl selected by the faculty committee to lead the senior class into the auditorium for the Sunday baccalaureate graduation service. She went on to say that Eddie White, one of the top academic and athletically talented boys in the class, would be my partner. Would I like to do this?

The bright light flowing through the windows made it difficult for me to focus on Miss March's face; she appeared almost mystical to me, and for a moment I thought it was a daydream. My response was a nod of my head, and in a whispered voice I replied with a faint, "Yes, I would." Miss March went on to say I would be required to wear a white dress; she hoped that would not be a problem.

I got off the bus that evening and raced up the drive, calling to Mom, "You will never guess what I was asked to do today in school!" My parents were equally thrilled for me. Mom saw to it I had not one but two white dresses. She made the one that I wore for the rehearsal. It was a white eyelet fitted dress, with lace framing a modest square neckline. The dress buttoned down the front. Somewhere Mom found the money to buy the dress I'd wear for the Sunday processional. This dress was simple in its elegance—a princess-cut cotton chiffon. I felt so proud that Sunday afternoon as I stood next to Eddie; together we led the senior class processional down the center aisle of the auditorium to the school orchestra's strains of the traditional graduation march, Elgar's "Pomp and Circumstance."

ADMITTEDLY, ACADEMICS WERE NOT MY PRIORITY throughout my high school years. Boys took a lot of my attention. Proms were a big event in the spring, but I never had a date to either my junior or senior proms. In my junior year the boy from Lennox, Howard March, who helped me get through my freshman geometry class, asked me to be his date. I declined. If I had a reason it was because I didn't think of him as being "glamorous" enough. My senior year I was going steady, dating a boy who had already graduated from high school. Due to school policy, he was not eligible to attend the prom with me. He did drive me to the prom, I went in alone, stayed for the dinner, and left early when he came to pick me up. I made adolescent mistakes, first when I declined Howard's invitation to be his date my junior year and amplified that mistake by dating an older boy during my senior year.

———————·+++++·———————

GRADUATION FOR THE FORTY-FIVE MEMBERS OF OUR CLASS was held in May of 1947 in the high school auditorium. Viola Kaipainen, my best friend, was the commencement speaker. My parents were there to see me walk across the stage and receive my diploma from the president of the school board; afterward we drove home. I did not have a graduation party—there were no family members or friends to invite. No special meal was prepared; animals needed attention and other chores had to be done.

The *J-HI-LIFE* staff responsible for writing the "WE PROPHESY" section of the publication wrote with tongue-in-cheek:

> Henrietta Schumann has at last gotten her law degree.
> I heard that Harvard had given her an honorary
> degree after Princeton chose her as their dean.

Reading on in the same publication, "AND NOW WE LEAVE YOU":

> Henrietta Schumann and Betty Eaken leave their abil-
> ity of getting and holding on to their men to Martha
> Wolfe and Jean Connelly.

Obviously, the prophecy is a satire on my high school academic and leadership achievements; the bequeath part had a truer ring.

After graduation, class reunions were held. I attended most of them. The first reunion was held five years after we graduated; then celebrations of the twenty-fifth, forty-fifth, fifty-fifth, fifty-seventh, and the sixtieth in 2007—at this writing, the last.

Almost the same people came each time, and at each reunion more classmates' names were added to the "in memory of" list. Most of those who came continued to act like they did in high school, especially the women who reverted to cliquish, giggling high-school-girl behaviors.

The men were somewhat more subdued, but still socialized and grouped together as they did in high school.

———— ++++++ ————

NEGATIVE FEELINGS OF INADEQUACY AND EXCLUSION remained with me long after graduation from high school. It was about 1970 when I read a book written by Ralph Keyes, *Is There Life after High School?* This book provided me with an insight that was the catalyst for a profound positive change of attitude. In his book, Keyes poses questions related to high school. Class president? Leadership position selected by popular vote of the student body? Cheerleader? Editor of school publications? Date to the prom? Recognized star athlete? Are memories of high school…enduring? Pleasurable? Painful? But the question that smacked me head-on was, were you an "innie" or an "outie"?

I pondered the questions related to academic achievement, leadership positions, athletic prowess, extracurricular-activity involvement, and social acceptance. The question that stood out, and overshadowed all others, was the one related to the "innie" versus the "outie" groups. I was an "outie" always wanting to be included with the "innie" group. The "innies" in my class, for the most part, were the kids that lived in town; those of us who were bused in from the "boonies" were the "outies." There were several of us who had talents, but due to whatever extenuating circumstances that stood in the way, we were never called on or found ourselves in a position to use those talents during our high school years. Oh, there were exceptions! My friend Viola Kaipainen was an "outie"—one of the Lennox students. She was smart, recognized not only by her teachers, but by her peers, for her superior intelligence. It didn't bother her that she was plain-looking and overweight. For me, being selected by the faculty committee to lead the senior baccalaureate processional was the highlight of my high school years. Had this been a position voted on by the junior class, I know I would not have been chosen. I was not that popular with my classmates.

———— ++++++ ————

IN 1947, WHEN I GRADUATED FROM HIGH SCHOOL, I was still very young and very immature. I did not realize that about myself at the time. I moved on to the next chapter in my life with that albatross of inferiority weighing heavy around my neck.

+ + ◆ ◆ ◆ + +

SIX

MOVING ON, LIFE AWAITS

URING HIGH SCHOOL, roller-skating became my passion. Tall girls were not in vogue in the 1940s. I never learned ballroom dancing. I was too self-conscious, being taller than most of the boys in my age group. I did roller-skate. I could slouch when skating with a boy, and my height was not so apparent—at least it seemed so to me.

I distinctly remember the first time I entered a roller rink. A neighbor girl invited me to go roller-skating with her. I was about twelve years old. When I walked into the Jefferson skating rink, I was awed by the building size, the crowd, the music blasting over the loudspeakers, the skaters gracefully gliding round and round. I was mesmerized, and I was hooked on skating.

When they could, Mom or Dad would drive me to the rink, but my skating opportunities were very limited until I was allowed, at the age of fourteen, to drive (albeit unlawfully) the six miles of back roads from our farm to the skating rink located on Route 46 north of Jefferson. On most Wednesday nights, which was ladies' night when admission for the girls was only four cents, I could be found at the roller rink. The rink was always packed with kids and young adults from the rural farm areas as well as from Jefferson and Ashtabula.

As time went on, I progressed from the rental clip-on skates to owning my own white shoe skates adorned with red yarn pom-poms tied onto the laces of the shoes' toes. By the time I was sixteen, a senior in high school, I could skate with the best in the crowd. I endured fanny falls, skinned knees and elbows, and black-and-blue marks that became semipermanent tattoos on my arms and legs. Miraculously, through it all, I never had any broken bones while learning to skate backwards and turning on one foot both to my right and to my left—skating skills that were a prerequisite to being a graceful partner for the Couples Waltz, the Fourteenth Step, and most challenging of all, the Flea Hop skated to the tune of "Pistol Packin' Mamma."

———— ·•••••· ————

WITH MY ACQUIRED SKATING SKILLS came my popularity. I think it was the summer between my junior and senior years in high school that I met Van Arvid Musgrave—tall, blond, with blue eyes, son of a prosperous dairy farmer. The romance lasted for only a short time. He never made it to the skating rink until after the cows were milked, and that was close to the eleven o'clock closing time. When we dated on a Saturday night, I would lie on my bed looking out of my south bedroom window watching for headlights that would signal his approach. Due to the lateness of the hour, dating involved a drive, seldom a movie, finding a quiet place to park, and some smooches before taking me back home. Sometime during that fall of my senior year, we broke up. It was Van Arvid, not I, who ended our brief romantic encounter.

Shortly after my failed romance with the dairy farmer's son, I met Lee Henderson. He was a regular at the Wednesday night skates. He was about my height, dark-haired, and average-appearing. Lee was a good skater and had a pleasant way about him. We became regular skating partners, and from that evolved a romantic relationship that led to our engagement. Lee was ten years my senior, divorced, and a father of three—a girl age three, two boys ages four and six. He was given full custody of his children by the courts; apparently his ex-wife was deemed an unfit mother.

In hindsight I ponder how I ever allowed myself, a young girl of seventeen, to get so deeply involved with an older man. The fall of my senior year, I took Lee home to introduce him to my parents. He was accepted by Mom with open arms. At the time my dad said nothing. The introduction to his children took place a few weeks before Christmas. Mom, always sensitive to the needs of others, bought gifts for the two boys and the little girl. I don't recall what she gave to the boys, but for the girl it was a doll with a complete wardrobe—the same as she had done for me when I was a child. Lee was an electrician, and later that year when my brother was home on leave from the navy, he helped Lloyd wire our house for electricity.

I was never comfortable introducing Lee to my friends. In fact, I didn't. I was self-conscious about his age and his children. Nevertheless, I went ahead with making plans for our wedding. We were to be married in the West Side Presbyterian Church in Ashtabula. The wedding date was set for June. To keep costs down, Mom offered to make my wedding dress. A pattern was selected, the satin material and trimmings purchased, and Mom sewed for hours on her Singer treadle machine, and I watched as the dress took form. The dress shimmered in its elegance as I tried it on for the final fitting. Wedding invitations were printed, addressed ready to be mailed, and the cake was ordered. The wedding would take place in the church with a cake-and-punch reception following the ceremony in the church social hall.

Throughout the month of May, as I prepared for graduation from high school, feelings of misgiving about the marriage mounted within me until I could contain them no longer. I remember asking Mom what she thought of my marriage to Lee. Her response remains with me to this day: "Henrietta, God puts us on this earth to serve others. Perhaps your reason for being here is to be a good wife and mother to this family."

It was just another day close to the end of the school year. I got out of bed that morning; Dad had already gone to work. Agonizing over the pending marriage, I had slept little that night. Mom was seated at the kitchen table having a cup of tea when I came down to breakfast. I unburdened my feelings to Mom—my doubts, my apprehensions, my fears. I wanted a dialogue that would help to quell the disquiet I felt. Mom had little to say. After her previous advice, she refused to help me with my decision. She said it was mine alone to make. Mom and I had had many long and intimate teatime talks during my growing-up years. When I needed her counsel, she was strangely quiet.

I was not able to make myself go to school that day. I stayed home, hunkered in the kitchen by the stove, trying to rid myself of the gnawing feeling that was destroying my stomach. By afternoon I knew I could not marry Lee; I could not be his wife and a stepmother to his three children. Late that afternoon, I drove to Lee's home in Ashtabula. I had a key to his house and let myself in. Mercifully, no one was at home when I entered. I placed the house key, my engagement ring, his picture, and my written note that I could not marry him on the dining room table. Later that evening, Lee drove out to the farm to confront me regarding my decision. I saw him but stood firm in my resolve that I could not marry him.

A weight was lifted from my young shoulders, and with it I felt a new freedom.

--------------- ++++++ ---------------

AFTER GRADUATION FROM HIGH SCHOOL, I got a job in Ashtabula as a waitress in the dining room at the Hotel Ashtabula. Mom and Dad secured a room for me in the home of Miss Martin, a lady who lived on our egg route. Her house was located across the Ashtabula River ravine on East Forty-Seventh Street, about three fourths of a mile from the hotel.

The dining room was open for lunch from 11:30 a.m. to 2:00 p.m. and again for dinner from 5:00 to 9:00 p.m. Most of the staff was required to work a split shift to accommodate these hours. To save money, I walked the distance twice a day across the iron bridge that connected Main Street to the East side residential area. I liked working in the hotel dining room. I served lunch and dinner to a classy clientele, and tips were good. It was not long before I wearied of the split shift, and when I learned there was a waitress position open at the Jack Mintz Restaurant just up the street, I applied and got the job. My shift assignment was to start at 3:30 p.m. and end at midnight.

The dining room at the hotel was light and airy with large windows; the tables were covered with white tablecloths and matching napkins. By comparison the Jack Mintz Restaurant was dreary. There were no exterior windows; there was dark woodwork throughout and large floor fans were used to circulate the hot, stifling air. Wooden booths, an eating counter, and a bar made up the seating areas. A jukebox stocked with popular records was played by the diners who inserted change into the money slot. Patti Page, Frankie Laine, Glenn Miller, Bing Crosby, and Perry Como were a few of the popular singers of the day. I heard the songs "Peg o' My Heart," "The Whiffenpoof Song," "Now Is the Hour," "Sixteen Tons," and "How Much Is That Doggie in the Window" so often that I still recognize and can hum the tunes to this day, albeit off key.

Our uniforms were white starched dresses, white shoes, and a mandatory hairnet. Management discouraged social conversation with customers, and waitresses were always directed to stand at attention monitoring their assigned stations (specific areas in the restaurant), even if there were no customers to serve. Management ignored the fact that I was only seventeen and the legal age for drinking or serving liquor was twenty-one, but when no older waitress was on duty, I was instructed to serve the customers at the bar. I made a fast trip climbing the learning curve to familiarize myself regarding alcoholic beverages. I came from a family that, to my knowledge, did not drink—at all! I soon learned about beers, both bottled and draft, and how to make mixed drinks.

————————++++++————————

THEN IT HAPPENED! From the first time the handsome tall, blond, blue-eyed nineteen-year-old man with an engaging smile sat down at the bar, ordered a beer, and spoke in a soft, melodious voice, I was twitterpated. His visits to the restaurant became nightly events that I anticipated with a shortness of breath, a rapid heartbeat, and a pain in my stomach.

I ignored the rule not to converse with the customers. When my assigned station was booths in the restaurant area, I used every excuse to be at the bar so I could have brief conversations with him. His name was Sidney (Sid) Nelson. He lived with his family in Swede Town in Ashtabula where all the Swedish immigrants settled. Sid was a sailor who had a job as an oiler on the Ashtabula Carferry—a lake-going vessel that traversed the waters of Lake Erie between its home port and Port Burwell, Ontario daily, carrying railroad cars filled with coal and/or ore.

Apparently, our feelings were mutual, because after a few nightly visits to the restaurant, Sid asked if he could drive me home when my shift ended. My answer of "yes" was a no-brainer. It was near closing time, so he remained seated at the bar sipping a beer while I finished the assigned duties of my shift. Together we walked out of the restaurant. To my amazement, he guided me to a beautiful dark-green car parked in front of the building. He opened the passenger side door and beckoned me to get in. That night I did not walk the three-fourths of a mile across the bridge to the house on East Forty-Seventh Street. I rode in style, seated next to this handsome young man, in a 1940 Packard sedan.

It became routine for Sid to be there each night when I finished my shift. Before taking me home, he would drive around Ashtabula, and on warm nights the destination would be Walnut Beach. We would take midnight swims in the warm waters of Lake Erie, then lay out on the sandy beach, and looking skyward, identify the constellations in the heavens. We were two young people falling in love.

The Carferry did not run on weekends. Sid lived at home, and I didn't have to report for my shift at the restaurant until midafternoon.

That gave us the opportunity to explore the city in the daytime. I knew nothing about the harbor area of Ashtabula. On one of our drives, he took me into this area, to Walnut Boulevard, where the stately lakefront homes were located. Sid stopped the car in front of a lot where there appeared to be a formal garden located between two of the grand homes that lined the street. Without saying a word, he got out, came around, and opened the car door for me. Taking my hand, he started to walk toward the garden. I protested, saying this looked like it was private property. Sid just smiled and continued to walk into the garden and along the manicured paths lined with a variety of flowers, flowering shrubs, and towering arborvitae bushes. Sid told me the property was owned by the Topkey family, who also owned and operated the hardware store on Bridge Street in the Harbor.

It was known that the Topkeys encouraged the local residents to visit and to enjoy their garden. I clearly remember that as we walked, Sid remarked, "Someday I am going to own a house here on Walnut Boulevard." I was stunned, yet impressed, by this apparent show of confidence. I lacked such confidence, and to be with someone who expressed belief in himself electrified me. I realized I was with a young man who held dreams for his future.

Our times together were as frequent as our work schedules permitted. We were in love. Our drives in the Packard took us to remote areas where we parked, and I put no stops on our caressing that quickly moved to intimacy. It was in August that I realized I was pregnant.

In the conservative 1940s, what did a respectable single pregnant girl do? She got married.

◆◆◆◆◆

SEVEN

MARRIAGE TO SIDNEY NELSON
(1947–1960)

IT WAS IN AUGUST OF 1947 that I told Sid I was pregnant. He immediately made plans for us to be married. Somehow he knew that if we
eloped to Kentucky, we could be married the same day that we applied
for our license. In Ohio, prior to 2001, there was a five-day waiting period.
We looked at a map, and the city of Covington was selected for our wedding destination.

The city is located south of Cincinnati, just across the Ohio River.
The interstate corridors did not exist in 1947, and it was about 330 miles
using state routes.

Both Sid and I managed to fabricate stories that gave us the needed
time off from our jobs. We set Friday, August 29, as the day we would
leave. The Ashtabula Carferry did not run on weekends, so Sid needed to
take only Friday off; for me it was three days, because I always worked the
weekends.

My immediate concern was my wedding dress. Sid said he liked black;
morbid as it may seem, I shopped and selected a black satin knee-length
dress for my wedding. (That dress is preserved in my hope chest.) How to
tell our families? I don't recall how Sid told his mom or dad, or if he did at
all. I had confided in my mom that I was pregnant and Sid and I were going
to elope. Mom advised me not to say anything to Dad but to leave a note
on my pillow. The morning I was to leave, she would conveniently find it
and in turn tell Dad. I did as Mom requested. The short note I wrote said
something to the effect that I was pregnant and Sid and I were going to

elope to Covington, Kentucky, where we could get a marriage license and be married the same day. I would be back on Sunday night and would stay in Ashtabula in my room at the house on East Sixteenth Street. Sid would go on to the Carferry.

The 1940 Packard, that grand dark-green car that impressed me the first time Sid took me home, served us well on our elopement trip. We stopped that Friday night at a house with rooms for rent just north of Cincinnati. Saturday morning we got up and dressed for our wedding. Sid wore a gray suit, white shirt, and tie; I put on my black satin dress and black pumps. We did make a good-looking couple. Sid drove through Cincinnati, crossed the bridge into Kentucky, and immediately we were in Covington. As I recall it was not a large city. Sid had no trouble finding a place to park on what appeared to be the main street. We got out of the car and started to walk. We needed to find a place to get information on how and where to get married.

We must have had a sign on our backs that read "Want to get married" because we walked only a short distance before a man came up to us and inquired if, in fact, we were looking to be married. Nodding our heads yes, he offered to take us to the courthouse. I have no memory of how we provided the required proof of identification. But we got the marriage license and left the courthouse with our self-proclaimed escort, asking no questions when he took us to a lab for our blood test. Once inside and seated, I looked in horror as a woman came toward me with a syringe aimed at my right arm. Given no time to protest, I closed my eyes and felt nauseated as the large needle was plunged into my vein; when it was Sid's turn, he did not even wince. (I question the validity of that blood test made in the few hours between getting our marriage license and being married.) It was with relief that we left the lab and walked the final distance to the waiting minster.

At this point my mind is a mishmash of memories. We entered a building (minister's house?), stood in the middle of what could have been the living room, and before the Reverend W. H. Hale of the Church of Christ and two witnesses (Janet Hale and Alvis Honeycutt—our escort?), we repeated our vows. Sidney placed a ring on the fourth finger of my left hand, and we were pronounced man and wife. There must have been fees for the marriage license, the blood tests, the minister, and a big tip to the "escort," but I have no recollection of what they were.

I can only surmise as we left the building with our marriage certificate in hand that we breathed a collective sigh of relief and found a place to eat and lodging for the night. We left early Sunday morning and drove directly home to Ashtabula. Sidney had to report to the Ashtabula Carferry on Monday, and I needed to be at my waitress job at the Jack Mintz Restaurant that afternoon.

The first time we visited our parents as Mr. and Mrs. Sidney Nelson there were awkward moments of embarrassment and of dialogue, at least for me. An announcement was to be placed in the *Ashtabula Star Beacon*, and Mom insisted that our marriage date be August 2, not August 30. That was for the benefit of the nosy neighbors who would count the months between our marriage and the birth of a baby as eight, not seven. The Nelson family accepted me with open arms and open hearts. From the very first, his family became an indispensable part of my life. For this reason, I consider it important to make known the members of my husband's family.

PETER NELSON (PA) WAS BORN ON FEBRUARY 20, 1873, in Gulofov, Sweden. As was the custom of the time, Swedish boys at a young age took to the sea. Pa sailed around the world several times on the tall ships, and would proudly tell about when he "rounded the horn" (Cape Horn) off the tip of South America. He fell overboard and had to be rescued.

Some years later he sailed on the Great Lakes and established a residence with other Swedes in Ashtabula. It was here he brought his young family in 1912, to their house on Pacific Street, later buying a home on Sibley Street (renamed E. Sixteenth Street). As his family grew, and wanting to be near his home, he found employment with the Ashtabula Carferry and later the New York Central Railroad.

Pa was retired when I married Sid. I have no visual memory of Pa as a younger man; the earliest picture I have of him is from 1927. He is with his family standing next to his wife, Anna. His hat covers his head, and the brim casts a shadow over his eyes. He stands straight and projects a picture of strength. This was not the Pa I knew for the few years before he died. I remember a man of medium build, slightly hunched, possibly five feet six inches tall, with blue eyes, partially bald, who spent his summers tending his vegetable garden and looking after the goats and chickens that inhabited the barn on their property. In the winter he could be found in his basement chewing Copenhagen snuff while crafting models of some of the tall ships he sailed on. All the model ships he hand crafted were created totally from memory. A model of the *Flying Cloud* was featured in a March 15, 1927 article that appeared in the *Cleveland Plain Dealer.* It is unfortunate for the family that this model was sold for a paltry sum during the Depression years. The family needed the money.

After we were married, Sid told me his dad put this question to him, "You don't have to marry her, do you?" Sid, out of concern for me, told his dad, "No." I'm certain his dad knew his son was telling one of those save-face white lies. Pa died at the veterans' hospital in Cleveland of age-related complications on July 3, 1951. The only time I knew Sidney to cry was at the time of his father's death. I cried as well—for my husband's loss, and because I too had grown to love this quiet, gentle man.

Anna Nelson, née Rosengren was born on October 6, 1885, in Skane, Sweden. Anna and Peter were married in Viby, Sweden, on May 22, 1909. In May 1912, Anna, with her toddler-aged daughter, Margit Gunborg, immigrated to the United States. Pa met them at Ellis Island and brought his young family to the house on Pacific Street in Ashtabula.

Ma was steadfast in her principles, firm in her beliefs, impervious to the vicissitudes of life. She was unequaled in her culinary talents. Her home was a testament to the mantra "Cleanliness is next to godliness." At first, I was intimidated by her. It was evident that I had grown up on a farm and my lifestyle was diametrically opposite to what she stood for and tolerated in housekeeping. If Ma detected any of this, she never let me know, for she accepted me, encouraged me, and cherished me. During that first year of marriage to her son, my feelings of inferiority and intimidation soon were transformed into respect and awareness that I had much to learn from this remarkable woman. Ma died on May 6, 1981.

The oldest of the Nelson siblings, Margit Gunborg (Gunne) Martin, née Nelson was born on May 15, 1910, in Sweden, and was brought by her mother to the United States in 1912. She married Richard (Dick) Martin, and they had one child, Karin. Gunne divorced Dick in January 1943. Anna raised her granddaughter while Gunne supported her family working as a nurse in the US Veterans Hospital in Brecksville, Ohio. Gunne died on January 14, 1984.

Evelyn (Nin) Brandenburg, née Nelson was born in Ashtabula on March 10, 1913. After graduating from high school, she and a friend went to live and work in Chicago. She was an executive secretary with the Brunswick Corporation. It was there she met her husband, Robert

Brandenburg, who worked for the Pure Food and Drug Division of the United States Government. Nin died on January 10, 2008.

Verner Nelson was born on October 22, 1914, and worked as an engineer for the Boland and Cornelius American Steamship Company. He married but later divorced. The couple had several children. I knew little of Verner or his family. He died on October 23, 1976.

Dorothy (Dot) Nelson was born on April 11, 1921, and after graduating from high school lived in Cleveland where she was an executive secretary for several companies with corporate headquarters in the city. Dot never married and, at a cost to her personal life, was resolute in her devotion to her mother and later, when I became a widow, to me and my sons. She died on May 2, 1979.

It is very possible that Sidney Nelson never would have been conceived if Ma and Pa, accompanied by their four children, had not taken a trip to Sioux City, Iowa, in September 1927 to visit Pa's sister and family. Nin tells the story that due to the number in their family, and the available beds in her aunt's home, Ma and Pa were made to share a bed, which they didn't normally do. It was nine months later, May 21, 1928, that Sidney was born.

Karin Lovell, née Martin, born on March 31, 1942, was raised by her maternal grandmother. Karin was five years old when I married her uncle. She was a polite, beautiful, petite, blonde child. After Sidney and I established our home in Ashtabula, Karin would spend a week or two with us each summer. She was the daughter I did not have. As of this writing, Karin is the only surviving member of the Nelson family.

There is a Nelson family four-grave lot in the Edgewood Cemetery in Ashtabula. The bodies of Ma, Pa, Gunne, and Sid are interred there; the urns containing the ashes of Nin and Dot are buried on two of the grave sites. Verner died in a San Francisco hospital and was cremated; his cremains were spread at sea.

At the suggestion of my son Bruce, in 1993 I had a plaque placed on The American Immigrant Wall of Honor at Ellis Island recognizing the Anna and Peter Nelson Family who in 1912 emigrated from Sweden to the United States.

AFTER OUR WEDDING, both Sid and I returned to our jobs, but only for a short time. We had no place to live as husband and wife and little money.

Facing this reality, I quit my job at the restaurant and returned to live on the farm. Sid terminated his job on the Ashtabula Carferry and, having sailed on the Great Lakes, was able to get a job working as an oiler in the engine room on the *George F. Rand*, one of the steamships in the fleet of the American Steamship Company headquartered in Buffalo, New York. This was not a satisfactory arrangement for a newly married couple, but it did provide a place for each of us to live and, more important, to save money.

Both of our parents were supportive of our decision. Within a few weeks of our marriage, Ma Nelson and daughters Gunne and Dot had a shower for me at the family home on East Sixteenth Street. This was the first time I met their friends in the close-knit Swedish community. Over these many years, their names have faded in my memory but not my feelings connected with the friendly warmth that was extended to me that day.

Second in priority to Ma's mantra "Cleanliness is next to godliness" was the importance she placed on setting a fine table. The Nelson family gave Sid and me a starter set of Franciscan Desert Rose china; over the years this fine china has been completed with service for twelve, including all serving pieces. Another gift was marked from "Skipper" and was a recipe box containing Swedish recipes. The puzzled look on my face brought laughter from those present until it was explained to me that Skipper was a cat, the house pet of the Stone sisters who were neighbors. To this day the recipe box is referred to as the "Skipper box." These two gifts are now with my granddaughter Candice Nelson Hayes. My mother gave us bed linens with an original poem about "line-dried, soft and fresh, sheets of white, comfort the weary body at night." Her poem is lost, but not her loving gesture of acceptance of our marriage.

Our baby was due in April, and for that first winter together, Sid was able to make arrangements to be a shipkeeper on the *Consumers Power* that was docked in Sandusky, Ohio. (The shipkeeper is a watchman in charge of a ship in the absence of officers and crew.)

On December 17, Sid was discharged from his duties on the *George F. Rand*, came to the farm for me, and together we drove the 130 miles to the Sandusky waterfront and the boat that was to be our winter home. We arrived at the dock where the boat was moored, and as we got out of our car, I stood in shock as I looked up at the huge vessel—605 feet long, with 24 feet of freeboard above the waterline! How was I to get to the top deck?

Sid took my hand, walked me over to a metal ladder attached to the side of the ship, and told me the only way to get there was to climb that ladder. Given no other option, I started up with Sid following directly below me and made it to the top deck, only to face the fierce winds off Lake Erie that lashed my body. We hurried to the aft end of the boat, and with key in hand, Sid unlocked the door and we entered the frigid interior of the ship's galley. I found myself facing a huge, black cast-iron stove, refrigerators, freezers, cupboards, sinks, and counters—all standard equipment found in a kitchen, only much larger in size. Sid immediately started a fire in the stove, which soon provided some warmth to counter the frigid temperature of the room.

All of this was new to me, and it took only a short time to tour what would be our living quarters. There was a large pantry stocked with canned and boxed foods, meats in the freezer—all ours for the using. When we left for home in the spring, we did take some of the food from the pantry and meat from the freezer. Sid made sure he took all the cans of Folgers Coffee for Ma Nelson, her favorite brand.

That winter, we never strayed far from the warmth of the kitchen as there were no other provisions for heat on the ship. In fact, the galley became our multipurpose living quarters—kitchen, living room, and bedroom. There was a toilet not too far distant. Due to the fact there was no heat on the boat, all pipes were drained for the winter. There was a large tank in the galley area filled with potable water, and that was where Sid would draw our water supply, bucket by bucket, for drinking, cooking and washing dishes and/or self. A bucket filled with water for flushing was placed in the room with the toilet. We found a laundromat not too far from the boat where we did our laundry. We wore clean, but wrinkled, clothes that winter. I made no effort to search for an iron or ironing board.

Sid's main duty as the shipkeeper was to test the water level in the ballast tanks daily to ensure that the boat remained stable in its moorings at the dock. This allowed him many idle hours during the day. Ever conscious that earning and saving our money was a top priority, Sid knew that he could make extra dollars by identifying a needed project. The officer's dining hall was located just off the galley. The wainscoting in the room was in dire need of scraping, staining, and varnishing. Sid took on the job, and it provided him with additional work and income for the remainder of the winter. I think I helped some, not a lot. My time was taken up with cooking and routine household tasks.

We stayed to ourselves that winter. The *George F. Rand* was tied to the starboard side of the *Consumers Power*. The shipkeeper of the *Rand* had to cross the deck of our boat to get to his. I have no recollection of this person. We had no social life other than the companionship of each other. Our entertainment was a radio and reading books or the newspaper. We had mail delivery, but not to our door. Sid would walk to the watchman's booth on the dock to get it. At night as I lay in bed, I would listen to the creaking of the boat giving way to a slight movement caused by the fierce winds or the lapping of the water on the ship's hull. These were musical sounds, and they lulled me to sleep.

I vividly remember the Sunday that Dad came with my younger sister, Brenda. Dad had sent a letter telling us he was coming and the approximate time of his arrival. That Sunday morning Sid and I kept stepping out on deck to view the expanse of the dock below, hoping to see the red Chevy coupe Dad would be driving. We missed seeing Dad drive in, but he found the *Consumers Power* and, with Brenda, climbed the ladder. The first we knew of their arrival was their shouts from the deck to get our attention. It was a joyous visit.

Spring came and with it Sid's orders to leave his shipkeeper duties and report to the *George F. Rand* on April 1 for the 1948 shipping season. By now I was comfortable using the ladder attached to the side of the boat, and it was a good thing because by then I was nine months pregnant and my belly was quite large. In fact, I had paid no attention to my food intake that winter—glazed donuts were my favorite. It was with a sense of relief, and yet sadness, that Sid and I descended the ladder and waved goodbye to our first "home" and drove back to Ashtabula.

++++++

Sɪᴅ ᴄᴀᴍᴇ ᴡɪᴛʜ ᴍᴇ ᴛᴏ ᴛʜᴇ ꜰᴀʀᴍ, and we had a week together before he had to report for duty on the *George F. Rand*. Dr. Lynn, a general practitioner, was my doctor, and I immediately went to see him for a prenatal checkup. Much to my horror, I had gained fifty pounds and was directed to immediately go on a restricted eating plan. I did and managed to lose a few of those pounds before the birth.

On April 9 my labor started, and when the contractions were a few minutes apart, it was Mom who drove me to the hospital in Ashtabula. I was not made for having babies because my contractions continued over the next thirty-six hours, and the baby was finally taken by use of forceps. To this day, I give thanks to God that our beautiful red-haired, eight-pound, eleven-ounce baby boy appeared to be perfect in every way.

Mom kept in touch with the Nelson family, and it was Sid's sister Dot who used the radioship-to-shore telephone to let Sid know he was a father. Sid wanted desperately to be with me, to meet his son, and he expressed this so poignantly in his letter that read in part, "I can't be with you. If you only knew how much I'd like to. But as I said these boats are a little better than a prison."

I was in the hospital for several days, and when released, sent home in an ambulance. Mom, driving her car, followed with Brenda holding the baby on her lap. Once home I was directed to remain in bed for ten days, and it was during that time that Sid was able to leave the boat in Toledo and remain home for three days before again connecting with the boat when it docked in Toronto. It was while Sid was home that we decided on the name Vernon Jack: Vernon was the Americanization of his brother's name Verner, and Jack was my choice. Throughout my son's adult life, he chastised me for giving him the nickname of Jack as a middle name.

Living at home with my folks was a blessing. Mom took over Vernon's care. He was bathed every morning, there were frequent diaper changes, and his bottom was washed and powdered so that he never developed a rash; his bottle feedings occurred when he cried. I tried to nurse but it was so painful I gave up. Dr. Lynn, an old-fashioned country doctor, would not circumcise a boy baby until nine weeks. I still remember the day I took my son for the procedure and waited in the entry room, hearing his cries. Leaving his office that day, I vowed that if I were to have another baby, I would find another doctor.

———————

FOR WHATEVER REASON during the summer of 1948, Sid transferred from the *George F. Rand* to the *Adam E. Cornelius*. The boat docked in Manitowoc, Wisconsin, for the winter. On December 10, Sid was discharged from his duties and able to come home in time for Christmas. I rented a two-room apartment in a house on Route 20 east of Ashtabula that would be our "family" home for the winter. The living room was also our bedroom, and we set up Vernon's crib in the kitchen. This seemed to be a satisfactory arrangement until one night we saw a rat in the kitchen! Sid set traps, and we moved Vernon's crib into our living space. We never saw the rat again, but did have great apprehension for the safety of our son.

Sid received his orders to report to the *Adam E. Cornelius* on March 21, 1949. I returned to live at the farm. The boats that Sid sailed on carried ore from the Mesabi Iron Range, located in Northeast Minnesota, to ports along the Great Lakes. Whenever the *Adam E. Cornelius* would come to a port in Sandusky, Fairport Harbor, Ashtabula, Conneaut (all in Ohio), or even as far as Buffalo, New York, I would make the effort to meet the boat so I could be with my husband for the few hours the ship was in port.

It was a demanding and frustrating lifestyle, but it was the only way I could see Sid during the shipping season. Living with my folks on the farm, Mom assumed the responsibility for Vernon's care, and I returned to waitressing, this time working second shift at Clampitt's Restaurant in Ashtabula. Wages were almost nothing, but tips were good, and each night when I returned home, I would unload the change from my pockets and stack it neatly on the dresser in my room. Sid and I were saving every penny we could with the dream of building our own home.

Sid was discharged from his duties on the *Adam E. Cornelius* in Manitowac, Wisconsin, in December of 1949 and took a train home to be with us for Christmas. That winter we lived with my folks on the farm. My brother had been discharged from the navy and started a TV business, which involved building TV towers in the garage on the farm. When needed, Sid helped Lloyd while also collecting his unemployment payments. I continued working at the restaurant. Sometime that winter, the three of us decided a trip to Florida would be a delightful relief from the demands of our work. Mom agreed to care for Vernon. I was able to get a week off from my job, Lloyd controlled his own work schedule, but Sid needed to be at his weekly sign-up time to remain eligible for his unemployment benefits. That gave us precisely one week to the day and hour we could be gone.

Realizing we were planning a 2,600-mile trip in seven days that would take us as far south as Miami, and would be spending much of that time in the car, Lloyd removed the back seat from his Ford coupe and put in a mattress. This makeshift bed would give at least one of us a place to stretch out on our arduous adventure. On Tuesday, March 1, at 2:00 p.m., Sid signed in for his unemployment benefit. We immediately headed south stopping only for gas, food, or any other required comfort stops.

During that week on our drive south, we made stops at the Marine Studios in Marineland, the Oldest Wooden School House in the United

States in Saint Augustine, and the Everglades south of Miami. On our return trip north, we swam in the Atlantic Ocean, sunned ourselves on the beaches, thrilled to the melodic sounds of the Singing Tower in Lake Wales, and visited the beautiful Cypress Gardens. As we left Florida and continued homeward-bound, we embraced the spectacular scenery of the Appalachian Mountains. Back in Ashtabula on Tuesday, March 7, precisely at 2:00 p.m., Sid walked into the office and signed in for his unemployment benefit. I never asked him how he justified the "seeking work" requirement for the previous week.

Lloyd had seen a lot of the country the two years he was in the navy; Sid had plied the Great Lakes on the ore boats. The greatest distance I'd been from home was Cleveland, Ohio. For me, our weeklong adventure was exhilarating. I saw new places, new scenery, and I realized there was a life outside of Ashtabula, Ohio.

------- ++++++ -------

IT WAS ON JUNE 8, 1950, a little more than two years after Vernon was born, that an event occurred which changed the direction of our lives. The *Adam E. Cornelius* had docked in Fairport Harbor, forty miles from Ashtabula, and I was there at the dock to meet the boat. As Sid came toward me, I knew something was wrong. His normal gait had become an awkward limp, he appeared much heavier, and as he came closer, I saw that his skin tone was yellow! He was obviously sick, and he carried a discharge paper granting him a medical leave.

We immediately returned to his parents' home on East Sixteenth Street. Ma knew the time we would be arriving. She was there in the kitchen, ready to make her son one of his favorite dishes, her thin Swedish pancakes. She took one look at Sid and knew, as I knew, something was wrong. Realizing he was ill, Ma immediately contacted her oldest daughter, Gunne, a nurse who had connections with the Cleveland Clinic. Gunne was able to get her brother an appointment at the clinic within the week. I drove to the farm and informed my folks what was happening. The decision was made that I would stay with Sid at his parents' home so I could be with him and also be able to continue working at the restaurant. Mom would take care of Vernon.

A letter from Dr. Robert D. Taylor of the Cleveland Clinic reads, in part:

> Mr. Sidney H. Nelson first came to the Cleveland
> Clinic on 6-15-50. He demonstrated evidence of
> severe acute glomerulonephritis and inactive rheu-
> matic heart disease with aortic insufficiency, and
> mitral stenosis insufficiency. His heart was well com-
> pensated at all times. The acute glomerulonephritis
> responded admirably well to treatment.

Sid's prescribed treatment plan was mandatory bed rest and a very stringent, 3,500-calorie, portion-controlled diet, high in carbohydrates, low in protein and fat, and drinking adequate fluids. No medications were prescribed. Since I needed to continue to work, it was Ma who lovingly took over the total care for her son. The plan prescribed by the clinic and carefully prepared by Ma worked, for in a letter dated August 3, 1950, Dr. Taylor wrote to us:

> We are delighted with the tests performed this week.
> Your kidneys are back to almost normal. They con-
> tinue to show signs of inflammation but they are
> indicative of the healing phase. We would like you to
> stay away from work for another week. There is no rea-
> son though while [sic] you cannot go on a normal diet.

Nine weeks after being placed on medical leave from the *Adam E. Cornelius* in Fairport Harbor, Sid was able to rejoin the crew in Conneaut on August 9. I took him to the boat, and as we parted, I gave thanks to God for my husband's recovery, but with it was an intense sadness that we had to part once again. He finished the remainder of the shipping season, and the boat was docked in Manitowac, Wisconsin, for the winter. With layup completed, Sid was discharged from his duties on December 6, 1950, and took a train home.

--------- ·+++++·+ ---------

SOMETIME DURING THAT WINTER OF 1950–'51, Sid, with my support, made the decision not to return to his job on the lake ore boats. Instead he was able to get a job as a deckhand on the Ashtabula Carferry. The money wasn't as good, but at least he would be home at night and on weekends. I continued at my waitress job, and we lived with my folks on the farm.

By now we had saved enough money to begin building our house, but where to build? We learned that A. H. Talcott, who owned property just off Route 20 on Vineland Avenue, one mile east of the Ashtabula City limits, had divided the acreage planted with peach trees into lots, and they were for sale. The first time Sid and I drove down the street, we knew this was the right location for us to build our house. Vernon would soon be old enough to attend kindergarten, and the lots were located within the Edgewood School District, one of the best in the county. We had selected our house plan and needed enough land to accommodate a ranch-style house and a double garage. In the absence of a sewer system on the street, we would need a septic tank, and that required enough area to accommodate a leach bed. That May we purchased two fifty-foot lots, giving us one hundred feet of frontage and 175 feet of depth, at the cost of $1,400.

In the 1950s, the building codes in Ashtabula County were very lax. Sid and I noticed that some families lived in garage homes or basement homes. Our first thought was to build a two-story garage home. We consulted a contractor, and his sage advice was to build the basement home. He observed that people who built garage homes lived in them, never building a house.

That summer we contracted for the construction of a basement home. Once the concrete walls were up, septic tank and leach bed in place, and street connections made for the water and wastewater hookups, Sid took over. With no previous carpentry experience, he constructed the subfloor for the house, covered it with tar paper, sealed the seams with hot tar, built the basement entry stairs, covering them with a fourteen-by-thirteen-by-ten-foot structure that we referred to as the "conning tower" entrance. Lloyd did the wiring, plumbing, and erected a seventy-five-foot TV tower. I painted the interior concrete block walls. We purchased appliances, furniture, and basic household items needed to set up housekeeping. In the fall, with our son in tow, we moved into our humble abode—a cavernous basement home.

During that first year in the basement, Sid installed an oil heating stove, partitioned off areas for the laundry/work room, bedroom, living room, kitchen, shower/toilet, built cabinets, and for insulation purposes, covered the subfloor joists with ceiling tiles. The concrete floor was painted but remained bare of carpets.

It didn't take long before we found out that our basement home had its idiosyncrasies, just like people. When the first heavy rain came, we experienced leaks that originated in the seams along the flat, tar paper–covered roof. This required us to strategically place multiple buckets to catch the dripping water. It soon became evident that our contractor had not provided the correct pitch to the basement wastewater floor drain; every few months the drain backed up into the laundry room. Sid bought a plumber's "snake," and regular as clockwork, he would snake out the drain to open it up. The septic tank was deep enough to accommodate the toilet in the basement, but this caused problems with the leach bed not draining the tank properly. Every year the tank had to be pumped out or the toilet would back up. Sid had built a closet in our bedroom, and much to our dismay, I discovered holes in Sid's best suit. Crickets had invaded our subterranean living quarters, and we think they were the culprits.

Despite it all, life was comfortable for us. Vernon enjoyed watching TV, and each weekday morning when his favorite show came on, he would grab the metal support post located in the middle of the living room and swing around it as he watched the antics of Captain Kangaroo. Not wanting Vernon to be an only child, I gave birth to his brother Bruce in October 1952. One night there was a torrential rainstorm, and we were awakened by Bruce's crying. We saw that a steady stream of water was coming from the ceiling above his crib. The rubber sheet covering his crib mattress retained the water, and Brucie Brumber (his Dad's favorite name for his son) was lying in the middle of a large puddle.

When Bruce was a little more than two years old, he wanted to play outside in the sandbox that his dad had built for him. I would let him go out, but every few minutes I would run up the stairs to check that he was safe. He never wandered off, but such were the risks I took as a young mother.

We planted a garden, and from it I would harvest and can tomatoes, corn, and green beans. The peach trees on our lot gave us an abundance of fresh peaches to eat and can. Blackberries grew in profusion in the vacant field behind our lot, and I'd be out in the hot sun, filling my basket with the delicious fruit. Each season I would make blackberry and strawberry jams. The shelves that Sid had built in the laundry/work area of the basement were filled with quarts of peaches and pears and the surplus vegetables from our garden. We had a freezer, and as was the custom when I lived on the farm, I bought beef in quantity and froze it. All of this amounted to a lot of work but saved many food dollars.

Ma Nelson would come to visit, always when the peaches were ripening. She would stay for a few days, helping me with my canning. The first few years our peach trees provided fruit for us, for my folks, and for the Nelsons. We soon learned that, if not properly cared for, peach trees have a short life. Such was the case with us. Gradually, we lost our peach trees and with it the savory taste of the tree-ripened fruit.

While we were saving the needed dollars to move ahead with the upward expansion of our house, Sid made bunk beds for the boys. Bruce would soon be out of his crib, and there wasn't space in our "family" bedroom for two single beds. However, before Bruce was old enough to be moved out of his crib, my sister came to live with us. She was eleven years old at the time, and for whatever the reasons, Mom thought it would be best for Brenda to attend the Edgewood Schools. At first it was she and Vernon who occupied the bunk beds; Bruce remained in his crib, and Sid and I shared a double bed. It was an intimate family relationship, but no one seemed to mind. I fondly remember those two years my sister lived with us in spite of my immaturity in dealing with the mood swings that are a part of the preadolescent's maturing. Brenda loved Sid. She later told me that he was the only person who really "listened" to her.

Our next basement project was to tile our concrete floor. We choose red and black asphalt-asbestos tiles. The floor was not level, and Sid dealt with this by using an acetylene torch to warm the inflexible tiles before laying them. Brenda was there looking over Sid's shoulder; he put the torch in her hand, and she dutifully performed the warming task. Brenda slept on the top bunk bed, and that night Sid and I heard her gabbling in her sleep. We turned on the light and saw her waving her right arm back and forth as she had done for hours that day warming the tiles. All the while she kept muttering unintelligible sounds. The day must have exhausted her.

———————— ·+++++· ————————

WHEN SID WAS DISCHARGED from the Carferry in January of 1953, he adamantly stated that his sailing days were over. He had a house to build. It was while I was working at Clampitt's that I met Hilma Fassett. Hilma became one of my best friends, and this was fortuitous for Sid. Her husband, Bernie, was president of the carpenter's union. It was he who encouraged Sid to consider carpentry for his livelihood, and it was under Bernie's tutelage that Sid acquired the necessary skills to pass the test and was initiated into the United Brotherhood of Carpenters and Joiners of America union on November 23, 1955.

Between the time Sid left the Carferry, and before he was certified to work as a union carpenter, he did odd jobs as a handyman and worked for Lloyd. Once we saved enough money, Sid bought the materials to construct the house frame and roof. Bernie devoted many hours to advising Sid how to proceed with this part of the construction. Once the shell of the house was completed, we applied to the Ashtabula County Building and Savings Company for a loan of $4,000, enough to finish the house. Looking back, I recall two of the bank executives coming to the house, making a brief tour, and as they were leaving, assuring us our loan request would be approved—it was apparent we had the required equity in the structure. The words "pride" and "joy" only partially describe our feelings of elation when we heard the news. We had sacrificed so much, worked so hard to get to this point in building our home.

We now had the money to buy the materials and pay for any needed labor. We had friends who donated their weekends to helping us. It wasn't work; it was a bonding with people who cared. Anderson windows were installed, the house was sided, and the exterior doors were put in place (in the process the "conning tower" that served as the entrance to our basement came down). Sandstone from a New England quarry arrived, and we hired a mason to build the fireplace, chimney, and lay the exterior sandstone. The mason built the fireplace and chimney and then disappeared. There was no word from him, and all our efforts to locate him failed. (We later learned that when this man got some spending money in his pocket, he would go off on a drunk, not to be seen again for weeks.) Sid decided he had learned enough that he could do the remainder of the masonry work himself. He put down his hammer and, with trowel in hand, proceeded to lay the remaining sandstone. I was the mason's helper, mixing and carrying the mortar to set the stones.

There are smells related to construction that are unforgettable. I haven't smelled new plaster for decades—now all homes have drywall. Our house was plastered. When the base coat of gray plaster was applied, I remember entering the house and a gritty smell tickled my nose. Not so with the finish coat of plaster. The smooth, white plastered walls emitted a clean smell that was pleasant to the senses. But the sweetest smell of all is cut wood. The spinning saw blade cutting into the wood and the flying sawdust emit a rich odor both soothing and homey to one's senses. Sixty-five years after the construction of our house, I can still conjure up these smells and the associated memories.

Sid took pride in selecting only the best materials. He wanted tongue-and-groove, random-width, pegged-oak hardwood floors. When he priced this product, he learned it was way over our flooring budget; he settled for solid oak boards, reluctantly giving up on the early-American pegged look. The fireplace wall in the living room was paneled with knotty pine, as well as the kitchen cabinets. We had attended a home-and-garden show and saw a pink corner-bathroom tub that we became enamored with. We gave no thought to the size of the tub in relation to the size of our bathroom. The tub was delivered along with the pink sink and commode. Lloyd installed the bathroom fixtures and did the plumbing for us, inadvertently reversing the hot and cold water faucets at the sink. Once installed we saw how totally out of proportion the tub was in our small room. Over time we became adept at gingerly stepping around the tub to get to the commode, but as long as I lived in that house, I never successfully adapted to the hot-cold reversal at the sink.

Sid was a perfectionist as he moved from room to room installing the baseboard, cove molding, closet shelving, door and window trim—his mitered corners so perfect the wood appeared to grow at a ninety-degree angle. Sid invested in only the best tools, and his miter box and six-foot level were his pride and joy. He used the level when hanging the interior doors. The door placement was so perfect within the doorframe that the width of a dime was his criteria for clearance. As the finish work was completed in each room, I made the curtains and drapes for most of the windows in the house, including the large picture windows at the front and back of the combined living and dining room. I wanted to have wallpaper in our hallway. Neither of us had hung wallpaper before, but we had worked so well together throughout the total building process we knew we could do it. It wasn't that easy. Getting those few rolls of paper on the wall caused such disharmony between us that at times I thought it would cost us our marriage.

It was all worth it—the long days and nights in all kinds of weather, the personal inconveniences, the sacrifices. It was a day of celebration in the summer of 1955 when we totally moved out of our basement quarters into our grand home.

Two years later we were ready to construct our double garage. Sid had heard of a lumberyard in Warren, Ohio, that sold lumber at discounted prices. He rented a truck, and with the garage plans and lumber list, we headed the fifty-two miles south on SR45 to Warren. We found the lumberyard, gave the lumber list to the employee who proceeded to direct us around to the different locations on the lot for the materials. Sid paid no attention to the loading of the truck, thinking the employee knew what he was doing. With all items on the list checked off, we paid for the lumber and started home. SR 45 was not a smooth road. As Sid drove and the truck bounced along, it became evident to us that our load of lumber was shifting on the truck bed. Sid pulled over to the side of the road and attempted to reposition the lumber, but found it was impossible unless we unloaded the truck and started over. Sid chose not to do this. Instead he got back in the truck, and driving much slower, we managed to make it home with all the lumber, although some of the long boards were half off the truck bed and dragging on the road by the time he pulled into our driveway. It was a harrowing experience.

Building the garage was almost that proverbial "piece of cake." Sid was now an experienced carpenter and had acquired enough masonry skills to supervise the digging of the footer and the concrete pour. He laid the blocks for the foundation and built the garage himself. According to my records, the actual dollars spent for materials and labor for the house amounted to $13,356.72. I have no records for the cost of the garage. I sold the home in June 1964 for $17,700 to Ron and Phyllis Ulshafer. Counting the donated labor that went into the construction, no money was made on the house.

Over the past fifty-plus years, I have remained friends with the Ulshafers. They added a bedroom wing to the south side of the house and made other improvements to accommodate their growing family of four children. Ron died at home in 2007. At the time of his death, I wrote to Phyllis, and my letter dated December 18, 2007 reads in part:

> To me the Vineland Avenue home is a symbol of faith, love, family, strength, and determination. You and Ron have personified these values. You have taken good care of what became "your home," and I will be eternally grateful to both of you for that.

--------++++++--------

Now given the opportunity, Sid was an amazing full-time dad. He wanted the boys to have a dog. One Christmas while still living in our basement home, Bowser, a boxer, joined our family. Bowser was a friendly dog, but he loved to wander. If we didn't keep him tied up, Bowser would stray, but fortunately he was always brought back by concerned neighbors.

We didn't have the money for vacations, but Sid thought that camping would be a fun family activity. Our first camping trip, using borrowed equipment, was to the Cook Forest State Park in northwestern Pennsylvania. We had such a good time that, two years later, planning for our next trip to Cook's Forest, we purchased our own camping equipment. The Army and Navy surplus store in Ashtabula had all that was needed, including an eight-by-twelve-foot cabin tent.

This time, being experienced campers, we tried as many outdoor activities as would fit into our long weekend. At the suggestion of a ranger, we climbed the hundred-plus steps to the top of the fire tower. As we climbed higher and higher, we had to hang on tighter and tighter as the tower seemed to dangerously sway from the strong wind. At the top, the view of the forest below was spectacular. While hiking the Clarion River Trail, the boys spotted a heavy grapevine attached to a high limb of a tree. A grapevine is an invitation to grab hold and swing, which the boys took turns doing. Vern spotted chipmunks along the trail. When we returned to our campsite, he used some string, a cardboard box baited with food, and his brother's help to set a trap to capture a chipmunk. He waited patiently, but the chipmunk came, stole the food, and scampered off before Vernon had time to spring his trap. That weekend we enjoyed roasting marshmallows over our campfire, singing together, and attending an open air church service where we sat on makeshift pews that were huge logs. Our Cook Forest experiences are chronicled in a book I wrote for one of my college English classes titled *Rugged Weekend*.

The following season we planned another trip to Cook's Forest for the Memorial Day weekend. Vernon and a neighbor boy, Billy Edixon, were good friends, and Vernon asked if he could invite Billy to come along. It turned out the entire family wanted to join us. We left on a Friday and told the Edixon family we'd get the campsite; they would not be able to join us until Saturday morning.

We had no problem on Friday when we checked in and selected a prime campsite. By Saturday morning, when the Edixon family arrived, the campground was filled. They were not allowed to enter even to share our campsite; the ranger did allow the children to remain with us. That day Sid injured his knee. It swelled three times its normal size, and he spent most of his time sitting on a campstool with his leg elevated. I spent my time cooking and washing dishes. I wouldn't allow the children to venture too far from the campsite, although we did take them to climb the fire tower.

Fortunately, we had some board games with us. When we left on Monday, Sid was in pain, I was exhausted, but the children were jubilant.

———————— ·•••••· ————————

BEGINNING IN THE SPRING OF 1956, Sid had regular employment as a union carpenter, and this provided a substantial improvement in our financial status. By now, with my work as a waitress and Sid's regular employment, we had earned enough money to pay off the $4,000 mortgage on our home. On November 27, 1957, we purchased a four-door Custom Royal Dodge. What an extravagance! We paid $3,936.56 for the vehicle and took out a $2,200 loan, and fortuitously for me, we took the insurance option of "paid in full upon death."

Sid had a seasonal job with a construction company that was building one of the chemical plants on Lake Road in Ashtabula Township. He was laid off in February of 1958, and with the boys in tow, we took a leisurely trip to Florida. It was nothing like the 2,600-mile one week trip we had taken with Lloyd ten years earlier. I packed our camp stove and cooked our meals as we stopped along the way, giving everyone a respite from the many hours in a car. We did stay in motels. This time our trip took us only as far south as Tampa, where our former neighbors the Forsbergs lived. We stopped in St. Augustine to revisit the Oldest Wooden Schoolhouse in the United States, stopped again at Marine Studios in Marineland, and took pictures by the heaters in Cypress Gardens to prove to the folks back home that it does freeze in Florida.

The following summer we decided to take the family to see Niagara Falls. My sister, Brenda, and my niece Karin joined us. The tent was left at home; we spent the two nights in tourist homes. I did pack the cooking equipment and filled the ice chest with food, hoping there would be little, if any, need to stop in restaurants along the way. We remained on the American side of the falls, took a ride on the Maid of the Mist, and visited Fort Niagara. What I remember most about this trip was gashing my ankle on a sharp object when we stopped at a picnic site. I didn't seek medical attention. Instead, with Sid's help, we cleaned and closed the wound as best we could with supplies from the first aid kit. Thankfully, it healed with no complications, but I carried a scar for years.

On June 26, 1959, her majesty Queen Elizabeth II and President Eisenhower officially opened the St. Lawrence Seaway. This marked the completion of the joint US–Canadian St. Lawrence Seaway navigation project that linked the Great Lakes region to world markets. In celebration of this event, service personnel at the Coast Guard Station in Ashtabula gave tours of the lighthouse that guarded the harbor. Sidney and I, with the boys, took advantage of this event and were ferried from the dock to the lighthouse. We climbed the ladder to the top where the beacon light was mounted. A fascinating fact learned from this tour was that women in France were employed to polish the lens using their fingertips, literally rubbing away any trace of their fingerprints.

THE NELSONS WERE A WELCOME PART of my life. With great patience, Ma taught me two Swedish phrases: "Tack sa mycket" (Thank you so much) and "Var so gut" (You are welcome). I loved to listen to Ma speak; her Swedish accent was pleasing to my ear.

I stopped to visit with my mother-in-law as often as time permitted. Ma would sit across the kitchen table from me and pour real cream into her coffee. She would place a sugar cube between her back teeth, and as she sipped the rich, hot, creamy liquid the sugar cube would melt, sweetening her coffee. She encouraged me to do the same; I tried, but it was not to my taste—too rich and too sweet. I did learn to drink coffee, but black. There was always a pastry on the table to enjoy with the coffee. One of my favorite treats was Ma's *skorpa*—any stale sweet bread thinly sliced and dried in the oven.

Other pastry delicacies that Ma made were *Klenators* and *Mandelmusslor*. She made rye bread, and her Ice Box Rolls recipe was basic to other sweet breads. Ma was always willing to share her recipes with me and, best of all, to instruct me in how to make them. I never seemed to be able to master the art of making rye bread. After I moved out of the area, whenever I baked bread, I would send Ma a loaf to critique my effort. She would promptly write back with, "Henriet, you use too much rye flour, use more white flour." Or "Henriet, you need to knead the bread more for better consistency." One day I sent her a loaf and her response was, "Henriet, this is gut [sic]. You have mastered the art of making the bread." I felt so proud. When Ma gave me her Ice Box Rolls recipe, she told me she called them "Bride's Rolls" because even a bride could make them. She was right. Ingredients were stirred together and placed in the refrigerator overnight to be used the next day in whatever sweet bread recipe was selected.

There was one of Ma's dishes that did not appeal to my palate—*lut-fisk*, a dried, salted whitefish that is prepared by soaking it in a lye-water solution, rinsing thoroughly, baking, and serving with a white sauce. This dish is traditionally served on Christmas Eve. To me it was tasteless.

The same as with my mother and our teatime talks, I had lengthy coffee-time talks with Ma. It was during one of these talks that I mentioned to Ma that my dad would be butchering. She asked me if I would collect some of the blood so she could make a Swedish delicacy, a *blodpudding* (blood pudding). I was dumbfounded! I'd never heard of using blood for cooking. She assured me it was a taste treat that Sid would love. It was a convincing argument, and I agreed.

On the day I knew Dad was going to butcher, I arrived at the farm, steeling myself with the knowledge that I would have to observe, for the first time, the slaughter of a pig. Equipped with a white enamel basin, oatmeal, and a large stirring spoon, I walked with Dad to the barn where the pig was tethered for the slaughter. Dad directed me where to place the basin to catch the blood, and then proceeded to hit the pig over the head with a firm blow of the sledgehammer, knocking it to the floor, and immediately slit its throat. Blood gushed into the enamel basin. I stood there carefully pouring a steady stream of oatmeal into the basin from the container I held in my left hand, while at the same time stirring vigorously with my right hand to keep the warm blood from coagulating. I did admirably well at my assigned task. I didn't faint, I didn't vomit, I didn't get light-headed. I surprised myself. As soon as I could, however, I left the barn.

Best I recall, I covered the blood-oatmeal mixture with a fresh towel and immediately drove into Ashtabula to Ma's home and handed her the precious consignment. Ma made the *blodpudding* adding nuts and fruit to the contents in the basin. She poured the mixture into oblong tins, refrigerated it, and later fried slices of it in butter for her son who covered it with maple syrup as he ate the culinary delicacy.

There were times of social involvement between our families. One time Pa Nelson went to the farm and stayed the night. He followed my dad as he tended to the farm chores. Apparently on his visit, the chicken house roof needed repair. I have a picture of Pa on the roof with Dad. Over the years, my mom and dad were dinner guests in the Nelson home. Mom would reciprocate and have the Nelson family come to the farm for one of her famous chicken dinners.

In July 1951, Pa Nelson died. It was not a prolonged illness, and he died in a veterans' hospital in Cleveland. The night Sid learned of his father's death, he wept. The year after Pa died, Ma sold the house on East Sixteenth Street and moved to Parma to live with her daughters Gunborg and Dorothy. Whenever possible we would visit the family. I know our visits exhausted the girls, but Ma always looked forward to seeing us. I know she missed her Ashtabula friends.

On several of our overnight visits, we would play "Rise Table Rise." To us, this was a frivolous, fun activity. We would sit around a card table, leaving one side open (I don't recall which side), placing our hands flat on the table top with fingers spread, lightly touching the extended finger of the person beside us. In unison we would chant, "Rise, table, rise." Within a few minutes, one leg of the table would rise, and then we would begin asking, "Yes" (two taps) and "no" (one tap) questions. We never tried to analyze why the table leg could levitate, nor did we attribute what was happening to the occult. It was innocent family fun, and then on one Sunday morning...

We attended the Church of God there in Ashtabula. We had mentioned to someone in our church what we did for entertainment when we visited Sidney's family in Parma. That Sunday morning during one of Rev. Bentley's hour-long hellfire-and-brimstone sermons, he referred to a family in the church who had been communing with the devil. Didn't we know that anything that went UP must come DOWN? And as he uttered the word **up**, he threw the heavy pulpit Bible up in the air, and as he shouted the word **down**, he dramatically fell silent as the Bible thumped to the floor. The effect of this revelation reverberated throughout the small congregation! I never could understand this analogy to our game. Of course, we knew what went up, gravity brought down.

It was at my urging that we started going to this church. Our neighbors, the Forsbergs, attended there, and it was they who invited us. Sid would reluctantly accompany me, and I do remember that he always chose to sit in the back row of seats (no pews). Just as Rev. Bentley would begin his sermon, Bruce, who was sitting on his father's lap, would begin to cry. Sid immediately got up and took Bruce outside for the remainder of the service. I am certain Sid pinched his son's bottom, causing him to cry, so the two of them would be relieved of the ponderous message.

After she moved to Parma, Ma looked forward to coming to our home on Vineland Avenue for extended visits. I loved having her with us, for she took over the cooking, cleaning, washing, and ironing. Sid and I kept to our work routines. By then I was a full-time employee in the office of the Reliance Electric Company in Ashtabula, Vernon was in school, and Ma cared for Bruce. When I came home from work, I was treated as a "guest" in my own home.

We had two bedrooms, the boys occupying one and we the other. We gave our bedroom over to Ma, and we slept on a daybed. On one of Ma's visits, we were sitting on Bruce's bed chatting when Bruce came into the room, climbed up on the bed, and sat down. He suddenly began screaming. He had sat on his grandma's knitting, and one of the needles was stuck in his butt. Terrified, I pulled it out; the needle had not penetrated too deep. The puncture wound was cleaned and carefully watched. Thankfully it healed without complications. After that incident, Ma was very careful where she placed her knitting.

Ma's "cleanliness is next to godliness" caused some irritation in the family. In the winter Bruce would set up his Lincoln Logs, Indians, and soldiers on our living room hearth, and there they stayed until spring, or until Ma came to visit. Ma would have Bruce pick up his toys each evening, to be brought out again the next day. I never said anything. Ma was our guest. I loved her and respected her; she was the matriarch of the family. Looking back, this was unfair to the boys; it was their home too.

———— ++++++ ————

BY NOW I HAD ACHIEVED MY YOUTHFUL DREAM of getting married, having children, and establishing my own home. Sid and I had worked hard to attain that goal, many times at the expense of nurturing our children. I clearly remember the occasion when I knew it was time for me to quit my job and be home with my boys. Over the years, placing my children under the care of others presented some emotionally disquieting situations. As a toddler, Bruce would cry when he was left with a neighbor. Later a kind elderly lady, a minister's wife, cared for Bruce. She would not let him play with his cowboy and Indian toys, saying it was too warlike. Bruce was so agitated when staying with her that, he tells me, one time he wet the bed. Then there was the time Vernon was ill while we were living in the basement and a neighbor agreed to care for him. Vernon wanted to stay home rather than go to her house; she agreed to this arrangement, walking over at regular intervals to check on him. It was on one of her checkup visits that Vernon, hearing and seeing feet pass the basement window, thought I was coming home early to be with him. These were heartbreaking times for me as a mother.

It was on a Saturday that we were shopping and stopped at a furniture store. While in the store, Sid noticed a painting hanging on the wall. It was a turbulent waterscape scene. Looking at it, I found it to be depressing, but to Sid it represented a time of warm feelings connected with home. This was what the lake waters looked like in late fall, when the boat went into winter layup, and the men were discharged upon completion of all duties. The price tag on the painting was $50. Reluctantly I agreed to the purchase, which I thought to be extravagant. Once home, Sid hung it above the living room sofa. As the days passed and I looked at the painting, I thought, "If we can afford this, I can afford to quit my job and be home with the boys." That very week, I turned in my resignation, and with few exceptions, for the first time since my marriage, I was able to be a full-time wife and mother.

———— ·+++++· ————

THAT FALL OF 1958, the boys were both in school, Bruce in the first grade and Vernon in the fifth grade. I thought it would be good if I could get a job with the school district that corresponded with the boys' school schedule. I remember interviewing with the principal of one of the Edgewood elementary schools. I was vague during the interview as to what I wanted, saying I could be a school secretary, a playground helper, maybe work in the cafeteria. At this point I was interrupted and heard the principal say, "You really don't know what you want to do, do you?" That ended the interview.

Yes, I did know what I wanted to do, and that was to be a teacher, but I had no college training. Kent State University opened its Ashtabula extension in 1958. The first campus was located in the then-vacant Ashtabula Junior High School building located at North Park. Here was my opportunity. Instead of getting a job, with Sid's support I enrolled at KSU's branch and started taking college classes. In high school it was boys who took my attention—not academics. Now that I had my husband, children, and home, I gave serious thought to my studies. At the age of twenty-eight, I enrolled as a freshman carrying a partial load of six credit hours. I continued this part-time academic program throughout the 1959 school year. In the winter quarter of 1960, I took on a full academic load.

Caring for my family and finding time for study presented a challenge in time management. Sid was very cooperative, extremely so when I had papers to write or was studying for exams. He would take the boys with him to Parma to visit his family, letting me stay home to luxuriate in uninterrupted study time. Ma and the girls always welcomed these visits and did all they could to entertain the boys there in the city. Ma had fresh-baked cookies and for Bruce "clean Jell-O," not "dirty Jell-O" (for some strange reason, Bruce thought his grandma put carrots in the Jell-O). I later learned that the boys loved going with their dad to Parma because he would stop and get them ice cream cones at an ice cream store a mile from the house. When I was with them, I never would let Sid stop, saying we were too close to our destination.

One of my freshman classes was speech 101. One class assignment was to give a speech using a visual aid. To this day I benefit from the speech given by one of my classmates. She demonstrated how to properly fold a contour sheet. I chose the topic of "capital punishment." Sid crafted a hangman's platform out of balsa wood, complete with thirteen steps to the top, a figure with a rope around its neck, and an operational trapdoor. I presented pros and cons related to capital punishment. At the conclusion of the speech, I manipulated the trapdoor lever, causing the figure to fall. It was a dramatic conclusion and earned me an A for the course.

——————— ✦✦✦✦✦ ———————

IN 1952, WHEN SID HAD TO LEAVE HIS JOB on the *Adam E. Cornelius* and come home on a medical leave, he was diagnosed at the Cleveland Clinic with acute glomerulonephritis. He was given a strict diet to follow and mandatory bed rest. It was noted in his medical records at that time that his heart was extraordinarily well compensated for the rheumatic heart disease that kept him out of school for the second semester of his fourth-grade year.

In July 1958 we again contacted the Cleveland Clinic, this time regarding Sid's symptoms of tiredness, poor sleep, and chest pain. Dr. David Humphrey, Division of Medicine, saw Sid and scheduled him for an electrocardiogram. The result of this test revealed an overworked, enlarged heart. An appointment for September was made for a heart catheterization with Dr. Earl Shirey in the Department for Cardiovascular Disease.

In the weeks between seeing Dr. Humphrey and the September appointment for the heart catheterization, Sid changed jobs. The union carpentry jobs that he worked were short-term and fraught with many weeks of unemployment. All of this created internal stress for Sid. He quit the carpenter's union and got a job installing furnaces with the Ziegler Furnace Company of Ashtabula. This provided regular employment, and the stress was minimal. Sid immediately regained his energy and slept very well at night. He conveyed this in a letter to Dr. Shirey in early September, stating he felt so much better he wished to cancel his appointment, but went on to say that he would keep the appointment if this was in the best interest of his health. A response came in a letter dated September 11, 1959, from Dr. Shirey:

> Despite your improvement I still strongly feel that you should go through with the tests that we have previously arranged because it is always better to make every attempt to prevent trouble rather than wait until the problem presents itself. I believe I discussed with you the fact that your heart is markedly enlarged and even though you are feeling well at the present time your heart is working quite hard and "overtime" which results in gradual and progressive weakness of the heart muscle.

With this dire warning, Sid decided to go through with the procedure, which required two days in the hospital. The day Sid was sent home, we met with the doctor in a consultation room to learn the results of the test. Dr. Shirey was kind, sensitive, and professional as he explained to us the catheterization process that supported the previous diagnosis of an enlarged, overworked heart. He went on to explain that Sid was one of the first at the clinic to have this done, and any further open-heart procedure was not yet developed that might help him. As I remember, we were both stunned and speechless by the prognosis but had no questions and got up to leave. It was then that a young red-headed intern, who had been in the room all the time, asked me to please follow him. Thinking he wanted to give me some further information related to Sid's care, I dutifully followed. He took me to another room, motioned me to sit down, and proceeded to tell me that my husband probably had no more than a year to live. I needed to go home and be certain all of our business matters were in order.

I don't remember this doctor's name. I was twenty-nine years old; Sid was thirty-one. Dying was for old people—not us! What I had been told was surreal; it wasn't happening. I left the room, returned to my husband, and together we went home to Ashtabula. Sid only knew the prognosis as given to him when I was in the room. When he asked me why the red-headed doctor took me aside, I responded that I was only given more verbal information about his care. I never shared with Sid that he might have only a year to live.

Naturally, both of our families wanted to know the results of the catheterization. We told them pretty much what they already knew, that Sid had an enlarged heart—a result of the childhood rheumatic fever.

It was September, and fall was our favorite season of the year—sunny, low humidity, with warm days and cool nights—the season when one could view nature's palette of leaf colors dominated by the red maple and the golden-yellow elm leaves. Halloween would soon be here, a time for fun and pranks; Thanksgiving and Christmas would be celebrated with our families.

We were financially sound. Our years of penny-pinching frugality, and the lax zoning laws, had allowed us to construct our home on a pay-as-you-go basis. The small mortgage that we had taken out to finish the house was paid in full. The chattel mortgage that we had on the 1957 Dodge was covered with an insurance policy. Sid and I had seen an attorney the previous June and made out our wills.

We took this medical interruption to our lives in stride and went on with living. It was traditional that we celebrated Thanksgiving with my folks on the farm. Christmas morning was always at home. Bruce and Vern were allowed to get up any time after midnight—my childhood tradition—and open their gifts. The remainder of the day was divided between a visit to the farm and a drive to Parma. That year we felt affluent enough to have a New Year's Eve party and serve Glogg—a mulled liquor of sorts made with wines and cognac.

On New Year's Day the Christmas decorations were taken down and stored in the attic. The boys returned to school, Sid to work, and I resumed my college classes. All was well as we entered the New Year. On a Sunday morning like any other, I was awakened from sleep by what I thought was Sidney snoring. I poked him, imploring him to turn over. The snoring didn't stop. By then I was fully awake, and when I looked at my husband, I knew it wasn't snoring that caused him to make that sound. He looked like death. I jumped out of bed and called our neighbor who was a nurse. She came over, took one look at Sid, went to the phone, and called for an ambulance. I called my mom and dad, and it was Mom that answered the phone.

"Mom, come quick, something has happened to Sid."

When Mom relayed my message to Dad, he wanted to finish the chores before driving to Ashtabula (Dad always took care of his animals before self or family). Mom emphatically told Dad, "No, Henry! Henrietta said to come right away."

My folks arrived within a half hour. I met them at the door and told them Sid had been taken to the hospital. I didn't know what was happening. Dad immediately left for the hospital; Mom stayed with me and the boys, who were awake. In a short time Dad returned. When he walked in the door, he was crying, and I knew. Sid had a heart attack; he was dead. I took Vern and Bruce into the living room, sat on the sofa beside them, and told them their father had died. It was Sunday, January 17, 1960—only four months after that red-headed young intern told me my husband had no more than a year to live.

The day was one of confusion that moved in slow motion. I called Parma. Gunne answered the phone, and I told her that Sid had died; I couldn't bring myself to speak with Ma. How does one tell a mother her youngest child is dead, one she had nurtured through serious illnesses, a son she dearly loved?

Within two hours their car came into the drive. I went outside to greet Ma. As she got out of the car, I went to her and hugged her. I heard her moan.

"My Sidney! My Sidney! Why didn't I die instead?"

I clearly remember answering, "You have me, Ma, and the boys. We need you."

It is interesting the memories that remain in one's mind from an emotional event of this magnitude. The days between Sid's death and his service are a blur; somehow plans were made. The service was held at the Richmond Ross Funeral Home in Ashtabula. The family gathered prior to the calling hours on Monday. We were standing by the casket, and Vernon placed his hand on the white satin lining on the top edge of the casket. His Grandmother Nelson, ever at the ready to avoid dirt, admonished her grandson to not dirty the cloth. Vern obediently moved his hand. I said nothing but thought, "My god, what does it matter? His father is dead and will be placed in the ground." As I write this, however, I cannot fault dear Ma, for at that moment, she was expressing her grief in the only way she knew how.

Sidney had lived in Ashtabula all his life, as had I. He was young, leaving behind a wife and two children. There was an outpouring of loving support from all who knew us; the room overflowed with flowers, and the solid receiving line lasted for over two hours.

The service was the next day, Tuesday. I placed the record player that my mom and dad had given the family for Christmas on the floor by his father's casket. It softly emitted the melodic voice of Tennessee Ernie Ford singing hymns, hymns that for the weeks since Christmas Sid and I played each night as we went to sleep. For me, the soft music was comforting and reassuring. Bruce tells me to this day he can't stand the name of Tennessee Ernie Ford, let alone his singing. Interesting how differently events in our lives, as children or as adults, are imprinted in our brains.

Sidney's body was laid to rest in a grave on the Nelson family lot in the Edgewood Cemetery. He was a member of the Harbor Masonic Lodge, and he wore on his body a white lambskin apron, the symbol of purity of life and conduct that assures admission into the celestial lodge. I returned to the cemetery the next day to visit the grave site. I was embraced by sounds of silence, a ground covering of fresh-fallen snow, the grave mound veiled with floral wreaths of fresh flowers.

———————— ++++++ ————————

ON THE MONDAY FOLLOWING THE SERVICE, the three of us went back to what we knew—school for the boys and college classes for me. Meaningful activity is the best antidote when tragedy strikes.

EIGHT

✦ ✦ ✦ ✦ ✦

A BLACK YEAR

CHRISTMAS 1959 WAS SPECIAL in a way that we did not know at the time. Vernon was thrilled to get his erector set, Bruce delighted with his ice skates from his Aunt Dorothy, and Mom and Dad gave Sid and me a multiple-changer record player. After the Santa Claus gift opening at home, we drove to the farm and spent a few hours with my parents. Leaving the farm, we drove to Parma to celebrate Christmas with the Nelson family. We arrived back home late, exhausted, and happy; it had been our best Christmas ever!

The week between Christmas and the New Year was filled with activity. For the first time, we were going to host a New Year's Eve party. Guests arrived, and New Year's Eve was spent in conviviality with family members and friends. Precisely on the stroke of midnight ushering in 1960, Sid entered the living room with a tray of glasses filled with warm Glogg. All present took a glass and toasted in the New Year with "skoal"—a Swedish toast for good fortune that means whatever one wants it to mean.

Sid returned to work at the Ziegler Furnace Company, the boys to school (Bruce in the first grade and Vernon in the fifth grade), and I resumed my college classes. All was well in our world.

Seventeen days later, on a Sunday morning, our secure world fell apart. Sidney's death profoundly affected all family members; even in my sorrow, I felt a deep compassion for his mother. In her unique style, Ma wrote in a letter dated January 28:

> I can see him sitting…by the radio he always pleased
> himself there, I have the pichers on my desk he look

so worry I am wondering what he was thinking if he felt he was not so well is he shhould be. I never got to talk to him about his health. I was so satisfied he could be in our lot. I always draid to be up there but now when he is there I am ready to join him. Love Ma

Another heartrending letter that Ma wrote was dated April 5:

It is your birthday and I wish I was with you just for a day. I could bake you a cake, but aguss it has to be to next year. I hope you are getting along alright. I also thank you for the note you sent.

I am satisfied just with a note just so I hear from you. I hope Bruce is ok. He sertenly get it all in ones. I wish I had lots to write about but here is not much to say when a person is all by yourself day out and day in, well try to take care of yourself and the boys. Love to you all.

Vernon expressed his grief differently. His friend, Teddy Ball, had spent the Friday night before Sidney died at our house. Traditionally, Friday was Sid's night out. He'd go to Gabe Mello's steam bath, and later to a local bar to drink beer and fraternize with the guys. When he arrived home about midnight, the boys were still up; they had built some contraption with Vernon's erector set. When Vernon heard his dad enter the house, the boys proudly showed him what they had built. After carefully looking at the structure, Sid commented, "That is something. Does it move?" The boys admitted, "No, we just built it for the fun of it." Within hours after Vernon learned his dad had died, he came to me crying and said, "I wish I had made something that moved."

Bruce was only seven years old, and I have no recollection of how he felt at the time. As an adult he finds it difficult to talk about his father's death.

———— ++++++ ————

SIDNEY WAS A BOY WITH DIVERSE INTERESTS. He collected stamps; his artistic ability was evidenced in portrait drawings of his sister Evelyn; in his sketches of explorers, presidents, airplanes and ships. He was a kid who belonged to a gang of boys who called themselves The Secret Six and met in the barn at the back of the Nelson lot. Sidney, the tallest kid in the class, quit school at a young age and joined his dad on the lake boats. This was the man I married. I expressed my grief in writing. Shortly after his death, I wrote in my diary:

> I know that time will dim many things in my memory. For this reason I want to write down a few of the more important things that made our lives so compatible... The last few years of our marriage were perfect years. The devotion we had for each other, the love, the desire to share unselfishly... You taught me too much of the good in life for yours to end so abruptly... I put myself in the other fellow's shoes, when I am tempted to become angry. This is what you taught me. You taught me to live, and I will live.

Lloyd loved Sid like a brother. Every day after his death, Lloyd came by the house at suppertime to fill that empty place at the table. Throughout the winter, on Sunday afternoons, we went to Lloyd and Gertrude's home. When we were with them and their three children—David, Peter, and Jill—it provided me with a sense of family that helped to ease our loss. Sometimes the boys (but most of the time it was I) spent the afternoon in the garage helping Lloyd to refinish his 1946 Lyman wooden boat. (Years later Peter told me he totally refinished the boat when he returned to Ashtabula after graduating from college.) Gertrude would prepare the evening meal that always included foot-long hot dogs roasted over the fire in their fireplace. Lloyd had his own family and a business to run, but he freely gave of himself to me and the boys. Bruce was in Indian Guides, and it was his Uncle Lloyd who assumed the "dad" role at events.

My folks were there for me. Mom was working, but Dad had retired. I was carrying a full academic load both winter and spring quarters. Some of my classes were at night, and it was Dad who would come and stay with the boys. On one occasion, much to my delight, he washed my very-dirty garage windows. Other times Dad would stop by the house during the day. If I were in class, he would leave me one of his scratchy, handwritten, almost-illegible notes directing me, "Call home if you can't come out," or commenting, "Strawberries and eggs are in the ref."

The Nelson family—Ma, Gunne, and Dot—made every effort to support me and the boys with telephone calls, letters, visits, and monetary contributions for music lessons and needed clothing items.

Letters and cards of concern and sympathy continued to fill my mailbox. There were communications from the boys' teachers and classmates, Vineland Avenue neighbors, neighbors on the farm, as well as family members. Notes from the Swede Town friends were especially touching. My former neighbor and dear friend Esther Forsberg, at the time living in Florida, came to be with me. A comment made by my sister-in-law Evelyn touches the very essence of such an outpouring of sympathy when she wrote, "It is comforting to know that others do care."

My life was filled with the boys, school, and the immediacy connected with business matters. Social Security claims were filed and approved. As Sidney's widow, I was awarded $225 per month and was able to manage the home on that amount, with additional financial help from my folks and the Nelson family.

----------·+++++·----------

WINTER BECAME SPRING, and spring became summer. There was a teacher shortage in the 1960s, and the state of Ohio granted cadet teacher certificates to those completing two years of academic work. Although this certificate was good for four years, enabling the student to work toward their four-year academic degree, Mom advised me to get my degree before I applied for a teaching position. She would pay my college tuition, which at that time was $84 per quarter for a full academic load. With this goal in mind, I carefully outlined the required courses needed to complete the bachelor of science degree. I noted what classes were offered at the KSU extension in Ashtabula and what classes I needed to take on the main campus in Kent.

Plans were made for the care of the boys during the weeks I would be at school in Kent that summer. They would spend time on the farm with Mom and Dad, with the Nelson family in Parma, and with Lloyd and Gertrude in Ashtabula. My car was in need of repair, and Lloyd took the responsibility to get it done, so it was Dad who took me to Kent that first week in June 1960. We arrived at the KSU campus, and Dad drove up in front of Engelman Hall, where I was assigned a room for the first summer session. It was all so strange to me, and not knowing if men were allowed in the women's dorm, I had Dad leave me at the curb. He unloaded my two suitcases from the car and placed them on the walk beside me. As he turned to leave, he gave me a hug—the only time I ever knew my dad to hug me. I was left standing there on the step with my two suitcases. Tears blurred my vision and made it difficult for me to watch the car as Dad drove away.

That first weekend I rode back to Ashtabula with someone who took me directly to my brother's home. My car was repaired, and I immediately drove out to the farm to see Vernon and Bruce. I spent the weekend with my folks. When it was time to leave on Sunday afternoon, I remember standing by my car under the maple tree behind the house—the very tree that held the tire swing of my childhood. I sobbed uncontrollably. I knew I had no choice; I had to return to school. The first of that week I received a letter from Mom:

> When you left last nite I got their minds off their troubles by having them get some rhubarb and I made 2 pies. Bruce got tired and didn't stay up to get some but Vernon wanted to stay up as long as I did so he got his piece of pie be-4 he went to bed.

I must have communicated to Mom how homesick I was, and how much a letter meant to me. In that same letter, she closed by writing, "I didn't realize a letter from me meant so much to you… If a letter from me will help a little I will try to find something to write about."

Not only did Mom write often, but she had the boys write. Those letters were my lifeline that black summer of 1960. The boys wrote of work and fun activities there on the farm with their Grandpa and Grandma. They wrote about helping their grandpa with farm chores—Vernon driving the tractor while cultivating or pulling the manure spreader, feeding the chickens, and gathering the eggs. Bruce wrote, "Grandpa and I just got done cleaning the barn. I pushed the hay around, and Grandpa put it in a pile." They worked with Grandma picking strawberries and preparing food for preserving. Vernon helped wallpaper an upstairs bedroom. Their summer wasn't all work-related though. The boys wrote of fun activities too: fishing, swimming, chasing a two-and-a-half-foot snake, playing with the kittens. At the time Brenda was married to Paul and they were living at the farm. They took the boys on a picnic to the Ashtabula Gulf and roasted foot-long hotdogs over an open fire, washed their car in the shallow part of the river, and at other times went roller-skating.

There were accidents. Mom wrote of Vernon cutting his finger (not serious) and the boys' escapade crawling under a barbed-wire fence. "We checked on Bruce and he'll live I guess. They were crawling under fences and he didn't crawl low enough. Scratched his back and they gave him a tetanus shot."

I was never concerned about the boys being content staying with my folks on the farm. I knew there was always something to do. When the boys stayed with Lloyd and Gertrude, they, as well, kept them busy. Gertrude took them to Bible school with their cousins, and they wrote of fun times in the craft class and at the picnic. Vernon wrote, "We played baseball today also. Bruce was hit in the head with the baseball once but it didn't hurt too much. We might go water-skiing tonight." Bruce helped his Aunt Gertrude bake cookies, but the best news for me was when they reported, "Aunt Gert has been very nice to us."

It was a challenge for the Parma family to care for the boys. Grandma Nelson would cook and bake some of their favorite dishes; Aunt Gunne would let Vernon wash the car. It was Aunt Dorothy who, through grit and determination, did the most in entertaining the boys. She got them a pass at the local swimming pool; she took them to the local ice cream parlor; they went roller-skating. A highlight of their summer was a trip on the boat the *Aquarama*. Vernon mentioned this in a letter, adding that, "Bruce got gum on the seat of his pants." The local Catholic church had a carnival each summer, and Dot took them to enjoy the rides and other attractions. Again, Bruce commented, "I am having lots of fun in Parma." Vernon added, "We're having lots of fun here."

After my emotional breakdown that first week standing under the maple tree at the farm, knowing I had to leave the boys and spend my summer in Kent, I developed an inner resolve that bolstered me to deal with the situation. Knowing the boys were well cared for reassured me and allowed me to immerse myself in my studies. All family members knew how important letters were to me, and no matter who Vernon and Bruce were with, there were letters in my mailbox several times a week.

————— ++++++ —————

We had all settled, as best we could, into our new lifestyles—that is, until the morning of August 4. I had signed out from the dorm to go to the library located in Rockwell Hall. I was there studying in one of the cubicles when I heard my name announced over the loudspeaker and the message to report immediately to the nearest phone. I was dumbfounded. When the phone connection was made, I heard Brenda's voice saying, "Dad died." I sat down on the top step of the second floor and held my head in my hands. My entire body was overcome with a feeling of numbness. I had no awareness of what was happening around me, until a classmate came over and asked what was wrong. When I told her, she offered to accompany me back to the dorm. I refused. I needed time alone. Somehow I managed to walk the short distance over the tree-lined, shaded paths back to Engelman Hall. I filled out the necessary emergency forms, gathered a few belongings, and drove home. Brenda was there with Mom and Vernon. I don't know where Bruce was at the time. I think I stayed at the farm with mom. Brenda reminded me recently that three of our dad's sisters—Sophie, Minnie, and Dorothy—came from Chicago for the service. Their effort to be with us was a testimonial to their love for their brother, but I have no memory of them being with us. I was in a stupor the days between learning of Dad's death and his funeral.

Vernon was very close to his Grandpa Schumann. He was the oldest grandchild, and it was my parents who were primarily responsible for his care the first three years of his life. At the time of Dad's death, Vernon was alone with him at the farm. Dad, who was working in the barn, asked Vernon to wash the dirty dishes so Grandma would not have to do it when she came home from work. Vernon did not wash the dishes but instead went into the living room and watched TV.

Brenda was working at the Carlisle-Allen Department Store in Ashtabula. When she came home that afternoon, she found Dad's body in the back shed where he had fallen. Vernon was still in the living room watching TV. Vernon carried guilt into his adult years that he was responsible for his Grandpa's death, even though we assured him over and over that it had nothing to do with his behavior.

I missed four days of classes. There was class work to be made up, with the exception of geography. Mr. James Rinier, my professor, told me no makeup work was necessary; it would not affect my final grade. Consulting his online obituary dated 2013, I read that he was awarded the KSU Teaching Excellence award in 1969, and the comment was made that he "touched and changed lives of many hundreds of students." I was one of those students. His kindness and understanding was balm for my grieving soul.

——————— ++++++ ———————

Now it was my mother who must deal with the shock of losing her mate as well as the news that Lloyd was selling his business, moving to Columbus, and enrolling in an engineering program at Ohio State University.

Shortly after Dad died, Mom wrote to Vernon, who was again staying with his Parma family. Her letter of August 13 gives an insight into the depth of her loneliness:

> Bless your heart. You didn't forget to write to me and I was glad to hear from you. Uncle Lloyd has been out every day to see me but that doesn't take the place of my bed partner. I have gone up stairs and sleep in your bed. It is so lone some [sic] down stairs.

Just three days after the above letter, Mom again wrote to Vernon on one of the cards supplied by the funeral home:

> I am sending you a card too. The flowers were so pretty for the small fry. Not that you are small but you are our oldest grandchild. Your Mom said she had been over to see you. She called me last nite and it seemed good to hear her voice. It is so good your Grandma Nelson will take care of you now.

About this same time, Mom wrote to me as well:

> Henrietta I wonder just what we are going to do. Your Dad gone and I just learned Lloyd is pulling up stakes. He never will be home again… Just so long as I can keep the day by day program I am all right but when I start looking into the future there is when I get shook.
>
> I hadn't ought to write to you like this and I'll try and not to do it again but when I learned about Lloyd and especially right now, it is a little more than

I can take but I won't lay a straw in his way. He has his life to live. I am asking myself now, why in the name of God did I get married.

———— ·+·+·+·+·+·· ————

SOMEHOW I MANAGED TO FINISH that second summer quarter and made plans for returning home. The boys were in Parma when I wrote to them on August 15:

> Since we have made plans to go camping I am getting excited about it. I think we will have a lot of fun. Pymatuning State Park isn't too far from home. One day we can go to Conneaut Lake Park and ride on the roller coaster (you can ride the Dogem cars, Vernon)…

———— ·+·+·+·+·+·· ————

THERE WAS A SHORT BREAK between finishing my classes and before the boys started school after Labor Day. Plans were made for a three-day camping trip to Pymatuning State Park, located thirty-five miles to the south and east of our home. Aunt Dorothy came from Parma to join us, and I asked Mom if she would like to try camping. I was pleased when she accepted.

With everyone's help, we packed the tent, camping equipment, and food. Once at our destination, we must have set up camp with no big snafus, or I would have remembered. As promised, we took the boys to Conneaut Lake Amusement Park, near Conneaut Lake, Pennsylvania— only a few miles from the campground. At the campsite there was plenty to entertain the boys, but the fascination for all of us was standing on the dock, feeding the carp that were so numerous in the water that the ducks could walk on their backs. Mom, Dot, and I made every attempt to be cheerful, but for the boys, it was not the same without their dad.

———— ·+·+·+·+·+·· ————

WITH THE BEGINNING OF SEPTEMBER came school for the boys and for me. I signed up for a full academic load at the Ashtabula campus. My concern was night classes; someone needed to be with Vernon and Bruce. Mom offered to come and live with me. Brenda and Paul were at the farm and could keep it going. I eagerly accepted. Mom moved in with us and continued with her position as a cook at the Longview Hospital, allowing her to be home at night. Life was not to our liking, but we all made the best of it as that black year of 1960 came to a close.

◆ ◆ ◆ ◆ ◆

NINE

MARRIAGE TO ALLAN DICKIE KENT (1963–1965)

T HE DEATH OF SIDNEY impacted all family members. Between 1961 and 1962, the boys spent time with my mom, the Parma family, and in Columbus with my brother's family. In a letter dated July 4, 1961, Lloyd wrote, "Bruce has been a big help. He worked right along all the time we moved and he was here two weeks before he and Pete even had an argument. Must be some sort of a record."

Everyone did their best for me and for the care of Vernon and Bruce, while I doggedly continued to pursue my bachelor of science degree. Each quarter I carried full course loads, managing the home while taking as many classes as possible at the KSU Ashtabula campus.

THE YEAR OF 1961 was significant in my life. On May 13 the KSU Ashtabula Student Education Association sponsored a May breakfast and I was the master of ceremonies. That evening the third annual dinner dance, Jamaican Holiday, sponsored by the student council, was held at The Swallows Restaurant in Ashtabula. I had invited my mom to be my guest at both events. Much to my surprise, Professor Allan Dickie, with his attractive wife, Nancy, was there. I was in Professor Dickie's physical science classes and had commented on several occasions to Sidney that he was my favorite professor. Paramount in my memory was his unannounced "Dickie's Quickie Quiz" involving ten questions. Quizzes were graded in class, and each student had immediate feedback regarding their grasp of information covered in class lectures. This method of testing was amusing, but more important, it was effective in preparing the student for comprehensive exams.

The after-dinner program was devoted to student recognition. It was a proud moment for me, and my mom, when my name was called and I walked forward to receive an award for academic achievement—a trophy inscribed "K.S.U. *SCHOLASTIC AWARD 1960–61 HENRIETTA NELSON.*"

That summer I was again taking classes on the main campus in Kent. I lived in Terrace Hall and ate all my meals in the dorm cafeteria. One evening, as a classmate and I entered the dorm, I was enveloped in a refreshing fragrance. Looking about, I saw several arrangements of colorful summer flowers. Curious, I asked, "Why the flowers?" I was dumbfounded when my classmate answered, "Professor Dickie's wife died." My immediate visceral response was one of unmitigated compassion for Professor Dickie. The classmate who related this sad news to me knew where he lived, and together we made plans to drop by his home at 210 Linden Road to express our condolences.

The next afternoon we met at the appointed time and walked the short distance to his house. Professor Dickie was in his backyard mowing the grass; his daughter Janet Fincher (née Dickie) was with him. Janet offered us lemonade. We sat for a few minutes talking and sipping our drinks. We rose, said our goodbyes and walked back to campus in silence. I felt such empathy for this man. I was still in a raw emotional state from the loss of Sidney.

In the fall of 1961, I was able to live at home. I did my student teaching with Miss Farley Pruitt, an esteemed fourth-grade teacher in the Ridgeview Elementary School located only half a mile from my house. I took one evening class at the Ashtabula campus, and on my way to class, I again saw Professor Dickie.

By then, I was close enough to graduation that I had started to think about dating. It had been a year and a half since Sidney died. Prior to this, I wore academic blinders; my goal was to get my degree and get a job so I could support my children. I knew myself well enough to know that if I were attracted to someone, an intimate relationship could develop, and for that reason I was not interested in casual dating. I missed the companionship of a mate, and I was beginning to consider the possibility of marriage. But in harboring the thought of marriage, I vowed it must be someone who could open doors for my children that I felt I was unable to open. I came from a working-class family, and there were no professional mentors to give me guidance.

———————— ·+++++· ————————

SEEING PROFESSOR DICKIE THAT FALL, I realized he was the one. How to get this handsome medium-height, blue-eyed, white-haired man, twenty-seven years my senior, to notice me? My first line of offense was to be in my car in the parking lot so that I could see when he arrived for his class. Then I would just happen to be walking toward the building at the same time. This provided the opportunity for casual conversation.

I knew he ate dinner at The Swallows Restaurant before returning to Kent. My goal was to get an invitation for dinner. On a parking lot encounter near the end of the quarter, my plan worked. Professor Dickie asked if I would be his dining companion the last night of the quarter. Outwardly I accepted the invitation with a poised calm; inwardly I was elated. Arrangements were made to meet at the restaurant. It was a memorable dining experience. His favorite before-dinner drink was bourbon and water, and I nodded in agreement to join him. I didn't drink, but I didn't want to appear unworldly even though I was concerned how the liquor might affect me. Slowly sipping the drink with my dinner, I remained in control of my senses. I did my best to be pleasant while at the same time carry on an intelligent conversation. Dinner over, Allan walked with me to my car and opened the door. As he bade me a casual good night, he commented that if I were on campus for the winter quarter, to stop by his office in McGilvrey Hall; there might be a job for me in the physical science department. His comment provided me with a glimmer of hope. A job in the department would keep me in touch.

Winter quarter, I was back on campus and planned to complete all requirements to graduate in June. The quarter got off to a rocky start. I had signed a lease for an efficiency apartment in a house at 525 Park Avenue, a mile and a half from the campus, but there was a fire in the house that destroyed my apartment. The woman who owned the property made arrangements for me to use a room in the home of her sister-in-law while repairs to the apartment were being made. Fortunately, before the quarter ended, I was able to move into the apartment that served as my residence for the spring and summer sessions.

———— ·˖˖˖˖·· ————

ONE OF THE FIRST VISITS I MADE when I came to Kent that winter of 1962 was to stop by the physical science office to inquire about employment in the department. I was interviewed by Dr. Gerald Chapman, the department head. He offered me the job of grading papers, and I accepted. The money was not my motivation. For me the perk that went with the job was the fact that I would be in physical proximity to my favorite professor. It worked, and I had many dinner dates with Allan throughout that spring quarter.

Another professional recognition event came my way the middle of March. I was contacted by a reporter from the Ashtabula newspaper, *The Star-Beacon*. An appointment was made to interview me and have my picture taken with Dr. Roy W. Caughran, head of the Elementary Education Department. The article, "15 Years, Two Children Later, Mrs. Nelson Will Get Degree" was published in the March 21, 1962, special tribute to **Ashtabula Kent Center** *Ashtabula's Link to Higher Education*. The recognition was humbling, but inwardly I was proud.

I was now in my final quarter for my undergraduate degree, and I took steps to apply for graduate school. With this in mind, I asked Allan if he would write a letter of recommendation for me. He agreed, and I have saved in my memorabilia file the page from his calendar of Friday April 6, 1962: "Letter of Recomm: to Dean Wilbur for H.N. to enter Grad. Sch." That spring I received a letter of acceptance to begin graduate studies in the summer.

On June 9, 1962, I graduated *magna cum laude* from Kent State University with the degree of bachelor of science. Mom's health was failing, but she was able to be there. I couldn't see her face when I walked across the stage of the Memorial Gymnasium to receive my degree, but I felt her eyes on me, and I knew she was proud. Vernon and Bruce were there along with several other family members. When the ceremony was over, we left the campus and drove to Parma. In celebration, Ma had prepared one of her special luncheons. I don't recall the menu (that is not important), but once again there was an outpouring of love for me and the boys. Sacrifices, both personal and financial, were made for me by my mother, my sons, my Parma family, my brother's family, and my sister; all played a part that allowed me to stay the course to experience this watershed moment.

IN 1962 I WAS HIRED BY BUCKEYE SCHOOLS at a salary of $4,500 to teach fifth grade at Lincoln Elementary School. A teacher orientation day was scheduled for the Tuesday after Labor Day. Lloyd was on break from OSU; he and his family were staying with me that Labor Day weekend. I had broken my glasses at the nosepiece, but unfortunately, there was no place to get them repaired before my Tuesday meeting. Realizing my predicament, Lloyd offered to fix them. I handed over my glasses, and when returned, they were "fixed." He had soldered the two parts together, leaving a big glob at the center over the nosepiece. Tuesday morning my vanity got in the way of me wearing my glasses, and I never put them on. I got in my car, drove to the end of the street, and started to make a left turn to pull across Route 20 on my way to the meeting. It was a foggy morning, and I did not see the approaching white car. It collided with my car on the driver's side. Fortunately, damage was not extensive to either vehicle, and neither of us was injured. The police came. I was at fault and was delayed getting to my meeting on time. Obviously, I was badly shaken—not a good way to begin my teaching career.

The boys started school the day after my accident—Bruce in the fifth grade and Vernon in the ninth grade. Professor Dickie again taught the physical science class at the Ashtabula extension. His late-afternoon class met on Tuesday and Thursday. We were now steadily dating. After class he would come by my home and take me to The Swallows Restaurant for our dinner. Mom was not living with me at the time; she had returned to live on the farm. Again the boys were left on their own, eating prepared frozen dinners while their mom pursued her quest.

I knew it was not wise for me to take a graduate level class that fall just as I was beginning my teaching career. However, I did register for one class offered on the Ashtabula campus for spring quarter of 1963. The requirements for the class made it necessary for me to spend weekends in Kent utilizing resources in the KSU library.

Allan and I had discussed marriage. On that first weekend in April, I was in Kent. I had rented a motel room. Allan took me out to dinner, and afterward we returned to the motel. He stretched out on the bed, reading. I was seated at a small table with books scattered about and my calendar open before me. As I broached the subject of a wedding date, Allan became evasive. No matter what date I suggested, he had a commitment: with his son George, attending dental school at Western Reserve University, who lived with him; scheduled golf outings; bridge engagements; etc. I became so exasperated that I abruptly put the calendar aside and caustically said, "I don't think we have anything further to discuss." I knew right then if he didn't want to marry me, I would move on with my life and not compromise myself in a one-sided relationship.

To this day I am not certain how it happened, but Allan suddenly came up with the date of Saturday, April 20, for our wedding. Plans were made, and we were married by the Reverend Fred Vermeulen, pastor of the East Side Presbyterian Church in Ashtabula where I was a member. Brenda was my matron of honor; George was Allan's best man. Vernon, Bruce, and the spouses of the wedding party were the only guests who witnessed the ceremony. Afterward, on the way to The Swallows Restaurant for a celebratory dinner, Allan and I stopped by the local hospital where my mom was a patient. She had met Allan on several occasions and, aware of the age difference, supported my decision to marry. There was no honeymoon. We returned to our teaching schedules on Monday morning. It took time for the students in my class to accept that their teacher was now Mrs. Dickie and no longer was to be called Mrs. Nelson.

Prior to marriage, I had not talked with Allan about combining our two households. I naively thought that we would buy a house and the boys and I would move to Kent that summer. Before I had a chance to discuss this with Allan, we attended a wedding at a local Catholic church. After the ceremony, we were standing on the steps of the church waiting for the bride and groom to emerge. The woman next to me was the mother of one of my students, and she turned, saying to Allan, "Congratulations, but we are sorry that Mrs. Dickie will be leaving us." Allan, not missing a breath, replied, "No, Henrietta won't be leaving her job this year. We're going to give our marriage a trial year before living together." I was shocked and speechless, but Allan was serious. I taught for another year at Lincoln Elementary. Allan continued to teach the physical science class at the Ashtabula campus, allowing us to be together two nights a week and on weekends.

The Christmas of 1963, Allan made arrangements for us to spend the holiday on Long Boat Key—an island off the west coast of Florida, south of Tampa. In anticipation of his pending retirement, Allan had scheduled an interview for a position in the science department at the

University of Florida in Gainesville. He made the decision to drive, taking Vernon with him. They left on December 16. Due to my teaching schedule, I could not leave until the following week. On December 21, Bruce and I boarded a United flight to Tampa where it was prearranged that Allan and Vernon would be at the airport to meet us—a first plane ride for both Bruce and me.

Allan was not offered a physical science position at the university. Later he commented to me that the interview did not go well. The person who interviewed Allan had authored a text of which Allan was unaware. He admitted he had been careless and not learned as much as he could about the department or its staff.

THAT FIRST YEAR OF MARRIAGE presented us with challenges. For Allan, it was a major adjustment in lifestyle that included a young wife with two young sons—one a preadolescent, the other a teenager. For me, it was once again adapting to being a wife and beginning a career in teaching, while at the same time remaining a mother to my sons. These loyalties often came into sharp conflict.

We were married on April 20, 1963. My mother died on May 28 of that year. Allan told me he would not be with me the day of the service for Mom. He had to meet with his morning classes on campus. That afternoon he and three of his golfing cronies played a round of golf at the Oak Knolls Golf Course. Allan scored a hole-in-one on the fifteenth par 3 green. It was bittersweet when I learned that my husband had achieved every golfer's dream on the day of my mother's funeral service.

The summer of 1963, we divided our time between Allan's home in Kent and my home in Ashtabula. The boys spent time with us as well as with other family members. Allan's home on Linden Road needed painting, and that was a job he gave to Vernon. Allan, ever the Scotsman, refused to buy Vernon new brushes for painting. That was very distressful to me, but I didn't challenge my husband. I do remember that Allan's neighbor, a professor in the physical science department, remarked to Allan, "A workman is only as good as his tools." It didn't faze Allan. Vernon was made to paint the house with bristle-shedding, worn-out brushes. Combined with his tendency to make decisions without informing me, and his lack of support when my mother died, I was beginning to question my decision in marrying this man.

--------------------- ·+·++++·+ ---------

THE 1963–'64 SCHOOL YEAR started for all of us. Allan supplemented his position on campus by continuing to teach the extension class in Ashtabula two nights. I returned to my fifth-grade classroom at Lincoln Elementary. Bruce was a fifth grader at Ridgeview Elementary, and Vernon was now a sophomore in Edgewood High School. In my 1963 diary, on November 15, I had made this entry. "Allan told me he wrote to Jan (his daughter) saying, I am anxious to get my source of irritation under one roof." The boys and I passed our "first year marriage test."

Our lives progressed smoothly until the day of November 22 when the announcement came over my classroom loudspeaker that President Kennedy had been assassinated. His death profoundly affected the nation. President Johnson declared November 25 as a national day of mourning. We, like most of the nation, watched on television in shock and sorrow as the funeral cortege proceeded down Pennsylvania Avenue, bearing the body of the fallen president to the US Capitol where it would lie in state.

Allan started making plans in the spring of 1964 for us to move to Kent in the summer. My opportunities to be in Kent were limited, so Allan did most of the house hunting. He found a three-bedroom house on Wolcott Avenue, and I was given little choice but to agree. What mattered most to me was that we would finally be living together as a family. The house was ideally located for all of us—a mile and a half from the campus, within walking distance of the boys' schools, and one half mile from Franklin Elementary School where I would be teaching the fourth grade.

Allan continued to join his golfing buddies for their semiannual golf outings at Oglebay Park in West Virginia. Allan would be away a weekend in May, and I made arrangements for Ma to come for a visit. I wanted to make the weekend a memorable one for her, as it would be the last time she would be able to be in the house her son had built. I invited Ma's Swede Town friends to come for a *coffee klatch*. After returning home to Parma, Ma wrote in her loving Swedish-English:

> My Dear Henrietta and family. I want to thank you
> for the suprising weekend I spent with you, and thank
> you Allan for lending me your sleeping plese. How

nice it was of you all to get me to Ashtabula and to entertain me beside. I sopose it will be the last apertunity. I always injoy to come to you and longing to go not only for Ashtabula but for my kids I have there it will be all togetter different now after you go because I don know where to go, but it well be nice to have you so nere to take a trip out here anytime and now when Vernon is driving you can just sit and rest when you come. The days you have left in Ashtabula will go so fast you will be out this way before you know. Love Ma

In her letter, Ma refers to the distance from Ashtabula to Parma (seventy-five miles) being so much more than Kent to Parma (forty miles).

I completed my second year of teaching the fifth grade in the Lincoln building. My class presented me with a pair of Auguste Rodin's *The Thinker* bookends. The gift was the suggestion of a mother of one of my students. Her daughter told her I was always saying to the class, "Now think!"

Word spread rapidly among the staff that I was leaving and moving to Kent, and I would be selling my house. Ron Ulshafer, a French teacher, approached me about the sale. No real estate agent was involved—the Ulshafers and I reached a financial agreement. The house Sidney and I so lovingly and laboriously built was transferred to Ronald and Phyllis Ulshafer on May 15, 1964. The following month, the moving van came, and my children and I moved to our new home in Kent.

———— ·+++++· ————

I found it to be a different lifestyle living in Kent. Our home at 453 Wolcott Avenue was functional, not fancy. The eight-room, two-story house, with a finished third floor and full basement, was similar in architectural style to the farmhouse in which I was raised. Once the furniture was in place and the boxes unpacked, like many women I had to make my own nest. Fresh paint, new wallpaper, and window coverings were necessities. When not teaching or on the golf course, Allan helped with the redecorating.

Everything was new to me. I had an instant circle of acquaintances—friends that Allan had made over the years were very accepting. Jessie, who had cleaned Allan's house on Linden Road, continued to work for us. The university and community were a wellspring of events and activities: athletic events, faculty wives, international students, lectures, music and theater productions. I took advantage of the adult-education classes offered through the Kent City Schools. In a woodworking class, I made a maple-wood king-size headboard and a set of three candelabra candlesticks. I had a weekly standing appointment at Evelyn Dickerson's Beauty Salon. Allan sent me to a local optometrist to have me fitted for contact lenses. I shopped at O'Neil's and Polsky's Department Stores in Akron. Allan and I would drive into Cleveland to the Hannah Theater and on our way home stop for a cocktail and a leisurely dinner at a Brown Derby. At times I was overwhelmed living in this stimulating environment; it was intoxicating and heady medicine for this unsophisticated girl from Ashtabula.

Before moving to Kent, I had applied for a position with Kent City Schools and was hired at a salary of $5,200 to teach the fourth grade at Franklin Elementary School. My teaching assignment was different from what I had experienced at Lincoln Elementary School. Instead of a class size of fifteen students, there were thirty. There was no storage space for books or student supplies. The room was already crowded with student desks but made more so by a coat rack needed to accommodate the students' outdoor clothing. The room was in the old part of the school, directly above the furnace, and it became unmercifully hot in the winter. I taught there for one year and resigned, but not because of dissatisfaction with my teaching assignment. Allan planned to retire the spring of 1966, and we would move to Florida. My goal was to complete the required course work for the master of education degree before we left the area.

———————— ++++++ ————————

LIVING TOGETHER AS A FAMILY, I got to better know the man I had married. He was born in Pontiac, Michigan, on March 11, 1904, one of five children. He graduated from Pontiac High School in 1921 and attended Alma College for two years before entering Michigan State Normal College, located in Ypsilanti, where he graduated with a bachelor of science degree in 1925. He taught science for three years in Morenci at the local high school, then left Michigan and moved to Ohio where he was employed by the Cleveland City Schools. Here he taught science in John Adams, John Marshall, and East High School, later becoming head of the science departments for East and John Marshall. The summers of 1935 through 1939, he took his wife and two children to be with him in New York City while attending Teachers College, Columbia University. He earned a master of arts degree from the college in 1940.

December 7, 1941, the day that Japan attacked Pearl Harbor, was proclaimed "a day which will live in infamy" by President Theodore Roosevelt, and on December 8, the House of Representatives, with only one dissenting vote, placed in the president's hands a declaration of war. Allan, along with a multitude of his countrymen, volunteered for the service in 1943. He was commissioned a lieutenant in the navy and assigned to the Naval Air Navigation School in Hollywood, Florida, where his family joined him. Upon completion of the program, he was sent to the US Navy Pre-Flight School in Iowa City. Here he served as a navigation instructor until 1945. The war ended on September 2, 1945, and Allan was given an honorable discharge. He returned to civilian life, became a lieutenant commander in the USNR, and resumed his teaching career. It was Dr. George L. Bush, professor of chemistry at KSU, who recommended Allan for employment in the KSU Science Department. He was hired in 1946 during the presidency of Dr. George A. Bowman. While at Kent, Allan pursued a life dream of becoming a pilot and used his GI Bill to that end.

Allan was a prolific writer. He coauthored a science text with two of his colleagues, *A Biology of Familiar Things*. He wrote letters to the editor on diverse topics. The summer of 1962, he took a three-week holiday in Scotland playing several of the famed golf courses. He documented his experiences in an article featured in *Golf Digest*.

Allan retired in 1966. In a letter written on April 4, 1969, and signed by President White, it reads in part, "It is my pleasure to have known you personally. Our recent action is overdue but nonetheless sincere and heartfelt." Allan was granted emeritus professor status.

++++++

AFTER MARRIAGE I HAD NO IDEA WHAT TO EXPECT regarding our personal finances. I was used to living on Social Security and my widow's benefits that were supplemented by Mom, Dad, and the Nelson family. After I started teaching and received a paycheck, I felt suddenly rich.

There was no need for a prenuptial agreement with Allan. I had no cash reserves. My assets were a home and car that were debt-free.

Once in Kent, Allan assumed all responsibilities for our living expenses. I was able to save almost all my salary. With this in mind, Allan counseled me regarding investments, suggesting that we purchase stock together, placing it in survivorship. But on our first trip to see his financial adviser, Allan made it clear that any stock I purchased was to be in my name; stock he purchased was to be in his name—another shock! It didn't take me long to accept that our finances would be kept separate. Now with 20/20 hindsight, I realize the wisdom of this financial arrangement. Over the twenty-three years we were married, there never were any financial misunderstandings between us, with his children, or with mine.

Early in our marriage Allan advised me to plan to work and earn my own retirement, commenting that due to our age difference, he would not be able to provide me with the financial resources needed for my golden years. When Allan retired, he opted to reduce his monthly annuity and designated me as his beneficiary. This provided me with a monthly income, even if I remarried, until my death. Allan kept all his financial affairs in what he referred to as his "empire desk"—an antique washstand that I repaired and refinished for him.

Shortly after marriage, I came to realize how important bridge and golf were to Allan. Wanting to adapt my lifestyle to meld with my husband's, I attempted to learn how to play bridge. What was I thinking? I didn't even know the four suits in a deck, had no "card sense," but I persevered, taking a series of beginner bridge lessons at the local YMCA in Ashtabula. When one of my teaching colleagues learned about my interest in bridge, she invited Allan and me to their home for a social Saturday evening bridge foursome. At best, in the bidding process, all I could attain was the status of revolving "dummy." For me, the evening was a disaster and ended any thoughts I had of becoming a bridge partner for Allan.

Golf was another matter. Allan had several golfing buddies in Kent, but he also maintained a golfing bond with three men he had taught with in the Cleveland City Schools. During the golfing season, the four men had a monthly Sunday afternoon date to play a round of golf at different courses in the area. Each took their turn at being the host and selecting the course. The wives came with their husbands, and while the men were out having a great time on the links, the women spent their afternoon sitting about, chatting, but mostly complaining about the hours their husbands spent playing golf. When the men returned, there was a lengthy cocktail hour while they rehashed, golf shot by golf shot, what had occurred during the eighteen-hole round. Finally we would eat, the evening ended, and the couples departed.

It took only one of these Sunday afternoon golfing events for me to realize I did not want to be a complaining golf widow. Allan had made an initial investment in the construction of the Oak Knolls Golf Course located on Route 43, a short distance north of the Kent city limits. His stock "dividend" was a life membership for him and his nuclear family. It was on this course that I attempted to learn how to play golf and jokingly renamed the game "croquet." Every time I hit the ball, it rolled a few yards along the fairway. I couldn't get it off the ground.

Allan, ever the Scotsman, did not believe in golf lessons; he was self-taught and carried a low handicap. I defied Allan's directive and signed up for golf lessons with the course pro, John Wegenek. I scheduled lessons with him those first two summers that I lived in Kent and, under his tutelage, developed a respectable game of golf.

Within the first weeks of our living together in Kent, I found that Allan would schedule a golf foursome seven days a week. I had some unsettling conversations with him about this. As I improved my golf game, Allan enjoyed playing with me. I knew I had achieved as a golfer when I overheard a conversation he had with one of his Kent golfing buddies. Allan was asked to make the fourth for a Sunday round of golf. He replied, "Can't do it, Ralph, Henri and I play golf on Sundays." My golf lessons and hours of practice were a contributing factor in the nascent harmony developing in our marriage. Yes, golf is addictive. Now I was "one of them," not a complaining golf widow.

———— ·+·+·+·+·+· ————

SEPTEMBER OF '64 ARRIVED and with it the beginning of the school year. I was scheduled to attend a staff meeting, and Allan suggested that I make myself known to Betty Brinkerhoff, commenting that she was someone I might like to have as a golf partner. What began as a casual acquaintanceship developed into a very competitive bond between two friends. It didn't take long for me to realize that my purpose in life was to lower Betty's golf handicap and raise her bowling average. No matter how good a golf round I had, Betty would best me by a couple of strokes. We bet a nickel a hole, and she took more nickels from me than I from her.

Kent City Schools did not have a women's bowling league, so Betty, known for her ability to organize, sent out a memo to all teachers encouraging them to attend an organizational meeting. I went, not knowing anyone. Due to the number of women there, the decision was made to set up the league in teams of three. Betty was one of four teachers who were close friends; Betty opted to be the odd one out. I knew no one, and when all teams were formed, I was the odd one out. Betty came to me and suggested that the two of us make up a team and she would get the third person from the high school. She persuaded Mabelle Apley, who had never thrown a bowling ball in her life, to be that third person. It was Betty's suggestion that we call our team the "Left Overs." Mabelle managed to throw gutter ball after gutter ball, and our team established the highest handicap in the league. Under Betty's tutelage, Mabelle did acquire basic bowling skills, and when Mabelle got "hot," we were unstoppable. In the short time I bowled with the Kent teachers, the Left Overs were the league champions twice. In bowling, I'd have an outstanding three-game series, but Betty would best me there as well. We bet a dollar every time we played. That dollar went back and forth, many times. I did win the last series we rolled; that worn-and-torn dollar bill, encased in plastic, is now a memento in my cedar chest.

———————— ✛✛✛✛✛ ————————

BRUCE WAS EIGHT WHEN HIS FATHER DIED, ten when I married Allan, and eleven the summer we moved to Kent. That fall we enrolled him at sixth grade in the Central Elementary School. Bruce was still young and had not yet entered the willful, tumultuous teenage years. He had time to get to know and accept his stepfather as his "dad." Bruce was a hard worker. Soon after moving to Kent, he took over a daily paper route, delivering the morning *Cleveland Plain Dealer*. Like the postman's pledge, that was Bruce. "Neither rain, nor sleet, nor gloom of night stays these couriers from the swift completion of their appointed rounds." In the winter, he would get up extra early on school days so he could deliver his papers, come home, and crawl back in bed to get warm before going to school. A Boy Scout troop, sponsored by the United Methodist Church in Kent, took a lot of Bruce's time. He earned merit badges, achieving the rank of Life Scout; but when other interests intervened, he dropped scouting. While in Kent he built and flew model airplanes, doggedly accepting crash after crash and rebuilding the planes to fly, and crash, yet again. Bruce and his friend Chuck Kish wanted to raise a hamster. Allan would have no part of it, but he did allow Bruce to raise mice and a rabbit he named Thumper. Bruce's interest in music persuaded both Allan and me that a saxophone would be a wise investment. It was, until it was determined Bruce needed braces and the orthodontist recommended that he not play a reed instrument. That led us to purchase a guitar for him that temporarily satisfied his musical interest. Overall, Bruce adapted well to our move to Kent.

Vernon was eleven when his father died, fifteen when I married Allan, and sixteen the summer we moved to Kent. Bruce accepted my marriage. It was much more difficult for Vernon. In a December 25, 1963, entry in my diary, I wrote, "Allan expressed his growing fondness for Bruce. *He* expressed his inability to relate to Vern, a teenager." From the time of his birth, Vernon was the cynosure of adult attention. I lived with my mother, Sidney was an absent father, and being the first grandchild, he was the center of his grandparents' world. This attention was amplified after his father died. When I married Allan, all of this changed. Vernon could be pleasant and engaging when he wanted something. If events did not go his way, like many teenagers, he became sullen, gloomy, and moody, isolating himself from the family. Allan would have none of Vernon's disrespectful behaviors. I loved my children; I loved Allan. Sometimes the internal stress I experienced was more than I could bear; but the storm cloud would pass and a degree of normalcy would return. I had long talks with Vernon about his relationship with his stepfather, mostly to no avail.

Vernon entered Theodore Roosevelt High School (commonly called Kent Roosevelt) as a junior. He did well academically. He tried sports: first football, dropped that; then he took up wrestling, which he previously had done when attending Edgewood Senior High School. He got a job at the local Phillips gas station, working after school and on weekends. Vernon's interest in cars led him to apply for a General Motors co-op scholarship his senior year. His first interview was with the Euclid General Motors plant in Cleveland, and we all shared in his disappointment when he was not accepted. However, the General Motors plant in Lordstown was interested. Vernon interviewed with them and received his letter of acceptance on January 25, 1966. The following March, as a family, we visited the General Motors Institute at Flint, Michigan.

I loved this handsome, tall, red-headed manipulative, intelligent son, but Vernon had a phobia that no one liked him—that is, no one except Roberta (Bobbie) Jalali, an attractive petite, dark-haired girl in his class. They were romantically attracted to one another, and serious dating ensued. This added to Allan's displeasure with Vernon. I did note in a March 1966 diary entry that, at my request, Allan had a "man-to-man" talk with Vernon about the consequences of a romantic involvement. I can only assume this had an impact on Vernon because, although they continued to date after high school, each pursued their own career track.

In hindsight, I realize my youthful parenting skills were inadequate when it came to my oldest son. In a diary entry from November 20, 1965, Allan coldly observed to me, "I notice you and Vern aren't very close as a mother and son." Dear God, Allan's perception hurt, but it was accurate. Looking back, I should have made arrangements for Vernon to see a professional therapist; in that neutral setting perhaps he would have spoken openly regarding agonizing thoughts kept to himself. I realized, only later in my life, that my move to Kent when Vernon entered his junior year in high school was one of the worst conscious decisions that I ever made. Vernon did not easily make friends, and I forced him to leave his familiar surroundings and his best friend, Bob Lee. After Vernon's father died, he spent a lot of time with the Lees, and I often commented that they served as surrogate parents. Perhaps he could have stayed with them for his final two years of high school.

—————·+++++·—————

As previously mentioned, I was drawn to Allan Dickie as my most outstanding undergraduate professor. Later my attraction to him was sexual, with the goal of husband and stepfather needed to complete my family circle. Now as his wife, I found myself in awe of his achievements, and my feelings of inferiority again surfaced. Would I measure up as Mrs. Allan Dickie? A comment made to me by KSU President George A. Bowman strengthened my self-esteem. Allan and I were attending the funeral of Dr. Gerald Chapman, Allan's boss in the physical science department. We were seated next to the Bowmans, and Allan introduced me to them. As we were leaving the service, President Bowman took my hand. I recorded his words in my diary of April 3: "You know I'm responsible for Allan's being in Kent.

I hired him. I'm glad you two got together. You look good together. You look like you belong together."

————— ⊹⊹⊹⊹⊹ —————

THE TWO YEARS WE LIVED IN KENT provided me with the opportunity to begin to get to know Allan's children—George and Janet. George was married to Lucille (Lou), and they had one daughter, Nancy. They lived in an apartment in Cleveland, close to Western Reserve University where George was enrolled in the dental school. George and his family made frequent Sunday afternoon visits to Kent. George was quiet, comfortable to be with. Lou was an extrovert, clever in her use of words, making me feel uneasy that I wasn't as quick with the repartee. Nancy, five years old when we moved to Kent, was in constant motion, and that tired her grandpa more than eighteen holes of golf. George graduated from Western Reserve with his degree in dentistry. Lou loved the French Quarter in New Orleans, and it was decreed that George establish his practice in the New Orleans area of Louisiana. Lou's claim to fame was that she could always get a front-row table at Preservation Hall, a venue dedicated to protecting, preserving, and perpetuating New Orleans Jazz. (My awe of Lou's claim to fame evaporated when I later saw her surreptitiously slip one, maybe two, $20 bills to the *maître d'* who seated the incoming guests.)

Janet (Jan) was married to Royce Fincher, an attorney by profession and a lieutenant in the Army serving a tour of duty in France when Allan and I were married. Their daughter Renee was born there. On July 11, 1964, Jan, with Renee, returned to the States, and Allan and I met them at the Cleveland Airport. Jan was exhausted from a fifteen-hour prop flight from Paris, holding a fretting toddler on her lap all the way.

Jan and Renee stayed for a short time with us in Kent while waiting for Royce to be mustered out of the service and join her there. I had briefly met Jan prior to my marriage to her dad and before she ventured to France to join her husband. Our days together in Kent gave me an opportunity to get to better know this attractive, talented, poised young woman. Renee was a delightful child, whose care Grandpa mostly left to her mother and me. Royce was from New Orleans, and it was a given that, when out of the service, they would settle in that area.

With both of Allan's children living in Louisiana, Allan arranged for us to visit them in September of 1965. What was to be a routine flight to New Orleans on September 8 turned out to be an adventure. We boarded our flight in Cleveland, with a scheduled stop in Atlanta. After the plane was down in Atlanta, we learned Hurricane Betsy had hit the New Orleans area. Our flight was delayed until further notice due to this category four storm. For us it was a pleasant interruption in our trip. United Airlines sent us to a deluxe hotel where we spent the night and toured downtown Atlanta the next day. Twenty-four hours later, we were back on the plane and headed to New Orleans. Our flight was the second one in after the airport opened. The runway had been cleared of debris for landing, but there were few lights, and despite the darkness, one became aware of the devastation. Walking through the deserted airport, there was an eerie silence. A bathroom visit was impossible; sewage covered the floor. The telephone in the airport worked, as well as the phone at the apartment of Jan and Royce. Royce came for us, and we spent the next few days with them in their stifling hot apartment with no electricity. Royce's parents lived in another section of town where power had been restored, and we sought refugee with them during the day. Royce borrowed his dad's car and drove us around the area in air-conditioned luxury as we observed firsthand the devastation caused by the high winds—trees and utility poles down, flooding, homes demolished, broken glass and trash everywhere, makeshift evacuation areas teeming with displaced people. That was the traumatic side of my first visit to New Orleans. The romantic side of the visit was a drive into the French Quarter where there was only minimal storm damage. Royce and Jan took us to the famous Brennan's Restaurant on Royal Street, a New Orleans dining tradition featuring a Creole menu influenced by French and Spanish cuisine.

We had arrived at Jan and Royce's home on Friday, September 10, and stayed with them for four days. On Tuesday we rented a car and drove to Thibodaux, about sixty-five miles to the southwest of New Orleans. To me the drive was frightening. We drove for miles without seeing another car; the roadway was barely visible above the level of the water filling deep roadside drainage ditches. On each side of the road, live oak and cypress towered above the dense undergrowth, adding to my sensation of being cut off from civilization. We arrived safely at the home of Allan's son. They as well were without electricity. After a short visit, Allan, satisfied his son and family were safe, headed back to New Orleans. We stayed the night with the Fincher family, and the following morning Royce took us to the airport where we boarded our flight for home. It was a gutsy trip for me, my first to the area, but for Allan, the seasoned traveler, it was all taken in stride.

--------++++++--------

THERE WERE OTHER TRAVEL EXPERIENCES that I had during those first two years we lived in Kent. Allan's retirement dream was to move to Florida where he thought he would be able to enjoy golf year-round. We had agreed that the Emerald Coast in the Pan Handle area of the state would be ideal for us—far enough north to avoid the intense heat and humidity of the lower peninsula. In the 1960s, there was a teacher shortage, and jobs were as plentiful as picking cherries off of a tree. In January I had contacted school districts in Pensacola, Fort Walton Beach, Destin, and Panama City and made appointments for interviews in each. My objective was to visit each city and select the place I thought best for me professionally.

Vernon took the week off from school so he could accompany me on the trip. Allan had recently purchased a 1966 green Ford Galaxy with air-conditioning, and he loaned us his car. We left on my thirty-sixth birthday and drove straight through to Thibodaux, staying with George and family for two days. George and Lou were gracious and generous hosts, taking us into the French Quarter so that Vernon would have the experience of dining at Brennan's Restaurant. Better yet, the evening before we left, they treated us to an elegant repast in the Tchoupitoulas Restaurant, a stately southern plantation house located at the end of a long drive lined with live oak trees. I was impressed, and for years Vernon spoke of this dining experience.

The next morning we bid our goodbyes to the family. Driving east we stopped on our way to the Fincher home in LaPlace to tour George's dental building in Vacherie. Our overnight visit with the Fincher family was short as I had an interview scheduled in Pensacola the following morning. The interview went well, but Fort Walton Beach was a smaller city and the scenic beauty of its location on a bayou was impressive. I accepted a position there to teach a fifth-grade class. I canceled all other interviews. Mission accomplished, Vernon and I headed north, arriving home on April 16. For the most part, it was a pleasant ten-day trip with my son.

--------++++++--------

JUNE OF 1966 WAS AN EVENTFUL MONTH in the Nelson-Dickie home. Allan retired, mother and son graduated. Two other professors from the physical science department retired and were recognized, along with Allan, at university functions: Dr. George L. Bush, with whom Allan taught in the Cleveland Schools and who recommended him for the position at KSU, and Professor Clarence L. Cook, his neighbor and friend. All three men were presented KSU chairs affixed with the university seal.

Vernon graduated from Kent Roosevelt High School on June 7. He was accepted in the General Motors Co-Op Engineering Program at Flint, Michigan, with a field assignment in the Lordstown assembly plant. Knowing he would need reliable transportation, his graduation gift was a 1966 Chevelle SS, and arrangements were made for him, when in the area, to live at 422 Park Avenue in Kent.

I had received the acceptance letter for admission to graduate school on August 23, 1962. From that day forward, I had my academic plan in place to get my M. Ed. as soon as possible. My second year living in Kent, relieved of teaching responsibilities, I was able to carry full course loads that enabled me to graduate on June 11, one week after my son's graduation from high school. The afternoon of my graduation, family members gathered at our Wolcott Avenue home to celebrate, lifting their glasses to the retiree and the mother and son graduates. Ma was there, and I wrote in my diary that when she left that day, she took Allan's hand and thanked him for all he had done for her family. Allan was noticeably touched.

———— ++++++ ————

IT DIDN'T SEEM THERE WERE ENOUGH DAYS on our calendar that spring and summer before our scheduled moving date. In May our realtor was successful in finding a buyer, Gordon and Nancy Waters, for our Wolcott Avenue house. Bill and Jan Hoover hosted a farewell party for us, inviting all the golfing gang and close faculty friends. The Cleveland foursome, with whom Allan had played so many years, wished us well and composed a doggerel verse that read in part, "At Fort Walton Beach, in the Land of the Sun, There'll be those occasions, when you'll want to have fun…" and gave us a dozen Spalding Air-Flyte golf balls. Allan wanted to visit his childhood home, so the four of us took a few days and drove to Pontiac, Michigan, where several family members still lived in the area.

Allan had contacted a real estate agency in Fort Walton Beach, and a realtor from the agency telephoned, informing Allan that a rental house on Pocahontas Drive was available for a one-year lease. The moving truck was scheduled to come on July 30, but a telephone call from the moving company put us both in shock when we were told it would be there on the twenty-eighth. We canceled our farewell golf outing, pitched in, and managed to stay ahead of the men loading the truck—that is, until Allan's briefcase came up missing. Allan insisted the men search for his attaché case on the partially loaded truck—important documents critical to our move were in that case. The truck had to be partially unloaded, and the driver made no effort to conceal his annoyance; but for Allan it was with relief and gratitude when the briefcase was uncovered and placed in his hands. He locked it in the trunk of his Ford to ensure its safekeeping.

We spent the next two nights with friends, returning to clean the house and pack our cars. We departed midafternoon of July 30. Saying goodbye to Vernon was difficult for me. I was leaving my son to fend for himself as he entered a new chapter in his life. I drove the Ford, and Bruce rode with me; Allan drove my Corvair (the car that Ralph Nader said was "unsafe at any speed"). We did some sightseeing on our eight-hundred-mile journey to our new home: the first night we stayed in Covington, Kentucky (the city where Sidney and I were married); on our way to Nashville, Tennessee, where we spent our second night, we toured Mammoth Cave; leaving Nashville we stopped in Birmingham, Alabama to view the Vulcan Statue. As fate would have it, the Ford had a flat tire just a hundred miles north of Fort Walton Beach (Allan and Bruce changed the tire). We arrived at our house at 538 Pocahontas Drive early in the evening. The key was in the mailbox. Entering the vacant house, we found the utilities had not been turned on. We had the foresight to bring our camping equipment with us. Our neighbor supplied us with potable water. We set up our cots, fell onto them, and slept!

TEN

MARRIAGE TO ALLAN DICKIE
FORT WALTON BEACH (1966–1967)

WE AWAKENED EARLY that first morning in our new home. Allan, Bruce, and I donned our bathing suits and drove the short distance to the beach on the Gulf of Mexico for a refreshing swim. It was the first time my fourteen-year-old son had seen the Gulf. As we trudged toward the water, we had to climb the sand dunes to reach our destination. After our swim we stopped at a coffee shop for breakfast. Bruce kept chattering about those huge sand dunes. These phenomena of nature impressed him more than the buoyancy of the salt water.

Back at the house we dressed for the day. The priority was to arrange to have the utilities turned on. Next on Allan's list was to locate the golf course, which he did and signed up for the eighteen-hole men's league at the Fort Walton Beach Golf Course. We found a nearby grocery store, stocked the ice chest with ice and food, and now exhausted from the heat, returned to the beach for an afternoon swim.

THE CITY OF FORT WALTON BEACH is an area of 8.2 square miles, seven feet above sea level, with a population of about ten thousand in the mid-1960s. It is in the panhandle area of the state, thirty-six miles to the east of Pensacola, and 140 miles to the west of the state capital of Tallahassee.

The climate of the area is subtropical. The summers are hot and very humid, autumn and spring are warm, winters are short and mild.

The average yearly rainfall is sixty-nine inches. Extremes of temperature were recorded at 107 degrees Fahrenheit on July 15, 1980, and 4 degrees Fahrenheit on January 21, 1985. I mention this because, for the short time that we lived there in the mid-1960s, it seemed we experienced near-record temperatures and rainfall. I recall getting up one winter morning to see cascades of ice formations where residents had neglected to turn off their sprinkling systems.

Tribes of native Indians lived in the area when it was first colonized by the Spanish and English in the sixteenth century. During the time that I lived there, I became aware of the diversity of ethnic groups: 70 percent were Caucasian; the other 30 percent were African American, Asian, Hispanic, and that catch-all category "miscellaneous." Due to the Hispanic population in the area, I was required to take a conversational Spanish class at the local junior college. This was required to have the "conditional" removed from my Florida teaching certificate.

One much more poetic than I is needed to describe the natural beauty of this area known as the Emerald Coast. The oval-shaped grains of white-quartz sand found along the beaches of the Miracle Strip are known to be the cleanest in the world. This is due to the headwaters of the Chattahoochee River originating in the Appalachian Mountains in Georgia. The river delivers this quartz sand material to the Gulf of Mexico. Once the river crosses the Georgia-Florida border, it becomes the Apalachicola, named after the Indian tribe that lived along the river. Gentle offshore breezes caress the sea oats that flourish on the sand dune mounds that rise in humpbacks along the beaches. The blue waters of the Gulf of Mexico invite one to wade or to swim. Azure skies and billowy white clouds complete this microcosm of nature's paradise.

While waiting for our furniture to arrive, the three of us daily visited the beach to swim and to take long walks. On the second day we were swimming, I was stung by a Portuguese man-o'-war. At the time I did not realize what had happened; the sting, although painful, had no medical repercussions for me. I had yet to learn that those living in the area would do the "Shalimar stomp" when entering the water to frighten off this floating terror with the venomous tentacles.

———————— ·++++·+ ————————

Our furniture arrived on August 5. The next few days were chaotic, as we attempted to fit the three floors of furniture that we brought from our

Kent home into a one-story house with eight small rooms. The house was located across the street from the Cinco Bayou. We learned from our neighbors that the bayou teemed with nonthreatening sea life, so this became our favorite place to swim. In the heat of the summer, I found it to be like swimming in a large tub of warm bathwater, not refreshing to the body. Later the bayou provided opportunities for water-skiing and sailing.

FWB was a small city in the 1960s, and it didn't take us long to acquaint ourselves with the location of services, shopping, and entertainment. Restaurants were plentiful in the area, mostly known for their seafood specialties. Our favorite fish restaurant was Fisherman's Wharf located in Destin less than ten miles to the east. Their menu featured fresh, honest-to-goodness-just-off-the-boat seafood. In the dining room picnic tables were covered with newspapers, and many times we ate our choice fish entrée with our fingers. Due to the informal ambiance of the dining room setting, this became our favorite place to eat. If we wanted to be entertained while eating, we would go to the Club Continental where there were dancing go-go girls. There were high-end restaurants as well, the Bayview Supper Club being one. Soon I found that we cooked less and dined out more.

Allan golfed almost every day at the Fort Walton Beach Golf Course. I frequently joined him in the late afternoons. Golfing and swimming were not all that we did. The local movie theater featured many films to our liking. And I persuaded Allan that we should sign up for square dance lessons, but after the second lesson, Allan said, "Enough!"

Area attractions did pique our interest, and all were visited while we lived there. The FWB Gulfarium Marine Adventure Park was a top-notch marine science center. Visitors were able to closely observe sharks, dolphins, sea lions, turtles, even penguins, and other forms of life native to the area. Venturing a few miles to the east on the Choctawhatchee Bay was Eden Gardens State Park, located on 115 beautifully landscaped acres that featured a Greek-revival–style mansion. Further east, on the Santa Rosa Beach, was the Heritage Park and Cultural Center; its purpose was to preserve and interpret the history of the community. Further on near Panama City the Museum of the Sea and Indian was located, featuring marine and Indian relic collections. This variety of attractions offered interesting entertainment for visiting family and friends.

There were two military bases in the area—Hurlburt Field (home of Air Force Special Operations Command) and Eglin Air Force Base (geographically one of the country's largest bases). While we lived in FWB we took advantage of resources available to the public. Allan, Bruce, and I had the opportunity to visit the Air Ground Control center at Eglin to observe the radar screen as military personnel directed planes in taking off and landing. We thrilled to the Thunderbird precision flying shows. We visited the Eglin Air Force Armament Museum.

As a teacher, my class was given a guided tour of base resources. But best of all, it provided Allan the opportunity to play golf on the challenging and picturesque base course.

——— ++++++ ———

THOSE FIRST WEEKS WE BECAME SO ENAMORED with the area that we inquired about real estate there on Cinco Bayou. By then we were acquainted with several of our neighbors. All were friendly, and we thought this was the right place for us. There were several waterfront lots available on Pocahontas Drive. We contacted a real estate agent and experienced sticker shock when we learned the asking price. Lots between sixty feet to one hundred feet were going for $12,000 to $14,000 with no room for negotiating. We contacted a local builder and learned that the cost for a no-frills three-bedroom house would run about $20,000 (over $150,000 in 2015 dollars). It didn't take long for Allan to realize that he didn't want to invest in any real estate; admittedly with my Depression-era upbringing, I agreed with him.

Before school started for Bruce and for me, to get our minds off of the aborted real estate venture, Allan offered to take us on a deep-sea fishing trip. Bruce had become friends with Wolfgang Kreitz, a teenager who lived next door, and we invited him to join us. The fishing boats docked in Destin. Arriving at the docks, the first thing we noticed was a boat emblazoned with the name *Sun Fisherman* that had a seven-foot shark suspended from its bow. This was unusual; the fish most commonly caught were red snapper, grouper, and flounder.

The ole salts of the sea had their weathered scows anchored there in the harbor, alongside the fancy glass-enclosed, air-conditioned boats equipped with electric reels on the fishing rods. We chose to get our passage on a wooden no-frills fishing boat, thinking we would have a more realistic deep-sea fishing experience. We followed some men as we walked up the gangplank to board the *Marathon*; the skipper was there to take our money. Another crusty crew member with leathery skin etched from the sun and biceps like small logs, provided us with life jackets, rods, and bait. As the boat pulled away from the dock, the four of us were wired with nervous excitement in anticipation of what was to come. Once the boat was out in the open waters, we observed flying fish with long, winglike fins that enabled them to glide for a distance above the water's surface. Two hours and twenty-two nautical miles later, we reached the fishing grounds. The captain slowed the boat, and the deckhand reeled out the anchor line until the boat stabilized. (I later learned the length of the line must be a minimum of three times the depth of the water to set the anchor.) No words were spoken as the other passengers, evidently experienced fishermen, baited their hooks and dropped their lines over the side. Observing them, we followed suit, taking a small fish from our bait bucket and impaling it on the hook. We dropped our lines over the side, freeing the rod reel to spin as the weighted fishhook found its way to a depth of 120 feet. (Red snapper are a bottom fish, and in hot weather this is the depth where they swim.)

The captain found a good fishing spot. The pro fishermen were reeling fish in as fast as they could bait and drop their lines. Allan, Bruce, and Wolfgang did admirably well. Allan caught several red snapper, but his thrill was being awarded the prize for the catch of the day, a twelve-pound bonito. Bruce had a decent catch of snapper and a rockfish. Wolfgang caught a number of fish. And then there was me. I couldn't snag (hook) my fish at the first awareness of a tug on my line. My arm ached from reeling my line in, again and again and again, only to find a bare fishhook. Now I knew why the tourist fishing boats were equipped with electric reels on the fishing rods. Before the day's end, I did manage to snag one decent-size snapper to add to our fish bucket.

We knew this would be an all-day fishing excursion, so we brought our own food and water. Hours passed, and I felt the call of nature and was told the head (toilet) was below. I navigated the narrow, rough-hewn steps to what I thought, by the smell, was the bilge well of the boat. This was far worse than any outhouse experience I ever had while living on the farm.

Late afternoon the captain started the engine, the deckhand pulled in the anchor, and all settled in for the run back to Destin. As our boat cut through the gentle swells of the Gulf waters, we observed a school of dolphins gamboling off the bow of the boat. Back at the dock, we walked down the gangplank of the *Marathon* at the same time the tourist boat came in and disembarked its passengers. A few carried off their catch of fish, but most were laughing and cavorting about. It was obvious there was more than water and food available to them on their daylong fishing expedition. Did any of us regret our choice choosing this seaworthy relic? Fishing rods equipped with electric reels, air-conditioned lounges, and pristine "heads" would have given me memories much different than the ones I have from the rustic conditions we faced on the *Marathon*. I think it might have spelled only **boredom**.

Once home Bruce, with the help of Wolfgang, cleaned the fish. That evening we had baked snapper for our dinner. The remainder we froze. I salivate as I write about this, as our fresh-caught red snapper was a savory taste delight never again experienced.

SEPTEMBER CAME, and we settled into our respective responsibilities. Allan visited the Okaloosa/Walton Junior College to inquire about a teaching position in the science department. He was hired immediately to teach classes in the physical sciences. When he was not teaching or playing golf, I benefited by his assuming all responsibility for managing and running the household.

We enrolled Bruce in the eighth grade in the local district school. Overall the school year was a lost cause for Bruce. The methods of instruction and curriculum did not meet the standards we were used to in Ohio. Bruce played on the junior high basketball team but was disappointed that he did not get more court time during games. He did make friends and took part in school extracurricular activities. I noted in a May 20 diary entry, "Bruce went to a school dance. He came home walking on air because he'd danced with a real-live-girl and even 'touched' her in the slow dances." His previous dance lessons were paying social dividends. On May 26 I noted, "Bruce had a blast at a party playing spin the bottle." (No further details were given.)

A lot of Bruce's after-school time was spent swimming in the bayou. We gave him snorkeling equipment; he fashioned a gig by bolting a three-tined metal spear with sharp barbed points to a broom handle and built a catamaran. He was well equipped for crabbing and fishing. One evening, soon after the beginning of the school year, when Allan was not home, I entered the house only minutes before Bruce came racing in with the gig embedded in his left hand. He'd misjudged the distortion property of the water when he attempted to thrust his gig, not at a fish, but at a beer can lying on the bottom of the bayou. His left hand got in the way. I had the presence of mind to saw the wooden handle off of the gig before rushing him to our doctor's office. I wanted to remain with Bruce. I must have appeared very pale because the doctor started to insist that I leave while he removed the gig. I assured him I would not faint. I watched fascinated as he took a pair of cutters and, with effort, snipped off part of the metal end of the gig, freeing it so he could push it out of Bruce's hand. My son's hand healed, no tendons were damaged, nor was there any infection. Bruce made himself another gig and used it with greater accuracy, especially when spearing beer cans.

When not in school or swimming in the bayou, Bruce spent hours in his bedroom with the door closed building model airplanes. He grew several inches during that year, and we attributed his weight loss to his height gain. At the time, neither Allan nor I had carefully read the warning label on the glue bottle stating that if used in a closed area, the fumes could be harmful to one's health. Years later, I came to the realization this could have been the explanation for my son's weight loss.

The Shalimar Methodist Church near us sponsored a scout troop and Bruce joined, but there were times he wanted to drop out. A note I made in a February 17 diary entry read, "Bruce went camping with the scouts out to Eglin AFB—Allan seems to have magic to persuade Bruce to 'keep at' and 'stay with' a commitment." At a troop campout in October, Bruce was a squad leader, but a few months later in April, I wrote, "…at the boy scout jamboree on Eglin Reservation he was not elected for the tap out of the Order of the Arrow." Bruce's eighth-grade year was plagued with disappointments, accidents, and illness, but through it all he persevered.

I was hired by the Board of Public Instruction of Okaloosa County to teach the fifth grade at Wright Elementary School in Fort Walton Beach. My salary for the year was $5,500. My first day of school was September 6, and for the next several weeks, I made daily entries in my diary that it was "hot, hot, hot and I am always tired!" Many afternoons I would come home, immediately don my bathing suit, and go for a swim. If Allan were home, he would join me. But the warm temperature of the bayou water was not refreshing; at least I was wet from something besides sweat.

My class size was limited to thirty students. Dealing with this number of students presented me with a major professional challenge. Symbolically speaking, my classroom had a revolving door. Due to the military influence in the area, students were constantly coming and going. I had only five of the original thirty students on the last day of school.

With the lack of air-conditioning and my ever-changing student roster, it was a rough year for me, but I made the best of it. I was with my students from the time they arrived in the morning until they left in the afternoon. I ate lunch with them. I took my bathroom break with them. I taught all subjects, including conversational Spanish and music. The only special-area teachers that gave me some relief were for the physical education and art classes. I must have concealed my inner frustrations, because I wrote in my diary on September 20, "Dee Davis, art teacher, commented I had a beautiful face; if she were a portrait painter she'd paint it…I always seemed to look so happy." I went on to say, "I sure must put up a good front because I don't feel 'happy' this move down here is getting me down." Again, on December 16, I made a diary entry that read, "I'm so depressed all the time. I don't like my teaching; I don't like this house; I miss family and friends."

I soon learned that these children of military families were world travelers and had many experiences that could be incorporated in my classroom teaching. I used instructional methods that encouraged active student participation in their learning. Classroom elections were held. The class wanted an aquarium and assumed all responsibility for its care. Current events were of great interest to the children; I used this interest to develop a weekly TV newscast.

For me, the most rewarding projects I did with my students were in language arts. The curriculum required teaching a unit on our flag. This evolved into a play, *History of Our Flag*, which they wrote, produced, and performed for the school. Their playwright and acting talent became known, and the class was invited to perform their play at another local elementary school—a proud moment for all.

I wanted them to write about their varied life experiences. It was an interesting project for the children, and they did remarkably well. I went to a local publisher and had each child's work bound into a book. I had not told the students I was going to do this. The day the books were returned and they realized they were an "author" was exciting for them, but for me as their teacher, it was professionally rewarding.

One of the students in my class, Kathy Alkema, had lived for a time with her family in Japan. She wrote about this experience and included the part of crossing the International Date Line in her story. Her book was, by far, the most outstanding one written by any of the students. I asked Kathy if I could borrow her book, have it copied, and bound into a book of my own. She was delighted and gave her consent. I was so involved with other aspects of my personal and professional life that I did not take the time to have this done and returned the book to Kathy with only a "thank you" and no further explanation. I remained in touch with the Alkema family, and years later I received a letter from Kathy saying that in one of their family moves, her book had been lost. She wanted to borrow my copy, promising to return it. It is difficult for me to describe my heartfelt sickness as I wrote to Kathy and told her I did not have her book. It was only then I realized the impact my lying by omission would have on a former talented student.

My school year ended on May 26. Despite all my frustrations and misgivings, I had persevered. In my mind I had done my professional best.

------------+++++------------

I WAS NOT THE ONLY ONE HOMESICK and missing family. The first indication that Vernon was unhappy with the career path he chose with General Motors came in the form of a letter on August 29, telling us he was lonely and homesick. The very next day, we received a phone call, informing us that after only one rotation in his co-op program, he realized that working for a large cooperation as an engineer was not for him. Further, he said he had quit GM and wanted to transfer to Kent State University and pursue a liberal arts education. We were shocked! We persuaded Vernon to get on a plane and come down to see us so we could discuss the matter face-to-face. Using a farm metaphor, "This might be like closing the barn door after the horse had run off."

Vernon arrived the next day, and we met him at the FWB Airport. My memory is murky regarding the next few hours. I do recall that Vernon was adamant about not returning to GM. My son said he knew he had to be his own person, and as he saw it, he could not fit into the collective mold required by the company. These were cogent thoughts coming from one so young and not understood by either Allan or myself.

The Vietnam War was raging, and Vernon had a low draft number. He was exempt as long as he was in school. Allan pointed out that if he started to jump from one college to another, he could end up being drafted, and he went on to say that Vernon had no choice but to enlist in the service, advising him to volunteer for the navy. Again, this was anathema to Vernon's ears, knowing the service would give him little to no opportunity for self-expression. The dialogue became so heated between my son and his stepfather that Allan took Bruce and left for the weekend to visit his daughter in LaPlace, Louisiana.

Vernon stayed with me for five days, and during that time we took long walks on the beach and had unending hours of conversation. My son did agree that when he returned to Ohio, he would investigate joining the navy. I took him to the airport on September 5. It was raining that day as I walked with him across the tarmac to the plane. We embraced; he ascended the steps and entered the fuselage. I continued to stand there and watch as the plane my son was on taxied down the runway, took off, and disappeared into the mist of the sky. It was not until years later that I fully comprehended the wisdom of this young man in knowing himself.

Vernon returned to Ohio, gave up his room in Kent, and went to live with his grandma and aunts in Parma. He visited the Navy recruiting office, but in the near term their quota was filled. His visit to the Air Force recruitment center was successful; he was accepted in the Air Force and left on January 3 for Lackland AFB near San Antonio, Texas. Vernon completed basic training on February 15 with a "highly qualified" rating. He was assigned to Kessler Field in Biloxi, Mississippi, and there he was trained as a digital computer repairman. I credit Allan with the emotional strength required to redirect my strong-willed son's career path.

FWB is only 140 miles from Biloxi, allowing Vernon to make frequent weekend trips home that spring. His time in the service gave him cause to reflect and count his blessings. We received a letter from him dated 6 March '67:

> You don't know how much I enjoyed this weekend. It was really great just coming home. I guess a person really doesn't know what he has until it's gone. I know in things gone by I've probably disappointed you both. I only hope it won't happen anymore. At least I'm really trying to make everything come out alright.

On one of his first visits home, Vernon went to the Eglin AFB BX and was checked out on the operation of the ski boats that were available to service personnel. Every weekend thereafter when he was home, he would get a ski boat and equipment from the base BX. As a family we would spend hours water-skiing on Cinco Bayou. Allan was successful in getting up once on his skis. As he ended his short run and came into shore, he briskly said, "Been there, done that, and it's enough!" I had heard one of the locals comment that when the water was smooth as glass on the bayou, you could hear a screech when you made a sharp turn on your slalom ski. When conditions were right, Bruce, Vernon, and I tried it, and experienced this thrilling phenomenon. There were several weekends that spring that the Fincher family drove over from LaPlace to join us for family times of fun in the sun.

When Vernon was home on weekends, we did a lot more than ski. He joined Bruce in flying model airplanes, and the brothers went to Destin for a fishing adventure. At home we played badminton and grilled many of our evening meals outdoors.

We were aware that the relationship between Vernon and his high school sweetheart, Bobbie Jalali, was serious. We invited her to come to FWB one June weekend. Allan took Bobbie with him to Pensacola to meet the bus that Vernon would be on. Allan later commented to me, "I thought Bobbie would jump out of her skin before Vern got there." Their time together was short. Bobbie arrived on June 2; Vernon took her to her plane for a two o'clock flight home on June 4. It was a very special weekend in the lives of two young people in love, for Vernon told us they both cried when they parted.

———————— ·+·+·+·+· ————————

WHILE LIVING IN FWB we enjoyed frequent visits from family members and Kent friends, while at the same time we made new friends who lived in the area. Our neighbors to each side of us, and another who lived across the street on the bayou, were especially friendly. Allan met a number of men at the Fort Walton Beach Golf Course. I became friends with some of the members of the Wright Elementary School teaching staff. Almost all of our new friends were connected to the military bases in the area.

Allan and I observed two phenomena related to our military friends. First, they extended a hand in friendship soon after meeting us. Second, they were precisely punctual. Allan and I had a cocktail party, and on the invitation we specified the hours of 7:00 to 9:00 p.m. At the appointed hour it was as if a bus pulled up in front of the house and all the passengers got out; at nine o'clock everyone left. I asked my closest friend, Carol Mitchell, a sixth-grade teacher, about this. Her reply has remained with me to this day. Carol said in words to the effect that, "In the military we never know how long we'll be in one place, and we feel the need to make friends immediately. We are conditioned to being punctual and strictly abide by specific time constraints." How different from what Allan and I were used to in civilian life.

New Year's Eve we were invited by Terry and Carol Mitchell to be their guests at the Eglin AFB Officer's Club. It was a black-tie affair, and like every woman, I was concerned about what I would wear. My favorite dress shop in the city was the Cover Girl, and it was there I found a white, floor-length sleeveless crepe Grecian-style dress. It was elegant. Allan and

I were dressed for the occasion, ready to leave the house, when to our horror, the toilets backed up, spewing sewage onto the bathroom floors. Allan grabbed anything he could find that would absorb the filthy mess, and we vacated the house, our clothes still intact. We weren't going to miss the festivities of New Year's Eve.

By the next morning the city had made the needed repair to the sewer system, and we cleaned up the mess. We learned that the county central sewer plant pump had malfunctioned, causing the problem.

We welcomed visits from Allan's children and their families. George and Lucy lived in Thibodaux, Louisiana, with their three children, and their visits were less frequent than Jan and Royce's, who lived in LaPlace with their two children. We lived less than 250 miles apart, a comfortable day trip by car. When the families came to FWB, water-skiing on the bayou was the major attraction, coupled with cookouts and relaxed family times together. We gathered as a family for special holidays—Thanksgiving and Christmas. I missed my own families but thoroughly enjoyed all the times we shared with Allan's children.

It was in October that Allan arranged an adult weekend in the French Quarter of New Orleans. George and Lucy, Janet and Royce, Allan and I met at the Bourbon Orleans on Orleans Street. During the day we took in the sights and sounds of the Quarter. We walked to the French Market to the famous Café du Monde for the café au lait (my preference was coffee black) and beignets (square pieces of dough, fried, topped with powdery sugar so thick that one dare not breathe while eating it). During the day artists populated Jackson Square displaying their paintings, some making charcoal caricature drawings of willing tourists. We walked Bourbon and Royal streets soaking up the French ambiance and architecture. We dined at Arnaud's, afterward stopping for drinks at Pat O'Brien's. Allan had, indeed, orchestrated a memorable weekend for all.

Friends from Kent, Ralph and Marie Hartzell and Betty Brinkerhoff, came for a visit in March of that year. Betty arrived on the eighteenth, and the Hartzells followed on the nineteenth, making it wall-to-wall people in our small house. We filled their six-day visit with golf, dining out at the seafood restaurants in Destin, or relaxing at home with drink in hand while preparing our evening meal on our outdoor charcoal burner. Allan was free to give our friends a tour of interesting places in the area. I was limited to three days of personal leave, and took one sick day, but the other two days of their visit, I had to teach. I noted in my diary that I played a total of eighty-five holes of golf with Betty, we bet our usual nickel a hole, and I took Betty for thirty-three holes, or $1.65. Betty bested me for total score, and true to form, I again aided in lowering her golf handicap.

We knew we would be moving back to Kent after the school year ended. We shared this with our friends and explained why. Our decision was primarily based on my unhappiness with the public schools of the state. As a teacher I was used to better curriculum resources. Allan did admit that his dream of enjoying golf year-round was shattered by the extreme heat and the rain. We both preferred the temperate climate of Ohio. When we bid our friends goodbye, there were only smiles, no tears. We would return!

IN PREPARATION FOR MOVING BACK TO KENT, I contacted Ken Cardinal, a member of the central office staff of Kent City Schools, and inquired about elementary teaching positions. In April I heard from Dodie Snyder, a golfing buddy, encouraging me to apply for a position with the Hudson schools, the district where she taught. She gave me the name of the person to contact, William Pletzer, and I applied there as well. I was successful in scheduling an interview on April 20 with Mr. Pletzer and on April 21 with Mr. Cardinal.

Once again, I embarked on a job-search journey. This time it was by plane, not by car, as it was when Vernon and I drove to Florida. My flight was on April 19 via Atlanta, where I needed to change planes for Cleveland. I had a layover in Atlanta and had neglected to change my watch to accommodate the different time zone. FWB was on Central Standard Time; Cleveland was on Eastern Standard Time. While browsing about in the shops along the concourse, something clicked in my brain. I checked my flight schedule and realized I had only minutes before my plane departed. I raced down the concourse, arriving at the gate just as the entry door to the walkway was about to be closed. Once in Cleveland, I rented a car and drove to Parma to see Sidney's family. We stayed up into the wee hours of the morning talking. Ma was thrilled when she realized I would be returning to the area.

I met with Mr. Pletzer one day and with Mr. Cardinal the next. I was offered a teaching position in both districts. A specific assignment in Kent would not be made until later in the year, but I was offered a sixth-grade language arts/social studies assignment in the McDowell Elementary School in Hudson. The pay and benefits were better in Hudson, and I liked the curriculum setup. I signed with Hudson and informed Mr. Cardinal of my decision.

Allan did not accompany me on this trip; now it was my turn to do a house search for the family. I contacted Bob Paton, the realtor who had sold our Kent home, and spent two afternoons with him. The only house I liked was located on the corner of Fairchild and Woodard Avenues. It was a nine-room, two-story colonial-style house with finished attic, full basement, and screened-in side porch with a double-car garage situated at the end of the driveway. There was a tall, black cherry tree located just off the side porch in a formal landscaped area I immediately named the Versailles Garden. The asking price was $30,800 dollars. I called Allan, describing the house, and he advised me to offer $28,500. The owners countered with $29,800, and we came back with $29,500, which they accepted. I was elated! My trip north was a success. I had a teaching position, and I had found a house. My flight home on April 23 was smooth to Atlanta, but from there to FWB, it was a rough flight. Allan was at the airport to welcome me back.

———— ·+++++· ————

Now the process was reversed, and we started our packing to return to Kent. In the days that followed, a few of our friends entertained Allan and me in their homes. Bruce had social involvements as well. A few days before we were to leave, he invited a dozen or so of his friends to the house for a cookout. The afternoon of the party gave way to one of the torrential rainfalls that frequented the area. That did not dampen the spirits of those energetic teenagers; they went to the beach and frolicked in the rain and returned dripping buckets of water. Allan charcoaled hamburgers over the grill he had set up in the garage. The group ate and talked, talked and ate some more, listened to records, and it was obvious everyone was having a good time.

We had received a letter from Bruce's Aunt Nin, who lived in Falls Church, Virginia, inviting him to come for a visit. As time permitted, she would take him on a tour into Washington, DC, and show him a few of the national sights. This seemed like a good idea. It would remove Bruce from the chaos created by another move. We scheduled him on a Delta flight into the Dulles International Airport on June 12. On June 11 Bruce made unending phone calls to friends. Apparently leaving was bittersweet for him as well.

Packing does not get easier no matter how often one does it. I think I was more efficient, but it remained a lot of work. The movers were supposed to inventory our load on June 10 but instead appeared with the truck, ready to load our earthly possessions. There was no repeat of the heart-stopper that happened in Kent when Allan's briefcase was buried under the furniture on the truck. Nevertheless, it was an exhausting day.

On June 11 Vernon came for his last visit before we moved back north. He rented ski equipment, and we enjoyed an afternoon skiing on the bayou. We dined at our favorite fish place before driving him to Pensacola for the bus that would take him back to the base. Parting was sorrowful for all, but not with the heavy emotional undertones of previous times.

We left the morning of June 12 driving two cars. I drove the Ford. Allan was in the Corvair. We traveled as far as Chattanooga, Tennessee, the first night. We got up the next morning and went to Look Out Mountain, and before leaving the area, we toured Rock City, and I noted in my diary, "Worth every penny of the $2.50 entry fee." We left the area early afternoon and drove to Lexington, Kentucky, where we spent our second night. Weary from the morning's activities and driving, we were fortunate to find a charming off-the-beaten-track motel. We arose early the last morning of our trip and were on the road by 5:00 a.m. As fate would have it, we again experienced car trouble on the final leg of our journey. We were thirty miles south of Maysville, Kentucky, when the Corvair refused to run. It was a remote part of the state. Allan had me use the Ford to push him in the Corvair over the miles of curving roads into Maysville. Fortunately for us the first service station we stopped at had a mechanic on duty and diagnosed the problem as a faulty generator. The repair was made in a short time, and we were back on the road headed north and home.

Exhausted, we drove into Kent at 4:00 p.m. Ralph Hartzell had been out on the golf course, and within five minutes of our arrival, pulled in the drive. Ralph had a bottle of bourbon at the ready, and we lifted our glasses, enjoying a welcome home drink with a good friend. Ralph left. We went to the Short Stop for a quick sandwich, and then returned to our house, relieved that the utilities had been left on. We unpacked our camping equipment, set up our cots, fell onto them, and slept the night through. Tomorrow would be a new day.

ELEVEN

MARRIAGE TO ALLAN DICKIE
RETURN TO KENT (1968–1972)

EXHAUSTED, ALLAN AND I SLEPT SOUNDLY on our cots that first night in our house the summer of 1967. It wasn't the morning light shining through the windows that awakened us but a knocking on the side door. I peered out the window to see my golfing buddy, Betty Brinkerhoff, standing there. Not concerned about modesty, wearing only my pjs, I opened the door and ushered her in. It was 8:30 a.m., and Betty wanted me to join her in a round of golf. Allan had insisted we bring our golf clubs with us, perhaps more for his benefit than mine, but with equipment at hand, I readily accepted her invitation.

We had arrived in Kent on June 14 and received notification that the mover would be there with our furniture on June 17. The truck arrived as scheduled; the furniture was unloaded and placed throughout the house. The only mishap was a broken glass in the dining room dish cabinet. That afternoon we drove to Parma to visit Ma, Gunne, and Dot. Nin and Bob had arrived from Washington, DC. Bruce was with them, and he was one excited young man to see us and to return home to Kent.

A TWO-STORY COLONIAL-STYLE HOUSE, with detached double-car garage, was built on the approximately quarter-acre lot located on the corner of Fairchild and Woodard avenues. The lot appeared to have been professionally landscaped with a small formal garden, sloping lawn, and a concrete drive with the painted markings of a shuffleboard court. The years that we lived there, we carefully maintained the grounds. Each season we planted lobelia, impatiens salvia, and begonias in the formal area that we named our Versailles Garden. On the larger sloping lawn, we erected a twenty-four-foot flagpole and planted a pink dogwood tree. The branches of the large, black cherry tree, located just off the porch on the east side of the house, was a roosting place for many songbirds that would devour the delicious black clusters of ripened fruit. Soon after we moved there, we noted the tree's large trunk had split, endangering our house, and regretfully had to have it taken down.

The house was well kept, but I again felt the desire to decorate and make it our home. To that end, I contacted the O'Neil's Department Store in Akron and met with an interior decorator. Mrs. Collins visited the house and made excellent suggestions for wallpaper, paint, window coverings, and furniture placement. Following her directives, Allan painted while I fashioned curtains for the windows; a seamstress at the department store made our drapes. But it was at my urging that we hired a paper-hanger. I still had dreadful memories of Sidney and me attempting to hang wallpaper in our Vineland Avenue house in Ashtabula, and I didn't want to jeopardize my marriage to Allan by making it a do-it-yourself project.

A small basement room, originally a coal bin, was dedicated to be the workshop. Hand tools were organized and made readily available. The Craftsman table saw was mounted on its stand, ready for use. My plan was to hang louvered shutters in a small window in our bedroom closet. The shutters needed to be cut to size. I recall the Sunday afternoon I attacked this project, carefully measuring the window opening. In the basement shop, I marked and cut the shutters to size. Confidently I returned to the bedroom closet and placed the shutters at the window to check for fit. Much to my horror, I had cut them too small. There was a gap of two inches at the top and the side. I realized too late that I failed to account for two inches for the case that housed the retractable tape measure. All was not lost—only my time; wood strips, glue, clamp, and with great patience, the shutters were made to fit.

Bruce's assigned project was to paint the steps off of our screened-in porch. He discovered dry rot in the wood; the steps were not safe and needed to be replaced. We tore them out, estimated the wood needed for replacement, and made a trip to the local Carter Lumber Company. I set up my saw horses under the cherry tree in the Versailles Garden and started to build the new steps. While I was wielding the skill saw to cut the wood, one of Allan's golfing buddies came by. He was impressed with my use of the saw, and I will admit his amazement made my day.

That first summer I traded in my Corvair for a Mustang. Allan contacted his previous cleaning lady, Jessie, to clean for us. She had a full-time position at a retirement center in town but did find another person, Ruby, to take her place. We were settling in, and I was very content, for in August I wrote in my diary, "I love being back in Kent."

--------++++++--------

Allan seamlessly settled back into living in Kent. He was contacted by KSU to teach physical science classes at the Warren and Salem extension centers. He resumed his membership with the Kent Lions' Club and participated in their annual Pancake Breakfast, golf tournaments, and floral fund-raiser events. He became politically involved as a precinct worker, distributing voter information and staffing the polling place the day of elections. He applied to and was hired by a company that provided drivers for cars. He selectively drove cars to destinations in Louisiana and Texas, where he had family. Unfortunately, Allan also faced temporary health issues related to back problems and hiccups that were resolved with minimal medical intervention.

All the while he was involved with these diverse interests, he wrote a book expounding on his philosophy of life. The book published by the Carlton Press in 1971, *Finished at Sixty, Hell NO*, was a fulfillment of a longtime interest of Allan's to share his beliefs about life with people in their fifties and older. It was an exhilarating day in February when a box of his books was delivered on our doorstep.

A few days later, the morning of February 24, the phone rang, and it was Loris C. Troyer, editor of the *Record-Courier*. He had received a copy of Allan's book, read it, and liked it. Mr. Troyer said he wanted one of the staff writers, John Hayes, to interview Allan for a feature article for the paper. The article appeared on February 26, and Allan is quoted as saying:

> Some of my family has read the book. I haven't received too many comments yet, but my wife said before it was published that she didn't like it. She's

changed her mind now, but maybe she's just being polite!

It is true. I didn't like the book when I first read it. His book was written for people in their fifties and older. I was still in my "immature" forties. Now, having recently reread the book from the mature perspective of an octogenarian, I can sincerely say I do like what Allan wrote. It is as if he is directly speaking to me—this wise man who accepted the responsibility for a young family and provided us with the stability of the rock of Gibraltar throughout his life.

———————

WHEN IT CAME TO EXERCISE, Allan preferred golf. William Pounds, a local businessman, solicited funds in the late 1950s for the development of the Oak Knolls Golf course to be built on State Route 43, located just north of the Kent City limits. Allan and a number of his golfing buddies each invested $1,000, making them original stockholders. No dividends were to be paid on the stock, nor was it transferable, but it did offer the perk of free play to the original stockholder, as well as to their immediate families.

The Oak Knolls Golf Course opened in 1961 and became the home course for Allan and his golfing friends. This group made semiannual weekend trips to Oglebay Park in West Virginia to play golf. They would bunk in one of the semiprimitive log cabin cottages, enjoying the freedom that comes with leaving the wives behind.

———————

MANY OF ALLAN'S FRIENDS became my friends. Ten couples made up the golfing group. The husband of one of the couples was a Sikh from India. Avtar and Ginder Singh provided a cultural awareness that enriched our lives. On many occasions we entertained in our home—cookouts during favorable weather and cocktail and/or dinner parties during the winter months. Of course, there was reciprocity, and we enjoyed being with our friends in their homes or dining out together.

On one occasion, Allan and I, with three other couples, made plans to spend a golfing weekend at Oglebay Park. It could have been a disaster for me. In our rush to leave on Friday evening, I mistakenly grabbed the wrong bag. It was not until we were in our room at the cabin that I discovered my mistake. As soon as I opened the satchel, my nose alerted me I had a problem. There was a pungent odor coming from the bag that held Bruce's sweaty basketball clothes. A phone call home to Bruce, and his contact with a couple who had not yet left, saved my day. I would have found it difficult to negotiate the rolling, sloping hills of the golf course in my sandals and wearing a too-tight dress that would not allow for a free golf swing.

We had other friends who were not part of the golfing group. Leonard and Alma Bush readily come to mind. Dr. Bush served as a mentor, colleague, and close friend to Allan; he encouraged him to attend Columbia University in New York City and recommended him for a faculty position in the science department at KSU. Allan coauthored a book with Dr. Bush, *A Biology of Familiar Things*. Leonard and Alma traveled widely, and on several occasions, we were entertained in their home by Leonard's informative and interesting travelogues.

An embarrassing, yet amusing, incident comes to mind regarding two other couples, not to be identified. It was a Sunday, and the six of us were in a car headed north to the Olive and Grape Restaurant near Willoughby for brunch. Casual chatter, punctuated with laughter, was being bounced back and forth among the six of us, when suddenly a fetid stench filled the car. I was seated in the middle of the back seat; Allan was next to the window. He immediately rolled it down to neutralize the odious smell. Silence! Not one of the other four occupants of the car made a sound or any effort to open a window to provide cross ventilation—apparently paralyzed by the foul odor. Someone in the group had silently farted. I know I didn't do it; I don't think Allan did it. Who the "somebody" was remains an unknown, lingering there in my memory bank of unusual happenings.

⁕⁕⁕⁕⁕

FAMILY CONTINUED TO BE VERY IMPORTANT in Allan's life. Living again in Kent, Allan took advantage of opportunities to visit his Michigan family. When I accompanied him on one of his Michigan visits, he drove me by the homestead in West Bloomfield. As we stopped by the house, he related a proud moment for his father. Many years earlier, Henry Ford, driving by the house and noting the original leaded-glass windows, stopped, expressing an interest in owning one, maybe several, of the windows. Allan said his father accepted no money from the auto magnate, honored that an object like a window was of interest to this man. He had no knowledge of what

Henry Ford did with the window(s) but basked in the thought that it was among Ford's possessions.

On another visit to Michigan with Allan, we visited his brother Ed and sister-in-law Olive. After dinner the men vanished, leaving me in the parlor to visit with Olive. Hour after hour passed, and the men did not reappear. It was late. Olive and I had run the gamut of conversation. We went looking and found the men in the basement bent over stacks of old family pictures. I did get Allan to leave, but reluctantly and very peeved with me. That was one visit he should have made alone.

Visits by his children continued but were not as frequent as when we lived in Florida. George and Lucy, Janet and Royce would come with the grandchildren in tow. The visits were welcomed, and all efforts were made for everyone to have a good time. Whenever children are present the adage goes, "When the children are unhappy, everyone is unhappy." Swimming at Pine Lake, visits to the Akron Zoo, Sea World, and Cedar Point Amusement Park were entertainment destinations. After one visit by Lucy and the three grandchildren, I wrote in my diary on August 11, 1968, "Lucy and traveling circus left at 5:00 p.m." I did enjoy the family visits, but I will admit that on most occasions, it was "headlights and taillights."

Due to my working schedule, Allan routinely traveled solo to visit his children in Louisiana. Bruce and I took advantage of the times we stayed at home. Bruce wanted to remove a built-in desk in his room, but his dad thought it unnecessary. I think Allan was still backing his car out of the driveway to leave for Louisiana when Bruce and I, with crowbar and hammer in hand, were already in his bedroom starting to demolish the desk. My thinking was, "It is better to beg forgiveness than to ask permission."

Another time that Allan chose to visit his children, this time by plane, I suddenly had the strong impulse to give in to my desire to purchase a wig—the fashion of the day. I selected what I thought to be an auburn-hair wig with a stylish cut. I wore the wig when I went to the airport to meet Allan on his return flight. I was standing at the gate watching the passengers as Allan emerged from the walkway and entered the concourse. He stood there looking, his eyes sweeping past me. I walked up to him, an expression of puzzlement on his face, and it took him a few moments to realize the tall woman with the auburn hair was his wife! He was not particularly complimentary regarding my wig. In truth I soon found out I wasn't that taken with this uncomfortable fashion statement on my head. It was too much like wearing a too-tight hat.

There were times I was able to travel with Allan on visits to see his children. In February 1972 we went to visit his daughter and family. Jan and Royce took us to the French Quarter for the Mardi Gras celebration on Fat Tuesday. This is the official day before the start of Lent. We took our place there on Bourbon Street and watched the colorful parade of floats as they passed by. We did as Royce directed, holding our hands high and shouting to the costumed figures on the floats, "Throw me something, mister," as purple, green, and gold beaded necklaces, doubloons, and candy came flying. We scrambled with others in the crowd to retrieve some of the worthless, but treasured, items that fell to the sidewalk. As I looked around me, I saw we were in a crowd of people of all ages. Many were drinking Boone's Hill Farm wine, the empty bottles littering the street. The rowdiness and vulgarity of a few in the crowd were unsettling, and I was relieved when the last of the floats passed and the crowd dispersed.

On another visit to Louisiana, Bruce was with us; it was Christmas 1968. Janet and Royce were living in LaPlace, a small community near the Mississippi River. On Christmas Eve they drove us along the Great River Road to observe the traditional burning of the bonfires on the levee. The bonfires are built by the locals and for the most part are tepee-shaped; a few are shaped to pay tribute to the river's heritage—miniature plantation homes or tiny replicas of paddle wheel steamships. All are made of logs, cane reed, and bamboo—Cajun folklore has it—"to light the way for Papa Noel." As we watched the burning tepees, I could only think of it as a spectacular fireworks show.

NOT ALL OF MY FRIENDS were Allan's friends; some were people I met under other circumstances. I learned that the international student office on campus needed volunteers to serve as surrogate families for international students. Allan reluctantly agreed when I approached him about volunteering to be a surrogate family. We were introduced to Kojiro Kaihatsu from Japan and Henrique Suplicy from Brazil. I have little memory of Henrique; our interaction with him was very brief. I do remember Kojiro; he spent many Sunday afternoons in our home. Allan did not like Kojiro, so most of the interaction with him was left up to me. During Allan's time in the navy during World War II, he was indoctrinated with propaganda about the Japanese, and these memories remained with him throughout his life.

When the men took off on their semiannual golfing weekends at Oglebay Park, we "golfing widows" would get together and enjoy our time sans husbands. Dining out was always an option, but my preference was to entertain at home. A dinner party that included twelve guests was a challenge to manage by oneself. As the women arrived, they would invariably ask, "How may I help?" I came up with the idea of a "help jar." Prior to their arrival, I wrote out and dropped into a ceramic jar all the ways I needed help. Some examples: fill and place water glasses on the table; oversee drinks; oversee hors d'oeuvre tray; assist with final food preparation; clear the table; rinse dishes; load the dishwasher, etc. This idea worked very well, everyone participated, and it made entertaining an enjoyable time for all—best of all for me, the hostess.

Another group that I socialized with was the potluck-dinner-Tripoli gals. This group was made up mostly with Kent Roosevelt High School teachers. I was included because I was a friend of Betty Brinkerhoff, who taught at the high school. We would meet at a different home one Saturday evening each month during the school year. We would arrive with a potluck dish in one hand and a jar of pennies in the other, prepared to eat, play Tripoli, and just have fun.

———————++++++————————

BACK IN THE KENT AREA, I was able to enjoy frequent visits with the various branches of my family—a welcome happening after my year's hiatus in Florida. Sidney's family from Parma and my brother's and sister's families from the Geneva/Ashtabula area were frequent visitors. Food preparation was social and fun, with Allan in charge of many meals prepared outside on the grill located in our Versailles Garden. Adult entertainment was to everyone's liking—golf, shopping, meals eaten out. The children enjoyed our driveway shuffleboard court, croquet on the sloping side lawn, swimming at Pine Lake where there were slides, swings, and rings all strategically placed to assure the swimmer a dunk in the lake. A SeaWorld Park was located a few miles to the north of Kent that provided interesting entertainment for all.

I enjoyed having my sister's daughters, Kellie and Shellie, come to visit. In June of 1968, I noted in my diary that I took them to the children's zoo at Perkins Park in Akron. A few days later I scribbled in my diary, "Today I took Kellie and Shellie home, they were so good." On another visit, several years later, I noted that we played miniature golf and I survived the heat and the hard-rock music that blared over the loudspeakers.

On January 12, 1970, tragedy struck my sister's family. Brenda telephoned and told me her husband, Paul, had a major stroke. He was in a coma, taken to the Cleveland Clinic, where surgery was performed to remove a large blood clot from his brain. He remained unresponsive for three weeks and was transferred back to the hospital in Ashtabula where he died on February 22. His funeral was held three days later. But following great sorrow comes great happiness, and the following year Brenda was married to Theren Gibson. Gibby adopted the girls, and Brenda told me their union was truly one where two people found one another, one of soul mates. I liked both Paul and Gibby, but I did not know them very well. I lived out of the area during those years. When they died, it was emotionally devastating for me because I knew what my sister was facing; I too had lost a husband. I shared in her happiness when she remarried, for I, too, had walked that path.

It was a rare happening that summer of 1970 when my brother's three children—David, Peter, and Jill—came for a week's visit. There was tournament play in shuffleboard, table tennis, and croquet. I vividly remember the croquet battles. Jill and Allan were teamed against Peter and me. They were unmerciful. Whenever they had the opportunity to send one of our croquet balls out of the court and down the side hill, it was done to the sounds of their gleeful laughter. My nephew and niece did present me with some challenges. Preparing meals was not a problem, except for David, the oldest who was a picky eater. I soon learned the best thing I could do was to put a loaf of bread and a jar of peanut butter on the table, and then he would eat. I didn't have a daughter, and it was a delight for me to take Jill shopping. I took her into Akron to one of the department stores to select her birthday present—a school outfit. It was the year she turned twelve, and nothing, absolutely nothing, I suggested in the way of clothes was to her liking. We left the store empty-handed, returned home, and the moment I walked into the kitchen, Allan knew something had happened. I uttered to him in total disgust that I would never, never take that girl shopping again—and I didn't! She was maturing and developing a very determined mind of her own.

Years later Jill had graduated from OSU and was working in the Columbus area. Allan and I visited her at her apartment. This time she took me shopping. We went to the Lazarus Department Store in downtown Columbus. Ever conscious of the latest in ladies' couture, Jill persuaded me to purchase a full-length ultra-suede coat and a wide-brimmed, black straw hat. I enjoyed wearing the coat, but the hat was another matter; I never wore it. I felt it was too ostentatious, not my style. If the subject came up in a family gathering, I'd comment, "Yes, Jill persuaded me to buy the hat, but she never was able to persuade me to wear it."

+++++

I ENJOY WORKING WITH MY HANDS, as was evidenced by helping Sidney build our Vineland Avenue house. Allan had little interest in handyman projects but was supportive of me in my woodworking interests. I joined an adult education woodworking class at Kent Roosevelt High School. We needed a headboard for our king-size bed, and I found plans for one at the library. Under the tutelage of Mr. Pierson, the industrial arts teacher, I selected oak for the project. I cut, sanded, stained, and buffed the pieces to a rich sheen, fashioned the fabric insert, assembled it, and to my eyes the headboard was magnificent. Years later, in one of my moves to a smaller house, my bedroom was too small to accommodate the king-size bed. It was a sad day when I donated it to the Salvation Army.

My adventures in woodworking did not end with the headboard. I had an interest in learning how to use a lathe, and that was what prompted me to make a set of three wooden candlesticks. These candlesticks grace the landing of my present home. I have informed Bruce that if they are ever donated or consigned to a garage sale, I will come back to haunt him.

To this day I can close my eyes and see Ma Nelson placing a sugar lump between her back teeth, slowly sipping a cup of hot coffee into which she had poured a generous amount of rich cream (espresso latte?). I would be seated at the table in the dining nook; Ma would seat herself in a captain's chair placed to the side in the dining area. This was her favorite chair, and before she died, she gave it to me. I repaired and refinished it before passing it on to Bruce—a memento of his grandmother.

Although I never became an accomplished pianist, I did miss having a piano. For a few dollars I bought an old upright piano. It was painted a dirty white; chipped-scarred-ugly; and screamed to be refinished. I attacked this project with Zip Strip at the ready. I poured the paint and varnish stripper into an unstable plastic container. In my clumsiness I knocked over the container, and the liquid went "splotch" everywhere but on the intended surface. With Allan's help, and hours of work, the situation was rectified.

The old finish was stripped off and a new finish applied. We did enjoy that upright piano, especially when friends dropped by who could play it.

I have always felt the need to be physically active, and to this end I participated in different types of sports while living in Kent. I had a bicycle and used it for errands and recreational riding. I took advantage of the ice-skating rink on the KSU campus, signed up for skating lessons, and when my skating skills were good enough, I took a class in ice dancing. But I was told I had to provide my own partner. That ended my dream of gliding double over the ice to the strains of a Strauss waltz.

The short time I lived in Kent, before moving to Fort Walton Beach, I was a member of the Left Overs bowling team. My two teammates did find a replacement for me the year I was away. But, as luck would have it, the year I returned, this person quit the team and my place was there for the taking. I was welcomed with open arms by Betty and Mabelle, but my new teaching position in Hudson presented me with a problem. The community of Hudson was located about eight miles from Kent. I would need to leave school at least thirty minutes early to get to the bowling alley in Kent on time. I approached my principal, explained the situation, and to my delight, he gave me permission to leave early on my bowling night but with the caveat, "Be discreet." I was very discreet, but it came with a price. I never mentioned to my teaching colleagues being a member of the Kent teachers' bowling league. I never mentioned any high games when I bowled over 200, nor did I mention my high series ranking in the league. I had to zipper my mouth not to brag that the Left Overs won the league championship for two years in a row. Such is the price of being circumspect.

Over the years I remained in close touch with my bowling buddies— the original Left Overs. Betty died in the 1990s; Mabelle died ten to fifteen years later. Now, an octogenarian, I am the one "left over."

Golf has always been the focus of my exercise-related activities. I resumed taking golf lessons from the pro at Oak Knolls, and I joined the women's eighteen-hole league. I participated in league championship play-offs, never to win, but always to place in the "character-building" spot.

The greatest pleasure that I got out of golf was my social interaction with friends. Betty and I played many rounds on the home course. I consistently lost and had to pay up whatever amount our bet of five cents a hole cost me. Sidney's sister, Dot, would come for weekend golfing visits. Dot was a smoker. I recall we were playing a slow round of golf on a Saturday afternoon at Oak Knolls. We were waiting to tee off on one of the fairways, and Dot lit up a cigarette, offering one to me. I accepted, lit up, sucked in, but couldn't manage to draw the smoke into my lungs (thankfully, probably kept me from acquiring the habit) to exhale it through my nose. As we sat there waiting, I kept sucking on the "weed" and, to Dot's amusement, blowing the smoke out of my mouth. It was obvious my sister-in-law was easily entertained.

Oglebay Park holds a special place in my life when it comes to golf. Allan had promised me a new set of golf clubs when I was able to break fifty on nine holes. (He made no mention of course yardage.) One weekend we went to Oglebay Park, and our golf clubs were a standard part of our luggage. Much to my surprise, Allan suggested we play the par-three course, and that was the day I broke fifty for nine holes of play. I came in with a score of thirty-four (par was twenty-seven), and with it came the new set of clubs.

The fellows made their semiannual, long-weekend pilgrimage to Oglebay Park to play golf; we gals started to do the same. We rented one of the large log cabins that provided dormitory-style sleeping and a common area with kitchen and fireplace. Our days were given over to playing on one of the four challenging golf courses built into the hilly terrain of the area. In the evenings we wined and dined at one of the local restaurants. Like the fellows, we had a great time, and for us, it was sans husbands.

ALLAN AND I ENJOYED THE THEATER. We attended KSU performances at the School of Theater and Dance on the campus, and in the summer we enjoyed the Porthouse Theater venue located on the Blossom Music Center grounds several miles to the north of Kent. On numerous occasions we drove in to Cleveland to the Hannah Theater. But the most thrilling for me were the few times that we went to New York City to see a Broadway show.

In March 1970, Allan planned a theater trip for us to NYC. He had lived there for several summers while pursuing his master's degree at Columbia University. On weekends he and his family would explore the boroughs of the city. He knew Manhattan well, so the weekend we were there, I was introduced to some of the major attractions: the Metropolitan Museum of Art, Grant's Tomb, St. Patrick's Cathedral, and the Empire State Building.

Our visit to the Stock Exchange on Wall Street is one that remains with me to this day. As we entered the building, Allan signed us in as guests, and we took the elevator to the observation deck where we could look down on the trading floor below. We had arrived prior to the day's opening, the ticker tape was already on, moving across the screen above our heads, and on it we read, "Welcome, Mr. and Mrs. Allan Dickie." Almost immediately the opening bell rang, and the brokers on the trading floor below burst into what appeared to be a chaos of activity. Fascinated, I watched the trades on the ticker tape. It was a memorable moment.

That evening we attended the preplanned Broadway show. I have no recall of the show, or the theater where it was performed. What I do vividly remember are the happenings of the next day. We ate breakfast in the hotel dining room, and when finished, we went outside to walk the streets of the theater district. We were walking on Forty-Sixth Street when I glanced up at the marquee of the Forty-Sixth Street Theater and noted that *1776* was playing. I knew nothing about the show, but I loved history, and the title commanded my attention.

We had no plans for that day, so I asked Allan if we could stop by the theater box office and find out if we could get tickets for either the matinee or evening show. Reluctantly Allan agreed, and we took our place at the end of the short line queued up at the box office window. When it was our turn, Allan stepped up to the window and inquired about available seats. He was told the evening performance was sold out but there were a few matinee seats available in orchestra seating and the price was $12.00.

Hearing this, Allan started to turn away. I grabbed his arm and pleaded, "Oh please, I must see this show." The ticket seller and those near us heard. To save face, Allan had no choice but to purchase two tickets. As we exited the box office area, I realized Allan was attempting to control his anger for my brazen behavior. The frigid silence of my husband remained with us the rest of the morning and even until the time we returned to the theater and were shown to our seats.

The lights dimmed, the curtain went up to the sound of fife and drums, and my eyes focused on the scene onstage. Members of the Continental Congress were seated. John Adams was standing, and his stentorian voice was heard saying:

> My god I have had this Congress for ten years, King
> George and his Parliament have grilled, cullied, and
> diddled these Colonies and still this Congress refuses

to grant any of my proposals on Independence even
so much as the courtesy of open debate. Good god
what in hell are they waiting for?

I sat mesmerized as the drama unfolded. It was performed without
intermission, and it must have been midway through that Allan nudged me
in the ribs and said, "Boy, am I glad I insisted that we see this play."

The impact of that statement remained with both of us throughout
the years of our marriage. There were other times when one of us would
have reason to nudge the other and say, "Boy, am I glad…"

++++++

UPON OUR RETURN TO KENT, I had accepted a position with Hudson City
schools. On September 5, 1967, I met with Mr. Gerald Reeves, principal
of McDowell Elementary School. I was favorably impressed. On Friday,
September 8, a staff meeting was held, and it was at that time that I met
with my sixth-grade team-teaching partner. I was to teach the language arts
/ social studies block, and she taught the mathematics/science block. That
evening I made a note to myself, "Splitting headache, got to learn how to
get along with this person."

The following Monday I met my students, and at the end of the day
I wrote, "All went very smooth my first day. Think I'll like this teaching
situation." The euphoria of the first day was short-lived because one week
later, I made several notations in my diary. On Wednesday I wrote, "Lousy
day in school; I let down on good planning and everything turns to shit."
Then on Thursday I wrote, "Days aren't going well in school." The week
ended on Friday with, "One hell of an afternoon at school."

It was evident the teaching methods I had found so successful in
Ashtabula, Fort Walton Beach, and Kent were not working. Hudson was
known as the bedroom community for the families of executives who had their
corporate offices in Cleveland. My students came from very privileged homes.

The sophistication of the lifestyle in the homes of some of my students was made evident to me in the form of a book report by a young
lady named Merrill Wood. Rather than tell the students what I expected
from them in their book reports, I demonstrated by acting out the part of
Jolanda in Lois Lenski's book *Cotton in My Sack*.

When I asked the students who would like to be first to give their book report, Merrill, without hesitation, raised her hand. The following day she asked to be excused from class; she needed to go to the restroom to dress for her presentation. The eleven-year-old that exited my classroom had very little resemblance to the sophisticated young lady who entered a few minutes later wearing a sleek-fitting, black cocktail dress, high heels, eye-and-face makeup, cologne, hair in a sophisticated upsweep, delicately balancing a champagne glass in her right hand. She immediately requested the "guests" in the room to be silent. "I want your attention. I have just read the best book, *The Little Leftover Witch*, by Florence Laughlin, and I just have to tell you about it." Wow! I was speechless!

I did modify my teaching methods to incorporate more resources from the community and engage the children in activities such as class elections, plays, debates, and choral readings. The class presented two school assembly programs: one, a citizenship project involving the police and the mayor; the other, a study of Russia that culminated with the class performing folk dances to the Russian music of the Korobushka and Troika.

In January of 1969, I was assigned a student teacher, Linda Greene, from KSU. Linda had a natural talent for teaching, and soon she was able to take charge of class instruction. I was elected to represent the teachers from McDowell on the district's negotiating team with the board of education. That experience was an eye-opener for me. It was difficult for me to support my fellow teachers in the hard-line negotiations related to salaries and benefits when I could readily understand the board's position related to operating levies needed to pay for their demands. I also served as a representative to the Ohio Education Association and attended a convention in Columbus where I had the opportunity to meet Senator Oliver R. Ocasek.

I drove the back roads between my home in Kent to the school in Hudson. One warm, sunny afternoon in mid May 1969, I was on my way home, enjoying the return of spring—the green splendor of the grasses, bushes, and trees and the occasional wildflowers that bloomed along the roadside. I did note the four-way stop sign at the intersection as I slowed and cautiously turned right, heading toward Kent. Almost immediately I noted in my rearview mirror the flashing lights of a police car. There was a side road off to my right, so as soon as I cleared the intersecting road, I stopped. The young police officer walked up to my car, and I rolled down the window to hear him say, "Are you aware you did not stop at the intersection?" Well, yes, I was aware that I had only slowed, not stopped, but I didn't admit that to him. I was chastising myself for failing to notice his police car parked off to my left and partially hidden by bushes at the intersecting roads. The officer's harsh directive pulled me out of my reverie when I heard him say, "Ma'am, I'm asking for your driver's license." I dutifully removed my license from my billfold and handed it to him. He studied it for a moment and then said to me. "Dickie, I was in Professor Dickie's physical science class at KSU. Would that be your father?"

Breaking the icy silence for the first time, I replied, "No, sir. That would be my husband."

"Oh no," exclaimed the law, "this man is much too old to be your husband."

Again I said, the ice in my voice reaching glacier proportions, "I repeat, sir. He is my husband."

The impact of my last statement finally sank in. Realizing his faux pas, a crimson flush gradually started to flow from his collar upward, turning his cheeks a rosy red. Mumbling unintelligible sounds, and avoiding my steady cool gaze, this embodiment of the law glanced up just in time to see a car approaching from the side road and turning left onto the main road without stopping. The confused policeman instantly tossed my driver's license back to me and took off in hot pursuit as I heard him say, "Now that guy is really going to get it!"

During my undergraduate years in college, I took as many electives as possible in history. I enjoyed teaching the social studies to my sixth-grade classes and considered pursuing a minor in history that would enable me to teach at the secondary level. Then I learned of an opening in the district at the junior high school for the 1969–'70 school year. The teacher of the World of Work class was transferring to another position. I expressed an interest in applying for the position, and arrangements were made by the building principal, Mr. Mottice, to visit the eighth-grade class. I learned the curriculum was developed to introduce students to different career opportunities through guest speakers, field trips, and films. The purpose was to provide the students with a background of knowledge for their selection of high school classes in pursuance of a technical or a college preparatory education.

I applied for the position. On April 22, 1969, Mr. Mottice telephoned to inform me the job was mine. I was elated, and that day I noted in my diary, "Hope I'm not sorry." Little did I realize the changes this decision would bring about in my life. That summer I took part in a Cleveland Community Teachers Resources Workshop through KSU. The group visited factories, businesses, and professions in the Cleveland and Akron areas. This gave me a rich resource of information for my new position.

I began the school year with great enthusiasm. My teaching day was structured so that I had the mornings for planning and met with classes in the afternoon. I scheduled field trips, invited guest speakers, selected appropriate films. The students' reactions ranged from boredom to rebellion. I was beginning to realize why the previous teacher had opted for another assignment. Questions came to mind. Was the basic philosophy and/or purpose for the course wrong for this age of student? How could the curriculum be adapted to the students' needs?

All through that tumultuous and frustrating year, Allan listened and advised. It was he who suggested I might benefit by enrolling in classes at KSU that would aid me in the development of a revised course curriculum. And it was Allan who also suggested that if I were going to do this, I should apply for acceptance in a PhD program. This idea was totally foreign to me and had never entered my mind. I never thought of myself as PhD material, whatever that means, but Allan reassured me I was of that caliber. Knowing I could count on his professional expertise, and willingly providing me with financial support, I requested a leave of absence for the 1970–'71 school year. I applied and was accepted in a PhD program in the College of Education and signed up for a full load of classes beginning fall quarter of 1970. I was notified that my request for the leave of absence was approved by the Hudson Board of Education, ensuring me of a position should I return to the district.

———— ✛✛✛✛✛ ————

Allan knew, but I had yet to realize, the doors that would open for me with the achievement of an advanced degree. One of the classes I took that fall was Education and Modern Social Issues, taught by a young professor in the College of Education. My reason for taking the class was to develop a revised curriculum for the World of Work class. As best I can recall, the end-of-course assignment was to choose a topic and write a paper that reflected the philosophy of the course title. This was a daunting assignment for me, every bit as vague as the class lectures I had sat through during the quarter. I chose to develop a revised curriculum for the World of Work program and submitted it with those of the other students. The last day of class arrived, and papers were returned to students, many receiving complimentary comments by the professor. All papers were returned but mine. At the end of class, the professor summoned me to his desk at the front of the room and requested that I meet with him in his office on Saturday morning at ten o'clock. No further comment was made. I left the room with a feeling of euphoria as I sincerely believed I had written an outstanding paper outlining the problem and providing a solution. Saturday came, and I appeared at the appointed place and time.

The professor, my paper in his hand, sat behind his desk. His first words to me were, "You are not a student with PhD ability and should remove yourself from the program." His tirade went on for an hour, belittling both me and my writing. He instructed me to rewrite the paper and resubmit it to him no later than the first week of the winter quarter. About the only comment I was able to interject was to ask him to give me a C. My grade point average was good enough to absorb it. He would have no part of it, insisting I resubmit the paper. I left his office as confused as I had been in his classes, not knowing what he expected. I managed to get home before I started to cry. Allan was there, and with great emotional effort, I told him what had happened. It was Allan who encouraged and emotionally supported me those bleak days over the Christmas holiday. I rewrote the paper; I don't recall that I made any major changes, but I resubmitted it as directed. It was returned to me with no verbal or written comments; I noted the acceptable B.

Many times over the years, I have pondered this incident. What was so wrong with what I wrote? My mind works along practical, not philosophical, paths. I had written a practical, not a philosophical, solution to the problem. I never approached the professor for an explanation. Drawing heavily upon the confidence that Allan had in me, I did overcome the trauma of the Education and Modern Social Issues class. My prescribed course work for my PhD program introduced me to new ideas in education; challenged me in areas where I was weak (statistics, where I had to hire a tutor); and gave me the opportunity to make many acquaintances and one dear, influential friend, Sister Frances Flannigan, with whom I remained very close until her death in 2010.

During those years of study, my life was enriched through travel and attendance at national curriculum conferences. I took advantage of the opportunity to join Dr. Gerald Reed's Comparative Education seminar in November 1971 and visited four Communist countries in Europe—Hungary, Romania, the USSR, and Poland. My course work at KSU gave me the opportunity to study with a variety of professors—some poor to mediocre, others outstanding and influential in my life. Dr. Roy Caughran was one of those professors whose classes honed my critical thinking skills and who became my dissertation adviser.

Once the requirements of the academic classes were met, I embarked on the steepest climb in the road toward achieving my goal. My year's leave of absence was up. I had to decide whether to teach the World of Work class or resign. Again, with Allan's support, I choose the latter, and it was a watershed moment for me when I cut my professional ties with Hudson City Schools. I am not good at departmentalizing my life or multitasking. I needed to devote full time to the research and writing of the dissertation.

The fall quarter of 1971, I continued taking the required classes, all the while studying for my written minor exams, which I took in March of 1972. On April 3 I received a note from my adviser that read, "Henrietta, you have passed your minor exam with flying colors—I rated you as outstanding. Congratulations! Roy Caughran." On July 11 of that same year, I received a letter from J. W. McGrath, dean, Graduate School and Research, informing me I had passed the written major PhD candidacy exam. I consulted with Dr. Caughran, and my dissertation proposal, "Critical Requirements of Administrative Instructional Leadership Behavior of Elementary Principals," was approved. It took me a year, many hours spent in the library and in my home office writing.

I'm not sure how I learned about Nancy Stevens, wife of an architecture student, who advertised she was available to type dissertations. I met with Nancy, liked her, and our yearlong working relationship was one of mutual benefit—professional support for me and financial gain for her. Nancy was open, honest, and pleasantly outspoken in the months we worked together.

The date of July 26, 1973, is of great significance in my life. After a sleepless night, literally quaking and shaking, I entered the room in White Hall where I was to defend my dissertation before my committee. Questioning got underway, and I began to relax as my answers smoothly flowed based on my research and findings. Then Dr. Rudolph O. Buttlar, the "outside discipline" person from the science department appointed to my committee, asked a question. Dr. Buttlar asked me to explain my "Individual Interview" research method using the Chi Square statistical categorical analysis. I recall answering his initial question to the best of my ability, praying he would ask no follow-up question. I had told him all I knew when I responded to his first question. Recall, statistics were my weakness, and I paid a tutor to help me get through my Statistics 2 class.

My prayer was answered—there were no further questions related to my research.

I'm not certain about the sequence of events that followed the conclusion of my defense. I think I was asked to leave the room, the committee consulted, I was called back and informed by Dr. Caughran that I had passed my defense with flying colors. I had a feeling of euphoria as I exited the building and drove home to tell Allan that "we" had done it! That evening Ralph and Marie Hartzell joined us in celebration. The champagne flowed freely, and toasts were made to my success. All of this never would have happened without my mentor, my husband.

August 25, 1973, was a perfect summer day for the commencement exercise to be held in the KSU Stadium. It assured all family members in attendance the opportunity to witness the ceremony; for the first time Allan's children and mine were together. Following the directive, I went to my assigned place with the other PhD candidates, carefully carrying my folded hood over my arm. I stood there waiting to have someone in the group aid me in putting on and adjusting the hood that draped down my back, revealing the satin chevron of deep blue with a rich background of gold, the colors of KSU; but I was proudest of the velvet dark blue edge signifying the PhD degree. When my name was called, I proudly walked across the stage, stopped before Dean James W. McGrath, and accepted my degree in my left hand, extending my right hand for the congratulatory handshake. The moment was surreal. Was this really happening?

That afternoon family and friends gathered at the home of Matt and Lavina Resick to celebrate with me. There were many congratulatory toasts made and captured on film for posterity. I savored it all, experiencing the ultimate joy of a goal achieved.

+ + + ◆ + + +

TWELVE

MARRIAGE TO ALLAN DICKIE
PENNSYLVANIA (1973–1977)

A LLAN AGREED THAT I DID NOT NEED TO RESTRICT MYSELF geographically in my job search. That spring of 1973, I spent many hours in
the Placement Bureau at KSU looking through the postings of job
opportunities in curriculum or administration. I applied for employment
in Ohio, Pennsylvania, and Indiana.

Ohio is a conservative state. In the seventies, I knew that women were
a rare breed in leadership positions in the public schools of the state. Still,
I was disappointed when there was no response to any of my applications.
Disappointment instantly changed to excitement when I received a call
from the superintendent of Red Lion Schools in Red Lion, Pennsylvania,
where I had applied for the position of elementary supervisor. An on-site
interview was set for me to meet with him in April.

Allan and I checked in at a motel in the Red Lion area the evening
before my scheduled interview. At the appointed time, I met with Dr.
Grissinger; the interview lasted for an hour. Leaving his office, I felt a
professional satisfaction that all had gone well. We planned to return to
Kent that day. As we were leaving the small town, I glanced up and saw
the name Henrietta Street on a signpost. This had to be a good omen,
and I left with a feeling of optimism that this was the place for me. A
week later, we were back in Kent when I received a phone call from Dr.
Grissinger requesting me to return for a second interview, this time with
the board of directors and the administrative team—a total of about fifteen people.

The interview was scheduled for late afternoon. We left Kent early in the day, and on the drive to Red Lion, my anxiety level exponentially increased. We arrived at our destination with time to spare. It was Allan's calming influence that enabled me to appear confident when I entered the room and was directed to the one vacant chair. The interview seemed interminable. Finally it was over, and as I was leaving, Dr. Grissinger directed me to stop by his office the following morning. Exhausted, I left the building and walked to the car. I was too drained to say much about the interview. It was all a blur.

I spent a restless night at the motel. The next morning I presented myself at the superintendent's office, hoping for the best but steeling myself for the worst. The secretary announced my arrival; as I entered Dr. Grissinger's office, he rose from his chair, walked around his desk, shook my hand, and with a broad smile congratulated me. I was to be the next K–6 elementary supervisor. My relief was palpable, my excitement visible, and my impatience controlled as terms of employment were discussed and necessary papers signed. Arrangements were made for me to meet the retiring elementary supervisor, Ms. J. Elizabeth Hake, who would take me on a tour of the district's nine elementary schools that afternoon. At last I was free to leave the office. I rushed out of the building, impatient to share the news with my husband—my mentor and adviser.

IT WAS BITTERSWEET for our family and friends, but not unexpected, when once again they learned we would be leaving the area. Arrangements were made with a real estate agent for the sale of the house. My dissertation defense was still before me, and on July 26, 1973, I appeared before my committee and successfully defended my thesis. In between golf outings, and family and friends farewell parties, Allan and I managed to pack and arrange for a mover the last week in July. On July 30 that we left Kent and drove east to our new home.

With the help of Dr. Grissinger's secretary, we were able to secure a place to live in Red Lion. On the appointed day, we were at the townhouse to meet the movers. I was to begin my duties on August 15, with permission to return to Kent to take part in the graduation ceremony the weekend of August 25.

When Nancy Stevens, the gal who typed my dissertation, learned that my job was in Red Lion, she made and presented me with a stuffed red lion. Nancy also wrote two letters on my behalf. The first was a "letter of reference" to Mrs. Carol Jamison, secretary to Miss Hake. In it Nancy sang my praises. She gave me high marks in professionalism and working relationships, but she noted my weakest areas were in grammar and punctuation. I quote from that letter dated June 22, 1973:

> You will notice that her weakest areas are in grammar. She is learning to split not the infinitive, to keep prepositions away from the ends of sentences, and that singular nouns take singular verbs. She still does not understand the intricacies of colons, semicolons, and commas; but this is, perhaps, my fault, as I have not tried to explain them.

Nancy's second communication was to me in the form of a memo with the topic noted as "Care and Feeding of Secretary." I knew I would have a personal secretary, and I asked Nancy for her advice regarding how to develop the best working relationship. Her one major point embedded in the content of the memo was, "Thou shalt always tell thy secretary where thou art going." She ended the memo with a PS: "I hope it doesn't take old Carol too long to realize how lucky she is." As events unfolded, all the complimentary things that Nancy had to say about me, as well as her advice that I took to heart, did not quell the tide of resentment that Ms. Hake's secretary soon built against me.

RED LION IS LOCATED thirty-five miles southeast of Harrisburg, the state's capital. From our first visit in April, Allan and I were impressed with the beauty of the area. Farms dotted the gently rolling terrain that included steep hills, making driving hazardous. I was asked by a resident if Ohio had steep, narrow roads like those found in the area, and my answer, without hesitation, was, "Not paved."

The borough of Red Lion covered an area of 1.3 square miles and in the 1970s had a population of approximately 5,600 residents. The area in York County, in which the school district was located, had a population of about 32,000 people, mostly descendants of the Pennsylvania Dutch and Scotch Irish with a few African American families.

The Red Lion Area School District was a total of 140 square miles with 11 schools—senior high, junior high, and 6 elementary buildings. There were approximately 5,200 students; 2,700 of those students were in grades K–6 with instruction provided by 110 teachers. Each elementary building had a designated head teacher. There were three regional principals, each responsible for three schools. Head teachers reported to the regional principals, RPs reported to the elementary supervisor, and the ES reported to the superintendent.

————— ⁘⁘⁘⁘⁘ —————

If I had a honeymoon period in my new position, it was so short-lived I do not remember it. The retiring elementary supervisor had been with Red Lion Schools all of her professional years, holding a place of esteemed respect in the community. She was the personification of Miss Dove, the beloved schoolteacher in Frances Gray Patton's book, *Good Morning, Miss Dove.*

A major change was set in motion the first month I was on the job. My phone rang early one morning, and it was my secretary's husband, informing me his wife would not be in the office that day; she was ill. She did not return to work. I was mystified. Carol gave no overt clues that she was unhappy. I can only surmise that she had developed a close working bond with Ms. Hake and she could not, or would not, adapt to working with me.

Dr. Grissinger took the news in stride and secured a temporary secretary for me. June Grove was about my age, tall, slender, attractive, articulate, very competent, and a native of Red Lion. From day one, June stated she was not interested in the position but would stay until a replacement was hired.

The position was advertised in the local newspaper, in the schools, and by word of mouth. There were several applicants; interviews were scheduled and completed. I was given a penurious budget for the secretarial position—an amount inadequate to attract one of the better-qualified applicants. As a temporary secretary, June was doing an exemplary job. On the final day that applications would be accepted, I approached June and asked her if she would reconsider and apply for the full-time position. She did. I hired her, and it was the best decision I made during my tenure as elementary supervisor. She knew the community, the school, the parents, and the children. She served in the capacity of a miner's "canary in a cage" that alerted me to what could have been disastrous decisions had I not altered my course. She called it as she saw it.

Regular meetings were scheduled with the regional principals, and June attended all. Another person who helped me was Leah Brant. Leah, a fourth-grade teacher in the district, was reassigned by Dr. Grissinger to function as the K–6 mathematics resource person. June, Leah, and the three regional principals made up the team whose counsel became indispensable to me.

My priority was to keep the interests of students and teachers in the forefront. I tried, in fairness, to enforce written policies, only to be compromised by the superintendent when a parent bypassed me and went to him. Case in point—a parent approached me one day in the corridor of one of the elementary schools and requested that her child be assigned to a specific teacher the following year. I listened and told the parent I would need to refer to the policy related to student assignment and would get back to her. I read the policy and informed her that requests of this type must be put in writing and given to the supervising regional principal. Learning this, the parent went directly to the superintendent; her request was granted. Soon after, I was advised by Dr. Grissinger that in the past, many policies were handled in a very informal way. He told me that I needed to be willing to make policy concessions.

When it was time to prepare the budget, I asked the teachers to submit their instructional material requests. As elementary supervisor I controlled the elementary budget and became acutely aware of the adage "unlimited demands on limited resources." I spent many weekend hours in my home office coordinating the requests with the schools' defined performance objectives. The day came to present the budget to the superintendent. I arrived with meticulously prepared information in hand and made my presentation, my plea for additional funds and requested supplies. Dr. Grissinger, in his stickler fashion, dismissed my carefully prepared information, informing me there were no additional funds available for the elementary schools. It was my job to stay within the budget and please the teachers.

I managed to leave Dr. Grissinger's office before the tears started to flow. I drove home. When I arrived, my niece Jill was there with Allan. She was sixteen at the time, and her parents had let her drive alone to attend an engineering conference for high school students at Lehigh University in Bethlehem, Pennsylvania. On her return trip, she stopped to spend a few days with us. I recently asked her about her observation of this incident. Her response follows:

> Allan and I were sitting at the kitchen table in that little townhouse you were renting… You came in and immediately launched into telling Allan exactly what you thought of your boss and his unreasonableness. You referred to the "good old boys network" of Red Lion. Looking back as an adult, I think you were trying to make changes to the curriculum…and he wanted nothing to do with it. I think he shut you down completely…and I do not think he wanted you to have any power. He was in charge.

How perceptive Jill was at the age of sixteen. Her memories of that incident ring true.

Not too long after the budget incident, the father of a kindergarten child came to my office and requested round-trip transportation for the half-day kindergarten students. I listened as he presented his arguments—child safety and parent need. Mentally I agreed with him. I knew Dr. Grissinger opposed kindergarten round-trip transportation. It would require buses to take the morning children home, then pick up and deliver the afternoon children to their schools. Clearly it was a budgetary matter. I had to walk the fine line of listening to the parent while at the same time supporting the superintendent's position. I sat there feeling powerless. I felt like I was a puppet on a string manipulated by Dr. Grissinger.

On another occasion, building administrators and the superintendent were to attend an area conference. The morning of the conference, I carefully selected my outfit, what I thought to be a very fashionable pantsuit. On the appointed day and time, the car, with the men already accounted for, pulled up in front of my office. As I walked out, Dr. Grissinger got out, opened the back door of the vehicle, and motioned for me to get in. Just as I passed by, he whispered, "Don't you know when you want to impress a group of men, you wear a skirt?" I gave no response to that sexist remark.

Allan was my sounding board, my release of pent-up emotions and frustrations. He listened, advised, and counseled me to the best of his ability. One evening when I was unloading on him, he stopped me by saying, "Henri, I've done all I can for you. I think you need psychiatric help." I was speechless, but I sensed he was right. I scheduled to meet with a psychiatrist. I think it was on the third session that the doctor said to me, "Listen to yourself. Do you realize how much time you spend in dwelling on past events and behaviors? Those can't be changed, but learn from them and focus on the future." I left his office, and on my drive home I tried to internalize his advice. Words from Henley's poem *Invictus* came to mind—"I am the master of my fate: I am the captain of my soul." In the vernacular of the day, I needed to just "suck it up" and move on. When I arrived home, Allan greeted me at the door with a newspaper in his hand. He proudly showed me an article in *The York Dispatch* with the headline "HENRIETTA DICKIE EXCELS IN MAN'S WORLD." Janice Fitzkee, a reporter for the paper, had recently interviewed me in my office. I inwardly glowed as I read her complimentary article. It strengthened my resolve to move on, to be my own person.

What I thought would have teacher support and be recognized by the parents as an effective means to ensure purposeful instruction the last two weeks of the school year turned into a report-card fiasco. Report cards in the junior and senior high schools were mailed to students after the close of the school year. It made sense to me to mail the elementary report cards as well. The previous protocol in the elementary schools was for instruction to be discontinued one to two weeks before the end of the year, allowing time for the teachers to complete school reports and have the cards ready to hand out on the last day of school.

At one of the regularly scheduled meetings with the administrative team, I presented the new report card plan and received their support. I then requested, and was granted, approval from the superintendent. A memo was sent out to all teachers informing them of the change. They were not happy with this directive that gave them no choice in the matter—they had to comply.

After the close of school at the June board meeting, I became aware of the full impact of my decision. A group of angry parents in attendance spoke vociferously against this policy, stating it was a waste of money (about $280 in postage) better used to purchase needed instructional supplies. The superintendent had approved the plan but bent to the winds of opposition and assured the parents it was not a permanent thing. The brouhaha was short-lived with only one article appearing in the local newspaper. The following school year, elementary students were handed their report cards on the last day of school.

My second year with the district, I attempted another change. In the 1960s and '70s, there was interest in nongraded schooling based on the book *The Nongraded Elementary School* authored by John Goodlad and Robert Anderson. The nongraded concept eliminates grade-level structure and allows for children to learn at the pace of their unique abilities. I consulted with the regional principals, then developed and presented a pilot plan to Dr. Grissinger, which he approved. The school, the grade levels, and the teachers were selected; parents were contacted for their approval. Informational meetings were held with all parties concerned, and the nongraded pilot plan was enthusiastically received. It was during the first semester of the school year that I realized the nongraded concept was not working. The major hurdle was the need for additional instructional supplies necessary for the individualizing of instruction. Dr. Grissinger turned a deaf ear to my request for additional dollars, reminding me I had not submitted the budget request with my original plan. The program limped along the remainder of the year and was aborted the following year. The elementary graded structure remained intact. I failed the teachers, but more importantly, the children.

Looking back on my years in the district, I realize I attempted too much, too fast. Admittedly, I had not always put the best interest of the students and the teachers first; I wanted to make a name for myself. In the report-card fiasco, I did not ask for teachers' comments. Regarding the nongraded pilot program, I knew it was fruitless to have a budgetary request embedded in the plan because the superintendent would not approve it. I placed my hope for success with the dedication of the teaching team involved with the project. Again, "Vee get too soon olt und too late schmart."

WHEN WE FIRST MOVED TO RED LION, Allan and I knew the town house would be only a temporary residence. Searching for a house was a pleasant diversion from the demands of my job. There was not a house for sale in the borough to our liking. We rapidly arrived at the decision to build. In the process of looking for a lot, we met Mr. C. Orville Delbaugh, a local contractor/builder. When we found a lot in the Country Club Estate area there in the borough, we contracted with Mr. Delbaugh to be our builder. We soon learned he was a man of character. He was a perfectionist. He held anyone who worked for him to his own demanding standards. His integrity was not to be questioned. Allan and I commented that had we known he possessed these exemplary qualities we would have willingly accepted a handshake to seal any verbal contractual agreements made. To us he represented the personification of the values held by the Pennsylvania Dutch.

The house plan that we selected was easily adapted to the sloping lot. It was a one-story, L-shaped, eight-room house with a full walkout basement and enough space for a two-car garage. The house proper had 1,600 square feet of living space. We were required to submit our house plans to the zoning board. Approval was given with one proviso; all exposed concrete block must be covered with a brick facade. Construction started in early spring, and the home was completed that fall.

Allan and I both liked the Williamsburg decor—painted woodwork and white walls. But in my office, a room in the walkout basement with a large window overlooking the rolling hills, I went wild with color. I had selected a multicolor carpet imprinted with board game designs. It required six panels of wooden shutters to cover the windows span. I wanted the shutters painted in the brilliant colors of the carpet—red, yellow, blue, green, and orange. I was within earshot, but not visible to the painters, when I heard one remark to the other, "Well, guess I better go down to that room where this crazy lady is having me paint the shutters those ridiculous colors."

Sticks and stones… I liked it.

The house was finished on schedule, and we were able to move in before the beginning of the school year. Once our family and friends learned we were in our new home, the guest room was continuously occupied. Vernon drove his VW bug, with his bicycle securely attached on the car's roof top carrier, cross-country from Reno for a visit. Bruce was in the Air Force and spent some of his leave time with us.

We had only been in the house a short time when Allan's son-in-law Royce visited. Royce and I were standing in the kitchen looking out of the bay window when he remarked, "Those utility poles are hideous." Up until that time, I had never noticed the utility poles, only the picturesque view of the rolling countryside. But from that day forward, all I could focus on when seated at the table in our breakfast nook were those "hideous" utility poles, wishing the lines were buried and not obstructing my view.

Within a mile of our home was the Red Lion Country Club. The locals termed it "the poor man's country club." The clubhouse was unpretentious, there were tennis courts, no pool, and a nine-hole golf course carved out of the rolling hillsides. We joined and found it very much to our liking. Allan made full use of our membership; I enjoyed playing a few holes of golf at the end of my day's work. It served as a conduit for us to meet local residents as we took part in the Sunday afternoon couples' golfing events.

We did stay in close contact with our Kent golfing friends. It was they who suggested finding a golf resort midway between our homes. We could schedule biannual golfing holidays, much the same as the Oglebay crowd had done. The Summit Inn Resort in Farmington, Pennsylvania, was identified as our meeting place.

Four couples made up the group that would meet. The men spent their days in continuous golf play. We women golfed but not to that extent, using some of our time to explore the Alleghany Mountain area. On one of our visits, we learned that Falling Water, the house designed by Frank Lloyd Wright, was located outside of Mill Run not far from where we were staying. We visited the house built over a waterfall on the Youghiogheny River. As we toured the levels of the house, we could hear the flow of the water, but we had to walk out onto the cantilevered balcony and peer over the barrier to view the waterfall. It was only then our guide related the philosophy of this famous architect. Frank Lloyd Wright believed in the preservation of the natural world and designed his buildings to be integrated with nature. He also believed that to truly enjoy something of extraordinary beauty, one had to make an effort to see it; if it was always in your visual presence, it became commonplace and unnoticed. Many times, in the years since my visit to Falling Water, I have pondered this slice of wisdom.

Allan did much more than manage our home, entertain family and friends, and play golf. He was curious about the Indians who had inhabited the area and was a frequent visitor at the Indian Steps Museum, located in the southern part of York County. Due to this interest, he was invited to speak to groups, mostly school children, who visited the museum. Allan enthusiastically accepted, and ever the teacher, he delighted in telling stories about the Indian tribes who inhabited the area—Conestoga, Delaware, Susquehannock, Iroquois, Lenape, Shawnee, Algonquian. I know he took literary license to enhance his storytelling, much to the delight of his listeners.

WE SOON REALIZED we were living in the middle of history and culture—Philadelphia; Washington, DC; and what became two of our favorite destinations, Gettysburg National Park and Williamsburg. During the

Christmas season of 1973, we were able to secure tickets through our congressman that allowed us to tour the White House. I was fascinated as I walked through the rooms and noted the unique ornaments decorating the Christmas tree. At the time, Richard Nixon was president, and our guide explained that the president's wife, Pat Nixon, herself a teacher, had requested that these ornaments made by the school children of America be used.

The place that was a "must-see" for all who came to visit was Gettysburg National Park, located only forty miles to the west of Red Lion. The first time we visited the park, we went to the information center and inquired about available brochures that would aid us as we drove through the battlefield. Better than brochures, we learned that for a nominal fee, we could have a person, a battlefield guide, with us in our car who would provide information and answer our questions. Allan agreed to the "extravagance," and we met Mr. Terry G. Fox. Terry was a fount of information and most personable. When the tour finished, he gave us his card and instructed us that on future visits, if we would like a personal guide, to call him directly to make the necessary arrangements.

As instructed, on subsequent visits to the battlefield, I would call Terry's home, identify myself as "Henri Dickie," and make the request. Most of the times I called, it was Terry's wife who answered the phone and took the message. Terry would meet us on the appointed day and time. The last time I arranged for us to meet Terry, we saw him standing in front of the information center. Allan stopped, Terry got in our car, and with a twinkle in his eye and laughter in his voice, he remarked, "My wife said that if Henri Dickie calls one more time for me to meet her, she will be joining us."

About a year ago I was sorting through my stack of contacts and came across Terry's card. Out of curiosity, just to find out if the telephone number was still valid, I called. I couldn't believe my good luck when Terry answered the phone. I identified myself as Henrietta. He immediately remembered me—it was my unusual name that did it. We had a delightful time reminiscing. Terry is now retired from his teaching position and has kept up his credential to be a tour guide. Like many of us who have experienced change in our profession over time, and found it to be unsettling, so it is with Terry. He commented, "It isn't the fun it used to be."

Equal in priority with our interest in Gettysburg was the Historic Triangle of Williamsburg, Jamestown, and Yorktown located on the Virginia Peninsula. But the distance of 180 miles prohibited frequent visits to the area. Of these three historic places, Colonial Williamsburg was our favorite, a living-history museum. I have two vivid memories of visits there.

The first was a weekend with Allan when we dined at the King's Arms Tavern. A waiter in period costume ushered us to a table for two in front of the fireplace where an inviting fire blazed. The ambiance was romantic; flickering candlelight and soft music filled the room. My memory of that evening of dining was not the entrée, it was the first course—the peanut soup. I had never heard of peanut soup. It was recommended by our waiter. I tried it, and it was surprisingly delicious.

My other memory involved June Grove. I was pleasantly surprised when she invited me to accompany her on a weekend bus trip to Colonial Williamsburg. I accepted. The Friday evening before our Saturday morning departure, Allan and I relaxed at home in front of our fireplace and enjoyed sipping champagne and eating Oysters Rockefeller. I felt no ill effects when I retired.

The next morning when the alarm rudely awakened me from my sleep, I knew something was amiss. When I attempted to rise from the bed, I could not stand up. My head whirled; my digestive tract was in rebellion. What to do? June would be waiting for me. I couldn't let her know I was suffering from the delayed effects of drinking too much champagne. With Allan's help, and whatever medicinal remedies it took to quell the pounding in my head and settle my stomach, I managed to arrive on time for the scheduled departure. The remainder of the trip is lost in oblivion.

———————— ++++++ ————————

I CONTINUED TO EXPERIENCE an unsettled feeling in my position as elementary supervisor. I had not had a "stepping-stone" experience as a building principal, and I felt the void. This was my first position with the professional title of "Dr.," and the respect that accompanied it was heady stuff for me to handle. I was able to talk the talk in the interviews that got me the job, but I sensed I fell short in walking the walk to fulfill the expectations of the superintendent. I wanted a change.

Over the previous years, I had attended professional conferences related to curriculum and administration. The serendipity that came from my conference attendance was creating a network of like-minded colleagues. It was through this network that I learned of a central-office curriculum position open in the West Shore School District in Lemoyne, a city located thirty-five miles to the north of Red Lion on the west side of the Olentangy River, just across from the state capital of Harrisburg. The contact person for the position was Superintendent Dr. J. Wentzel. I applied and was informed that Dr. Wentzel would be attending the annual meeting of the Association for Supervision and Curriculum Development in Miami, Florida. A preliminary interview could be scheduled for me there with Dr. Wentzel. I was elated with this news, for I had already received permission and made plans to attend this conference.

It was at the ASCD conference that I first met with Dr. Wentzel. When the interview was over, I left with ambiguous feelings. I was unable to "read" my interviewer's professional assessment of me. But within a short time after I returned home, I received a call. It was Dr. Wentzel's secretary, and she informed me that Dr. Wentzel had scheduled an interview with the district's board of directors and administrators. The prospect of another interview before a large group was not as agonizing as the Red Lion experience. I left this second interview with the feeling it went well. When the call came, informing me I was to be the next K–12 curriculum director for the West Shore School District, I luxuriated in an unabashed feeling of professional accomplishment.

I submitted my letter of resignation to Dr. Grissinger; it was placed on the July board agenda and approved. Allan contacted a realtor, and our house was listed for sale but had not been sold when the movers came in July. We secured an apartment in Lemoyne and were semisettled in time for me to begin my duties with the West Shore School District (WSSD) in August.

I had survived my two years in Red Lion with the support of my administrative team. I found leaving to be bittersweet. Well-wishes for my success came from teachers, parents, and the five that I had worked with so closely over the previous two years. June and I had moved beyond a working relationship to one of friendship that endures to this day. This was also true for Leah, until the time of her death a few years ago. Of the three regional principals, Mike is the one who continues to remain in communication with me. Over the ensuing years, I have visited Red Lion and met with these dear friends. Our conversation over lunch always centers on our families and reminiscing about the time we worked together.

❖❖❖❖❖

MY LAST DAY WITH RED LION SCHOOLS was September 10, 1975. Our house had not been sold when the movers came to transport our worldly goods to the apartment in Lemoyne. (The house finally sold on February 3, 1976.) Allan no longer wanted the responsibility that goes with home ownership, and I had no time for it, so an apartment was a viable solution.

We signed a lease with the Westgate Garden Apartments, a complex that had about sixty buildings with neatly landscaped grounds and a swimming pool for residents and guests. It was located within a mile of the administration building for the WSSD. Our eight-room apartment, located on the ground floor at 1105 Columbus Avenue, provided us with 1,100 square feet of living space. As apartments go, it was luxurious.

There were four units in our two-story building, and we soon met the occupants of each. But it is Betty Compton, the octogenarian who lived across the hall from us, that I remember the best. Betty was polite the first months that we lived there; she spoke when we met in the hallway but nothing more than that. But one Sunday afternoon, when Allan passed her in the hall, he invited her to join us for our cocktail hour. She accepted, and we found her to be a delightful person, well traveled and conversant on any topic that came up in conversation. As she left that afternoon, she thanked us for our hospitality and commented, "One has to be very careful before making social contact with others when living in such close proximity." I have never forgotten the profound wisdom of those words.

———— ·+++++·· ————

THE BOROUGH OF LEMOYNE covered 1.61 square miles and in the 1970s had a population of about four thousand people. It is located on the west bank of the Susquehanna River, directly across from the state capital of Harrisburg. Lemoyne was advertised as the "little town that has it all." Allan and I found this to be true. There were parks, adequate shopping, a variety of restaurants, as well as cultural and entertainment venues. On an island located just south of the borough in the Susquehanna River, the Three Mile Island Nuclear Generating Station had been built in the early 1970s. (On March 28, 1979, a partial nuclear meltdown occurred at this site. There were no deaths or injuries reported.)

Physical activity was an important part of our days. Allan soon became familiar with the golf courses in the area and connected with a coterie of golf partners. For myself, in warm weather, I found running and swimming to be the most convenient means of exercise. There was a ski resort in the area. Allan had no interest in skiing, but that winter I signed up for ski lessons. One Saturday I was gliding down the bunny hill when suddenly, out of nowhere, a skier knocked me down and paid no heed, nor did any other of the skiers on the slope. I managed on my own to get up; my body was bruised, but nothing appeared to be broken. Once home, Allan was there to console me with hot-packs and aspirin. That ended my desire to ski.

Allan and I enjoyed the cultural and entertainment venues in the area. On July 3, 1976, that we stood in line for two hours at the Army Depot to see the American Freedom Train painted red, white, and blue. The train celebrated the United States Bicentennial, and as we walked through the cars, we noted the displays of Americana and related historical artifacts. On another occasion, we attended a Victor Borge show at a local Harrisburg theater. One of Borge's famous quotes is "Laughter is the shortest distance between two people." Without exaggeration, his show was so funny we, with others in the audience, had to hang onto our seats to keep from rolling in the aisle laughing.

Hershey, Pennsylvania, lies fourteen miles to the east of Harrisburg and is known as Chocolatetown USA. It is here that Milton S. Hershey built his chocolate business. Driving through the city, one observes the lamppost lights that are shaped like candy kisses. The city itself, and especially the Hershey United Hotel, became a favorite destination for us to take any family members or friends who came to visit.

DURING THE YEARS WE LIVED IN LEMOYNE, we continued to enjoy contact with our families, but now it was mostly by telephone or letters. As time permitted, especially on holidays, we made efforts that extended near and far to visit family and friends.

Vernon was in medical school in Reno, Nevada, when I received a telephone call informing me that he was to be married. Judy Poulsen worked in the offices of the medical school and had her own home where she lived with her preschool-age daughter, Kim. Her mother had recently died; her father was a well-known optometrist in the city. This attractive, tall, slender blonde had captured my son's heart. The wedding date was set for December 21, 1975.

At the time of their wedding, the demands of my new position, further complicated by pending airline strikes, prohibited me from attending. But different circumstances made it possible for Allan and Bruce to be there. We had recently sold our Red Lion house, and Bruce came to help Allan load a U-Haul trailer with the items I wanted him and his brother to have—

childhood toys, bunk beds made by their father, and some of his tools. I failed to designate who was to get what, naively thinking the brothers would arrive at an amicable decision. Months later I learned this did not happen.

On the drive to Nevada, Allan and Bruce had a near-death experience. Bruce was driving, passing a semitruck on an uphill grade near Flagstaff, Arizona, when he hit "black ice." The U-Haul trailer jackknifed. Fortunately, there was no oncoming traffic, and due to Bruce's skillful driving, he managed to regain control of the car and trailer. (I recently asked Bruce about this incident, and he claims the imprint of Allan's fingers can still be detected on his right-leg Sartorius muscle.) Badly shaken, Bruce continued driving, and they safely reached their destination in Las Vegas.

It was April of the following year before I was able to make arrangements to be in Reno. The WSSD Board approved my request to attend a Middle School Conference in Saint Louis. After the conference, I continued on to Reno. I was looking forward to meeting my new daughter-in-law, her daughter, Kim, her twin sister, Ann, and her father, Dr. Poulsen. I arrived on Friday, April 9.

Prior to my visit, I asked Vernon if I could invite Bruce to join us as I would not have time to visit him in Las Vegas. Vernon gave his permission but, unbeknownst to me, never discussed it with Judy. Consequently, Bruce's arrival on Saturday was a surprise to Judy. But she was gracious in her acceptance and made reservations at a local restaurant for all family members to attend a Sunday brunch in celebration of Vernon's (April 11) and my (April 7) birthdays.

Sunday morning a conflict erupted between Bruce and Vernon regarding who got what was in the U-Haul trailer. Ever the mother, I tried to calm the animosity between the brothers. I spent two hours with them behind a closed door in Judy's home, while Judy and Kim waited patiently for us. When we finally emerged, it was too late to keep the brunch reservation. The foul mood of the brothers affected us all; the birthday celebration was ruined. Bruce and I, on different flights, left Reno the next day. My behavior had destroyed any favorable feelings my daughter-in-law might have felt for me.

Vernon spent the first two years of medical school in Reno. He transferred to the University of Washington in Seattle to complete his MD program. In June 1976, Allan and I were met at the Seattle airport by Vernon, Bruce, Judy, and members of her family. We were there to celebrate Vernon's graduation.

After the graduation ceremony, after family pictures were taken, and after we returned to the hotel, it was only then that Allan and I were made aware of plans for a four-day family trip into Canada. To this end Judy's father had rented a seven-passenger vehicle to accommodate all of us. The highlights of that trip for me were the visit to the famous Butchart Gardens on Vancouver Island and the relaxing ferryboat rides that relieved me of the boredom of extended hours in the vehicle.

At the end of the four days, we again crossed the border returning to the United States. Vernon headed the car east to their home in Spokane where we spent the night. The following morning, refreshed from a good night's sleep, Vernon took us to the airport for our afternoon flight home.

It was years later before I learned that what I thought was a joyous family time of celebration created a misunderstanding with Judy that added to the undermining of my relationship with her. Apparently, Judy's father had made the comment to her that Allan and I had not contributed our fair share to the four-day Canadian trip. Resentments were building that did not bode well for any future accord I might have with my daughter-in-law.

On July 25, 1976, the call came from Vernon informing me of the birth of my granddaughter, Darci Ann. It was not until November 24 of that year that I was able to arrange a trip to Spokane to meet Darci. It was Thanksgiving, and reservations had been made at Clinkerdagger, Bickerstaff, & Pett's Public House for dinner. Darci wore a red-and-white polka dot voile dress with white tights and black patent leather shoes. She was picture perfect, but as soon as we arrived at the restaurant and were seated, she started to cry. Nothing calmed her; Darci's crying was disturbing others. Vernon, having driven separately, took his daughter home. Judy, Kim, and I finished our dinner. When we arrived back at the house, we found Darci contentedly lying on a blanket in front of the fireplace. Her father had removed her party dress and replaced it with soft baby wear. My first meeting with my granddaughter made it a Thanksgiving to be remembered.

Vernon had applied for, and was accepted into, a residency in family practice, but he did not find the program to his liking. Instead he accepted a position as emergency room physician in a local Spokane hospital. I was not surprised with his decision. Ideally, physicians in family practice need to relate to their patients in a caring manner. As Vernon's mother, I had found he could be aloof, cold, uncaring in family relationships as well as with friends and acquaintances; at other times he revealed a depth of loving sensitivity that astounded me. Ever since he had abruptly resigned from his co-op program with General Motors, telling me he could not be "organization man," I respected my son for living the maxim "Know thyself."

Another graduation that took place during the time I was at WSSD was that of my nephew Peter Schumann. Peter had completed his pharmacy program at Ohio Northern University in Ada, Ohio. The graduation was on May 22, 1977. I was close with my brother's three children and looked forward to attending the graduation, for I knew David and Jill would also be there.

The distance from Lemoyne to Ada was close to five hundred miles. The limited time we had to be with my two nephews and niece was worth the hours we spent in the car. We attended the graduation ceremony, dined together, and enjoyed hours of conversation related to family and other topics of interest. I remember saying to Allan on the long drive home that I was certain the town of Ada had been moved further west since our arrival.

On December 24, 1975, I met Flo Beth Geiger, Allan's niece, in New York City. We would travel together to the USSR to participate in a week-long Winter Festival Seminar in Comparative Education. This would be my second trip with Dr. Gerald Reed. Allan was not interested in joining me and chose instead to spend the holiday with his children.

The tour took us to two cities—Leningrad and Moscow. The focus of the tour was more on Russian culture than education. One outstanding memory survives from the two days I was in Leningrad. I was able to spend hours in the Hermitage Museum, one of the oldest and largest museums in the world, founded in the mid-eighteenth century by Catherine the Great.

We traveled by train from Leningrad to Moscow; there we spent the remaining days of our tour. Lenin's Mausoleum, in the shape of a large, black box, had been constructed in the middle of Red Square. I recall entering the tomb, walking for a distance through a maze of corridors, turning a corner, and suddenly seeing the well-preserved body of the man who is known to be the architect of the Communist State. It was a startling, eerie experience.

St. Basil's Cathedral is located next to Lenin's Tomb. It is a structure so magnificent it is almost too much for the eyes to behold and the brain to comprehend. The cathedral was closed the day our group was there—a disappointment. As I stood gazing in reverence at this architectural wonder, I heard our guide tell us that it was built in the mid-sixteenth century, during the reign of Ivan the Terrible. The architect was Yakovlev. When the building was finished, the czar had him blinded so he would never again create such a thing of beauty. To me it was a terrifying, sobering, inhumane action that caused me to tremble.

One evening our group attended the ballet at the Bolshoi Theater. I do not remember anything about the performance, but I do remember the long, steep escalators. The stairs underfoot moved so rapidly that I gripped the moving banister and held fast for fear of being hurtled into the cavernous space of the atrium.

I had heard of the beautiful stations of the Moscow Metro subway system. I was curious, but I could not persuade any of the group to venture there with me. I went alone to the station at Red Square, entered at street level, and walked down several flights of steps before I reached the train platform. I gazed about and gasped. I thought I had entered an underground palace—huge marble columns, a vaulted ceiling with massive chandeliers, walls covered with picturesque designs made from exquisite tiles. I made no attempt to board a train. I could not speak Russian, nor could I read the Cyrillic script on the information boards. I was terrified at the thought of not being able to return to my point of origin. My curiosity somewhat satisfied, I retraced my steps to emerge into the welcome daylight of Red Square.

The last day of our stay in Moscow, Flo Beth and I went shopping. We learned of a store that accepted dollars, and that was where we spent our time and money. The item that fascinated me, and at the time could not be purchased in the United States, was the nesting Matryoshka doll. My luggage space was limited, but I did purchase several of these dolls for the children in my family.

My first trip to the USSR had been in 1971, but now, years later, I found I benefitted equally from this trip in a different way than the first. The more relaxed emphasis that was placed on the arts did not require the disciplined attention I had given to the earlier three-week comparative education study tour.

On January 2, 1977, Bruce called and introduced Allan and me, by phone, to his fiancée, Linda Gripentog. But it was February, when I attended a curriculum convention in Las Vegas, before I met Linda and her parents.

The Gripentogs had a business in Las Vegas, the Dry Dock Boat Sales, where pleasure boats were sold. A second arm of the business was the Las Vegas Boat Harbor located on Lake Mead about twenty miles from the city. Bruce drove me out to the lake and gave me a tour of the marina that included a boat ride to Hoover Dam. Back in the city, we visited the boat sales where Linda worked with her mother.

In late June, I again made the trip to Las Vegas to attend Bruce and Linda's wedding. Allan was not able to come due to health reasons. Dorothy, Brenda, Royce, and children were there with me to represent Bruce's side of the family.

The evening before the wedding, we gathered at a local restaurant. Toasts were made; Bruce recognized his family and ended with his father's toast of "skoal." When it was my turn to make a toast, I passed on his step-dad's sage advice. "Getting married is easy, staying married takes effort."

The day of the wedding, June 24, was perfect—made golden with Las Vegas sunshine and a comfortable temperature. The wedding took place at the home of Linda's parents. The minister and couple stood under an arch decorated with flowers and ivy. Bruce spoke so tenderly to Linda that it brought tears to my eyes. The wedding reception followed with all of the traditional festivities—cake cutting, garter and bouquet toss, and gift open-ing. The following morning, I was on a plane headed east to Harrisburg and home. (As I write this, Bruce and Linda have now been married for thirty-eight years. My son chose well, and at the same time, he gave me the gift of a loving daughter-in-law.)

----------+++++----------

FRIENDS CONTINUED TO BE AN IMPORTANT PART OF OUR LIVES. A dear friend from Kent that I had met during my graduate study days at KSU, Sister Frances Flannigan, came to visit in July 1976. At the time of her visit, I was not able to take days off from work, and it was Allan who functioned as tour guide during the day. Late afternoons when I returned home from the office, Sister Frances would join me at the pool, but only as an observer. One late afternoon, as I was about to get in the pool for my evening swim, Sister Francis silently motioned for me to look at an overweight lady, face covered with heavy makeup, wearing a two-piece bathing suit revealing rolls of belly fat and whispered, "Apparently, that gal hasn't looked at her birth certificate recently!" This "bathing beauty" was a painful study in vulgarism.

I met Helen Goodman at work. She owned a handwriting company and was contracted by the school district to come at periodic intervals to enrich third-grade handwriting instruction. Helen mesmerized the children as she presented her handwriting lessons forming perfect cursive letters on the chalkboard and, as she did so, further captivating their attention with stories about birds, animals, and flowers related to the letter formations

Helen and her husband, who went by the moniker "Goody," were golfers. Allan and I developed a close friendship with them and enjoyed many golf foursomes together. Helen had many talents, but her cuisine was top of the list, and we were guests in their home for many a meal. After we left the area, we remained close friends, meeting for golf as often as schedules permitted. Helen and Goody have both passed on, friends who are irreplaceable.

We continued to meet with our Kent golfing friends too. In August of 1976, the Dickies, Resicks, and Livelys gathered in Fairfax, Virginia, to be house guests of Clayt and Winnie Schindler. Clayt had been able to secure tickets for the Professional Golfers Association tournament played that year at the Congressional Country Club in Bethesda, Maryland. Being a golfer of sorts, I did enjoy watching the pros as they walked past us on the fairways. Our group was not there the day of the final round to see, and then hear the crowd roar, as Dave Stockton sank a ten-foot putt to save par and win the tournament. But, as we bid our goodbyes when leaving Clayt and Winnie's home, I could only think how fortunate we were to have friends who added so much to the enrichment of our lives.

For me, personally, there is one golf outing that stands above all the rest. Soon after graduation, I joined the Educational Administration of Kent State University alumni group. In June 1975 I was in Kent to take part in the group's annual SCHOOLZ-OUT golf outing played at the KSU Golf Course. My partner was my dissertation adviser, Roy Caughran. We didn't win any of the golf prizes, but that night at the banquet, I was recognized for being "the first woman to have joined the Alumni Committee for Educational Administration of Kent State University for their annual SCHOOLZ-OUT Golf Outing." This certificate of recognition, dated June 13, 1975, and signed by Robert E. Wilson, PhD, Director, is framed and hangs on my home office wall—evidence of one perk for entering a man's world of school administration.

———— ++++++ ————

THE ACTIVITY IN OUR PERSONAL LIVES would appear to eclipse my position with the West Shore School District—the reason we moved to Lemoyne. That was not the case; my job responsibilities were paramount in my mind when I reported for duty on August 28, 1975.

The WSSD covered an area of seventy-eight square miles in Eastern Cumberland and Northern York counties. At the time I was there the population of the district was about forty thousand—96 percent white with the remainder representing various other races. There were thirteen schools (two high, two junior high, and nine elementary) scattered throughout the district serving a student population of 7,500.

There were major contrasts between WSSD and Red Lion. The area was one half the geographical size, more densely populated, and served one third more students. As curriculum coordinator my office was in the administration building with the superintendent and assistant superintendent, not in an elementary school as in Red Lion. I soon learned that the leadership style of Dr. Wentzel was a polar opposite to that of Dr. Grissinger. Dr. Wentzel gave me a job to do with little to no supervision; Dr. Grissinger gave me a job to do with rigid supervision. I was assigned a secretary from the secretarial pool who resented having to work for a woman (previously the position was only held by men), whereas in Red Lion I had a private secretary. In WSSD as curriculum coordinator, I held a central-office position that did not allow time for working closely with principals and staff; as elementary supervisor in Red Lion, my days were given over to close communication with the regional principals and teachers.

I knew when I accepted the position that I would serve as an assistant to Dr. Gerry Brinton, the district's curriculum coordinator who had announced his retirement to become effective the following year. Dr. Wentzel had convincingly persuaded the nine members of the board of directors that it would be beneficial to the district to have someone in place when Dr. Brinton retired, and I was that person.

The Pennsylvania Department of Education (PDE) had recently passed an edict requiring all public-school districts in the state to develop a long-range plan (LRP). WSSD was listed as one of the first districts to submit their plan, and for this reason, there were no prototypes to use as a guide.

The first year I was with the district, Gerry provided me with direction and urged me to take the time to get to know the district. I did this but with a sense of apprehension. I was aware of the deadline for the development of the LRP, and Gerry made no effort to begin work on it. He was retiring and the torch would be passed to me.

Gerry retired, and that summer of 1976, July 23 to be exact, I met with Dr. Wentzel and the assistant superintendent, Peck Purnell. In this meeting they made clear my responsibility for the development of the LRP.

The plan had fourteen sections, requiring involvement by the board of trustees, administrators, principals, supervisors, teachers, and nonprofessional staff. I was overwhelmed! The words of one of my professors came to mind when asked by a fellow student to define curriculum. "Why, it's the universe, and other things."

I developed a timeline to complete the plan. As I methodically made out the schedule for the various groups, I was met with degrees of feigned interest, from barely concealed boredom to total disdain. Realizing I was like a ship without a rudder, I requested a meeting with Dr. Wentzel and Peck Purnell for the purpose of soliciting their advice regarding the vagueness of the state's directive and how to proceed. During this meeting I was told, "You're taking the LRP too seriously. Just back off, get it done, it will receive almost no attention by the board." Given this directive, I simplified the format for some of the sections and requested a meeting with the PDE for approval.

On the appointed day and time, I appeared in the state office and, in true bureaucratic form, was made to wait for almost an hour. The person with whom I had made the appointment finally appeared, impatiently listening to my explanation and request for a change of format. With little further thought, he peremptorily denied it. I had put my professional heart and soul into the development of the plan, took to heart Dr. Wentzel's blunt statement to "just get it done." This bureaucrat's disdain for my request brought me to tears. Apparently, my tears were too much for this personification of power. He abruptly left the room and returned with his superior. This gentleman gave me the courtesy of his full attention, and with it, approval for the change.

The plan was completed on schedule. The night of July 14, 1977 (one year after I was given my initial directive), I presented the plan to the board. My introduction was short, the board members appeared indifferent, and several inane questions were asked. Then one of the members blindsided me by commenting that the LRP was too voluminous and redundant, requesting that it be tabled for future discussion. I cowed at this unexpected attack; the room went silent. The following day Dr. Wentzel came into my office (a rare happening) and apologized for the attack. I stoically accepted the apology while thinking, "Where were you when I needed your help?"

In a letter I received from Dr. Wentzel, dated September 12, he wrote:

> I want to thank you for accepting the responsibility to
> develop the long range plan. I know that you became

totally involved and that you devoted a great proportion of your time to this project. You provided the
organization and direction to get the job done. You
accomplished what is always very difficult; getting a
lot of other people to do their part. The format of the
long range plan was new to all of us and I know Peck
and I gave you little direction. You got the job done
in spite of that and I am very thankful.

As curriculum coordinator, I did have job responsibilities other than
the LRP. The art, music, physical education, and reading K–12 supervisors reported to me. It was during an evaluation conference with Ron, the
music supervisor, that I asked if he had any hobbies. His reply was, "Sure
do, skeet shooting. It is what I do almost every weekend when the weather
is favorable." In return, he asked me what I did on weekends, and I truthfully said, "Work." Ron looked me in the eye and retorted, "That is sick."
He was right, and truth be told, my demanding work schedule did not
bode well for me in my marriage.

Although not specifically stated in my job description, I did make an
effort to get out among the teachers. I attended special art displays, band
and music concerts, theater productions, and accepted invitations to classroom programs.

One unplanned event in a first-grade classroom had me totally flummoxed. In January I scheduled a meeting with a principal of one of the elementary schools. During the night a snowstorm made driving conditions
treacherous, but that morning I managed to make it to the school and was
surprised to be met at the door by the principal. He grabbed my arm and
then set a pace between a jog and a run down the long hallway that led to
the primary wing of the building, all the time explaining the dire need for
teachers. I was ushered into a first-grade classroom, introduced, and left
standing before the children. What to do? I never felt so helpless in my life!
I knew I needed to come up with an activity, because bedlam was about to
pour forth. Sensing I needed help, the teacher from across the hall came to
my rescue with ideas supplemented by worksheets. From that experience
I gained a deeper respect for the challenges that face first-grade teachers.

Another experience I had, of a different type, was serving as a judge
for the county spelling bee. The contest was sponsored by the local newspaper, the *Patriot News*. I sat there and listened carefully as each word was
pronounced and noted the student's nonverbal behavior, expressing relief

when the word was noted as "correct" and he/she returned to their chair. Contrasted with that were the dashed hopes when the judge would say "incorrect" and the student dejectedly exited the stage leaving a vacant chair behind.

Life with the WSSD was not all work. The administrators took advantage of opportunities to socialize—a rare happening in Red Lion. After board meetings, a few of the board members, with some of the administrators in tow, shoved forth to a local pub to share a few pitchers of beer and relaxed camaraderie. Not to be intimidated by the men, I tagged along, drank beer, listened to their give-and-take chatter, but cringed at their telling of off-color jokes that too often were demeaning to women.

I had occasional lunches with Jean Rowland, the only female board member. On one occasion we had agreed on a time and place to meet. Jean was late; she was delayed in leaving her house as her husband had gone to the post office to register a letter—a birthday card to his elderly uncle. Register a letter containing a birthday card? That piqued my interest, and I inquired of Jean why. Her answer astounded me. Her husband and his uncle had been exchanging the same card for twenty-five years, and to them it was too valuable to risk being lost in the mail.

In 1982, the idea came to me to ask my sister if she would be willing to try this. She agreed, and thus the tradition of the annual birthday card exchange was born.

There were other opportunities to socialize together. The central office personnel would leave the cares and responsibilities of their positions behind the locked door of the office and venture out to enjoy a game of friendly, fierce volleyball with teams from the district's schools. Without question, this promoted better professional understanding within the district hierarchy.

An annual event, enjoyed by many of the administrative team, was the invitation by school vendors to be their guest at the local country club for a round of golf followed by dinner. There would be couple's events for evenings of dining and the theater, or one in the group would host a party in their home. It was all fun, in marked contrast to the demands of our jobs.

My position with the WSSD gave me the opportunity to attend national conferences. This enabled me to keep abreast of the latest developments in school organization and curriculum design. It was at a curriculum conference in Las Vegas that I first learned of career opportunities available in the Clark County Schools of Nevada. Following the fiasco of the LRP, combined with the fact that Allan and I took advantage of every opportunity to travel to the west to visit our children living in California, Nevada, and Washington, the thought of resigning my position with WSSD and moving to the west appealed to me.

———————— ·+++++· ————————

DURING THE TWO YEARS I WAS WITH THE WSSD, both Allan and I had major surgeries. In April 1976, I requested, and was granted, a five-week leave of absence. An incontinence problem had plagued me for several years, and upon the advice of my physician, I opted to have a hysterectomy as the best course for the needed surgical repair. My eleventh-floor room at the "Harrisburg Hilton" hospital on First Street faced west. I could look out of the large window at Riverside Park below that paralleled the Susquehanna River. My eyes took in a breathtakingly stunning view of greenery, water, bridges, and the low skyline of Lemoyne. There were no complications from the surgery, and as hospital stays go, it could not have been better, providing me with the opportunity for a good rest.

In May 1977 Allan and I attended my nephew Peter's graduation from Ohio Northern University in Ada. On our way home, Allan was driving and experienced numbness in his right arm that caused him to immediately pull over to the side of the road. I drove the remainder of the distance to Lemoyne.

The following day an appointment was made with our family doctor who referred Allan to a neurologist. X-ray tests revealed blockage in his left carotid artery. The diagnosis was a transient ischemic attack (TIA) that deprived his brain of oxygen causing the numbness. Allan was admitted to the Harrisburg Hilton on June 19; his surgery was scheduled for the following morning. Janet arrived from California to be with her dad. (Bruce was to be married to Linda on June 24. Janet's being there allowed me to attend the wedding in Las Vegas.)

Janet and I were with Allan the morning of his surgery, scheduled for noon. We passed the time talking and playing checkers (Allan kept winning) when my good friend Helen Goodman stopped by. The minutes and hours of waiting that Allan, Janet, and I were experiencing seemed interminable. Helen's cheerfulness brought me to the realization of the role a friend can play at such stressful times. It was her presence that helped us through that tense morning until the nurse arrived with the gurney and wheeled Allan away.

Allan's surgery over, he spent two days in the ICU, two more days in an intermediate care unit, and on June 23 was moved to a room with a river view. There he stayed, day after day after day. Janet stayed with her dad until my return on June 25. Allan was regaining his strength and was ready to come home. The doctor refused to sign his release; apparently the incision had not healed to the doctor's satisfaction. Finally, on the twenty-ninth, Allan informed the nurse he would sign himself out of the hospital if the doctor would not do so. His ploy worked. The doctor appeared, removed the stitches, wrote a prescription for an antibiotic, and signed Allan's release—all in stony silence. It was with great relief we exited the Harrisburg Hilton, ten days after he was admitted.

DUE TO EXTENUATING CIRCUMSTANCES (that will be explained), it was only a two-year span between the *alpha* and the *omega* of my time with the WSSD. On September 9, 1975, the newspaper headline in the *Metro West* read, "WOMAN GETS A TOP POST IN WEST SHORE DISTRICT." My resignation was accepted by the board at the June 17, 1977, meeting. The same newspaper reported on June 20, "CURRICULUM COORDINATOR RESIGNS IN WEST SHORE."

My resignation did not go unnoticed. At a county administrator's meeting, a colleague came up to me and remarked, "You're a local folk hero." I asked him to define "folk hero," and he said, "Assessed values and decided job wasn't worth it."

The district administrative staff gathered for a farewell luncheon in my honor. One of the high school principals remarked how impressed he was with me the night I was interviewed for the position. Jean Rowland telephoned to wish me well, but more to the point wanted to discuss the board's reaction to the LRP. Ellie Stanton, the art supervisor, invited me to have lunch with her and during our luncheon conversation related that Dr. Wentzel had said to her that he was impressed from the time of his first interview with me in Houston. He was sorry to see me go.

In Shakespeare's play *Romeo and Juliet*, Juliet says to Romeo, "Parting is such sweet sorrow." So it was for me.

IT WAS MORE THAN JOB DISSATISFACTION that caused me to resign from WSSD. Soon after we moved to Lemoyne, I began to have feelings of unrest with my marriage to Allan. Apparently, I was good at "talking the talk" but not "walking the walk" and found the pressure of my new position—which required long hours spilling over into my weekends, evening meetings, and limited vacation—to be burdensome. I attended conferences and conventions where I was exposed to stimulating ideas and information, networking with professionals at vendors' social events where few women were present. It was all heady stuff and, in my thinking, exacerbated the twenty-seven-year age gap with my husband.

Apartment living was Allan's choice. He no longer wanted the responsibility of house maintenance or lawn care. He was content with managing the home, golf, reading, dining out, and select movie and theater attendance. We were experiencing a role reversal. In our life up to the time of our move to Pennsylvania, I was known as "Allan's wife." The change started with my job in Red Lion, when Allan became known as "Dr. Dickie's" or "Henrietta's husband," and became more pronounced in my position with WSSD.

The metamorphosis from being a homemaker and a mother to that of professional woman was still unfolding. Somehow during this unstable time, I thought I would do better to go it alone. I couldn't be a wife to Allan and yet fulfill the demanding responsibilities of my position—or so I thought. I asked Allan for a divorce.

Reluctantly Allan agreed, and our children were made aware of our decision. He also respected my wish that the divorce proceedings, for professional reasons, not be filed in Pennsylvania but rather in California. His son-in-law, Royce Fincher, an attorney, had apprised Allan that the divorce laws of California were lenient and the residency requirement could be easily met by using their San Jose, California, address and filing in Santa Cruz County.

In January 1976, Allan established a California residency, using Janet and Royce's Santa Cruz address. Technically he was not required to physically live in the state. For family reasons, Royce referred Allan to another attorney who processed the papers. I signed the Interlocutory Decree of Dissolution on October 9, 1976. Thirty days later, Allan appeared in court for the dissolution filing on November 12. The uncontested procedure that would dissolve our marriage lasted only fifteen minutes. A waiting period of six months was required before a Judgment of Dissolution, the divorce, would be final. Ironically, the projected date was April 7, my birthday.

Our separation became a reality when Allan signed a lease for an efficiency apartment at the University Inn in Kent and left Lemoyne on September 23, 1976. When I returned to the apartment that evening, there was a note on the kitchen table from Allan that read, "This Isn't a Goodbye Just a Hello to a new life for us both—Au Revoir, Sweetheart—Allan."

We both had the nonjudgmental love of our families. Bruce called me the first day I was alone; my sister and brother made frequent telephone contacts. I heard nothing from Vernon, and I knew my son well enough to know he could not process any emotional upheaval related to my marriage. Janet, Royce, and George wrote to let me know they wished to remain in touch.

Living solo impacted me in ways I never could have imagined when I first asked for the divorce. I couldn't tolerate being in the apartment except to sleep. I signed up for dance lessons. I contacted the Tri County Singles group. Nothing worked to fill the void of Allan's absence.

We parted the end of September, and Allan took little with him. He was returning the first week of October to get needed items for his apartment. In preparation for this, I was in the kitchen sorting dishes and cooking utensils, going through the pantry sorting out Allan's favorite food items, when I noticed an unopened box of Kellogg's Corn Flakes that replaced a box of Wheaties. I didn't like Wheaties and had asked Allan to exchange it at the grocery store for me. Such are the small acts that symbolize love. I sobbed. Already my daily diary entries were filled with references to missing Allan, needing Allan, living without Allan, being sad, being depressed, overeating—what had I done?

Filing for the divorce in California was only part of our agreement to keep our separation quiet. There were several professional and social commitments that would have proved embarrassing if Allan were not with me. For that reason, the first weeks and months of our separation found us apart/together, apart/together, again and again. Thanksgiving I spent in Spokane with my son and his family, while Allan took a trip to Hawaii with friends and stopped over in California to visit his daughter and family. We kept our December Bermuda vacation plans that were made the previous summer. The times we were together were civil, with rational discussions related to our separation, but during these times we experienced moments of intense emotion with many a tear shed by both of us.

We had been separated for three months, but somehow I couldn't let go. A short time after our Bermuda vacation, I telephoned Allan at his apartment and invited him to come for an extended visit. During our hour-long conversation, he advised me I had to "think single."

I had one friend in whom I confided—Charlie Ryder, principal of the junior high school. He gave me his undivided listening attention. When I seemed to have finished talking, he offered me this sage advice: "Call Allan, and tell him you want him to come home."

I did call, and Allan came to be with me the first part of February. While together we had long talks, and only then did I regain my emotional equilibrium and realized I did not want the divorce. We arrived at what we felt was a solution. On February 14, 1977, I noted in my diary "Allan leaves tomorrow. We've done a lot of talking and I feel basically good about our future. For me, I believe it is necessary to move into a less demanding professional position."

On March 24, Allan closed out his apartment in Kent and returned to live with me in Lemoyne. We had been separated for six months. In celebration of Allan's returning home and his seventy-fourth March birthday, I baked a three-layer chocolate cake and placed it on the traditional pedestal cake stand. On April 20 we celebrated our fourteenth wedding anniversary. I noted on my anniversary card to him, "the one we almost didn't make."

Knowing that we were going to move yet again, and realizing I needed to continue to work, where was the best place for us to relocate? Moving back to Ohio did not hold a strong appeal to Allan or to me. Many of Allan's friends had retired and left the area. Over the years we had made frequent trips to Louisiana (George and family), Nevada (Bruce and Linda), California (Janet and family), and Washington (Vernon and family). We immediately ruled out Louisiana and Washington but considered either Nevada or California—two states that were more centrally located for visits with our children. California was ruled out due to the cost of living in urban areas. Nevada was our choice.

I contacted Clark County Schools in Nevada regarding certification requirements and employment opportunities. I received a letter informing me that I would be required to teach in the district for three years before I would be eligible to apply to be a building principal. As directed, I applied for a Nevada teaching certificate and at the same time completed the necessary application forms for classroom teacher. In May I received both my

Nevada teaching certification and a contract to teach mathematics in the Quannah McCall Sixth Grade Center in Las Vegas. In June, when I was in Las Vegas for Bruce and Linda's wedding, I signed a rental agreement for a town house that was under construction near the University of Nevada Las Vegas, which would be ready for occupancy by the middle of August.

I COMPLETED MY JOB RESPONSIBILITIES AT WSSD in July, allowing Allan and me adequate time to visit family and friends in Michigan and Ohio before moving to Nevada. My visit to Parma to see Ma Nelson before our move was tinged with sadness. I made this entry in my diary on August 7: "As I left Ma took my hand and said 'Thanks for all the good years.'" Her comment brought tears to my eyes and a deep emotional feeling of sadness. Would I see her alive again?

Back in Lemoyne we made arrangements with the Mayflower Moving company and were packed and ready when the truck arrived on August 16. We spent the night in our almost-vacant apartment. Awakened the following morning at two fifteen, we gathered up our few remaining belongings, closed and locked our door, dropped the keys in the drop box at the office, and driving separately, departed 1105 Columbus Avenue and headed west. That first day we drove for fifteen hours, covering 530 miles, stopping only for fuel, food, map study, and exercise breaks. We were headed west and into the unknown of a new beginning.

THIRTEEN

MARRIAGE TO ALLAN DICKIE
LAS VEGAS (1977–1979)

ALLAN AND I LEFT LEMOYNE before sunrise the morning of August 17, 1977, each driving our own car. The distance between Harrisburg, Pennsylvania, and Las Vegas, Nevada, is 2,085 miles. Driving over the next four days, I marveled at the beauty of the ever-changing landscape and vegetation as we left the green rolling hills of the east, crossed the Mississippi River onto the breadbasket flatlands of the Midwest, noted the sparse vegetation as we climbed the long grade up to the Continental Divide in the Rocky Mountains near Flagstaff, Arizona, and descended onto the arid land of the Western states before crossing the Colorado River at the Hoover Dam bridge, entering Nevada the afternoon of August 22.

The Las Vegas Boat Harbor on Lake Mead, which was (and still is) owned by Betty and Bob Gripentog, was where Allan and I met Bruce on that hot summer day. With Bruce in the lead, we caravanned into the city, stopping at Dry Dock Boat Sales, another part of the business, to greet Bruce's wife. Linda's parents were on vacation, so we spent our first nights in Las Vegas with Bruce and Linda in Betty and Bob's home.

The following day Bruce took us to the newly constructed town house complex at 5156 Golden Lane, where we had previously signed a contract to rent one of the units. We were anxious for our furniture to arrive; I wanted to help Allan get us partially settled before I reported on August 29 for my first day of work at the Quannah McCall Sixth Grade Center. It didn't happen as we had planned. Due to delays en route, it was August 30 before Mayflower delivered our possessions. Furniture damage was minimal, but after carefully checking the packing list, I discovered my mother's little rocking chair was missing. (I had rebuilt the chair from pieces found in the attic of the farmhouse, turning a missing spindle on a lathe and weaving the caned seat to complete the restoration project.) This was emotionally traumatic for me. The little chair was irreplaceable, and the insurance settlement was slight compensation for my loss.

Despite Nevada's low humidity, I found the hundred-degree temperatures to be stifling, draining my energy, and limiting the time I could devote to getting us settled in the apartment. Shortly after we moved in, one of the area's rare torrential rainstorms hit. The townhouse roof leaked, dripping water onto our bed in the second-floor master bedroom. Adding to our misery was the rise in humidity. The torrential downpour also flooded the garage floor, requiring dozens of unopened cardboard boxes to be moved.

The delayed furniture arrival and the extremes of weather were challenging negatives we had to overcome those first days in Las Vegas. This was the place that Allan and I chose for our "new beginning."

LAS VEGAS, SPANISH FOR "THE MEADOWS," is in a basin on the floor of the Mojave Desert, ringed by majestic mountain ranges. It is a rocky, arid region supporting desert vegetation and wildlife. The earliest visitors to the area were the nomadic Paleo-Indians, followed by scouts and traders using the Spanish Trail. In the mid-nineteenth century pioneers settled here, having learned about the area through the writings of John C. Fremont. In 1855, the Church of Jesus Christ of Latter-day Saints (LDS Church—the Mormons) chose Las Vegas as the site to build a fort halfway between Salt Lake City and Los Angeles. The construction of the Hoover Dam (1931–1935) and the coming of Nellis Air Force Base (1941) were contributing factors to the growth of the area.

People came in droves to this subtropical, hot desert climate that averages 310 sunny days a year, where temperatures in the summer range from 90 to 115 degrees and in the winter drop into the 40s. In 1911 Las Vegas was incorporated as a city. When Allan and I moved there in the late 1970s, the area supported a population of around 130,000 people. Today there are approximately 600,000 residents within the city limits; the population of the metropolitan area is more than two million.

The above information may be known by a few of the old-timers, but it is of little to no interest to the multitudes of tourists who visit the city.

Anyone driving north on the Strip (Las Vegas Boulevard), four miles south of the city limits, is greeted by a lighted sign that reads "WELCOME to *Fabulous* LAS VEGAS Nevada." Today Las Vegas is a mecca for weddings, divorces, gambling, shopping, fine dining, entertainment, and recreation. But it is much more than "sin city"; it is becoming known as the cultural center of southern Nevada.

Living in Las Vegas required me to adapt to a different lifestyle. I was accustomed to jogging at the end of my workday. The heat made that impossible. Even the air-conditioning in my car gave way to the heat and needed to be repaired. It wasn't practical for me to run in the morning even though we lived near the University of Nevada Las Vegas (UNLV) where there was a rubberized track. With limited exercise, I found I was overeating, gaining weight, sleeping poorly, and given over to sudden emotional outbursts for no apparent reason.

It was different, and challenging, to make needed financial connections. We came from the Midwest where, for the most part, one's integrity was a "given." Neither Allan nor I could understand why the bank required a two-week waiting period before approving our initial checking account deposit, drawn on our bank in Lemoyne. Establishing medical connections was much easier with the help of Bruce and Linda.

We visited the Division of Motor Vehicles (DMV), took a crash course in Nevada law, and passed the written test only to find ourselves standing in long lines to be issued a temporary license. Weeks later our permanent driver's licenses arrived in the mail. With residency verified, Allan and I returned to the DMV and stood in more long lines to exchange our Ohio car license plates for shining new Nevada plates. It took time for us to become accustomed to driving in the city; fortunately, neither one of us had any fender benders.

———— ++++++ ————

THE TOWN HOUSE WAS NOT TO OUR LIKING. With Bruce's help, in early October we started house hunting. New homes that were within our price range were being constructed in the Forest Park allotment located in the southwest quadrant of the city. We looked at a one-story house with three bedrooms, two baths, living room with fireplace, family room/kitchen, and attached double garage. We liked what we saw, and this made our house hunting short-lived; on October 16 we made an offer of $42,950 that was accepted. We moved into our new home at

7176 West Enterprise Drive in early December, just in time to be partially settled for Christmas.

Allan and I immediately became aware we were living in a multiracial neighborhood made up of Asian, black, Hispanic, and white families. Like us, all had moved to Las Vegas from different parts of the United States, with a few emigrating from other countries. We found our new neighbors to be quite friendly, and our exposure to different races and cultures enriched our lives.

With few exceptions, homes in Las Vegas have solid fences that define property lot lines. I never inquired as to why, but living there I came to the realization that fences provided much more than privacy. They were sound barriers muffling street noise, as well as minimizing the force of the constant winds that blew across the desert carrying dust and debris.

That winter our first house project was to build our lot line wall. To this end, Allan appointed me negotiator-in-chief to speak with our neighbors. (Allan's rationale was that I had been on both sides of the negotiating table—as a teacher with Hudson City Schools and as an administrator with West Shore School District.) I approached each of our three neighbors with whom we shared a contiguous lot line regarding the feasibility of building the wall. Two of the neighbors willingly shared in the construction cost; the third neighbor was not interested. When completed, the bluff slump stone used in the construction provided a solid, good-looking wall.

In the summer of 1978, one of my home projects was to build a brick deck with a latticed wood cover off our family room. Allan had no interest in helping. With a *Better Homes & Gardens* book in hand, I optimistically forged ahead. With needed supplies, water bottle, and my how-to handbook ever at the ready, I worked in hundred-plus degree temperatures. Granted, I did get help from Bruce and willing neighbors. When finished, I noted in my diary entry on July 7, "If I knew what I were doing it would have gone a lot faster."

There was no basement in our house, no place to store tools and other miscellaneous equipment. A storage shed would solve this problem. In August I took on the project of building an eight-by-ten-foot metal toolshed. This time Allan was willing to help and the project moved faster. It took the two of us only six days in the heat of August to assemble the metal shed. As we worked, Allan and I became fully aware of why construction workers did not "burn daylight." Their day would begin as soon as the sun rose over the mountain peaks and their workday ended in the early afternoon before the heat became unbearable.

LAS VEGAS AND THE SURROUNDING AREA provided Allan and me with abundant choices for dining, recreation, entertainment, and cultural activities. One could choose from restaurants of every ethnic type and price range, but our favorite place was Marie Callender's Restaurant and Bakery. Their soup-and-salad bar were to our liking, and the price was right.

Allan and I were no different than all the tourists who came to town—we, too, were drawn to the Las Vegas Strip. The unique architecture of the casinos, at night emblazoned by thousands of lights, was a sight to behold. Our weekly Friday evening entertainment was walking through the vast interiors of the different casinos, all the while observing the peoples' dress (or the lack thereof), the ostentatious building designs, eating in one of the restaurants, and gambling. Allan's game was blackjack. My game of choice was craps. I lost more times than I won, so my itch to gamble was short-lived.

We did enjoy the entertainment offered in the casino theaters. At Caesars Palace we saw Andy Williams and the Lennon sisters. At The Tropicana we enjoyed Rodney Dangerfield's "I get no respect" stand-up comedy routine, which, to my disgust, turned lewd when the audience failed to respond to his humor. Linda was able to get us VIP tickets to see Wayne Newton at the Sands. There was also a movie theater located in the MGM Grand. It was there, sitting on one of the plush theater sofas with Bruce and Linda, sipping a Tequila Sunrise, that we enjoyed *The Adventures of Huckleberry Finn* and, on another occasion, *Dr. Zhivago*.

I vividly remember the Liberace performance at the Hilton. Liberace was seated at his grand piano with his trademark candelabra in place. When I lived in Ashtabula, I treated my mother and mother-in-law to a sold-out Liberace performance at the Palace Theater; I was unable to get a third ticket for myself. Now in Las Vegas, my unfulfilled dream to see Liberace in person was realized. Seated there with Allan beside me, I closed my eyes and just listened as the strains of "Send in the Clowns" reverberated throughout the theater. It remains for me a magical moment in time.

Allan maintained his interest in golf and played whenever one of his golfing friends came to visit. I played very little—too hot! Allan's daughter,

Jan, arranged for us to have a once-in-a-lifetime golfing experience. As a combined birthday gift from our four children and their spouses, Jan made a reservation for us to play the famous Pebble Beach Golf Course on 17 Mile Drive in Pebble Beach, California. Included in our birthday package was a two-night stay in an alluring bed-and-breakfast, reservations for dinner with Jan and Royce joining us at the famous L'Escargot Restaurant—all there in Carmel.

It was a test of our golfing ability to play the championship Pebble Beach Course. We had caddies, which was a distraction to me. As we walked along the cliffside fairways, we had little time to gaze in wonderment at the wide-open ocean vista before us. We were too busy avoiding the sand traps and out-of-bound hazards that held a magnetic drawing force for our golf balls. Despite the myriad distractions, Allan scored a 116, and I came in with 123 on the par 72 course. Forget the score—we had played one of the world-famous golf courses!

Lake Mead is about twenty miles to the east of Las Vegas. Allan and I (truth be told, it was my idea) were interested in sailing and in September of 1977 registered at the Clark County Community College (CCCC) for the course offering "Skills of Sailing." We took part in the classroom sessions and passed the required written test. On Saturday October 1, we were at the Las Vegas Boat Harbor on Lake Mead to meet with our instructor, Art Johnson. There were several small sailboats (Sunfish) moored at the dock, enough for each of the class participants to venture out on the water alone. As directed, I seated myself on a Sunfish and was pushed away from the dock. Once out on the water, I immediately capsized the boat and struggled to crawl back on. I managed to sail for a short time, then capsized the boat again. But this time it exhausted me to crawl back onto the Sunfish, and with almost no breeze, I somehow managed to make it back to the dock.

The next day we appeared for our second sailing lesson. As directed by Art, we got on our Sunfish and sailed out on the water. Within a short span of time, I saw Allan return to the dock. Not sure why he had gone in, I attempted to follow him. There was a stiff breeze, and I was not able to maneuver the Sunfish under full sail and slammed into the dock. Art was standing there; he was enraged, insolent, and arrogant as he berated me for my inept sailing skills. I crawled off the Sunfish onto the dock, and with Art continuing his harangue, Allan joined me, and together we turned our backs on our irate instructor and walked away—our sails furled forever.

Mount Charleston, located in Kyle Canyon northwest of Las Vegas, is within an hour's driving distance of the city. It is the highest point in Clark County with an elevation of 7,500 feet and is a popular all-season destination. In the summer it provides relief from the heat of the desert and in the winter the opportunity to ski. On occasion Allan would be out of town visiting his children during the winter. That was when my teaching partner and I would enjoy a day of skiing on Mount Charleston, albeit spending most of our time standing in long lift lines.

In February 1978, Jan and Royce with children, Renee and Royce III, Bruce and Linda, and Allan and I attempted a family skiing adventure. Our destination was Brianhead, a ski resort located 165 miles to the northeast of Las Vegas in Southern Utah. I had rented a condo for the weekend. We arrived on a Friday evening. The next morning, with poles and skis in hand, we walked to the ski lift and took the fifteen-minute chair ride to the top of the mountain. Allan remained behind; the extremely cold weather was not to his liking. His job was that of resident chef. Late afternoon we returned from the slopes and, with voracious appetites intensified by the cold, devoured the chili and stew set before us. The next morning the weather report made skiing less desirable. It was thirteen degrees at the bottom of the ski lift, with blizzard conditions at the top. Jan and Royce had suffered ankle and knee injuries on the previous day; they remained in the warmth of the condo with Allan. The rest of us braved the blizzard conditions and managed three runs before returning to the sanctuary of our abode.

It was Renee's birthday; the condo was decorated with streamers and balloons. Placed in the center of the table was a cake with fifteen candles. Earlier in the day Bruce, Linda, Royce III, and I, at the top of the ski run, in competition with the howling wind, had bellowed out the "Happy Birthday" song to Renee. That evening we were in much better voice as we serenaded her once again in front of the inviting fire in the living room fireplace.

On Monday Allan returned to Las Vegas with the Fincher family; the cold and high altitude made him ill. I stayed on with Bruce and Linda. We rented cross-country skis and spent the morning gliding over the pristine snow in the winter wonderland of the mountain, enjoying the beauty and peace away from the noise and confusion of the ski runs—that is, until the snowmobiles invaded the area and destroyed nature's serenity. We returned to Las Vegas that afternoon by way of the beautiful Virgin River Gorge of Arizona.

Fifteen miles to the west of Las Vegas is Red Rock Canyon, named for the iron oxide in the area rock formations. There is a one-way, thirteen-mile loop road that runs through the canyon. Located within the canyon is Spring Mountain Ranch where one can visit an authentic ranch house, bunkhouse, blacksmith shop, two-hole outhouse, observe horses in the corral, and walk through the cemetery. The Bonnie Springs Ranch Restaurant is located there, where tables are adorned with red-checkered tablecloths. If fortunate enough to be seated by a window, one can look out and observe ducks and swans on a nearby pond. In the meadow a local nonprofit theater group provided seasonal entertainment. Allan and I took advantage of the beauty and the amenities of this area when we hiked some of the trails, toured the ranch, ate at the restaurant, and enjoyed Broadway musicals and Shakespearian plays at the outdoor theater.

Located 165 miles to the east of Las Vegas in northern Arizona is one of the seven natural wonders of the world, the Grand Canyon. I telephoned the number I took from a roadside billboard that promoted the north rim of the Grand Canyon and made a reservation for two nights in June. The year was 1979, and we had invited my niece Jill Schumann to come for a week's visit to celebrate her recent graduation from The Ohio State University.

Before leaving for the canyon, we did the tourist routine with Jill, taking her to the Strip where we stopped at casinos to gamble. We went to the top of the Landmark Hotel (designed after the Space Needle in Seattle, Washington) for a view of the city while enjoying a drink in the lounge on the thirty-first floor. Another time we went out to Lake Mead for a cruise to Boulder Dam, but the water was rough, and we didn't make the distance.

On our way to the Grand Canyon, we drove through scenic Zion National Park. Arriving at the north rim, we checked in at the lodge and were given directions and the keys for our cabin. I know the stars must have been in alignment when I made our reservation. Cabin number 306 was located within a few feet of the canyon's rim with no protective fence to keep one from stepping off into space. My immediate thought was— don't sleepwalk! What I espied from the cabin's front porch was majestic. Whenever I close my eyes and visualize that first view of the canyon, Antonin Dvořáks *New World Symphony* plays in my mind, especially the lyrical second movement theme "Goin' Home." For me, the music validates the beauty of the canyon, for words fail me. I want this played at my memorial service.

I had made reservations for the three of us for a twelve-mile rafting trip through the Glen Canyon Dam on the Colorado River. We left early the next morning to drive the hundred miles north to Page, Arizona, and the rendezvous point. We boarded the raft and, as directed, donned our life vests. I had hoped we would experience the thrill of white water, only to be disappointed. The raft floated lazily along between the majestic cliffs of the canyon, but after the first thirty minutes, it became an endurance test for survival. The extreme heat, made worse by the confinement of the canyon walls, was unbearable. I noted in my dairy, "Glad I did it once, never again."

While at the cabin, we prepared most of the meals on our Coleman stove and ate at a makeshift table placed on the cabin's front porch. The day we were to leave, Allan fixed bacon and eggs for our breakfast. After we ate, Jill and I remained seated, not talking, just absorbing the beauty of nature's wonder when a sudden movement in the periphery of my vision brought me out of my reverie. A chipmunk had scurried onto the table. I silently caught Jill's attention, and we watched, enthralled, as the chipmunk sniffed, licked the plate containing the remaining piece of bacon, took a delicate bite, then snatched the piece in its mouth, and ran off without so much as a tail wiggle to say thanks. Just one of the many serendipities experienced while at the canyon, and I felt a deep sadness when we left to return to the glitz and glitter of the city.

To celebrate my forty-ninth birthday, Allan made reservations for us at the Furnace Creek Resort in Death Valley, California, one hundred miles slightly northwest of Las Vegas. This is the lowest, driest, hottest area in North America, but also one with a unique beauty of colorful rocks, desert sands, and seasonal desert flowers. There was no radio or television reception in our motel room; the area is below sea level. We were there in April, so the daytime temperatures were comfortable. Our first day we played an eighteen-hole round of golf on the course near our motel, giving little thought to the extravagance of water needed for our recreational pleasure.

While in the area we drove about fifty miles to Scotty's Castle, located in northern Death Valley. Walter E. Scott was a gold prospector who struck up a friendship with a Chicago millionaire, Albert Mussey Johnson. It was Johnson, not Scotty, who owned the land and developed the site. But due to the friendship that developed between these two very different men, the house (not a castle) that Johnson built was affectionately named Scotty's Castle. It is here on Windy Peak Hill overlooking the castle that Scotty was buried alongside his beloved dog. We visited the burial site, and on Scotty's tombstone these words are engraved:

> Don't say anything that would hurt anybody.
> Don't give advice no one will heed it.
> Don't complain,
> Don't explain.

Words of wisdom, very difficult to live by—I've tried.

In 1979 an oil crisis occurred in the United States as a result of a decreased oil output in the wake of the Iranian Revolution. Las Vegas was no different than the rest of the country; there were long lines at the gas pumps. People joined car pools to conserve their gas supply. At the close of school that year, a teaching friend and I planned to take a white water rafting trip on the Colorado River. When we realized the rendezvous point was more than a tank of gas away, we canceled the trip, not knowing if we would be able to find a gas station en route or, worse yet, be able to fill the car's tank to return home.

The gas lines did not deter Allan and me that May from our planned trip to Lake Havasu City, Arizona, 150 miles to the south of Las Vegas—less than a tank of gas away. Lake Havasu was an Army Air Corps rest camp during World War II. After the war, the area was acquired by Robert P. McCulloch, and in 1963 Lake Havasu City was established. This Missourian entrepreneur, known for McCulloch chain saws, learned that the city of London planned to replace its famous London Bridge, built in 1930, that spanned the River Thames. He purchased the bridge for $2.5 million in 1967. It was disassembled and each stone marked; for another $7 million it was shipped to Arizona and reassembled on Lake Havasu, a body of water formed behind Parker Dam on the Colorado River.

After my workday ended on Friday, May 5, Allan and I drove to Lake Havasu. We stayed at the Ramada Inn, spent a delightful Saturday viewing the partially reconstructed London Bridge, walked through the shops of an old England village, and dined in an English pub. We left our motel on Sunday morning anticipating a relaxed drive back to Las Vegas. It was one of those 310 beautiful sunny Nevada days. We rolled down the car windows and, as we drove along Interstate 40, reveled in the transformation of the desert into a blanket of colorful flowers revealing shades of purple, blue, yellow, orange, and red. We learned this phenomenon was not an annual occurrence; there had to be the perfect combination of winter rains and warm daytime temperatures before the desert would bloom.

Traffic was light as Allan leisurely drove along, occasionally stopping so I could get out of the car to take pictures. Somewhere along Interstate 40, one of us came out of our reverie to realize we had missed the Route 95 turnoff at Needles that would take us north into Las Vegas. Allan glanced at the gas gauge; it registered below the half-full mark. Consulting a map, we saw no alternate route. It was then we realized we must continue west into Barstow, California, hoping we had enough fuel in the tank to get us there.

We made Barstow and stopped at the first gas station that came into view. We took our place in the long line of cars and inched car length by car length toward the pumps, all the time praying the station would not close before we replenished the fuel supply. We made it to a pump, purchased the amount allowed, headed east on Interstate 15, and covered the 162 miles back to Las Vegas in record time. Home never looked so good. Being stranded in the desert did not appeal to either one of us.

———— ++++++ ————

Now living in Las Vegas, we experienced the luxury of being close to my son and his wife. We soon came to realize that Linda's parents also included us as part of the Gripentog family. Bob and Betty extended their hospitality in many ways. We were invited to join the family for fish fries at the lake. When Allan's son George came for a visit, Bob loaned us a twenty-two-foot Carver and suggested we take a cruise to view Hoover Dam from the waterside.

George, with limited boating experience, was at the helm, and the distance of fifteen miles to the dam was a pleasant ride. The water was calm, and the shoreline desert scenery was strikingly beautiful, revealing the lovely variegated colors of sand. Arriving at the dam, we marveled at this man-made edifice of concrete, stretched between the walls of the canyon, holding back the waters of the Colorado River that formed Lake Mead.

Our return was not so pleasant. Winds can rapidly whip up the waters of the lake, and so it was with us. The bow of the boat crashed through the choppy waters. I cowered below deck. Allan stayed above deck with George, who remained at the helm. George managed to return us safely to the dock and later admitted he was terrified.

Allan and I wished to reciprocate Bob and Betty's hospitality, so we invited them, along with Bruce and Linda, to enjoy dinner with us at our town house. A convivial time was had by all. It was late before Allan and I were able to go to bed. Allan crawled into bed first, and from the bathroom I heard him yell, "What the hell!" I ran into the bedroom to find him examining the sheets on his side of the bed. He had been "riced!"

Allan was flummoxed, but I knew what had happened. Apparently, Betty, prankster that she could be, was getting even with me. Bruce and Linda were married at Bob and Betty's home. Royce, Brenda, and I stole into their bedroom, and, in true Royce fashion, not able to pull a prank on the bride and groom, we instead targeted the bride's parents. In truth, I can't recall exactly what we did to Bob and Betty's bed, but it was enough that Betty remembered, and here was her chance to get even. The folly of her prank was that she chose the wrong side of the bed.

While living in Las Vegas, Allan and I had the opportunity to observe Bob in various roles—as an employer, as a friend, and with his family. It didn't take us long to realize that Bob was a self-made, strong-willed man, and I will add, with a keen sense of humor. We seized a devil-made-me-do-it moment when Allan and I found a wood sign with the words carved on it: "If I want your opinion I'll give it to you." We purchased the sign, gave it to Bob, and for many years it hung in the family room of their home.

⋅⋅+++++⋅⋅

WE WERE THERE TO CELEBRATE WITH BRUCE when he graduated from UNLV in May 1978. After the ceremony we took Bruce and Linda to the MGM Grand and enjoyed a champagne brunch, later returning to the convention center to take pictures, when a series of misfortunes prevailed. Allan opened our car trunk, somehow had possession of Bruce's keys along with his own, placed both sets of keys down on the floor of the trunk when he picked up the camera, and without thinking, slammed the trunk lid just as Bruce yelled, "Dad, wait!" Confusion reigned; keys to both vehicles were locked inside the trunk. Our house was closer than Bruce and Linda's, so we got a cab, went home, returned to the convention center with our second set of keys, and the problem was solved—well, almost. Allan's Scotch nature reared its objectionable head when he had to pry open his billfold to pay the taxi driver the $8 fee. The following May, Linda graduated from UNLV, but her graduation was not enlivened with the same excitement we experienced the previous year.

Allan and I had other memorable times with my son and his wife. Bruce and Linda's first home was a trailer located on the Dry Dock Sales lot. After Linda graduated, they purchased a small two-bedroom house in Las Vegas. It was our delight to be invited to share a meal with them in their home. There was the occasion when Bruce asked me if I'd like a ride in his recently purchased Datsun 280 Z. I eagerly accepted and was enjoying the ride until I realized he was driving at a speed on the plus side of a hundred miles per hour. Albeit the road was straight, no traffic, but at my insistence, he reduced the car's speed and returned me safe to my home. Another time, after the fact, Bruce came by our house with a bandaged left hand. When I asked what had happened, he informed me his hand got too close to the blade of the wood planer he was operating. The doctors at the Henderson Hospital ER were not able to reattach the end of his middle finger, giving him a shortened digit. These are only selected incidents making me acutely aware it is best a mother does not know everything; distance had its advantages.

Bruce and Linda took us out on Lake Mead on numerous occasions to water-ski. It was exciting to crisscross the wake of the boat as I skimmed over the water on my skis. Better yet, my most challenging achievement in water-skiing was when I was successful in being pulled up out of the water on a slalom (single) ski, remaining upright to skim over the waves until fatigue compelled me to drop the towline and sink gradually into the water, to be picked up by the boat.

Another adventure with Bruce and Linda was a two-and-a-half-day cruise on the lake in August. We arrived at the Las Vegas Boat Harbor and stepped onto the deck of a twenty-five-foot Carver with Bruce at the helm. Linda and Gary (brother) followed in a Boston Whaler that would be used for skiing. The boat ride took us through a canyon to our destination of Sandy Point in the Upper Basin, approximately sixty nautical miles. The two boats were beached for the night at the base of a sand mountain. The fresh air had whetted our appetites, and the cabbage rolls that I brought were quickly devoured along with beverages of choice. That evening we entertained ourselves climbing, sliding back, and climbing again until we were successful in reaching the summit of the sand hill, then, to a cacophony of hoots and hollers, trying again as we repeated the fun.

That first night Allan and I were comfortable in our sleeping bags placed on inflated air mattresses in the bottom of the Boston Whaler. The gentle rocking of the boat by the waves lapping the shoreline, the stars overhead, and the fresh air combined to make a potent tonic for tired bodies in need of sleep. The next morning, rested, fueled with a hearty breakfast of bacon and eggs, the helmsmen of the two boats backed off the beach at Sandy Point, and as we made our way into the Lower Basin, those of us so inclined enjoyed the chance to ski. The second night we docked at an island, continuing the camaraderie of a shared family experience before returning the following morning to the marina and the routines of every-day living.

AFTER ACHIEVING MY PHD and leaving Kent to embark on what became a biennial job odyssey, we were able to make good friends wherever we lived. This was primarily due to the fact that neither Allan nor I had fam-ily in the area and had time to devote to friends. It was different when we went to Las Vegas. Our priority was given over to time with our nuclear families.

I did make friends with two of my colleagues—Kris Nielson and Bill Partier. Kris and I enjoyed snow-skiing together. Bill's family came from California. They had a two-year-old daughter, and on numerous occasions we enjoyed having them join us for a Sunday afternoon dinner at our home. As mentioned before, our neighbors were friendly, and we had casual social interactions with them.

In March 1978 Vern and Judy with their girls, Darci (one and a half years old) and Kristen (four months), came to spend Easter with us. I had rented cribs, high chairs, and other baby equipment to make the family's stay as comfortable as possible. It was a novel experience for Allan and me. We offered to take care of the girls so their parents could enjoy a few hours sans children. While they were gone, both Darci and Kristen pooped their pants, reminding me how demanding it was to take care of babies. I invited Judy to have lunch with me, and I noted in my diary on March 25: "We ate lunch at Marie Callender's Restaurant. We talked for two hours. Judy is a very fine, sensitive person. I really like her." (Reading this makes me very sad, because little did I realize what was to come.) I had made a stuffed mother bunny with three baby bunnies for the girls' Easter baskets. We enjoyed Easter dinner together, and the following day the family returned to Spokane.

That fall Jan, Royce, and children joined us for Thanksgiving. Prior to Thanksgiving Day, we all went to the Silver Slipper for breakfast. After breakfast I took young Royce with me into the casino, and he was watching while I played the slots. A casino guard came over and informed me there was a $500 fine for gambling in the presence of a minor. With Royce in tow, I hurriedly left; that ended my gambling losses for the day.

With my demanding teaching schedule and little time to prepare food for the Thanksgiving feast, Allan ordered a takeout Thanksgiving dinner from a local restaurant. The turkey was very good, the trimmings tasteless. Nevertheless, it was a joyous time together.

The notable family event for the year 1979 was the celebration of Allan's birthday. In February Jan came for a short visit to help me plan the events that would take place honoring her dad. The weekend before Allan's birthday on March 12 was set for the party. Our four children and their families would be with us—a family portrait was a top priority. The sandstone quarry at Red Rock Canyon was identified as the ideal site.

The first of the family arrived on Wednesday. On successive days all others followed. On Friday a few of us, with cameras at the ready, were at the airport to welcome and record for posterity my nephew Peter Schumann's first flight as he walked off the jet way. It was Brenda who persuaded Peter to be a part of the family event. On Saturday morning, with all family accounted for, we assembled at a scenic spot in Red Rock Canyon selected by the photographer. This became a two-and-a-half-hour ordeal, taxing the patience of the parents with young children. That night the family gathered at the Dunes Hotel to enjoy dinner while watching the spectacular Folies Biegere show from our table next to the theater walkway. When the birthday cake appeared, many voices from the audience joined us in serenading Allan with "Happy Birthday."

Sunday was the day of the party at our home. Vernon took charge of the food preparation, and the conviviality that followed mellowed everyone for the reading of *An Epic Poem Honoring Allan Dickie's 75th Birthday*. The talents of the siblings, the editing expertise of Royce, and the reading by all contributors provided merriment difficult to surpass. It was the verse near the end of the poem that brought everyone to a degree of merry hysteria:

> *And now in Las Vegas—1979*
> *The whole clan together thinking it's fine*
> *Celebrating Allan's birthday, number 75*
> *Who'd 'a thought that old bastard would still be alive?*

The merriment continued; many left for the Strip—some to gamble, others to enjoy the Don Rickles show at the MGM Grand. I later learned that Peter, Brenda, and Kellie did not find their way back to their motel room until four thirty the next morning. On Monday everyone departed. That night I recorded in my diary: "What a wonderful four days! Allan was 'king.'"

———————————+ + + + + +———————————

OUR FIRST SUMMER IN LAS VEGAS, we scheduled two out-of-town trips—one to visit Vernon and family in Spokane, the other to Ohio. The August visit to Spokane provided me with the opportunity to become better acquainted with my granddaughters Darci, Kristen, and Kim (Judy's daughter). It was during this visit that I learned the parents planned to have the girls baptized at Christmas. I asked Judy if I could make their baptismal dresses. I was delighted that she agreed, and together we spent time looking for a dress pattern and material.

One morning Vernon took us to a local park and over an open fire prepared bacon and eggs, served with coffee and sweet rolls—just like his Grandma Nelson used to make for us when we would go to the Ashtabula Gulf. Vernon had previously mentioned that he and Judy had purchased property in Spokane. It was on this visit that he proudly showed us the four and a half acres of undeveloped land located in the middle of the city where he planned to build his dream house. Another day he took us on a scenic drive along the Priest River to Sandpoint, Idaho (about eighty miles), where we enjoyed lunch at a quaint restaurant on Lake Pend Oreille.

In December we returned to Spokane to spend Christmas with the family. We attended the christening ceremony for the girls at the Unity Church. I was a proud grandmother to be there and see the girls wearing their christening dresses that I had made. Christmas morning Santa appeared (Vernon in disguise) and distributed gifts to all, including Allan and me. Our gift was an eight-by-ten-inch glass etching of Don Quixote that was handcrafted by Vernon and Judy. It hangs in my living room window in my home in Kent.

Later that August, we were able to schedule a visit to Ohio before I returned to work. Arriving at the Cleveland Airport, we rented a car and drove immediately to North Kingsville to be with Brenda and her husband, Gibby (Theren Gibson). They had a recreational vehicle (RV) business and let us stay in their luxurious fifth-wheel RV trailer.

We spent a week in Ohio, and while there I experienced the emotional extremes of the height of happiness and the depth of sadness. The previous April, Brenda telephoned and told me Gibby had surgery at the Cleveland Clinic; he was told he had inoperable lung cancer. In June Gibby started chemotherapy treatments at the Roswell Cancer Research Hospital in Buffalo, New York. Brenda revealed little of the depth of her sadness, but loving my sister as I did, I felt some of the pain she was experiencing, and it overwhelmed me. They had just opened an RV refrigerator repair business, Torchlight Inc. Now that would change, and I grieved for them. One morning Brenda made us a "hillbilly breakfast" (Gibby was from Kentucky) of biscuits, fried eggs, tomatoes, bacon, and gravy. Brenda did all she could to maintain a functioning lifestyle for her family, realizing the inevitable.

Visiting Lloyd and Gertrude was always a blithesome time. My brother had acquired another "toy." He had attached a front-loader bucket onto his tractor. When I inquired as to how the hydraulic system for the bucket worked, he was delighted to show me. For the remainder of that afternoon, I entertained myself and my brother, seated on his tractor in front of a small mountain of dirt manipulating the hydraulic system that controlled the bucket, scooping and dumping as directed. I had only a modicum of success in the scooping but total success in dumping.

Another vivid memory recorded in my diary happened on the afternoon of August 14 when I drove to Parma see Ma, Gunne, and Dot. I was seated in the dinette area enjoying a cup of coffee and one of Ma's mouthwatering pastries, visiting with Ma and Gunne, when Dot came in the side door and entered the kitchen. She failed to speak as she rushed past us and upstairs. Gunne expressed grave concern regarding her sister's behavior; she knew Dot had an appointment with her doctor that afternoon. Shortly Dot appeared with a pack of cigarettes and a lighter in her hand. Sobbing she threw both in the wastebasket, regained emotional control, and told us the doctor had informed her she had polyps in her throat. An uneasy silence invaded the room. When I left that afternoon, it was with a foreboding feeling of sadness for them, and for me.

———— ++++++ ————

ALLAN AND I RETURNED TO LAS VEGAS prepared to settle into our routine, but that was shattered when I received a telephone call from Brenda on August 26 that Gibby had been admitted to Ashtabula General Hospital with pneumonia. Gibby's condition was critical; they desperately wanted/needed more time together, and the joint decision was made to have Dr.

Millberg, with whom Brenda had professional connections, perform the surgery that might buy Gibby more time. Gibby had an unfulfilled dream—to see Hawaii. His surgery was on Monday, September 11. Brenda called me on Wednesday, September 13. Her brief message was "Gibby is at peace." He had died at two thirty that morning.

I hurriedly made the necessary bereavement arrangements at school. My flight into the Cleveland Airport arrived the afternoon of September 14, and Peter was there to meet me and take me to Brenda's home. Calling hours were scheduled for that evening at the Ross Funeral Home; I went there with Brenda, Kellie, and Shellie. Many Schumann and Gibson family members were there—some quite emotional. Brenda was in complete control, but this did not surprise me, for I knew she had given in to her grief from the day she learned of Gibby's diagnosis and their precious moments together before his death. She had done her grieving and now was able to be strong for the many well-wishers who came to give their last respects.

The service was held at the funeral home the following day. The Rev. Fred Vermeulen, pastor of the East Side Presbyterian Church, lightened the sadness with his words, "Comfort in Memories." A long procession of cars followed the hearse to the cemetery for the graveside service. After everyone departed, Brenda remained behind. Gibby insisted on a bronze casket, and he wanted Brenda to be certain that he was interred in that casket.

Later that evening, when all had departed, Brenda and I sat up late into the night—sisters just talking. It was then she shared with me that Gibby had planned his service. He insisted it be a happy time, and that was why the Statler Brothers music played both at the calling hours and at the service. She observed people tapping their feet to the beat of the music, and she knew then she had fulfilled all of her husband's final wishes.

Many floral arrangements filled the room at the funeral parlor where Gibby lay, providing a contrast of the warmth of nature's beauty with the coldness of death. Some of the flowers were used to cover the bare earth at the grave site—the remainder shared with family, friends, and the church. There were two arrangements that Brenda wanted to place on the graves of family members. Gibby loved to play his guitar, and it was an arrangement in the shape of a guitar that she placed on Sidney's grave in Edgewood Cemetery. It was then I learned how much she and Sidney loved singing together. The other arrangement was a broken wheel, a favorite of our mother—the missing wheel piece and spoke symbolizing the absent family member. We drove to the Gageville Cemetery where our parents and grandmother were buried and placed it there in front of the Shuart/ Schumann family monument.

I spent the next few days with Brenda and my nieces. Brenda treated us at a Samurai Restaurant in the Cleveland area where we enjoyed being entertained by a Japanese chef, the fastest knife in town, who prepared our meal on the grill in the center of our horseshoe-shaped table.

My return flight was on September 22—eight days after my arrival. Brenda took me to the Cleveland Airport, where I boarded the plane. When we landed in Las Vegas, Allan was there to greet me with a loving embrace. It was good to be home.

SOME RESEMBLANCE OF ROUTINE returned to our life that fall/winter of 1978–'79. But sadness again reared its grotesque head when I received a telephone call from Gunne on March 25 to let me know that Dot was diagnosed with lung cancer and the prognosis was six months to live. Dot's fifty-eighth birthday was on April 11, and I called her. During our conversation, it became evident that Dot had accepted her fate. She told me that if she had known this would happen, she would have given up cigarettes years ago. I responded, "I am so sorry," and her reply was, "So am I."

The call came from Gunne on May 3 that Dot had died. Her body was cremated. Months later, there was a private memorial graveside service at the family plot in Edgewood Cemetery in Ashtabula. After Dot died, Gunne made arrangements to sell the house and join her daughter in Houston, Texas. Ma was placed in the Aristocrat Nursing Home in Cleveland. Events with my Ohio families were happening too fast for my mind to comprehend. I felt both an emotional as well as a geographical distance from them. A feeling of helplessness took hold of me and would not let go.

IN 1956 THE NEVADA LEGISLATURE had mandated consolidation of the public school districts into seventeen county districts in the state. Within Clark County there were fourteen separate districts that, when consolidated, became one large district—the Clark County School District (CCSD). At the time of consolidation, the CCSD had an enrollment of just over twenty thousand students. This was prior to the area's population explosion that was soon to take place.

A Supreme Court decision in 1971, *Swann v. Charlotte-Mecklenburg Board of Education*, ruled that federal courts had the discretion to include busing as a desegregation means to achieve racial balance. Based on this ruling, many school districts in the 1970s implemented mandatory busing plans. The Supreme Court ruling impacted the schools in Las Vegas. The black population was concentrated in North Las Vegas; to desegregate these schools, a cross-town busing plan was implemented.

When I signed the contract with CCSD, I was assured that my request to teach in the Las Vegas area would be honored, but I would not know what grade or where my assignment would be for the 1977–'78 school year until late summer. It was just before we left Lemoyne that I learned I would be teaching mathematics in North Las Vegas in the Quannah McCall Sixth Grade Center.

For their sixth grade year, selected black students from the school to which I was assigned were bused to predominately white areas in Las Vegas, and students from the predominately white areas of the city were bused into North Las Vegas. This concept of the sixth-grade center dealt a death blow to the elementary community school and was totally foreign to any of my past professional experiences.

———— ⊹⊹⊹⊹⊹ ————

MY FIRST DAY OF SCHOOL was Monday, August 29, 1977. That week was spent in orientation meetings: completing a multitude of personnel forms including information that required me to take a course in Nevada history; meeting with members of the school staff; and when time permitted, I cleaned and decorated my assigned classroom. I was given a packet of information that contained the rosters for my six classes, along with a duty schedule for playground supervision and teacher lounge cleanup. I noted there was no time allocation for instructional planning. I remained optimistic. I had chosen to exchange the pressures of high-level administrative positions for the classroom. How naive I was.

Tuesday, September 6, was the first day for students. My diary entry that day read, "First day of school with the children; six classes, just one blur of kids after another."

As the week progressed, conditions only worsened: "What a nightmare at school today. I'm teaching classes of twenty-five students and I am unable to get them to pay attention."

"Kids, papers, lunch count! A nightmare—home exhausted."

"Realize I must be much stricter with my students."

Adding to the inattentive and disruptive behavior of my students, the room air-conditioning didn't work. It was hot! The students had thirty minutes for lunch, followed by thirty minutes of activity on the playground. When my first class after the noon break entered the room, their body odor was so strong it nauseated me. I placed air fresheners around the room by the dozen, but to no avail. Finally the air-conditioner was repaired and that provided relief from the heat, but not the odor. Mother Nature took care of the body odor problem with the advent of cooler weather.

I managed to survive those first weeks at Quannah McCall. I soon learned I could not reason with the black students; they were too argumentative. The Asian students were like sponges, so eager to learn. All the rest were somewhere in between. Some days were better than others. One diary entry reads, "A real miracle day at school—six classes and I didn't have to speak sharply to one student." Contrast that with a statement I wrote a few days later. "Really 'blew' with my homeroom class and my ill-humor consumed me—a bad day."

Parental involvement was minimal. There was an open house at the end of September. I taught 125 children, and only thirty parents came. I did my best to keep parents informed/involved regarding their children's academic and behavior problems, but I faced the constant conundrum of limited time and unlimited student needs.

December came, and with it Christmas vacation; a number of the children wrote notes/presented small gifts expressing their appreciation for me as their teacher. Their endearing thoughts somehow made all the past months of frustration fade to naught. I left smiling for my Christmas break. Classes resumed the first week of January, and with it the ever-constant problems related to student discipline. The feeling of euphoria I had experienced was destroyed the morning I found an anonymous hate note on my desk. That evening I wrote in my diary, "All the obscenities I have ever heard are in it, along with some unfamiliar to me. I am shocked."

Like the weather, it seemed all I had to do was wait, and the comments made about my days would change. After my probationary conference, I received a permanent teaching certificate, in spite of my students' poor performance in the mandated district mathematics test. Testing was paramount in the district, and my classes ranked below the 25th percentile. This was a blow to my professional ego, but I was not surprised. Many of the students did not know their basic facts of addition and multiplication, had no clue as to how to subtract or divide, fractions and prime numbers held the same mystery as speaking a foreign language. Parental interest was almost nonexistent. As their teacher, I was ineffective in keeping their attention, and class discipline was a problem. When I had the chance to review the district test, I realized how ineffective my classroom instruction had been. Something must change, and I knew I was it!

Fortunately CCSD provided opportunities for professional growth. It was in January that the principal of the school approached me regarding a curriculum conference that was in San Diego. I was delighted to take advantage of this opportunity. I attended special sessions, listened to keynote speakers, and perused the vendors' booths. I acquired new ideas and learned about new materials that could be used in my class instruction.

Allan came with me to San Diego. One evening we took advantage of the opportunity to board a bus and cross the Mexican border to Tijuana. Once in the city, walking the main street, we noted a building where a jai alai (a form of handball) competition was in progress. I had played some handball with my niece Beverley Schumann while living in Ashtabula. My curiosity was piqued. Together we entered the building to observe a fast-paced game played on a three-walled court. Players used a long, curved wicker basket that was strapped to their wrists for catching and throwing the small, hard ball. Fascinated we watched as the ball bounced off the walls of the court, almost as fast as the speed of light. Our interest gradually waned, not from the game, but our necks were tired from the constant swiveling required to follow the play.

We left the viewing stands to again walk outdoors and meander through the streets of the city. It was Allan who noted an arena where cock-fights were advertised. Curious, Allan purchased tickets, and we entered the building to face a large room with stadium seating. We selected a seat high up that enabled us to look down on a cockpit where two cocks, with metal spurs attached to their legs, were fighting. I knew nothing of the betting that took place, but the cacophonous, ear-piercing noise of the crowd and the bloodbath that was taking place in the cockpit below were too much for both Allan and me. Fortunately, it was time to return to our bus that would take us back to San Diego.

The four-day conference ended, and I returned refreshed and energized to face my classes. The special sessions that I attended were excellent, and I revised my lesson plans to incorporate many of the ideas that were presented. The instructional supplies that I had previously ordered arrived. I was ready! In huge block letters, I made a banner that read **BE A PARTICIPATOR NOT A SPECTATOR** and mounted it above the chalkboard in my classroom. I appointed student tutors to work with their classmates in small groups. I developed a quiz method similar to what Allan used in his physical science classes (Dickie's Quickies). It was a daily quiz that tested the mastery of material taught in the previous day's instruction. Quizzes were graded by classmates and provided instant feedback. I utilized multisensory math manipulative materials I now had available to me. All of the above required hours of preparation, but discipline problems lessened, and I could actually teach.

In May, a day near the end of the school year, a choir from one of the junior high schools was scheduled to perform at Quannah McCall. There was no place for an all-school assembly within the school complex, so chairs were set up in the courtyard. It was hot; there was no shade. Order was difficult to maintain. The choir walked out and stood in formation before the student body. It was difficult for me to focus on the program. I was stupefied by the provocative dress of these young girls, revealing their cleavage along with a disproportionate amount of bare skin. My Midwestern values were obviously in conflict with the culture of the area.

It was a daunting challenge to keep the attention of students the final days of the school year. On the last day, as I stood before my first class of the day, whatever I attempted to do wasn't working. One of my students raised his hand and asked, "Could we play cards?" I had many decks of cards in the classroom (cast-offs of the casinos) that I had previously used to teach math concepts. I saw no harm in students' playing cards, so I replied in the affirmative. To my amazement, faster than mice can scurry, students moved into groups of four with playing cards in hand. Once seated, a designated dealer shuffled and distributed the cards with the nimble dexterity of a casino dealer. I was flabbergasted; I stood there with mouth agape, realizing how little I had immersed myself in the culture of the students I taught, for I knew many of their parents were casino dealers.

WHEN I REPORTED FOR DUTY my second year with the district, I was relieved to learn I had a reduced teaching load—five classes, not six. I had shed the mantel of the novice and acted accordingly. But there were still too few positive entries in my diary like, "A really great day at school" and "Teaching was truly a pleasure." One notation read, "Nine days in succession, children worked industriously, no discipline problems," only to read the following day's entry: "Kids are back to being their obnoxious selves. I'm exhausted. I came to Nevada for this?"

I persevered. I had no choice. I used my hour of planning time to contact parents, issue unsatisfactory notices, make telephone calls, but best of all, I was able to schedule more one-on-one parent-teacher conferences. These methods helped, but parent disinterest and parent criticism came with the territory. As I remarked to Allan one evening, "The school board doesn't even allow us time to pee during the day, so how does one satisfy?"

There were two happenings that winter, albeit totally different, that were quite exciting for me. From day one of that second year with the district, I taught to the test, ignoring the sixth-grade mathematics curriculum guide that contained material not measured by the test. The sixth-grade mathematics test was administered early in the second semester, and when the district results were back, my classes ranked in the 90th percentile and above. It was a proud moment I shared with my students.

The other event happened on Sunday, January 28, 1979—it snowed! By Wednesday of that week, enough snow had fallen that everyone was flummoxed. The transportation department said, "No school." The head-shed (administration) said, "Yes school." Confusion reigned. Some buses delivered children, others didn't. The children who were in school that day had a grand time building snowmen, snow forts, and having snowball fights. The following day school was canceled; a total of eight inches of snow had fallen. At our house, Allan set our snow shovel out on the front lawn with a sign that read "For Rent"—there were no takers.

The confusion over to cancel / not cancel school was minimal compared to the decision the board of education faced in how to make up the missed school day. Nevada school law made no allowance for missed instructional time due to an act-of-god phenomenon. To make up the time missed, the school board, in their collective wisdom, opted not to add a day to the school calendar. There were thirty minutes added to the end of fourteen successive school days in the month of April. Chaos prevailed! The lengthened school day required the internal revision of daily building schedules, and bus schedules were modified to accommodate the change.

This had a profound effect on student employment, athletic programs, childcare, and any other activities that marched to the beat of the school day schedule. In spite of it all, school employees and parents alike survived to live another day.

----------·+++++·----------

I EXPERIENCED CRUMBS OF SUCCESS my second year with the district, but I did not accept employment with the CCSD to remain a classroom teacher—my goal was to be a building principal. When I initially applied to the district, I was told I would need to accept an entry-level position as a teacher, teach for a minimum of three years, and then I would be eligible to apply for an administrative position. Much to my disappointment, it was during my first year with the district that I learned the board had changed the requirement from three to five years before one could apply for a position in administration. I can only surmise that this change of policy was due to the influx of out-of-state talent.

I already had K–12 reading certification. I applied at three schools where there were openings for reading specialists and was granted interviews at each. My first interview was with the principal at Deskin Elementary School. I arrived at the school and was directed by the secretary to take a seat in the waiting area. Shortly, I was greeted by a very disheveled-looking middle-aged man (the principal?) who beckoned me into his office and motioned for me to be seated. The interview lasted fifteen minutes, and his body language communicated boredom with not so much as the courtesy of stifling his yawns. As I left his office, I said to myself, "He is either totally incompetent or already has someone for the position."

My second interview was with the principal of Paradise Elementary School. My interview with Mr. Hall lasted for one and a half hours. Within a few days, I received a call; four people had been interviewed for the position. I was one of two finalists. That gave me hope, only to have it shattered when I learned I was not the chosen one.

My last hope was the reading position advertised for Kenny C. Guinn Junior High School. I was interviewed and invited to attend a building staff in-service. I left the meeting impressed with the leadership and staff of the school. Again, I received disappointing news—no reason was given.

It was evident that CCSD was overflowing with talent. Allan agreed that I should expand my job search to other places in Nevada. Previously I had met the superintendent of Reno public schools at a convention and was invited to serve as a consultant related to their transitioning from a junior high school to a middle school structure. I contacted the district and was told there were no administrative jobs available; they promoted only from within—similar to the CCSD policy.

Bill Partier, a teacher friend at Quannah McCall, had applied to teach in Carson City Schools and encouraged me to do the same. The thought of moving to Carson City appealed to us. It was the capital of Nevada and located close to the Lake Tahoe recreational area. I called and was granted a preliminary interview. I was told that if I were serious about wanting employment in the district, I would need to fill out an application and wait in line. The location of the city, near Lake Tahoe, made it a desirable place to live, and I sensed the competition for employment there was greater than in Clark County. Albeit my job dissatisfaction weighed heavily on Allan, but he continued to support me in all my endeavors.

———— ++++++ ————

ALTHOUGH WE HAD LIVED IN THE CITY for almost two years, neither one of us had shed our Midwestern conservative ways. Without realizing it, I put Allan to a test. I had always cut his hair, but this one time I encouraged him to come with me to the beauty salon and have his hair styled by a professional. I assured him I had seen several men at the shop each time I'd been there. Allan reluctantly accompanied me. Once seated in the barber chair, a young curvaceous stylist proceeded to cut his hair. I watched from afar and noted that Allan's eyes were laser beams on the woman's cleavage. Granted, her low-cut, skin-tight dress made it appear that her breasts would pop out at any moment. I detected Allan's embarrassment. When we left the shop, my husband's remark to me was, "I didn't know where to look, never, never again!"

Allan experienced some health issues that were very disconcerting to both of us. There were times that spring of 1979 that he became very weak and nauseated. Another time we went to the Flamingo to enjoy a champagne brunch. Allan fainted, came to, and was placed on a makeshift bed where he rested for a short time before I was able to bring him home. Allan attributed it to drinking too much champagne.

Soon after that, a very alarming incident occurred one morning when I was at school. I was called home. Allan had a severe nosebleed. A neighbor who was a medical doctor came to Allan's help and stopped the bleeding. That afternoon our family doctor scheduled urine, blood, EKG, and X-ray tests to diagnose the cause. It appeared it was high blood pressure.

Fortunately, Allan responded well to the prescribed medicine and rest. There were no more fainting or nosebleed incidents.

At times I was very happy with our life in Las Vegas, but more often my dissatisfaction was expressed in outbursts of anger, overeating, constant complaining, and feelings of utter exhaustion. Perhaps it was I who, unknowingly, contributed to Allan's health problems. I had resigned my central office position in Lemoyne and accepted the position of classroom teacher with CCSD, thinking it would lessen my job stress. Obviously, it hadn't worked. I only changed the scenery.

———————— ‡‡‡‡‡‡ ————————

FROM THE GET-GO, Allan and I were always able to openly discuss challenges to our marriage. After my failed efforts to secure a different position in the district, as well as my attempts to find employment in towns outside of Las Vegas, Allan took a serious look at my retirement. He was very direct in telling me I must earn retirement in my own right. Due to our age difference, he had made limited financial provisions for me after his death, readily admitting it would not be enough for me to live on. He analyzed the benefits of Nevada's retirement system and compared it with Ohio's system; it was to my advantage to consolidate my years in the Ohio system. I faced the caveat that if I wished to vest (buy in) my out-of-state years in the Ohio system, I must be actively employed in Ohio. It appeared there was an overriding reason to return to our home state, and that reason involved the pocketbook.

I contacted KSU and spoke with Dr. Robert Wilson, educational administration department head. Dr. Wilson informed me of an opening for a middle-school principal in Painesville, a city about twenty-five miles to the west of Ashtabula. Dr. Fritz Overs was the superintendent; he was in the doctoral program at KSU the same time as I. An interview was scheduled for me on July 2 that summer of 1979.

On June 30 I boarded a plane for Cleveland. Landing at the airport, I rented a car, drove to Parma, and spent the night with Gunne. The next day I drove into Kent, met with Dr. Roy Caughran, my dissertation adviser, who obligingly helped me prepare for my interview the following day. The interview with Dr. Overs and assistant superintendent Mr. Britt lasted more than an hour. I left the interview and drove to my sister's home in North Kingsville, with the feeling that all had gone well, only to have my hopes dashed the next day. A man who had eight years of middle school administrative experience was the one chosen.

The morning following the disappointing phone call, I grasped at the proverbial straw and stopped in at the office of Mr. Jerry Peterson, superintendent of Buckeye Schools. Mr. Peterson was not in, but his secretary informed me interviews were being conducted for someone to fill the combined position of Lincoln Elementary School principal / director of community education. I was interested. My first teaching experience was at Lincoln—a K–6 neighborhood school with an enrollment of about 225 students. I was aware that community education programs were promoted through the schools, and this position presented an interesting challenge for me.

I expressed my interest, and an interview was scheduled with Mr. Peterson and his assistant, Mr. Taylor, for Wednesday morning, July 11. My excitement was palpable as I returned to Brenda's home and telephoned Allan with the encouraging news. The interview seemed to go well, and I left with the admonition, "We'll call you, don't call us." I telephoned Allan again, and he informed me no matter what the outcome, he had made the decision to join me in Ohio. I filled the days waiting for Allan's arrival visiting friends and family and painting my sister's garage.

Allan arrived on Tuesday. I still had not heard from Mr. Peterson, but the next day, Wednesday, July 18, the call came. Mr. Peterson informed me that he was recommending me to the board. I was scheduled to meet with the full board the following Monday, July 23.

To pass the time, Allan and I finished painting Brenda's garage and started to paint her house. One evening my niece Shellie got out the Ouija board, and the four of us sat around the card table, our fingers placed lightly on the planchette as the teardrop-shaped device spelled out the answer to our question: Would I get the job or wouldn't I? (Mr. Bentley, pastor of the Church of God, would have brought hellfire and brimstone down on us for consulting with the occult.) When the planchette spelled out the answer YES, our whoops and hollers could be heard outside the walls of the house!

The interview was scheduled for 7:00 p.m. I appeared outwardly composed but inwardly felt a crunch of fear that I would again be rejected. The board members asked questions centered on my willingness to enforce the terms of the teacher contract and establishing my residence in the district. Interview over, I was directed to wait in another room while the board went into executive session. I noted in my diary that it was 10:05 p.m.

when Mr. Peterson emerged and informed me of the board's unanimous decision—the Ouija board was right!

It was late when I returned to Brenda's home, but she and Allan were still up. I was unable to conceal my excitement, and the moment I walked through the door, they knew! The bourbon flowed freely, keeping our throats moistened, as I joyously described in great detail the happenings of the past few hours.

The following day the education reporter for the *Ashtabula Star Beacon* contacted me and scheduled an interview. Within the week an article with my picture—"LINCOLN PRINCIPAL HAS EXPERIENCE"—appeared in the paper announcing my employment.

Allan and I immediately started house hunting. I had committed to establishing residency within the Buckeye District, and within a few days, we settled on a house located on Ridgewood Avenue that was for sale by owner. The Hoskins were asking $69,000; we offered $65,000, which they accepted. I think it was on my sister's birthday, July 22, that we signed the contract. We returned to Las Vegas on July 29—mission accomplished.

BACK IN LAS VEGAS we shared the news with our children. My excitement might have clouded my eyes and made me insensitive to any feelings my son had about our leaving. (The following summer his daughter was born, and I know he was disappointed I could not be there.) However, I resigned my position with the CCSD and felt no remorse, only relief, as I cleaned out the personal belongings that were in my classroom.

I tolerated the heat as I prepared yet again for our move. I noted in my diary that many days, temperatures reached 115 degrees. Allan arranged with Allied Movers to transport our belongings—nine thousand pounds at a cost of $3,500. Having lost my mother's little rocking chair in the move to Las Vegas, I insisted that we rent a U-Haul trailer and pack our irreplaceable memorabilia in it.

We placed our house with a realtor, but it had not been sold by the time we were scheduled to leave. A daughter of a teacher friend was looking for a house to rent. It was fortunate for us as she rented the house and liked it so much that she later bought it.

A few days before we were to depart, Bruce and Linda invited us to their home for a farewell dinner. When we arrived, we were greeted by the entire Gripentog clan—Bob and Betty, their children and spouses, grandchildren, other family members. It was a party! We drank, ate, laughed, and were "roasted" in the unique Gripentog way. We were chided that it was "Ohio or Bust."

THE EXCITEMENT OF A NEW JOB and the return to Ohio masked any sadness I might have felt that August day as I pulled out of the driveway on West Enterprise Drive with a loaded U-Haul trailer hitched behind my Olds. Again we caravanned, with Allan following in his Plymouth.

The first day of driving went without incident. I drove across desert flatlands onto the buttes in Utah under an azure sky dotted with white fluffy clouds. As I covered the miles over Interstate 15, I detected a noticeable change in elevation as the automatic shift on the Olds would drop into second gear. We made 340 miles that day and stopped our first night in Green River, Utah.

The second day of driving along Interstate 70 presented sights of land and sky indescribably spectacular—the mesa and the buttes. It was when I approached the Rocky Mountains that I had a grave concern regarding the loaded U-Haul trailer I was pulling. The automatic shift dropped into first gear. The engine labored, and I noted on the speedometer the car was traveling at only fifteen miles per hour. Heart racing, white-knuckled, and with a prayer, the car continued its climb to an elevation of eleven thousand feet where I looked out and saw tree-covered mountains so high their peaks were in the clouds. When the car made the grade at Loveland Pass, I breathed a prayer of thanks. (Later I learned the carburetor on the Olds should have been set to operate in high altitudes.) I felt only relief as we descended the mountain and continued our drive to Idaho Springs, Colorado, where we spent the night. We were both exhausted from the tension of the 325 miles driven that day.

The next morning we were on the road before daybreak. There were more grades to conquer, but none as daunting as the previous day. I enjoyed the scenery of the rolling flatlands of Nebraska—the fields of hay and corn, the cattle ranches, the wonder of America's breadbasket. Our third day we drove 425 miles before stopping for the night in Grand Valley, Nebraska.

We drove for thirteen hours that fourth day, 505 miles, through Iowa into Illinois where we spent the night in Princeton. The next morning, determined to make our "Ohio or Bust" destination, we left before 5:00 a.m. in a rainstorm. We crossed Indiana and entered Ohio. We arrived in the Cleveland area during the afternoon rush-hour traffic but made it safely to Brenda's home in North Kingsville by six thirty that evening. We drove 525 miles. We had arrived!

The distance between Las Vegas and North Kingsville was 2,160 miles; the Olds used 192 gallons of gasoline, averaging 11.25 miles per gallon. The most I spent for gas was in Saint George, Utah, paying $1.08 per gallon; the cheapest gas I purchased was in Toledo, Ohio, at $.94 per gallon. Neither Allan nor I had any mechanical problems with our vehicles. We spent long days in our cars in solitude and experienced exhaustion, but it was to God that we gave our thanks for an accident-free, safe journey.

FOURTEEN

MARRIAGE TO ALLAN DICKIE ASHTABULA (1979–1984)

A FTER ALL OF THE PROFESSIONAL TRAUMA that I had faced over the previous seven years, I returned home. There I would work in professional bliss completing the needed years for my retirement in the school district where I was first employed as a teacher. I was so naive. Allan and I would live in our Treehouse for only five years, and it was during those years I experienced the (almost) worst times of my professional life. But I get ahead of my story.

THE CITY OF ASHTABULA had changed little since my childhood. The racial/ethnic makeup remained the same—predominately white, a small percentage of blacks and Hispanics, with a smattering of others. Main Street was as I remembered it. The chemical industry still thrived on Lake Road, as did other manufacturing industries throughout the area. Employment was high, and population loss was minimal; according to the 1980 census data, down only 1,500 from the 25,000 of the postwar years.

IT WAS ON A FRIDAY, August 17, exhausted after our long drive, that we pulled our cars into the driveway of my sister Brenda's home in North

Kingsville. She was there to greet us and had prepared a meal for our arrival. Food never tasted so good to two road-weary travelers.

Our date of arrival was by necessity, not choice. I was to report for my position with Buckeye Local Schools on Monday, August 20. We would not have possession of our house until the end of September. For the interim weeks, Brenda provided us with lodging in a fifth-wheel travel trailer parked in her backyard.

Living in the trailer, we enjoyed the conveniences of home, albeit within limited space. The shower stall was small, and if you dropped the soap, you had to open the shower door to pick it up. We took turns experiencing the delight of honey-dipping (emptying the sewage reservoir). This brought back childhood memories of living on the farm, when one of my daily chores was to empty the pot located in the hallway on the second floor of the farmhouse.

One unhappy memory involved an accident with Brenda. She was standing on a step ladder, repairing a leak in the trailer roof with tar, when a wind shear caught her and knocked her off the ladder, causing her to break her wrist in the fall, requiring a trip to the ER.

On the last day of September, we vacated our trailer home and were given the keys to the home at 3120 Ridgewood Avenue. The Victorian-style, double-L-shaped, 2,708-square-foot house was built in 1950 on 1.3 acres at the top of a hill populated with cherry, oak, maple, and black walnut trees. The house was built into the hillside and had a single-car garage off of the basement under the east wing of the building.

Our furniture was delivered on October 2 by Allied Movers, who provided service to our full satisfaction in stark contrast with the handling by Mayflower when we moved to Las Vegas. During all this confusion, Fred Vermeulen, pastor of the East Side Presbyterian Church, stopped by to welcome us. We were surprised to see him at our door, but we invited him in. As he carefully stepped among the boxes into our living room, he looked about and candidly remarked, "You have got to do something about all this green wall paint." Fred had married us in 1963, but this was our first opportunity to converse informally with him and in a very unorthodox setting. During the few years we lived in the area, we got to know and respect him for his intellect, leadership, and wry sense of humor.

Fred's comment prompted us to action. Our first task was to cover up the green walls with either paint or wallpaper. The woodwork and floors were cherry, to our liking. But it didn't take us long to realize that the house wiring was a disaster (house inspections were not yet in vogue) and prompted us to hire an electrician.

Living on the top of a hill, almost totally secluded from prying eyes, the many windows in the house provided us with breathtaking views—a large picture window to the front and back of the living room, as well as the twenty-four windows on the three exterior sides of the sunroom at the east end of the house. Seated in our living room and looking to the north, we would see only the tops of the trees, and this was what promoted us to name our home the Treehouse. On early mornings when I would be seated at the breakfast table in the sunroom, I could watch the brilliant yellow-orange ball as the sun rose above the silhouette of the trees. Totally immersed in the beauty of the natural world that surrounded us, Joyce Kilmer's lyric poem "Trees" would come to mind.

The long approach drive from the street climbed upward until, cresting the hill, the driveway sloped down into the garage located under the house, where I parked my car. We had an automatic opener installed on the garage door. I will always remember the first afternoon I drove home from school in a heavy rain, pulled up in front of the garage door, hit the opener button, the door went up, and I drove into the garage, escaping all exposure to the elements. I thought, "This is how it is to be rich!"

That feeling of euphoria soon vanished as I stepped out of my car and observed that a river of water had surged down the sloping drive and flooded the garage floor. Being a do-it-yourselfer, I convinced Allan we could fix the problem. We used our recently purchased, secondhand utility trailer to haul stone, rocks, sand, and asphalt materials to construct a speed bump on the drive connected to a sluiceway we built in the yard that carried the water away from the basement of the house. Not professional, perhaps not aesthetically pleasing to the landscape artist, but it worked, and we were proud.

That first fall we lived in the Treehouse, we gave our attention to cleaning up the natural debris that had fallen in the yard. Aware that any burning might cause a fire, Allan cleared a large circular area and called it his leaf-burning pit. He filled it with the yard debris. One item placed at the bottom of the pile was a large rotten hollow log. One sunny calm day, Allan set the pile ablaze, and as we carefully monitored the burning, to our amazement, a squirrel raced out of the hollow log. Allan pulled the log from the fire and upon close examination found a nest of three newborn squirrels. The mother squirrel never returned to her babies, so we took over the task of feeding. We named them Cinderella, Sylvester, and

Rumpelstiltskin. Using an eyedropper, we fed them sugar water and milk. The first-week feedings went very well, and Cinderella advanced to drinking from a dish. We were thrilled, only to have our joy smashed to despair when one morning soon after, Allan found Cinderella dead; the two males became sickly, and they, too, soon died. We buried them in the yard. We were distraught that our cleanup activity had robbed the baby squirrels of their mother's nurturing.

There were two other buildings on the property. A small barn was located at the base of the hill. The former owner's daughter had kept her horse there. Located about thirty feet from the house at the top of the hill was a large utility building. This building needed painting, and it was here I had an accident, which miraculously did not result in a serious injury. I had raised an extension ladder to rest in the front peak of the building, a height of twenty-four feet. The ladder had rubber foot pads, which I mistakenly thought would keep it in place. I stepped onto the ladder's bottom rung with paint bucket, scraper, and brush in hand, testing the ladder's stability as I made my way to the top. Once in position, I started scraping and immediately felt the ladder sliding down the building. To my horror, I realized the ladder's rubber foot attachments were not holding on the concrete pad below. I distinctly remember telling myself to "relax, relax, relax" as I smashed into the concrete. Our one neighbor on the hilltop was Don and Roz Moulder. They, along with Allan, heard the crash and came running. I was badly bruised but not broken. Once in the house, Roz packed my face, hands, and knees with ice. I refused medical attention. Lloyd, when learning of my foolhardiness, wryly commented, "Henri, you need to take Ladder Safety 101."

Due to the trees that shaded the lawn, the grass was sparse and easy to mow. Allan used a push, rotary mower. On many an occasion, I would be sitting in a comfortable chair on our front porch that was inset between the two L-shaped rooms on the house, with feet up on the stone planter where busy lizzies (impatiens) grew in abundance. I loved listening to the hypnotic sound made by the whirring blade of the mower, accompanied by the songbirds that inhabited our trees. We had no desire to search for gold on our land, for we had found our own variant of Erskine Caldwell's *God's Little Acre* there on the hilltop.

The 250-foot, 15 percent grade that was our asphalt driveway connected our lot to Ridgewood Avenue, and asphalt requires maintenance. One summer, I took the odious task upon myself of applying the asphalt sealer and, before doing so, failed to check the weather report. I started at the top of the drive with a long-handled brush, evenly spreading the smelly black liquid as I worked my way down the driveway toward the street. The sun was shining when I finished, but Mother Nature hit the toggle switch, and a dark cloud sailed overhead, releasing a heavy rain. The asphalt sealer had not yet "set," forming a river of black water that gushed to the street. It was a hard lesson learned, but this time, no after-the-fact advice from my brother.

In the winter, heavy snows would cover the grass and the boughs of the trees, transforming our home into a picturesque winter wonderland. Nature's beauty, however, brought with it problems. A snowblower was not practical to clean our expanse of asphalt. The length of our driveway, and the large parking area at the top of the hill, required us to contract with a local person who had a truck with a blade to plow the snow. Most of the time, we were able to navigate the hill, but there were occasions when the snow would be deep and the drive not yet plowed; or worse yet, the drive would be covered in ice. When these conditions occurred, the only option was to park at the bottom of the hill and plod our way to the top.

There was one other house, located about a hundred feet to the south of our home. Bob and Rose Germaine lived there. We did not get to know them as they sold their house and moved shortly after we arrived. The house was purchased by Don and Roz Moulder. Don was a local dentist; Roz worked for a travel agency and was very active with the Ashtabula Art Center where she starred in several shows. Don passed away after we moved off the hill, but Roz and I remain friends to this day.

OUR FIRST OUTREACH EFFORT was to take care of financial matters. We selected a local bank and, with proof of residency, set up our checking and savings account services—nothing like the long delay we had experienced in Las Vegas. Our main reason for returning to Ohio was for me to earn enough years in the State Teacher Retirement System (STRS) to assure me an adequate income in retirement. Proof of employment with Buckeye Local Schools was all that I needed, along with a $10,000 buy-in, and five out-of-state years (maximum number allowed by law) were credited to my STRS account.

I had no problem transferring my Nevada driver's license and car plates for an Ohio license and plates. For Allan it was quite another matter. He had his Nevada car registration but had lost the car title. In Ohio,

no title equals no car plates—a catch-22 conundrum. Phone calls and letters involving the bureaucracy of three states and seven months later, Allan
succeeded in securing Ohio plates for his 1972 Plymouth. This ordeal
prompted Allan to write a letter to the editor of the *Ashtabula Star Beacon*
relating the bureaucratic nightmare. His letter and picture were featured in
the Saturday, March 22, 1980, paper with a heading that read, "Lose title
and you may lose mind." Allan was prolific in writing letters to the editor;
this was one of his best.

———————— ⋅⁺⁺⁺⁺⁺⋅ ————————

AFTER WE PURCHASED THE HOUSE from the Hoskins family, they held an
auction as they prepared to move. Two items in the auction of interest
to me were a player piano with accompanying rolls and eight old empty
trunks. Brenda came with me that sunny autumn day. We arrived early and
stayed late. It was hours into the sale before the trunks or piano came up
for bid. I successfully bid on all eight trunks—flattops as well as roundtops,
known as humpbacks.

The humpback trunks were of special interest to me. Humpback
trunks appealed to the traveling rich; they could not be stacked and therefore were placed on top in the luggage cars of trains, giving them protection
from damage. It took many hours to restore those trunks; it was a labor of
love, and when finished, it was difficult for me to part with them. But part
with them I did. I gave a small stagecoach-sized one to my daughter-in-law
Linda and another to my granddaughter Renee as her high school graduation gift. The remainder of the trunks I passed on to interested family
members.

The player piano was another prize, or so I thought. When Allan
and I toured the house, prior to purchase, Mrs. Hoskins demonstrated the
player piano to me. I was fascinated as I watched the no-hands keys playing
songs off the moving perforated rolls. I wanted to purchase the piano outright, but the Hoskins said it would be in the auction. I gave it no further
thought, and when the piano was put up for bid, I was the highest bidder.
The piano was mine, but its purchase was pure folly. It played for Mrs.
Hoskins; it didn't play for me. After the fact, I did have a knowledgeable
person look at the piano and was told I had purchased a piece of junk. Now
I had not only an irate husband (out of town at the time of the sale) but this
piece of junk to deal with.

Not to be deterred, I took on the project of rebuilding the player piano. I purchased a how-to book, ordered supplies, and set to work. I started by replacing the decomposed bellows' fabric on the eighty-eight pneumatic keys. I spent Sunday afternoons in my shop, and after many months of tedious work, I had covered only thirty-three of the bellows. Due to time constraints, I packed up the supplies and pushed the piano into the corner of the shop where it remained untouched for years.

I started the project with great enthusiasm, telling others what I would accomplish. Fred Vermeulen never let me forget my abandoned undertaking. Whenever he saw me, with a twinkle in his eye and a mischievous tenor in his voice, he would ask, "Now tell me, Henri, just how are you progressing with your player piano?"

I worked alongside Allan in maintaining our home, but we still stayed physically active in other ways. Friday evenings we could be seen playing golf at the local North Kingsville Village Green Golf Course. I jogged, and one Thanksgiving I ran the Main Street Mile and earned a trophy—only because I was the only person over fifty in the race. I joined the Ashtabula County office bowling league. The first time I bowled, I left my common sense at home (should have sandbagged) and rolled a 529 series. It was all downhill after that. I took up racquetball with my niece Beverley. I did enjoy the game, even though she would best me every time. I was disappointed, while at the same time elated, when she told me on February 4, 1983, that she was pregnant and would stop playing until after the baby was born. I lived dangerously and would roller-skate with students from Lincoln Elementary whenever the PTO sponsored a fund-raising activity at the rink. Allan and I also enjoyed walking together.

THE EAST SIDE PRESBYTERIAN CHURCH is located on the southeast corner of the intersection of State Road and Route 20 just east of the Ashtabula city limits. The Wallace H. Braden Junior High School is located there as well. I was a member of the church when I lived on Vineland Avenue, so it was a given that this would be our church home. We transferred our previous church memberships in December 1979. Two years later, Allan was invited to be an elder in the church.

My involvement with the church was minimal. I joined the bell choir, and much to my embarrassment, in my first performance as a bell ringer, I missed at least half of my "rings." Wisely I resigned from the choir before I was asked to leave. Allan and I did enjoy the monthly Wednesday-evening adult potluck suppers.

Allan and I were guests at the wedding of Fred and Myra's son, where Fred officiated. The ceremony was beautiful. The guests slowly moved through the reception line and were directed to the social hall, then seated at long tables to await the appearance of the bride, groom, and bridal party. We waited, and we waited, and we waited. We sat with Marilyn Shipman, church organist and a friend. Marilyn wearied of the waiting and left. Allan and I attempted to follow her and were outside the church, walking toward our car, when Fred raced out the door of the social hall, calling to us to return, saying the wedding party would soon make their appearance. Embarrassed, we did Fred's bidding, realizing our behavior was rude, yet resentful that we were held hostage by the lengthy photography session.

This incident did not destroy our friendship with Fred and Myra. We were part of their social circle that enjoyed frequent dinners together. Fred served his church for thirty-eight years, and we were in attendance on Sunday, October 18, 1981, when he announced that he would be retiring on February 28 of the coming year. His announcement sent an emotional shock wave throughout the sanctuary.

Allan and I remained close friends with Fred and Myra. They moved to Charlotte, North Carolina, to be near their son, his wife, and two grand-daughters (the son whose wedding reception we tried to escape). We visited them on more than one occasion. Myra died in 2004; Fred died in 2011.

WE TOOK ADVANTAGE OF THE ENTERTAINMENT and cultural opportunities in the area. The Shea Civic Theater on Main Street was remodeled around 1980 with the promise of providing live professional performances. Allan and I subscribed to the upcoming season's program. It was a perfect evening in September when we attended the first of the season series featuring the Cleveland Orchestra. At the conclusion of an electrifying performance, as the audience was leaving the theater, they were greeted by tables set with an elaborate choice of hors d'oeuvres and drinks in the foyer that extended out onto the sidewalk. Apparently, this lavish display on opening night did not bode well for those in charge of the promotion. Ashtabula residents did not subscribe in large numbers to sustain the season. In November, much to our disappointment, we read in the local paper that the theater declared bankruptcy. No money was refunded.

There were community theater venues where local talent was used in live stage performances—Ashtabula Art Center, Rabbit Run Theater (fifteen miles to the west in Madison), and the KSU Ashtabula Campus. We would also drive into Cleveland to enjoy performances of the Cleveland Orchestra at Severance Hall.

Locally we attended the annual Ashtabula County Fair in August, and in the fall the Geneva Grape Festival. Here anyone willing to remove their shoes could step into a vat to stomp and experience the squishy feel of the grapes between their toes. The Perry Nuclear Power Plant in Lake County opened in the early 1980s. Allan, of a scientific mind, found the tour of this facility to be of great interest.

There are eighty-eight counties in Ohio. An interesting geographical fact is that Ashtabula is the largest county, and contiguous to the west is Lake County, the smallest county in the state. Ashtabula is known for its covered bridges. At the time we lived in the area, we made Sunday afternoon jaunts throughout the county and visited thirteen of the present-day seventeen bridges. The first Covered Bridge Festival was held in 1983; we were ahead of the times when we set up our own self-driving tour.

It was never my goal to be a joiner, or gain public recognition, but there were a few social and professional organizations in which I wanted to be a part. Mom was an active member of the Daughters of Union Veterans (DUV). Brenda and I were inducted into this august society in September 1982. I became a member of the local American Association of University Women (AAUW) in 1981. Once I had returned to the area, I was invited to be a part of the "Big 30" group made up of area administrators, all men and mostly KSU graduates. The group met monthly on the Kent campus. I was the only woman in the organization and said little during the meetings, but I enjoyed the association with kindred professionals and the networking opportunities it provided. A fringe benefit was being a part of the annual spring Schoolz Out Golf Tournament. I would partner with my dissertation adviser, Roy Caughran, for an enjoyable-but-competitive eighteen holes of golf.

On Memorial Day of 1980, I was invited to be the speaker at the Kellogsville Cemetery's Memorial Day service located ten miles to the east of Ashtabula. When I arrived, the size of the crowd unnerved me. There were 250 to 300 people gathered there. Allan had helped me in the preparation of my speech. I spoke of my maternal grandfather who served in the Civil War, my father who served in World War I, and to all veterans—those living and those who had died—in the service of their country. That evening I wrote in my diary, "My speech was well received. It was worth all the angst I experienced in preparing it."

The following year I was again invited to speak at the Memorial Day service, this time at the Gageville Cemetery located a few miles from my childhood home. I felt humbled, for this was where my parents and grandparents were interred—where, as a child, I helped my mother place flags on the graves of the deceased members of the DUV.

Shortly after that, Fred asked me to speak on a Sunday he would be away and needed someone to fill the pulpit. At the conclusion of the service, I stood by the door, greeting the parishioners as they filed past; a few made dutifully respectful comments. I found it a challenge to relate to groups outside of my professional role.

ALLAN AND I TRAVELED the years we lived in Ashtabula. We made frequent visits to our out-of-state family and friends. In the summer of 1981, Allan, being of Scottish ancestry, planned our trip to Scotland. We rented a car (my first experience of driving on the wrong side of the road), stayed in bed-and-breakfasts, took a boat ride on Loch Lomond (no monster), enjoyed bagpipe music whenever possible, and browsed the shops in the small towns. We soaked up the culture during our two-week adventure touring the southern part of the country.

Our trip was enjoyed to the fullest, and once home, Allan immediately made arrangements for us to return the following summer. That time we took our golf clubs and our travels were in the northern area of the country. It is in St. Andrews, Fife, that the Old Course at St. Andrews is located, considered by many to be the home of golf; and the highlight of the trip for me was to play golf on those hallowed fairways. We were in St. Andrews on a Sunday morning and attended the Holy Trinity Church—a memorable experience because it was here, for the first time, we took Communion from the common cup.

—————·+·+·+·+·+·—————

HEALTH ISSUES DID BECOME A CONCERN for us. I learned that I had an arthritic condition in my right hip, and I gave up jogging. Due to my age, the dreaded symptoms of menopause reared their ugly heads—hot flashes, poor sleep. But estrogen came to my rescue. Otherwise, my overall health was very good.

Allan's health was another matter. In July of 1982, Allan collapsed on the sunroom floor of our home; he could speak, but his left side was numb. Dr. Altier admitted Allan to the hospital, and tests revealed he had a transit ischemic attack (TIA), the same as had happened when we lived in Pennsylvania, when the right side of his body was affected. This alarmed me as well as his children. The attacks could happen at anytime, leaving Allan alone and helpless for hours. Allan agreed to wear a medical alert button, and in the initial stage of use, he inadvertently set off the alarm and was surprised when the EMR squad appeared at our door.

Allan's hiccoughs, although not life-threatening, drained his energy. On one occasion Allan experienced ten days of continuous hiccoughing. Doctor visits, shots, cough syrup, decongestants, hiccough pills, antacid— nothing worked! It was Peter, my nephew and a pharmacist, who suggested to Allan that he drink eight to ten glasses of water each day. According to my diary notes, it was three days later that the hiccoughs stopped!

The following spring, Allan experienced fluid retention, a serious health problem fluid retention. He spent several days in the hospital in the ICU wearing a heart monitor. After numerous tests were completed, his blood pressure stabilized, and his Coumadin increased, Allan was able to return home. That was a joyous day for him and for me.

———— ++++++ ————

FOR THE YEARS THAT WE LIVED IN THE TREEHOUSE, our lives overflowed with activity. We lived close to my family. Each of the three Schumann siblings had property frontage on Route 20. Brenda lived six miles to the east of me in North Kingsville, I lived in the middle in Ashtabula, and Lloyd lived fifteen miles to the west in Geneva. Due to our geographical proximity, there was a lot of family interaction.

Shortly after Gertrude married Lloyd, she invited me to join her friends when they drove to a theater in Cleveland, and I experienced opera (*Carmen*) for the first time. Gertrude and I shopped and lunched together, attended Weight Watchers together, laughed and cried together, and traveled together. She was more than just my sister-in-law; she was my friend.

I have a vivid memory of the Thanksgiving that she and Lloyd hosted the family gathering. Allan and I were not living in the area at the time, so we came the day before the event. That evening Gertrude and I consumed a bottle of wine (Lloyd didn't drink, and Allan had his scotch), and this loosened her tongue. Usually, when the family gathered, Gertrude was the quiet one in the group, but we all recognized that when she spoke, she meant it. Seated next to me on the sofa, she turned and blurted out, "I don't like my name, from now on I want to be called Trudy." The pronouncement was given; it took some getting used to, but from that day forward, she was our beloved Trudy.

By and large, Lloyd was "need-driven," and whenever we needed help, Lloyd was there. But times with my brother were not all work-related. Lloyd, Allan, and I enjoyed many a game of golf together. Lloyd and Trudy, as much as possible, included us in the lives of their three children—David, Peter, and Jill.

Brenda enriched my life in many ways, from the imaginable to the unimaginable. She drove by my house each morning on her way to work at Reliance Electric in Ashtabula. I recall many days she would stop in for a cup of coffee. The visit was brief, fifteen minutes at most, but it meant a lot to me. Our lives were so busy we grabbed at any precious minutes that we could be together.

In December 1979 Allan and I planned to go to Las Vegas to be with Bruce and family for Christmas. We saw no purpose in putting up a Christmas tree. The night before we were to leave on our trip, there was a knock on the door. When Allan opened it, he was greeted by a young man holding a silver tree decorated with old socks (holes in the toes), tin cans, lids, broken light bulbs, and worse yet (or best, depending on one's perspective), rotten oranges and bananas. Our delivery boy was Brenda's messenger, and he greeted us with, "Hey, is this where the Scrooge lives that doesn't want a Christmas tree?" The rotten fruit was garbage and treated as such; all that remains of that gussied-up tree are the holey socks, saved in my cedar chest.

During the years I lived in Ashtabula, I met all the men my sister was dating. She almost married one of them, but his bizarre behavior on New Year's Eve caused her to call off the wedding. Then, one day in May of 1984, she came "floating" into our house on the arm of a good-looking, tall, dark-haired man and introduced us to Walter Spadaro. He was the one, and they married shortly after I moved from the area.

I have always had a special relationship with Brenda's daughters, Kellie and Shellie. I have been, and remain, a part of their lives. Allan and I, with Brenda and Shellie, attended Kellie's practical nurse pinning ceremony. Allan remarked that if he were ever ill, he hoped Kellie would be his nurse. He felt she had a special sensitivity in caring for people. Shellie was a competitive roller skater. In high school she starred on the volleyball team. We were able to attend only a few of these events, but I was still living in the area when Shellie graduated from Edgewood High School and was able to contribute a part to the celebrations.

Shortly after Allan and I left Pennsylvania, my niece Jill accepted a position with the Quaker Oats Company in Shiremanstown, located close to the area we had left. On our first visit to her apartment in Dillsburg in the early 1980s, I learned she only stocked her refrigerator with hot-dogs and beer. Our second visit was in 1983 to her second-floor, one-bed-room apartment, in an old house in New Cumberland. This time I came prepared with a well-stocked ice chest. Jill had broken her foot but was mobile enough that we were able to take her to dinner at the Riverboat, our favorite dining place in that area. In the spring of 1984, Jill moved again, this time to an apartment in Mechanicsburg. It was on an overnight visit that we met her future husband, Garvin Rumberger. To this day, Garvin delights in telling how Allan introduced himself, shook his hand, and said, "Hi, I am Allan Dickie, a registered Republican."

We saw a lot of our four children those years we lived in Ashtabula. George's son was a dentist; Allan's trips to Louisiana combined a family visit with needed dental work. Janet (Jan) visited, but we saw her and Royce more often when we traveled to the West to visit Bruce and Linda in Las Vegas or Vern and Judy in Spokane.

Vernon brought his family to Ohio in March of 1983. He showed his children the places of his childhood, visited with other family members, and enjoyed an open house that we held in his honor, inviting neighbors and friends who remembered him from the years when he lived on Vineland Avenue.

One year later to the month, we gathered with our four children and their families in Santa Cruz to celebrate Allan's eightieth birthday. Jan and Royce hosted the celebration. The activities were centered in a large beach house rented for the occasion. It was a four-day extravaganza of family camaraderie, culminating with a Saturday-night catered dinner and a Sunday afternoon roasting of the honored guest.

That summer we were again in the West, this time in Las Vegas where Jan, Royce, and children, with George and his recent love, Rita (he and

Lucy had divorced), joined us at Bruce and Linda's home. My son and his wife had been able to get tickets at the Sands for the popular stand-up comic Gallagher. We were seated close to the stage and provided with appropriate protective gear, and with good reason. Gallagher adroitly wielded a large wooden hammer that he termed his Sledge-O-Matic. Throughout his show, he would smash food items, culminating with the signature watermelon, spraying the screaming audience with garbage, who laughed and begged for more.

To me, a funnier incident occurred the following day. We had eaten brunch at the MGM Grand and were walking through the parking lot to our vehicles when we observed a black man jumping out of a car, chasing a black girl. As he gained on her, we noticed she tossed what appeared to be a billfold in his direction. This stud put on a show of superhuman agility. He was running with his pants down around his ankles. Wow! Only in Las Vegas and in broad daylight.

+++++++

A FEW YEARS EARLIER, Dorothy had died and the care of Ma was more than Gunne could handle alone. In the fall of 1979, Gunne had Ma placed in the Aristocrat Nursing Home in Cleveland. The following spring, Gunne sold the Parma home and moved to Houston, Texas, to be near her daughter Karin and family.

I had just returned to Ashtabula, and knowing Ma was alone in a nursing home sixty miles away troubled me. As best I could, I made monthly Sunday afternoon visits to see her and always left with a feeling of helplessness. I communicated with Gunne my desire to have Ma moved to a nursing home close to me. She gave her approval, and along with it signed the necessary papers that gave me the legal authorization for Ma's care.

I pursued finding a place for Ma. Both Lloyd and Fred Vermeulen were most helpful. Lloyd, in his television repair business, was in and out of local nursing homes at unexpected times and had a good feel for where the residents were provided the best care. Combining that with Fred's insight as a pastor, I settled on Inn Conneaut located ten miles to the east of my home in Conneaut, Ohio.

Ma was a Medicaid patient, so I had to deal with all relevant bureaucracies—State of Ohio approval, Cuyahoga County release, and Ashtabula County acceptance. All of the bureaucratic i's were dotted and t's crossed, approval was granted, and Nin came from California to be with her mother the day of the transfer on September 12, 1980.

It was a joy to have Ma near me. The first weeks she was in the home, Ma had a private room. I would visit her every Sunday afternoon and bring with me a thermos of hot coffee, a small container of heavy cream, and sugar lumps. We would sit together, sipping our coffee and reminiscing about days and people long gone. Those were joyful, quiet hours that we spent together.

A number of people visited Ma. One time Brenda came with me and gave Ma a mani-pedi. On another occasion Allan, Ma's niece Helen Hausen, and her longtime Swede Town friend Jennie Brown came with me to celebrate Ma's ninety-fifth birthday. Ma looked queenly. The nurse had styled her hair, and over her nightdress she was wearing a blue bed jacket—a gift from her daughter Nin. We sipped champagne, drank coffee, and enjoyed the angel food birthday cake that I baked for the celebration. It was a delightful party.

As the months moved along into 1981, Ma's condition worsened. She experienced kidney problems, bed sores, diarrhea, and fell into a state of depression, refusing all liquid and solid nourishment. On Saturday, April 25, I brought Jennie Brown with me to visit Ma. Her room was empty. Upon inquiry, I was told she had been transferred to another wing of the building. I was so distraught that evening, I recorded in my diary:

> When I finally found Ma she was sitting in the line-up
> in front of the nurses' station and was crying, 'ai, yai,
> yai, yai' and drooling. I was appalled. I pushed her in
> her wheelchair back to her assigned double room. I
> wanted help to get her into bed, but the nurse refused.
> Ma had no socks on her feet, wearing only a thin gown,
> nothing over her shoulders. She would not take any of
> the hot broth I had brought with me. I left her that
> day, totally devastated, thinking what have I done?

The call came on May 6 while I was at school. Ma had died. The funeral home listed on her intake papers was notified, and Ma's body had been taken there by the time I got to the nursing home. When I walked through the front door of the Inn Conneaut, I was ushered into the office and directed to sign several papers. I inquired about Ma's personal belongings and was handed a black trash bag. Somehow the mental image of Ma sitting half naked in a bleak hallway crying, coupled with the black trash bag that contained her personal items, remains with me to this day and causes me to ask the question, "What happened?" I expected much more based on the recommendations of Lloyd and Fred, my assessment of available facilities, and the initial care Ma received.

The family was notified; funeral arrangements were made with Rev. Fred Vermeulen presiding. Ma was laid to rest with her husband, Peter, son Sidney, and the ashes of her son Verner and daughter Dorothy in the Edgewood Cemetery family plot. After the graveside service, family and friends returned to my home for a time to reminisce and share memories of this most noble lady. To me she will always remain my dear Ma, whom I deeply loved.

Ma's two surviving children, Gunnebourgh (a.k.a. Gunne) with daughter Karin, and Evelyn (a.k.a. Nin) with husband Bob came, along with my son Bruce, wife, Linda, and daughter, Candice. Vernon and family, for their own reasons, were not able to be with us.

Bruce stayed on after the funeral with his family. Candice was ten months old, and this was my first opportunity to meet this precious child. One afternoon I was sitting in the living room looking out of the north window at the tops of the trees swaying in a gentle breeze. Candice was on my lap, face snuggled against my bosom, asleep. I was alone in the room, seated in a low, armless rocking chair. Not wanting to disturb my granddaughter and luxuriating in the joy of holding her, I remained in the chair for almost two hours, hoping my bladder would not burst before she awakened. (She did wake up in time before my bladder gave out.) The week that Bruce and Linda stayed with us helped me to escape the sadness of the previous weeks and months.

In January of 1984, members of the diminishing Nelson family again gathered at our home. Gunnebourgh Margaret Martin (née Nelson), the remarkable woman who wrote the most interesting letters describing the mundane happenings in her day, died on January 14. She was laid to rest in the family plot at Edgewood Cemetery next to her brother Sidney, who died on January 17, 1960, almost twenty-four years to the day. The ground was covered with snow, and a cold wind sent a chill through the small group that included her daughter, Karin, assembled by the graveside. I studied the granite grave markers—Pa, Ma, Sidney, Verner, Dorothy, and now Gunne. Evelyn stood beside me, the last remaining of the five siblings.

RETURNING TO MY HOME AREA, I was able to reconnect with people who at one time played a significant role in my life. There was Betty Shore, my fifth-grade teacher, now married and living in Ashtabula. Viola Scribben (née Kaippainen), my best friend from high school. Esther Forsberg, my former neighbor on Vineland Avenue, made annual visits from Florida to visit her nonagenarian mother. Hilma Fassett, whom I first met as a waitress at Clampitt's Restaurant. Another, previously an acquaintance, became a good friend. Rev. Vermeulen was my pastor when I lived on Vineland Avenue. I sought his counsel before marrying Allan. Now Allan and I enjoyed many social times together with him and his wife, Myra. Individually, or coupled with Allan, all added some form of enrichment to my life.

In 1963, my own dear mother died; eighteen years later, death took my beloved mother-in-law. Now it was Ma's friend Jennie Brown who filled a mother role in my life. One Mother's Day, Allan and I loaded our trailer with rich topsoil and mulch, hitched it to the car, and drove the short distance to Jennie's home on East Fifteenth Street. We removed the subsoil from along the foundation on the east side of her house and replaced it with topsoil, then planted busy lizzies, carefully mulching the plants. With Jennie's daily TLC, the flowers bloomed profusely.

On her birthdays we celebrated with the traditional three-layer cake placed on the pedestal cake stand. We shared many Sunday meals together, and to our delight, Jennie enjoyed a before-dinner scotch and water.

Jennie's only family were two nephews, one living in California, the other in Cleveland. As Jennie's health weakened, it was very distressful to her that she heard little from the nephew in Cleveland, and rarely from her California nephew, to whom she had given her health-care power of attorney. It was the California nephew who gave me the authority to secure at-home care for Jennie when she became too weak to manage for herself.

Later, when I found it necessary to move from the area, it was with deep regret that I had this dear eighty-eight-year-old lady placed in a nursing home in Jefferson, Ohio. I stayed in touch with Jennie through letters, telephone calls, and occasional visits. Sadly she died within two years after being placed in the care facility.

WE CONTINUED TO HAVE as much involvement as time and distance would allow with our Kent friends. As church deacon, Allan's responsibility was to provide the music for special church services. One Sunday Allan invited Ralph Hartzell, his long-standing golfing buddy to sing. Ralph and Marie came for the weekend. On Sunday morning, Ralph's tenor voice reverberated throughout the sanctuary as he sang those sacred words of "The Lord's Prayer." When he finished, a prayerful hush fell over the congregation. After the service, the pastor, deacons, and spouses gathered at our home for a brunch to meet Ralph and Marie and enjoy a social time together.

Three couples of our Kent golfing friends lived in Florida. In April of 1981 we drove to the Orlando area to stay with one of those couples, the Resicks. It was more than a golfing holiday. Matt and Lavina drove us to Cape Canaveral on the East Coast to watch the launch of the Columbia space shuttle on April 12. Matt chose a place along the beach south of the launch site as our observation spot. I recall standing on the sandy beach, under a cloudless blue sky, listening to the quiet lapping of the waves to observe this huge, white object thrust into the sky and within minutes disappear from our sight. The thrill of this real-time experience has no equal to watching it on TV.

Golf was the magnet that kept bringing us back to visit our friends in the Red Lion / Lemoyne area of Pennsylvania. When there, we took full advantage of all friendships that were made the few years we lived there. On one of our visits to Red Lion, we stayed with Roy and Neil McCliment. Roy had made arrangements for us to play golf at the local (poor man's) Red Lion Country Club. It was a nine-hole course built into the rolling hillside of the area. Roy had reserved carts for our foursome, and trying to concentrate on one's golf game while at the same time driving, or worse yet, riding shotgun in a golf cart teetering along the sloping hillside, was not my definition of fun! That evening we were dinner guests of Leah and Wayne Brant. They had invited those who knew us to their home for a most pleasant social evening.

Our visits to see West Shore School District acquaintances and friends in Lemoyne always included golf with the Goodmans, and on one visit a cocktail party hosted by the Bernsteins at their home attended by central office staff and school administrators.

As I reflect on these visits, it is gratifying to me that during my short tenure in each district, I had made many acquaintances, but most importantly I formed lasting friendships with a few of my colleagues.

Buckeye local school district serves the children in the northeast corner of Ashtabula County in Ohio. The district had the reputation of being one of the best in the county. School funding was not a problem. The Cleveland Electric Illuminating Company, chemical industries built on or near Lake Erie, along with other businesses and area real estate, provided a sound tax base to support the schools. But with the passing of time comes change, and change was to come to Buckeye Local School District.

My first teaching position was with the district in 1962, when I was hired by the board of education to teach fifth grade at Lincoln Elementary School. Lincoln was a small neighborhood school (about 250 students) built in 1954 and located in a blue-collar residential area of moderately priced homes. There were two classrooms per grade in the building, and Ron was my fifth-grade teaching partner. I mention this because his presence caused me major problems when I returned as principal of the school.

I reported for my first day as principal of Lincoln School on August 20, 1979, and as I walked through the side entrance used by staff that led into the boiler room, I was greeted by a cheery voice singing out "Hi, sweetheart." I turned, and there stood Tony Bernardo, the same custodian who helped me as a neophyte first-year teacher seventeen years ago. There are two employees in a school on whose right side one should always remain—the building custodian and the secretary. Pleasant, smiling Tony had been a fixture in the school from the time it had opened.

That first week of school, all county administrators were mandated to attend a three-day conference at Hiram College, located forty-three miles to the southwest of Ashtabula. We left on a Wednesday; I was a passenger in the car with four other Buckeye principals. This was my first exposure to my colleagues, and my impressions of them were...a clown, a restrained one, a judicious one, and a male chauvinist.

On the first day of the conference, after the morning session, we adjourned to the dining room for lunch. Seated around the table, as we were eating, I wanted to interject a comment into the repartee and started to say, "Let me tell you..." only to be rudely interrupted by Jack, principal of Ridgewood Elementary School. He pointed his finger at me and loudly said, "You don't tell me anything." I am guessing that in his eyes, I was the token female administrator, and for the moment he silenced me.

That was my initiation into the Buckeye administrator's "Ole Boys" club, but the remaining days of the conference were valuable after that disastrous moment. Keynote speakers and breakout sessions were both inspirational and helpful. I became acquainted with other county administrators, one a woman. The afternoon of unscheduled activities, I joined with others and played eighteen holes of golf at the nearby Sugar Bush Knolls course in Garrettsville.

++++++

I HAD MOVED UP THE LADDER in education from that of classroom teacher to head of elementary schools with the Red Lion School District, to a central office curriculum position with West Shore School District, both in Pennsylvania. I had skipped the rung of building principal, although my dissertation topic was "Critical Requirements of Administrative Instructional Leadership Behavior of Elementary Principals."

Despite all my scholarly learning, little did I realize what was really involved in being a building principal. None of my previous professional experiences prepared me for what was ahead. Over the span of the next three years, I was to be tested by fire.

A myriad of disruptions required my attention. Lunchroom disturbance—call the principal. Playground accidents—call the principal. Problems on the bus—call the principal. Medical emergency—call the principal, who in turn called the rescue squad. Students with cigarettes (fortunately no drugs at that time)—call the principal. School grounds vandalized—call the principal. Mechanical problems in the cafeteria—call the principal. And on, and on, and on. It left me little time to be that "instructional leader" I so eruditely wrote about in my dissertation.

Most of the interactions I had with parents were good, but there were some parents who were more difficult to deal with than their offspring. Behavior problems that required disciplining the student, almost without exception, resulted in a call from an irate parent. If I could not satisfy the angry parent and justify the disciplinary action taken, their next step was to go to the superintendent. This happened in only two cases, and to Jerry's credit, he stood by me.

There were few direct complaints from community members. The most common were children trespassing on the property of older residents. But the one that seemed the most bizarre to me came from the precinct judge who presided over workers for precincts four, six, and ten that voted at Lincoln School. Previously, the gymnasium was used for voting, which required gym classes to be outdoors or confined to the classrooms in inclement weather. There was a large, empty classroom in the building, so at the request of the gym teacher, and without consulting the precinct judge, I changed the voting place from the gym to the classroom. Not realizing I did not have this kind of authority, I was directed to immediately remove the voting booths from the classroom and return them to the gym. I had done the forbidden. I lost that one.

In the many roles I assumed, communication was the key. Communication with individuals, however is entirely different from communication with groups, be they small or large. Overall I was relatively successful with individuals, but with groups, it was another matter. Each person in a group may understand the message in a different way. When this happens, there is little to no opportunity to correct misconceptions, and confusion can rear its ugly head.

Such was the case when the directive came down from the superintendent that the principals in the elementary schools were to initiate assertive discipline (AD) in their respective buildings. The AD plan was based on a "take-control" approach to classroom management. Behavior rules were made clear to the children, with consequences for repetitive misbehaviors. Should a child's misbehavior continue, the parent and/or the principal would then become involved.

Classroom discipline is unique to each teacher and cannot be effectively implemented by a one-size-fits-all set of rules. But who was I to argue with the superintendent? I attended the required AD informational workshop with the other three elementary principals. Then, with supportive materials in hand, I scheduled meetings to inform the staff. A few staff members were receptive, but others rebelled, knowing it was just another fad—and silently ignored the AD.

I met with the executive committee of the Parent-Teacher Organization (PTO) to explain the AD program. Their response was one of approval. But when I called an all-school assembly to explain the plan to the children, I got into serious trouble. The consequence for the child who exhibited recidivist behaviors was isolation. To this end I had placed in the gym a large refrigerator box, made to look like a telephone booth, and explained that it was an isolation booth for the boy or girl who kept misbehaving. I knew the children would have concerns, and in my closing comments, I encouraged them to direct questions to their teachers. The presentation was over, and the teachers, with children in tow, left the assembly in an orderly manner, and I naively thought, with relief, that the AD program was launched in Lincoln Elementary School.

The next morning I arrived at school to find a group of six irate mothers of first-grade students seated around the table in my office. The previous evening the children had come home from school telling horrific tales of being confined in a box if they misbehaved. During the following days repeated phone calls and parent visits to my office required my full attention. When I was able to respond one-on-one to the parents' concerns, they were, without exception, receptive to the AD plan. Communication was the key, and I had failed with the young children.

In my interview with the board of education, I was asked the question, "As principal of the Lincoln School, will you enforce the teacher contract agreed upon by the Buckeye Teachers' Union and the board?" My mother and father did not raise an idiot, and I wanted the job. My obvious answer was "Yes." I had not been given the contract to read, so I did not know the full impact of what I agreed to do. Prior to the opening of school, the superintendent informed me that the previous principal had been lax in enforcing the contract, especially the hours teachers were to be in the building. I was expected to change that.

The school secretary was Sandy. She walked a narrow professional line as she fulfilled her duties in providing for the needs of students, teachers, and parents, while at the same time supporting me in my role as principal. She was another June Grove, ever loyal to me in spite of the difficulties I incurred those three years I was principal of the school.

I met with the teachers on Tuesday, September 4. I recognized several from when I taught in the building in the early 1960s. My fifth-grade teaching partner Ron was there—still teaching fifth grade, still teaching in the same classroom. The students came the following day. The school year was off to a smooth start.

My honeymoon as principal ended on Friday when I met Ron in the hall and confronted him about being fifteen minutes late every morning that week. His only comment at the time was that he had been doing this for years, but Ron did not accept the reprimand well. Within the hour he was in my office, pounding his fist on my desk and informing me I was out of line. Apparently, the teachers never expected I would enforce the policies laid out in their contract, but the board of education did.

Later that day I met with Jerry and mentioned the morning's incident with Ron. Jerry made no effort to conceal his delight. Little did I realize what the consequences would be for me when I answered "Yes" to the board member's question. I did it, and now I had to live with it.

My action created a storm that lasted for the entire first year I was at Lincoln, and never totally subsided during the following two years. There was support in the community for Ron's plight. I learned that someone circulated a petition to have me removed from Lincoln. The intermediate-grade teachers on the second floor of the building rallied behind Ron. The primary teachers on the first floor remained neutral, some brave enough to express support for me.

Through all the ensuing months, I could not fault the teachers, both those against me and those with me. They all fulfilled their classroom teaching responsibilities. It was in the extracurricular events that the defiant teachers did whatever could be done to obstruct my effectiveness as building principal. They refused to support the science fair exhibit, the PTO carnival fund-raiser, the spring junior Olympics—all annual events that were special to parents and community alike. Staff from other buildings and willing parents came to my rescue as needed.

During that first school year, I had endless meetings with the angry teachers, listened to all their grievances, attempted to explain and reason with them, but it was pointless. Two parties cannot arrive at agreement when they function from a different base of reason. Ron filed a grievance against me. It was the following fall before the grievance was heard before a binding arbitration agent. It was a relief to me that the ruling was in my favor, but little to no help in my role as principal. Ron, believing he was right, continued to stir the pot of teacher resentment and the clique that ran the Lincoln School was not to be denied.

There were other incidents with the Lincoln teachers—some good and some not so good. The kindergarten teacher, Nancy, was an outstanding teacher. I wanted to nominate her to represent Buckeye in the Ohio Teacher of the Year competition. Jerry gave his permission. I worked with Nancy as she completed the required forms, but with no further support from the superintendent, and no newspaper coverage, it went nowhere.

It came to my attention, through an anonymous note, that a fourth-grade and a fifth-grade teacher (both married to others) were having an affair. I was given credit for handling this situation in a creditable, professional manner with no repercussions to any of the parties involved.

The physical education teacher suffered from epileptic seizures. He was forthright in directing me how to handle the situation in the event he had a seizure while instructing one of his classes. It did happen, and knowing what to do, the incident was resolved without frightening the children.

Tragically, the young man died not too long after, leaving a young wife and little girl who was in the second grade in the Lincoln School.

The most difficult situation I had to deal with, apart from Ron and the defiant teachers, was the first-grade teacher who could not maintain classroom control. Concerned parents, as well as special-area teachers, approached me regarding the problem. I spent considerable time helping and supporting the teacher, but nothing worked. I came to realize her health was an issue, and for that reason she took a leave of absence. She retired at the end of the school year.

———— ✦✦✦✦✦ ————

THE MOST REWARDING EXPERIENCES were those I had when I was able to interact with the children. I grasped at any and all opportunities available to me. On Halloween it was a tradition that the children and teachers would dress in costumes and walk through the neighborhood. I delighted in joining the parade, and when we returned to the school, Sandy and I would trick-or-treat our way through the building. One year I borrowed the George and Martha Washington costumes that Brenda had made. I was George, and Sandy was Martha.

Tony the custodian was a good friend during those first months I was principal. Sadly, he died unexpectedly on December 29 during the Christmas holiday. When the students returned from their Christmas break on the second day of the New Year, I planned a flag ceremony to honor Tony. The students, accompanied by their teachers, formed a circle around the flagpole. With hands placed over hearts, the Pledge of Allegiance was recited as two students solemnly raised the flag then lowered it to half-staff. The somber mood remained as all reentered the building.

In February of 1980, two months after Tony had died, the children of the school, under the able direction of their teachers, presented a program of memories that were a *Tribute to Tony*. In attendance were his widow, parents, and community members, four of the five board of education members, the superintendent and his assistant, and the former building principal. All in attendance that day came away with the realization that Tony had made a profound and lasting impact on the lives of the Lincoln children.

Another program, directed by talented members of the staff, was a *Musical Review of the 1890s*. The day of the performances, there was standing room only in the gym. Early arrivals got the chairs. In fact, the program was so outstanding it was featured two weeks later on a Cleveland television channel.

There were many student programs. The kindergarten classes performed for the PTO. The physical education teacher had a special program for parents demonstrating activities that developed physical strength and agility. Christmas was special when the stage was decorated with poinsettias and the traditional Christmas tree. This was the time when the music teacher featured each grade in special songs and readings. There were other opportunities when the children were able to showcase their efforts—science fair exhibits, end-of-year awards assembly, and the Junior Olympics. I was a part of it all, but for the most part only the cheerleader. It was dedicated staff, parents, and community members who made it all happen.

The parent-teacher organization was a dynamic group that supported the school. Each fall there was an open house and, at the end of the year, a school picnic. Throughout the year there were potluck suppers, parent-guest lunches, and homeroom mothers who aided the classroom teachers for special in-room parties. It was the mothers who did the grunt work that made all these events successful.

Parents and community members enthusiastically supported their school but were found wanting when it came to supporting the board of education. An operating levy was placed on the ballot the fall of 1981. The superintendent requested that I set up a community informational meeting whereby he and a member of the board would explain the need for the upcoming levy. The meeting was held in October prior to the November 3 voting day. Teacher support was lacking, and only a few from the community were in attendance. The levy failed by a margin of two to one.

I had a very good working relationship with the PTO. When the nurse or teachers needed to make phone calls, their only options were to use one of the two telephones in the school, both located in the office area—one in my office, the other on the desk of the secretary.

Teachers, or the nurse, were reluctant to ask me to vacate my office and would use the telephone on the secretary's desk, allowing for no conversational privacy. I approached Jerry regarding the need for a telephone in the school clinic. Pleading frugality, he refused the request. I then went to the PTO executive committee and presented the need to them, explaining that the superintendent had refused. They agreed with the need for an additional phone. A contract was made with the phone company, and the phone was installed. My act of defiance, albeit in the best interest of the staff, did not bode well for my continuing relationship with Jerry.

The PTO spearheaded numerous fund-raising events. To mention a few, there was the annual school carnival; skating parties (that I attended to the delight of the children); and when an empty classroom was designated as a central library to replace the room libraries, the PTO took on the fund-raising task to carpet the room. Thousands of dollars were raised for school supplies that otherwise would not be available through the school budget.

I was hired not only as the principal of Lincoln School but also the Director of Community Education. This was a time when school districts were actively promoting the development of programs that would utilize school facilities in an outreach to the community. Buckeye had no community education (CE) program. To this end Jerry sent me, with representatives from the teaching staff, to a conference in Columbus on CE. Following this conference, I prepared and presented to the board of education the bylaws that would govern the program. As soon as the bylaws received board approval, I proceeded with a community survey and selected interested community members to serve on various committees. Based on survey results, the program committee identified the first CE classes that would be offered to the community.

Immediately I became aware of the central office staff's need for help with the mailing of the Buckeye Report—the district newsletter that was periodically sent to all area residents. My most successful task as CE director was when I set in motion the Buckeye Report mailing committee. Allan was a willing member of this group. It was made up of thirty people, who met in the social hall of the East Side Presbyterian Church. As they collated, folded, addressed, and stamped the report pages in preparation for mailing, they drank coffee, many pleasant, snacks, and spent enjoyable productive hours together.

The program committee aided me in the task of identifying CE class offerings. This was the easy part; my task was to find instructors for the classes. I promoted CE through mailings, radio presentations, telephone calls, and by word of mouth. In the end, the only classes of interest were those dealing with fun, food, and fitness. CE died a natural death after its second year when I was removed as CE director.

⸻ ++++++ ⸻

It took the Lincoln teacher clique one year to "whip" me into shape. During my brief tenure as principal, there was an unspoken truce; the clique did not blatantly defy the terms of the teacher contract, and I was able to fulfill the responsibilities of my role as principal. Then it happened. In the spring of 1983, rumors floated about that Lincoln students would be reassigned to Ridgewood Elementary School, located one mile to the east. In March Jerry informed me that the board had taken official action to close Lincoln Elementary. I would not be offered another administrator contract, but I would have a tenured teaching position in the district. I have no memory of how the community and the staff were informed of the school's closing. The responsibility was not given to me, but I do know it all went without any major negative incidents.

I'd made mistakes, but had done my best to correct them and move ahead as the building principal. It was gratifying to me that some took time to recognize my efforts. One individual I'd approached to teach a CE class commented that I'd done a good job in getting along with those "creeps" at Lincoln School, and those who counted respected me. His words rang true, for I received the following written notes from a few members of the Lincoln staff.

From Nancy, the kindergarten teacher whom I had recommended for Buckeye Teacher of the Year:

> Dear Henrietta,
> I want to thank you for the insight and support you have given me during the past two years. You were always available for information and supportive in situations which were troubling to me. We both know that there have been some difficult times and it wouldn't be right to overlook these. However, out of every unfortunate experience there is something positive to be gained. (Ahhh, where did I hear that before?!) I've always felt communication is important, in good times and in bad. It is for this reasonthat I wanted to share these few thoughts with you.
>
> It is difficult leaving Lincoln and I know things will be different, however it will also offer me many new experiences that will help me grow. I thank you for the experiences you've provided me...
>
> Sincerely yours,
> Nancy

From Kathy, a second-grade teacher:

> Dear Henrietta,
> I will miss working with you next year, and I wanted to say that I've enjoyed your short stay at Lincoln. You've done a fantastic job, and I do hope you plan to stay in Buckeye. We need dedicated, efficient, positive and fair people. Should you become Buckeye's first female superintendent, I'm sure you will apply yourself in the same manner, not forgetting the elementary school as some do when they reach the pinnacle. Good luck this year on your momentary pause. You'll go on I'm sure.
>
> Sincerely,
Kathy

From Sandy, a third-grade teacher:

> Dear Henrietta,
> I hope you enjoy your new position next year, even though it will be quite different for you.
> Thank you also for giving <u>100%</u> to make things better for the staff. I realize some of the staff can't be happy no matter what. I just wanted you to know that I appreciated your efforts.
>
> Love,
Sandy

The notes made it apparent the primary-grade teachers recognized my leadership role in the school. I was not able to sway the negative attitudes of the intermediate-grade staff—win some, lose some.

MY HONEYMOON IN THE EYES OF THE SUPERINTENDENT lasted a bit longer than it did with the staff at Lincoln School. In late October of that first year, Jerry met with me in my office and told me he was pleased with my work. Almost immediately following that favorable meeting, it was more than a slippery slope with Jerry; it was a fast downhill slide. Speaking in my own defense, I was loyal to the superintendent but at the same time stood for what I believed to be in the best interest of the students and staff of the school.

It was a telephone incident that caused the greatest upset with Jerry. At the end of that school year in 1981, when I asked to see my personnel file, I found a letter of censure written by Jerry, and at the bottom of the letter was stamped "COPY Hand Delivered 10/22/80 JMP." To my knowledge I never was given that letter. During my evaluation conference in May of 1981, I told him the circumstances under which I'd seen the letter but that I never received it. He offered no explanation.

Building principal and CE director were both time-consuming tasks. The message I got from Jerry was, just "do it" and accept mediocrity—the same message I got from the superintendent in West Shore School District when I was given responsibility for the long-range plan. It was not in my nature to make only a pedestrian effort when given a job to do; perfection is a heavy cross to carry.

I have no idea what the working relationship of the other administrators in the district was with the superintendent. Perhaps given more time, mine would have improved, but it was not to be. I was hurt and disappointed that day in June 1982 (the last day of work for administrators before summer break). They gathered for their traditional golf outing. I was not invited, as I previously had been. It was perhaps another decade before women were accepted in administrative roles, and not simply the token female administrator.

I was given tenure as a teacher in the district; I had no choice but to accept a teaching position for the 1982–'83 school term. I was to teach eighth-grade reading at Braden Junior High School. My teaching assignment included homeroom responsibilities and six classes. Someone once made the wry remark that the adolescent should be provided with needed supplies and sent to a remote island, not to return until they had matured— at least to the point where they realized that someone other than their peers knew something. It didn't take me long to come to the realization that I was a total misfit when it came to dealing with children this age.

In October I requested, and was granted, a leave of absence beginning the first of November for the remainder of the school term. I needed time to explore other job opportunities. My involvement in CE piqued my interest in that field, and when I learned of a CE seminar at Columbia University, with Allan's encouragement, I attended. Visiting the campus of this Ivy League institution was an event in and of itself. For the most part, the featured speakers and the breakout sessions were good, but I do recall one speaker took sixty minutes to make her presentation, and when she finished, I had no idea what she said—too erudite and not practical.

I wanted to remain in the area, and when I learned there was a position for a coordinator of developmental studies open at Kent State University Ashtabula Campus (KSUAC), I applied and was interviewed in May. I knew the interview did not go well. The letter came in June informing me that a person with collegiate experience was awarded the position.

There was an opening for an elementary supervisor in the office of the Ashtabula County Educational Service Center (ACESC). I interviewed for this job on June 3, only to receive a call on June 7 that I was not their first choice. That same day a call came from a school district located in the county informing me I had been recommended by the ACESC (remorse on their part?) as a candidate for the position of principal in their middle school (grades 6, 7, 8). I had no interest. My recent teaching experience provided me with the insight to know I did not relate well to adolescent children.

It was Brenda who learned about a position at Lakeland Community College—a two-year institution located thirty-five miles to the west of Ashtabula in neighboring Lake County. In January I met with the president of the college, only to be told the position was filled, but in turn he introduced me to the associate dean for curriculum. Through him I was able to arrange an internship in which I would be actively involved in senior citizen program development.

The dean was interested in a historical perspective on previous college program offerings for the elderly. He assigned me the task of interviewing relevant retired personnel and documenting my findings. There was an old mansion on the college property; I developed a position paper recommending the building be made a senior citizen center. I worked with others in preparation for a Gerokinetic Conference to be held at the college that spring. During the few months I was at LCC, I was given the opportunity for professional growth in an area of great interest to me. When my internship ended in May, I departed with a feeling of sadness.

My excitement was palpable when I was informed the following November that a new position for Lifelong Learning Director at LCC had been approved and job applications were being accepted. I applied, and my interview was scheduled for November 16. It did not go well for me. When a member of the committee asked me what a "loss leader" was, I had no idea and should have said so, but instead I stammered about, giving some inane answer. In December the letter arrived; the committee felt they had not interviewed any person qualified for the position and had reopened the job application process.

While all the above was going on, I registered for classes at KSU and Akron University (AU). At KSU I met with Dale Cook and expressed my interest in pursuing a concentration of studies in the field of CE. He agreed to be my adviser and identified a curriculum that included classes in school community relations, microcomputers, and finance. At AU I met with personnel in the Lifelong Learning Institute, and a program was developed that would lead to a certificate in higher education. I was multitasking in my career goals.

When I was at KSU I spent overnights with our friends the Singhs, whose home was located close to the campus. My class at AU met only one night a week, and Allan always accompanied me on the 140-mile round-trip. The hours we spent together in the car were pleasant times, discussing my career goals and what we would do if nothing worked out for me in the Ashtabula / Lake County area.

⊹⊹⊹⊹⊹⊹⊹

CAREER-WISE NOTHING MATERIALIZED FOR ME. My leave of absence from Buckeye was granted for only the second semester of the 1982–'83 school term. That fall I had to either report for teaching or resign. Not one to throw caution to the wind, I returned to Buckeye as a classroom teacher. My first day back, when I stepped into the school office, the principal was standing there, and his first remark to me was, "I never expected to see you here."

My teaching assignment for the 1983–'84 school term was modified due to a recently enacted state requirement that reading instruction be available to students in grades 1 through 12. It was my misfortune that I was the only teacher in the district who had K–12 reading certification—ergo, by default, the position was mine. To meet this state requirement, the board adopted the resolution that the reading classes for grades 9 through 12 were to be remedial—that is, available to students not reading at grade level.

I divided my time between the junior and senior high schools. In the morning I taught three classes at the high school, in the afternoon three classes in the junior high. At the junior high I was assigned my own classroom where I had ready access to teaching supplies. Not so at the senior high. I was a roving teacher, using whatever classroom was empty and any supplies I needed were kept on a rolling cart.

It was left to me to search through the dust-covered books in the high school book room to find whatever materials I thought would aid me in getting my classes started for the year. On my first day with my high school students, I passed out the books. One six-foot, burly freshman opened his book, glanced at the front pages, raised his hand, and said to me, "Teacher, this book is older than I am!" There was nothing wrong with this student's comprehension skills. I was required to teach groups of twenty to twenty-five students in forty-eight-minute blocks of time. This was not the best solution for the student who needs remedial reading help. I barely survived that year. I might have helped some of my students, but if I did, I am not aware of it.

There were forces at work that gave me hope for a job change which would again place me in a leadership position. Reed Taylor, who worked as an assistant to the superintendent, retired. Learning this, I did some "politicking." Ever aware of the hierarchy of position and authority, I first met with Jerry to let him know I was interested in the job. Jerry was noncommittal. As the opportunity presented itself, I spoke informally with board members.

It was not until March of 1984 that the board acted to fill the vacant position, identifying it as administrative assistant (AA). At that time I was approached by two board members and urged to apply. On May 3, I met with Jerry for the mandated preliminary screening interview. It did not go well. A month later, on June 4, Jerry informed me the board wished to interview me over his objection. I met with the board on June 8 and wrote in my diary, "Met with the board at 8:00 p.m. and was interviewed for the position of AA. The two-hour interview went very well. JP was not in attendance. If I am not offered the job at least I had the opportunity to let the board know my areas of expertise."

While all of the above was in motion, another career opportunity presented itself. A colleague and friend who lived in Columbus called me in December of 1983 about job openings with the State Department of Education. Floyd (Skip) Shipman worked there in the Department of Elementary and Secondary Education (DESE). Skip was aware of my job situation at Buckeye. He had spoken with Mary Poston, the head of the DESE, on my behalf. In April of 1984, Skip called and said Mrs. Poston wished to interview me.

My interview was on April 20, and I felt it went very well. I wasn't aware at the time, but Jerry knew Mary and had approached her on my behalf regarding a position for me in the department (desperate to hand me off?). It is a moot point as to what forces were at work, but I received a telephone call in early June informing me that I was the one selected for the job. Allan and I drove to Columbus. I spent some time with Skip and he gave me a good idea of what it would be like working for the department.

That night Allan and I stayed in the Columbus area, talking well into the night. Should I remain in Buckeye, with the possibility of regaining a position in administration? Or should I accept the position in Columbus, totally uprooting our lives yet again? Together we made the decision, and the following day, June 12, I met with Mary Poston and accepted the position with the State Department of Education.

Back home, I telephoned the president of the Buckeye Board of Education on June 13 and informed him I was withdrawing my application for the position of administrative assistant. The following day a telephone call came from a member of the board expressing his disappointment that I had withdrawn. I noted in my diary, "I know I had two votes on the five member Board. I will never know if the third vote was there and I would have been offered the position. It is best this way."

In the middle of June, I submitted my resignation to the superintendent for the 1984–'85 school term. Later that summer, in a chance meeting with a board member, I did learn that the position would have been mine for the accepting. I noted in my August 4 diary entry, "Saw Fred today. He said I would have been offered the job. So be it."

In hindsight I know it was the right decision. There is no way I could have succeeded in the position with the superintendent against me and with an underlying current of animosity held by influential members in the teacher's union.

Again, after the fact, I received a note from a Lincoln teacher:

> Dear Henrietta,
> I hear you are leaving us and I wanted to write and tell you I hope Buckeye hasn't lost you permanently. You have a lot to offer our school system and should really be our new Director of Curriculum. You certainly did well as a principal at Lincoln and I should have written you concerning that this summer. The best of luck to you.
>
> Fondly,
> Audrey

WHEN ALLAN AND I WERE IN COLUMBUS for my acceptance interview with Mary Poston, we contacted a real estate agent. Skip and Marilyn lived in Worthington, an upscale community, north and contiguous with Columbus. We limited our search to that area and looked at only three homes. The location and the price were right; we purchased a two-and-a-half-story New England cottage–style house, located at 170 East Selby Boulevard in Worthington.

Back home in Ashtabula, we were now faced with selling our Treehouse. We contacted my nephew Peter and his wife, Beverley. They were interested in the house, and after some negotiating, the sale were finalized. A caveat connected with the sale was that they must host the annual Thanksgiving family gathering and that they did over the next thirty-two years. They made unbelievable improvements to the home before selling it the spring of 2016 when they moved to Mentor to live close to their son, wife, and granddaughter, Macie.

Allan and I loved the Treehouse, but neither the love for it nor the love of family could keep us in the area. We were off on another adventure.

FIFTEEN

MARRIAGE TO ALLAN DICKIE WORTHINGTON (1984–1986)

W ORTHINGTON IS A CITY located in the northern area of the meg-
alopolis that surrounds Columbus—the state capital. Settlers
who moved west from Connecticut and Massachusetts set-
tled here, dedicated land for a Publick Square, built their homes, church,
school, and library. It was 1803, the year Ohio became a state.

Today's buildings along High Street of Old Worthington, as well as
the town, evidence a charm that perhaps belies the sacrifice and hard work
of those original settlers. In season there are weekly concerts on the green
of the Publick Square; for the interested shopper there are specialty shops
located along the main street. For the weary, refreshments may be savored
in the unique ambiance of eateries like the Old Bag of Nails. The historic
Old Worthington Inn still stands, offering both fine dining and lodging.

In 1984, when Allan and I moved to Worthington, the population
was about thirteen thousand consisting of 93 percent white, 2 percent
African American, 3 percent Asian, and the remainder other races. It is a
white-collar community with many of the residents employed in government offices in Columbus.

Our home at 170 East Selby Boulevard was in the Colonial Hills
subdivision of moderately priced houses. We paid $77,500 for the one-
and-a-half-story bungalow on a quarter-acre lot. The 1,400 square feet of
living space comprised three bedrooms, one and a half baths, living room,

kitchen, and a full basement with finished recreation room. A single-car garage was attached.

Our furniture arrived on August 6. Immediately Allan and I set to work unpacking; I was scheduled to report for work the end of August. Much to our dismay, the full-length sofa was too large for our living room and was relegated to the recreation room in the basement. We found a reclining love seat to our liking that was a better fit for the small living room. The purchase of a drop-leaf table provided a place for us to eat in the kitchen. There was no dining room in the house. The previous owners had taken one of the two bedrooms on the main floor and converted it into a dining room. With no other option available, we followed suit. We brought with us furniture for two bedrooms. The first-floor bedroom accommodated our king-size bed, but the second-floor bedroom presented a challenge; it was a head-knocker. The room ran the full length of the house following the pitched roofline. This allowed for an adult to stand upright only in the center of the room. At one end of the room was a half bath. Any guests would have to make do.

We purchased the house in haste. Soon after we moved in, we realized a lot needed to be done that would require a handyman. We found one. His name was Paul Garrison, and he could do it all—electrical, plumbing, woodworking, painting, and wallpapering. The paint on the ceiling in our bedroom was peeling, and Paul pointed out the drain pipe from the second-floor half bath was leaking. That was the first of many projects Paul did for us.

The second-floor bedroom needed redecorating, and I wanted it wallpapered. When we lived in the Treehouse, I had one bedroom papered, and when I learned that Bev was going to redecorate the room, I asked if she would try to remove the wallpaper (high-quality, vinyl-coated) so I could have it. She was able to do this and passed the wallpaper rolls on to me. I had Paul hang that paper with the blue poppy flowers in the stairwell to our second-floor bedroom. I loved that paper, and it provided me with a sense of continuity in our new home.

There was also outside work that needed to be done. The concrete in the front steps and walk had cracked. I persuaded Allan that we could take on this project. He reluctantly agreed, and repair progressed smoothly until Allan spotted what appeared to be a tree root alongside the front walk. He took a hatchet and severed the dastardly "root," only to realize he had cut the underground wire to the front walk light. That repair required the attention of Paul.

There were several large oak and maple trees on our lot, providing areas of pleasant shade in the summer, but covering the ground with layers of leaves in the fall. The city provided leaf pickup and posted an area pickup schedule. One fall, when Allan's daughter, Jan, was visiting, the leaves needed to be raked to the curb for pickup. Allan, Jan, and I spent the better part of two days raking leaves, and Jan lamented, "The next time I visit, I am going to first check your leaf raking schedule." Such are the joys and the responsibilities of home ownership.

I thought moving 175 miles south, we would experience a more moderate climate. True, the trees leafed out and the daffodils bloomed two weeks earlier. But there were times in the winter when the snow equaled or exceeded what fell in the snowbelt, and the temperature plummeted to extremes unusual even for Ashtabula County. On January 20, 1985, a record-breaking temperature of 18 degrees below zero was officially recorded, endangering the safety of anyone who ventured outside.

OTHER THAN THE SIZE AND PRICE OF THE HOUSE, the location was perfect. We were one block from High Street, the main north/south artery of the city that provided reliable bus transportation. Within a three-mile radius, we had access to all services necessary for one's daily living needs—medical, financial, and shopping.

Overall, our neighbors were friendly, but I do recall a conversation I had with the neighbor who lived on the east side of our house. I was working in our yard; the man came out his side door and walked toward me. Rather than introducing himself, the first words out of his mouth were, "I hope you don't have any young children." I was dumbstruck; my only thought was, "What a way to greet a new neighbor." I don't recall the neighbor's name. He repaired bicycles, and when I learned there was a bike path close to our home, I bought a rebuilt ten-speed bicycle from him for $35.

On the west side of our house was the home of Dewey and Susan Fisher. Susan's two children, Heather and Mike Reeve, lived with them. Heather was tall and slender, delicate as the flower of her name—artistically talented, voracious reader, writer, and painter. She graduated from high school and entered OSU with all the promise that falls to youth. Tragically she developed cancer and fought a courageous battle, but died in January 1991 during her sophomore year at OSU. Her parents selected a few of her favorite writings, assembled them in a booklet, and distributed them to family and friends. I am privileged to have a copy.

Mike was in junior high school at the time we were neighbors. I remember him as a very active teenager who, on occasion, would come over to visit and regularly borrowed my bicycle pump. I benefitted from his friendship; several years later my husband and I visited him on an island off the coast of Sitka, Alaska, where he worked in a salmon hatchery.

Our relationship with Dewey and Susan got off to a shaky start. Allan and I were invited to visit a neighbor whose home was on the street behind our house. Our lot was fenced in on three sides. Allan and I did not want to walk around the long block to get to their street. We noted by walking along the fence line on the side of Dewey and Susan's home we could access the street that ran behind our house. It was dusk when we trespassed on their property and were observed by them. The following day, a comment was made to us, requesting that we respect their privacy. Fortunately they held no resentment from the incident. Susan and I bonded in a friendship that continues to this day.

Art and Helen Romig lived across the street. They were retired missionaries who had lived in China for many years. Our social interaction with them was interesting and informative; they provided an insight into a culture totally unknown to us.

The area provided easy access to different types of physical activity. My favorite exercise was swimming at the high school pool complex, where there were three pools designed to accommodate all age groups. As soon as I arrived home from the office, I would change into my bathing suit and drive the short distance to the pool. In season, I would swim laps in the outdoor adult pool alongside the youth frolicking in their designated pools. In the winter there was the natatorium pool.

There were golf courses in the area, but Allan made no effort to play golf. He was experiencing the ravages of age and had not the energy to pursue, or the desire to make, new contacts for the game he loved so much. To compensate for this loss in Allan's life, we took many enjoyable walks throughout our quiet neighborhood.

I had my bicycle, but rode it very little even though there was a scenic bike trail near our home that paralleled the Olentangy River. My job took me out of town during the week. When I was home, I enjoyed swimming and walking with Allan. It was later that bicycle riding became an important part of my life.

Wherever Allan and I lived, except for Las Vegas, we became affiliated with a church. Worthington was no exception. Our first church visitation was with the Romigs, who took us with them to the magnificent Broad Street Presbyterian Church in Columbus. Our goal was to find a church closer to our home, and to that end, we visited both the Methodist and Presbyterian Churches in Worthington. We liked them both, but based on our backgrounds, we joined the Presbyterian Church in April 1985. It was the right decision, for in the not-too-distant future, the assistant pastor, Jane Mykrantz, was there for me when I needed spiritual support.

The area overflowed with entertainment that included cultural activities and interesting places to visit, all within fifteen miles of our home. On summer evenings, Allan and I would walk the mile and a half to the public square and enjoy Sunday evening concerts performed by local artists.

In August we would spend an exhausting day on the grounds of the Ohio State Fair. The cotton candy or the antics of the barkers on the midway were of little to no draw for us. But the performances in the stadium were outstanding, and one year we enjoyed the country and gospel music of the Statler Brothers. We both had grown up on farms and held a common agrarian interest; therefore a must-see for us was to visit the livestock exhibits.

Through our friends, Skip and Marilyn Shipman, and my niece, Jill Schumann, we were able to enjoy both high school and The Ohio State University marching bands. Skip and Marilyn's youngest daughter, Stephanie, was a majorette with the Worthington High School Band. It was a delight to attend a football game and watch the half-time show when Stephanie performed as the lead majorette. Jill, an OSU graduate, was able to get us tickets for the September 1985 football game between OSU and Washington State. My only interest was the halftime show, but for those who bled scarlet and gray, the Buckeyes won 48–32. My thrill was being seated in a place where I could see the designated band member with the sousaphone prance out and dot the "*i*" at the conclusion of the Script Ohio maneuver.

German Village, the historic neighborhood south of the city's downtown, is an area settled by German immigrants in the mid to late nineteenth century. They built sturdy, redbrick homes on brick tree-lined streets. Their small home lots were defined by wrought iron fences. To this delightful neighborhood, Allan and I would venture to enjoy the annual home and garden tour. If we were fortunate, we would be able to go through at least five of the ten homes on the tour before the lines became prohibitively long. Inside the small houses we marveled at the interior design that gave a feeling of spaciousness to the rooms. The perfectly groomed flower gardens that covered the small earthen areas were ablaze with flowers—aster, daisy, poppy, and yarrow to name a few.

There were several restaurants in German Village. It was on our first visit, only by chance, that we sauntered into Schmidt's Sausage Haus. We enjoyed the food and the ambiance; it became our favorite place to dine. Our second eatery choice was Max and Erma's (the original restaurant of the chain now found throughout the eastern and Midwestern United States).

A must-stop place each time we visited the village was The Book Loft—an independent bookstore in the heart of German Village that covered a city block. To enter, you walked up a tree-shaded brick path paralleled by planters overflowing with begonias and busy lizzies. Along the path were conveniently placed benches where you could sit, rest, or just people-watch. Once inside the store you could wander through rooms filled with books and stocked with CDs, DVDs, posters, racks of greeting cards, and other miscellanea. Soft music played over the sound system, providing an unspoken invitation to sit and browse with a book. On more than one occasion, we found it a challenge to wind our way back through the maze of rooms to the main exit.

A living history museum, the Ohio Village (depicting life in the 1860s), opened in 1974 on fifteen acres adjacent to the Ohio Historical Society. Of the twenty-two buildings on the grounds, the ones of special interest to Allan and me were the town hall, general store, blacksmith shop, cabinetmaker, schoolhouse, weaver, and Colonel Crawford Inn. In December the Madrigal Dinner at the Colonel Crawford Inn was a must-do event. When possible, Jill and Garvin Rumberger would join us for this traditional feast. At Christmas time we enjoyed the Ohio Village carolers who sang in the candlelit town hall.

In summer there were a variety of outdoor events. It was fun to watch an Ohio Village Muffins baseball game played according to nineteenth-century Knickerbocker Rules—e.g., in 1857 the length of the game was changed to nine equal innings; prior to that the first team to score twenty-one "aces" (runs) was the winner. Another time we sat under a large canopy on the center green and enjoyed watching and listening to an exceptionally talented jazz piano player.

I enjoyed visiting the Weaver's Shop to observe the person working the loom, with hands deftly interlacing the threads of the warp and the weft to produce intricate designs. I purchased several placemats in the Weaver's Shop for myself and as gifts.

My own nascent woodworking hobby made visiting the Woodwork Shop an experience in sensory pleasure as I inhaled the aroma of newly sawed, shaved, or sanded wood. It was here Allan and I bought a small Shaker-style cherrywood stand for Jill and Garvin's wedding present.

The Ohio Theater in downtown Columbus, across from the State House, was a favorite venue. Built in 1928 as one of Lowe's movie palaces, it was saved from demolition in 1969 and restored to its original majestic Spanish Baroque style. The Mighty Morton organ was a part of the theater restoration. Here Allan and I enjoyed Broadway shows and Columbus Symphony Orchestra concerts. During one Fourth of July celebration, we attended a rousing concert of John Philip Sousa marches. At Christmastime we took part in a Messiah sing-a-long in the theater.

———————————

FREQUENT AND LENGTHY TELEPHONE CALLS were the main means of communication with our families and friends, but some were persistent enough to follow us, and their visits were always welcome. My brother's oldest son, David, lived with his family in Atlanta, Georgia. On occasion David and Susy would visit Lloyd and Trudy in Geneva with their young sons, Matthew and Christopher. On their return trip to Atlanta, they would stop at our home in Worthington. Susy has since remarked that Worthington was a traveler's haven for them. A stop at 170 East Selby Boulevard meant an open-arms welcome, a meal, and freedom for the boys to run about before again being strapped into a car seat for the eight-plus-hour drive home.

Bruce and Linda, with children Bruce Allan and Candice, planned a visit. We knew the day of the family's arrival and were told to expect a call sometime in the late afternoon. We were at home waiting for their call when a knock came on our front door. Bruce and Linda, ever the ones for a surprise, had rented a car and located our house with no help from us. Imagine my astonishment when I opened the door and there stood

Candice and Bruce Allan, but no Dad or Mom. Bruce was behind a tree, taking pictures.

The previous owners left a large doghouse on our lot—a pitched-roof three-by-five-foot building. I had the great idea to make it into a playhouse for my grandchildren. The metamorphosis of the doghouse into a playhouse came about with a good cleaning, a coat of paint, and indoor/outdoor carpeting installed on the floor. It was dusk, that first night of the family's arrival before I had the opportunity to show my grandchildren their backyard playhouse. Candice's first remark, rather than enthusiastic, was one of disappointment. "It doesn't have any lights." Their dad went into the garage, found an extension cord with a light, and presto, lights illuminated the playhouse interior to the amusement of Candice.

The following day, Candice explored every room, every closet, every nook and cranny in our house; she even found the entrance to the small storage area, accessed only by walking under the basement stairs. It was her find, and she called it her "secret place" and admonished me not to let her brother know.

A visit to the Ohio Village was on the list. Candice and Bruce Allan attended class in the schoolhouse, where girls sat on one side of the room and boys sat on the other side. They shopped in the general store. Now living in Kent (where there is an annual black squirrel celebration), the black iron nutcracker squirrel that Bruce Allan bought for me is perched on my kitchen window shelf. I named him Samkin, and he looks out at his flesh-and-blood kin cavorting on the ground, scampering up the tree trunks, and nimbly hopping from branch to branch in the fir, oak, maple, cherry, and sassafras trees of my backyard.

Their ten-day visit was a whirlwind of activity. We also visited the Columbus Zoo and the Center for Science and Industry (COSI). We drove to Ashtabula/Geneva where Brenda planned a family gathering for the Schumann clan at her home. We spent the night with family members, and the next morning, before we returned to Worthington, Pete and Bev treated everyone to breakfast at the Treehouse.

I had in my possession a little brown suit that Sidney had worn as a child. Both Vernon and Bruce had worn their father's suit, and I wanted a picture of Bruce Allan wearing it. It was an effort on the part of Linda and me to get Bruce Allan (age two and a half) into the suit. His father managed to get one picture before his son's cries demanded that the suit be taken off.

Allan's son George with his wife, Rita, came to visit us in May 1986. Their home was in Thibodaux, Louisiana—Cajun country. Rita's reputation for preparing delicious Cajun food preceded her, and to our salivary delight, she brought with her the makings of a delicious crawfish-over-rice dinner that we enjoyed that first evening of their visit.

We spent Sunday touring the area, and for their wedding present, we treated them to a night's stay at the historic Worthington Inn. It was the Memorial Day weekend; on Monday we joined with hundreds of others who lined High Street in Old Worthington to watch the parade. Late that afternoon, we took them to the airport for their flight home.

Prior to George and Rita's May 1986 visit, George had visited us in July 1985. It was on this visit that George sensed his dad's health was failing. He made it possible for each of his three adult children (Nancy, twenty-seven; Scott, twenty; Georgia, nineteen) to come one by one for a weekend visit with their grandfather.

Scott was the first to come in October 1985. Each year Jill was able to get us tickets for one OSU football home game. That particular year, our tickets were for the Ohio State vs. Purdue game, and it was on the Saturday of Scott's visit. Allan did not feel well enough to attend the game, so I went with Scott.

We took Scott to the Book Loft in German Village, and from there to Ohio Village where we dined at the Colonel Crawford Inn. Sunday, Scott and his grandfather enjoyed watching some sporting events on television before we took him to the airport for his late afternoon flight home. I commented in my diary, "A wonderful weekend. Scott is a sensitive, considerate, intelligent young man—a grandson who makes his grandfather very proud."

Nancy's visit was next, in January 1986. Most of the hours of her weekend visit were spent with me, and we did "girl" things together. I took her to get her hair styled, and we shopped. We ate lunch at Schmidt's Sausage Haus in German Village and spent time in the Book Loft. Saturday evening, Nancy treated us to dinner at the Worthington Inn.

On Sunday morning, Allan and I attended church; Nancy remained at home. In the afternoon Nancy watched football with her grandfather. She asked if she could smoke, but Allan gave no reply. There, in the living room, watching TV, Nancy lit up her cigarettes, annoying the hell out of Allan. I know Allan thought his subtle nonverbal behavior would get the message across to Nancy. It didn't work, and I maintained neutrality during the ensuing frigid hours of her visit. (There had been too many incidents with Allan where I had tried to intercede on behalf of my sons that ended up with my being the emotionally distraught person.)

Georgia, the youngest of the siblings, visited in April 1986. She wanted to visit the OSU campus. Susan Shipman, the daughter of Skip and Marilyn, was a student there. We met her on campus, and she gave us a tour through some of the buildings. Georgia bought OSU sweatshirts at the bookstore and I treated the girls to lunch. That evening we again dined at the Worthington Inn. Sunday afternoon I took Georgia to see Meryl Streep in *Out of Africa*. Allan again remained at home, but he did come with me when we took Georgia to the airport.

George was thoughtful to provide a one-on-one opportunity for each of his three children to visit their grandfather. Tragically, Allan's failing health depleted his energy and did not allow for him to fully enjoy their visits. The serendipity for me—I did.

FORTUNATELY OUR FRIENDS CONTINUED TO VISIT. Gladys Bannister, a colleague who worked for the Ashtabula County Board of Education, came, so I requested a personal leave day, and the two of us played golf at the local Minerva Park course. When our neighbors on the hill in Ashtabula, Roz and Don Moulder, came for an overnight visit, the four of us enjoyed a Picnic with the Pops concert on the spacious lawn of a local industry. Fred and Myra Vermeulen surprised us by accepting an invitation to join us for the graduate organ recital of Susan Shipman at Hughes Hall on the OSU campus. We were thrilled when Sister Frances Flanigan, my friend from graduate school days at KSU, scheduled a visit. Her previous visit was when we lived in Ashtabula. We kept moving, and our friends kept following.

VISITING IS A TWO-WAY STREET. Allan and I knew this, and efforts were made to visit our family and friends. Whenever my school visitation schedule took me into northeastern Ohio, I would try to see my brother and sister and members of their families. In November 1984, when Pete and Bev hosted the traditional Thanksgiving dinner, Allan and I were invited to the Treehouse for the gathering of the Schumann clan.

Over the next two years, our out-of-state travels to visit family members were limited. Christmas of 1984 we were in Las Vegas. That was the year four-year-old Candice would say over and over, "I have the greatest idea." Then we were treated to the unique insight of a child's mind. We returned to Las Vegas the following Christmas. One year the California Fincher family came to Las Vegas to be with us; the next year Allan and I traveled to San Jose to be with them. In July of 1985, we took a few days to visit Allan's brother and sister-in-law in Michigan. The memorable event of that trip was the flat tire on our way home.

———————✦✦✦✦✦———————

I WAS EMPLOYED BY THE OHIO DEPARTMENT OF EDUCATION (ODE). It was housed in the Ohio Departments Building at Sixty-Five South Front Street. It is a magnificent building, and I think it important to digress and provide the reader with at least some scant information about this impressive edifice. In attempting to do this, I found myself at a loss for words. I am indebted to Mr. Jay Wuebbold, an employee of the Supreme Court of Ohio, who provided me with a copy of the *Thomas J. Moyer Ohio Judicial Center* booklet. (In 2004, more than a decade after I retired, this building became the permanent home of the state Supreme Court.) The information that follows was taken from this publication.

Funds were approved for the building prior to the stock market crash in 1929; construction started in 1930 and was completed in 1933. A prominent Cincinnati architect, Harry Hake, designed the building. Sculptors, artists, and artisans contributed their talents in the construction. When completed, the building became known as "Ohio's pride." Carved into the building's exterior facade are symbols depicting education, the arts, and sciences. Inside are grand hallways and august hearing rooms with wall murals that display the development and growth of late-nineteenth- and early-twentieth-century industry, construction, and agriculture. Throughout the building are bronze panels with bas-relief figures of Ohio government leaders, US presidents, and Ohio and Supreme Court justices. My favorite place was the entrance lobby off of Civic Center Boulevard where intricate mosaic designs cover the ceiling, and on the bronze elevator doors are life-size bas-relief figures of American Indians.

The ODE set the Minimum Standards for the schools. The responsibility for determining a school's compliance with the standards came under the auspices of the Department of Elementary and Secondary Education (DESE). Mary Poston was the director of this department. It was she who hired me.

My first day on the job was August 31, 1984. Floyd (Skip) Shipman, my friend who recommended me for the position, guided me through my first day in the office, introducing me to personnel and acquainting me with my new surroundings. One large room on the sixth floor accommodated most of the DESE staff. This room was sectioned off by moveable four-foot-high partitions that formed cubicles for the employees. I was delighted when Skip directed me to what would become my cubicle. It was in a row next to the windows, and I was amazed at the panoramic view I had overlooking the Scioto River.

My first week on the job was given over to endless meetings for new staff. We were inundated with stacks of paper forms that we would use to evaluate a district's compliance with the Minimum Standards. The standards were all-encompassing. They covered the physical plant, health and safety, school year, subjects, time allotments, and professional certification. The final day of that week, all DESE staff assembled. It was then I became aware there were about fifty personnel in the department.

Our house in Worthington was ten miles north of the building where I would work in downtown Columbus. Most days I drove, using the express route number 315. When there were hazardous driving conditions caused by heavy rain or snow, fearful of the irresponsible and aggressive drivers that used 315 as a speedway, I took High Street into the city.

I would park on the west side of the Scioto River and walk a half mile to the office building. I soon found the stairs that connected the floors and enjoyed climbing the 323 steps to the sixth floor. (Yes, I counted.) Days I didn't drive, I would walk from my home to High Street and take the express bus downtown. When in the office, seated at my desk all day, the walking and stair climbing gave me the opportunity for needed physical exercise.

As I became acquainted with my colleagues, on occasion I would join them for lunch. Eateries were in abundance in the midtown area, which was overrun with government employees. My favorite place to dine was the relaxed atmosphere of the dining room in Lazarus Department Store. Eating lunch with colleagues was a pleasant, but costly, social activity. There was a YMCA located three blocks from the office. Our lunch hour gave us a degree of flexibility (no time clocks) if not blatantly abused. I found I could walk to the YMCA, swim for thirty minutes, shower, dress, and return to the office in a little over an hour. Then, while working, I would eat lunch at my desk. I got my exercise and saved money—both to my liking. During the summer, I would walk a block to the State House, join the crowd seated on the lawn, and eat my lunch while enjoying the weekly concert featuring local talent.

There are 611 school districts in Ohio's eighty-eight counties. All school districts within a county were evaluated the same year. DESE evaluator teams would be assigned to schools within a county. Prepped by hours of meetings, loaded down with Minimum Standard materials, assigned to a two-person team—I was ready.

My first school assignment was in Ashtabula County in the Geneva School District. My teammate was Jody Wallace, another new hire. We were to be mentored by Lee Majesky, a man who had been with the DESE for many years. Lee introduced us to the evaluation protocol. We would first meet with the superintendent and relevant central office staff. Next Lee walked with us through a school pointing out what to look for when evaluating building safety and health standards. We visited each school within the district, met with the principal, and visited classrooms. All the while we carried our clipboard with the Minimum Standards checklist, making notes as we went. Before we left a district, we met again with the superintendent and gave a brief oral report of our findings.

Back in Columbus we wrote our report, which would be mailed to the superintendent regarding the district's compliance, or noncompliance, with the Minimum Standards. For me, it was difficult to check a noncompliance item when I knew a school district had a meager tax base and little money. Examples of this might be an inadequate school library, or special classes held in broom closets. These were referred to as unfunded mandates required by the state. (In *DeRolph v. State*, a landmark case in Ohio constitutional law, the Ohio Supreme Court ruled 4–3 on March 24, 1997, that the state's funding system for public education was unconstitutional. In part, the decision reads "fails to provide for a thorough and efficient system of common schools" and directed the state to find a remedy. Despite this landmark court decision, the underlying problem exists to this day.)

When schools were in session, my workweek would be given over to one day in the office and four days in the field. This meant three nights in motels. I was given a stipend for meals and lodging. With careful budgeting, it was barely adequate to cover expenses. I had the choice of using a state vehicle, requiring planning and paperwork, or driving my own car and reimbursement for mileage. I chose the latter.

My professional involvement in the schools that I visited was one-dimensional in my evaluator role with staff and students. I was from the state department, and my only job was to determine the school's compliance with the Minimum Standards. A consequence of this sterile relationship was a lack of incidents that made for good stories.

The one exception to this was with my colleague, Jody Wallace. Of all the people in the department with whom I worked over the years, it was Jody who became my best friend. Jody was a vivacious dark-haired, moderately tall, slender woman with a ready smile and infectious laugh. During our first school evaluation experience in Geneva, an incident occurred that we chuckle about to this day. We would spend our mornings working in the buildings, leave the school grounds at noon, and find a local restaurant where we would eat lunch with our mentor. This provided Jody and me with the opportunity to ask Lee questions and discuss compliance issues.

On this day, Jody and I ordered a salad; Lee ordered a burger. Our food arrived. Jody and I were savoring our salads, and it went unnoticed that Lee had scarfed down his burger. Suddenly Jody threw down her fork, salad veggies flying everywhere as she screamed, "A worm!" pointing at her hand. I looked, and sure enough, there was a tiny worm making its way up her index finger. The waitress rushed over, assessed the situation, immediately removed our food plates, and called the manager. He appeared, solicitously apologizing, and offered to provide us with another lunch—no charge. Lee had devoured his burger, so he wasn't hungry; Jody and I had lost our appetites and refused the offer. We hurriedly exited the restaurant with the unspoken question in our minds, "Was that the only worm in the lettuce?"

With any job, there are advantages and disadvantages. The same was true in my position with the DESE. On the plus side, there was diversity in my work. I traveled throughout Ohio and observed the beauty in the changing vegetation and topography that ranged from the flatlands of the northwest to the hilly south, where I drove on roads so narrow, steep, and winding that I feared for my safety. I visited schools that served children living in rural areas, small towns, and cities. I met administrators and teachers of all stripes.

The disadvantages were there too. During the school year, I was away from home three to four nights a week. I drove in very hazardous conditions—torrential rains, blinding snowstorms, and icy roads. The interaction with professional staff was fleeting. I missed the involvement with students. Staying in a motel and eating in restaurants was not to my liking. My job was incompatible with my marriage. Allan was home alone;

I was in a motel alone. Allan assured me he managed while I was away, but I knew in my heart he was lonesome.

In January 1986, I learned through Skip of a consultant position open in the nonpublic-school sector. I knew that only one consultant worked in this area and reported directly to Mary Poston. That appealed to me. Also, for the most part, visits to a nonpublic school could be made in one day. That meant I would not have to spend nights away from home. Immediately I contacted Mary Poston and told her I was interested. Then I waited. It was March before I learned the position was mine. Another month passed before I assumed my new responsibilities.

Nonpublic schools fall into two categories—religious or nonreligious affiliated. I worked with Catholic, Protestant, nondenominational, and Jewish religious-affiliated schools. In the nonreligious sector, I was involved with private schools—Montessori would be one example. Nonpublic schools in compliance with the Minimum Standards received a charter and were eligible for tax-funded state support.

I enjoyed the opportunity to be a one-person "department" within the DESE. Overall my job responsibilities were the same. Many nonpublic schools, especially those connected with churches or synagogues, started small with one, two, or three grades—K, K–1, K–2. Once a school was chartered, and as the children progressed, a request would be made to add grades to their charter. This gave me the opportunity to work closely with the staff of the school, and that was to my liking.

Again, there are few anecdotes I can relate relevant to my working in the nonpublic sector, but two do come to mind. The first involved a meeting I had with the principal of a small school. The day was cool, and rather than wear a coat, I chose my beige ultra-suede coat-style dress—loosely fit, buttons down the front, with a matching cloth belt. When I entered the principal's office, he motioned me to a chair but before I was seated offered to take my "coat." I thanked him, saying I was quite comfortable and sat down. Once seated, he again offered in an insistent voice to take my "coat." His insistence made me uncomfortable, but I again declined. No third offer was made. To this day I wonder what his reaction would have been had I replied, "Sir, this is not a coat, it is a dress. Do you want me sitting here in my slip?"

The second incident involved my contact with the rabbi of a synagogue where there was an interest to charter their school. My husband came with me on this visit, and Allan was invited by the rabbi to join us in his office. I presented the information and answered his questions. At the conclusion of the meeting, we stood, and as a professional courtesy in leaving, I extended my hand. He refused to take my hand, saying, "I can touch no woman but my wife, but I can shake your husband's hand." Then turning, to my embarrassment, he shook Allan's hand. I had failed to do my homework. It was an orthodox synagogue and the rabbi was an orthodox Jew.

‑‑‑‑‑‑‑‑‑‑‑+++++‑‑‑‑‑‑‑‑‑‑

ALLAN'S HEALTH WAS A CONCERN when we lived in Las Vegas, and again when we lived in Ashtabula. Had I used common sense—which 20/20 hindsight confirmed—I would have realized that the move to Worthington was one move too many for Allan. But my husband agreed to my career move, and I forged ahead. When I was in the field evaluating schools, Allan was home alone. Until his vision weakened, he managed the house and relaxed by reading and watching television. We talked by phone each evening and shared the interesting happenings of our day. It was a poor substitute for being together, but that was how we coped the fall of 1984 and through January of 1985.

On February 1, Allan appeared to have what I thought might be another TIA. His left side was partially paralyzed. We had no family doctor, so I went to our neighbor, Helen Romig, for help. Their doctor was not accepting new patients, but his young associate Dr. Ringle was. When I telephoned the office, I was able to speak directly with Dr. Ringle and explained to him that Allan was adamant about not going to the ER. Dr. Ringle came to the house and entered the bedroom. He gave Allan a cursory physical examination. Then sitting on the edge of the bed, he quietly explained what he thought needed to be done.

Allan was calmed by Dr. Ringle's presence and agreed that I could take him to Riverside Methodist Hospital (three miles from our home) where he was admitted on February 2. Over the next three days, tests confirmed there was a blockage in Allan's right carotid artery; the left was clear due to a previous surgery in 1978 while living in Harrisburg, Pennsylvania. Allan came home on February 6, and on February 9 we met with the cardiovascular surgeon. He showed Allan an X-ray of his blocked right carotid artery that convinced him surgery was necessary. We returned home, and over the next few days Allan and I had soul-searching talks related to his end-of-life wishes. Allan also consulted an attorney to be assured his financial wishes were legally documented.

Allan's surgery was scheduled for Monday, February 11. I telephoned Brenda, who still lived in Kingsville, and asked her to be with me. There was a severe snowstorm on Sunday. Allan had been admitted to the hospital for his surgery, and I was with him that evening when Brenda walked into his room. We both heaved a sigh of relief, knowing she had driven over hazardous road conditions to be with us. After a short visit with Allan, we drove home. I poured Brenda and myself a drink; we sipped our bourbon and talked well into the early morning hours. It was calming for my troubled soul to have my sister with me.

The morning of Allan's surgery, I packed up the projector and several carousels of slides with the hope it would entertain as we whiled away the hours waiting. It worked. Allan asked the time only twice during our two-and-a-half-hour slideshow. It was twelve forty-five when the nurse came and wheeled Allan off to surgery. Knowing it would be several hours, Brenda and I left the hospital. I treated her to a leisurely lunch at the Worthington Inn. We returned to the hospital waiting room at two thirty. At three fifteen the surgeon appeared and informed me all had gone well, Allan was resting comfortably in recovery. The surgeon went on to report the artery was 95 percent blocked; Allan had missed the bullet of a major stroke. I would not be able to see my husband until he was in his room, so I used the time to telephone our children to let them know everything went well. We were waiting in Allan's room when he was wheeled in at seven thirty. Brenda and I spent a short time with him before returning home. It had been a long day.

Brenda stayed the night and left in the morning. Allan's recovery was rapid. When I visited him the following afternoon, I took with me two freshly baked brownies that he inhaled with a cup of hot tea. It was the third day after his surgery that I brought him home. Entering the house, I settled Allan comfortably on the love seat in our living room. As I turned to leave, he asked me to sit for a moment beside him on the sofa. Allan took my hands, tenderly held them, and told me of his love for me. It was an affectionate moment, one I recorded in my diary that Valentine's Day, 1985.

THE SURGERY WAS MINIMALLY SUCCESSFUL, which gave us a "new normal." Allan's hiccoughs returned. This time they lasted for fourteen days. No medications worked. Dr. Ringle prescribed a tranquilizer that gave Allan some relief so he could sleep. It was during this time that a telephone call came from George and Rita. They were married at Lake Tahoe; Jan and Royce were with them. It was difficult for Allan to convey congratulations or speak with enthusiasm in his voice due to the hiccoughs.

My job required me to be in the field, but Allan could not be left alone. I used the services of an at-home care group, but he was uncomfortable with a stranger in the house. Jan came and stayed with her dad for a short time. It was during her visit that Allan had a night consumed with fantasy and nightmares that scared Jan. She telephoned me the next day at the school where I was working, and I immediately went home.

Jan needed to leave, but Allan would not have a caregiver in the house. How could I continue to work and at the same time care for my husband? My prayer was answered when Lloyd telephoned and said he and Trudy would like to have Allan come and stay with them during his convalescence.

Allan readily accepted. He stayed with Lloyd and Trudy from February 28 through March 8. While with them, Allan regained enough strength that he was able to make a flight from Cleveland to New Orleans on March 9, where he then stayed with his son and family for a week. I was at the Cleveland Airport on March 16 to meet Allan's flight. I stood at the end of the concourse waiting for him to appear. When I saw Allan, I was amazed at how well he looked. It was apparent he had regained much of his strength. The week spent with his family out of the cold of the north, basking in the warmth of bayou country, held beneficial healing powers.

--- ‡‡‡‡‡ ---

I REALIZED ALLAN NEEDED TO BE WITH ME when I was in the field evaluating schools, but that was not a good solution. We were at dinner one evening when Allan fainted. Another time he went for a walk during the day while I was at a school, became confused, and needed help back to the motel.

The most disconcerting episode of all happened at a motel Jacuzzi. I had finished swimming; Allan was enjoying himself in the Jacuzzi and was not ready to leave. I returned to our room, showered, and started to dress before I realized he was not there. Concerned, I hurriedly walked back to the pool area to find Allan sprawled out on a poolside lounge chair. His skin was ashen. Somehow, he had gotten out of the Jacuzzi before collapsing; no one in the pool area had noticed. An ambulance was called, and the EMR team appeared. By then Allan had semirecovered and, against medical advice, signed the paper refusing to be taken to the hospital. We returned to our room. The water in the Jacuzzi was too warm, and Allan had stayed in too long.

The new normal was not an easy adjustment for either of us. Allan's health continued to decline. His vision weakened; he no longer enjoyed his lifelong habit of reading. He lost hand/finger coordination that, combined with weakened vision, made it a challenge to press the small buttons on the TV remote. He gave up watching television. He stopped taking solo walks in the neighborhood. Allan just existed. There were no activities/interests to replace what he had lost. Sex became an issue. Allan's disorientation worsened. He grew depressed.

In July 1985, I scheduled an appointment for Allan with Dr. Ringle that resulted in his wearing a heart monitor which confirmed his heart was not working properly. Dr. Ringle prescribed a blood thinner, explaining it should increase blood flow and minimize his confusion and lack of coordination.

In October, Jan again came to spend time with her dad. Her presence lifted both of us out of our days of endless despair. Prior to leaving, Jan took me aside and shared observations made during the time she was with her dad—constant chatter, confusion, dependency, lethargy, no "fight." It only confirmed what I had been seeing.

We both had hoped the right carotid artery surgery would be as beneficial to Allan as the left surgery in 1978. In truth it did not happen, but we lived life to the fullest, accepting his limitations. On July 3 Allan joined me after work in downtown Columbus to view the fireworks display. We found a place to sit, along with thousands of other spectators, on the banks of the Scioto River. There we enjoyed musical and theatrical entertainment until darkness fell. Then, with faces turned toward the sky, the crowd remained transfixed for the next thirty minutes as the heavens became ablaze with dazzling colors and shapes. The fireworks ended as Tchaikovsky's *1812 Overture* played over the loudspeakers, and the entire sky burst with the unexplainable energy of the grand finale.

Another musical venue that summer took place on the manicured grounds of a local industry. We enjoyed pleasant evenings dining from our picnic basket while listening to the Columbus Symphony Orchestra perform their monthly Picnic with the Pops concert.

We ignored the health problems that Allan faced and went to New York City in April of 1985 to celebrate our twenty-third wedding anniversary. We strolled Fifth Avenue, admired the recently constructed brass and glass of Trump Tower (today very much in the news as Donald Trump was elected the forty-fifth President of the United States in 2016). We boarded a double-decker bus and enjoyed the tour through Central Park, China Town, the Battery, with a stop at the First Presbyterian Church (often referred to as Old First). That night, too tired to enjoy dinner in a restaurant, we bought food in a deli and returned to our hotel room, then put our feet up, relaxing with a drink, to reflect on our glorious day in NYC. Our visit to the city included the Rodgers and Hammerstein musical, *The King and I.* It was a getaway weekend, and we both were thankful that Allan experienced no health problems to mar our enjoyment.

———— ·+++++· ————

AFTER HIS SURGERY, Allan continued to drive his car, but an incident occurred in October 1985 that gave both of us cause for grave concern. Allan had driven to the grocery store, purchased groceries, and returned to the parking lot, but could not locate his car. A good Samaritan came to his rescue. I was outside washing windows when I saw Allan drive past our house, apparently not realizing where he was. I anxiously watched for his return, wondering what to do, when five minutes later he pulled in our drive. It was then Allan realized it would be best if he gave up driving.

His 1972 Plymouth sat in our garage for months. Allan would wait for me to come home, and then we would take care of any shopping and business errands. When we stopped for gas, our in-joke with the pump attendant was, "I pump, Allan pays." Allan was taking a blood thinner and needed to have regular blood draws. I would be at work, and he would take a cab. This dependency on others was difficult for Allan to accept.

March 2, 1986, was a sad day in our lives. With Allan in agreement, I made the arrangements to donate the 1972 Plymouth to the Volunteers of America. I wanted us to do this together, so it was on a Sunday afternoon that we drove to their downtown used-car lot. I parked the car; we got out and walked the short distance to the lot office. It was Allan who dropped the car's keys into the secure deposit box by the office door. We joined hands as we left the lot and silently walked the two blocks to High Street. We boarded a city bus that took us the ten miles north to Selby Boulevard. Once there we exited the bus and continued our silent hand-holding walk the long block to our home. For the first time in our marriage, we were a one-car family.

—————— ‧+++++‧ ——————

EASTER SUNDAY, MARCH 30, 1986, Allan and I attended the breakfast and service at our church. It was a beautiful day, and as I drove home, Allan suggested we go to the local driving range to hit some golf balls. We hurriedly ate our lunch, changed our clothes, and were off. On our way to the range, Allan asked me to detour into the Worthington High School parking lot. He wanted to drive our new car. (After we donated Allan's car, I sold mine and purchased a 1986 four-door Polar Silver Jetta). Allan got behind the wheel of the Jetta, and for a short time enjoyed maneuvering the car around the vacant lot. It was the last time he drove. We continued to the golf range, rented two buckets of balls, stood on the practice tee, and amused ourselves as we sliced, hooked, dribbled, even whiffed, and occasionally watched as one of our shots sailed straight and far out onto the practice range. When our buckets were empty, we returned home to savor the Cornish hens I had prepared for our dinner. We shared a pleasant day together, and it was that evening that Allan took my hand and said, "We expect our wives to be miracle workers." No further explanation was given, nor was it needed.

In truth I was not a miracle worker. I did my best, but the stress of my work and Allan's health took their toll. Each morning my prayer was, "God, give me strength and patience for this day." I was facing a health problem of my own. My right hip became very painful (bursitis). It was then I came to the realization that when pain and pride collided, I should pocket my pride and use the cane. I consulted an orthopedic specialist and learned I was a candidate for a hip replacement within the next five to ten years. I was advised to keep my weight under control (I had dealt with this problem all my life), use a cane, and take pain pills.

—————— ‧+++++‧ ——————

IT WAS NOT TOO LONG after our move to Worthington that we received a letter from Bruce inquiring about our retirement plans. Bruce and Linda were discussing the possibility of communal living for interested family members, and this would include Allan and me. With Allan's weakening condition, the idea of returning to Las Vegas was of interest to both of us.

But the need for me to independently assure my financial security reared its ugly head. It was something we could not consider until I had more years in the Ohio retirement system.

———— ++++++ ————

I CONTINUED WITH MY WORK at the DESE and hoped that the status quo would be continue. Unfortunately, on Saturday, May 3, 1986, Allan fell down the basement stairs. He landed at the bottom, bent but not broken. I was able to move him to our bedroom, made him comfortable in bed, and placed ice on his bruised body. That night he was restless. Sunday morning when he awoke, I could not get him out of bed; he felt cold and clammy to my touch. I called the emergency squad. He was taken to the Methodist Hospital ER where he was examined, medications prescribed, released, and I brought him home.

A bright spot in our lives was a call from Bruce to let us know he'd be coming for a visit prior to attending a June 2 seminar with IDS American Express in Chaska, Minnesota. Bruce arrived on May 29, and over the Memorial Day weekend, together with Allan's help, we constructed a fifty-foot-by-four-foot brick walk along the side of the driveway in preparation for a blacktop resurfacing. What would have been backbreaking work for me was fun with Bruce's help. He left on Sunday to attend the seminar.

I was in the process of having dental implants, and my next implant was scheduled on June 6. Knowing I would be sedated and not able to drive home, I called a cab to take me to the dental office. Later I recorded in my diary, "Allan felt so bad for me. When the taxi came, as I was going out the door, he hugged me and cried." The implant procedure took about two hours, and while I was in the chair, the assistant told me my husband had called to ask how I was doing. She assured him I was okay. Allan didn't feel well enough to come with me, but his telephone call was a poignant reminder of the feeling of helplessness that consumed him and the deep love he felt for me.

I had purposely scheduled the procedure for a Friday, allowing myself the weekend to recover before work on Monday. Saturday was a pleasant day at home. I rested, Allan and I watched movies, and that night I slept very well. On Sunday I fixed a manicotti and meat casserole for Allan, soup for myself. As we sat down at the dining room table, Allan said, "I think we should give thanks," to which I responded that I would like him to. We bowed our heads, and Allan, in his slow, halting, methodical way, gave a beautiful prayer thanking God for his family, his children, and his life with me. His life was full, and I was to him all a man could want in a wife. It was a sentimental moment. As a couple we had overcome personal, professional, and marital challenges to become inseparable as husband and wife.

Not wanting to disturb Allan, I had been sleeping on the sofa bed in our basement recreation room. One Sunday morning I had awakened early, went upstairs to the bathroom, and noted Allan was still asleep in our king-size bed. Still sleepy myself, I crawled in beside him, and what followed was one of those tender, unplanned beautiful moments of intimacy.

On Monday, June 9, I planned to go into the office for only half a day. I went home at noon. Allan wanted to go to the bank. We did, and then on to the grocery store where we followed our routine of each taking our own cart—Allan to find the mark-down items, while I picked up the needed groceries. Back home, both quite tired, we rested for a time before I went out to work on the brick patio project at the back of the house. Allan joined me, handing me the bricks as I placed them on the sand-bed base of the patio. About five o'clock we'd finished one section, and I went into the kitchen to fix a snack. I looked out the kitchen window and saw Allan shoveling sand from the pile into the wheelbarrow. Thinking this would be a good photo op to capture for posterity, I grabbed the camera and went outside. In my first attempt to frame Allan in the picture, the sun was shining directly into the camera's lens. I started to reposition myself to take full advantage of the sunlight, when Allan suddenly dropped the shovel, grabbed his sides, and cried, "I've got to sit down."

He sat on the patio chair and complained of pain in his chest. I managed to get him into the house, through the kitchen, into the bedroom, and onto our bed. I immediately telephoned Dr. Ringle. He came to the house, examined Allan, and was not able to determine the cause of his pain. He directed me to take him to the ER at Riverside Methodist Hospital. He assured me he would shortly be there himself.

We arrived at the ER; Allan was immediately taken in for evaluation. Once he was settled, the medical staff informed me there were orders for several tests that would take up to two hours. I was feeling quite faint from lack of nourishment (my mouth was healing from the dental surgery) and wanted to return home and get some soup for my supper. As Allan was about to be wheeled away for the first of his tests, I tenderly kissed him and told him I loved him before we were parted. As I left the ER, I was given a direct-line number to call so I could check on Allan's condition.

Once home, I enjoyed a bowl of soup before calling the hospital. I spoke with a nurse who told me Allan's tests were completed (X-ray, EKG, and blood work); he was resting comfortably. Just as I was about to leave the house to return to the hospital, the telephone rang, and it was Bruce. He called to find out how I was doing from my dental surgery. I assured him I was okay and then told him about his dad. We talked for about fifteen minutes.

I left the house and drove to the hospital. When I entered the ER, I was met by a member of the ER staff, who ushered me into a small waiting room. The hospital chaplain came in. He told me the doctors were with Allan and continued by saying it would be best if I called someone to be with me. Dr. Ringle entered and informed me that. Allan had been "coded." He asked if any life-sustaining procedures should be used. Although my head started to spin, my mind was clear on this issue, and my immediate answer was, "No." Allan and I had discussed this at length, and Allan's living will verified this decision.

Dr. Ringle left, only to return within five minutes to tell me that Allan had died. The cause of death was a dissecting aneurysm of the aorta. This was surreal. It could not be happening. I was emotionally paralyzed. Someone asked me whom they might call. I gave the name of my good friends, the Shipmans. Floyd and Marilyn came. Marilyn, driving my car, took me home and stayed the night. It was June 9, 1986.

———— ++++++ ————

AT SOME POINT I must have made the necessary phone calls. The following morning Jane Mycrantz, assistant pastor of our church, stopped to see me. Her strength, her calming presence, was solace for my weary body and soul. George was the first of the children to arrive; Bruce's plane was due about the same time, so we waited together at the airport. Jan and Royce with Renee arrived that evening.

The funeral service was scheduled for June 11 at the Jack W. Ross Funeral Home in Ashtabula. Few knew us in the Worthington area, and Ashtabula was close enough to Kent that Allan's friends could be at the service. Fred Vermeulen, although retired, was still living in Ashtabula. He officiated, delivering a powerful tribute to Allan's life. Brenda prepared a buffet for family and guests, and we assembled at her home following the service. I spent the night in the Treehouse with Pete and Bev.

We remained in the Ashtabula area the following day and left on Friday the thirteenth (a day that was anathema to you, dear Allan) for Michigan. Allan's childhood home was on Fourteen Mile Road out of Farmington. His ashes were to be interred in the Dickie family plot at the Farmington Cemetery.

Allan was the youngest, and the last living, of the seven Dickie siblings. There were other family members who joined us for the brief graveside service. I spoke first, and my words were, "We honor Allan Dickie by gathering here today. First you were my teacher, then my husband, father to my sons, but best of all, my friend and soul mate."

Bruce spoke next, "You came into my life at a time when I needed a father."

Allan's children were there and they spoke lovingly of their father, but I did not record their words. As we left the graveside, our love for this talented man was evidenced by our tears.

We left the cemetery, and the families parted. George, Jan, Royce, and Renee drove to the Detroit Airport for their respective flights home. Bruce and I were together in the Jetta on our drive back to Worthington. I recorded in my diary one especially cogent comment that Bruce made during that drive. "Had we written the script for Allan's passing we couldn't have done it better. All, with the exception of Vern, got to be with Dad the last months of his life. I was the fortunate one; I was the last to be with him."

—————————

Prior to leaving for Allan's service in Ashtabula, I had made arrangements for the drive to be blacktopped. Now back home, Bruce drove the Jetta over "The Allan Dickie Memorial Parkway" into the garage. Bruce stayed with me for two more days. On June 16 I took him to the airport. I noted in my diary, "We must get on with our lives." I slept well that night, and on Tuesday, June 17, I returned to work.

—————————

Allan knew an unfulfilled heart's desire of mine was to own a string of pearls. It was in April 1986 that he gave me an opera-length string of uniform cultured pearls—a combined fifty-sixth birthday and twenty-third wedding anniversary gift. Allan must have had a premonition that he would not live for us to celebrate our silver anniversary.

SIXTEEN

+ + ◆ ◆ ◆ + +

LIVING ALONE

I WAS TWENTY-NINE YEARS OLD when Sidney died. The shock, the agony of loss, the heartache was all there, but not the loneliness. I had two young sons to raise—Bruce age seven, and Vernon age eleven. I had family in the area who supported me emotionally, helped me maintain my home, and provided financial assistance as needed. A third-year student at Kent State University, it was important that I complete my undergraduate degree, enabling me to support my children. There was no time to be lonesome.

I was fifty-six years old when Allan died. The shock, the agony of loss, the heartache were all there, and added to that was the loneliness. My sons were married and living in the West; other family members lived miles away. Several had died. For the first time in my life, I experienced the reality of living alone. I missed Allan. I missed his companionship—he was my soul mate. At the time of Allan's death in June, due to poor sleep habits related to my dental surgery, I slept in the basement recreation room. It was not until November that I was able to return to sleep alone in our king-size bed.

When Sidney died, our finances were simple. Good financial planning, miserly frugality, and hard work provided me with a home, personal items, and a car, all debt-free. When Allan died we were debt-free; I had an adequate income as long as I worked and was also assured of financial security in my retirement. Allan had made a distribution of assets to family members prior to his death, relieving me of any misunderstandings that might have arisen. It was left to me to do what I thought best with his personal items. These I distributed among his two children and five grandchildren.

At the time of Allan's death, it was requested that donations be made to the KSU Chemistry Department. In August I received a letter from Norman V. Duffy, department chairman, thanking me for contributions received and informing me the funds would be used for a onetime Allan Dickie Scholarship Award. Decades later, wanting the memory of this dedicated professor to live on and to recognize Allan's roll as my mentor, I funded the Dickie-Nelson Scholarship in Education and the Sciences in January 2013.

Eight days after Allan died, I returned to work. As it happened, Marilyn Shipman walked in the building the same time as I. Seeing her, I was overcome with emotion and became so weak I was barely able to stand. Marilyn's soft-spoken words were a comfort, but I needed time to regain my composure, and for that reason did not ride the elevator with her but took the stairs. Once seated in my office cubicle and looking out of the window at the panoramic view of the river, calmness returned.

Prior to Allan's death I was reassigned to the nonpublic-school sector. I liked this position in the department; I was able to function independently, responsible only to the director. I spent a lot of time, either in the field or in the office, working with individuals who wanted to charter their start-up schools. The idea came to me that I could develop a New School Workshop. I would meet in the office with interested groups, answer their questions, and supply them with informational materials. The workshop was a success and enabled me to devote needed hours to other demands of my position.

In the nonpublic schools I was able to have a closer working relationship with teachers and administrators than I experienced in the public schools. It came to my attention that the nonpublic schools were being given short shrift by the secretarial pool in the preparation of required paperwork for their charter. I made my annoyance known to Annie, the head of the secretarial pool. Annie did not take this lightly, as it was she who assigned what work was to be done and who was to do it. I'd stepped on her professional toes, and her professional nose was totally reconfigured.

Due to this incident with Annie, I had to appear before the secretarial grievance committee. Nothing came of it, other than I was censured for challenging the secretarial pool protocol by questioning the authority of the person in charge. Lesson learned. After that I carefully followed protocol and avoided Annie.

My compulsion to overeat under stress returned and with it another vice—an increased amount of alcohol consumption. In my struggle to regain discipline with my eating and drinking, I resorted to intense physical activity.

Being a do-it-yourselfer, I filled the hours of the long summer evenings with maintaining the house and lot. There was the lawn to be mowed, windows to be washed, gutters to be cleaned. I seal-coated the driveway and painted the recently erected utility barn. I ordered shrubs from the nursery, and when the variegated dogwood, smoke bush, and chokeberry were delivered, I planted them along the back property line.

On rare occasions I would take time to sit on the patio and watch the birds flutter from tree to tree, seemingly not disturbed by the ever-present squirrels. One morning as I was sitting and enjoying my cup of coffee, I suddenly became aware of the large pile of dirt in the middle of the yard, left over from the patio excavation. Immediately I visualized a flower garden.

Supplies were needed. I learned of a source for used railroad ties, made the necessary contact, and ordered enough ties to form the periphery of a raised garden that would measure approximately eight by twelve feet. I rented a sod cutter, and with the help of friends, the sod was removed and the ties were placed. To help enrich the soil of the dirt pile, I purchased peat moss and cow manure. The weekend that I planned to work on the raised garden, Bobbie Jalali, my former daughter-in-law, and her children (from another marriage) visited. As we worked together to layer the soil with the peat moss and manure, ten-year-old Shanna remarked, "This is like making a lasagna." Somehow the recipe of dirt, manure, and peat moss as lasagna ingredients elicited peals of laughter from her mother and me, and it was immediately christened The Lasagna Garden.

About this time, I read in the local paper that bricks were being removed from a city street in Old Worthington and were available for any interested resident. This was a piece of Worthington history, and the thought came to me that I could use the bricks to made a path in my garden. I got up at dawn for several mornings, drove to the brick pile, filled my trunk, and returned home to unload the bricks, all before going to the office. It was exhausting work, but I did get enough bricks for the garden path. A specialist from the local nursery aided me in the selection of plants that were color and size appropriate. As summer turned to fall, the Lasagna Garden became a blaze of beauty, but the greatest benefit to me was the intense physical activity that helped me cope with Allan's death.

The Worthington Presbyterian Church filled a needed spiritual place in my life. Neither Allan nor I wore our religion on our sleeve or proselytized, but I wrote in my diary on January 11, 1987, "God, I am thankful Allan felt the desire to express his thoughts to you in prayer that last Sunday of his time on this earth. I thank you for being there when I need you. You are a source of comfort in times of grief; you are there to share my times of joy."

An uncontrollable emotion surfaced the first time I attended church after Allan's death. I remember walking into the sanctuary, looking about for a place to sit, and observing a lady seated alone. Looking up, she greeted me with a welcoming smile. I sat down next to her. During the service my grief silently surfaced. The lady, Lynn Porter, noticed and, in a comforting gesture, placed her hand on mine. When the service ended, Lynn introduced herself and invited me to join her and others for lunch at a nearby restaurant. That was the beginning of a lasting friendship.

I took part in a Bible study class at the church, but a more spiritually rewarding experience was to become a Stephen Minister (SM). Stephen Ministry is a lay caregiving ministry that supplements pastoral care in the church. Laypersons provide one-on-one support to individuals who request help in times of loneliness, death, or for any personal need. To become certified as an SM, one must take part in fifty hours of study that are divided into weekly sessions over the period of one year.

When I completed the course, I was assigned to a lady who requested SM help. Peggy had an alcohol problem, and I went with her to weekly AA meetings. Over the course of the year, I found the SM experience not only beneficial for Peggy, but beneficial to me as well. It gave me a sense of helping another human being—a feeling of being needed.

Family, friends, and colleagues were there for me by means of telephone calls, notes, and visits. I felt their love, their concern, but my deepest feelings of loneliness remained unspoken as I did not want to add to their worry.

Plans had been made for Trudy, with Beverley and Adam, to visit Allan and me in June. Trudy was reluctant to come, but I did persuade her that their visit would be welcome. Trudy and Lloyd had lived in Worthington in the 1960s when Lloyd attended OSU. It was interesting to drive through an area familiar to Trudy as she pointed out some of the changes that had occurred. We browsed the shops in Old Worthington. In one of the shops, Beverley noted some Southwestern Indian prints that were to her liking.

(Beverley had lived with her parents in the Southwest.) I was pleased she allowed me to purchase them for her home. We visited the Columbus Zoo, Ohio Village, German Village including the Book Loft, and spent time in the Park of Roses. When they departed on Sunday, my feeling of sadness returned, but it was a good feeling in the sense that their visit confirmed the close connection I had to ones who loved me very much.

Allan's children and their spouses visited, and our time together was spent in enjoyable activities and meaningful conversation. Jill and Garvin came at the end of November, and with Jody, the four of us enjoyed the Madrigal Dinner feast at the Ohio Village Colonel Crawford Inn.

Whenever possible, I arranged my school visitation schedule to be in Northeast Ohio so I could attend family events or just enjoy a weekend visit with my siblings and families. I was there in July 1986 for my niece Shellie Gibson's wedding (it was hot). On other occasions, I spent time with my brother and his family, enjoyed a friendly (but competitive) game of golf, or a Saturday night square dance.

Thanksgiving 1986, the traditional Schumann Thanksgiving dinner was held at Lloyd and Trudy's home. The extended family was seated around the table. Prior to dinner, it was traditional for each person to give a short statement of thanks. When it came my turn, I had in my hand a small replica statue of the American eagle, one I had purchased in 1976 at the time of the country's bicentennial celebrations. For me the eagle represented Allan's place as the family patriarch—one who nurtured and had vision. After Allan's death, I wanted Lloyd to have the statue. I always thought of my brother as having these same character traits. Now he was the oldest family member—the patriarch. I began my eulogy for Allan and the feelings of my loss surfaced and, with it, the emotion. At that moment I felt a small arm placed around my shoulder by Stephanie Van Buren, a five-year-old member of the extended family. In her childish loving voice, she whispered in my ear, "I know how you feel. My cat died."

WHEREVER I LIVED, I made the effort to remain in touch with past friends. After Allan died, I needed all my friends—past as well as present. My former daughter-in-law Bobbie was no exception. She'd remarried and had two children, Shanna and Michael. A detailed explanation is unnecessary as to why or how, but I did become the children's surrogate Gran Henri. Bobbie lived in Kent, and I encouraged her visits. Shanna spent weekends with me. We would play board games, swim at the pool, and visit area places of interest. One weekend we baked rye bread, and when Shanna left on the bus for home, she took several loaves of bread with her that were proudly shared with her family. I enjoyed Shanna's visits. When she was with me, there was no time to be lonesome.

I welcomed all visits from my friends; they kept the loneliness at bay. Sister Frances Flannigan, my KSU graduate school friend, spent a night with me. Gladys Bannister, Ashtabula County supervisor, brought her golf clubs that made her weekend visit most enjoyable. I traveled to Kent and played golf with my Hudson School friend Dodie Snyder, enjoyed lunch with Mabelle Apley from the Left Over Team bowling days with Kent City Schools, visited with longtime friends Ralph and Marie Hartzell, and stayed with Janet Hoover.

In September I was in Ashtabula and visited my dear friend Jennie Brown at the nursing home. She was on oxygen, catheterized, so weak she could hardly speak, but it was obvious she enjoyed the hours I spent with her. The nurse informed me that her cancer had metastasized to her lungs, and they were filling with fluid. She died in October. I did not attend her funeral; I sent a dozen yellow roses and requested that one of the roses be placed in her casket. In this way I mourned the loss of a dear friend.

I had two neighbors who were especially attentive. The Romigs (retired missionaries) invited me to their home on numerous occasions for dinner. Just being in their presence, their nonverbal support that communicated their inner strength, gave me a feeling of comfort. I also took long walks and had long talks with Susan Fisher, the mother of Heather and Michael. Susan was a good listener.

I was pleasantly surprised by the support I received from many of my colleagues. Hazeldean Stent belonged to a quilt group, and she invited me to join them one evening. I had not quilted for years, but I accepted the invitation and took with me an unopened box that contained a Thirteen Colonies quilt kit. I remember that first meeting. The gals were seated in a circle, and each, in turn, shared their needlework projects. When it came my turn, I picked up my box, removed the lid, and tore off the paper covering, revealing hundreds of pieces of precut material. There was no way I could start my needlework project that evening. The gals made some innocuous comments and returned their attention to their own projects. Later, it was Brenda who told me to just start and "not get tied up in your underwear." With that sage advice, I threaded my needle and took the first stitch. It was many years later before the Thirteen Colonies quilt was finished.

When one of my coworkers in the department learned that the Chippendales (a touring dance troupe of men known for their striptease performances) were appearing in one of the area night spots, a group of us decided to go. It promised to be a risqué evening, so I eagerly agreed to be part of this ultimate girls' night out. Six of us, giddy with excitement, arrived early and commandeered a table directly in front of the stage. Drinks were ordered; we sipped, laughed, chatted as we anxiously waited for the show to begin. The houselights dimmed, the music reached an ear-shattering pitch. With spotlights dancing on the stage, several sexy, muscular, partially clothed young men pranced out.

Amidst this pandemonium the lights went out—total blackness and then total silence before an undercurrent of panic erupted. A man with a flashlight walked onto the stage, announced there was a power outage, and admonished us to stay calm and remain seated. One of the girls in our group began to gasp, terrified of the dark. We were unable to help her regain her composure. There were no lit exit signs. It was not total darkness outside, and I noted an open doorway and escorted her out. She would not return; her forebodings of disaster were too real. The other four gals joined us outside. We assessed the situation and, for the first time, realized we were in a converted warehouse building, and left. Disappointed I didn't see the show? Of course, I'd be lying if I said I wasn't. Relieved for my safety? Yes, yes—a thousand times, yes!

Jody Wallace and I bonded in friendship from the beginning, from the time of the incident with the worm found in her lunch salad. One Saturday in April, Jody and I were to go biking in the afternoon, but the weather was threatening. Jody telephoned and suggested I come by her home at two thirty, and we could go to the antique show at the fairgrounds. When I rang the doorbell, and Jody opened her door, I was flabbergasted to see a room filled with my colleagues. Jody had planned a surprise birthday party for me. I was deluged with crazy gag gifts. There was a table laden with refreshments and placed in the center of the table was a birthday cake on a pedestal cake stand (her grandmother's). Jody knew of my families' birthday cake tradition—a three-layer cake on a pedestal cake stand, or it wasn't a birthday cake. My fifty-seventh birthday celebration in 1987 is a memory I cherish to this day.

Years later Jody was diagnosed with histoplasmosis—an infection caused by breathing in spores of a fungus often found in bird and bat droppings. The disease affects primarily the lungs, but for Jody it was her eyes.

Jody was unable to drive, and many times I was able to be of help to this special friend.

————— ++++++ —————

SOLO TRAVEL WAS DIFFICULT FOR ME, but that did not keep me at home. In August 1986, Bruce and Linda invited me to join them in Boston. Boston Whaler boats were sold by their family owned company, Dry Dock Boat Sales, in Las Vegas. Bruce and Linda were the sales representatives for the business at the boat show in Boston. I eagerly accepted their invitation and met them the evening of the nineteenth (Tuesday) in their hotel room.

On Wednesday morning, I went with Bruce and Linda to tour the Boston Whaler factory and saw firsthand how the boats advertised to be "unsinkable" were built. That afternoon we boarded a tourist trolley, and our first stop was to view the USS *Constitution* (Old Ironsides); back on the trolley we continued our tour to Beacon Hill. Here we ate lobster at a restaurant on the wharf. The venue was perfect, but the dinner only confirmed my dislike of lobster.

Thursday morning, we checked out of the hotel and spent our second day being tourists. We walked to Paul Revere Park (Allan and I had been there many years ago), entered the Old North Church and sat in one of the pews, toured Paul Revere's home, and listened to a lecture at Faneuil Hall. Here Bruce asked a question about the state of Nevada, and the guide was quick to respond that Nevada was a territory, not a state, at the time related to the question. The three of us were equally impressed with the guide's knowledgeable grasp of history.

Leaving Faneuil Hall, we shopped in the Quincy Market and ordered lunch—Boston clam chowder and Boston Cream Pie—at one of the street-side kiosks. Late that afternoon, we took a water shuttle to the airport where Bruce and Linda waited with me for my 6:00 p.m. flight.

Another travel experience involved a different family member that fall. My sister-in-law Trudy and I made arrangements for a weekend visit to Carlisle, Pennsylvania, where Jill and Garvin lived. We left on a Friday morning, and the three-hundred-mile drive, mostly on the Pennsylvania Turnpike, gave us hours to talk, enjoy the scenery of the forested hillsides, and marvel as we drove through several tunnels, entering the blackness that required using the car's headlights before exiting into daylight on the other end.

This was Trudy's first opportunity to visit her daughter's home. On Saturday Garvin drove us north to spend the day on the family island in the

Susquehanna River—a small island homesteaded by his maternal grandfather. Apparently at one time wild turkeys were in abundance in the area, and the island was appropriately named Turkey Island.

I took most of Sunday to give Trudy a tour of the Lemoyne and Red Lion areas where I had spent several years of my professional career. Returning to Jill and Garvin's home that evening, Trudy retired early, soon to be followed by Garvin. It was then that Jill got out the bottle of Frangelico and filled our delicate liqueur glasses with this nectar of the gods. We talked of family, of relationships, of life, and as we talked Jill kept refilling our glasses. I paid no heed to the time, or to the fact that Trudy and I would be leaving in the morning. The hours passed; we continued talking and sipping until the bottle was empty. In the wee hours of the morning, I staggered to the sofa bed, hoping to get a few hours of sleep.

Morning came and with it a formidable hangover. Somehow, with the stimulation provided by strong coffee and some food, I was able to manage the secondary hilly roads north to connect with I-80 where Trudy willingly (probably fearing for her life) took over driving. I immediately went to sleep. Beverley was there to meet us at a predetermined McDonald's in the Youngstown area. Miraculously, I did get myself safely home to Worthington that evening. It was a good weekend. I know Trudy enjoyed the visit to her daughter's home. For me, it was a rare Frangelico bonding experience with my niece.

Christmas 1986, I was again with my son and his family, but this time at their home in Las Vegas. It was a difficult trip without Allan. After the celebration of Christmas, the gifts and the dinners, we traveled as a family to Ojai, California, for a short visit with their dear Aunt Nin, Sidney's sister, and her husband, Bob.

On New Year's Eve, I joined the family for the traditional party at the Lake Mead Boat Harbor Restaurant. Admittedly, the '50s music and the gayety were too much for me. I found a quiet place to regain my composure and, wearing a fake smile, returned to the party in time to celebrate ushering in the New Year to the singing of "Auld Lang Syne."

The second day of the New Year, I wanted to make rye bread for the family, but I was missing some of the needed ingredients. Linda, with six-year-old Candice in tow, volunteered to walk with me to the grocery store. On our return trip we decided to take a route through a neighborhood park only to find the far-side gate locked. We searched for a place that would allow access to the sidewalk a few feet below. Linda found a place and was in the process of climbing over the wall when suddenly a dog barked. I heard crying and screaming. I turned and was horrified to find Linda sprawled on the sidewalk four feet below me. Candice, crying, was with her mother. I managed to drop down to them. Linda was able to sit up, but her arm appeared to be broken. Hearing all the commotion, a nearby resident came to his door to assess the situation, and we frantically asked him to call Bruce. Bruce arrived and immediately took Linda to the emergency room. I returned to the house with Candice. To fill the time, and to calm Candice, I started the bread-making process. Bruce returned with Linda. Her wrist was broken in three places, but she was wearing only a temporary cast. She needed to return to the hospital the following day to see an orthopedic specialist. I did make the rye bread, and it was delicious. To this day whenever Linda has the opportunity, she makes it clear to anyone that will listen, "Don't walk with Henri, it is dangerous."

Jill received her MBA from Shippensburg University in May 1987. All of Jill's family was there—Lloyd and Trudy, David and Susy and children, Peter and Beverley with Adam. It was bittersweet for me. I was happy to be included with my family and be part of the celebration, but it made me poignantly aware I was no longer a couple. I was a solo.

It was June 1987, when I was once again in Las Vegas. George and Rita, Royce and Janet joined me at Bruce and Linda's home. We spent five wonderful family days together. With drink in hand, enjoying the warmth of the water in their pool spa, we shared Allan stories.

Bruce and Linda treated all to a two-day cruise on a twenty-nine-foot Carver boat. During the day, we ate a delicious crawfish stew that Rita had brought, we swam, and we lounged the hours away. We spent the night on the boat docked at a favorite beach. It was hot, and I couldn't sleep. Neither could Candice. At three o'clock in the morning we went skinny-dipping together. The following day we returned to the dock, helped to clean up the mess we had made on the boat, and returned to the city.

The final day of our stay, we found relief from the heat of the desert by driving to Mount Charleston for a picnic. It was Bruce Allan's fourth birthday and a time for celebration. That evening the families parted— George and Rita to Louisiana, Royce and Jan to California, and me back to Ohio. I enjoyed those days with the family. For me parting was a time, not of sadness, but for reflection and giving thanks for what I had experienced. Fortunately I was moving on with my life.

Les Misérables had recently opened and was playing at the Broadway Theater in New York City, and I wanted to see it. In the spring of 1987, I purchased two tickets for a July performance and was optimistic that I could find someone to go with me. It was a newfound friend, Vernie Mellott, who agreed to join me and to share expenses. I was fortunate, for it turned out she was a good traveling companion.

We arrived in New York City the morning of July 3 and checked in at the Drake Hotel, near the theater district. On our first afternoon in the city, we took a bus tour through China Town to the Battery. From there we took a ferry to Liberty Island to visit the Statue of Liberty. Once on the island the long line, with an estimated wait time of two and a half to three hours, discouraged us from entering the statue to climb the steps that would take us into the crown. We returned to the mainland on the ferry and browsed the quaint shops in the Southside Seaport complex of the Battery before returning to our hotel.

We spent the morning of July 4 touring Rockefeller Center and Lincoln Center. That afternoon we were in our seats at the Broadway Theater, fully engrossed in *Les Misérables*. As the final curtain came down, we expressed to each other the powerful emotions we felt during the performance—the story of the convict Jean Valjean, his redemption, his sacrifices, and a bloody glimpse into the time of the French Revolution.

That evening we positioned ourselves below the Franklin Delano Roosevelt Bridge and enjoyed the Fourth of July fireworks display with thousands of others gathered along the banks of the East River. It was a fitting finale to our weekend in New York City.

———————+++++———————

DURING THE FIRST MONTHS I WAS A WIDOW, I purposely kept myself busy with work, family, friends and travel. But the emptiness was there—the primordial need for a mate. I had opportunities; some men approached me, others I was the subtly assertive one.

Shortly after Allan died, I received a telephone call from a former colleague. He had made it big-time climbing the professional ladder and was superintendent of a large urban district. It was nine years since seeing or hearing from him; he had learned of Allan's death, would be in the Columbus area, and invited me out to dinner. I knew of his reputation as a rake through previous professional connections, but lonesome as I was, I accepted his invitation. I was wined and dined at a fashionable restaurant in German Village, Engine House No. 5, and with no coercion on his part, I spent the night with him in his hotel room.

My daughter-in-law Linda knew more about me than I was willing to admit to anyone but my inner self. She said the family had identified a traveling partner for me (age sixty-one), a lifelong friend of her mother Betty. Nothing came of this. I never met the gentleman.

I did admit to my dear friend Jody that I would like to meet someone. Realizing this, she assumed the role of Cupid and introduced me to a colleague who worked in another department in the building. Shortly after our introduction, Bob invited me to lunch. When he learned of my interest in purchasing a new bicycle, he directed me to a local bicycle shop owned by one of his friends. That contact prompted me to buy a Cannondale touring bicycle.

Over the following months, I enjoyed several activities with Bob. On Sunday afternoons we visited the Columbus Metropolitan Art Museum. We went to the Columbus Zoo and took in the annual Art Festival, where he purchased a set of handcrafted earrings for me. He invited me to a wine-tasting dinner at the Colonel Crawford Inn. Bob was a pleasant person to be with, but our relationship remained platonic. I wanted more.

AT THE END OF A WORKDAY, it was difficult to go home to an empty house. I was experiencing a deep emotional pain from the loss of two husbands; now I searched for ways to possibly use my pain to help others recently bereaved. To that end, I contacted the Riverside Hospice to pursue becoming a hospice volunteer, only to learn that volunteers were not accepted within one year of the death of a family member. To alleviate the cutting pain of disappointment, I immediately pursued other ways to fill my evening and weekend hours.

Worthington Schools offered classes for adults. I signed up for swimming and yoga lessons. My swimming lessons were on Saturday morning. My instructor Theresa was a pleasant, knowledgeable, and patient teacher. She asked why I wanted to take lessons, and my response was to improve my freestyle stroke, learn the breaststroke, and do a flip turn. Of my three goals, learning to coordinate the arm and leg movements of the breaststroke was, for me, the most difficult.

The beginner yoga class met in the evening at one of the district's elementary buildings. I found even the beginner poses to be a challenge.

The last fifteen minutes of class were devoted to a time for meditation that was so relaxing I would go to sleep. I benefitted from yoga—physically, spiritually, and emotionally.

Through bicycling I learned about the American Youth Hostel (AYH) organization. I was interested in their program offerings; I was not interested in the hosteling part. My first AYH class was bike maintenance. I learned how to repair a flat tire (a basic for any cyclist), clean and lubricate the chain, and listened to talks related to proper clothing (colorful to be seen, always protective headgear) and riding etiquette.

It was the emphasis placed on wearing protective headgear that saved me from a serious injury. One day on my way to the store, my route took me down a steep hill. Without thinking, I pressed the left handlebar lever that controlled the front-wheel brake. The brake pad grabbed the wheel and instantly stopped its rotation, upending the bike. I was projected over the handlebars. I took a nosedive onto the street, and my head took the brunt of the fall. Sprawled on the pavement, I realized I was badly shaken, but nothing seemed to be broken. My bike helmet had absorbed the impact. I managed to get back on my bike and finished my errand. I learned my lessons: never use only the front-wheel brake and always wear a helmet. Over time I signed up for other bike maintenance classes, but they were more frustrating than helpful. I preferred taking my bicycle to the bike shop and having the pros do the work.

AYH also offered classes in canoeing, and I signed up for the basic course. The first class met at a local health club where there was a large pool. We were required to demonstrate our ability to tread water, stay afloat, and climb into the canoe while in the deep end of the pool. Not easy, and certainly not graceful, but I did it! As I recall, all in the group passed the pool test. The remainder of the course was taught on the flat water of the Scioto River that flowed through the city.

With a beginner's mastery of basic strokes and canoe maneuverability, I qualified to enroll in the Canoe River School. This advanced class was held on the Mohican River near Malabar Farm State Park, sixty-five miles to the northeast of Columbus. Members of the group assembled for the weekend at the Malabar Hostel. We spent Saturday afternoon on the river, stayed the night in the hostel, then returned to the river on Sunday where we experienced the excitement of running one of the river's rapids. We ended the day by portaging our canoes up a thirty-foot embankment to stow them on the rack of the AYH trailer. In a state of semiexhaustion, yet invigorated, we climbed into the vehicle, rode back to the hostel, gathered up our belongings, said our farewells, and returned to our homes.

Overall, AYH membership benefitted me in several ways. There was instant camaraderie with others who held the same interests. In club-sponsored bicycle rides, over a short period of time, I was able to increase my strength and stamina, enabling me to ride faster and longer distances. I became familiar with the bike paths and the secondary roads in outlying areas.

Canoeing classes were fun, and I gained enough confidence to paddle my own canoe on the flat water of the Scioto River. On July 4 that summer of 1986, I was one of a group who advantageously positioned themselves in canoes on the river for an unobstructed view of the fireworks display.

I wanted to dance, but growing up, I was too self-conscious of my height. Most of the boys were shorter than I, and for that reason I chose to roller-skate. I always had an interest in square dancing though. As a young girl my dad danced with me at the informal Grange square dances; later my brother would take me to area Saturday night dances. But I never learned the standardized calls of Western square dance. When I read in the local paper that a square dance club in Delaware, a small town fifteen miles to the north of Columbus, was offering a thirty-week series of Western square dance lessons, I signed up. I didn't have a partner, but upon inquiry I learned the club provided angels (members) to partner with singles.

Lynn Porter, my friend from church, was interested because she had always wanted to wear one of those full-skirted dresses with layers of petticoats. For thirty weeks, on Sunday nights, Lynn and I dutifully attended the square dance classes. With the help of our angel partners, we learned how to circle, promenade, allemande-left, do-si-do, and much more. At the end of the lesson series we passed the test, graduated, and to Lynn's delight, immediately went shopping for proper square dance attire.

Newly graduated from square-dance school, properly attired, we ferreted out square dances in neighboring communities. If a guy didn't ask me to dance, I approached any likely-looking single to be my partner. I knew how to sit; I wanted to dance. It soon became obvious to Lynn and me there were cliques at these dances, and without a partner, it was difficult to break in and be made welcome. We didn't seem to "fit," and our interest in square dancing soon waned.

Ohio State University had a Community Adult Program (CAP) that offered a variety of activities. I signed up for a wardrobe planning class that was helpful regarding color and style in making one's wardrobe selections. Another part of the class was given over to makeup; that was totally useless as I never used much makeup.

Dance lessons were listed. I joined a clogging class that left me exhausted at the end of the sessions. There was a waltz and polka class, and for this I needed a partner. Not to be deterred, I asked an acquaintance from another dance group to fill this role. It soon became apparent I had to tenaciously hang on to my partner because there were a number of women in the class who signed up as a single.

A six-week wine-tasting class was of interest to me. We were provided a checklist to aid us in critiquing the wine's complexity and character. The first night of class, I tasted and swallowed each sample pour as it was presented, oblivious to the necessity of the "big spit," never asking why I was provided an empty container. I left class quite tipsy and was fortunate to drive home without an accident. In the weeks that followed, I tasted and dutifully spat.

On the last night of class, our instructor informed us he had made arrangements for a six-course dinner to be served at a local restaurant. A different wine would be featured with each course. I invited my dear friend Jody as my guest; we decided it would be nice to have a male escort. We knew a bachelor colleague, and when invited, he accepted without hesitation. We three had a delightful evening of gluttonous dining, sipping, and socializing.

In late spring 1987, I learned folk dances were held every Monday night in the Whetstone Center, located in north Columbus within a few miles of my Worthington home. I knew folk dancing did not require a partner. It was with a feeling of trepidation that I joined the group the first night but was relieved to be greeted with welcoming smiles by the group's twenty or so dancers. Immediately I was reassured that this was a no-fault dance group, and I would learn the steps as the dances were taught. It was true. I became a regular, and I looked forward to the Monday night dances.

One gentleman caught my attention. He was a quiet unassuming man, liked by everyone. I learned his name was Charlie Gass, and within the past year his wife had died. Learning this, my immediate gut reaction was one of empathy. Over the next weeks I subtly made my presence known to Charlie. I might chat with him during the refreshment break, or position myself to dance next to him in the line dances.

A member of the folk dance group, Laurel Tigner, was especially friendly to me. She was a good friend of Charlie's and had astutely observed that I appeared to be attracted to him. I felt comfortable with Laurel and soon confided my desire to get to know Charlie better. She willingly assumed the role of go-between.

Charlie would invite me to be his dance partner for the couple dances. As much as I wanted to dance every dance with him, I was aware that there were several women who wanted him for their partner. I wisely backed away, knowing I was the new kid in the group and did not want to antagonize.

My moment of epiphany came on the Monday evening I walked into the gym of the Whetstone building where the folk dances were held and spotted Charlie wearing a dark blue, long-sleeved cotton T-shirt covered in lint. My immediate thought was, "That man needs help, and I'm it!"

OUR FIRST DATE WAS ON JUNE 5. Friends of Charlie, Art and Jane Baz, were moving from the area, and he wanted to treat them to an evening out. Charlie invited me to complete the foursome for dining and dancing at the Hilton North in Worthington. My diary notation that night read, "I am strongly attracted to Charlie. He gave me a 'slight' goodnight kiss. I didn't pursue any further—perhaps there will be other opportunities."

The "other opportunity" came the next morning. It was Saturday; I was sitting on my patio sipping coffee, reflecting on the previous pleasurable evening, when the phone rang. It was Charlie, inviting me to attend the Art Festival in downtown Columbus. Without hesitation, I accepted.

My diary note for that day read, "Charlie appears to have the attributes of a person I could care about; but Laurel told me he is 72." Months later, when I told my son Bruce I had met a gentleman to whom I had a strong romantic attraction, his first question was, "Mom, how much older is he than you?" When I replied fifteen years, Bruce, ever at the ready with the smart quip, retorted, "Good, at least you are closing the gap." Allan was twenty-seven years older than I.

June 9 was the first anniversary date of Allan's death. A colleague, Linda Mercer, had noted on her calendar the significance of this day for me and invited me to lunch at Jimmy's Upstairs, an upscale restaurant in downtown Columbus. This was a thoughtful gesture, and I was grateful, but knowing I would be alone that evening, I invited Charlie to come over. I explained why, and he graciously accepted. We spent a pleasant evening sipping our drinks and reminiscing about our mates.

Charlie was a member of the Sheraton Health Club in Worthington. It was the middle of June when he asked me to join him for a swim at the club, followed by dinner. When he escorted me to my door that evening, I invited him in. We sipped liqueur while we enjoyed listening to the music of Neil Diamond. When he was about to leave, I asked him to spend the night with me. He did, and it was the beginning of a loving relationship between two consenting adults. Perhaps at first it served to ease the pain of losing one's mate, but soon it caused me to ask myself—have I again been fortunate to find love?

After that the frequently asked question was, "Your house or mine?" Exciting as my life had become, I grew short on sleep. Charlie was retired. I went to work every day, and I soon came to the realization that I had to slow my pace or I would be no good to anyone.

——————— ++++++ ———————

CHARLES E. GASS WAS BORN ON MARCH 25, 1913, in Henderson, Kentucky. Charlie stood an erect five feet nine inches, slender, with blue eyes partially concealed by his sexy bushy, white eyebrows and a full head of white hair. His calm, unpretentious mannerisms were evidenced in his ever-engaging smile. He was a World War II veteran, retired, and made his living in sales. He and Betty had raised two children, Richard and Barbara, both recently married. There were no grandchildren.

Charlie had diverse interests, and he included me whenever possible. In turn, knowing that he liked to swim, I invited him to join me at the Worthington Pool. I had always wanted to slide down the high slide in the adult pool. With Charlie swimming beside me, I asked him if he would be a daredevil and use the slide with me. His eyes lit up with a mischievous twinkle as he agreed. We swam to the base of the ladder, and as we started our climb to the top, we both noticed the three pool lifeguards quickly walking to the area at the base of the slide. Once at the top of the slide, in turn, Charlie and I flew down the steep slope and into the water below. Not sure, but I thought I noticed disappointment, or maybe relief, on the faces of the lifeguards when there was no need to rescue what they apparently thought was a foolhardy venture of two senior adults.

Charlie's game was tennis, and he played three afternoons a week at a local tennis club. He wanted me to play well enough that we could enjoy a game of doubles with other couples. Charlie was a patient teacher but I was not a good pupil, and it came to naught.

Music was another of Charlie's interests. He belonged to a barbershop quartet, and I enjoyed attending their concerts. During the summer we spent Saturday evenings picnicking while we listened to the Columbus Orchestra's performance at Picnic with the Pops. On another occasion, a jazz pianist performed at the Ohio Village. We were fortunate enough to be seated where we could watch with fascination as the pianist beat out jazz rhythms on the keyboard with his nimble fingers.

Charlie was acquainted with several local artists—painters and sculptors. This made it more interesting when we attended their special exhibits. My understanding of art was minimal—one quick look and I either liked or disliked an art piece. When I went with Charlie to the art exhibits or to the Columbus Art Museum, I learned to patiently stand and study an art piece in-depth before forming an opinion. This gave me an entirely new perspective on the understanding and enjoyment of art.

Charlie took me to the Scioto Downs harness racing track south of Columbus—a thrilling first-time adventure for me. We dined in the penthouse restaurant, where we could place our bets and watch the races all the while enjoying our drinks and dinner in the comfort of air-conditioning. I placed only small bets and won a few dollars, but lost it all by evening's end.

I became a regular with the Whetstone Folk Dancers. In the summer the group would vacate the building's hot gymnasium and travel to Alum Creek Park, a few miles north of Columbus. There we would dance barefoot on the sandy beach. At other times the group would dance at the gazebo in the nearby Park of Roses. That summer I took vacation time to travel to Brunswick, Maine, with Charlie, to attend a two-week International Folk Dance Camp. The camp was located in the woods. We were assigned one of the rustic cabins, ate in the dining hall, and danced in a large pavilion. During the fourteen days we were there together, Charlie and I experienced total harmony, and it was during this time our mantra became, "We deserve one another."

In October we spent three days in New York City. Charlie was interested in the theater, and I was able to get us tickets for *Cats* and *Les*

Misérables. After the matinee performance of *Cats*, we left the theater and walked into Central Park to the Tavern on the Green Restaurant. Our dining experience was elegant, memorable, and extravagant—our check came to a bit more than $100.

The three days we were in New York allowed us time to explore other parts of the city. We took a Gray Line bus tour of Upper Manhattan, walked Fifth Avenue, and ate lunch in one of the Trump Tower restaurants. We took a boat trip around Manhattan Island, and to my amazement, we passed a little red lighthouse under the George Washington Bridge. This was the lighthouse featured in the book by Hildegarde Swift illustrated by Lynn Ward, *The Little Red Lighthouse and the Great Gray Bridge*, which I read to my fifth-grade class when I taught in Buckeye schools.

It was a phenomenal weekend, outstanding in every way with theater, sightseeing, and dining. Unfortunately, Charlie's new shoes were too tight, blistered his feet, and caused him great discomfort.

———— ·++++·+ ————

As summer became fall, we each felt the need to meet the other's family. In August Charlie took me to Okemos, Michigan, to meet his daughter Barbara (Barb), and her husband, Terry Rosenbaum. We arrived at their house late afternoon, to find neither home from work. Barb arrived first about six o'clock; Terry came much later. They were both very pleasant, Barb more so than Terry, who by nature was not social. Terry was a chef, and much to my stomach's dismay, a late dinner hour was a lifestyle at the Rosenbaum house. We ate at eleven o'clock.

I met Richard (Rich) and his wife, Marcy, in November. They lived in Chicago and drove to Columbus to visit their dad. I prepared dinner at my home and later noted in my diary, "Rich and Marcy walked through the door and in our first meeting their eyes remained very cold. They appeared uneasy, but the evening went well and we maintained a civil dialogue." The next day, I arrived at Charlie's home just as Rich and Marcy were leaving. Rich hugged me goodbye; Marcy made no similar effort. I was warmed by Rich's apparent acceptance of me. Over time I realized Marcy was not a socially demonstrable person.

We drove to Carlisle, Pennsylvania, in October to attend my niece Jill's marriage to Garvin Rumberger. It was a festive occasion, and Charlie was warmly received by all of my family in attendance.

We left Carlisle and stopped at the home of Charlie's niece in Pennsylvania for an overnight stay. Irma Jr. taught French at a nearby college and had lived for a year in France. We arrived midafternoon and were greeted by a rumpled appearing lady. This was one of the strangest family visits I ever made.

Irma Jr. had prepared a multicourse gourmet dinner that lasted for four hours. The first course, served with the proper wine, was tartare—raw ground beef—and I managed a polite bite or two. The following courses were delayed. Irma Jr.'s oven was not working, and she kept treading back and forth between her house and the neighbor to use theirs. Each course was served with a different wine. I was very hungry, ate what foods my palate would accept, and drank too much wine. The dinner ended about eleven o'clock. I excused myself and went to bed. Charlie remained behind to visit with his niece. During the night I awakened and had to pee, went to the bathroom, and was horrified to find Irma Jr. asleep in the tub. We left the following morning after breakfast and returned to Columbus.

That first meeting with Irma Jr. was somewhat bizarre, but as the years passed and I had other occasions to interact with her, I came to respect her intelligence and her unrivaled uniqueness.

Charlie's mother, a widow, had remarried and had a devoted stepfamily. Over the years I met a number of these family members. Everyone I met was successful in their vocation, talented, interesting, and exceptionally kind to me.

———— ++++++ ————

OVER THE SUMMER MONTHS SINCE OUR FIRST DATE IN JUNE, Charlie and I spent a lot of time together. In September I asked him where he thought our future might be headed. Charlie responded that he was content with the present "special friend" relationship we had. I noted in my diary on September 4, 1987, "Guess I better cool it. I'm not sure I want more myself." A week later, Charlie accompanied me on a school visitation to Ashtabula. I treated him to dinner at Tiffany's Restaurant on Main Street. I loved the ambiance of this former bank building. The interior featured engraved mahogany paneling, and a portion of the ceiling incorporated a Tiffany stained glass skylight. It was during dinner that Charlie commented something to the effect that if our relationship continued, he would consider marriage.

With this conversation in mind, I brought up the subject of Painte, Charlie's cocker spaniel. Up to that time, whenever Charlie was with me at my home, he brought Painte and I would help with walking and feeding the dog. Painte was an undisciplined cocker spaniel and, when anyone came to the door, would start barking and not stop until removed to another room.

House dogs were not to my liking. I was used to a farm dog that lived in the barn. I had a house dog when the boys were small, and Bowser, our boxer, gave me no end of grief because he was always running off. Then there was my mother's feisty little Mugsy, a mixed breed bulldog / cocker spaniel that she brought when she came to live with me and the boys on Vineland Avenue. In those days, dogs usually were not neutered and were allowed to run loose. The memorable event with Mugsy happened when he met up with a bitch in heat and got stuck, to the neighborhood children's education and amusement.

No, I did not want to cope with the antics of another house dog. I put the question to Charlie, "Would you be able to part with Painte?" His reply was, "Yes, but only if I can find a good home for him." Charlie asked his son Rich if he would take the dog. In return, Rich pointed out to his dad that Painte was in a kennel for two years before Charlie became his owner and provided the dog with loving care. Sending him on to someone else would be cruel, and he encouraged his dad to keep Painte. Although I did not agree with this logic, I had no grounds to pursue the subject further.

On September 23, I had dinner with Charlie's friend, Laurel. We talked on and on about Charlie and me, and in this conversation, Laurel commented that she could see us married. As I returned home, I pondered Laurel's remarks. About nine o'clock the phone rang. It was Charlie inviting me to come over and spend the night. I was tired, almost ready for bed, but I couldn't say no. I thought it would be good for him to see me when I wasn't all sweetness and light.

When I arrived, Charlie had a nightcap ready, and as we sat sipping our drinks, I remarked that I must get more rest. Our arrangement was draining me. My diary entry for that night read:

> I suggested three alternatives (1) confine our time together to Friday through Sunday, (2) live together leading to possibly (3) marriage. Charlie opted for (1) with possible future discussions of (2) and (3). The long talk with Laurel about Charlie and me was still

fresh in my mind; I was disappointed and remained silent. Charlie prodded me to 'talk.' I told him I had nothing to say, he'd opted not to discuss the options that I wanted to discuss. Charlie was quiet for a few moments and then said, 'Are you saying you would consider marriage?' I replied, 'I haven't been asked.' Charlie sat up straighter, looked me straight in the eye, and slowly said, 'Henrietta, would you marry me?' So there it was, I could hardly conceive the magnitude of the question but I answered 'Yes' thinking we could work out the details later.

My excitement was short-lived, for when Charlie and I were together the following evening, the consequences of his proposal had hit him, and he was having second thoughts. Fortunately, it had happened so fast I felt it unwise to mention it to anyone. When Charlie expressed his "proposal remorse," I assured him it was okay; I did not hold him to the proposal.

Over the next few days, Charlie did reconsider and assured me he wanted to marry me. I noted in my diary entry of September 26 that he took me to the Diamond Cellar on Henderson Road, there in Columbus, and together we selected an emerald-shaped diamond to be placed in a white gold band. At the same time, we selected matching wedding bands.

Leaving the Diamond Cellar, we stopped at the nearby Hai Lai Restaurant, ordered a Jack Daniels with our lunch, and raised our glasses in a toast, giving our mantra frequently spoken at the folk dance camp: "We deserve one another." Once home, now that the engagement was official, I called Bruce and Linda to share the joyous news. I no more than hung up the receiver when the phone rang again. It was Candice, a giggly seven-year-old, and when she learned her grandma was going to get married, she said to me, "I want to meet him first." Bruce and Linda had not met Charlie in person, but they supported me in my decision.

Charlie informed his children of our marriage plans. Since the first meeting, there had been other opportunities to become better acquainted with me. They gave their approval in words to the effect that they were happy their dad had met someone with whom he could share his life. My estrangement with my oldest son, Vernon, continued; I did not inform him of my plans. All other family members were happy for us, realizing we were adults who knew what marriage was all about.

On October 3, Charlie and I were having dinner at the Kahiki on East Broadway when he presented me with my ring. Events moved rapidly from that date forward. We saw an attorney regarding a prenuptial agreement. Charlie had planned to be with me in Las Vegas for Thanksgiving. Linda suggested our marriage take place while we were with them, and she would plan our wedding.

When Jody learned of my engagement, she and Linda Mercer immediately planned a personal bridal shower for me. This would be my third marriage, but my first bridal shower. I did feel like a bride when my colleagues gathered, and amidst good-natured teasing, sprinkled with sounds of laughter, I opened my gifts.

Not only Charlie had apprehensions about marriage; I did as well. He was seventeen years older than I. How long would he have his health? But by the same token, how long would I?

———— ✦✦✦✦✦ ————

SEVENTEEN

MARRIAGE TO CHARLES GASS
COLUMBUS (1987–1991)

B RUCE MET US AS WE EXITED THE JETWAY into the McCarran
International Airport in Las Vegas on November 24, 1987—one
day before Thanksgiving. I lovingly embraced my son and, in the
same moment, introduced him to Charles E. Gass, my future husband. As
soon as the excitement of the meeting subsided, and because time was of
the essence, Bruce took us directly to the Clark County Marriage Bureau
for the required marriage license.

The day following our arrival was given over to food preparation for
Thanksgiving. Early afternoon of Thanksgiving Day, our arms loaded with
food, Charlie and I with Bruce, Linda, Candice, and Bruce Allan, navigated
the wooden walkway from the parking lot of the Las Vegas Boat Harbor to
the dining area in the marina. Charlie was introduced to members of the
Gripentog family and welcomed by all. Prior to eating, as was the family
custom, everyone seated around the table gave a brief statement of thanks.
For Charlie and me, it was our marriage that would take place in two days.

With the predinner formality concluded, the overabundance of food
was served and eaten amidst constant chitchat, interspersed with teasing
and laughter. Much to my surprise, the after-dinner entertainment was
provided by my husband-to-be. During the dinner repartee, Charlie had
commented he could walk on his hands. At the conclusion of the dinner,
one of the younger family members called Charlie's bluff and said, "Show
us." To everyone's delight, Charlie stood, moved to an open area and, to the
amazement of all, demonstrated that he could invert his body and walk on

his hands. Following this amazing feat, and to further delight the children, Charlie led a conga line in the ludicrous Chicken Dance.

Saturday, November 28, was not just another typical sun-filled Nevada day—it was my wedding day. The previous evening we celebrated with our children, dining at the Sam's Town Casino lavish buffet, followed by a performance of the Folies Bergere at the Tropicana Hotel. It was late when we parted. The family was slow to assemble for our 2:00 p.m. appointment at the Mitrani Photography Studio for the wedding pictures (the same photographer who ten years earlier took the Dickie family pictures for Allan's seventy-fifth birthday celebration).

My feeling of internal angst was for naught as the entourage made the appointment on time. I was wearing a floor-length, purple, soft, flowing Grecian-style jersey dress. Adorable Candice (age seven) wore a white ruffled organdy dress. Bruce Allan (age three) appeared so grown-up in a suit, vest, and white shirt, set off with a bow tie. The women wore street-length dresses, and the men dressed for the occasion in suits, white shirts, and ties. Charlie's children—Richard and Marcy Gass, Terry and Barbara Rosenbaum—were there. My family was represented by Allan's children, Royce and Janet Fincher, and granddaughter Renee with her future husband, Scott LaBar. Bruce and Linda, Candice, and Bruce Allan were there by my side.

The wedding ceremony took place in the home of Bruce and Linda. They had converted their living room into a chapel. An arch covered with artificial flowers and greenery was placed at the front of the room filled with rows of chairs. Soft strains of Pachelbel's "Canon in D" played over the home speaker system as the guests seated themselves for the late-afternoon ceremony. My daughter-in-law Linda, my matron-of-honor, and Charlie's son Richard, his best man, positioned themselves on each side of the arch. The minister took his place under the arch. As the first strains of Wagner's "Bridal Chorus" were played, I took my son's arm, and together we walked the short distance up the aisle. Bruce stepped aside to sit with Candice and Bruce Allan, I took my place beside Charlie, and the minister intoned the sacred words of the wedding ceremony that united us as husband and wife.

Later that evening, an informal reception was held at the house. Members of the Gripentog family and a few close friends were there to congratulate us. Charlie and I opened our gifts to the merriment of the assembled group. The minister was one of the guests at the reception, and even I noted that he remained much longer than protocol dictated. It was not until later that Charlie and I learned the reason for his delayed leaving. Prior to the ceremony, Charlie had given Rich an envelope containing $50 for the minister. Rich forgot; that explained why the man stayed so long. The following day Rich realized his oversight and passed the envelope over to Bruce. It was Bruce and Linda who went to the parsonage, found the minister, and gave him the AWOL envelope, hopefully removing any negative thoughts the man might have harbored that he had been hoodwinked by two freeloaders in Sin City.

Bruce and Linda provided us with a full-monty honeymoon that included two nights at the Mount Charleston Resort, thirty minutes from Las Vegas. Linda's parents loaned us their white Lincoln Town car, with tin cans attached to the back bumper that made a cacophonous sound as we drove away, and to his dismay, Charlie noticed the gas gauge registered on empty. We had no choice but to pull in at the first available service station. Charlie ordered "fill-'er-up" and got out of the vehicle to dispose of the clanking cans to face a snickering service attendant. Finally we arrived at the resort, ensconced in our room, exhausted from the frenzy of activity since our arrival in Las Vegas, and opened our suitcase to have rice pour out on the bed! Was there no end to the Gripentog's penchant for pranks?

Bruce took us to the airport on Wednesday, December 2, escorted us to our gate, and watched as we entered the jetway to board the flight that would take us back to Columbus. At home, the celebrations continued. The Whetstone Folk Dancers, at their December 7 Monday night dance, honored us with a "Welcome Home Honeymooners" banner displayed above a chock-full buffet table of tasty treats that would satisfy any palate. Throughout the evening, there was socializing and dancing, with Charlie and me privileged to dance our favorite couple dance—"St. Bernard's Waltz."

Later that month, we attended Charlie's tennis group Christmas party and were introduced as the newlyweds by the president, who made a sly quip to a previous incident. "Charlie may need his donated baby furniture returned." Really, did our newly found love make us appear that young?

Before our marriage, I discussed my concern about having a dog with Charlie—our travel plans would require extended periods of time away from home. He agreed that after we were married, he would make the effort to find a home for his dog, Painte. Through one of his tennis friends,

Charlie learned that a man who lived on a small farm had recently lost his dog and was looking for another. He assured Charlie that the farm would be a good place for Painte.

The arrangements were made, and I noted in my diary the sad day when Charlie said goodbye to Painte. It was December 17, 1987, less than a month after we were married. Charlie was in the kitchen preparing bacon and eggs for breakfast. The sadness that pervaded the house was palpable. After breakfast Charlie took Painte out for their walk. As I backed the car out of our driveway to go to work, I waved goodbye, and Charlie lifted a listless arm in response. He could not bear to take Painte to his new home; he asked his friend to do it instead.

There was an eerie silence when I entered the house that evening—no barking Painte. Charlie was there, subdued, but he greeted me with a hug and a kiss. No greater sacrifice can be made by a man than to give up his dog for the love of a woman.

———— ++++++ ————

COLUMBUS IS THE CAPITAL OF OHIO, founded in 1812, nine years after Ohio became a state. The city is named after the explorer Christopher Columbus, is located at the confluence of the Scioto and Olentangy Rivers, and was named the state capital in 1816. The population of the city in the 1980s was about 565,000; at the time I am writing this (2016), the population has increased by almost 300,000 people.

The city supports a diverse economy that includes education, government, corporations, industries, and businesses. *Forbes'* list in 2013 recognized Columbus as one of the "Best Places for Business and Careers" in the United States. This utopian city was where Charlie came as a young man, married, established his home, and raised his family in a neighborhood located in north-central Columbus called Clintonville. Developed as the center of Clinton Township, Clintonville was named for United States Vice President George Clinton, who served with both Thomas Jefferson and James Madison from 1805–1812. The area was part of the bounty land warrants issued to Revolutionary War soldiers in lieu of a pension and at the time was Wyandot Indian territory.

Clintonville has NO official existence and boundaries are a matter of opinion—Worthington to the north, Indianola Avenue to the east, Olentangy River to the west, and Glen Echo Ravine to the south. The area is interspersed with ravines—Walhalla, Overbrook, Beechwold, Delawanda,

Bull Moose Run, and Glen Echo—providing picturesque vistas for a number of fortunate property owners.

There are four distinct areas within Clintonville; three are residential with identifiable housing trends. North Broadway is a major east/west artery that divides the community. South of North Broadway, single- and multiple-family homes were built in the 1930s. Here one finds the basic American foursquare alongside catalog kit homes sold by Sears and Montgomery Ward. In the two residential areas north of North Broadway, one can see the Cape Cod influence in home construction, and in the heavily forested Beechwold area, a number of high-end palatial homes are on large lots where stone walls identify boundary lines. The Graceland Shopping Center, along with the School for the Deaf and the Ohio State School for the Blind, are north of Morse Road.

Charlie's home was in a residential area north of North Broadway. Whetstone Park, rich in cultural, educational, and recreational resources, is within one mile of Charlie's house. There one finds bike trails, open fields, tennis courts, a pond, buildings housing a library and a recreation facility, and the famous Park of Roses—thirteen acres inside Whetstone Park that opened in 1953. Within this area are walking trails and strategically placed trellises, where one is submerged in sensory overload with the sights and fragrances of more than 350 different varieties of roses in season, each cluster area clearly marked for identification.

A large shelter house for community events is directly in front of the entrance to the park. Located within the park is a large gazebo where entertainment events are held in season. In June there is an annual Rose Festival, and on the Fourth of July, a celebrated fireworks display. The park is a "destination" for anyone living in or visiting the Columbus area.

In times past a person, or group, with a keen sense of humor poked fun at this unique area within the city limits of Columbus; on the corner of Torrence and Brevoort Roads there is a plaque encased in the concrete sidewalk that reads "On this Site in 1897 Nothing Happened."

⁘

At some point in our courtship, we made the decision that I would sell my home in Worthington and move into Charlie's Richards Road house. In January1988, I listed the house at 170 East Selby Boulevard with a realtor. An offer was made the first part of March, close enough to the $78,900 asking price that I accepted it. I noted in my diary on March 2, "I'll be glad to sell. This is physically and emotionally draining on me." My furniture was moved on March 18.

I can best describe the Richards Road house as a modified Dutch colonial style. Built in 1939, the lower front facade of the two-story house was limestone; the remainder of the exterior walls was a blue/gray aluminum. There were single-pane double-hung windows, a wide exterior brick chimney, and a traditional front door. Three large deciduous trees—one in the front and two in the back—provided shade in the summer and the need for leaf raking in the fall. The living space, divided between two floors, included a large living room with fireplace, dining room, kitchen, breakfast room, family room, and bath on the first floor. A large screened-in porch was located off the back of the house and accessed through the French doors of the living room. There were three bedrooms and a full bath on the second floor.

The first time I entered Charlie's home, I observed that every flat surface in the house was covered with books, magazines, newspapers, and miscellaneous items never discarded or stored. It was evident that his housekeeping standards were far different than mine. Nevertheless, as I looked about and noted the carving in the wood fireplace surround, the oak balustrade leading to the second floor, the feeling of warmth in the layout of the rooms, it was evident that the house held the promise of a comfortable home. Charlie went along with my ideas, and the redecorating/remodeling process took a priority those first years in our marriage.

We were able to find a cadre of skilled workmen. The first-floor carpet was removed, the solid oak floors exposed, and when sanded, stained, and varnished, the beauty of the grained wood gave a mellow golden radiance to the rooms. Both bathrooms were gutted and all fixtures replaced. The original single-pane double-hung windows were replaced by Andersen double-paned windows. A new furnace was installed. The electrical system of the house was updated.

The kitchen was gutted. This required setting up a temporary basement kitchen, where my Coleman camp stove was put to good use. The efficiency and the beauty that came with our new kitchen was luxury to behold: birch cabinets, granite countertops, tile backsplash, and all new appliances that included a subzero refrigerator freezer.

Not as romantic, but requiring attention, was the basement west wall. Several H-irons that extended from floor to ceiling were embedded in the cement floor and firmly attached to the rafters above, shoring up weakened wall sections. Added to that, termites were discovered and the necessary precautions taken to keep the pesky critters from devouring the wood in the house.

The cosmetic changes covered every square foot of the interior and showcased a modified Williamsburg décor—off-white walls and Williamsburg-blue painted woodwork. The trim and the wood of the new windows were primed and painted white; hardware was removed from the doors, cleaned, and reinstalled.

The lot and garage received attention too. Trees were trimmed; the lot was surveyed, and a six-foot-high wooden privacy fence installed on all sides but the front. A brick patio was built. The lean-to on the back of the garage was cleaned out and became the ideal place for our bicycles and equipment. The chimney leaked. It was tuck-pointed and sealed. A section of the house roof was replaced. The dust, dirt, inconvenience, ongoing shopping for materials, as well as the workers' presence in and about the house, prohibited establishing any daily routine.

EIGHT DAYS AFTER OUR WEDDING, on December 5, I returned to work. The routine of my days in the office was the same—lunchtime walks with coworkers, swimming at the YMCA, and too many days with hours of boredom lacking meaningful work. But one incident happened that might have ended it all in forced retirement. The director of the department informed me that a Bob Rausch would be calling, needing information about what is involved when a nonpublic chartered school changes location. The call came within the week, and when I answered the phone, the operator said, "Collect call from Bob Rausch, will you accept the charge?" I almost replied, "Who is Bob Rausch?" The heads-up alert given to me by the department director came to mind, and I meekly answered, "Yes." I realized in the nick of time that Bob Rausch was the vice president of the state board of education. It was he making the collect call; he lived out of the area.

I must have related this incident to some of my coworkers, hinting in jest that I might be targeted for early retirement. Within a week of the incident, I was standing in the lobby of the Huntington Bank, waiting in line to use the ATM. A colleague acquaintance from another department came up and remarked to me that he had heard I was asked (forced) to retire.

Shocking! His comment made me starkly aware of the gossip and political maneuverings that went on in the department.

There was variety in the nonpublic schools in which I was privileged to work. Schools were located in buildings ranging from the Spartan to the extravagant. I visited a small one-room school house in the Springfield area that was reminiscent of my childhood. At University Circle in Cleveland, I entered a school held within the Covenant Church building, which was constructed in the Gothic architectural style with stained glass windows—one a Tiffany. By and large most of the schools were traditional in the sense that one would be hard-pressed to tell them apart from the public schools in the district.

Nonpublic schools existed to serve specific student groups. A number were called academies, serving mostly students from the homes of professional parents. Others were named in reference to church or synagogue affiliation. There were schools for black children and schools for developmentally handicapped children. A Par Excellence school was dedicated to teaching poor children in an effort to break the welfare cycle. There were Montessori schools that had a hands-on, individualized approach to learning developed by Maria Montessori—physician and educator.

Working in the nonpublic sector, I met interesting people who enriched my professional life. There was Stella Moya, who emigrated from Romania in 1979 at the age of forty-two. She arrived penniless in the United States. When I met her in 1990, she was the owner of four profitable day care centers. Another was the headmistress of a private school in Wooster—a delightful petite lady, infused with energy, whose age appeared to range someplace between seventy-five and ninety-five.

As much as I disliked driving, I never tired of the changing scenery of the seasons as I traveled the highways and byways of Ohio. The greening of the trees and the landscape as spring turned to summer and with it the blossoming of the flora, the maturing of the corn and grain crops planted on the farm acreage. Fall, with its Indian summer, was my favorite time of the year, when the leaves changed their colors to rich reds and multicolored golds. With winter came vistas of snow-covered hills and early-morning scenes of ice-laden trees that the sunbeams turned into a sparkling fairyland. But there was a dread that came with winter—the ice and sleet storms made for hazardous driving conditions.

I enjoyed the flexibility that came with being the only person in the department assigned to the nonpublic-school sector. I set my own school visitation schedule, which, when possible, made it convenient to visit my family and friends in Northeastern Ohio.

There were occasions when a school visitation did not fill the hours of my workday. This allowed me time to take care of personal errands, stop at the YMCA to swim, or return home to work on house projects. On one occasion, when I finished early, I decided to stop by the YMCA to swim. I found a space close to the Y, parked my car, put money in the meter, and entered the building. An hour later I exited the Y, walked the short distance to where I remembered parking my car, only to find the street parking lane empty of cars. I had failed to read the warning posted on the meter that clearly stated "On street parking restricted between the hours of 4:00–6:00 p.m." It was now four thirty, and my car had been towed. Charlie was not home; he was at his scheduled afternoon tennis match. It wasn't until forty-five minutes later that the cab I was riding in entered through the gate of the police car pound. I paid the $75 fine, claimed my car, and drove home. It took two glasses of wine and a venting of my frustrations before my saneness returned.

On several occasions Charlie accompanied me on school visitations. He would drive, which was luxury for me, but beyond that, we took advantage of special events unique to an area. When we were in Marietta, we toured this village that was the first settlement in the Northwest territory. In the Toledo area, we went to the zoo and saw Nan Nan and Le Le—two pandas on loan from China. When I was in the Euclid/Cleveland area, we stopped at the Cleveland Art Museum to view the Impressionist exhibit of Van Gogh and Monet.

Major changes were afoot in the department that would affect my idyllic position. Mary Poston, the director of elementary and secondary education, announced her retirement effective January 1, 1989. On January 6, Dr. Osborne, school superintendent from a nearby district, was hired as her replacement. Within the year, the supervisor to whom I was directly responsible moved to another position in the department and Ms. Betty Drummond, from the public-school evaluation pool, was hired as her replacement.

None of this boded well for me. Soon after Betty's appointment, she and Dr. Osborne met with me. They had developed a list of policy suggestions related to changes (edicts) in the nonpublic-school sector. I would no longer work alone; nonpublic-school evaluations would become a team effort. The state board of education had recently approved a home education policy, giving parents the right to teach their children at home.

The responsibility for monitoring this program was given over to the local school districts with no guidelines developed for oversight. I was given the directive to develop these guidelines in keeping with the standards as set forth by the state board. The good news that came out of the meeting was that a secretary from the office pool would be assigned to work only with the nonpublic-school team.

The wheels of a bureaucracy turn slowly, and it was a year later, in September 1990, that a former elementary teacher was hired and assigned to work as a member of the nonpublic-school team. Sherry was younger than I, smaller in stature, a dynamo of energy, assertive, and at times could be abrasive.

I prided myself on my monthly New School workshops held in the conference room. Relevant materials were passed out and questions answered to help interested parties meet the state standards to charter their schools. At my direction, Sherry prepared informational booklets for an upcoming workshop. Unbeknownst to me, she used a smaller font size and printed information on both sides of the paper, congratulating herself on reducing needed supplies by more than half. At the meeting, the print was so small that a number of those attending could not read it, and the front-to-back printed pages were difficult to read due to the thin paper. Confusion reigned. From that moment forward, my professional relationship with Sherry was on a fast downhill track.

About this same time, some bureaucrat in the facilities department decided to change the configuration of our cubicle partitions in the office; the six-foot-high partitions that provided a modicum of privacy were replaced with four-foot-high partitions using the rationale that this would encourage more professional interaction and aid communication (socializing?). Walls torn down, the dust, the noise, the chaos that ensued planted the idea in my head that retirement was looking better all the time.

That fall of 1991, I started to inquire into the feasibility of retirement. In October, I visited the State Teacher Retirement System (STRS) in Columbus. I met with my financial adviser, and she assured me my portfolio reserves, supplemented with STRS annuity funds, should be adequate for my retirement years. I filed my application for retirement with STRS on November 26. The following day I submitted my retirement letter to the department director, Dr. Osborne.

I met with Betty, my immediate supervisor, and asked that no retirement recognition be planned for me. I had attended several retirement luncheons only to listen to snarky, catty comments from coworkers that they had to make a mandatory appearance at a retirement luncheon for someone who meant nothing to them. I would not give anyone that opportunity.

I had made several good friends from among my colleagues, and I knew they would celebrate with me in a meaningful way, but the secretary who had been assigned to the nonpublic-school sector could not see me leave without some memento to take with me. On my last day, she and another secretary presented me with a Reflections quartz desk clock inscribed with the date of my retirement. I don't know where they obtained the funds to buy the clock, perhaps out of their own pocketbooks. Their gesture touched my life, and to this day, I have that clock on my desk and think of them each time I look at it.

When the time was close for my son Bruce to be mustered out of the Air Force, he would refer to coming up "short" and count the days. The evening before my last day in the office, I telephoned him, and our conversation went something like this:

Me: "Bruce, I am so short I need a ladder to get into bed."

Bruce: "Did you have to jump up to get to the buttons on the phone to dial me you are so short?"

Me: "I am not going folk dancing tonight I am so short I might get trampled on."

Granted, the conversation was nonsensical chatter, but when I arrived at the office the following morning, Tuesday, December 31, the impact of my decision to retire was made clear. I found a vase of eleven yellow roses on my desk with a card that read, "Count the roses, oh no, there are only eleven, they must be SHORT! Love, Bruce, Linda, Candice and Bruce Allan"

My last day in the office was memorable. Charlie drove me to work, and he took with him the remaining personal articles from my desk. I made the rounds at the office and said goodbye to my colleagues. I stopped by the desk of Annie, the head of the clerical pool, and reached out the olive branch to her in farewell. Her icy demeanor thawed enough to smile and wish me well. My good friend and coworker Emily Schuh took me to lunch and when she brought me home, placed a package in my hands with the directive to open it later. Her gift was a Goebel Hummel figurine of a boy and girl, arm raised in a farewell wave—a fitting tribute to my twenty-seven years in education.

++++++

MOVING TO CLINTONVILLE, I maintained contact with old friends and made new. A year after we were married, on December 31, 1988, we held an open house for our Richards Road neighbors, folk dance friends, and coworkers. Emily came with her alert petite ninety-eight-year-old mother. The evening was a success as the guests came and went. I was able to move about and chat with each in a relaxed, informal, social environment. All told, there must have been forty to fifty people that came to meet and greet and share in our happiness.

In early June 1989, I hosted a dinner party honoring Linda and John Mercer. Linda was the department's music consultant and was selected to travel to China later that month with a group of educators. She was the official representative for the Ohio Department of Education. But the Tiananmen Square uprising on June 4 happened and the US government canceled the group's visas to visit China. Although it was not a bon voyage party as planned, we went ahead with the Chinese-themed dinner. The fun that would have accompanied the dinner was dampened by the visual images of the slaughter of Chinese protesters as seen on our television sets.

January 1991, I experienced a deep sadness for my former neighbor in Worthington, Susan Fisher. I always enjoyed my visits with the family, and on one such occasion, I gave her daugther Heather an amber ring that I had purchased in Moscow in 1974. As she thanked me for it, she placed in my hand a finely detailed beaded necklace she had made. She died on January 20. I have the necklace and each time I look at it, it is a poignant reminder of the valiant battle she fought against the cancer that invaded her body.

Perhaps it is because I moved so often that I made the effort to get to know my neighbors. So when Charlie and I planned a ninetieth birthday party in May 1991, for our neighbor Myrtle Kelly, I was flabbergasted when some of the neighbors told me they had never met her. With my niece Shellie Gibson's help, we planned the party to be a surprise. As prearranged, Charlie took Myrtle to visit Shellie in her new apartment. I remained at home and greeted the neighbors as they arrived, asking each to pause at the video camera and speak a few words of greeting for Myrtle, as they were being taped.

At the appointed hour, with the neighbors sequestered in our dining room, Charlie and Shellie arrived with Myrtle. As she entered the living room, the neighbors appeared, lustily singing "Happy Birthday." Myrtle enjoyed her party, and all got to know the delightful white-haired, petite lady with the engaging smile—their neighbor.

In August 1991, Charlie and I drove to Steubenville, a small town located on the Ohio River, to attend the Greek wedding of the daughter of Charlie's former neighbor. As a spectator I found it to be an interesting but exhausting ceremony. There were crowns, candles, a common cup, with the bride and groom making endless walks around the center altar—all traditional rituals of the interminable ceremony. At last we were able to exit the church and blindly navigated our way over unfamiliar streets in a heavy rainstorm to the place where the reception was held. By the time we arrived, the hall was filled with boisterous guests enjoying the open bar, gorging themselves on plates piled high with delicacies from the buffet table, others forming a circle on the dance floor and moving to the rhythmic strains of the traditional Greek music. I never saw the movie *My Big Fat Greek Wedding*, but it may be that I was privileged to be part of one.

Frank and Laverne Fust lived in the Lexington, Kentucky, area and had firsthand experience with the Kentucky Derby. Those fortunate enough to be friends of Frank and Laverne received one of the coveted invitations to their annual Kentucky Derby party held at their home on Richards Road. Saturday May 4, 1991, Charlie and I, along with perhaps fifty other people, crowded onto their lot, invaded their home, and overflowed into their garage where the "official" betting took place. Knowing nothing about horse racing, but egged on by the raucous partying crowd, and with mint julep in hand, I placed some bets—win, place, or show I don't recall. The short note I recorded in my diary reads, "I won one race." I do recall that I gorged myself on crab cakes and shrimp, finishing with the "death by chocolate" delight, Devil's Food cake. It was an afternoon to remember and, to the disappointment of all, the Fust's Kentucky Derby swan song.

It was not long after I moved onto Richards Road that I experienced a flooding phenomenon which occurred when there was a heavy rain. The street drains were inadequate to carry away the volume of water that fell during a torrential rainstorm. A cloudburst could leave one to two feet of standing water in the street, overflowing the curbs and encroaching on lawns, coming close to the front steps of homes, ours being one of them. As soon as the downpour subsided, the children in the neighborhood would be out cavorting in the street, good-naturedly splashing one another or playing on their float toys, with the older children gleefully riding their bicycles through the high water. The curbside drains, not covered with a grate, presented a real and present danger to the smaller children. Adults would position themselves by these drains, where the suction from the escaping water was so powerful that a small child could be pulled in. Frank Fust wrote a letter to the county/city officials clearly warning them of the water hazard. All neighbors, including Charlie, signed the letter. The wheels of a bureaucracy, with limited resources, turn very slowly. It was twenty-five years before the street was torn up and the drainage problem on Richards Road was fixed.

THOSE FIRST YEARS OF MARRIAGE TO CHARLIE included additional family involvement. My relations with the families of my siblings, Lloyd and Brenda, as well as Allan Dickie's children, remained intact. Adding Charlie's children and their spouses along with his half-brother Mac left few open dates on our social calendar.

It was in July 1988 that Charlie took me to Chicago to visit Rich and Marcy. Admittedly I was apprehensive about the visit. We arrived late on a Friday afternoon, and that evening Rich and Marcy prepared a delicious picnic dinner which the four of us enjoyed sitting on the grass at the Michigan lakefront near their home while enjoying a live performance by the Chicago Symphony Orchestra. The following day we visited the Great Barrier Reef at the Museum of Science and Industry, and in the evening we dined at a restaurant specializing in French cuisine. We left early Sunday morning to return to Columbus. I was made welcome and left feeling that it was a good family visit.

A year later, Rich and Marcy telephoned to announce the birth of Kevin Brendan Gass. Charlie was a grandfather! We celebrated the joyous news with champagne glasses raised in a toast to parents and child. Three months later, Rich and Marcy came for a week's visit, and Charlie met his grandson. We managed quite well the week they were with us. One evening we watched Kevin while Rich and Marcy went out to enjoy a well-deserved romantic dinner. Fortunately, Kevin was a good baby, and when the parents returned, there were no telltale red eyes that would require an explanation. Each year, Rich and Marcy made it a practice to spend a week with us and with their visits came the opportunity for Charlie and me to bond with Kevin.

The first year of our marriage, our visits to Okemos, Michigan, to be with Charlie's daughter, Barb, and her husband, Terry, were short and pleasant, centered around family activities. It was on October 1, 1989, that a telephone call came that Allen Louis Rosenbaum was born. In November Barb came with one-month-old Allen for a visit. I enjoyed taking long walks with Allen in his stroller that gave Barb some time for rest and relaxation. It wasn't long before Charlie and I came to realize that, like Rich and

Marcy, Barb and Terry were of the modern persuasion that the child was the cynosure of attention, their slightest whim not to be denied—the child reigned supreme.

At the time of my marriage to Charlie, his half brother, Vernon McCoy (Mac), was a widower living in Clearwater, Florida. Mac was older than Charlie, a child of his mother's first marriage. At the time I knew Mac, he was in his eighties, blind and lived alone, requiring only the help of a daytime caregiver. He was fiercely independent and managed very well in an apartment where everything had its place, and must be kept in its place—even the food dishes in the refrigerator. Mac spent hours listening to recorded books that he borrowed from the government's library for the blind. We visited Mac in his Clearwater home, and on what became our last visit, Mac complained of his cold feet. Upon returning home, I sent the white wool socks knitted years ago by Ma Nelson to Mac. In subsequent phone conversations, I was thanked several times for the wool socks that made his feet so comfortable. Mac died peacefully at home on September 22, 1991.

Charlie was in Mac's will, and a few months after his death, when the estate was settled, a moving truck arrived at our home with his earthly possessions. In one of the bureau drawers were the white wool socks. I was profoundly moved by whatever communication must have taken place with his caregiver in the last days of this gentle, dignified man's life that the socks that meant so much to me were returned.

Charlie and I traveled to the West to visit my son Bruce and his family more often than they were able to travel east to visit us. But there was a memorable visit in June 1990 when my granddaughter Candice, who was ten years old, came by herself to visit. It wasn't the visit, per se, that was memorable, but rather her arrival and departure that stays with me in memory. Candice was on a Delta flight out of Las Vegas to Cincinnati where she was to change planes for Columbus. As a minor, an employee of the airlines was assigned to monitor Candice. Nevertheless, there were hours of intense anxiety for me when I learned the flight out of Las Vegas was forty minutes late. The connecting flight in Cincinnati was held, and Candice, along with several others, made their assigned flight and arrived in Columbus only a few minutes late—much to the relief of one Grandma Henri.

It was a delightful week's visit. We spent three days in Ashtabula visiting with family. When in Columbus, we went to places familiar from previous visits—the Center for Science and Industry and the Columbus Zoo. The days passed too quickly, and the time came to take Candice to the airport. I was able to board the plane with her and get her settled. Before I could leave, we discovered I had placed her in the wrong seat and she was embarrassed when asked to move.

For me, it was distressing that in my final minutes with my grand-daughter, I had caused her this upset.

Visits from Allan Dickie's children and their spouses were always welcome, but another connection with his family brought enrichment to our lives. Ralph and Sue Mitchell, Allan's niece and her husband, lived in Lewiston, Michigan. The area was a destination for tourists who enjoyed the seasonal activities of golfing, fishing, camping, and boating. In the winter there was cross-country skiing, and this was what appealed to Charlie and me. We were guests of Sue and Ralph on different occasions and enjoyed the opportunity to ski the groomed trails in the area parks. To reciprocate, Ralph and Sue were our guests in Columbus, where we enjoyed taking them on a walking tour of the downtown that included the Statehouse and lunch in a restaurant at the top of the Riffe Tower, named for Vernal G. Riffe Jr., who served as speaker of the Ohio House of Representatives from 1975 to 1994. From there we would drive to the Ohio or German villages and take in whatever sights and sounds of the area piqued our interest.

Lloyd and Trudy had always been a mainstay in my life and now became a part of Charlie's life. At the end of September in 1990, Charlie and I drove to Geneva for a weekend visit. The annual grape festival was in progress, and that Friday evening we enjoyed watching Lloyd and Trudy perform with their square dance group. I think that was the time Charlie and I took off our shoes and did the grape-dance-stomp. We jumped around in a large tub of grapes, feeling their softness squish under our feet and slip between our toes, turning our feet shades of purple. We cavorted in the large tub, clinging to one another for fear of sliding down into the slith-ering mix of grape skins and fleshy centers. All this to the cheers and laugh-ter of those watching, and perhaps thankful they were not participating.

It was during these years that those of us who played golf took part in what we termed The Schumann Open. The competition was friendly but fierce—especially between me and my nephew Peter and his wife, Beverley. It was a rare occasion when I had the low score. Although, to this day, the gentleman that Peter is will declare I won more than I lost—which causes his nose to grow just a wee bit.

On January 12, 1991, I received a disturbing telephone call from my niece Jill, telling me she had lost her right index finger in a wood-splitter accident. The severed finger was recovered, but the prolonged effort of the surgeon was not successful in establishing a blood flow sufficient to save the reattached digit. After Jill's unfortunate accident, the family adopted the Schumann wave—raised hand revealing only a "stub" of an index finger.

Living in Columbus we were fortunate to have family members come to combine a social visit with a professional need. Such was the case when my nieces, Kellie Peine and Shellie Gibson, stayed with us for a few days in July 1989. While the sisters took advantage of visiting the Columbus Art Museum to view the Son of Heaven exhibit, I took care of my great-niece Courtney, age four, with a three-minute attention span.

Later, Shellie returned to take the state board test for her nursing certificate. She survived the two days of marathon testing and was elated to learn in September that she had passed. To the delight of Charlie and me, Shellie accepted a position at Riverside Hospital in Columbus and rented an apartment in the area. However, she warned us never to visit her unannounced (she told us housekeeping was not high on her priority list), and it was almost six months before we received an invitation to come for dinner and see her very neatly furnished apartment.

It was a delight for me that Shellie lived nearby. One Saturday, the weekend before Thanksgiving in 1991, we enjoyed a girls'-day-out-shopping spree. I wanted to treat Shellie to lunch at the restaurant in the top of the Riffe Tower. As we exited the elevator, we were disappointed to find the restaurant closed to the public and, upon inquiry, learned that the patrons seated inside were FBI advance agents for President Bush's visit the following Monday. We turned to leave, but the maître d' motioned us to stay, checked with the owner and the chef, and returned to inform us we could be seated and served—one of those interesting serendipities that happen in one's life.

⁺⁺⁺⁺⁺⁺⁺

THANKSGIVING AND CHRISTMAS were holidays that we always shared with family. The Thanksgiving of 1988 was special for several reasons. Bruce and Linda, with Candice and Bruce Allan, were driving to Ohio and then continuing on to see Linda's family in Kentucky. Bruce wanted to claim the antique rolltop desk that I had given to his stepdad Allan, who in turn had willed it to Bruce. For Linda it was heirloom furniture from her mother's side of the family.

Knowing my grandchildren would be spending long hours over several days in the vehicle, I purchased a number of items, wrapped them as gifts, and labeled them as to when to open—for example, "Open this one first when you are a hundred miles from home," or "Open this one when you feel like singing," or "Open this one when you are tired and ready to sleep," and perhaps most helpful, "Open this one when you are BORED." I marked the items for Bruce Allan or Candice, packed them into a very large box, and sent them out to Bruce and Linda to be a part of the luggage. As I look back, I think this was one of the best ideas I had in connecting with my grandchildren.

Their visit was special for other reasons. They were there to join the Schumann clan for the Thanksgiving dinner hosted by Pete and Bev in the Treehouse, and they were with us to celebrate our first wedding anniversary.

For Thanksgiving in 1989, we were back in Las Vegas. We arrived by plane on the morning of the twentieth, three days before Thanksgiving, in time to meet Candice and Bruce Allan at their school. We were greeted with broad smiles, hugs and kisses, and my "Grandmother's fix begins." It was a week of family events, celebrating our second wedding anniversary by dining with Bruce and Linda at Tillerman's Restaurant on the strip. This time it was our treat, and not being used to Las Vegas prices, we felt the $400+ dinner check was outrageous for value received, but sharing the event with my kids was priceless.

To celebrate Thanksgiving with family in 1990, we chanced driving into the snowbelt region along the southeastern shore of Lake Erie to be with my brother and sister and their families. We stayed with Lloyd and Trudy. Dinner was at their home that day, and that evening I played two games of checkers with my brother and WON—unbelievable. For certain, Charlie's checker lessons were paying off.

Being newly married, Charlie and I had no holiday traditions to uphold. During our first years together, we enjoyed the beauty of the Christmas season as evidenced in the light displays at the Columbus Zoo, the Ohio Village, the white light bus tour of the city, and a walking tour of the churches in the university area where the architectural styles of Gothic to modern were enhanced by the Christmas lights.

Our first Christmas together in 1987 was in Columbus, and Barb and Terry joined us. For the first time in many years, I got out my Christmas ornaments and decorated a tree, cooked, and entertained. I did my best to make it pleasant for all, but I found it to be very stressful and was relieved when it was over.

Christmas 1989 was meaningful for the gift Charlie gave me. The desk I used in my second-floor office was the refurbished shop desk my father salvaged from the Electro Met in Ashtabula—the desk where I spent hours studying for my college degrees. Charlie replaced this with a rolltop desk that he had purchased unfinished, then stained and varnished, bringing out the mellow luster of the oak. He completed this project during the two months prior to Christmas, and his loving gesture was made more special because Charlie was known to be a procrastinator.

Barb and Terry, with four-month-old Allen, again joined us for Christmas. I wanted the family to have an enjoyable time together, but when I found myself chief cook and bottle washer, the entertainment committee, and added to that, babysitter, I lost my composure. That year I was more than relieved when the holiday was over.

Christmas 1990 was with Bruce and Linda in Las Vegas. Barb and Terry, with one-year-old Allen, joined us. Linda was used to large family gatherings and much better able to calmly manage the chaos of it all than I.

Linda's dad, Bob Gripentog, had recently purchased an ultralight plane and offered to take Charlie and me for a ride. We welcomed the opportunity. Three days after Christmas, we met Bob at a small airport in Boulder City. It was cold—thirty-two degrees—but we had dressed warmly for the adventure. The plane was an open cockpit two-seater. Charlie took the first ride. As I observed the plane taxi down the runway, it reminded me of a walking-stick insect with fixed wings. I watched as the fragile machine lifted into the air and flew out of sight, to return fifteen minutes later, land, and taxi close to where I was standing. Charlie, smiling, climbed out of his seat, and it was my turn.

While waiting, I felt apprehensive but not to the extent that I was going to pass up this opportunity. I took my place in the seat behind Bob. As he taxied down the runway, the roar of the engine was so loud it was impossible to communicate, if I had wanted to call off the ride. The flight seemed interminable. I was close to frozen in the open cockpit when Bob landed the plane fifteen minutes later. I felt more than relief; I gave a prayer of thanks as I pried my frozen fingers loose from the frame and managed, with help, to get my semiparalyzed body out of the seat and to the ground. Indeed, it was a flight to remember. But all the while I was airborne, I could not shake a feeling of foreboding, yet I had no idea why.

———— ✦✦✦✦✦ ————

THERE WERE MANY INTERESTING EVENTS that took place in Columbus. It was through folk dancing that Charlie and I learned of the Living Theater, an outreach program through The Ohio State University, for senior citizens. A member of our folk-dance group was in an upcoming production, and it was for this reason in April 1991 that Charlie and I went to see the play, *Once I Was Young, Now I'm Wonderful,* written by senior citizens who doubled as actors. To this day, I vividly recall one scene in the play: an elderly gentleman, his voice filled with emotion, saying, "The worst thing about growing old is one exists on the periphery of family life, no longer able to be a dynamic participant." I have never forgotten that statement, for I find it rings so true now that I am an octogenarian.

In August 1991, Charlie and I were among the many visitors to the statehouse lawn where a blaze of color made up an 80'-by-180' carpet of begonias that had been planted on the statehouse lawn. This was the kickoff event for Ameriflora, scheduled to open on April 20, 1992, on an eighty-eight-acre site two miles to the east of downtown. It was to be a world's fair for gardeners celebrating the five hundredth anniversary of Columbus' arrival in the New World. We purchased badges that were our passes for all Ameriflora events. This included the onsite bus tours that gave interested persons the opportunity to observe firsthand the progress of this massive project.

It was folk dancing that brought Charlie and me together, and it was folk dancing that provided us with unique experiences. A Scandinavian folk dance group was coming to Columbus, and our club was asked to provide food and lodging for several of the members of the group for the six days they would be in the city. That was when we met Dan Henriksen and Goran Skogfors, two young men with family ties in Sweden. We housed, wined, dined, and entertained them, and enjoyed their exhibition dance performances. We felt a sense of regret when they departed. We had formed a friendship that continued until 2005 through letters and later e-mail exchanges. It was I who allowed the communication to lapse; my life kept changing and, as so often happens, failed to give this a priority.

Charlie also joined me in my enjoyment of bicycling. He took a bicycle repair class with me and supported me in other bicycle adventures. It was in May 1988 that Kathy Wolken and I decided to take part in the bicycle ride known as The Tour of the Scioto River Valley (TOSRV). The ride originated in 1962 when a father and son team followed a route along the Scioto River Valley from Columbus to Portsmouth on the Ohio River, a distance of 105 miles. The annual Mother's Day weekend ride became one of the largest noncompetitive rides in the United States, later sponsored by the Columbus Outdoor Pursuits (COP). The year Kathy and I made the ride there were close to six thousand registered riders.

The 210-mile weekend ride required the cyclist to camp overnight in Portsmouth, returning to Columbus on Sunday. Kathy and I decided in advance that the ride down on Saturday would challenge our cycling endurance to the limit. We needed Charlie's help. He agreed to drive to Portsmouth and bring us back to Columbus. We left the morning of May 7 at 5:45 a.m. The weather was perfect—sun, no wind, and temperatures in the high seventies and low eighties. We biked along at an average of ten to twelve miles per hour, stopping as needed for food and comfort breaks. The last twenty-five miles of the ride, we both were so tired we didn't dare stop for a rest; we never would have been able to get back on our bicycles. Shortly after four o'clock that afternoon, close to exhaustion, we rode across the bridge onto the campgrounds and saw Charlie there to meet us. I almost fell off my bicycle, barely able to walk, and staggered into the waiting arms of my husband. On the drive back to Columbus, neither Kathy nor I were able to provide Charlie with much detail about the ride—that would have to wait for another day. We slept.

When Allan and I moved from the Treehouse to Worthington, Pete and Bev said it would be all right if I left the player piano in the basement to be claimed at a future time when they needed the space. The request came five years later, in October 1989, to move the piano. Charlie and I temporarily stored it in our garage. I had no time, and little interest, to resume the restoration project. The player piano eventually met the ignominious fate of a sledgehammer. I was able to break it into small enough pieces that it could be disposed of in the weekly trash pickup.

The piano was gone, but there were occasions when we would visit my former pastor in Ashtabula, Fred Vermeulen. Inevitably he would chide me, "Now tell me, Henrietta, just how are you progressing with your player piano restoration?"

I was called for municipal court jury duty in January 1990. This was a first-time experience for me, and I found it quite interesting to be seated as a member of a jury. The case before the court was a forty-four-year-old woman arraigned on criminal charges of trespassing, assaulting an officer, and resisting arrest. As I listened to the evidential arguments made by the prosecution and the defense attorneys, mentally I questioned why this dispute ever made it to the court. It was evident the defendant in the case was a hotheaded individual. The jury deliberated two and a half hours before reaching the verdict of guilty on all counts.

At the conclusion of jury duty, we were given a tour of the Franklin County jail. The tour lasted for one and a half hours. As I walked through the cell blocks, I saw the inmates confined like caged animals, and for me it was a bleak, melancholy, and alarming experience. It was with relief that I exited the jail and welcomed the sunlight.

CHARLIE AND I HAD INTERESTING and varied travel experiences during our marriage; our first was a trip to New Zealand with Trudy. The first year after Allan died, I searched for ways to compensate for the loneliness that I experienced. I wanted to travel and asked my sister-in-law Trudy if she would be willing to travel with me. I commented that I had no place in mind and was amazed when Trudy told me of a dream she had ever since her junior high school years. The teacher of her social studies class required each student to choose some country in the world and write a comprehensive report about it. Trudy chose New Zealand and from that time forward dreamed of one day visiting the country. Given the opportunity to travel, the fact that she had never been on an airplane did not deter her; we were going to New Zealand.

In the interim between the initial planning of our trip and the actual doing, I met and married Charlie. He had served in the Pacific theater during World War II, and his travel dream was to visit Australia. He wanted to join us, so our twosome became a threesome, and our travel plans were expanded to include Australia.

Arrangements were made through Brendan Tours. Our flight departed from Cleveland on Saturday, January 2, 1988, to Los Angeles. There we boarded our international flight to New Zealand. Eight time zones later, and crossing the International Date Line where we lost a day, we arrived in Auckland on January 4.

Over the first several days of our trip we toured the north and south islands of New Zealand. On North Island, we spent considerable time in Auckland, where it appeared sailing was the pastime of the masses. While there we spent an afternoon on a catamaran enjoying the sea breezes, the sun, and the beauty of the city's natural harbor. Leaving Auckland, we traveled south by bus to Rotorua, en route stopping at a kiwifruit orchard, where we enjoyed eating the succulent vine-ripened fruit. At a restaurant we sipped a glass of kiwi wine—not to my taste as it was more sweet than dry. We enjoyed a Maori festival. This is also an area of thermal geysers, spewing steam into the atmosphere somewhat similar to our Old Faithful in Yellowstone National Park.

While in Rotorua, we stayed at the Hyatt Kingsgate Hotel, and here I took the opportunity to do some laundry. I strung my clothesline across the small deck off our third-floor room and hung my clothes out to dry. The telephone rang, and the voice on the other end politely requested that the clothes be taken down; they were visually displeasing to members of Her Majesty's Government, housed in a palatial building across the canal from our room. I reluctantly acquiesced to the request, brought them inside, and hung them in the bathroom.

Four days after our arrival, we left North Island and were taken by plane to South Island where we divided the remainder of our time between Queenstown and Christchurch. While in the Queenstown area, we hired a guide, Struan McDuff, who drove us to Milford Sound where we boarded the luxury vessel *Milford Haven* to cruise the waters of the fiord and observe the beauty of the ice age wonder of Milford Sound. On our return drive to Queenstown, Struan stopped beside a sparkling brook. As we exited the car and walked toward the stony brook, he handed us each a cup and directed us to fill it with the clear, sparkling water from the brook, assuring us it was pure enough to drink. My first reluctant sip was an invitation to drink my fill, and I did with no ill effects. Later we stopped at a teahouse, and it was here, taking part in the English formality of afternoon tea, that I enjoyed my first scone.

From Queenstown we traveled to Christchurch, which had the appearance of a quaint English city. The Avon River meandered through the city center. Charlie rented a canoe from the livery, and we spent a pleasurable hour canoeing. Another adventure was a plane ride to Mount Cook, the highest mountain in New Zealand, just over twelve thousand feet. As we stepped from the plane onto the ice that is known to be three hundred to five hundred years old, our eyes took in the spectacular views of the glaciers and snow fields that surrounded us.

Trudy's dream fulfilled, we left Christchurch on January 12 and took an Air New Zealand flight to Australia. We divided our time between Melbourne and Sydney. Just outside of Melbourne we visited a sheep ranch and had the opportunity to enter the shearing shed to observe the shearing process up close. I flinched each time I saw the shearer nick the sheep's skin and draw blood. I stood there and observed the rapid movement of the shearer's hands and his ability to position the sheep's body as he sheared away its wool, leaving it standing naked and shivering. I chatted with a shearer, ran the newly shorn wool through my fingers, and was revolted by the obnoxious smell. It was a real-life experience, not a sanitized one as viewed on a movie screen.

In Sydney we took a relaxed boat tour of the city's harbor, but the highlight for me was attending a performance of *Fascinating Aida* at the Sydney Opera House. When time permitted, Charlie and I walked the streets of the city near our hotel. There was a street performer playing his harmonica. Charlie and I stopped to listen. He took my hand, put his arm around my waist, and the two of us danced there on the sidewalk to the melodious harmonica music of "Waltzing Matilda." For me, that moment encapsulated the magic of our trip.

The final night of our travel was spent enjoying an evening of dining at the Waterfront Restaurant overlooking the harbor. On January 17, thirteen days from the date of our arrival in Auckland, we boarded our flight for home and gained a day when we crossed the International Date Line, arriving in Los Angeles the same day. We endured a layover of eight hours and arrived in Cleveland the evening of January 18. As Trudy exited the jetway, she fell into the welcoming embrace of her husband.

Charlie had an interest in sailing. When he read an advertisement in my bicycle magazine for a bike-sail adventure out of Camden, Maine, sponsored through Open Road Bicycle Tours, he requested the brochure. The information captivated our interest, and we signed on. For Charlie it would be an adventure on a sailboat; for me it would be the opportunity to bike in a picturesque area of the country.

On August 19, 1989, we were in Camden harbor and boarded the windjammer schooner *Rosemary*. We descended the circular metal stair common to maritime boats and, once below deck, located our six-foot-by-eight-foot stateroom furnished with a double bunk. Under the bottom bunk were built-in pullout drawers for storage, and a small sink with cold running water stood in one corner. The showers and the "head" were on the main deck.

The trip was advertised as a working vacation. There were sixteen in our group. The first evening we gathered in the mess hall and seated ourselves on the benches. We listened attentively as the first mate explained our duties for the coming week. There would be deckhands helping with the sails and other on-deck duties. There were mess hall duties of table setting, serving, and cleanup. Last was the ship's galley, and anyone drawing this duty would be washing dishes and scrubbing the pots and pans. Charlie was delighted to be assigned the duties of a deckhand. I was assigned to work in the mess hall.

We sailed out of Camden harbor on Sunday, August 20, to return the following Saturday. Our northern destination was Acadia National Park, the onetime estate of John D. Rockefeller. The six days alternated between sailing and bicycling. The first day of our bicycling, we were divided into two groups of eight, seated in rowboats, and told to row to shore. (This was a muscle-power vacation, devoid of mechanical power.) Our group attempted to row, but for anyone watching, it was slapstick comedy—each rower had a different cadence, and it was with great effort that we eventually made it to the rocky beach.

There were three days we bicycled, and the highlight for both Charlie and me was the day we cycled the crushed and rolled stone carriage paths of Acadia National Park. The paths were lined with stone walls that followed the contour of the land and provided beautiful vistas of the Atlantic Ocean. The cycling days drained our strength, and we welcomed the days we remained on the sailboat and could rest.

During the six days of sailing/biking, a communal camaraderie developed. We worked comfortably together to complete our assigned duties on the *Rosemary*, chatted, shared stories, and laughed as we cycled together along the scenic byways. One member of our group was a Navy pilot, and he refused to wear a helmet. I was inquisitive and asked him "why" as some of the downhill cycling was extremely dangerous. He commented that he was a NAFOD—a pilot stationed on a Naval Aircraft Carrier. When you took off and returned in your plane to land on a bobbing speck in the ocean, you needed to have an attitude of "no apparent fear of death." Now I had a glimmer of understanding why he refused to protect his head with a helmet.

Charlie was in a lobster lover's seventh heaven. When ashore, we ate our evening meal in area restaurants, and Charlie never looked at a menu; it was always lobster. On our final night ashore, there was a lobster bake, and Charlie devoured at least three, maybe four, lobsters. He earned the Lobster Lover award, bestowed on him by one of the buxom, winsome young ladies in our group. The following day the *Rosemary* sailed into Camden harbor. Our bike/sail working vacation was over.

A year later, in August 1990, we were in the Netherlands for an eight-day cycling vacation with Vermont Bicycle Touring. We arrived in Amsterdam on August 25, exhausted from lack of sleep on the trans-Atlantic flight that set us ahead six time zones. Once the group assembled, our guide took us on a walking tour of Amsterdam. It was morning, our hotel rooms were not ready, and staying awake would help us adapt to the current time.

My first impression of Amsterdam was a crowded, dirty city—pedestrians, bicycles, and dogs were everywhere. The first stop on our tour was the Anne Frank House. We entered the building and walked up the narrow, steep stairway to the second floor. In one of the small second-floor rooms, our guide pushed on the side of what appeared to be a built-in bookcase, only to have it move away from the wall. The opening revealed another narrow, steep staircase leading to a third floor. One by one we carefully navigated the stairs to stand in the cramped area where the Frank family lived in hiding from the Germans for two years during World War II. To say it was a sobering moment is an understatement. All remained silent as we descended the stairs and left the house.

The next stop on our walking tour was the Rijksmuseum where I stood awestruck before the twelve-foot-by-fourteen-foot painting of Rembrandt's famous *Night Watch*. When we left the museum, it was dusk, and the lights were coming on in the city. Walking to our hotel, we passed the city's famous red light district (RLD). This area was apparently not on our walking tour, but several of us persuaded our guide to allow us the chance to get a firsthand look. I had heard of the RLD and somehow had the visual image of a small, round window illuminated by red back lighting with only a woman's face visible. I was shocked to see buildings with eight-by-ten plate glass windows, with a surround of red lights, revealing women seductively seated for the curious passerby to gawk at or for an interested party to partake.

The walking tour had elicited feelings of deep sorrow in the Anne Frank House, a time for meditation in the museum, and now to be exposed to this degradation of women was abhorrent to me. It is no wonder the RLD was not on our scheduled walking tour.

We checked into our hotel, unpacked, ate, and finally to bed and sleep! The following day we joined the throngs of cyclists and left the city behind. During the next six days, our tour took us into all parts of the Netherlands. I cycled by pastures filled with sheep, cows, and horses. I observed fields of corn, turnips, and cabbages. Wild blackberries lined the country roads and were there for the picking. There were flowers—fields and fields of tulips of every color. But the sight that remains with me occurred when I topped a hill and a spectacular view of a meadow of purple heather unfolded before my eyes.

To cover the distances that took us to all parts of the country, we were transported on buses, trains, small and large planes, sailboats, canalboats, and ferryboats. In the large cities we stayed in luxury hotels with luxury accommodations; in the small towns our overnight accommodations were in small hotels, some with rooms so tiny that it was almost a wall-to-wall bed.

Biking through the countryside, I noticed a variety of home styles. There were homes large enough to be palaces. There were cottages. Along the canals there were canalboats converted into homes. On the levees there were windmill homes.

The food was adequate to gourmet. We savored the delicious soups, the variety of fresh vegetables, the myriad ways chicken was served, the occasional pork or beef entrée, the strong coffee and the dessert ices.

For most of the week the thermometer registered in the eighties. There was only one day when a torrential rain made cycling hazardous; in fact, Charlie was almost sideswiped by a lorry. But it was a daily occurrence to ride through swarms of small pesky insects.

Along the way we took in points of area interest. We visited the Kroller-Muller Museum, where many of Van Gogh's original paintings are hung—my favorites were *Self Portrait* and *Sunflowers*. In contrast, we stopped at the Jopie Heisman museum, where the artistic works of a self-taught scrap-dealer are displayed. At the Tichelaar Pottery factory, I looked but did not buy any of the beautiful expensive pottery pieces. Another stop was the Delft factory, where I purchased a few small vases for gifts.

Returning to Amsterdam, we biked along levees lined with the iconic windmill. During our weeklong cycling adventure, I noted the variety of materials used on the roads. There were brick, packed sand, clay, and worst of all, the "tire-sucking" asphalt experienced in the heat of the day.

On September 1 we were back where we started, in Amsterdam. The following day, baggage in tow, we were at the airport for our flight home. On the plane I made notes regarding a few of my impressions from the trip:

- Most annoying—dog poop on the sidewalks
- Second most annoying—pay to pee and then the mystery as to how to flush. Did I push a lever, pull a lever, pull a chain, or step on a floor pedal?
- Price of coffee—no refills
- Most spectacular—meadow of purple heather
- Most emotional—visit to Anne Frank House

- Most fascinating—glimpse of a Dutch wedding party, their limousine decorated with fresh flowers
- Most rewarding—hospitality of the Dutch people.

In August 1991, Charlie and I were in France to take part in a tour sponsored by Vermont Bicycling Touring, the same company that we cycled with in the Netherlands. Twenty of us gathered on August 31 for a week-long tour of the Bordeaux wine country. Our first day together was spent in orientation meetings familiarizing us with schedules, biking routes, points of interest, area topography, and practical suggestions related to challenges we might face as we cycled through the countryside. It was in this meeting that I learned the wines of France were identified by the region in which the grapes are grown; they are not identified by the name of the grape as they are in the United States.

One of our brochures described the French countryside as a symphonic landscape, blending the flora and the fauna together. Flowers were everywhere—marigolds, petunias, geraniums, and lilies. I cycled past fields planted with corn, tobacco, and acres of orchards and vineyards. There were pastures where cows and sheep grazed. On a pheasant farm, I observed the birds wore metal protectors on their beaks and was told it kept them from pecking one another. There were forests of pine, chestnut, cypress, and poplar. Throughout all the countryside the flatlands were laced with canals and streams that meandered around the hills.

Red-roofed farm buildings were common. Farmhouses in the southern part of the province were built in the Périgord style—an outside staircase led to the second floor where the family lived. Animals were kept under the house. The bucolic countryside suggested an idyllic rural life.

It was interesting that there were many stone buildings and cobblestone streets, but where did the stones come from? It did not appear that they were dug out of the fertile fields and pastures of the area. I learned the stones were used in English ships for ballast and unloaded in France, making space for a full cargo on the return voyage. I will add that the narrow cobblestone streets were hazardous for the cyclist.

In centuries past, the Romans had occupied the area now known as France. There was evidence of this in some of the buildings. Charlie and I visited a Romanesque St. Vincent Church where an original Rembrandt painting of the Crucifixion hung. Another day we passed a cemetery and saw monuments with ceramic plaques to memorialize World War I and II soldiers.

Each night our accommodations ranged from adequate to luxurious. Our luxury accommodations would include a large room with twin beds, huge pillows, shower, and a bidet. There would be a swimming pool where our group could gather at the end of our cycling day to swim, relax, and socialize with a drink in hand. The most interesting place we stayed was a restored abbey with stone walls, hand-hewn wooden beams, and large interior fireplace chimneys.

The French are known for their gastronomy. Steak with shallots, spit-wood-roasted pigeons, capon, goose, duck, baked stuffed salmon, baked whitefish, baked chicken, salads, vegetables, crusty rolls, the rich desserts of custards, crepes, ices, and cream puffs, enjoyed with demitasse coffee—I denied my palate nothing. French cuisine is to be enjoyed in a leisurely manner. Five-course dinners lasted upward of three hours. I was distressed to find that in spite of the day's physical activity, I gained weight; calories consumed were not balanced with calories burned.

Fortunately, our breakfast and lunch fare was in moderation. Charlie and I would select from the breakfast buffet crusty breads, a variety of cheeses, and fruit to enjoy during a midday rest stop. But the final day of our cycling included a gourmet lunch. Arrangements were made for the group to gather at the Chateau de Fournax for a tour of their vineyards. (This was where I learned why roses were planted at the end of each vineyard row. Roses are vulnerable to the same diseases that infect the grapevines, but evidence of the disease appears much sooner in the rose.)

After we completed the vineyard tour, we entered a building where the wine was processed and stored. At last our group was escorted to the dining room and lunch was served. The appetizer course was goose pate and cheeses, including brie. Next came the entrées of smoked duck, ham, and filet mignon with assorted salads and vegetables. A different wine was served with each course, the meal ending with dessert and cognac. By that time neither Charlie nor I were feeling any pain.

When we finished gorging ourselves, we left the dining hall and waddled back to our bicycles. The first twenty miles of our trip that morning were over flat terrain; unfortunately, the final ten miles were hills. We struggled, and when Charlie made it to the top of the last steep hill, he yelled, "Geronimo!" It was a fitting call—too much wine, stuffed on food, and we survived! Cycling through the countryside of the Bordeaux region was a thrilling experience. Once out of the cities, riding through the rural areas, we had the opportunity to interact with the bourgeois. The downside of this was, no one spoke English. I learned a few French words: *bonjour* ("hello" or "goodbye"), *s'il vous plait* ("if you please"), and because I loved coffee, *un café, s'il vous plait.* Otherwise, verbal communication was nonexistent, and I resorted to smiles and hand motions.

During the flight home, I reflected on the remarkable experiences of the past week. But I couldn't shake the melancholy feeling I had for not being able to speak the language. As I cycled along the byways of the Bordeaux region, the farmers would come out to greet me. But I couldn't speak French, or they English. Our nonverbal communication of smiles had to suffice. So many unanswered questions. It was my loss.

———————— ++++++ ————————

IT WAS I, NOT CHARLIE, who faced the most health issues during those first few years of our marriage. On one of Charlie's routine visits, his primary-care physician said to him, "You are as good as you can expect to be for a man of your age."

My right hip had bothered me off and on for a number of years. In March 1988, the severity of the discomfort forced me to give in to my pride and accommodate the pain by using a cane. I scheduled an appointment with an orthopedic surgeon only to be told I had an arthritic hip, to restrict my daily physical activities, and accept my condition. I was too young to have a hip replacement.

I was unwilling to accept this doctor's arrogant manner. I met with a second surgeon in July who confirmed the diagnosis and recommended a hip replacement; both my age and my good health were in my favor. The surgery was scheduled for October 24. A coworker of mine, who had just had a knee replacement, gave me a journal and encouraged me to keep a daily log of my surgery/recovery experience.

I filled the journal with thirty written pages, beginning with admission to the hospital on October 23, the afternoon before the surgery, through November 21. (It was Charlie who made the entry the day of my surgery.) On the fifth day after my surgery, I left the hospital. Charlie brought me home and for the next several weeks was a loving caregiver.

During those weeks of recovery, family members and friends were in touch through visits, telephone calls, cards and letters, flowers and food—all expressions of concern for my well-being. I had many sleepless nights, experienced pain, and also boredom from forced inactivity, but knowing there were those who cared helped me to endure.

Bruce and Linda came with Candice and Bruce Allan for Thanksgiving that year. Dear Candice served as my little nurse who would help me with my shower. I did have physical therapy in the hospital, but once home, Dr. Halley recommended only to walk, walk, and walk some more. This I did, and I walked for miles listening to books on tape. Having the hip replacement at a relatively young age was the right decision. The pain was gone, and I was able to resume my active lifestyle. It was a lot to ask of Charlie, that first year of our marriage. He was a patient caregiver with never a word of complaint or regret.

I had started the process of having dental implants when I was married to Allan. In June 1990, one of the implants in my upper jaw became infected. A call to Dr. Halley's office alerted me I must get the infection cleared up ASAP; there was danger that the infection would spread to my artificial hip. I had the implant removed, the teeth in my upper jaw extracted and a denture made. I have never regretted that decision either. Through all of this, Charlie was again patient and loving, sensitive to the anxiety and pain I experienced.

WITH MANY COUPLES, the initial attraction is physical. It takes years of living together to bond in marriage. The first year of our marriage, Charlie and I both recognized the necessity to address legal and financial interests and took the needed steps to ensure our wishes would be carried out, updating our general wills, our living wills, and our health-care powers of attorney. As we worked our way through this, we arrived at a better understanding of one another's wishes.

There was one area that was never discussed, and that was a change of my surname. When our first joint income tax forms came back from the accountant for our signatures, I was listed as Mrs. Charles Gass—not to my liking. I was Henrietta Dickie, professionally known as Dr. Dickie—my identity. In truth, I don't recall how the IRS forms were handled. Through all the years of my marriage to Charlie, I maintained the surname of Dickie. When people referred to us as Mr. and Mrs. Charles Gass, I accepted it and made no issue of the matter.

From day one of our marriage, I agreed to a financial arrangement that was different than any I had experienced in my previous two marriages.

I would pay Charlie one half of the appraised value of the Richards Road house to have my name on the survivorship deed. Also, I would contribute to one half of all expenses connected with the house. Allan had been very generous with me, assuming most of the household expenses, allowing me to save the major part of my earned income. Over time I grew accustomed to the arrangement. But it was not without incidents of irritation, too minor to mention, and were always resolved.

From the time I married Charlie, I rarely attended church. Admittedly, I was too involved with work and all the demands that go with daily living to be upset about it. I did fulfill my Stephen Ministry commitment—regular meetings with the young woman I was assigned to and the weekly Tuesday night meetings with the group. It was in August 1988 that I met for the last time with the group and with Peggy. I was relieved to have it end.

---------- ·+++++·+ ----------

I CAME TO REALIZE those first years of marriage how blessed I was to be Charlie's wife. We were physically compatible—that was evident from our initial attraction. But our union went much deeper than providing for one another's sexual needs. We communicated well, listened to one another, and intuitively knew how to respond.

Charlie understood my need to just "talk" through my problems and would patiently listen. In the process he became aware of some of his behaviors that irritated me and vowed to work to change them. Top of this list was his habit to procrastinate on things that needed to be done. With my nudging, sometimes gentle, other times downright brutal, he did modify this behavior.

Charlie had many interests. He enjoyed physical activities—tennis, swimming, dancing, and after marrying me, bicycling. He spent hours reading; he enjoyed cooking. He had a beautiful tenor voice, had sung with barbershop quartet groups, and when he traveled with me, we would pass the time singing together, he taking the harmony as all I could manage was the soprano.

He was liked by my family and interacted comfortably with them. He approved of, and supported, all my home-redecorating/remodeling plans—always willing to be the "gofer." Surprising to me was how neat he was with his personal care and items, given that when I first came to the house, there was not one flat surface free of clutter.

Truth be told, Charlie changed more for me than I for him. I know, due to my type A personality, at times I could be difficult to live with. But it was seldom that Charlie became angry with me. Early in the first months of marriage, I was overcome with fatigue and could not sleep. I arrived home from work one afternoon to find a vase with a dozen yellow roses on the dining room table. The note written in Charlie's hand read, "Because I love you." With Charlie's understanding and acceptance of the essence of my complex nature, our marriage survived.

In spite of it all, we must have communicated our love for one another in nonverbal ways. Otherwise, there would have been no reason for people to comment, "You are meant to be together."

EIGHTEEN

MARRIAGE TO CHARLES GASS
RETIREMENT (1992–1997)

M Y LAST DAY OF WORK was Tuesday, December 31, 1991. Charlie and I celebrated my retirement by joining the New Year's Eve festivities at Ohio Village. We dined at the Colonel Crawford Inn. As it neared midnight, we gathered with others around the crackling bonfire fed with evergreen sprigs—a symbol of destroying the old to make way for the new. As the clock in the town hall struck midnight, all voices joined in the singing of "Auld Lang Syne." Weary, we returned home, soon to bed, only to be awakened out of a sound sleep by the ringing of the telephone. It was 3:00 a.m., but for Bruce and Linda in Las Vegas, it was midnight, and they were making their annual mischief call to wish us a happy New Year.

The years of working provided a structure in my life. For a time, my body demanded I keep the rhythm of early to bed and early to rise, but otherwise, any resemblance of a daily routine was gone. Now I had the luxury of time to use as I pleased. Keeping up with local, state, and national happenings became a priority. I was finally able to take advantage of spur-of-the-moment events.

One morning I read in the *Columbus Dispatch* that the C-Span bus would be at the Ohio Historical Society that afternoon. I was an avid C-Span viewer. I got on my bike and rode the five miles to the site where I joined a long line and waited my turn to enter the forty-five-foot bus. Once inside, I took part in the interactive multimedia exhibit in the mobile classroom. As I exited the bus, I had a much better understanding of this nonprofit, nonpartisan network founded in 1979 by the cable industry to televise government proceedings.

I had time to continue familiar activities as well as explore others of interest. I enjoyed walking and persuaded Jody to take part in the annual New Year's Day 5K Couch Potato Walk. I joined a Volksmarch Club, purchased a fancy walking stick, and at times Shellie would accompany me to take part in the club's 10K hikes, but it was Emily and I who walked together each week. When the weather was favorable, we walked around Antrim Park; when unfavorable, we walked in a nearby mall.

In the winter Charlie and I took advantage of the snow to cross-country ski. The Park of Roses was close to our home, but it was the Ohio State University Golf Course, with its groomed trails, that was more to our liking.

We continued with our folk and English country dancing. Charlie arranged for us to take private dance lessons at the local dance studio owned and operated by his tennis buddy, Jimmy Rollins. We wanted to learn the Charleston—that uninhibited dance made popular in the 1920s. I tried, but the coordination wasn't there for those knee-knocking, arm-swinging, fast-paced dance movements.

Charlie attempted to teach me chess, but it didn't take; I stayed with the checker lessons. We both had an interest in art, so we signed up for an art appreciation class at the Columbus Art Museum, "Learning to Look at Art." The class centered on the Realism movement in France in the 1850s and the emphasis placed on *trompe l'oeil* (fool the eye)—interesting that I remember this. I am hard-pressed to come up with the names of the famous painters of the time.

Emily and I signed up for the Golden Girls Investment Club, but after attending only one meeting, we realized it wasn't for us. We would be required to analyze financial reports and make purchase recommendations to the group. This dulled our enthusiasm for making our fortune in the stock market.

There was a new YMCA in the area, and I used the weight room and pool facilities on a regular basis when Charlie played tennis. The serendipity for Charlie and me was my meeting Adam, the trainer in charge of the Nautilus room at the Y. He later became our at-home personal trainer.

Even with all that activity, I still had open hours in the day. I wanted to volunteer, but in my mind, any hours I gave over to volunteering must fulfill three objectives: (1) I wanted to use my talents; (2) I wanted to be valued; (3) and I wanted to learn something new.

I contacted Riverside Hospital. I went through the mandatory volunteer training program and was assigned to work in one of the satellite lunch cafeterias. Within a month I came to the realization that like any job, paid or volunteer, there was a built-in hierarchy, and I had entered at the bottom. But I did have a talent for my assignment, and it was needed, except I wasn't learning anything new. I was a dishwasher standing over a sink, isolated from all other activity in the cafeteria. I was bored, and I refused to be bored when volunteering my time. I quit.

On a number of occasions, I was in the Columbus Outdoor Pursuits (COP) office on biking business. The office employed two people—a director and the secretary, Ann. It was Ann I approached about volunteering. I was forthright in telling her my only experience with digital technology was using a word processor. Ann welcomed me and expressed a willingness to teach me whatever I needed to know—computer or otherwise. I volunteered one afternoon a week, and Ann's knowledge and patience made it a mutually agreeable arrangement for both of us.

The Wednesday afternoons that I spent at the COP office were enjoyable. I worked well with Ann and met many people who shared a common interest in a healthy, active lifestyle. Within the year I was elected to a seat on the board of directors.

There were perks that came my way through the COP office. The area Director on Aging had contacted Ann for names of older bicyclists to interview for a program on "Physical Fitness, Lifestyle and Aging." Charlie and I agreed to the interview. The thirty-minute program was viewed on the local public access channel, and we got our (Andy Warhol's) "fifteen minutes of fame." From this we were contacted by a person from Channel 6 and interviewed for their featured program, "How to Live to be a hundred." I think we got three minutes of airtime with that one.

FAMILY CONTINUED TO BE AN IMPORTANT PART in our lives—visiting us, visiting them. My priority was to make family visits to our home as pleasant as possible. I kept foremost in my mind the words of Lulu Thompson, a Shuart relative, spoken when Charlie and I were guests in her home in Farmville, Virginia. As we left, I thanked Lulu for her hospitality, and this slightly bent, white-haired, physically fragile octogenarian raised her eyes to meet mine and said, "I always try to treat guests in my home as I would like to be treated in theirs."

In the fall of 1993, Charlie and I took time for a relaxed drive to visit Rich and family in Chicago. We headed west on Route 30 across the flat farmlands of Ohio and Indiana, veering off to the northwest to connect with the scenic Lake Shore Drive into the city. On this visit we stayed in a motel near the condo of Rich and Marcy located in the northern section of Chicago.

We arrived a day early because we had made previous arrangements to meet a biking acquaintance, Maureen, at Lou Mitchell's Restaurant and Bakery, the "in" place to meet and eat for breakfast in downtown Chicago. It had been a year since we had seen Maureen, and she proudly announced that she had passed her bar exam and was now a practicing attorney with a law firm in the city. She went on to trump that announcement by telling us she was married. Her future husband sat next to her when they took their bar exams. There was electricity in that meeting, and subsequently they became engaged. Both were outdoor enthusiasts, and they chose to be married standing on the dock of an Illinois river canoe livery, with the owners of the livery as their witnesses. After the ceremony, they launched their canoe and paddled off on their canoeing/camping honeymoon. Charlie and I were both enthralled by Maureen's story, and I, for one, was thinking what interesting people one meets when traveling.

During the five years covered in this chapter, there were other visits to see the family in Chicago as well as their visits to Columbus. Entertainment always centered on the children and was dependent upon the seasons. In the summer there was the zoo, or visits to area Renaissance fairs, and in the fall visits were made to a farm to trek through a cornfield maze with shrieks of fear followed by laughter as we made the twists and turns to find our way out. Once released from our cornstalk prison, our final stop was at the pumpkin patch where the boys made their selection of the perfect pumpkin for carving.

Opportunities to see Barb and family were more frequent. Perhaps distance was a factor—Okemos was only 150 miles from Columbus, whereas Chicago was 350 miles. There were two major events during this five-year period that took Charlie and me to Okemos. The first was the birth of Allison in 1993; the second was the occasion when Barb, Terry, and four-year-old Allen went to the Winter Olympics in Lillehammer, Norway, in 1994.

Charlie and I had agreed to be with Allen when his sister was born. We were there on April 5, when Terry took Barb to the hospital. Allison was born the following afternoon, April 6, weighing in at seven pounds, twelve ounces. (I have always referred to Allison as my "birthday buddy" as my birthday is on April 7.) Late in the afternoon on the day of Allison's birth, we went to the daycare center to get Allen. Instead of taking him home, we drove to the hospital. On the way we stopped at the florist—a yellow rose for Allen to take to his sister and a bouquet for his mother.

Allison Jeanne Rosenbaum had dark hair, blue eyes, and dainty features—all of this female pulchritude contained within a tiny being twenty-one inches tall. Three-year-old Allen met his sister, touched her hair, her ears, her fingers, examined her toes, laughed and cooed at her, and was able to hold her while seated on Grandpa Charlie's lap—and me without my camera!

The next day Allen helped Grandpa and me decorate the dining room with streamers and balloons, but it was the banner that read "WELCOME TO YOUR HOME ALLISON, Love, Allen" that was best of all. Terry brought Barb and Allison home that afternoon. We were able to hold her and share in the joy and excitement of this new family member. Within two days the parents seemed to be able to manage on their own, and we returned to Columbus.

In February 1994, we were back in Okemos to care for ten-month-old Allison when Barb, Terry, and Allen left for Lillehammer, Norway, and the Winter Olympics. The family would be away for two weeks. Charlie and I were given detailed verbal and written instructions regarding Allison's care.

The first day Allison rebelled by not eating. Any food I placed in her mouth, she spit back at me. This lasted for one day, and then hunger took over. Fortunately for us, two factions came into play that ensured our survival—Allison slept through the night, and on weekdays she loved being in daycare. Charlie and I took advantage of these free daytime hours and used the facilities of the local YMCA. Overall the evenings went well with Allison. We would get her late in the afternoon from the daycare center. I would feed her, read her stories, and then to bed. It was the all-day Saturday and Sunday care that presented the challenge; she would cry, and nothing I did soothed her. I found that taking her with me grocery shopping, riding in the cart as I collected the groceries, would calm and tire her. By the time we were home, Allison would be ready for a nap.

One Saturday not even the grocery store experience calmed her. I tried another tack and took her to the nearby mall. With Allison in her stroller, I spent a good part of the afternoon meandering through the mall, acknowledging the approving glances of other shoppers, while stopping to gaze in the store windows. A hat store seemed to delight Allison. I pushed the stroller into the store, took hats off of the rack, and one by one placed the hat on her head. She loved it, laughing as she pulled or pushed at the brim of each hat. The clerks paid no heed, or if they did, it was only to be amused by the antics of this potential future customer.

On the appointed day her family returned home. I was in the kitchen preparing supper. Allison was in her high chair waiting to be fed. As Barb entered the kitchen, she saw her daughter and went toward her with out-reached arms, only to be startled by her cries. Allison turned and reached for me, much to the disbelief of Barb. However, within the hour, love pre-vailed, and Allison, smiling and laughing, settled herself in her mother's arms.

Most of Barb and Terry's visits with the children were to celebrate Thanksgiving and Christmas with us. Entertainment events were always selected to please the children. During the weekend following Thanksgiving, we would make an evening pilgrimage to the Columbus Zoo to observe whatever animals could be seen, but most of all to thrill to the multitude of lights that decorated the walkways, the trees, and formed interesting animal shapes.

Born and raised in the Upper Peninsula of Michigan, Terry was an avid hockey player. At a very young age, he introduced his son to the game. I think it was the Thanksgiving of 1992, before Allison was born, that Charlie got tickets for the family to attend a hockey game for the first time. The Columbus Chill was a professional ice hockey team in the East Coast Hockey League from 1991 to 1999. The team played their home games in the Ohio Expo Center Coliseum in Columbus. Five of us went to see this fast-paced game played on ice using long sticks and a puck. I didn't under-stand the rules and had no clue as to why the game appeared to be so bru-tal. Opposing team players engaged in fisticuffs. A referee would blow his whistle, and the offending player(s) were placed in a penalty box. Terry and son loved it; Barb enjoyed it; Charlie tolerated it; I was repelled by it. This became an annual Thanksgiving event as long as we lived in Columbus, and I eventually accepted it.

The following year, the family was with us for Christmas. On Christmas morning we were all gathered in the living room, the presents under the tree. Allen, in true childish fashion, had torn into two or three of his presents before his dad handed him the next gift—a long, wide, shallow box. Allen tore off the paper, and when the box was finally opened, to his wide-eyed amazement, there was a tabletop hockey game! In his excitement he shouted, "I don't want any more presents!" He meant it too. He did not open any of his other gifts and with his dad proceeded to play with his new game.

Allison and I did have a special bond. When she was old enough and had a vocabulary that enabled her to express her thoughts, she would have her mother place a phone call to me. One of her memorable calls came when she was perhaps three years old. When I answered the phone, Allison proceeded to tell me in her childish voice, "Gran Henri, I caught a fish, I have a boyfriend, and his name is Alex."

A crowning joy for me was when the family came for one of their Thanksgiving visits. They arrived late on Wednesday evening. I was up early Thursday morning preparing the turkey for the oven. I heard footsteps on the stair and turned to see four-year-old barefooted Allison standing there in her pajamas. She came to me and said, "I love you, Gran Henri. We are friends."

In August 1996, Charlie and I, along with Rich's family, met at Barb and Terry's home. Never having lived within what I termed a Sunday afternoon visiting distance from the homes of the children, I always placed great value in taking pictures. It was at this family gathering I managed, with help, to corral seven-year-old Kevin, two-year-old Darren, six-year-old Allen, and three-year-old Allison for a picture with their grandfather. I did not know at the time it would be my only opportunity to do so.

These pleasant memories, recorded in my diary, cause me to reflect on those Gran Henri years when I was young and physically able to fully enjoy the children. It minimizes the memories of my fatigue in preparation for the visits, the ensuing entertainment, or of my annoyance and impatience related to modern permissive parenting.

Charlie's life was enriched through the lives of his steprelatives, as was mine when introduced to them. Jim and Sara Whitaker lived in Middletown, Kentucky. Jim had served in the European Theater during World War II as a commandant of a POW camp. The location is unknown to me. On the mantel of Jim and Sara's home was a model sailing ship made by one of the POW detainees. Jim remarked that the prisoner made it from scraps found within the camp and had given it to him. I was impressed by something so beautiful created by one who had experienced the horrors of war. We enjoyed dinner with them, stayed the night, and the following morning, after breakfast, were sent on our way with a pecan pie—true Southern hospitality.

————— ·•+•+•+·· —————

Between the years of 1992 and 1997, there were visits to and from Bruce's family—they, to Columbus, and we, to Las Vegas. The summer of 1994 presented me with the challenge of finding age-appropriate entertainment for my grandchildren. In July, fourteen-year-old Candice came with her sixteen-year-old cousin Krystal (daughter of her mother's sister) for a visit. The following month Bruce Allan and his cousin Adam, both eleven years old, were with us for the better part of a week.

Upon the arrival of Candice and Krystal, Charlie and I gave over the large family room at the far end of the house to the girls. Here they would have a TV, a sofa that converted into a double bed, a bathroom, and best of all, their privacy. We filled the days with visits to COSI, the Columbus Art Museum, and the Santa Maria (a replica of the original ship, permanently docked in downtown Columbus on the Scioto River). We toured the recently renovated State House. Here, in a large vaulted room on the basement level, we observed the splendor of a map of Ohio embedded in the center of the room's floor. The map contained each of the state's eighty-eight counties cut to scale in multicolors of marble mined in the Marble Cliff Quarry in Upper Arlington, a suburb of the city.

It was Charlie who came up with the idea of giving the girls a two-thousand-piece puzzle that held no interest for him but might serve to fill some of their empty hours. This was a godsend because the girls enthusiastically spread puzzle pieces out on a card table and spent hours assembling it. Come time to leave, the incomplete puzzle was somehow secured and placed in one of their suitcases and finished at home. To their distress, when completed, they found one piece missing!

Son Bruce suggested we take the girls for a tour of the OSU campus. Neither was pleased with the idea, but once there, realizing we would have a handsome male undergraduate as our tour guide, the girls' attention moved to the top of the interest scale.

We made two trips out of the city during their visit. The first was to King's Island Amusement Park, a hundred miles south of Columbus. It was the second trip that gave the girls a new experience. We treated them to an evening of harness racing at the Scioto Downs Race Track just south of the city. For this occasion, the girls wore their cleavage-revealing sundresses (embarrassingly low cut for my Midwestern taste, but perfectly acceptable in the Las Vegas culture). They looked lovely and very grown-up. We were seated in the glass-enclosed, air-conditioned dining room and ordered our dinners. The races were about to start and Charlie gave each of the girls $20 and a racing form, directing them to choose their horse and make their decision as to bet win, place, or show. Being that they were underage, Charlie placed the bets. I think they lost more than they won, but that did not depress their enjoyment of the evening.

Krystal, two years older than Candice, was a quiet, unassuming guest in our home. In contrast, Candice's behaviors were more typical of the adolescent—giggling, punching, arguing, pouting, and at other times self-assured and sophisticated. I could see she was maturing. She was my granddaughter, and I wrote in my diary, "I love her dearly." The girls arrived on a Wednesday, and the following Monday, we drove to the home of relatives living in Kentucky where they would continue their vacation.

Adam had been visiting Bruce in Las Vegas, and the boys arrived together in Columbus on Monday, August 15. Their flight was due in the Port Columbus International Airport at 5:50 a.m., but weather and mechanical problems caused a four-hour delay. At 9:50 a.m., we met two very tired, hungry boys as they stepped out of the jetway into the concourse. We took care of the hunger need by stopping at Bob Evans for breakfast on our way back to the house.

Once home, both Adam and Bruce telephoned their mothers to let them know they had arrived safely. Adam immediately fell asleep on the family room sofa. I took Bruce with me on an errand. When I returned home, my voice must have awakened Adam because he came rushing out, hoping to see his mother. I will never forget his disappointed expression and his withdrawal back into the family room to cover his face so I would not see his tears. I knew there was no way I could comfort him; I respected his privacy.

Adam's feeling of homesickness, coupled with Bruce's confession that he lost his billfold containing $65, dampened what I hoped would be a delightful visit for the boys. But things improved the next day. I took them, along with some neighborhood children, to Leaps and Bounds— best described as a large McDonald's play area. They crawled through tunnels, laughed as they descended the enclosed spiral slides, ate pizza, enjoyed cake, and played some more.

On Wednesday, things were better for Adam; his mom and dad had arrived the previous night. Wednesday morning, we left to spend the day at King's Island and the Water Works Park. We rode the roller coasters— the Racer (very bumpy), the Beast (moderately bumpy), and the Vortex (smooth and terrifying). After the boys had their fill of adventure at King's Island, we traveled the short distance to the Water Works Park, cooled off in the pools, and exhausted ourselves climbing the steps to experience the thrill of the high-water slide before departing for home.

The Schumann family left the next day, and Bruce stayed on with us until Saturday. I took him to Vertical Adventures. He did all right on the slanted wall, but when he attempted the challenge of the vertical wall, he was not able to make it to the top. No matter. We returned home and enjoyed a ride on my tandem bicycle where Bruce proved to be a good stoker.

Laundry done, clothes packed, Charlie and I took Bruce Allan to the airport Saturday evening for his nine o'clock flight home, ending another enjoyable visit with a grandchild. I love Bruce and Candice equally, but I will admit, I find it easier to deal with the emotional makeup of boys than I do with girls.

There were a number of visits to Las Vegas during those years, but there was one that will always remain foremost in memory that took place in 1992. Flight reservations had been made weeks in advance; we were to arrive on Saturday, February 22, and sixteen days later depart on Tuesday, March 10.

Charlie and I had no inkling of what awaited us when we arrived on time at the McCarran International Airport. As previously instructed, we went to the baggage claim area, anticipating that Bruce would be there to meet us. We retrieved our bags off the carousel, looked about, and still no appearance of my son. Puzzled, we fashioned a makeshift seat with our suitcases and sat down to wait. It was not a long wait, for I glanced up and saw Bruce hurrying toward us. Instantly I sensed something was wrong by the pained expression on his face. His first words, so filled with emotion he could barely speak, were that Bob (Linda's father) was in an accident. It had happened two hours earlier when his ultralight plane, with son Gary in the copilot's seat, was caught in a wind shear as he approached the Boulder City Airport runway to land. Bob sustained massive injuries. He was taken to the University Medical Center in Las Vegas where doctors were doing all they could to keep him alive. Gary was badly shaken but sustained only minor injuries.

Over the next few days, Bob's life hung in the balance. Family members, to the point of exhaustion, remained at his side. Reports vacillated between his life ebbing away to hope when his condition appeared to stabilize. The few times that Bruce or Linda returned home, the emotional weight they were carrying created a tension that was palpable.

The best help that Charlie and I could give was to stay with the children. Candice and Bruce Allan needed some structure to their days. On Monday we saw Candice off to her junior high school. Bruce Allan's elementary school was on break, so he remained at home with us. That first week we grocery shopped, and together we made cabbage rolls—a family favorite. We took walks, played board games, and watched videos. I helped Bruce clean his room and took him for a needed haircut.

On the weekend Candice was home, and the four of us ventured to the Strip. We visited the Mirage and were mesmerized watching the tropical fish in their huge aquarium, and we stood for a time gaping at the dolphins in their pool. The white tigers, a part of the casino's Siegfried and Roy animal magic show, could be seen in their special habitat cage. We exited the building just in time to see the volcano erupt—a spectacular man-made sight.

In the evening we went to the Excalibur Hotel and Casino to dine with King Arthur and his Knights. The nine-hundred-seat dining/entertainment hall was massive, built in the round with tables placed on a level so diners would have an unobstructed view of the center arena where the entertainment took place. Keeping to the tradition of the time, we ate with our fingers. We dined on roasted Cornish hen, twice-baked potatoes, broccoli, pastries, and beverages that included wine for the adults. The entertainment was exciting to behold. Acrobats performed gravity-defying tricks from the backs of horses; knights took part in jousting encounters, the victor winning the hand of the King's daughter. The culminating event to the evening's entertainment was a lavish royal marriage ceremony. I, for one, regretted leaving this romanticized moment from English history to return to the tragic reality of the present.

Originally, our plan was to include a visit to Jan and Royce in California. Both Bruce Allan and Candice were back in school the second week. Bob was clinging to life. Bruce assured me he could handle the situation and insisted we keep our original plans. With apprehension, we accepted the loan of a car and drove to Santa Cruz. We were there for three days when the call came that Bob had died. It was a Thursday, March 5. The following day, we were back in Las Vegas with the family.

Bob's funeral was on Monday, March 9. Temperature-wise, it was a comfortable, sunny day common to the valley. There were more than three hundred people in attendance for the service. Bob and Betty were well-known in the Las Vegas area. Bob, well-liked and ever the "wheeler-dealer," had become a legend in his time.

We kept our original flight reservation to return home March 10. Bruce took us to the airport and waited with us until time to board our plane. On our flight home, I reflected on those sixteen days of our visit. It was surreal that the day we arrived Bob's accident happened, and the day before we were scheduled to leave was Bob's funeral.

Less than a month after returning home, Charlie and I took a road trip to visit family and friends living in the South. This gave us the opportunity to visit my nephew David Schumann, his wife, Susy, and their four children (nine-year-old Matthew, eight-year-old Christopher, six-year-old Eric, and five-year-old Kathryn) in Christiansburg, Virginia.

We arrived at their home on Thursday, April 2, to spend the night, planning to leave the next day. A freak snowstorm, an uncommon phenomenon to the area, delayed our plans. During the night, a half foot of snow fell that made the hilly roads unsafe for travel. We made the best of the situation playing board games with the children in the morning. When it came time to eat, thinking it would be good for all to get some fresh air and exercise, we offered to treat the family to lunch. That is, anyone willing to trudge the quarter mile through the deep snow up a rather steep hill to Long John Silver's, the nearest restaurant to their home.

All were up for the adventure. Their father, the tallest and strongest of the adults, broke the trail. We must have appeared to be a motley line of eight as we trudged up the hill. Arriving at the almost-vacant restaurant, we satisfied our voracious appetites on what to me was "greasy spoon" fare— but food never tasted so good. The downhill trek back to the house was much easier. That afternoon Charlie and I played outside in the snow with some of the children, including making a snowman. It was a memorable visit that is talked about to this day!

We did get to see Lloyd and Trudy's middle child, Peter; his wife, Beverley' and son Adam more frequently. Beverley was a square dance caller. There were several occasions when she would have a gig in the Columbus area, and much to our delight, they headquartered in our home. There were occasions when the youngest of the siblings, Jill, and her husband, Garvin, visited Columbus. But our opportunities to see them were mostly at Trudy and Lloyd's home in Geneva.

My sister Brenda and her husband, Walt, would make their annual pilgrimage to Columbus to celebrate Charlie's and my birthday with us. We would make it a special weekend attending a Broadway musical at the beautiful restored downtown Ohio Theater, returning to the house for a lobster dinner (Charlie's favorite) and the traditional three-layer cake.

Visits from my sister's oldest daughter, Kellie, and her husband, Kirk, were rare but most enjoyable. There was one occasion when we met the family in Mansfield, a halfway meeting place, and their daughter Courtney came to spend a few days with us. But the visit I vividly recall was the year the family came for a weekend in October. The leaves were rapidly falling and covered the ground with a thick carpet. Upon their arrival, Kirk grabbed a leaf rake and became a leaf-raking machine as he made huge piles on the stretched-out tarp, then methodically schlepped each pile to the backyard compost area to be sprinkled with lime and left to decompose over the winter. That was the only year we were fortunate enough to have them visit at leaf-raking time.

Brenda's youngest daughter, Shellie, had lived for a time in Columbus, and we became very close; she seemed more like a daughter to me. She was my buddy on the Volksmarch Club hikes. When she closed her apartment the fall of 1992, she stayed with us for several weeks before moving to Aliquippa, Pennsylvania, for her marriage to Dave Byrne.

When their daughter was born, they named her Natalie Elaine. It was the middle name that touched my heart; Shellie liked the name, and it became more special to her when she realized it was also my middle name. Charlie and I were with them in Aliquippa the Sunday in August 1994, when Natalie Elaine Byrne was baptized wearing the beautiful baptismal gown that her Grandmother Brenda had lovingly stitched for her.

With each marriage I gained new family, but always sustained the bond with the old. I have spoken often of visits to and from Allan Dickie's children. Those visits continued after I married Charlie. They welcomed Charlie and his children, and we became one extended family.

———— ++++++ ————

Now that I was retired, I took full advantage of all social opportunities to be with neighbors and friends. Marion and Frank Clover were in our folk dance group, and when Marion asked if Charlie and I would like to play bocce with them, we readily agreed. We regularly met one night a week and played on the rough ground of our backyard lawns. Marion always played in her bare feet; Frank was a stickler for precision. He carried a measuring device to determine which ball came to rest closest to the "jack." Our competitive, but friendly, competition that year of 1995 began as the winter snows melted and continued until the fall leaves covered the ground making play impossible. In November we decided to have a banquet celebration; losers treated the winners. The individual scores were close, but Frank and Marion came out the winners. They chose The Olive Garden as our banquet site. Charlie's artistic talents aided me with the making of a pink crown for Marion that featured colored paper cutouts of right and left bare feet, toenails painted red and sparkling with glitter. For Frank it was a meter stick decorated with a few of those pesky lawn impediments that always seem to knock all balls but Frank's off course, giving his ball the point advantage of nearest to the jack. Our bocce league lasted only one season, but the memory will last a lifetime.

In June 1995 we held a block party on our street. Over the years, the idea had been discussed, but no one took the initiative to organize it. It was Susan Fox and I who appointed ourselves a Richards Road Block Party committee of two and moved ahead with plans. The neighbors willingly signed the required city petition requesting permission to close the street. They volunteered to serve on food, entertainment, and equipment committees. The owners of a home with a large front porch offered to host the event. The afternoon and evening of the block party, the street was closed to vehicular traffic. First were the planned children's games, and then the excitement of free-play time with no fear of a child being hit by a vehicle. Adults milled about conversing with neighbors never previously met. Food was plentiful. After the evening meal, there was folk dancing in the street. The merriment went on well after dark. By all accounts it was a success. In following years, there were other block parties, but in truth, each year enthusiasm waned. By the time 1997 came around, my life had taken a dramatic turn. I was not able to take part in the planning, and our wonderful idea of an annual Richards Road Block Party died a natural death.

I HAVE OFTEN REFERRED to the variety of resources and events that made living in Columbus so enjoyable. During the years 1992 through 1997, there were four events that stand out in memory, given that it was for different reasons—sporting, commercial, natural, and man-made.

My niece Jill, an alumna of OSU, was able to get us tickets for an annual football game. My interest in football was nil, but I loved the band's halftime Script Ohio performance. It was in 1992 that our seats, high up in the bleachers, gave me my first-time, straight-on view of the consummate moment in the Script Ohio routine when I could follow the band member as he pranced out of the line formation to dramatically dot the "*i*" in Ohio with his sousaphone.

Each year in early December, a Winterfair craft show was held in the Ohio Expo Center on the Ohio State Fairgrounds. I read an article about the show in the Columbus Dispatch, and this piqued my interest. When I entered the large hall filled with literally hundreds of booths staffed by artisans showcasing their wood, glass, ceramic, cloth, and leather creations (to name only a few), I was overwhelmed. I sauntered the aisles, all the time browsing through the myriad of choices, experiencing such frustration I was ready to give up on my idea of selecting gifts for family members.

Just as I was turning to make my way to the exit, along the back wall at the far end of this blimp-sized room, I spied a display booth of dolls. Dennis and Jane Tressler, from Valencia, Pennsylvania, traveled widely to display their handcrafted ethnic dolls at juried craft shows. On display were Santa Claus dolls from Germany, Sweden, Ireland, England, Switzerland, France, Poland, Hungary, to list only a few of the countries represented. I was enthralled that the character we call Santa Claus came in so many personas, shapes, and sizes. Here was just the right gift for Candice and Bruce Allan. I selected dolls from countries representing a part of their genealogical makeup—Saint Lucia from Sweden for Candice, Knecht Ruprecht from Germany for Bruce Allan. Over the years I added to their collection until the time this talented couple, to my disappointment, ceased to make the dolls.

It is trite to say, "The best kept secret…" but when I speak of the Topiary Garden Park on the grounds of the original Ohio School for the Deaf, I speak the truth. Located in a restored neighborhood one half mile east of the Statehouse, James T. Mason, a local sculptor, and his wife Elaine, had a vision—to recreate Georges Seurat's Post-Impressionist painting *A Sunday Afternoon on the Isle of La Grande Jatte* in topiary art form.

In 1988 George Mason crafted framework out of tubing that formed the shapes in the painting—fifty-four human figures, three dogs, a monkey, a cat, and eight boats placed in the water of the man-made pond that depicted the Paris River Seine. Elaine, an artist in her own right with knowledge of horticulture, supervised the planting of the yew shrubs that, when matured, filled in the frames of the figures. Later she directed a cadre of park volunteers in properly trimming the shrubs. This is the only known topiary representation of a painting in the world. Now completed, it covers one-third of the park's nine acres.

Looking back, I think our Schumann Open pseudo-golf tournaments paved the way for our Schumann Huddle reunions. Our golf outings were mostly held at golf courses in Ashtabula or Lake counties where Lloyd and Brenda lived. Jill and Garvin would make annual visits home, and for Charlie and me, it was the opportune time to get to see everyone. In favorable weather, we would play golf and, at game's end, assemble at the home of one of the family members where a jovial replay of the game would take place—bragging about the unbelievable shot or lamenting a missed putt. This took place while the empty beer bottle pile became higher and the stories took on a life of inflated fabrication. Missing from all this family conviviality were Lloyd's son, David, and my sons, Bruce and Vernon, and their families.

Ameriflora, the international horticultural exhibition, opened in April of 1992 in Columbus. Now that I was retired, the thought came to me this would be a good time to host a family reunion. There was an ulterior motive in my wanting a family reunion. I was the middle child of the three Schumann siblings, and for the better part of my life, I lived apart from them, making an effort to visit each as often as possible. A family reunion would provide the opportune time for all to come together. I presented the idea to family members in 1991 during Thanksgiving dinner at Pete and Bev's home.

Anyone listening would have heard my deep sigh of relief when this family of chiefs and no Indians nodded their approval. A date was set for the weekend of June 12–14 for the coming year. I moved ahead with reunion plans—later given the moniker Schumann Huddle. All families but one responded. Those that would be in attendance were the following:

Lloyd and Trudy Schumann	Geneva, Ohio
David (Suzy) Schumann—Matt,	Christiansburg, Virginia
Chris, Eric, and Katy	
Peter (Beverley) Schumann—Adam	Ashtabula, Ohio
Jill (Garvin Rumberger) Schumann	Carlisle, Pennsylvania

Henrietta (Charles Gass) Schumann (Nelson, Dickie)	Columbus, Ohio
Bruce (Linda) Nelson—Candice and Bruce A.	Las Vegas, Nevada
Brenda (Walter Spadaro) Schumann (Dennis, Gibson)	North Kingsville, Ohio
Kellie (Kirk Peine) Gibson—Courtney	North Kingsville, Ohio
Shellie Gibson	Columbus, Ohio,
Dave Byrne	Aliquippa, Pennsylvania

We were sorry to miss the company of Vernon, Judy, and their children.

I spent the month of May planning the menus and assembling miscellaneous supplies. To some degree, the success of the weekend was weather-dependent. I never petitioned God regarding trivial matters, but this weekend held the necessity of importuning him to intercede with Mother Nature for sunny skies and a comfortable temperature.

The Las Vegas family was scheduled to arrive on Thursday, the day before the festivities were to begin. But Candice, wanting to help, came a week earlier on June 4. Her first assigned task was to make a banner that read "WELCOME TO THE 1992 SCHUMANN HUDDLE." Next I asked her to assist me in the food preparation. This she did, as much as possible with her limited culinary skills. Then she would sit on the wheeled office chair taken from the desk in the breakfast nook and roll about following me as close as space permitted in the small kitchen when she became bored or tired—a twelve-year-old's way of helping.

Candice's most embarrassing, yet comical, moment occurred when Shellie, Candice, and I were shopping in Sam's Club. We were in the beverage aisle, and Candice was helping load beverages in our already-chock-full cart. She attempted to lift a gallon jug of apple cider into the cart. It slipped from her hands and dropped to the floor. The top flew off, gurgling a sticky rivulet as it flowed out of the bottle. Shellie, standing near us and ever ready with a clever retort, called out in a loud voice, "Herb, clean up aisle 7!" (A famous line from the movie *Mr. Mom*.)

Some time ago, based on an article I had read in the *Columbus Dispatch*, I facetiously proclaimed myself to be a "FRUMP FAIRY"—frugal, responsible, unpretentious, and mature person. Pete and Bev heard me, and when they arrived presented me with a Frump Fairy Wand—a child's baseball bat turned on a lathe into the shape of a wand by Bev's brother-in-law, inscribed by Bev using a wood burner tool, and varnished to enhance and protect.

By three thirty that afternoon, all family members had arrived, and with wand held resolutely in hand, the Frump Fairy declared the first Schumann Huddle officially open. God must have heard my supplications, for weather-wise, it was a perfect weekend. On Saturday the family spent the day enjoying the Ameriflora attractions—flowers in abundance, the foreign country pavilions, and live entertainment on the stage of the ground's natural amphitheater. In the evening, all gathered back at our house to enjoy food and a time of camaraderie. Later the younger beer-drinking members departed to check out the downtown bars.

All told our first family reunion was a resounding success. There were subsequent reunions hosted in North Kingsville at the home of Kellie and Kirk, by Jill and Garvin in Pennsylvania on the Turkey Island family retreat in the Susquehanna River, and by Bruce and Linda at the Lake Mead Marina outside of Las Vegas. Over the years the enthusiasm for the Schumann Huddle waned—children grew up, nuclear families retreated unto their own, and no one took the initiative to carry the organizational torch to continue making it happen. Am I surprised? No. Am I disappointed? Yes.

———————+++++++———————

RELIEVED OF THE DEMANDS of my professional life, I was now free to travel—and during the years of 1992–1997, travel we did. We traveled within Ohio, visited distant places within the country, and planned one overseas adventure each year.

In May 1994, we took advantage of a three-day trip offered by the Ohio Historical Society to islands in Lake Erie, north of Sandusky. Our first stop was on Kelly's Island, where we carefully walked among the glacial grooves that were shaped by the ice-age glaciers, all the while observing the beauty and inhaling the fragrance of the lilacs that our guide told us were planted by German immigrants who settled there in the early part of the nineteenth century. A visit to South Bass Island followed. We visited Perry's Victory and International Peace Memorial commemorating Commodore Oliver Hazard Perry's decisive victory in a naval battle in the War of 1812. The final stop on our tour took us to Johnson's Island—a sobering event. We observed an ongoing Civil War prison camp archaeological dig. Here archaeologists were able to learn something of the lifestyle and conditions endured by the prisoners. Before leaving the island, our group traversed the sacred grounds of the Johnson's Island Confederate Cemetery.

Charlie did not share my interest in history, so he opted out of the Hayes Presidential Tour, also sponsored by the Ohio Historical Society. I was one of twelve who boarded the bus the morning of August 2, 1994, for a three-day adventure that took us to places of interest related to Ohio's nine presidents. The tour bus traveled through twenty-eight of Ohio's eighty-eight counties, covering 1,050 miles. The bus stopped in small towns and large cities. We visited past presidents' homes, their grave site memorials, and were privy to lectures by those well versed in their history. It was an informative and exhilarating trip. What follows is a list of the nine presidents in the order in which they served and includes an interesting anecdotal comment about each.

We stopped in North Bend on the Ohio River at the tomb of William Henry Harrison, the ninth president of the United States. At his March inauguration in Washington, DC, he refused to wear a hat and coat defying the frigid temperature, developed pneumonia, and died at the age of sixty-eight—one month after taking the oath of office.

The home of Ulysses S. Grant's birth is in Point Pleasant, also on the Ohio River, but his home state is given as Illinois. Grant lived to become the eighteenth president due to the fact that he declined the invitation of President Lincoln to join him at the Ford Theater on April 14, 1865. John Wilkes Booth's nefarious plan had included Grant.

The home of the nineteenth president, Rutherford B. Hayes, is located in Fremont on thirty-five masterfully landscaped acres known as Spiegel Grove. Hayes "squeaked" his way to becoming president in 1877. The popular vote was contested, and it was the Electoral College that gave Hayes one vote more than Tilden.

The twentieth president, James A. Garfield, ran a front porch campaign from his house in Mentor, named Lawnfield. In the months leading up to the election, more than seventeen thousand people came by foot, horseback, carriage, and train to hear him speak. His impressive monument is in the Lakeview Cemetery in Cleveland.

The twenty-third president was Benjamin Harrison—the only grandfather-grandson duo to hold office. History judged him to be ineffective. A song was written entitled "Grandfather's Hat Fits Ben." Ohio was his birth state, but Indiana was his home state.

The last of the Civil War veterans to become president was William McKinley. The William McKinley Memorial and Museum is in Canton, paying homage to our twenty-fifth president.

The twenty-seventh president, William Howard Taft, is remembered for his size. A custom-made bathtub was installed in the White House to accommodate this six-foot-two-inch man weighing 320 pounds. When asked the difference between a "fat man" or "a man who is fat," Taft replied, "In the second, the man dominates, not the fat."

The twenty-ninth president was the first to be elected when women were given the right to vote in 1920. The Warren G. Harding home and museum are in Marion. Harding is known to have said, "I have no trouble with my enemies. It is my friends who keep me walking the floor at night." Harding's undoing was he could not say "no" to friends, and he surrounded himself with his Ohio cronies. His administration is remembered for the corrupt Teapot Dome scandal.

Car trips to visit my cousins in Farmville, Virginia, provided Charlie and me the opportunity to become immersed in Civil War history. Louis Thompson and Della Mendez (grandchildren of Squair Shuart) lived near several Civil War sites. Louis and Della took us to Richmond, the capital of the Confederacy; to the Petersburg Battle Field where a ten-month battle raged that weakened the South; and to Saylor's Creek where five thousand died, marking the final battle of the war. The carnage that took place at these sites seemed surreal amidst the flora and fauna of the placid countryside. We also visited Appomattox Court House. Here on April 9, 1865, General Lee accepted the terms of surrender from General Grant.

An antidote to the horrors of the Civil War was our visit to the Light of Truth Universal Shrine (LOTUS), located outside of Buckingham, built on a majestic Virginia hillside that slopes to the James River. The edifice is shaped like a lotus flower, a symbol for the spiritual unfoldment of the soul. It is dedicated to all faiths and to world peace. We were privileged to meet the Reverend Sri Swami Satchidananda, the founder. Louis, general contractor for the construction of the shrine, was personally acquainted with the Reverend.

We chose to drive, not fly, to New York to take part in a five-day Elderhostel program held on the campus of Long Island University. I was the designated driver when we approached the city and had to drive through the Midtown Tunnel that took us onto Long Island. Not used to the aggressiveness of the New York drivers, or multilane highways, I found this a white-knuckle, nail-biting experience.

The theme of the Elderhostel program was immigration. In education, when completing a study, we referred to the "culminating event." Our culminating event was a trip to Ellis Island. I knew Ma Nelson had come through Ellis Island when she came from Sweden in 1912. When entering the main building, I rented a tape narrated by Tom Brokaw explaining the intake process conducted by government officials for the incoming immigrants. The first test was a preliminary health screening, and on my way up the stairs to the second floor, I tripped. I was so taken up in my mental time warp that I was momentarily paralyzed with fright, fearful an official had observed me and thinking I had a physical deformity would send me back on the first available ship. Fortunately for me, no uniformed officer took me firmly by the arm to lead me away. I virtually completed all the tests an immigrant had to pass before I came to the exit door and walked out onto the street. I was in America!

Our next trip was not by car but by train. The Ohio Railway Museum in Worthington sponsored a trip, Rails to Greenfield Village at Dearborn, Michigan. The Norfolk Southern Corporation provided the eighteen passenger, four club, and two snack cars that made up the train pulled by a steam engine. It was a pleasant Sunday morning in July when we joined the crowd of 850 people assembled at the fairgrounds, ready to board the train for the two-day excursion to Dearborn.

Greenfield Village was founded on eighty-one acres by Henry Ford in 1929 as the Edison Institute. Over the years, it has been expanded to promote and celebrate the spirit of innovation in America. Upon our arrival, we immediately realized there was too much to see and too little time. Charlie and I used our time wisely and spent most of the hours in Edison's Menlo Park Laboratory and the Wright Cycle Shop—home of the famous brothers Orville and Wilbur, who are credited with inventing, building, and flying the world's first successful airplane.

Charlie and I enjoyed travel and planned accordingly. On April 23, 1995, we backed out of the driveway in our Dodge van filled with clothes, camping equipment, tandem bicycle, and other miscellaneous items for an eight-week touring adventure in the West. Leaving Columbus, we drove southwest to cross the Mississippi River at Saint Louis and connect with nostalgic Route 66 that took us across the Southern tier of states. In Arizona we veered to the northwest to take scenic seaside routes north through California and Oregon into Washington. We headed east and home across the Northern tier of states, following around the Great Lakes into Ohio. Our seven-thousand-mile, accident-free trip took us through eighteen states. On June 23, 1995, after driving seven hundred miles on the final day of our trip, we uttered a prayer of thankfulness and relief as we entered our driveway at 247 Richards Road in Columbus.

As much as possible, we camped along our route, welcoming the activity involved in pitching a tent and cooking the evening meal. When location or inclement weather prohibited camping, we stayed in motels. I became very adept at setting up the motel room's ironing board to use as a kitchen counter, plugging in the hot plate and coffee pot and, with drink in hand, cooking our evening meal.

In Arizona, we visited the Grand Canyon. Previously I had made reservations for a campsite at the Mather Campground. It was early evening when we arrived, found our site, and set up camp. The next morning, we were up early, prepared breakfast, and when cleanup was complete, we unloaded the tandem bike from the van and set out to explore the area. We did get attention—two white-haired senior citizens cycling along to the strains of Grofe's *Grand Canyon Suite* playing on the cassette that was strapped to the carrier of our bicycle. We noted some taking our picture and heard comments—"Looks like fun"—and fun it was!

Our first stop was at the IMAX Theater featuring the 3-D film *Grand Canyon Hidden Secrets*. Leaving the theater, I was left with the feeling of the finiteness of one's life placed in perspective over eons of time. We got on our tandem and rode to Angel Point where I stood in silence and absorbed the magnificent, hypnotic spell created by the canyon's unspeakable beauty.

We planned for a two-night stay at the Grand Canyon; on the morning of the third day we were on the road again. Before leaving Arizona, we visited Lake Havasu, the town featuring the reconstructed London Bridge. Fifteen years earlier, when I lived in Las Vegas, I had been there. I remembered it as a quaint, friendly desert town; but the call of the London Bridge had transformed it into a rude, crude, tourist-gouging place. Our stay was short.

A few hours' drive north took us to Hoover Dam where we crossed into Nevada and the home of my son and family in Las Vegas. Our week with them was filled with family activities, casinos, shows, and a boat ride on Lake Mead. Reluctantly, we left Las Vegas and drove into California where we opted to take the scenic seascape Route 1 to Santa Cruz, spending a delightful week with Allan Dickie's daughter Jan Fincher and family.

Leaving Santa Cruz, we drove posthaste to Seattle, Washington, for our scheduled flight out of Sea-Tac Airport to Sitka, Alaska. Previously we had made arrangements to visit Mike Reeve, son of Susan Gardner, my former neighbor in Worthington. Mike worked at a fish hatchery on a remote island off the coast of Sitka. We arrived in Sitka on May 30 while a fishing derby was in progress, and my first impression of the natives was their hit-

or-miss comfortable, functional clothing (loose garments and bib overalls). The men were heavily bearded and best described as having that salt-of-the-earth look. We registered at the local hotel and noted that almost every guest had a dog, and dogs were welcome in the rooms.

We contacted Belair Flights and made reservations on a four-passenger float plane that would take us to the small island where the fish hatchery was located. The next morning we checked with the airport. Winds were favorable, and the plane would fly as scheduled. The forty-five-minute flight at an altitude of 1,400 feet provided us with spectacular views of small, rocky, pine-tree-covered islands with waves crashing at the shorelines and cobalt-blue water the likes of which I had never seen. Nearing our destination, the plane descended to glide over the water to the dock with nary a vibration.

Mike was at the dock to greet us. We followed him, carefully navigating the maze of wooden walkways, as he led us to the two-story house that was his home. As we lurched along, we noticed several of the men with a shotgun slung over their shoulder. Mike calmly informed us that brown bears came into the camp and one had to be alert and prepared.

Along with the other seven men who worked at the fishery, Mike had various duties in the care of the fish tanks and ponds. He took us on an introductory tour of the hatchery, stopping by a long, narrow tank measuring four feet wide by twenty feet long and three feet deep. I looked, and the water appeared to be solid with tiny fish. Mike commented this tank held upward of half a million of the baby coho—unbelievable to me.

We learned of the cyclical life of the coho salmon. As adults, the fish return to their original habitat to spawn. The released eggs are placed in metal boxes (incubators) and hatch in two and a half months. One month after hatching, they are transferred to a fresh water pond, and are now called "fry," where they are cared for and fed for one year. The "yearlings" are placed in salt water and referred to as "smolts." After one month, the smolts are released into the ocean to return one and a half years later, and the cycle repeats itself.

Back at the house, Charlie and I unpacked while Mike prepared our supper of ground bear meat, mixed vegetables, with an egg added, and served over noodles. I was in need of some food; I found the dish to be quite tasty.

The next morning, Mike took us out on a boat into the bay area to fish. No fish were caught, but the sea life was fascinating—jellyfish, seals, and a sunflower starfish with a large body and twenty legs. Mike's senses were accustomed to the natural habitat of the surroundings, and as we approached the dock, he pointed out a bald eagle in flight.

That afternoon Mike asked if we would like to climb the mountain to view the lake at the top that supplied the fishery with fresh water. We enthusiastically agreed and together started the quarter-mile climb. As we neared the top, the terrain became so steep that a rope had been installed to use to pull oneself up along the narrow path carved out of the dense undergrowth. All effort put forth in the climb was rewarded when I reached the top and my eyes took in the spectacular panoramic view of meadows, a freshwater lake, pine-covered hillsides, and below, the cobalt-blue waters of the ocean.

As we were slipping and sliding our way back down this small mountain, Mike pointed out pieces of a decaying twelve-inch wooden pipe wrapped with heavy wire. Decades ago fresh water from the lake flowed through this man-made pipe to the whaling station that was here on the island. Alongside remaining sections of the old pipe lay a modern-day water line that supplied the fresh water to the fish hatchery.

Back at the house, seated about the table relaxing with a cup of tea, I noted that Charlie appeared disoriented. The climb to the top of the mountain was too much for his compromised circulatory system. It appeared he was having a TIA—a slight stroke. The RN was summoned who was stationed on the island, but to my relief, and certainly to Mike's, Charlie appeared to slowly regain mental and physical control.

Following a restful night, I was up early enjoying my first cup of coffee of the day on the deck. A gentle rain was falling. I looked to the west, and there was a rainbow that began at the water's surface, arching against a background of pine trees, the apex of the bow reaching into the sky—a phenomenal farewell sight. The weather was favorable, our plane was on time, and we returned to Sitka. No travel agency could possibly replicate our experience on that tiny remote island just off the coast of Sitka.

Mike's mother had arrived in Sitka and was at the dock to meet us with a rented car. She gave us a tour of the area. It didn't take long, for there were few paved roads that extended beyond the city limits. We had registered for an Elderhostel program at the local Sheldon Jackson Campus. For the next six days, we were immersed in classes related to Alaskan history and culture. Much to our surprise and enjoyment, there was a class in chamber music staffed by local talented residents.

Much later we learned that no alcoholic beverages were permitted on the island. It was Susan who laughingly told us that shortly after our visit, she visited her son. She had filled her suitcase with six-packs of beer, and as the pilot loaded her suitcases, he remarked how heavy they were. Susan replied that she was taking books to the men on the island. It was then that Charlie and I realized the men must have been disappointed when Mike's anticipated guests did not come bearing suitcases filled with six-packs of contraband—our only regret on this most uncommon visit to Alaska.

As we were waiting to board our flight from Sitka to Seattle, I was fascinated to observe cartons of frozen fish loaded onto the plane. I entertained the thought that the additional weight might require some of us to forfeit our seat in favor of the fish, recalling that a fishing tournament was in progress when we arrived and the men were returning home with their prize.

We were not asked to give up our seats for boxes of frozen fish. The flight was uneventful back to Seattle, and upon landing at the Sea-Tac International Airport, we immediately got our car and headed east. Our first stop was to spend the night with family in Spokane and then continue east to Glacier National Park in Montana.

We had made reservations for two nights at the Lake McDonald Lodge. Stepping out onto the deck of our corner room, we had a spectacular view of the surrounding mountains with the tree-covered lower slopes beginning close to the water's edge and extending into the sky where one could see glacier-covered peaks. This view was complemented by the fauna of the area—birds and squirrels in abundance and deer drinking at the water's edge. Fortunately, we encountered no bears. When we checked in, we were warned there were bears in the park, and when hiking on the trails near the lake, we took the necessary precautions of carrying no food and made loud noises as we moved along.

On the morning of June 14, we left Lake McDonald Lodge and continued eastward to Yellowstone National Park located in the northwest corner of Wyoming. The day's drive was uninteresting (flat land in the middle of nowhere), but we entertained ourselves listening to Stephen King's spellbinding book *Dolores Claiborne*.

As we entered the park, we observed the devastation of the fire that raged there in the early 1990s. The slopes paralleling the Gallatin River were covered with blackened, charred trees. Some of the natural vegetation had grown out of the scorched earth, and we saw buffalo, elk, and deer grazing on the hillsides. Our destination was Old Faithful and the Mud

(Paint) Pots that gurgled and burped revealing multicolored bubbles—hypnotic to watch. We found lodging for the night within the park.

The next morning, we were up early and on the road for the day's journey that would take us to the Devils Tower National Monument in northeastern Wyoming. This rock formation, 1,400 feet high, juts out of a flat landscape and can be seen for many miles. It was formed by the cooling of molten rock and, incorrectly translated from the Indian word, given the name "God's Bad Tower" that further morphed into "Devils Tower" (no apostrophe) as it is known today. At the tower, we immersed ourselves in the folklore and artifacts on exhibit in the museum, opted not to climb the tower (I jest, but many do), but hiked the one and a half miles around the base.

As impressive as the tower was, it was our encounter with a couple we met when we stopped at a café for an early supper that remains with me. Seated in a booth, waiting for our order, Charlie and I were discussing Stephen King's book. Apparently, our conversation piqued the interest of the couple in the booth behind us for they spoke up, saying they were most interested in our comments, having not yet read the book.

Jan and John Moore spent their summers on a ranch in Wyoming, the remainder of the year in their California home. We invited them to join us as we ate and for the next thirty minutes engaged in the most spellbinding conversation. She was a professional photographer; he, a retired Rockwell engineer. They had traveled the world. As we parted, we offered to loan them the *Dolores Claiborne* tape so they could enjoy listening to it as they continued their drive. They graciously accepted and took our address with the assurance it would be returned. Within the month we received the tape in the mail with a note saying they had driven through the night to get to their home. The story was so compelling they had to hear it to the end.

The following day we drove to Sturgis in western South Dakota. Both of my sons owned Harley Davidson motorcycles, and it was their desire at some time in the future to take part in the annual Sturgis Motorcycle Rally. When we were there it was a quiet, sedate town with a population less than six thousand people. Not so when the bikers were in town. We promised Bruce we'd stop and, at the very least, buy him and his brother Harley Davidson T-shirts. We walked the Main Street and had no difficulty in finding a store where Harley Davidson memorabilia was sold. T-shirts purchased—mission accomplished. We left about noon the day following and continued to Mount Rushmore.

We had made a reservation for three nights at a campground located close to the Mount Rushmore National Memorial. Upon arrival we were told there was an available campsite with a tepee. The thought of living in a tepee for three days appealed to our sense of adventure. The tepee was twelve feet in diameter, a ten-foot lodge pole in the center, the frame covered in canvas (not skins) with an additional flap overlapping the peak that could be opened separately to provide ventilation. The floor was a raised wooden platform. The entrance was through a split in the canvas that could be secured with attached leather thongs.

At first our temporary home appeared quaint. Needed equipment was unpacked; sleeping bags spread out on the floor. Only then did I note the space between the floorboards and the overgrown grass under and around the tent. With great difficulty, I squelched any fear of critters that might invade our space. Our first night in the tent was without incident, but on the second night, there was a torrential rain and hailstorm. We had left the ventilation flap of the tent open. Rain and hailstones pelted our sleeping bags. Charlie got up, went outside, and used the long pole attached to the ventilation flap to close the opening. In the process, he was soaked. Living in a tent was anything but quaint.

In the 1930s, Gutzon Borglum and his son Lincoln supervised the carving of the heads of four presidents into the granite face of Mount Rushmore—George Washington (father of our country), Thomas Jefferson (author of the Declaration of Independence), Abraham Lincoln (end of slavery and preservation of the Union), and Theodore Roosevelt (conservation and completion of the Panama Canal). The final night of our stay, we were two among hundreds who stood in reverent silence watching the multicolored lighting ceremony that illuminated the memorial. The ceremony concluded with the singing of our national anthem—an emotionally moving experience.

We left the Black Hills and, now anxious to return home, connected with I-90 to cross South Dakota. Stopping at the first available rest stop, we learned we could rent a tourist tape for $20 and return it at the last rest stop before crossing the eastern border of the state to get a refund of $15. It was the best investment we made on our trip. For $5 we were entertained for the next three hundred miles learning about the history, famous people, legends, and interesting attractions in the state.

We stopped in Wall, South Dakota, a small town just off I-90. In the mid-1930s, Ted Hustead, a pharmacist, and his wife, Dorothy, purchased the town's only pharmacy. It was the time of the Great Depression, and no one had much money. Ted managed to hold on for five years but was ready to give up until Dorothy experienced a eureka moment. Over the years, she was aware of the number of cars that passed by on the main road, but few ever stopped. She inveigled Ted to make and post signs along the highway offering free ice water to the hot, weary traveler. Reluctant, and feeling foolish, Ted did as his wife directed and strategically placed "Free Ice Water at the Wall Drug Store" signs along the highway. (One might think it was a precursor to the movie *Field of Dreams* starring Kevin Costner. "If you build it he will come.") Hot, weary motorists saw the signs, pulled into Wall, and stopped at the Wall Drug Store to claim their free glass of ice water. Some made purchases. It was a miraculous marketing strategy that made what was once a small-town drugstore into a place that has become world famous.

When we were there in 1995, Wall Drug Store was a multibuilding complex, stocked with trinkets, tchotchkes, and gaudy merchandise—items that had tourist appeal. But one could find amidst the glitz and the glitter some mannequin displays that tastefully depicted the culture of the area. Before leaving we stopped in the coffee shop for refreshments. There we observed an elderly gentleman seated nearby, given attention by many people. Upon inquiry, we were told that was **the** Ted Hustead (1903–1999). I could not let this opportunity pass. I had purchased the book *Free Ice Water*, went up to where he was seated, introduced myself, and he graciously autographed my book, even consenting to allow his picture to be taken with Charlie and me.

Once again headed east on I-90, listening to the informational tape, we learned about the annual outhouse race held in Kadoka each summer. The rules were, each outhouse must have three participants—one seated on the inside and two on the outside manually propelling the building along the prescribed route. The visual image of this rollick brought back memories of my childhood and the outhouse pranks of the boys in the neighborhood. To my regret, the race was not on at the time we passed through. It would have been a hilarious sight to behold.

Before leaving South Dakota, we drove through the desolate Badlands and toured a sod house, recalling the *Little House on the Prairie* books written by Laura Ingalls Wilder. Our last stop before leaving South Dakota was the Corn Palace in Mitchell. The mural art that adorned the walls of the building, created by using different colors of corn, was incredible. We spent one more night in a motel, and the final day of our trip, we drove seven hundred miles to get home—an all-around spectacular trip.

————— ‡‡‡‡‡‡ —————

CHARLIE JOINED ME IN RECREATIONAL BICYCLING. We were members of several bicycle clubs. I had read a book entitled *Life in the Slow Lane*, and both Charlie and I came to the full realization of what that meant as we pedaled the back roads of scenic byways, explored small towns, met all types of people and experienced all kinds of weather—the extremes of the gratifying and the gnarly.

As members of the Columbus Outdoor Pursuits (COP), we took part in one of their annual June Great Outdoor Bicycle Adventure (GOBA) rides. GOBA is a weeklong event for 1,500 bicyclists—fifty miles a day, different campsites each night, porta-potty, lines for the gang showers, and food served mess-hall style. The primitive conditions combined with the extreme heat proved to be too much for us, and this was our onetime effort to take part in this ride.

In the fall of 1994 COP sponsored a GOBALUX ride. This three-day ride was planned for the less-rugged cyclist, no more than thirty-five miles each day, with lodging in upscale inns providing rooms with a comfortable bed, private bath, and a dining room menu that would please any palate. We took part in only three GOBALUX tours. By design, the ride catered to a small group of twenty people. Consequently, COP lost money and was discontinued.

I was a member of the Westerville Bicycling Club (WBC), located in Westerville, a suburb of Columbus. I often took part in their group rides, and on one ride, not able to keep up, I had fallen behind the group with whom I was riding. The day was hot, and the kerchief I had about my neck was bothersome. While riding, I attempted to untie the kerchief and reattach it to my handlebars. In doing so, I lost control of my bicycle just as a huge truck was passing. I can't in all honesty say that my life went before my eyes, but I do recall a feeling of horror thinking I would go under the truck's wheels and be crushed. Miraculously, I narrowly missed the truck as I hit the ground. The driver stopped and rushed back to my aid. I was able to get up and was relieved to find I had sustained only scraped knees, bruised elbows, and a humongous bruised ego. My helmet had saved my head. Lesson learned—from that day forward, I never took my hands off the bicycle's handlebars while riding. That annoying kerchief almost cost me my life.

Charlie was with me on another WBC ride. We drove to Lancaster, thirty miles to the southeast of Columbus, and joined three other couples for a weekend stay at Shaw's Inn. We arrived early on Saturday morning, enjoyed a day of biking in the hilly, picturesque area surrounding the town, then returned to our rooms to shower and rest before the others were to join us in our luxury suite for drinks before dinner. Charlie paid no heed to the fact that he was tired and hungry, drank three bourbons, one martini, and promptly fell asleep on the bed. We left him there and went to dinner. Now we both had an identity of ineptitude with the WBC. It seemed neither of us could stay upright—me on a bicycle, and Charlie with his imbibing.

———————————++++++———————————

OUR ENJOYMENT OF BICYCLING extended beyond the byways of Ohio. During those first five years of my retirement, we joined other groups. We learned about the Great Eastern Rally (GEAR) rides, offered under the umbrella of the League of American Wheelmen.

GEAR rallies were held in the summer at rural college campuses with ready access to flat, rolling, and hilly terrain—something for all ages and cycling abilities. The colleges opened their dormitories and cafeterias to the several thousand bicyclists who registered for the ride.

We attended our first GEAR in 1992 at Georgetown College in Georgetown, Kentucky, twelve miles north of Lexington. To arrive at our destination, we drove through the beautiful bluegrass region of central Kentucky. There the barns appeared to be larger and more luxurious than the houses. This left no doubt in our minds—we were in thoroughbred horse country.

Upon our arrival, we registered and were given our dormitory room assignment and packet of information—ride maps, meetings, vendors, food availability, and evening entertainment. All this for a nominal fee, if one were willing to tolerate cafeteria food, uncomfortable mattresses, and for many, bathrooms down the hall.

We found our room, unpacked, studied the route maps, and settled for a short ride before dinner. Charlie was a trouper, doing his best to keep up as we cycled along. But he struggled; his legs would cramp, requiring frequent rest stops. Previously, I have referred to our riding a tandem bicycle. It was at this GEAR ride that I first shared with Charlie the nascent idea I had harbored for some time—a tandem could solve the problem of our different riding abilities. I noted in the information packet a session "Introduction to Tandem Riding" offered the next morning. I suggested to Charlie that we attend. At the conclusion of the program, and at my insistence, we signed up for a test ride that afternoon.

At the appointed time, we were at the football field where a paved track provided a haven for the novice to attempt their maiden tandem ride. Charlie agreed I could sit on the front seat as the "captain," he behind me as the "stoker." The control of the bike was mine, and it gave me concern for our safety. Adding to my angst, I noted some of our biking buddies seated in the bleachers. I regretted, too late, that at lunch during our mealtime conviviality, I had mentioned our plans. They were there *en masse* to observe.

Our turn came. Charlie and I awkwardly mounted the tandem. I remembered from the class session that communication was critical between captain and stoker, so when Charlie told me he was seated, I resolutely said, "Okay, we're off." But we didn't move; we almost toppled over, saved by the instructor standing at our side. There were peals of laughter from the gallery. The instructor calmly said, "Try again, and this time, let go of the brakes."

The second try was successful, and we cycled the track twice to cheers from our biking friends. Several months later, our Santana tandem, pearl-white with black trim, a beautiful, finely tuned machine, arrived at the S. L. Lewis bike shop in Columbus. With practice, we became a finely tuned human machine, enjoying many hours of riding over the hills and dales, and at times our voices blended in song, singing "A Bicycle Built for Two."

Each summer over the next several years, we attended GEAR Rallies, some more memorable than others. In the summer of 1994, we had the opportunity to ride our tandem on the Assateague and Chincoteague Islands, located off the coast of Maryland and Virginia. This was the home of the wild horses that I had read about in Marguerite Henry's book *Misty of Chincoteague* to my fifth-grade classes at Lincoln Elementary School in the 1960s. As we cycled along, observing these beautiful feral horses, I recalled words of caution from the book and, unlike some of the apparently fearless tourists, heeded the posted signs. The first one said "Wild

Ponies Bite and Kick," followed by "Keep Your Distance," then finally "Do Not Feed."

There is one more noteworthy stateside biking adventure to relate. The morning of May 15, 1994, Charlie and I were at Battery Park in lower Manhattan to take part in the seventeenth BIKE NEW YORK: THE GREAT FIVE BORO BIKE TOUR. City dignitaries were there, and it was the mayor (I think), who at 8:00 a.m. fired the gun giving the signal to twenty thousand nervy, antsy cyclists to start pedaling. The ensuing movement of cyclists flowed like a lazy river up Fifth Avenue and Broadway.

We were in the middle of the pack, and when it came our time, I had a white-knuckle hold on the handlebars of the tandem. As we started pedaling, I kept my eyes focused on the bicycles in front of me, to my right, and to my left—this was no time to sightsee. The forty-two-mile course took us through Central Park in Manhattan, crossed the Madison Avenue Bridge into the Bronx, recrossed on the Third Avenue Bridge back into Manhattan, over the Queensboro Bridge into Queens, managed the Pulaski Bridge into Brooklyn, then took the Verrazano-Narrows Bridge, cycling the length of Staten Island to enter the New York Naval Station—the terminus of the ride. Here refreshments, live music, restrooms, first aid stations, and bike repair services were at the ready for the weary cyclists; and weary we were, for the forty-two-mile ride had taken us six hours. After resting, Charlie and I proceeded to the Staten Island Ferry dock and waited with hundreds of other cyclists to slowly walk our bicycles onto the ferryboat. Given that we were packed like sardines in a can, I still enjoyed the cooling sea breeze and the cityscape view before the boat docked at Battery Park and we rode the short distance to our hotel.

Bike New York was not a fun-filled experience. We saw little of the city. Riding captain, I had to be on the alert to avoid street hazards and other bicycles. Charlie was the navigator, telling me when it was safe to maneuver right or left as the need might be. Our teamwork paid off. We were not counted as one of the causalities along the route. There were too many people—long lines for food, for the porta-potties. With foresight, we carried our own water and food supply. When nature called, we found a secluded place to relieve ourselves. This was a memorable once-in-a-life-time cycling experience—one we did not choose to repeat.

++++++

OUR OVERSEAS TRAVEL centered on bicycling—England in 1992, China in 1994, and Greece in 1996. Previously we had traveled with Vermont Bicycle Touring (VBT) when we cycled in the Netherlands in 1990, and again in France in 1991.

VBT offered tours in England. We were extremely pleased with their services and joined their BIKE ENGLAND tour in August 1992. Our plane landed at Gatwick Airport/London, near the village of Horley. Here we met our guides Adam and Brett, joined with other members of the tour, and were taken by train to our hotel in Arundel south of London in West Sussex. Ensconced in our room, we rested and were refreshed when we appeared for the get-acquainted, informational meeting that gave us an overview for the next twelve days of the trip.

There were sixteen in the tour group, and all had opted to rent a bicycle. At the conclusion of the meeting, Adam and Brett, in turn, spent time with each of us adjusting our bicycle seat, handlebar, and brakes. A properly fitted bicycle is first and foremost a safer bicycle. That makes it a more comfortable bicycle to ride. Charlie and I were the last to be fitted for our single bikes, and as we were leaving the area, I overheard Adam remark to Brett, "It is much easier to be a guide on one of our walking tours. All we have to provide are extra shoelaces."

Our first order of business was to exchange dollars for pounds. The exchange rate of $1.92 for one British pound put us on notice to watch our discretionary spending. Traffic was another issue, but not unfamiliar; we had previously cycled in France where the cars drove on "the wrong side of the road." Here the cars were small, but it was comical to note that the license plates were large, covering almost one half of the bumper. Petrol sold by the liter and in dollars cost $2.99/quart. We were thankful to be on a bicycle.

Our adventure began in Arundel, took us west and northwest with overnight accommodations in Petersfield, Winchester, Salisbury, Oldfields, Gloucestershire, Stratford-on-Avon, Woodstock, and back to Horley. For the most part the terrain was undulating, allowing us to enjoy the picturesque English countryside. On rare occasions, we cycled along the ridges of the hills, on roads built by the Romans when they occupied

England from AD 100 to AD 400. We rode at a relaxed pace along narrow country lanes made secluded by hedgerows too thick to penetrate, serving as fences for the sheep, cows, and pigs. We saw fields of barley and wheat; acres of cabbages, lettuce, beans, and asparagus; orchards with trees bearing plums, cherries, and apples. Cycling through one village, we stopped in front of a home to admire flowers being tended by a lady. I commented how beautiful the impatiens were, and with a puzzled look, she replied, "You mean the busy lizzies." Never thought of plants that continuously flower all season as busy lizzies—but credit the English for giving them a most apt name.

Stone was plentiful in the areas through which we cycled. We noted the precision-cut flint used with brick in the thatched-roof farm buildings in the Sussex area to the south. To the west and north in the Hampshire, Wiltshire, and Gloucestershire areas soft, honey-colored sandstone was used in the buildings. There landscape and buildings complemented one another, predating the time of Frank Lloyd Wright's philosophy of organic architecture.

Villages were close together, so during a day's cycling, we passed through several. In our tour information, we read that the word village was derived from the Latin work *vicus*, and its meaning was "settlement without walls." In each village, the original medieval layout of manor house, church, farm, village green, pond, tenant cottages had been maintained. But with time comes change, and today one will find many small shops and pubs in the villages.

We always chose a pub as the place to eat our lunch. Each pub was unique and held a quaint English charm. On one day, before entering the pub, we read a posted sign on the door:

WARM WEATHER WARNING

GENTLEMEN:

During warm weather we operate a
popular policy of dignity and restraint in
order to keep the ladies calm!
Please refrain therefore from wearing
ultra-skimpy tops and T-shirts that reveal
bare mid-driffs (sic), armpits and other
unbecoming bits of you.

Gentlemen who display unseemly acres
of flesh, may not be served at the bar!

Remember—what you reveal today—
we'll be talking about tomorrow!

We thank you for your co-operation

Glancing at one another, giving an audible sigh of relief and with the
hint of a smile on our faces, we entered, knowing that Charlie was appropriately dressed and we would be served.

Our lodging accommodations varied. The bed-and-breakfast inns
typified Old England. Some were century-old buildings—small rooms,
uneven floors, stone fireplaces, original oaken beams embedded in the
walls, shared bathrooms. Their charm made up for physical discomforts.
The hotels were modern with private baths. Inn or hotel, too many nights
were spent on hard mattresses, somewhat compensated for by the down-
filled duvets that kept us warm. The names brought forth visions of the
gallantry of Knights of Old and the Hunt—The Kings Arms, The Royal,
The Hare and the Hounds, and The Bear.

No matter where we stayed, the evening dinners would please anyone's tastes—delectable hors d'oeuvres with drinks; sorbet to clean the palate; entrées of fish, poultry, beef, or pork; demitasse coffee and rich desserts
to complete the meal. Charlie and I would waddle back to our room and
to bed.

Each day of cycling rewarded us with unusual sights and experiences.
In Arundel, we learned of a Roman villa that was discovered by a farmer in
1811 when his plowshare struck a hard surface. Archaeologists uncovered
an area of two hectares revealing Roman construction (AD 100 to AD
400) of buildings, courtyards, walls, with elaborate inlaid colorful mosaic
designs of people and animals.

In Winchester, we visited the Winchester Cathedral, and the statue
of a diver in the church courtyard interested us. We learned this statue was
erected to honor the man who, for six years, worked submerged in water
under the cathedral to replace rotted timbers with bags of cement—thus
preserving the Winchester Cathedral tower.

Our group assembled at 4:45 a.m., the morning we were to depart
Winchester. Our guides drove us by van to Stonehenge, located on a tree-
less plane eight miles north of Salisbury. We were to be there at sunrise to

see the sun's rays dissolve the darkness and reveal the ring of more than a dozen monstrous stones. It didn't happen. A heavy fog shrouded the area, and as the sun rose, this prehistoric monument appeared in the mist as only as a ring of gargantuan ghosts. We did walk the periphery. A barrier prohibited us from exploring among the stones—tourists can be so destructive. I was disappointed but took with me the mystical experience of actually being there and seeing this famous British cultural icon.

As we cycled on a country lane from Winchester to Salisbury, we came to a railroad crossing and noted the sign: "Drivers of Large or Slow Vehicles must phone and get permission to cross—park and use phone at the crossing." Slow was defined as five miles per hour or less, and that didn't apply to us, so we started across. Just as we were crossing the track, a bell rang, gates came down, and within seconds a high-speed train flew by! I shuddered as the impact of the message on the sign sank into my brain.

In Salisbury, we visited the Salisbury Cathedral and learned there was a rooftop tour. We registered for the tour and signed the required paper stating that we assumed full responsibility for our safety. We were two, in a group of six, that entered the stairway to climb the 163 steps to the upper level of the cathedral, 140 feet above the ground surface. This tour was not for the acrophobic. Looking down into the nave below provided a magnificent, breathtaking sight that caused a queasiness in my stomach. Looking up fifty or more feet to the peak of the roof, our guide pointed to the queen-and-king system of heavy to light wood-beam braces as he explained how they were used to support the steep incline of the roof. The roof tour was an uncommon experience that provided us with an in-depth appreciation for this English Tudor building that took sixty years to build. Before leaving the cathedral, we stopped in the chapter house (a small room in the complex). Here we stood before a case where one of the four original copies of the Magna Carta, preserved and protected under glass, was on display. As we left the cathedral, the eventide service was about to begin. We seated ourselves in the nave and absorbed the celestial sounds that came forth from the organ.

Fishing is a sought-after pastime with the English. The streams and ponds abound with pike, perch, chub, and roach. Private fishing rights on area streams and rivers are expensive, and there are waiting lists of applicants. On our ride from Salisbury to Frome, we passed a small lake. Along the way, I noted fishermen seated at the end of narrow, twenty-foot piers that were evenly placed about the lake. We stopped and went over to talk with one of the fishermen; his name was Paul Haines. Paul told us he had purchased a one-day fishing permit (cost four pounds) and with it came the assigned pier. He fished with an eleven-meter pole and was hoping to catch pike or perch. It was early in the day, and no fish had taken his bait. We thanked him for his time and moved on. I have often wondered if his four-pound investment paid off and provided him with some fish for his dinner.

Our visit to Bath was fascinating, and again we became keenly aware of the Roman occupation. We walked through the meticulously restored buildings that were the famous Roman baths—public and private. The people and animals depicted in the wall and floor mosaics were like what we had seen at Arundel.

Our tour allowed us only one day in Stratford-on-Avon. This is the birth and burial place of William Shakespeare, known as the English national poet and the greatest dramatist of all time. With our self-guided tour brochure in hand, we walked by the thatched-roof, wattle-and-daub, timber-frame cottage of Anne Hathaway, the early home of Shakespeare's wife. We visited the Holy Trinity Church where Shakespeare is buried. In the evening, we attended a performance at the Royal Shakespeare Theater on the River Avon. There was way too much to see and not enough time to see it. The next day we reluctantly went on our way.

In the Woodstock area, we cycled by Blenheim Palace, the birth-place of Winston Churchill, on our way to Oxford. In Oxford, we took a self-directed walking tour, and it was while walking, unbelievable to my eyes, before us was a store with the name blazoned above the door in huge letters—Henrietta. Charlie and I went in and browsed a bit, for I wanted to make a purchase. But when I came to the realization it was an upscale women's dress shop, and we were running short of pounds and needed to be careful that we had enough money to get us out of the country, I bought nothing. But I did engage in a conversation with the saleslady. I was interested to learn why the shop was called Henrietta. I was told the shop opened in March 1963 and was named after the wife of the present Duke of Marlborough. I knew the name Henrietta was common in England, more so than in the United States; but to learn of this blue-blood-name connection was heady information for this little farm girl. I chatted a bit more and, before leaving, asked for a business card. Back out on the street, I took a picture of the front of the shop. To this day, I regret that I did not buy at least one small item, perhaps a handkerchief or a scarf.

Oxford was the terminus of our biking holiday. Our guide retrieved the rented bicycles and provided us with directions to the train we would take into the London Victoria Station. Once in London, we had only a few hours and used our time to walk by Buckingham Palace, hoping to see the changing of the Queen's Guard. It didn't happen. We missed experiencing this spectacular display of British pageantry. We returned to Victoria Station and, with help from a friendly Brit, managed to find the train stop that would take us to Horley, and from there to our hotel in time to meet with our group for a farewell dinner.

Packed and ready the following morning, we again found ourselves at Gatwick/London Airport for our flight home. Our plane landed at Boston Logan International Airport. We deplaned and found the line to be checked through customs. While standing there, the cutest beagle, wearing a green coat with letters USDA, stopped and sniffed my carry-on suitcase. The handler for this sniffer dog was with the United States Department of Agriculture, and I was taking contraband into the country. An orange was found and confiscated before I could proceed through customs. It was an innocent act on my part, but even this brief encounter with a government authority caused my heart to palpitate. From Boston, our connecting flight took us to Detroit, and from Detroit to Columbus. Seventeen hours after leaving England, two exhausted but happy travelers were home—another remarkable holiday to be remembered.

—— ·+++++· ——

My visit to the USSR in 1971 piqued my desire to visit China. It was in 1994 that I read about a cycling tour in China advertised in the League of American Bicyclists magazine *Bicycling*. Charlie and I signed up only to learn a few weeks before the scheduled departure date that the tour was canceled due to lack of participants. Disappointment!

Within the year, we received information from Charles Barton; he was organizing a China bicycling tour. He learned of our interest through our sign-on with the LAB tour. Hope sprang anew. Information was requested and received. We carefully read the tour brochure "Biking in a Changing China." The price was manageable—$3,480 per person for the sixteen-day tour (October 16 to November 1) that included round-trip airfare from Chicago to Beijing, hotels, meals, airport fees, tips, and bicycle rental. It was a relief to read no vaccinations were required.

On October 16, with passports and visas in hand, we boarded a JAL B747 in Chicago for Beijing, with a one-night stopover in the Narita Airport located on the outskirts of Tokyo. The purpose of the stopover was to aid us in adapting to the time zone change. Our 6,286-mile, fourteen-hour flight took us through twelve time zones, crossing the International Date Line and losing a day, to be regained on our return flight east.

Semirested, the following morning we left Narita and boarded our flight for Beijing—the cultural and political capital of China. Arriving in the Beijing Airport, we advanced through security and were directed to a bus that would take us into the city and to the hotel. My first sensual impressions made during the forty-five-minute ride were the air pollution and the noise. Black smoke spewed out of exhaust pipes, and there was a continuous cacophonous sound of horns. Apparently, vehicles ran only if horns sounded. Looking out of the bus window, I observed evidence of a changing China: horses and wagons shared the road with trucks and cars; men with picks and shovels worked alongside large construction equipment; hovels were crowded between buildings ten to twelve stories high.

Entering the city, I was awed by the mass of bicycles that filled the streets. The synchronized movements of the cyclists reminded me of a school of fish. I watched a family on a bicycle—father pedaling, child on the handlebar, another on the crossbar; mother sitting side-saddle on the carrier with a child on her lap. This was a common sight. (Charlie remarked that the Chinese must have a superior sense of balance.) Bicycles were used as taxis, as trucks, to transport people and all types of goods (grain, live fowl, boxes, even a refrigerator) lashed to and/or suspended from the carrier. One man was reading a book as he rode along. A few bicycles had a protective, colorful wrapping covering the frame. I later learned anyone affluent enough to buy a new bicycle did not remove the wrapping. Much to my amazement, I only saw one motorized bicycle. Our bus driver skillfully navigated the streets without incident and left us at our hotel.

That evening we gathered for the tour orientation. It was our first opportunity to formally meet the other eight members of our group. Previously, we met our tour guides—Charles Barton (frequent traveler in China, author, and fluent in Chinese) assisted by Jane Schnell (biking enthusiast, author). Charles introduced us to Mr. Cui Suyi. (It was stressed that surnames always appear first in Chinese.) Mr. Cui had connections with the China International Sports Travel Company and would accompany us on our travels while in China.

Charles provided us with information that would be helpful throughout our stay in the country. He explained the Chinese money system, and I understood it well enough to get by. His effort to explain the pronunciation of names and places was so foreign to me that I made no attempt to speak any Chinese during our entire trip. We were assured we would be housed each night in a first-rate hotel with hot running water (a luxury). He warned us never to drink water from the faucets; drink only bottled water or from a special container provided by the hotel. No tipping—when the occasion warranted a tip, we were advised to present them with an English slang/phrase book, T-shirts, cigarettes, balloons, stickers, pins that we had brought with us. Always carry identification and hotel information (written in both English and Chinese). Recommended shopping in the state-run Friendship Stores and stop at the street markets that became common following the Cultural Revolution. Charles suggested we taste all dishes served at our dinners. Given that we liked the taste, eat it—adding with a sly smile, "Best never to ask what you are eating!" (Later, when walking along the aisles of a street market, I observed live reptiles, dogs, cats, kittens, civets, field rats, fowl, insects, and fish in cages and tanks alongside the meat display. It was then I fully understood what he meant.)

Another scene, more poignant than the above, remains with me to this day. A seasoned traveler in our group bragged of his ability to bargain with merchants in foreign countries and planned to do so in China. The idea of bargaining intrigued me, and I made my first attempt at a street market fruit stand. I approached the booth of a tiny, bent woman dressed in peasant garb, lines of fatigue etched into her face, callouses on her work-worn hands. I pointed to the oranges and pantomimed I wanted four, showing the coins in my hand. She emphatically shook her head **no**, signaling they were twice that much. I refused to add the needed money; she disgustedly accepted my offer. As she dropped the four oranges into a paper bag, she turned to her companion, and with hatred in her eyes and disgust in her voice uttered the word "Americans" and **spat**. I was mortified. My fellow traveler, the braggart, watched the entire transaction and added insult to injury by asking, "Was that worth it?" No, it wasn't worth it. I was the personification of "the ugly American"—a term used to refer to the thoughtless, ignorant, ethnocentric behavior of Americans working and traveling abroad. To this day, I am flummoxed as to why I was so easily influenced by this individual to compromise my integrity.

While in Beijing, I walked past the world's largest McDonald's; I had no desire to eat there. I was in China to learn about the people, and food is a mainstay of a country's culture. To that end, I sampled all dishes served at our dinners and admit to savoring most of what I tasted. Breakfast was similar to a traditional western meal (toast, bacon, eggs, coffee with sugar), the table set with cutlery. Lunch was usually buffet-style with the choice to eat with chopsticks or cutlery. The beverage was beer. For dinners, the presentation was only Chinese cuisine again with a choice to use chopsticks or cutlery. Charlie, with several others in our group, opted to eat with chopsticks. Not me. I couldn't get the hang of manipulating two thin pieces of wood. The food never made it to my mouth. I was hungry. I used a fork. Courses were served on large lazy Susan platters placed in the center of the table (an assortment of green and root vegetables, eel, crab, shrimp, ribs, chicken, pork, liver, rice, noodles, dumplings). The final course was soup, on occasion with a whole fish in the bowl, served with steamed sweet bread, sweet coconut balls, and custards. Beverages were hot tea, beer, or sweet wine—gluttony to the extreme.

Our final dinner in Beijing included the famous Peking Duck. The chef entered from the kitchen carrying a large silver tray displaying the duck, plump and roasted to golden perfection. Mr. Cui related the tradition of the Peking Duck, giving us time to admire the chef's artistic culinary skill displayed on the tray before he whisked it away to be carved. A duck's life from egg fertilization to the table was forty-eight days, and during that time the duck was immobilized and force-fed to maintain tenderness. The duck, now carved for serving, reappeared; and Mr. Cui demonstrated how to eat it with caraway seed roll, onion, and plum sauce. For me, this was TMI. When the platter was passed, I took a very small portion and gingerly tasted what was supposed to be a delicate morsel. I don't recall how it tasted; my mind was consumed by the duck's trauma.

We were taken to the finest Chinese restaurants for our evening meals. Here, after dining, it was interesting to observe the ever-present toothpick that appeared in the hands of diners—at first used aggressively, then lingeringly, as it appeared to be almost an after-dinner entertainment. While there I, too, succumbed to this cultural idiosyncrasy.

Our group would be in Beijing for six days. On our first day, we were transported by bus about forty-five miles north of the city to the Great Wall of China. Construction of the wall began in the seventh century BC and continued over the next twenty-five centuries. At one time, it covered 13,171 miles in an east–west direction along the historical northern border of China, using the rivers and mountains as natural barriers. The wall's purpose was to protect China from an invasion by the nomadic Eurasian Steppe tribes, allow for the regulation of trade, and function as border control of immigration and emigration. (Today, President Trump uses a similar rationale for building a wall along the United States/Mexico border.) Most of the structure is in disrepair, but China has rebuilt, maintained, and enhanced portions for public use.

Arriving at the wall, our driver parked the bus in a lot close to the base. The area teemed with hawkers selling memorabilia. We bought nothing and came to regret not purchasing a T-shirt and Mao Zedong's *Little Red Book* published in 1964 and widely distributed during the Cultural Revolution. We mistakenly thought we would have other opportunities to purchase these items—not so.

Charlie and I rode a cable car to the top of the wall where we had access to a restored portion. At this point the wall stood thirty feet high and twelve feet across. I set foot on the wall but walked only a few steps before I stopped, looked about in amazement and viewed what, to me, resembled a giant anaconda snaking its way over hill and dale as far as the eye could see. We spent an hour on the wall—walking, stopping, and gazing. The surface was patchy, the steps uneven and rough; my eyes were constantly focused at my feet as I carefully moved along and descended the steep steps to ground level and back to the bus. The experience was surreal. I had read about the Great Wall in elementary school geography class, with nary a dream that one day I would visit China and set foot on the Great Wall.

That evening we were fitted with a Chinese bicycle. They appeared to be well used, with large balloon tires and hand controls for shifting gears and braking. My bicycle was heavy! I guesstimate twenty-five pounds. Our Santana tandem weighed thirty pounds.

Over the next four days, we made excursions to Tiananmen Square, the Forbidden City, the Summer Palace, and Temple of Heaven. We were transported by bus as needed but also experienced limited cycling in the city, which I found to be thrilling, yet dangerous, as I became one synchronized fish pedaling along in a school of fish.

Tiananmen Square, the largest city square in the world, is located in the center of Beijing. Mao Zedong proclaimed the founding of the People's Republic of China at this place on October 1, 1949. Mao's mausoleum is there. On June 6, 1989, the Democracy Movement by student and civilian demonstrators was forcibly suppressed, killing upward of a thousand people, and became known to the world as the Tiananmen Square Massacre. Visiting the site five years later, I observed a peaceful scene of people milling about and school children, dressed in uniforms, walking together through the square.

We left the square and entered through the Tiananmen Gate (Gate of Heavenly Peace) into the Forbidden City, so named because emperors allowed only members of their families and household to enter. Our visit was short, but enough to appreciate the size of the city (180 acres) and the palatial architecture seen there.

Another day we were taken by bus to the Summer Palace located to the northwest of Beijing. This was the imperial summer resort of the Qing Dynasty. What I vividly recall about this site was a huge two-story marble boat (one hundred feet long by twenty-four feet wide) that appeared to float in a small lake on the palace grounds. The empress dowager had embezzled funds, depleting the navy treasury, and ordered this boat to be built. The consequence of her action was an inadequate navy to defend China, and during her reign, Japan won a major naval victory, diminishing the power of China.

No matter where we went, the ever-present smog filled the air—my eyes smarted, and it irritated my throat—diminishing the pleasure of being outside. During our stay in the city, we visited craft industries where delicate figurines and silk paintings were made, but it was the open-air shops that held the most appeal for me. These shops were seen in the public parks and along the sidewalks. Here a man could get a haircut, a mechanical gadget fixed, shoes repaired, and the often-needed help at a bicycle repair shop.

Given that one had energy left after a day of bicycling, sightseeing, and indulging in a multicourse dinner, an evening of entertainment awaited us. One evening our group attended an opera, *Farewell My Concubine*. The commonality with opera as I knew it were the elaborate costumes. The acrobats, exaggerated body language, discordant music (to my ear), the sweets and tea served during the performance, were my introduction to a type of entertainment enjoyed by the Chinese.

On day eight of our tour, we turned in our bicycles and left Beijing by plane to Nanjing (south, 550 miles) to continue along the lower reaches of the Yangtze River—an area rich in history, agriculture, and industry. Our route took us along a section of the Great Canal, the second wonder of China, stretching for over one thousand miles to the north beginning in Hangzhou and ending in Beijing. The canal was built over the course of centuries to link the rice-rich area of the South with the food-deficient North. The weather was ideal for bicycling—sunny days with temperatures in the seventies.

Leaving Nanjing, we visited the cities of (pronunciations in parenthesizes) Yangzhou (*Yahn joe*), Zhenjiang (*Juan jiahng*), Changzhou (*Chang joe*), Yixing (*Eee shing*), Wuxi (*Woo shee*), and Suzhou (*Suchoa*), ending in Shanghai. For this part of our tour, we were issued Japanese-made ten-speed bicycles, better suited for road cycling. Each day's cycling was limited to fifty miles or less. A sag wagon carried our luggage, water, and refreshments, made hourly stops and, if needed, could provide a weary cyclist with transport.

For the most part in Beijing, our group was kept together and our contact with the Chinese people was minimal. Here we would be able to cycle at our own pace, observe, and take advantage of opportunities to interact with the Chinese peasants. In the rural areas, I saw no mechanized equipment to lessen the worker's burden. I observed women washing clothes by streams and ponds, men walking alongside their oxen hitched to plows in the fields, or on the roads hitched to sturdy two-wheel wooden carts heavily loaded with grain or wood. I saw both men and women as beasts of burden—balancing shoulder yokes used to carry buckets of water to irrigate the fields of rice.

One day, seeing figures with bent backs wearing conical hats on their heads, stooping over rows in a rice paddy, I stopped. Getting off my bicycle, I stepped and splashed over the rice rows, making my way to the workers in the field. I held a bag containing souvenirs (balloons, ornamental pins, stickers). As I approached the workers, I smiled in introduction and offered a GOBA pin to one of the children. Seeing this, all wanted one. I was mobbed. Chaos reigned. Tossing the bag, I made a hurried retreat to my bicycle and pedaled away. On another occasion, I stopped by a rice paddy and walked over to the workers. Using sign language, I communicated that I would like to take their child's picture. The woman (mother?) shook her head no. I blew up a balloon, placed it in their large work basket and left, respecting their privacy.

In rural areas, little effort was made by adults or children to conceal natural body functions. Small children wore nothing below the waist; older children's pantaloons were split at the crotch, making it convenient for them to pee. I was introduced to the floor-embedded ceramic urinals used by women at the Narita Airport in Japan. In rural areas, the toilets were primitive, and the urinal was a trench, sometimes flushed with a slow-moving stream of water. One day, cycling with two other women, we needed a toilet. We found one in a small village. Entering the mud-brick hut, we covered our nostrils to block out the stench, squatted, and peed. Upon leaving, one of the gals quipped, "Well, at least it was deep enough we didn't get splashed!"

In Nanjing we cycled alongside the Xuan Wu Lake where the shoreline was solid with blooming multicolored flowers of the lotus plant. We were on our way to the Sun Yatsen Mausoleum when a wedding caravan passed us by. I noted the cars were decorated with colorful paper lotus flowers and roses. We arrived at our destination and saw that a triangular-shaped mountain encircled by 325 steps (by count) must be climbed to access the mausoleum. There were options to get to the top. I opted to walk up; Charlie's choice was to ride in a chair with a colorful overhead fabric shade. The chair was mounted on horizontal poles that were shouldered by two coolies—one in the front, the other to the back—who would carry the chair's occupant to the top. Upon leaving the mausoleum, I wanted the experience of the chair ride and found it delightful to be carried down, marveling at the skill of the two men keeping the chair level on the descent.

On a stretch along the Grand Canal, I encountered men fishing with cormorants, noting the string tied around the birds' necks. Here was a way to catch fish not using a hook. I did take a picture of one fisherman who had several cormorant birds, feet tied together, suspended from his shoulder pole. There was no interpreter near that would have enabled me to have a conversation with the fisherman. The first question I would have asked him would have been, "How do you control your bird that it doesn't fly off with the fish?"

En route to Yangzhou, we boarded a ferryboat that took us across the wide, muddy Yangtze River. The river was crowded with various sizes of boats, also tugs pulling as many as six to ten barges loaded with commodities stacked, bailed, bundled, and boxed. In Yangzhou, we toured the Benniu Bicycle Factory and saw firsthand the monotonous process used in bicycle manufacturing. Our tour took us through the area of the factory where frames were welded and painted. The welded frame was placed on a belt. A young woman, with a spray gun in hand, sprayed black paint on each frame as it passed by on a continuously moving conveyor belt—drab, monotonous work. It was evident China had no Occupational Safety and Health Administration (OSHA) standards in place. I am not certain if protective eyewear was worn by the welders, but it was evident no protective face mask was used by the painters. It was at this factory that I observed a visibly pregnant young woman—the first I had seen on our tour. I had read about China's one-child policy, and it was evident it was strictly enforced.

We left the bicycle factory; our next visit was to a comb factory. In each of our factory visits, we participated in the Chinese tradition that before business is transacted, all gather in a conference room and are seated around a large table. Tea and sweets are served, while pleasantries are exchanged. We learned about the ancient tradition of comb manufacturing. Aged boxwood is used for the combs, which are believed to stimulate good health. There are nine acupuncture points in one's head, and properly stimulated two times each day will promote good health. Before leaving the factory, I purchased several of the combs in the gift shop to be given as gifts for family and friends. The combs took little space in my luggage and represented a true part of the Chinese culture.

In Zhenjiang, we visited the Ezhou Pagoda (home of monks) on Gold Mountain, so named because gold was found there. The pagoda, reached by climbing three hundred steps, provided us with a spectacular view of the mighty Yangtze. Leaving Gold Mountain, Charlie and I hired a bicycle taxi to take us back to our hotel. On the route back, the pedaler encountered a rather steep grade. Straining his leg muscles to the maximum, he admitted defeat, got off the bicycle seat, and laboriously pushed the conveyance, with us still in it, to the top of the hill. Feeling sorry for the man, Charlie and I attempted to get out and walk. Using exaggerated face and hand motions, he conveyed to us we were forbidden to step out of the taxi. Must have been a matter of pride. I guesstimated this man's age to be in his late thirties. Charlie and my combined weights equaled about three hundred pounds—difficult enough on a flat surface, impossible going up a steep grade.

We left Zhenjiang and cycled to Changzhou, noting the changing terrain evidenced in the undulating nearby mountains. The mild climate and the fertile land provide for a prosperous economy in this area.

Cycling on to Yixing, we noted the ever-present rice paddies lining the sides of the road. On this part of our tour, we stayed together as a group, and as we approached Yixing, our guide directed us to a commune. We saw the peasants threshing the rice stalks, the rice seed scooped up and placed in baskets. From the basket the seed was tossed into the air, allowing the breeze to winnow the chaff from the grain—a method used by my father on our small farm. There were several families who made up the occupants of the commune, each with their private living quarters. Charlie and I were invited into the home of one family. The mother served us tea and sweets. There was a little girl, perhaps five years of age, very curious as to who we were. Charlie and I were seated on the sofa in their living room. The little girl shyly sidled up to us, and Charlie inflated a balloon, handing it to her. I fastened a GOBA pin to her dress. We attempted to entertain her by singing "Incy Wincy Spider" with accompanying hand gestures. She did mimic our gestures as we sang—no interpreter needed. Finishing our tea, we reluctantly left, noting their smiles and hand waves as we cycled away. We had experienced a rare opportunity with a Chinese family, and I had a better (if only superficial) understanding of communal life. It was much different than I had envisioned—a large building where people ate and slept together with no privacy.

Yixing is famous for its red-clay pottery. Cycling along the streets of the city, I noted the light fixtures hanging from the utility poles were in the shape of elongated vases. (Reminded me of Hershey, Pennsylvania, where street light fixtures are shaped like Hershey kisses). While in the city we visited the Redpottery Artware Factory. Here artists and technicians create the designs that workers use in making tea sets, pots, vases, and a variety of other interesting pieces. One that caught my eye was a panda bear trash receptacle.

As interesting as the visit to the pottery factory was, another adventure held fascination of a different type. Leaving Yixing, we cycled past a bamboo forest on our way to a tea plantation. I was amazed to see a forest of trees that grew to be fifty feet tall and was so dense it appeared to be impenetrable. Arriving at the plantation, we were ushered into a large room for the traditional tea ceremony. Here we were greeted by our host, who spoke perfect English. As we enjoyed refreshments, he told us about work on the plantation. Three crops a year are planted and harvested. The first stage in the harvesting process is done by young girls with small, delicate fingers. They walk through the fields and pluck the tender leaves from the stalks. Tea made from these leaves is of the highest quality. Green tea is the more popular tea drank in China. Black tea is made by a fermentation process. Our host ended his talk by inviting us to walk into one of the fields on the plantation. As I did so, the aroma from the tea plants enveloped me, an experience I have never forgotten!

Leaving Yixing, we cycled the thirty miles to Wuxi. As we entered the city, we passed large rectangular tanks, each with netting, tied to buoys suspended in the water. We were looking at an oyster industry and learned each tank held literally thousands of oysters. An irritant was inserted into each oyster, then it was thrown into the net and remained there to feed on plankton for two to three years before being opened and the resultant cultured pearls harvested. We viewed an oyster demonstration. The oyster was opened and twelve to eighteen pearls, two to three millimeters in diameter, were removed from the shell. I strolled through the gift shop, giving only a cursory glance at the displays of exquisite art objects made from the pearls.

There were probably excellent buys, but I was tired from the morning's ride and went with Charlie to rest and enjoy a cup of tea with sweets.

In the afternoon we visited a silk factory. The first step in the silk-making process was to obtain the silk thread from the cocoons that were in vats of boiling water. I stood behind a worker watching as, almost too fast for the eye to see, she snatched a cocoon from the tank using only her bare hand. The cocoon was placed on a spinning machine used to extract the silk onto a spool—a fascinating process to observe. I collected several of the spent cocoons as souvenirs. We left the factory and were taken to the silk museum, where we observed the silk-weaving process. Our tour ended in the gift shop where the items on display were too beautiful to pass by. We left with silk jackets for ourselves and outfits for children in the family.

I think Charlie found our visit to the sports complex to be the highlight of our trip. We entered a large room filled with Ping-Pong tables where young children, barely able to see over the top of the table, perfected their Ping-Pong skills. Our guide told us these children practiced two and a half hours each day and invited anyone interested to play. Charlie immediately volunteered and was teamed up with a boy, maybe six years old. Charlie had some good shots, but overall, he was bested by his competition.

Our group was scheduled to leave Wuxi the following morning, and several of us wanted to visit the large farmer's market near our hotel. This venue was not scheduled into our day, and Charles suggested that anyone interested arrange to go early (5:00 a.m.) the next day. Three of us opted to do this. The following morning, when we walked to the front door of the hotel, we found it locked, as were all other exits. It was then we realized we had been locked in for the night—a terrifying thought. We awakened the desk attendant, and she sleepily retrieved the key from a desk drawer, staggered to the door, and let us out. Not too long after my return home, I read in our local paper that a fire took the lives of many people working in one of the factories in a Chinese city. The article went on to say that the workers were locked in and could not get out.

Our bicycles were locked up, so we walked the half mile to the market and were surprised to see it already teeming with life. We strolled through aisles where vendors had attractively displayed a colorful variety of vegetables, passed by tanks holding numerous species of sea life, cages with live poultry. Next, the area of processed meats—a few recognizable, most not. Vendors were friendly, eager to be photographed, and I took many pictures. The market seemed to represent the essence of the lives of the commoner. It was in recent years that government officials allowed the people to sell their products and keep the money they earned.

The next morning we cycled the twenty miles to Suzhou, known as the Venice of the Far East for its network of canals and many tranquil gardens. The focus of attention for our day in Suzhou was a boat tour on the canals. I was fascinated by the houseboats moored stem to stern along the sides of the canals. The population of the city was eight hundred thousand, and we were told a hundred thousand made their homes on houseboats. Women were seen washing clothes in the murky water of the canal then hanging them to dry on crisscross lines strung over the deck of the houseboat. Men were fishing. As I observed in parks and on the sidewalks of the cities we visited, here as well were seen a variety of repair shops on the decks of the houseboats. Garbage floated on the water, adding a stench to the air. But I also sensed beauty and a feeling of serenity in this "city" of houseboats. Planters filled with colorful flowers were attached to the gunwales, and gentle waves silently lapped at the boat's sides, giving it a gentle rocking motion.

During my time in Suzhou, I was not feeling well. Since our arrival in China, I had consumed a variety of foods; or perhaps it was the water I drank the one night from a designated pitcher in our hotel room, only to discover mud in the bottom of the container. Fortunately, with careful food consumption and drinking only bottled water, the illness was short-lived.

I felt excitement, coupled with exhaustion, as I boarded the train for the final stop of our tour. Shanghai is the largest city in China with a population today of twenty-four million. The city is located on the Huangpu River delta, close to the mouth of the Yangtze River. Arriving at the Shanghai train station, we were transferred to a bus that would take us to our hotel. As I boarded the bus, I took a seat next to a window and suddenly heard a tapping. I turned to look, and a woman in ragged clothes stood there holding a small child in her arms, with two others clinging to her skirts. She pantomimed eating and mouthed what I interpreted to be the word *food*, while holding up a small basket—a receptacle for coins. We were warned not to donate to these beggars as it would cause a riot. With this admonition in mind, I turned my head and looked away, but the tapping on the window continued until the bus pulled out. As I write this more than twenty years later, the image of this woman begging for food remains with me in my mind's eye.

Our introduction to Shanghai was by bicycle, and we would see the ancient, the modern, and the industrial. We rode through Old Shanghai, making frequent stops to listen as our guide pointed out portions of the restored old wall, moon gates, pagodas, and gardens. Leaving this area, we cycled along broad suburban streets, where in 1994 homes selling for $100,000 stood amidst multistory apartment complexes. Further on we entered the waterfront district, noting the low-lying skyline of warehouses broken only by loading cranes that reminded one of prehistoric birds. Here we also saw tall grain elevators that resembled huge smokestacks.

On the morning of the second day in the city, we visited a jade carving plant and a carpet factory. Charlie and I purchased a six-foot diameter wool rug woven in the factory. Cost of the rug, $400; cost for shipping, $200. We toured a cloisonné factory and left the gift shop with our shopping bag filled with elaborately decorated cloisonné hand exercise balls, small vases, chopsticks, and eggs.

Shopping was not the main event of the tour, but for those interested, the afternoon hours were open for shopping. Our tour bus took us to Shanghai's Fifth Avenue shopping district. We were left to our own devices with instructions on how to get transport back to the hotel.

There was a day in Beijing when it had rained during our trip, and it was a sight to behold—a street filled with cyclists wearing colorful ponchos that covered bodies, almost obliterating the person pedaling the bicycle. We wanted ponchos. It was with great difficulty that we managed to get directions to a poncho shop in Shanghai and purchased four—red, yellow, blue, and green. I still have these ponchos. I no longer ride my bicycle when it is raining, but they are good for walking.

It was our visit to the Yu Yuan Garden that remains the outstanding feature of our time in Shanghai. There are four elements in all Chinese gardens—rocks, water, plants, and buildings. These elements were readily visible in this Garden of Happiness. Upon entering the garden, we shuffled with the crowd over the ZigZag bridge, so named because the walkway was built over a lotus pond and constructed with nine forty-five-degree angles requiring right and left turns. To the individual, a different eye view came with each turn. Once over the bridge, we noted the sculpture of a six-hundred-year-old cast-iron lion (taken by the Japanese during their occupation, but returned). Another feature was a rock carving of a figure with a large forehead and its hand held a peach—the God of Longevity. (Charlie and I rubbed the head of this figure, hoping it would impart this gift of life to us.) We paused before a four-hundred-year-old gingko tree—the national tree of China. Before leaving we sauntered through some of the pavilions, all the time admiring and enjoying the fragrance of the flowers.

The evening before our departure for home, our group assembled for dinner at a Mongolian barbecue restaurant. We were shown to a round table, large enough to seat our entire group, then given instructions as to how to move along the self-serve bars. My entrée choice, made from the multitudinous variety of fish, fowl, and other meats on display, was chicken (my stomach was still a bit queasy, and I was taking no chances). One of the many chefs took the raw chicken and sautéed it, then with a flourish added bean sprouts and spinach, with a final sprinkle of seasonings. I continued along the bar and served myself rice and a sesame roll. Beer was my beverage of choice. It was all delicious.

By now our group had developed a camaraderie, and the table conversation dwelt on the nostalgic, regretting our time together was at an end. Julie, a general's wife who always inspected the kitchens before she would eat, rose to make a farewell speech. She included everyone; her speech was sensitive and sincere, to the point of being painfully accurate. She looked at Jane Schnell, our assertive tour director, and said, "Thank you for always telling me what to do." There was a moment of silence before everyone burst into laughter.

On day 16, Monday, October 31, 1994, we were taken by bus to the Shanghai International Airport. Charlie and I boarded our JAL flight to Narita, Japan, for an overnight before embarking on our transcontinental flight home. Allan Dickie introduced me to the value of travel as an educational experience having no equal. He was so right; the ten-hour flight home gave me time to reflect on the two weeks I spent immersed in a culture unknown to me. It sensitized me to respect differences, yet realize the common bond of humanity that binds us all together.

JOAN AND ED, FRIENDS MADE DURING OUR YEARS OF BIKING, had recently returned from a cycling tour in Greece. They endlessly raved about their adventure, and this piqued Charlie's and my interest to visit another country where people and customs were also unfamiliar to us. Dale Hart, a retired college professor knowledgeable in all things Greek, had for many years escorted academic groups to Greece. In retirement, he owned a company that sponsored bicycling tours in Greece. We requested a catalogue and selected a two-week tour priced at $2,189—plane tickets were extra.

On May 10, 1996, we departed the JFK International Airport for Athens. At the time of check-in, our coach seats were upgraded to business class. I was elated until I realized our newly assigned seats were located directly across from the loo—not pleasant. I endured the nine-hour flight that took us through seven time zones by eating, watching movies and, in desperation, pacing the length of the fuselage. I discovered an empty storage area, concealed by a curtain, at the back of the plane. Returning to my seat, I grabbed my pillow and blanket, strolled back to my secret place and surreptitiously slipped behind the curtain. Stretched out on the floor, I slept for four hours.

It was late morning on May 11 when our plane landed in Athens. Dale Hart was there to meet us and drove us to Ancient Corinth, located about fifty miles to the west, for the start of our tour. Upon arrival, we were fitted with our rented Trek bicycles. Before dinner we gathered for a brief orientation session and were given basic information related to our biking route to the west along the southern coast of the Corinthian Gulf that included Kalavryta, Nafpaktos, Zakynthos Island, Olympia, and finally returning east to Athens. Grateful the meeting was short, Charlie and I gave in to exhaustion and retired for the night.

We spent two days in Ancient Corinth. During that time we cycled throughout the scenic countryside and, when not cycling, meandered the streets of the city. We climbed the Acrocorinth (acropolis), the natural citadel that protected the city and was critical to control of the isthmus; visited an archaeological site where it was known that Aphrodite (goddess of love and beauty) was worshipped; and climbed partway up the 150 steps of a restored amphitheater carved into the side of the acropolis—a place where the ancient Greeks came for healing, and today is used for theatrical productions. I experienced a feeling of palpable excitement as I climbed over the slick stones of the uneven steps to access the entrance to the vaulted underground tombs dug into the steep slopes of the acropolis. Significant to me was the realization that I walked in the footsteps of Saint Paul.

Another site that took my total attention was man-made. In 1893, a French engineering company dug a canal four miles long, twenty-seven yards wide, and twenty-six feet deep between the Salonika Gulf to the east and the Corinthian Gulf to the west. A bridge was built over the canal that connected northern Greece to the southern Peloponnese region of the country. As Charlie and I cycled along the canal, we spied an ocean liner approaching the bridge. As we watched, the bridge did not lift; it submerged. Unobstructed, the ship steamed along, and once clear, the bridge reappeared. As I watched the bridge rise out of the water, it reminded me of a grotesque sea monster. It was a mesmerizing sight!

The morning of the fourth day, we left Corinth and faced strong westerly winds as we cycled the forty-five miles to the seaport town of Diakopto. Here we left our bicycles, boarded a cog rail train, and rode about fifteen miles inland to Kalavryta, our destination for the night. The Italians laid the cog rails in the years 1885–1895. The track bed was literally carved out of the side of the mountain; cog wheels were needed to negotiate grades as steep as 14 percent. Once in operation, the train was used to transport products to and from the area. The views on the ride were breathtaking, yet terrifying, as the train chugged ever upward over trestles and through tunnels traversing the sheer sides of the mountain.

A somber experience awaited us when we arrived at the top. Our guide took us to a shrine memorializing the Massacre of Kalavryta. During World War II, German soldiers roamed the mountainous area surrounding the town. Greek guerrilla soldiers managed to capture and kill seventy-seven of the Germans. In retribution, the Nazi supreme command ordered that all males in the town twelve years and older were to be rounded up. Five hundred boys and men were captured, placed in single file along the side of the mountain, and slaughtered with machine guns. Women and children were locked inside the town church, and the building was set ablaze. Miraculously, those inside, either by breaking windows or because of sympathetic soldiers who unlocked the doors, were allowed to escape. The town's main clock, located in the square, was recovered from the rubble. The town was rebuilt after the war, and the clock was installed on the facade of the church with the hands set at 2:35, the time of the massacre—a poignant reminder of man's evil.

I can only speak for myself when I say I was emotionally distraught as I stood at the memorial and learned of the massacre. The following morning, as I walked with the others in our group to the train station, I observed a vibrant energy among the townsfolks, and it lessened my sadness. I took my seat on the train with the others for the ride down, the beauty of the mountainside more breathtaking, more thrilling, more terrifying than the ride up.

At the base in Diakopto, I reclaimed my bicycle. By this time Charlie had come to the realization that this mountainous country was too much for his legs and instead rode with Dale in the van. Once again, I faced the strong westerly wind as I cycled to Navpaktos where our group spent the night. The next morning, refreshed, I continued to Kyllini on the west coast. Here we boarded a ferry that took us on a pleasant one-hour cruise to the island of Zakynthos.

In 1953 the small mountainous island of Zakynthos, an area of 240 square miles, was destroyed by an earthquake and fire. Four decades later, we visited a town that picturesquely appeared to hug the hillside. The buildings, covered in a white-and-beige stucco, were two to four stories high with red-tiled roofs. The church steeple commanded the view and, on that day, seemed to disappear in an azure blue sky. We spent three days on the island, cycling grades of 5–8 percent with distances of three to five miles. When we reached the summit, there was the thrill of coasting down the other side. Speed was not for me—the fastest I could ride on the flats was ten miles per hour; on the uphill stretches sometimes only three miles per hour, just enough to maintain my balance. I had the moniker of being the turtle in the group.

While on Zakynthos we boarded a sailboat and explored the sea caves found on the postage-stamp island of Keri just off the island's west coast. The largest cave was one hundred feet wide, three hundred feet deep, with enough height to accommodate the twenty-foot mast of the boat. The water's depth was unknown, but so clear one could see large rocks on the bottom. Leaving the subdued light and coolness of the cave, we were put ashore at a nearby sandy beach. Some went swimming, but Charlie and I opted to walk the beach with others in our group, and much to the revelry of the men, we ambled past an area where bare-breasted women were sunbathing.

Our three days on Zakynthos ended too quickly, and once again we were on the ferry back to Kyllini. Our destination for the night was Olympia, the original site of the Olympic Games, forty-five miles to the south. It was here the Olympic Games originated in 776 BC when Nike was known as the goddess of victory, not a registered trademark. But why here in Olympia and not the place where the Greeks defeated the invading Persians, at the Battle of Marathon in 490 BC? Or why not in Athens, located 186 miles to the east, to honor Pheidippides, the long-distance runner ordered to carry the message of victory who, upon arriving in the city, shouted, "Rejoice, we conquer!" and dropped dead?

The answer to the question "Why Olympia?" is linked with the fealty of the Greeks to their god Zeus. It was in Olympia that the Greeks built a temple to this god. The statue of Zeus, constructed of gold and ivory, stood forty-two feet high and was surrounded by fluted columns of marble measuring five feet in diameter. (The Temple of Zeus is known as one of the seven wonders of the ancient world.) When I was there, I saw only the broken remains of the temple's foundation and several scattered pieces from the fluted columns.

The marathon race, only one of the Olympic Games, was so named to honor Pheidippides. The distance he ran over mountainous terrain between Marathon and Athens is uncertain, but for the curious, it makes interesting reading and answers the question as to why in modern times the race has been officially set at 26.2 miles.

Given this background, we visited the archaeological site where the excavation of Zeus's temple was undertaken by the French and Germans in 1958. We toured the museum and viewed artifacts used by the ancient athletes—dagger-tipped javelins, weightlifting stones, and crescent-shaped stones held in the hands, with arms extended, used by jumpers to propel them a greater distance in flight.

I entered the grounds of the Olympic Games through a tunnel constructed of fieldstones, meandered about the grass-covered playing fields, placed my toe firmly against a starting stone, and pretended I was about to run a race. Realizing I, a woman, was allowed on these sacred grounds, in ancient times reserved only for men, was an electrifying experience.

Our brief visit over, I returned to my bicycle and began pedaling east toward Athens, the final stop on our tour. It was a relief to cycle on flat land as it gave me time to muse over what I had learned and observed. Only 25 percent of the land in Greece was cultivated. This land was used for orange and lemon citrus groves and small fields of melons, corn, and potatoes. There were vineyards and patches of fig trees mixed with gnarled olive trees. In the rural areas, it was the sights, smells, and sounds of Old Greece that fascinated me—farmyards with bleating goats and clucking chickens, or the occasional farmer herding sheep to pastures that made up another 40 percent of the land area. I saw a farmer leading a donkey pulling a loaded cart. I got off my bike, pantomimed I'd like to take his picture, and he nodded his head yes. This picture captured the essence of old, rural Greece.

The landscape provided breathtaking vistas, along with hazards for the cyclists. Small villages seemed to cling to the sides of the steep hills. Mountaintops appeared to be shrouded by clouds in azure skies. I recalled long, arduous climbs of 4-8 percent grades that almost sapped the strength of my leg muscles. There was the thrill of the downhill coast around hairpin turns, the ever-present potholes that spelled disaster if hit, and hands that ached from clenching brake levers to control speed.

Someplace along this stretch of undulating terrain, before reaching the hills of the first mountain, I motioned for Dale, driving the van that always "swept" our route, to stop. Before my bike was loaded in the van, I noted the odometer read 314 miles. Exhausted, I joined Charlie in the van for the final part of the journey into Athens.

Athens is known as the political, industrial, and cultural capital of Greece. Here one third of the country's ten million people (eleven million in 2015) lived. The streets were crowded with vehicular traffic, and there was gridlock at the city's intersections. Reminiscent of Beijing, the incessant, deafening honking of horns pained my hearing. Dale skillfully maneuvered the heavy traffic and deposited us at the door of the hotel that was to be our home for the final three nights of our tour.

That evening at dusk, our group gathered on the hotel's garden rooftop. As the sun was setting, I had my first glimpse of the Parthenon on the acropolis located a short distance away. The acropolis is a formidable rock, 450 feet high, with sheer cliffs on three sides. As the natural light faded a multicolored, soft light show illuminated the Parthenon. I shuddered with excitement as I gazed at this magnificent structure. It was built in the mid-fifth century BC and dedicated to the goddess Athena.

The following morning, our group walked from the hotel, approached the acropolis, and started the climb up the steep slope located on the only side with an accessible path. As we climbed, Charlie's legs became very painful, and we stopped for frequent rests. The group did not wait for us, but when we reached the top, we found them clustered around a large stone. We arrived just in time to hear the guide comment that this was the place where St. Paul spoke to the people—a sobering moment that brought the scriptures alive.

Our time and energy were in short supply. There were the remains of other buildings and statues on the acropolis, but we opted to center our attention on the one building that held our fascination—the Parthenon. We walked around the building's perimeter, defined by mammoth marble Doric pillars, before entering the open interior space that measured approximately 230 by 65 feet. As I stood there gazing about, I felt only frustration that I knew so little about this iconic building. In true tourist behavior, I bought a book.

It was early afternoon when we returned to the hotel. Several in our group wanted to visit a colosseum located in the center of Athens; it was not listed as part of our tour. Charlie declined, but I embraced the opportunity to view a venue similar to the one in Rome where the famous chariot race in the movie *Ben-Hur* took place. (I later learned a special arena was constructed where the action scene for *Ben-Hur* was filmed. But learning this years later did not diminish the memory of the goose-bump thrill I experienced that day.) We did not join an on-site tour but explored on our own. One arched entrance took us directly into the tiered seating area. I stood there in a daze of wonderment looking about this bowl-like structure built to hold upwards of eighty thousand people. Looking down on the field below, I imagined I could see gladiators in battle, and I thought of the Christian martyrs who died here to the roar of a bloodthirsty crowd. We knew there were tunnels and cavernous rooms under the structure, but we did not find a way to access them and returned to the hotel.

Our final day in Athens was unscheduled. Dale asked us to dress in Greek attire for the farewell dinner that evening. Charlie and I spent the day shopping, relaxing, packing, and planning our costumes. At the appointed hour, we appeared in white bedsheets draped about our bodies. On our heads were wreaths of bay laurel. Fortunately, we did not recline on couches but sat in chairs at a table as we dined.

Morning came. Packed and ready, we met Dale in the hotel lobby and drove to the airport. Here we descended into chaos. The terminal was crowded. Only with the help of a compassionate fellow traveler did we found the correct line for passport and carry-on luggage check. The plane was not full, and once airbound, Charlie and I were able to move away from our assigned seats across from the toilet.

On the eight-hour return flight to JFK, I was able to mull over the experiences of the past two weeks—the people, the food, the lodging, and always, the shopping. Cycling through the countryside, I experienced a glimmer of the country's religion and culture. In one of the small towns I entered a Greek Orthodox church and listened to the chanting of the Divine Liturgy. In another, I observed a priest siting with a group of men on a patio working their handheld beads—women were noticeably absent. Many mornings I would be awakened by the prolonged ringing of church bells. On one day, I stopped to rest in a small town where three young boys came up to me wanting to converse in English. Our conversation was slow, stilted, but understood. As we parted I gave each a GOBA pin for a souvenir. Near Kyllini I stopped to take a picture of several small, dirty ruffians playing by the side of the road. When they saw me, they raised their fists and shouted. For money? Obscenities? I was frightened and hurriedly pedaled off, concerned for my safety. I later learned I was near a Gypsy camp. Dale had not warned us of any possible encounters with Gypsies.

Food was plentiful. Breakfasts were informal, served buffet-style—brewed weak coffee and a variety of breads. Lunch was on our own. It was the dinners that were memorable. There were few bugs, and most dining was outdoors. One evening on the island of Zakynthos, our group dined on the patio. The sweet fragrance of mimosa trees filled the air. Greek cuisine was savory—soups, salads, entrées of fish, poultry, beef, lamb, and pork, dairy items made from cow and goat milks. A careful reading of ingredients used in the various dishes revealed no part of the animal went unused. Vegetables were plentiful, zucchini and eggplant dishes common menu items. There were luscious desserts, baklava being the favorite. Dale provided us with a listing of Greek dishes that included ingredients—a handy reference that added to my enlightenment and enjoyment of the food.

Overall our hotel accommodations were comfortable. The small rooms had patios, beds with firm mattresses, and bathrooms with corner showers and a handheld spray. There was limited hot water and no shower curtain (it was quick in and out), but there were flush toilets. Marble was everywhere—exterior and interior steps, floors and bathroom walls.

Each place I visited, I liked to purchase a few items relevant to the area. Greece was no exception, but shopping was not always convenient. Merchants closed their stores between one thirty and four thirty for an afternoon siesta. In Ancient Corinth, I visited the shop of a pottery maker and watched with fascination as he shaped a lump of clay into an item of delicate beauty using a foot-operated potter's wheel. Here I purchased several small vases. In another village, I visited a shop where handstitched tablecloths with intricate embroidered designs were sold. Jewelry could be found everywhere, and like most women, I added jewelry items to my shopping stash.

Our return flight landed on time at JFK. There were no delays through customs, and we made our connecting flight to Columbus and home. Two weeks in Greece gave me a deeper awareness for the degree to which their culture has melded with ours—in our architecture, food, drama, and sports.

<hr/>

OUR INTERNATIONAL TRAVEL did not end with Greece. Bicycle Adventure, operating out of Olympia, Washington, offered a weeklong tour in the Gulf Islands. We were in Seattle on October 7 where we met our tour guide who took us to Vancouver, British Columbia, Canada. At the time we were there border crossing was simple; a driver's license was all that was needed for identification.

We spent the night in Vancouver and the next morning made the ferry crossing to Vancouver Island. Over the next six days, we rode our rented bicycles on sparsely populated islands so small they are not listed in an atlas. Bed-and-breakfast accommodations were provided by local residents. No matter where one cycled, there were hills—steep hills and steeper hills, long hills and longer hills. It was too much for Charlie. After the first day, he turned in his bicycle and enjoyed the scenery from the vantage point of a comfortable seat in the van that served as the "sag" vehicle.

The only way I could enjoy the flora and the fauna of the area was to stop and get off my bike. Otherwise, my focus was to reach the top of a hill so I could coast down the other side. On Galiano Island I spoke with an old codger about the ruggedness of the terrain. I have never forgotten his response. It was in effect, "T'ain't hilly here. Don't ye know that one half up divided by one half down equals **flat**?" Even this mental crutch didn't help. To me it was hilly. At least in Greece we encountered stretches of rolling hills and flatland.

The final night of the tour, we were asked to dress in togas for the farewell dinner. Not sure why, for I was not aware of any Roman influence in the area. But in the spirit of cooperation, Charlie and I again fashioned bedsheets about our bodies, this time toga-style. I will say Charlie looked quite dashing in his above-the-knee toga that exposed his athletic tennis legs. His feet (sexy as described by one of his folk dance female friends) were clad in sandals, and on his head was a wreath fashioned from fresh carnations.

The morning of the final day of the tour, we boarded a ferry that took us to Victoria on the southern tip of Vancouver Island. The culminating event of our tour was to visit the world-renowned Butchart Gardens. Charlie and I spent the day meandering along the manicured paths. Our senses were on overload as we viewed the beauty of the gardens and inhaled the fragrance of the flowers. The hours passed too quickly, and it was time to rejoin our group and board the ferry that would take us back to Vancouver and the mainland of Canada. Another unique travel experience, but this time not totally unfamiliar to us.

When we were in Greece, we met Indiana Jane, an energetic cycling enthusiast in her midforties. Jane had cycled throughout the United States, and it was her animated account of a cycling adventure in Louisiana Cajun country that prompted Charlie and me to contact the Pack and Paddle French Louisiana Bike Tour Company.

Dick and Joan were the owners of the company—a couple who enjoyed cycling, were of Cajun descent and wanted to share their culture with others. We knew nothing about the Cajuns, but the information provided in the brochure was interesting and enlightening. Tour participants would stay in homes with bed-and-breakfast accommodations. Charlie and I found all this to our liking and signed up for a weeklong tour scheduled for April 1997. Louisiana is flat, and it would be ideal terrain for riding our tandem bicycle.

The distance between Columbus, Ohio, and Lafayette, Louisiana, is slightly over one thousand miles. Several members of Charlie's family lived in Kentucky. On our way south, we stopped for family visits in the towns of Henderson, Sturgis, and Paducah.

We arrived at Dick and Joan's home in Lafayette on April 20. On our first night, we were treated to a Cajun dinner. There were eight of us seated around the island in the large kitchen. As we sipped wine, we watched, listened, and were informed as the meal was prepared. After only a few bites, I realized it was heavily spiced. Charlie loved the cuisine; I survived it.

During that week we dined in restaurants with French names such as Cafe Lagniappe, Cafe des Amis, and Prejean's and savored a variety of Cajun foods: jambalaya, shrimp étouffée, pan-fried catfish, crawfish boil, alligator (tasted like chicken), grilled salmon, hush puppy balls, red beans and rice. Wine flowed freely with each meal.

We stayed in towns with French names like Bienville, Fausse Point, and Breaux Bridge. Our accommodations were in planation-style houses with two stories, including lower and upper porches, that also had French names: Grand Maison Bed and Breakfast, Chretien Point Planation, and Bienvenue House. Inside the houses, the wood used on the floors, doors, and bannisters invited me to touch, to caress, for a sensual connection to their visual richness. Some of the bedrooms were furnished with ornate four-poster beds. For breakfast, we would be served tasty nut breads, cranberry pancakes, sausage gravy and biscuits, and the Southern favorite, grits—not to my liking, an acquired taste.

One day Charlie and I stopped to rest in a park in historic and beautiful St. Martinville. It was here we learned of the Evangeline Oak, a living memorial to the tragedy of the Acadian exile from Nova Scotia in 1755. The oak marks the legendary meeting place of Emmeline Labiche and

Louis Arceneaux, the counterparts of Evangeline and Gabriel immortalized in Longfellow's epic poem *Evangeline*.

The week passed too quickly. I felt I had experienced only a trace of the Cajun earthiness, richness, and idyllic romanticism so visible in the lives of these people. Here was evidence of our country's "melting pot"—a place where there is a blending of races, peoples, and cultures harmoniously living together.

Charlie and I left Lafayette late afternoon on Saturday, April 25, for a two-day visit with my stepson George Dickie and his family in Thibodaux before we would head north and home. But it would be twenty days before we were back in Columbus under circumstances far different than I could ever have envisioned.

We arrived at George and Rita's home in the early evening. Conversation flowed freely, as well as the wine. Rita prepared a crawfish dinner that surpassed any cuisine eaten during the past week. We satiated ourselves with food and drink, exhausted ourselves from talking, and prepared to retire for the night. Charlie and I were in the guest wing of the house preparing to go to bed when suddenly Charlie complained of chest pains and nausea. I called George and Rita. George, a dentist, identified Charlie's condition as a possible heart attack and insisted we take him to the Thibodaux Regional Medical Center located less than two miles from the house.

We arrived at the ER. The next hours were a whirlwind of chaotic activity. The doctors confirmed that Charlie was having a heart attack. At all times Charlie was aware of his surroundings, and when told he needed open-heart surgery gave his approval. I was mystified, yet at the same time terrified, that he agreed to this. Over the past several years, Charlie had experienced recurrent leg pain and reduced stamina. His condition was diagnosed in Columbus as atherosclerosis by his cardiologist. His doctor had put the question to him that if further tests revealed the necessity for surgery, would he agree? Charlie emphatically told the surgeon **no**. Now, when I had a few minutes alone with Charlie, he assured me he knew what had happened, and he wanted the surgery. I signed the paperwork. An open-heart surgical team was immediately assembled.

It was 4:00 a.m. when Charlie was taken to surgery, and the painful hours of waiting began. At 10:00 a.m., the surgeon appeared and commented that Charlie's arteries were so calcified it was difficult to attach the heart/lung machine and equally difficult to find a healthy length of vein for the needed bypass procedure. The good news was that he survived the surgery and was being monitored in the ICU. I telephoned his children, Rich and Barb. Late the following day, Barb arrived. Rich would come later.

Charlie's condition was fraught with potential complications—poor heart and kidney function, blood clots, and possible neurological damage. He survived and improved to the point where, three days after the surgery, all invasive tubes were removed. When Barb and I visited that day, he knew us, and his first words were "I love you." But Charlie grew confused as to what had happened. We told him of his surgery and that he was in a hospital in Thibodaux. It was then he chirped, "I'll be damned. I'm not up to tennis today." Barb and I were elated. Hope springs eternal.

During those first critical days when he was in the ICU and visitation hours were restricted, I needed to fill those vacant hours with some worthwhile activity. Rita knew, when at home, I exercised daily and also practiced my piano. She directed me to a fitness center and a music store with practice rooms. I enrolled at the fitness center and rented a practice room. (A friend in Columbus sent my piano music.) During those critical days, I spent hours either exercising or practicing the piano—activities that provided some balance in my life.

Charlie continued to improve and was transferred to step-down and from there to a private room. Now there were no restrictions on visiting hours or visitors. Family members came and went. The granddaughters, Nancy and Georgia, were especially attentive, making a large get-well banner and, knowing he once had a cocker spaniel named Painte, found a small, cuddly replica to be his bedside companion. I spent hours with Charlie, and the time passed pleasantly for us.

On May 9, thirteen days after the surgery, the doctor signed a day pass for Charlie to leave the hospital—a test of his stamina. On our outing, I drove him by the stable where granddaughter Nancy kept her horse Judge, then by George and Rita's home for a short visit. Later that evening I received a call. Charlie had a relapse, vomited blood, and was back in the ICU. I expected the worst when I visited him the next morning, but as I walked in, he greeted me by singing "Happy Mother's Day to you." I cried—this time it was tears of joy, not sadness.

Charlie improved and was again placed in a private room, but he was restless and wanted to be home in Columbus even though it meant transfer to a hospital there. (For my part, I knew I had been a houseguest of George and Rita far too long.) Charlie's wishes were honored, and medical staff contacted Riverside Hospital in Columbus and processed the necessary paperwork for his transfer.

I arranged with Arcadia Medical Emergency Transport Service for air transport to Columbus. The morning of Thursday, May 15, twenty days after our arrival at George and Rita's home, we said our heartfelt goodbyes. Charlie was taken by ambulance to a plane waiting for us at the small airport in Houma. With a medical team aboard, the plane took off and soared into a blue cloudless sky. We were on our way north and home.

Three hours later the plane landed at the Columbus International Airport. Another ambulance ride, this time to Riverside Hospital. During the next several days, I spent my waking hours with Charlie and talking with doctors responsible for his care.

Four days after Charlie was admitted to Riverside, I spoke at length with Dr. Deep, the attending physician. Her compassionate, professional demeanor gave me the courage to ask her to give me a truthful prognosis for Charlie's recovery. Her answer was what I suspected, but did not want to hear. Charlie's heart was severely damaged. He would never be able to resume an active lifestyle. He would remain a semi-invalid. He would be kept alive with medicine. Soon, breathing and feeding tubes might be necessary. Knowing my husband, I knew it would be agonizing to him if he were imprisoned in this lifestyle.

My next question was, "What would happen if all medical support were removed at this time?" Dr. Deep's answer was honest in its brevity. "He would die." I shared with Dr. Deep Charlie's reason for agreeing to the surgery. He put his trust in the miracle of medicine and with the doctors, believing they could repair his heart and restore his health. He didn't understand that it wasn't just his heart; his entire circulatory system was compromised. Dr. Deep suggested that I share with my husband what she had told me. That I did not want to do; Charlie needed to hear this from her. Thankfully, she agreed.

I sat with Charlie while Dr. Deep quietly, and with compassion, shared the prognosis of his medical condition. Then she asked, "Do you want us to continue with further tests, more medicines, whatever it would take to keep you alive?" I sat there feeling the weight of the interminable silence that suddenly filled the room as Charlie processed what he had just been told. How would he answer? At last Charlie spoke. His answer was an unmistakable "No." He settled into a relaxed state and appeared to accept the inevitable that comes to all.

Later that day, Charlie spoke by phone with Barb, Rich, Bruce, and other family members. When sixteen-year-old Candice spoke with her Grandpa Charlie, he told her where he was going, he'd teach the Candice dance (Macarena) to anyone willing to learn. Candice replied, "Be sure you find Grandpa Bob and teach it to him." I needed emotional support for myself, and I reached out to Brenda, who immediately came with Kellie.

It was on May 21, after only a six-day stay at Riverside Hospital, that Charlie returned to his home at 247 Richards Road under hospice care. Charlie was brought into the house on a gurney and transferred onto the hospital bed set up in the dining room. Brenda, Kellie, Rich, and Barb were there. We began our round-the-clock vigil. A morphine drip kept Charlie comfortable. The following day Charlie became very agitated. Valium was added to the morphine. From that point on, Charlie was unaware of his surroundings or the presence of his loved ones. Rich said his goodbye to his dad and returned home.

That night, as uncomfortable as it was, I lay for a time with Charlie in his hospice bed. His irregular breathing was shallow and labored. At 3:41 a.m. on May 23, only two days after returning to his home, Charlie took his final breath—then silence. I called Barb, Brenda, and Kellie. The hospice nurse arrived. The funeral home was notified and came to remove Charlie's body. The four of us remained together in the kitchen area; it was Barb who requested we drink a toast to her dad, whose daily morning ritual was a glass of cranberry juice. Barb poured the ruby liquid into four juice glasses. It was 4:00 a.m. when we solemnly raised our glasses in a toast to this kind, gentle loving man who would now live on forever in our hearts and minds.

I recorded in my diary: "I am too tired to write anymore."

Word spread rapidly of Charlie's passing—people telephoned, some stopped by the house. Charlie was a member of the First Baptist Church, but he seldom attended. Barb's attempts to contact the minister were unsuccessful. We were not too disappointed, for we both wanted someone who knew Charlie to give the eulogy. I knew Brenda was a capable public speaker. With Barb and Rich's consent, I approached Brenda, and she agreed. Southwick-Good Funeral Chapel oversaw the service, and Walt and Brenda Spadaro were listed as the officiants.

Charlie's casket was on a bier surrounded by floral arrangements that gave a softened beauty to the solemn scene. He was a veteran, and a triangular folded flag was placed above his head in the open casket. Barb had assembled a meaningful picture display. The three of us (myself, Rich, and Barb) received a never-ending line of visitors during the Memorial Day evening calling hours.

The morning of Tuesday, May 27, held promise for one of those glorious days when it felt good to be alive—a blue sky, soft cumulus clouds, a breeze gently swaying the trees, spring flowers, and chirping birds. The family assembled, the limousine arrived, and we were driven to the funeral home for the chapel service. I had specifically requested Charlie's favorite Scott Joplin rag *The Entertainer* be played, and in the offbeat rhythm I felt his approval. Marcy, Charlie's daughter-in-law, read a prayer. Brenda and Walt officiated and incorporated in the eulogy thoughts from the family giving essence to Charlie's life.

Charlie was to be interred with his first wife, Betty, in an aboveground crypt at the St. Joseph Cemetery located several miles south of Columbus. I wanted to give the graveside eulogy. Bruce and Linda were not able to be with me, but she had sent me a beautiful poem—author unknown. For the eulogy, I shared this with the assembled group:

> *Do not stand at my grave and weep,*
> *I am not here, I do not sleep.*
> *I am a thousand winds that blow,*
> *I am the diamond glints of snow.*
> *I am the sunlight on ripened grain,*
> *I am the gentle spring rain.*
> *When you awaken in the morning's hush,*
> *I am the swift uplifting rush of quiet birds in circling flight.*
> *I am the soft star that shines at night.*
> *Do not stand at my grave and cry.*
> *I am not here. I did not die.*

We returned to the house where refreshments were served. My family, all from out of town, soon departed as did all others. Barb and children, Rich and his family, were to stay the night. Rich was executor of his dad's estate, so he immediately busied himself with business matters. Charlie's will gave all his furniture to his children. Terry was returning to Okemos that day and insisted the antique desk could be loaded in his van. I held up very well to that point, but somehow the removal of the desk and the mess it created caused a reaction in me that I can best describe as an emotional tsunami.

Like the weather, emotions too will change. I resumed my composure, and we were again all civil to one another. Barb, Allen, and Allison stayed with me in the house. Rich and family were in a motel. Barb and Allen slept late the next morning. Allison awakened early, came downstairs, slipped onto my lap, put her arms around my neck, and whispered, "Gran Henri, I love you"—balm for my weary soul. Later that day, they too departed for home.

Once again, I was alone.

+ + ✦✦✦ + +

NINETEEN

LIVING ALONE—AGAIN

E ACH TIME I RETURNED HOME, after parking my car in the garage, I would walk the few steps to enter the screened-in porch at the back of our house, open the back door, and call out, "Hello, honey, I'm home." Shortly after my marriage to Charlie, I acquired that habit, and it continued throughout the years. Now a widow, I felt the urge to continue making this announcement even though I knew Charlie was not there to return my greeting.

Charlie knew how, with just the right humorous quip, to defuse my explosive outbursts that resulted from an intense work ethic which brought me to a state of physical and emotional exhaustion. I could not envision my life without a husband, the one person who really knew me, loved me, and cared for me above all others. My children and their families loved me, as did my siblings and their families. I had close friends who loved me, but I found that only a husband could enhance that love by **knowing** me.

+++++

AFTER CHARLIE DIED, contact with his children and their families remained firm. Most of the visits took place in Columbus due to the necessity of settling matters related to the will. It was Barb's children, Allen and Allison, who always brought joy into my life. For Allen, it was the delight of attending a Blue Jacket hockey game and getting a Blue Jacket Stinger jersey—a blue bug-eyed critter with a big head. For Allison, it was our special times together and her telling me, "You are special. You are the only grandma I have left."

As executor, Rich's visits were governed by business matters related to the final settlement of the will. He would arrive with Kevin and Darren, and they referred to their visits as boys-on-the-go. The first hours of their visits were uncomfortable, but trips to the park and reading bedtime stories with them would ease the boys' anxieties. I kept reminding myself it was difficult for them not to have their grandfather there.

———— ‡‡‡‡‡‡‡ ————

I SOON REALIZED I MUST REDIRECT MY LIFE to give it purpose. The months after the funeral were taken up with acknowledging bereavement messages, taking care of financial matters that included innumerable medical bills, ensuring that I fulfilled my part related to the dictates of Charlie's will, and disposing of his personal belongings. My diary notation on November 4, 1997, read, "Right now I am adrift in a sea of activity."

Overall, what I was doing only darkened my emotional landscape, but I did engage in activities that brought me pleasure—something as basic as hanging the wash on the clothesline. This gave me the opportunity to be outdoors, feel the sun on my face, the breeze gently blowing my hair, listen to the song of the birds, and enjoy my backyard flowers.

Friend Emily joined me for morning walks around Antrim Lake in Worthington. I resumed my physical fitness program with Adam, the trainer who had worked with Charlie and me. One beautiful June evening, I treated my delightful ninety-something-year-old neighbor Myrtle to dinner at the River Club Restaurant, located at the fork of the Olentangy and Scioto Rivers. Seated at a table by a window, we had the perfect place to watch the synchronized rhythm of the OSU rowing team out for a practice session on the river.

Difficult as it was, I worked with the neighborhood committee to organize our summer block party. It was well attended, and many of the neighbors related humorous stories about Charlie that brought smiles to my face but tears to my eyes.

Music again became a part of my life. Marion and Frank, the couple who were Charlie's and my nemesis in our competitive bocce-ball games, remained a welcome presence in my life. Marion was learning to play the balalaika. We got together to play balalaika-piano duets that produced discordant sounds but provided us with hours of harmonious compatibility.

Playing the piano was a source of comfort to me. Marilyn, my piano teacher for the previous two years, was busy that summer and would not be available until fall. I needed to find a teacher. I inquired at the local music store and was put in contact with an older woman. The first month of my weekly lessons went okay, but it didn't last. One particular week, I was playing a difficult musical passage and kept hitting wrong notes. Out came the red pencil, and the troublesome notes were flagged in red. I stopped playing and asked her never to mark my music mistakes in red, as it reminded me of what my childhood martinet music teacher had done. She listened, but my warning was short-lived. I came to another difficult passage, again hitting wrong notes. This time she kept her red pencil holstered, but out came a purple pencil. It was a pyrrhic victory.

Bicycling provided me with much-needed exercise that relieved stress, boredom from daily routine, and was my main social outlet. I bicycled with different groups: two recognized bicycle clubs, one informal group of bicycling enthusiasts, and several friends. Jane Nickerson, whom I had met on a previous GOBA ride, introduced me to the challenges of biking and camping. That summer of 1997, Jane invited me to join her on the Bon Ton Roulet, a weeklong ride in the Finger Lakes region of New York. Charlie and I had taken part in a number of organized rides, where each night we were lodged in upscale hotels and dined in white-tablecloth restaurants. Not the case when biking and camping. After a long day of cycling, at times to the point of exhaustion, I pitched my tent, grabbed clean clothes and personal shower items, hiked an unknown distance to stand in line for the gang showers, hiked further to the dining hall to again stand in a cafeteria line, and finally with tray in hand, searched out a space at a long table where I could sit down and eat! In spite of it all, I found this semirugged cycling experience much to my liking. There was an instant, unsophisticated camaraderie among the cyclists, much different than the more-restrained aloofness Charlie and I had experienced on fully supported bike tours.

I resumed volunteering in the Columbus Outdoor Pursuits office and benefitted in a variety of ways. I was approached by a member of the COP board and asked to run for office. I reluctantly agreed and was quite surprised when elected. That summer, unbeknownst to me, when I signed up for the weeklong GOBA ride sponsored by COP, I was given the single-digit number 7. I was naive and did not realize this signified I was a member of the COP board. Not that I really cared for the honor, but it did answer an age-old question. How did a rider get one of the first nine numbers when there were 1,500 who registered? Obviously, it was a perk.

I resumed regular church attendance at the Worthington Presbyterian Church where I was a member. Charlie was a Baptist, Betty a Catholic. Rarely did Charlie attend church with Betty, rarely did he attend his own church, and very rarely did we attend church together. Dr. Hazelton, the senior pastor, preached sermons that were not only spiritually uplifting but had a practical application that helped me immeasurably in dealing with what I faced in life. His sermon, "In All Things Give Thanks," helped me to find hope. One Sunday I felt very sad, and the sermon "Make the Best of Life's Situations" uplifted my downcast spirit. When I found myself critical of unfilled expectations in others, the sermon "Living with Thorns" reminded me we all have imperfections and people are not perfect.

Tuesdays were especially difficult days for me. After my retirement in 1992, Charlie and I traveled extensively. At home we had routines, exclusive of one another, that filled our days. I suggested to Charlie that we set aside Tuesdays, when neither of us had scheduled activities, and plan to do something special together (currently referred to by couples as "date night"). We could take turns with the planning and keep it secret to infuse the event with a degree of mystery.

Charlie enthusiastically embraced the idea. It appealed to his enjoyment of practical jokes infused with mystery. There was variety in the places planned by Charlie—the Motorcycle Museum and the National Ceramic Museum both in nearby Westerville; the famous Columbus North Market and the Columbus Water Works Plant. But two places remain clear in my memory as top-of-the-list favorites. On July 9, 1996, we visited the National Road Zane Grey Museum, located sixty-seven miles east of Columbus in Norwich, Ohio. In January 1997, our destination was the two-hundred-year-old Clifton Mill Restaurant, fifty-three miles west of Columbus. For several nights prior to our dining there, the temperature dropped below zero. Seated at our table by the window, we were fascinated to observe the ice covering on the fifty-foot waterfall that cascaded over the steep bank into the gorge below.

I didn't totally slack off. My first Tuesday destination was the recently restored State Capitol Building. Another destination of a different type was a tour of the Anheuser Busch plant in Worthington. Beer was sampled at the conclusion of the tour. Sadly, my last diary entry for our Tuesday events was made on March 18, 1997. It was Charlie's choice, and we saw the movie *The Preacher's Wife* starring Denzel Washington and Whitney Houston.

We looked forward to our Tuesdays together. The excitement was not confined to just that day. Rather it provoked a heightened interest throughout the week, where through surreptitious questioning and observation we would attempt to solve the destination teaser being planned by the other. It was our special time to be together—a day replete with mystery and romance. How I missed them!

I HAD BEEN MARRIED AND WIDOWED THREE TIMES. Over my life span of sixty-seven years, I had surnames of Schumann, Nelson, Dickie, and Gass. Who was I? The one constant that remained with me were my sons, Vernon and Bruce, and their surname was Nelson. On April 16, 1998, I contacted my attorney, John Jones, and started the process to have my name changed back to Henrietta S. Nelson. On June 11, 1998, I appeared before a magistrate of the probate court in Columbus and made it official. It gave me back my identity as the mother of Vernon and Bruce. I liked it.

TRAVEL INVOLVING FAMILY AIDED ME in coping with my loss. In June 1997, I made the trip to Las Vegas for the Schumann Huddle, this time hosted by Bruce and Linda. I was the first family member to arrive, followed by Jill and Garvin—the only members of Lloyd's family to attend. Vernon came from Spokane, Washington—the first and only time my two sons were together for the Huddle. Brenda and Walt arrived with her daughters and their families—Kellie and Kirk with Courtney, Shellie and Dave with Natalie and Zach. We totaled seventeen.

In Las Vegas there is intergenerational entertainment for all. We rode the Manhattan Express roller coaster located on top of New York New York Hotel and Casino. Thrilled to the Siegfried and Roy show at the Mirage—magicians and entertainers famous for their animal show that included white lions and white tigers. We drove to the California/Nevada state line and experienced a ride on the Desperado Roller Coaster. The force of the 120-foot drop gave the rider a momentary feeling of weightlessness.

For me, the Sky Screamer ride at the MGM remained my favorite. Each ride mandated a group of three, so I rode with Vernon and Bruce. Ride participants suited up, something akin to the apparatus worn by parachute jumpers, then were hooked to a cable that pulled them to the top of a 250-foot pole to be released for a two-second free fall before swinging out in wide arcs as they descended to earth. It was thrilling! With feet planted on terra firma, my heart thumped from the excitement of the fall. I managed to walk back to the observation area where Linda waited with other members of the family.

Seated there, watching others experience the thrill of the Sky Screamer, two good-looking, athletically tanned young men walked by and asked if anyone wanted to buy a ride ticket at a reduced price. There were two of them, and they needed a third person to fill their ride. Linda teased, urged, provoked, and then volunteered me to be their third. I think they hoped for some curvaceous young blonde. What they got, thanks to Linda, was me—old enough to be their mother. They had to be disappointed, but they were gentlemen and attempted to conceal it. I observed their disappointed expressions and quipped, "You lucked out getting me for your third. I have age, wisdom, experience, so have no fear." It was true. I knew what to expect, was more relaxed, and bereft of fear. My second ride was more thrilling than the first.

Linda and Bruce arranged for us to spend a day on Lake Mead. With all members of the Schumann contingent aboard, a cabin cruiser and a speedboat left the dock at the marina and deposited us at one of the sandy beaches along the lake's shore. From there, those interested were given a relaxed ride to Hoover Dam, others went swimming, some opted to ride the wave cutter towed by the speedboat driven by Linda. I was one of several who straddled the wave cutter, thinking it would be a fun ride. Wrong! Linda revved up the motor, gained speed, swerved and circled and swerved some more, until she managed to dump some of us in the lake. I was one of them. Coughing and gasping, I crawled into the boat. One dump off of the wave cutter was one too many dumps for me. In the afternoon, the family gathered on the beach for the traditional family-huddle picture taking and gluttonous eating.

We were together for five activity-filled days. Bruce and Linda were outstanding hosts, although there were moments of disappointment and frustration for all. Lloyd and family members were not able to come due to illness. Kirk lost the keys to his rented van. Shellie and Dave were there with their small children, Zach (one) and Natalie (three). Upon arrival, I was stranded at the airport for about an hour before someone came to get me. I was disappointed when the official picture taken on the beach was not organized into family groupings (to aid in identification for future generations). My suggestion was shot down by a couple of discourteous voices.

I wrote in my diary on June 9, the day before we departed, "A wonderful Schumann Huddle. It had its tense moments, but I'll remember only the good times."

The fall of 1997 I received an informational brochure from Slater Tours promoting a four-night New Year's Eve adventure in New York City. It was Allan Dickie who introduced me to the thrill of the Big Apple, and knowing Bruce and his family had never visited the city, I wanted to treat them to this experience. They accepted my invitation and arrived in Columbus on December 26 to join me on our flight two days later to NYC.

That was the first of two mistakes I made related to the trip. I should have arranged their flights straight through from Las Vegas to NYC and met them there. They arrived in Columbus the day after Christmas tired from the intensity of preparations and family social events surrounding the holiday. Candice was ill with flu symptoms (although it might have just been exhaustion). Added to that, Linda took a fall down the two steps that led into the family room.

All recovered, and the five of us boarded our flight to NYC on December 28. Our lodging reservations were at the Hotel Edison on West Forty-Seventh Street, strategically located near Times Square and close to the theater district. We had tickets for my favorite Broadway show, *1776*. We missed the opportunity to get tickets for *Lion King* but thrilled to the precision dancing of the Rockettes at Radio City Music Hall.

On New Year's Day, we arose at 5:00 a.m. and walked to Rockefeller Plaza to secure a place in the first row behind the barricaded fence to view the *Today Show*. Bruce had made Las Vegas identity signs, hoping to make a nanosecond appearance on TV. Once there, we came to the realization that the New Year's Day show had previously been taped. Disappointed, Bruce hung his signs on the available fence, and on our walk back to the hotel, he was naively swindled out of twenty dollars by a sidewalk con artist who sold him two sleek NYC caps.

We visited the Empire State Building, only to learn it was a two-hour wait for an elevator that would take us to the observation deck. We aborted our hope for a bird's-eye view of the city, hailed a cab, and went to the Harley Davidson Cafe on Fifth Avenue for lunch.

Our bus tour of Manhattan was informative but did not have the element of excitement that we experienced on our subway ride south to Battery Park. We entered the subway station somewhere around Forty-Fifth Street. Standing on the platform, and not knowing any better, we took the first car available to us, and that was at the end of the train. Battery Park was at the southern tip of the route, and it was here the train did a sharp U-turn to head back north. Fortunately, one of the locals advised us that if we wished to exit at Battery Park, we needed to be in one of the first four cars of the train—explaining that platform space was limited due to the U-turn. There were no connecting doors between the cars. Realizing this, at each stop the five of us exited the train, ran along the platform as far as possible, reentered the train, rode to the next stop, and repeated our frantic run until we were in the third car from the front which assured us an exit at Battery Park. There we took the ferryboat to Ellis Island.

In January 1993, I had completed the paperwork and paid the $215 fee to have the Nelson family name inscribed on The American Immigrant Wall of Honor—a project initiated by Lee Iacocca. Once inside the main building on Ellis Island, we were directed to a kiosk that gave us the needed information to locate the name of our family. The day was bitterly cold, and a strong wind battered our bodies when we exited the building and walked along the waist-high wall that enclosed the plaza. Then we saw it—the plaque reading "The Anna and Peter Nelson Family." It was a tribute to Pa and Ma. To their strength, their courage, their determination, their resolve to immigrate to the United States with the hope of providing a better life for their progeny than was possible in Sweden.

For any tourist in NYC on New Year's Eve, it was essential to view the ball drop on the Times Square building ushering in the new year. What was to be the highlight of our trip was compromised by the second mistake I made. Our tour group had eaten dinner in a restaurant close to Times Square. We exited the restaurant about ten thirty, and the street was rapidly filling with people. We had dressed for the theater; our warm clothing was in our hotel room. We were limited in time to return to the hotel to change. I persuaded my family to take advantage of the police officer's willingness to allow us entrance into one of the sectioned-off areas on the street. Once inside the barricaded area, I immediately realized we were facing the west wall of the Times Square building, not the north wall that provided the best viewing of the ball drop. Too late to retreat. We stood there huddled among the mass of people, our feet, heads, and hands freezing, our bodies shivering uncontrollably, but we endured the wait for the ball to drop. I had been there years earlier with Allan, when security was not as tight, when people were allowed the freedom to move about, and when I stood in a place that gave me a full view of the ball drop. This time, when the ten-second countdown started and the ball began its slow descent, I attempted to mask my disappointment that our view was partially obstructed by other tall buildings.

The afternoon of New Year's Day, we boarded our flight back to Columbus. Bruce, Linda, Candice, and Bruce Allan stayed with me for another day before returning to Las Vegas.

In June 1998, I was again in Las Vegas to attend Candice's graduation from Grand Valley High School. The ceremony for the seven hundred graduates was held at the Thomas and Mack Center on the campus of the University of Nevada Las Vegas (UNLV). I had a special gift for Candice, purchased on a previous trip to Hawaii. It was a gold turtle suspended on a gold chain, with a circle of small diamonds embedded around the edge of the turtle's shell. The Hawaiians honor the turtle, recognized as their ancestral spirit guide whose wisdom protects and leads them throughout their lives. The turtle represents longevity, safety, and spiritual energy. I felt it a fitting gift for my granddaughter about to embark on whatever paths her life would take her.

———— ++++++ ————

IN APRIL 1998, I visited Fred and Myra Vermeulen. Fred was pastor of the East Side Presbyterian Church in Ashtabula who married Allan and me, now retired living in Charlotte, North Carolina. My brief visit with them was an introduction to Charlotte. We toured the restored historic area of the city where we stopped for refreshments at an enchanting tea room. Fred drove through an upscale residential area, evidence of the nouveau riche growth in the city. The day before I left we attended the Calvary Temple (referred to by Fred as the Pink Palace) with membership over six thousand. Fred commented that this was further evidence of the recent influx of young families who had moved into the city.

My brief visit with Fred and Myra ended, I was again in the Charlotte Airport, this time on my way to Savannah, Georgia, where I would be a houseguest of May Mahoney. May was the mother of Stewart Waibel, my neighbor and good friend, who lived near me on Richards Road. May, recently widowed, had moved from Washington, DC, to Savannah. She purchased one of the historic homes in old Savannah, located on a quiet residential street lined with live oaks swathed in picturesque drapes of Spanish moss. Typical of all homes on the street, May's two-story house was narrow and long (perhaps twenty-five feet by sixty feet). It was filled with a collection of memorabilia from their world travels—nautical items, brass figurines, intricately carved pieces of Italian oak furniture, and a harpsicord.

I commented to May how attractively the artifacts were displayed, adding it reminded me of a museum. I meant it to be a compliment, but due to May's icy response, I knew I had made my first faux pas—but it would not be the last of my visit.

May had prepared our dinner, and we engaged in interesting conversation while we leisurely sipped the wine that complemented the food. It was late when we finished dinner. May commented the kitchen cleanup could wait until the next day, adding that any guest not abiding by her request would not be invited back. Difficult as it was to get up from the table and leave the cleanup until morning, I obeyed her directive, excused myself, and went to bed.

When I awakened the following morning and entered the kitchen, dirty dishes, pots, and pans filled the sink and overflowed onto the counter. I noted May was working in the garden at the back of the house. Now thinking it was all right to be a helpful houseguest, I proceeded to clean up the dirty dishes left from the previous night. I finished just as May came into the kitchen. She noted what I had done, made no comment, and proceeded to fix our breakfast. At that moment, I suspicioned I was on her no-return-invitation hit list.

May remained the perfect hostess. We visited a nineteenth-century cemetery and sauntered among the tombstones, reading names and epitaphs that remained legible. We walked through the historic district and strolled into a few of the riverfront shops. It was here in a doll shop that I spied a doll about the size of a two-year-old child. She had curly red hair, wore a dress of blue-jean fabric, with a red-and-white Band-Aid on her knee. The doll had a mournful expression on her face and was seated on a small stool with a sign above her head that read "Time out." That doll looked just like Brenda when she was maybe three years old, and Brenda's granddaughter, Natalie Elaine, looked just like her grandmother when she was that age. I wanted that doll, but it came with a price tag more than I cared to pay.

May and I left the shop, but I couldn't shake my desire to purchase the doll. That led me to the third faux pas of my visit, when I inquired of May if she thought it proper to return and attempt to bargain the price. May replied with an innocuous comment that I needed to do whatever I felt comfortable doing. I returned to the shop, and my first attempt to offer less than the asking price was immediately quashed. I paid the price. Miss

Time-Out would have a new home with Brenda Louise and one day with Natalie Elaine.

The last full day of my visit, May drove us to Tybee Island. Taking off my shoes (acceptable) along with May, I enjoyed the feel of the sand and water between my toes as we walked the beach. The following morning, May drove me to the Savannah Airport for my flight back to Columbus. I sent May a gift and with it a heartfelt thank-you note. I never heard from her again.

+++++++

DURING THAT YEAR AFTER CHARLIE DIED, my travels were not confined to the continental United States. Tuesday, August 19, 1997, I was standing by my desk in my second-floor office when the telephone rang. Answering it, I was delighted to hear my niece Jill's voice. As I recall, her first words were, "Aunt Henri, are you sitting down?" I wasn't, but hearing those words, I carefully seated myself at my desk chair, expecting to hear a message of doom. To my total surprise, Jill invited me to join her and Garvin, Peter, Beverley, and their son, Adam, on their trip to Europe in celebration of her fortieth birthday. I was honored and humbled by the invitation. Jill took care of all arrangements, coordinating flight schedules and lodging.

On October 8, my flight from Columbus took me into the Washington Dulles Airport where I joined Pete, Bev, and Adam. From there we traveled together on the international flight to London. Jill and Garvin greeted us as we exited immigration at the Heathrow Gatwick Airport. My first impressions of London were the clean cabs, smartly dressed drivers wearing white shirts, ties, and suits and, in spite of heavy city traffic, an absence of the cacophony of sounding horns experienced in China.

We spent one day in London, visited the Waterloo Block at the Tower of London, and located the Jewel House to view the Crown Jewels. We sauntered through the display of priceless jewelry pieces. I squelched the desire to wear my sunglasses to shield my eyes from the brilliance of the diamonds, rubies, emeralds, and sapphires—attractively displayed on a carpet of red velvet. We walked by Buckingham Palace and observed the statuelike forms of the foot guards who stood at the front entrance doors, dressed in their eighteen-inch-high black bearskin caps, scarlet tunics with white belt and gold buttons, and dark blue trousers. We were fortunate to be there at the right time to watch the Changing of the Guard—similar to the ceremony at the Tomb of the Unknown Soldier in Arlington National Cemetery.

Our exciting, but brief, time in London ended, and the next morning the six of us, baggage and all, crowded into a taxi, and Jill directed the driver to take us to the Eurostar Station. We were off to Paris. Part of the trip was through the Chunnel on a smooth-riding bullet train that attained speeds of up to 125 miles an hour.

We arrived in Paris and checked in at our hotel located on the Avenue des Champs-Elysees, one of the most famous streets in the world. Soon after, we walked the short distance to the Arc de Triomphe. I purchased my ticket and then trudged up the one hundred steps to the top. I stood and gazed out over the city. The wide boulevards radiated from the central point of the Arc. I visualized a large pie, cut into many pieces, and I stood at the epicenter of that pie.

The six of us left the Arc and walked to the Eiffel Tower, constructed in 1889 as the main entrance to the World's Fair. We stood in line for thirty minutes to buy tickets before we could ascend the tower. This time, we used the lift for the first stage of the ascent, then continued our upward climb using the stairs, and finally reached the top level, 906 feet above the ground—the apex for the viewing public. Darkness came upon us. The city came to life as lights illuminated the boulevards and moving vehicles had the appearance of bright-eyed bugs. There was a feel of romance in the air.

It was Saturday, October 11, and we would be in Paris for only one full day. That morning we found a pastry shop where we ate a late breakfast. I ordered a flakey French pastry, coffee, yogurt, and berries, and after taking a few sips, found the coffee to be delightfully strong. Fortified with this nutritious food, I kept pace with the group as we walked the mile up the Champs-Elysees to the Louvre. Along the way Beverley saw a unique water faucet that was activated by turning a crank. Arriving at the Louvre, we all stopped and gaped at the controversial modernistic, glass, pyramid-shaped building that served as the entrance to the museum.

Cost to enter, $8. We stood in another queue and had to be cleared by security before we could go in. The place was mammoth. I stayed with Beverly and Peter, as Bev had mapped out how to navigate the corridors that would take us to Leonardo da Vinci's famous painting, the *Mona Lisa*. There, amidst the throng of people, I gazed at the enigmatic face of the woman in the painting. I didn't think. I didn't feel. I didn't have any emotional reaction to capture this moment in time. The crush of people didn't allow time for reflection.

We exited the museum. The next stop was the Notre Dame cathedral, made famous to many by reading Victor Hugo's novel *The Hunchback of Notre Dame*, or viewing the 1939 American film starring Charles Laughton as Quasimodo and Maureen O'Hara as Esmeralda.

No admission was required, but a donation basket was conveniently visible. Once inside, I stood and gaped as my eyes took in the grandeur of the interior—the high arches, the stained glass windows, and the carved mahogany pews. It was raining when we left, and I felt I was on a forced march that required me to maintain a fast pace to keep up with the group. Without umbrellas, we attempted to seek the cover of store awnings as we weaved and sloshed our way back to the hotel.

Jill had scheduled an evening dinner cruise, and we were short on time. Punctuality is part of the Schumann DNA. Dressed appropriately in dry clothing, we all reconvened in the hotel lobby and flagged a cab that took us to the wharf where our boat was docked on the River Seine. The five-course dinner, with wine to complement each course and superb entertainment, made for an unforgettable evening. My souvenir menu provided proof of our indulgence as we titubated off of the boat, got our land-legs, and made it back to the hotel before the witching hour of midnight.

Early the next morning we boarded a train for Salzburg, Austria. Jill wisely planned that the ten-hour, five-hundred-mile train ride would give us time to relax after the activity-filled days in London and Paris. Equally important was our opportunity to view the picturesque distant mountains and flat to rolling countryside of France, southern Germany, and Austria. None of this would have been possible had we traveled by plane.

In Salzburg, arrangements had been made to rent an eight-passenger van for the drive to the Marco Polo Club Alpena, fifty miles to the south. The next five days were spent at this luxury resort, and once there, the activity pace slowed. Our first day we enjoyed a swim in the pool. We exited the pool and, still wearing our bathing suits, entered the sauna bath where nude men and women comingled. Seating ourselves on wooden benches, we were just beginning to adapt to the hot, steam-filled room when a fleshy lady approached our group. She stopped directly in front of fourteen-year-old Adam and, with her pendulous breasts swaying about twelve inches from Adam's eyeballs, informed us we must leave as our bathing suits were a threat to the sanitary conditions of the sauna. Embarrassed by the unwanted attention focused on us for not obeying the "NUDE ONLY" posted rule, we left. Later, not to be deprived of the full sauna experience, Garvin, with Adam in tow, stripped to the buff and reentered the sauna to sweat it out!

All made appointments for a full-body massage. My masseur spoke only a few words of English, and the massage he gave me was as limited as his English. What I paid for, and what I received, were polar opposites. I was disappointed.

October 13 arrived, and with it the day to celebrate Jill's fortieth birthday. She survived the jibes, the black decorations in her suite, the drive to the restaurant located in a picturesque setting on a country road so remote it required the help of a local taxi driver. Our entrées were served in individual skillets—there were no dinner plates. We enjoyed tasting one another's entrée choices. It was a unique, communal dining experience.

One morning we awoke to see a blanket of freshly fallen snow that covered the fir trees and the ground. That day our destination was Zell am See, a town in the foothills of the Alps. A decade earlier Jill and Garvin visited the area on a ski vacation. The plan was to take the ski lift to the top of the mountain, but the lift was not operating the day we were there. When all else failed, we resorted to what most tourists do: we shopped.

Located not too distant from the resort was the Liechtenstein Gorge. This phenomenon of nature is a few feet wide, three miles long, with walls two hundred feet high. Legend has it that the devil, full of anger and rage over a failed plan, threw water onto the rocks with such force that it carved out the gorge. Slightly over a one-half-mile section is accessible to the public by means of a wooden walkway. As the six of us moved cautiously along the walkway, we felt the penetrating cold of the moist air and heard the deafening roar of the water that surged through the narrow passage below, making conversation difficult. As we approached the end of the walkway, nothing prepared me for the grandeur of the two-hundred-foot waterfall which thundered down the mountainside into the narrow chasm of emerald-green water that flowed beneath us.

On Saturday, October 18, we took our places in the van. With Garvin as chauffeur, we headed west the ninety miles to Munich, Germany, where we would spend the final two days of our trip. Garvin managed the narrow, winding roads that took us away from the spectacular beauty of the snow-capped mountains, past pastures where there were herds of sheep and cows, on to the Autobahn where vehicles are not restricted by speed limits. I don't know how fast Garvin drove, but he maintained a speed that allowed his navigator to read the exit signs for Munich.

Once in Munich, with no GPS navigational system, Jill directed Garvin through the miles of narrow, crowded streets to our hotel, map in hand. The Bavarian-style Hotel Han offered attractively decorated clean rooms with private baths and (for me) a bed with a comfortable mattress.

Almost 90 percent of Munich was destroyed during World War II. It was of interest to all when we took a two-hour walking tour through the historic area of the city. We viewed restored churches, statues, and political buildings—all the while listening to our knowledgeable guide spew out more information than one's brain could possibly retain.

Our tour ended in the Marienplatz, the city center of Munich. It was 11:00 a.m., and the chimes in the Rathaus-Glockenspiel clock sounded in the tower. The clock is divided into two levels utilizing thirty-two life-size figures and the musical sounds of forty-three bells during the twelve-minute show. The top half of the clock begins to turn, and the dancing figures depict the marriage of a local duke, ending with a joust between knights on horseback. Next the bottom half begins turning. Figures emerge and engage in a cooper's dance. The dance symbolizes warding off the 1517 Munich plague. As the dance ends, at the top of the Glockenspiel, a golden rooster comes out and crows three times, signifying the end of the performance—and what a spectacular performance it was!

Leaving the plaza, we stopped in a Hofbrauhaus microbrewery to quench our thirst and relax. Inside, the bar reverberated with an air of festivity and merriment. Patrons rollicked to the music of the musicians playing accordions, zithers, and dulcimers. Sipping my beer, I readily fell in with the atmosphere of the revelry that permeated the room. Jill and Bev were having a flirtatious conversation with a group seated at a table across the aisle from us and invited a tall, florid-faced German with a receding white hairline to join us. Their spurious motive was to hook him up with me. It worked. He joined our group, and I succumbed to his charms, even sat on his lap (captured for posterity on film by Bev). Jill later learned he was the local bookie. Another gentleman, cleaning his stein in preparation to store it in the locked cabinet reserved for club members, stopped by our table and spent a few minutes with us in animated conversation. He had interesting tales to share from his visit to the United States. What fun! One meets the most interesting people when traveling.

All good things come to an end. Monday, October 20, was travel day. Our flight from Munich took us to the London/Heathrow Airport. There we transferred to our international flight to Washington/Dulles. On this flight Jill, Garvin, and I encountered a most unpleasant situation. Seated behind us was a family from the mid-East, the woman garbed in traditional dress covering her body. Her head covering had only an eye slit that allowed her to see. A nauseating body odor filled the air space that surrounded them. Once airborne, the airline attendant alerted us there were two seats available several rows back. Jill insisted I take one of the seats. She and Garvin remained and endured.

At Washington/Dulles, I bid goodbye to Jill and Garvin and boarded my flight for home. There were relatively few tense moments during our twelve days together. Overall, I felt I was a good Indian in this tribe of Schumann chiefs. How blessed I was!

⁜⁜⁜⁜⁜

I MANAGED TO STAY IN A CONSTANT TRAVEL MODE. It was my way of coping with Charlie's death. An emotional hurdle I needed to face was our tenth wedding anniversary. I was going through Charlie's personal items in his desk when I discovered his 1997 appointment book. Nostalgically, I turned to the date of November 28, and there, penciled in, were the words *Hawaii—10th Aniv.* I couldn't believe my eyes. Charlie had died on May 23, and apparently weeks before that date, he noted on the calendar his plan to take me to Hawaii. He knew I had never been there.

Now I knew how I would celebrate our anniversary; I would join a biking tour. Bicycle Adventures, headquartered in Redmond, Washington, offered bicycle tours in Hawaii. Their catalogue description beckoned me. "Hawaii is always perfect. Pedal sparkling coastlines, explore coffee plantations, hike tropical volcanoes and snorkel with green sea turtles. Let Bicycle Adventures take you on a once-in-a lifetime experience." I signed up for their eight-day tour (November 22–30), knowing I would be doing something I enjoyed that included the day of my tenth wedding anniversary.

Saturday, November 22, 1997, I flew to the Dallas/Fort Worth International Airport to connect with my Delta flight to Hawaii. My seat was comfortable, the food tasty, and I spent the eight hours in flight eating, snacking, visiting, sleeping, making more bathroom visits than necessary as an excuse to move around the fuselage. The downside for me was the air of romance in the plane. The young couple seated behind me were to be married in Honolulu on Tuesday. The couple across the aisle from me were celebrating their twenty-fifth wedding anniversary. Although Charlie was with me in spirit, a feeling of sadness enveloped me. Fortunately, I came prepared to keep busy. I hunkered down, busying myself writing notes on previously addressed Christmas cards to family members and friends.

Arriving in Honolulu, a friendly Hawaiian directed me to the International Island Airport. There I booked my flight to Hilo located on the island of Hawaii—the largest island in the archipelago (four thousand square miles) comparable in size to Rhode Island. The tour leaders, Steve and Nancy, met me at the airport and drove me to the small, eight-room hotel where all members of the tour were staying. That evening, twelve of us met in the lounge for the orientation/get-acquainted session where the wine flowed freely, promoting a convivial atmosphere.

Once again, I had signed on with a tour company that provided top-of-the-line hotel and dining accommodations. Throughout the tour, I shared a comfortable room with Nancy, the tour guide. Most evenings we dined outdoors on patios surrounded by colorful tropical flowers. The food was tasty, and dinner plate presentations were artistic creations before I destroyed them with my fork. I recall eating papayas and remarking that it tasted like bland cantaloupe. I dined on Ono, a delicate whitefish in a sweet sauce with macadamia nuts. One evening I was served a dinner entrée that looked like green mud and tasted of coconut. More to my liking was an entrée of macadamia chicken. For dining entertainment, I enjoyed the soft, rhythmical sounds produced by the Hawaiian musicians on their drums, bamboo pipes, steel guitars, ukuleles, and flutes. The music aided digestion and promoted relaxation.

There are fourteen known climate zones on earth, and the island of Hawaii is listed as having ten of these zones, including extremes from tropical to periglacial climate. During the eight-day tour, I experienced most of them. There were days I cycled in heavy downpours, days I welcomed a gentle cooling rain, and days in the hot sun through barren areas where not a leaf of vegetation was to be seen.

The perimeter of Hawaii measures about three hundred miles. With some assist from Scott, who drove the van (a.k.a. the sag wagon), I rode 210 of those miles on my rented bicycle. What follows are some of my most memorable cycling experiences during the eight days of the tour.

My first heart-stopping cycling experience took place thirty miles south of Hilo along the southeastern coast of the island on the Kilauea Crater. Scott portaged us to the top. At an altitude of four thousand feet, I got on my bicycle, pedaled a few strokes, made certain my hands were in ready contact with the brake levers, and began the descent to the seacoast. The road was paved, no hazards, and I covered that distance in a breathtaking hour and fifteen minutes—a true NAFOD (no apparent fear of death) adventure.

We continued southward, riding through fields of lava flow, through tunnels of trees, all the time aware of the crashing surf on the shore. At one place along the top of the cliff, we stopped to view a black sand beach that was a haven for nude swimmers. Looking down, the swimmers' bodies were in stark contrast to the black sand. I joined the others as we ditched our bicycles and carefully hiked the narrow path to the beach. People of all ages were in a state of undress and total relaxation—sunning themselves sprawled on the sand, frolicking in the surf, or swimming. A family of four, adults with two children, were about to enter the water. The man nodded at me. That night I wrote in my diary, "I returned his greeting, careful not to let my gaze stray toward his groin area." I was definitely overdressed, and very uncomfortable, in that setting.

The road to the top of Kilauea Crater was smooth and hazard-free—not so with all roads we cycled. One day I biked on a road surface so rough it was easier to ride on the narrow berm at the side. Another day it was a gravel service road through a sugarcane plantation, later passing among ironwood and avocado trees, ferns, and tall grasses. The day our route took us to South Point Park required cycling eight miles of hills. I made the first hill, but when the sag wagon came along, I signaled for Scott to stop and asked to be portaged to the destination. Once there I got on my bike for the ten-mile coast to Ka Lae (South Point), the southernmost town in the United States, 18.9 degrees N latitude (Key West, Florida is 24.5 degrees N latitude).

My biking angel was with me the day I rode north in the rain on the west coast of the island. Traffic was heavy, and I stayed to the side of the road marked by a white edge line. My bike wheels lost their grip on the slick line. I crashed, hitting my head hard on the pavement! I was badly shaken, but nothing was broken. I got up without assistance from the kind motorist who saw me fall and stopped to help. I was able to ride off, and gave a prayer of thanks to my guarding angel and to the bicycle helmet that protected my head.

Bruised but determined, I attempted to ride the next day. Headed north, I felt the strong headwinds that battered my body and forced me to get off my bicycle and ride with Scott in the sag wagon. After lunch Scott took our group to a protected area along the Pacific Coast where we enjoyed a swim, followed by a hike along some scenic trails. As I tell it, I realize that was my Ironman Marathon Day—I biked, swam, and hiked.

I later learned we were in the area of Kailua-Kona where the annual Ironman World Championship is held. The Ironman consists of an open water swim of 2.4 miles, a bike race across the Hawaiian lava desert of 112 miles, and a marathon run of 26 miles, 385 yards—all to be accomplished in a twenty-four-hour period. Other than the memory of the strong headwinds and the awareness that I had actually cycled over some of the Ironman route, the only souvenir I came away with was a cycling jersey purchased in Kailua-Kona.

Back on the east coast, headed south, our route took us to the Wailuku River State Park. It was there I stood in wonder viewing a sheer wall of rock with a rush of water gushing over the edge forming an eighty-foot waterfall cascading into the gorge below. It was morning, and the sun's eastern rays created a perfect rainbow in the rising mist. Waianuenue, a.k.a. Rainbow Falls, is a tourist destination. Mesmerized by it, I understood why. On the final day of the tour, I cycled along rough roads through cattle country, followed by a rain forest, before returning to Hilo.

There were few opportunities to interact with the natives of the island. I did not note the location, but at one point on our cycling tour, we stopped at a Polynesian village. Here I observed a native shaping a canoe made from a koa tree (wood similar to black walnut) using a stone adz. When finished the canoe would be fitted with lateral support floats, making it an outrigger canoe that would be used in open water.

North of Kailua-Kona, on the west coast of Hawaii, Scott took us to the Puako Petroglyph Preserve. Petroglyphs are images carved in rock. We carefully trudged along a footpath through the lava field to observe hundreds of petroglyph designs—canoes with paddlers, dancers, family groups, deity symbols, dogs, chickens, and the sacred turtle with its four outstretched flippers as if swimming. Tragically only a few of these fields remain. Over the centuries many were destroyed by natural forces of earthquakes and lava flows. But the greed for the almighty dollar destroyed many more in the construction of land-consuming resorts and golf courses.

Not a place, but Hawaiian folklore required learning about Pele—the goddess of fire, lightning, wind, and volcanoes. She is recognized for creating the islands. There are many variations related to her legend, but the romantic one is that the goddess Pele shunned the amorous advances of the eight-eyed hog. In retaliation, the creature caused it to pour down rain and put out Pele's fire. Her final resting place is the Halemaumau Crater fire pit at the summit of the Kilauea Volcano.

I noted several places of interest—some man-made, others of nature. The Mokuaikaua Church was founded in 1820 by Congregationalist missionaries who arrived on the brig *Thaddeus* and settled in Kailua. The church was originally constructed of wood from the ohi'a tree and had a thatched roof, later rebuilt using stone and limestone. The interior of the church is replete with koa wood, beautiful and smooth to the touch. This is the extant church I visited.

The original Bad Ass Coffee Company, now with franchises in the continental United States, is located in Kealakekua on the west coast of the island. The climate there is favorable to growing some of the finest coffees in the world. I didn't get to visit a coffee plantation, but several of us enjoyed a demitasse seated at an outdoor table in front of the Bad Ass Coffee Company building. Fun! I bought a demitasse cup with the Bad Ass label. Unfortunately, this conversation piece has vanished from my kitchen cupboard.

In Kapaau, located near the northern most tip of the island, I visited an art store. The lava sculptures on display were life-size human forms. I asked the artist in residence how he produced these works of lava art. He welcomed the opportunity to relate the process. His first step was to use a human to form the mold. He then took the mold with him to the molten lava field. There he donned an asbestos suit, walked into an area of flowing lava, and used a shovel to fill the form with the hot substance. I failed to ask how he retrieved the heavy form from the field. He admitted his art creations were life-threatening endeavors. The cost of one of his art pieces? Upwards of twenty thousand dollars!

It was at South Point where I observed an art form of a different type. Here the dependable winds are conducive to the construction of windfarms. Tall towers topped with slowly spinning triple blades appeared before my eyes like dancers on a stage set on the water.

There is a United States Post Office at Volcano, Hawaii, located on the southeastern coast of the island. Because it was at the beginning of our tour, I didn't have any post cards to mail, but I was fascinated with the name, and one of my biking buddies took a picture of me standing in front of the building.

We were eating breakfast one day when I casually commented about the beautiful flowers and wished I could take some home with me. Scott overheard and remarked that the Akatsuka Orchid Gardens were nearby and they sent flowers all over the world. He offered to take all interested parties to visit the gardens. Once there I felt I had entered a tropical paradise. I was surrounded by chrysanthemums, hibiscus, dahlias, orchids, bromeliads, bougainvillea—all flowers familiar to me and many more that I did not recognize. It was the anthurium with its glossy-red, heart-shaped leaf and rodlike spike of tiny yellow flowers that caught my eye, and it was this flower I selected to send to family members and dear friends.

One afternoon we snorkeled off the western shore of the island near Kailua-Kona. I did take the advice of our guide and purchased an underwater camera. To the disappointment of the men in our group, this was not a nude beach, so all wore swimsuits. With snorkel, mask, and flippers in place, I entered the enchanting world of sea life. As I drifted, peering down into the warm waters of the Pacific, I saw fish of all sizes, shapes, shades, and combinations of color—blue, green, yellow, orange, black, and off-white. My knowledge of ichthyology is very basic—carp, pike, trout, and goldfish—but that did not deter me from the fascination of observing the fish that swam before my eyes. Well, that is, until I submerged to the point where my snorkel tube filled with water, forcing me to the surface gasping for air. I felt tired. Common sense prevailed, so reluctantly I forfeited any further pleasure to view this underwater Shangri-La and returned to the beach.

NOVEMBER 28, 1987—Charlie's and my tenth wedding anniversary. That morning when I awakened, Mother Nature seemed at her best. The sun, sky, breeze, temperature, birds, and flowers joined in concert orchestrating this to be a perfect day.

The morning cycling route took us north along the western coast of the island. There were challenging uphills and the bracing thrill of the downhills. Thirty miles south of Kailua-Kona we stopped to view the Captain Cook Memorial. In 1779, on the third of his exploratory voyages in the Pacific while attempting to kidnap the native chief of Hawaii, Captain Cook was killed. Historically significant as this place was, it held little interest for me as my mind was totally given over to the importance of the day to me.

I had been discreet and shared only with the tour guides, Scott and Nancy, why I had taken this trip. That afternoon they offered to abandon their responsibilities and drive me to a "graffiti field" located close to the highway. There, white coral rocks were used to outline messages on a bed of hardened black lava.

Arriving at the graffiti field, I was amazed to look out over a vast expanse of lava where messages and images (mostly hearts) made with the white rocks formed words and drawings. I frantically searched for an open area, Finding none, Scott directed me to "just pick a place and reuse the available rocks." As I scavenged for the needed materials, I felt sad to think I was destroying another's message, but I did it anyway as I knew, one day, someone would do it to mine.

The three of us worked together to outline a large heart with an arrow through it, and inside the heart formed the initials C and H above the numerals 11-28-97. It was a joyful time, and my heart sang with love as I gazed upon my graffiti message attesting to my ten-year honeymoon with Charlie. At that moment, I knew I had made the right decision to come to Hawaii.

My flight home left Hilo the morning of November 30 for Honolulu, where I connected with a flight to Las Vegas. The family was there to greet me as I walked out the jetway wearing my lei.

Linda's fortieth birthday was celebrated on December 2 with the obligatory, but humorous, decorations of black. I'd purchased a white Lladró bell in Hawaii for Linda. It seemed an appropriate gift for her to ring in her next decade. On December 5, I departed Las Vegas for home.

———— ++++++ ————

ON JANUARY 5, 1998, my friend Emily was at my door at 5:00 a.m. to drove me to Riverside Methodist Hospital for my scheduled incontinence surgery. She drove to the hospital's main entrance and stopped, commenting that she would call later to find out how I was doing. I opened the car door, stepped out, and walked through those foreboding hospital doors; I never felt so alone in my life. I accepted her offer to drive me to the hospital, thinking she would remain with me as long as permitted before I was wheeled off for the surgery. Her abruptness in dropping me off at the hospital's front door was totally unexpected and not planned for!

By 7:00 a.m. I was prepped and lay waiting for my 8:00 a.m. surgery. First I heard her voice, then I looked, and there stood Reverend Robyn Abel, the assistant pastor of the Worthington Presbyterian Church. She was there to give me comfort.

Surgery went well. I endured two days in the hospital. Nurse friend Jane took me home on January 7. I'd telephoned Brenda. She arrived that afternoon and was able to be with me for two days. When we parted, the stillness in the house reinforced that I was again alone.

I was blessed with many who offered help—neighbors, several friends, and church members. My needs were adequately provided for. Several brought food and remained to eat with me; some helped with the light housework; others served as my chauffeur until I was given the okay to drive.

Due to my type of surgery, there was a suprapubic tube inserted into the bladder through which urine was voided. During my convalescence, any medical questions I had were answered by the doctor's nurse—spiked temperatures and drug reactions. One month after surgery, after waiting one and a half hours, I saw my surgeon for only five minutes. It was a relief to me when he gave permission for the nurse to remove the tube. I found his bedside manner abusive in its neglect. On February 8, I wrote in my diary, "Being alone and sick is frightening."

Later that month I drove to northeastern Ohio to see my family, with the expressed interest of visiting Brenda and Walt in Madison-on-the-Lake. Walt was in the process of overseeing a major add-on to their recently purchased lakefront cottage.

On that particular morning, the three of us were seated on uncomfortable chairs in front of a bow window in their second-floor master bedroom. We engaged in lively conversation while sipping our hot coffee, all the while enjoying an unobstructed panoramic view of Lake Erie. I sat there mesmerized by the waves as they crashed along the shore, yet somehow tranquilized by the somber greyness of the sky and the starkness of the land. It was peaceful. At that moment, a nascent thought of the need to be near family became planted in my mind.

HOUSE MAINTENANCE PROBLEMS plagued me—termites, sewer, and furnace for starters. The euphoria I felt when I returned home from Hawaii soon vanished. On February 20, I wrote in my diary, "I am profoundly sad. Without Charlie, my life in Columbus is sterile."

In March, I again visited family in Northeastern Ohio. It was on this visit that Brenda suggested I look at properties in the area. I reflected back on my previous visit in February, when I sat with Brenda and Walt and felt the comfort of being with family. The idea of living there appealed to me. I voiced my interest to Brenda, making it clear I would only consider a place with a lake view, and it must be under $200,000.

When I visited in April to celebrate my sixty-eighth birthday, Brenda and Trudy had identified places that might interest me. We looked at several, but the only one I vividly recall was a condominium located at Geneva-on-the-Lake. One fast walk-through was enough that I gave it a thumbs-down—open architectural style, cathedral ceiling, with a restricted lake view. Disappointed, I returned to Columbus.

It was Saturday, May 2. My phone rang. When I answered, I heard the voices of both Walt and Brenda. They had found my house. It was lakeside, located within a quarter mile of their home, and priced at $198,000. I drove up on Sunday. The house at 7645 Lakeshore Boulevard was originally a summer cottage, winterized and upgraded to an attractive one-story house with an attached double garage. One walk-through and I knew this was the place for me. I met with the owners, Ted and Joan Dimon. Negotiations followed. I agreed to a cash deal, and the sale price of $185,000 was agreed upon.

I returned to Columbus and on Monday, May 4, telephoned a realtor, and placed the Richards Road house on the market to be listed at $164,900. The first open house was on Sunday, May 10. An interested couple, Scott and Shelby Passias, returned on Monday for their second house tour and made an offer $12,000 lower than the asking price. I accepted the offer. Somehow, in all house deals throughout my adult life, I managed to buy high and sell low. When the house inspector listed picayune needed repairs, I refused, with the exception of a change to the main fuse box.

Fortunately, the Richards Road home sale was finalized on June 30. I had money in hand when I appeared at the title office in Painesville on July 2 for the Madison house closing. I was blindsided when directed to sign an encroachment form regarding the shared driveway with the property on the east side of the house. Nothing had been said to me about this by the Dimons. After forty-five minutes of discussion, and a phone call to my Columbus attorney, a statement was written that I agreed to sign. Actually, all the statement did was kick the can down the road, and as the new owner, I had to deal with it later.

On July 6, I returned to 7645 Lakeshore Boulevard, this time to take possession of my house. I excitedly unlocked the door, entered, and there on the counter was a beautiful floral arrangement and wine in the refrigerator—compliments of Walt and Brenda. In hindsight, I realize I moved too fast when I agreed to a cash deal and was oblivious to the need for a lot survey. But the stars in my orbit were aligned, and it all worked out. I was again near family.

July 30 was the date the Passias's were given for occupancy of the Richards Road house. That gave me three weeks to pack up for the move. I contacted a mover, and an estimate of weight (thirteen thousand pounds) and cost ($2,300) was made.

Friends came to help me pack and clean. Charlie's family came—Rich with Kevin and Darren, Barb with Allison and Allen. It was an emotional time for them. This was their childhood home. Rich took many pictures to aid him in preserving memories. The morning Barb left, she said to me, "I was lying awake last night in my old bedroom and thought how this is the last time I'll see this room." The solemnity of her statement and the sad expression on her face brought tears to my eyes. Through all of this, I had focused inward on my own pain; I had not thought of how this would affect Charlie's children.

Moving day was Thursday, July 30. Brenda, with my great-niece Courtney, came to help. As the movers carried boxes and furniture out, Brenda and I followed, giving each room a final cleaning. Late in the afternoon, as the truck pulled away, I took a solitary walk through the house, paused in each room, and allowed memories to consume me.

When we were ready to leave, I asked Brenda to telephone Scott Passias. I knew they were anxious to take possession, but I could not bring myself to speak with them. Nothing must disturb the final memories that flooded over me as I walked through each room of the house—the house where I had spent ten wonderful years with Charlie.

Our vehicles loaded, we backed out of the driveway, caravanned to Madison, and stopped for dinner on the way. Exhausted, we arrived at Brenda's home about 10:00 p.m. A new chapter in my life was about to begin. What would it hold?

◆◆◆◆◆

TWENTY

LIVING IN NORTH MADISON

L EAVING COLUMBUS AND MOVING 185 MILES NORTH was a significant lifestyle change—from an urban to a semirural environment, from a two-story with basement to a one-story house, from community involvement to no involvement, from leaving friends to living near family.

North Madison is located in Lake County, the smallest of the eighty-eight counties in the state, originally a part of Geauga and Cuyahoga Counties. In 1840, the Ohio government authorized that 228 square miles of land be set aside to form a new county and named it Lake County after Lake Erie. I became aware of Lake County's size in my third-grade geography class. We had completed the study of Ohio's counties, and Miss Kister told us she would pass out a map of the state with the counties outlined and named on Monday. We needed a box of crayons with enough colors to vary the color of each county. On Saturday when Mom went into Ashtabula to do the weekly shopping, she somehow eked out enough money to buy me a large box holding thirty-six Crayola crayons.

That Monday I could not contain my excitement when Miss Kister placed the promised map on my desk and I opened my new box of crayons. I quickly identified Ashtabula County—right there in the upper right-hand corner of the map. I took out the sharp-pointed yellow crayon (my favorite color) and very carefully stayed within the lines as I colored my county. Done to my satisfaction, I then selected the tiny county just to the left of Ashtabula County. I have no recall of what color I chose for Lake County, but I do remember that the impression of big and small stayed with me, and I was duly impressed by **big**. It was this geography coloring assignment that brought me to the realization that I lived in the largest county in the state (702 square land miles, 1,368 square miles to include littoral water rights), and it was located next to the smallest county in the state (228 square land miles, 979 square miles to include littoral water rights). Now the reverse was true; sixty years later I was living in Lake County—the **smallest** county in the state. It was to this small, but dynamic, county where I moved in 1998.

Lake County was a part of the land area covered by the Pleistocene Glaciers. As the glaciers receded, clay, silt, and rocks were ground up, leaving a rich, loamy soil and major deposits of gravel. Glaciers were responsible for the final sculpting of the land. The depression dug out at the terminus of the glacier's advance is today known as Lake Erie. Three miles south of the lake is the lower moraine of North Ridge (US Route 20); another mile farther south is the higher moraine of South Ridge (US Route 84).

Bog iron was discovered in the early part of the nineteenth century, and a shipbuilding company, the Arcole Iron Works, was formed in 1825. The first steamboat was built here in 1828, and at the peak of production, two thousand men were employed. The last steamboat was built in 1860 as nature's supply of bog iron was depleted. What was a thriving industry vanished. Buildings became ghost remnants of a more prosperous time. Today the area, located a half mile from my home in North Madison, is known as Arcola Creek—one of the county's thirty-eight metro parks.

The lake and the fertile land provided the Mormons, the first settlers in the area, with natural resources for earning a livelihood by fishing and farming. Today Lake County is known as the nursery capital of the world, as well as a grape-growing industry recognized for its award-winning wines. Much of the twentieth-century growth in Lake County can be attributed to the advent of the automobile. With it came population growth and the expansion of opportunities to include jobs in industry and commerce.

Within the county are five townships, nine cities, nine villages, and one CDP (census designated place). The years before and during the Civil War, the area served as a terminus for the Underground Railroad, a conduit for fugitive slaves seeking freedom in Canada. The village of Madison (named after James Madison, fourth president of the United States, and located five miles south of Lake Erie) was incorporated in 1867 and covered 5.09 square miles. In the year 2000 approximately three thousand residents populated the village. Five miles to the north, located on the south shore of Lake Erie, is the CDP of North Madison, with an area of four square miles. This same year the population of North Madison was approximately 8,450. At the time I lived there, the racial makeup of Madison/North

Madison was 96 percent white with the remaining 4 percent being African American, Asian, Hispanic, Latino, and Native American. Residents of all municipalities in Lake County ardently support their public schools, with North Perry having the enviable position of benefitting from tax dollars paid by the Perry Nuclear Power Plant located in the northwest section of the county. Opportunities for higher education and vocational programs are available for high school students and adults through Lakeland Community College, Lake Erie College, and the Auburn Career Center.

It did not take me long to realize that I had moved to an area unique in its topography and climate, as well as rich in its history, presenting opportunities for community involvement and diverse venues for entertainment.

—————++++++—————

I MOVED INTO MY HOME ON JULY 20, 1998. The lot was small with fifty feet of street frontage and 195-foot depth to the edge of the lake frontage cliff. The eight-room house contained almost 1,700 square feet. The two bedrooms, two baths, and utility were defined rooms. The kitchen, office, living room, and dining room were an open space with one area flowing into the other. There was a surround of casement windows on the lakeside walls of the house, allowing for a panoramic view of the ever-changing lake scene.

I immediately put in motion the installation of a concrete driveway and the remodeling of interior spaces. Unfortunately, a very contentious situation with my neighbor Mary Jo Lilly to the east could have been avoided if the Dimons had been truthful with me about her use of a shared driveway. Based on my attorney's advice at the house closing, I contacted a surveyor and had my lot surveyed and the property lines identified.

For years Mary Jo had used a portion of the driveway. Now in July, after moving into the house, I was confronted by her request that I honor the arrangement she had with the Dimons. This presented me with a big problem. I wanted a concrete driveway that abutted the east lot line identified by the survey. A letter came from her attorney requesting that I recognize the long-standing gentleman's agreement she had with the Dimons. I would not yield and went ahead with the driveway installation. This resulted in Mary Jo having to use a few feet of lawn area to accommodate her car. I did relent to the extent that whenever necessary, service vehicles could use the narrow space between our houses to access her lakeside property. On this particular matter, I served as my own council.

Time heals wounds and changes attitudes. Fortunately for me, Mary Jo was forgiving, and we became good neighbors. During the years I lived there, I would say we became friends. I fault the Dimons for failing to disclose the shared driveway issue, but I fault myself for agreeing to a cash deal that did not require a lot survey. I further fault myself for being so pig-headed. I had foremost in my mind the aphorism "Give an inch an' they'll take a mile."

Brenda and Walt were helpful in directing me to people and places to facilitate the remodeling process. Walls and closets were removed, all wood-work including doors were scraped for refinishing. The laundry room and kitchen were relocated, ceilings and walls were insulated, and electrical and plumbing were upgraded. New appliances were purchased, a new furnace installed. When not involved with decisions related to the purchasing of supplies or supervising the work in process, I busied myself sanding, and applying walnut stain and two coats of polyurethane finish to the hundreds of board feet of baseboard, window trim, chair rail, crown molding, and the eleven solid oak doors. This was no small feat as I had to have materials ready on time for the finish installation.

The sixteen casement windows, located on the lake side of the house, were covered with a hideous orange stain. This was removed and replaced with the walnut stain and polyurethane finish. Although finishing the new wood and refinishing the window casings were laborious tasks, in the end it was worth the hours invested in the process. I took great pride in my work. The wood finish had the feel of a fine piece of furniture—smooth and satiny to the touch.

There were subcontractors who required my attention—plumbers, electricians, masons, and a kitchen planner. The plumber was a brawny, jolly fellow who alerted me to a potential problem. After running a snake through the sewer line, he informed me it was made of a product called Orangeburg—common to home construction in the 1950s to '70s. Orangeburg was made of layers of compressed coal, tar, and wood, and found to be too soft and apt to deteriorate underground. My house was built on a concrete slab, and all the years I was there, I lived with the fear of a sewer pipe cave-in and the necessity of tearing up the concrete floor. (It didn't happen to me, but it did to Brenda in the small cottage abutting their property, which she and Walt had purchased for an investment.) At the peak of the remodeling on February 7, 1999, I made an amusing diary entry: "No bathroom available, had to pee in a can."

Soon after I moved into the house, I had a clothesline installed on the lake side of the lot where I would hang out my laundry. As I listened to the gentle lapping of the waves on the shore and felt the warmth of the sun on my body, it seemed as close to heaven as I could get on this earth. On March 24, 1999, I noted in my diary that I saw a freighter on Lake Erie. That brought back memories of my marriage to Sidney Nelson, when he crewed on freighters for the American Steamship Company.

In the first stage of the remodeling project, son Vernon, who lived in Spokane, came for a visit. The first morning of his stay, he emerged from the bedroom, looked at the chaos, and asked, "Tell me, Mom, just **why** did you buy this house?" My answer was, "Location, location, location."

As work progressed, I was besieged with frustrations. Craig Shepp was the subcontractor responsible for the upgrade of the electrical system in the house. He put two young men in charge who mutilated a corner house support post while installing the new fuse box. (It was later reinforced by the contractor.) These young electricians took lengthy morning and afternoon rest breaks. I did not have a contract with Shepp—I was billed by the hour—but I never challenged him regarding the break-time issue. I'd already had one confrontation related to the job, and I wanted them done and out of there.

Jim Molnar was hired to be the contractor/carpenter for the project, also Jim Funk, a jack-of-all-trades, who worked tirelessly with Molnar. The mason, Jim Mack, did the ceramic floor and tile work. He was a delight to have around—industrious, cheerful, and meticulous. Ted Lyndell, the kitchen planner, was equally as professional. The new kitchen, with cherry cabinets and a Dakota mahogany granite countertop, was a highlight of the remodeling project.

Jim Molnar was unpredictable—one might say "moody." He came on the job that summer and soon started to take days off, even weeks, putting other jobs ahead of mine. Ted Lyndell related to me that Jim remarked to him that mine was "a winter project." True to his word, Jim returned in late fall and remained on the job into the winter. On February 14, 1999, I noted in my diary, "Jim finished! He was ecstatic, so was I!!!" Still, I need to be fair to Jim. He was a professional. The wood of his mitered corners looked as if it had grown in that shape, doors fit perfectly, new windows raised and lowered with ease, the laminate floating floor installed in the dining room and kitchen area was perfect. I wanted a counter, pub-table height, facing the lake. This required a cantilevered granite top extending from a pony wall. Jim had to rebuild the structure three times before he had the right support system to hold the weight of the granite. This he did with patience and no complaint.

As Jim completed the finish work in each room, Brenda came to do a major part of the redecorating. I liked the texture of wallpaper as opposed to paint. I asked, and she agreed, to paper the walls in all the rooms. The first "room" in the house to be papered was my bedroom closet. I was thrilled with the effect, and I recall that I sat down on the floor in the closet to fully admire the papered wall. The foyer in the house I came to refer to as the "happy" entrance. The floor was Italian stone. Ceramic tile covered the lower half of the room's walls. Above the tile, Brenda hung a celestial design paper. My sister used her sewing talents to make Roman shades for the casement windows on the northwest corner of the house—needed to control the afternoon sun.

In the bedrooms there were double-hung windows. Here Jim almost lost his religion when he installed the wood shutters, which required fabric inserts that I sewed myself. The bathrooms were modernized with new floor, wall tile, and bath fixtures. Everything was done to perfection, but as work progressed, my funds diminished. I needed to keep increasing my construction loan to the point where I spent an additional $110,000 on the house—two thirds of the purchase price.

Eight months after I took possession of the house, the interior work was completed. In February 1999, I retrieved my furniture from storage and began in earnest the process of a transformation that made the house my home. Some of the furniture and accessories did not fit into the available space. I did a lot of discarding, customizing, and replacing. The walls, floors, and cabinets were in earth tones, and when completed, the home radiated a serenity of calm, rest, and peace.

Without a basement, I needed more storage space. This time I opted for a different contractor, Bill Cesilinski. I requested he draw up plans for a garage extension, entry patio with privacy fence, and stairs from the lakeside deck to the beach. Bill completed all work in a timely fashion, and it was done to my satisfaction. He overestimated, by a large amount, the number of bricks needed for the patio. His brother-in-law could use the brick and would buy them from me at a discounted rate of 20 percent—the required restocking fee for returned materials. I agreed to the sale, later disgusted for not striking a better bargain. Hindsight is twenty-twenty, and I found being a single woman working with men was not in my favor.

No sooner was the garage/patio/stair project completed than I met with a landscape designer, requesting an irrigation system be part of the contract. The lawn and plantings were to my liking, but the irrigation system was a waste of my dollars. It was not properly installed. The following season I paid to have it redone, this time by a certified irrigation contractor.

A few years later, when I sold the house, after uncounted hours of hard work and an investment of thousands of dollars, the description written by the real estate agent was "Open and airy immaculate ranch on manicured sun-splashed Lake Erie lot." Time and money well invested.

———— ·+·+·+·+· ————

Living on Lake Erie, I became keenly aware of the beauty and the force of Mother Nature. The lake was ever changing. There were days when soft, cotton-fluffy clouds floated gently overhead, birds glided over the water, and in the cool of the morning a mist appeared to rise out of the lake. At times the lake looked like glass. There were soft and gentle breezes which contrasted to the nor'easter that was sharp and penetrating. I experienced strong winds that lasted up to twenty-four hours and churned the water into monstrous waves. On one such occasion, a storm deposited two large logs on the beach at the base of the stairs.

Another force of nature was only mildly frightening. Late afternoon on September 25, I felt the earth shake. It was reported as a 5.2 quake on the Richter Scale. This happening had residents, including me, checking their homeowner insurance policies for earthquake coverage.

Then there were the bugs—swarms of muffle heads (a.k.a. muckleheads or midges). These flying insects, about the size of a mosquito, neither sting nor bite. The muffle heads first arrive in June. The second infestation comes in September, and it is little comfort to man or beast that they are smaller. The insects are a plague to man but, as part of the food chain, are a bonanza for the fish. They swarm for up to 150 feet back from the lake's shore. Houses are covered with the bugs. When outside, humans must cover their mouths and noses to keep from ingesting them, and protect their eyes and ears. Little can be done for the animals but to keep them inside. Before leaving the house, I would take a deep breath and hold it until I was out of range of the swarming insects. Their existence along the southeastern shore was evidence that the lake was again a fresh body of water. For years this area of Lake Erie was polluted, and there were no muffle heads to plague man, or food for the fish. This is Lake Erie in the summer.

Lake Erie in the winter is its own force of nature. I had been told of a snow-effect phenomenon that I thought unbelievable until I experienced it. In the late fall, when the water temperature is warmer than the air temperature, the onshore winds carry moisture-laden air. Moving across the land for three miles to the south, to Route 20, where the air is forced to rise and cools, the moisture turns to snow, and it snows on North Ridge. One day, driving on Route 20 in a mild snowstorm, I turned north on Dock Road toward home. To my amazement, for the next three miles, there was no snow! Arriving at my house, the driveway was bare. I became a believer!

When subzero temperatures prevail long enough, the lake freezes, but it doesn't freeze smooth. The water solidifies first near shore, freezes out for several hundred feet, and the strong northerly winds bring in ice floes that build a mound of solid ice. One winter when I had houseguests, assured by the lake forecast that it was safe to venture out on the ice, five of us walked about a hundred feet offshore and climbed the rough ice mound to gaze out over a frozen wonderland. When the lake freezes, no waves hit the shore, and one feels a serenity in the white stillness that envelops the area.

Lake Erie provides the moisture that fuels nature's snow machine. My first winter in North Madison, I experienced the first snow of the season on December 17. From then until spring, it was snow, snow, and more snow! Fortunately, I had a four-wheel-drive Dodge Durango, bought while still living in Columbus. I purchased a snow blower but was not able to blow the snow on my driveway to the east; it would cover Mary Jo's driveway. I tried blowing it to the west, and the fierce westerly winds blew it back in my face. There were ice storms that made driving hazardous and closed schools and businesses.

I moved to the area at a record-setting time for the lake and the winter snows. When I purchased the property, I had no beach—the lake level was near its high mark recorded in 1988. But within two years after moving there, the water receded, and I had several feet of rocky beach. Winter made records as well. I noted in my diary on January 7, 2001, "This was the most severe winter since 1976." I was there and experienced it all.

LIVING CLOSE TO MY FAMILY was a new experience. Prior visits were always an event, but now proximity provided me the opportunity for more family involvement. My brother and his wife lived eight miles to the east on

Route 20. Lloyd helped when needed with house maintenance. The electric power often went out in our area. My brother built me a generator. For Lloyd, who understood electricity, it was a no-brainer to hook it up. For me it was terrifying. Hookup required more than just throwing a switch. Lloyd patiently instructed me in how to use it, I took pictures, carefully recorded all steps, and ended up with my very own "Generator User Manual for Dummies." There were occasions I used it, each time fearful I would make a misstep in the process and destroy the house wiring along with anything plugged into a convenience outlet. Fortunately, it never happened.

It was my sister-in-law Trudy's idea that the Schumann women get together for a monthly luncheon. I was delighted and took on the task of notifying family members and making the reservation at an agreed-upon restaurant. In Kirtland we enjoyed lunch at His Majesty's Tea Room. Another time we joined a Lake Metroparks tour into Cleveland. We ate lunch at a Cleveland hospital with Kellie, who was recovering from surgery. Pictures were always taken. Trudy was the one who recorded the when, where, and who attended, what we ate, and comments related to likes and dislikes. Trudy and I never missed our monthly luncheons. Most times Brenda was able to join us, otherwise the attendance of Schumann women varied based on work schedules and other commitments. It was fun.

Adam was a star basketball player with Edgewood Senior High School. Trudy and Lloyd attended their grandson's games along with parents Peter and Beverley. The first game I attended, I was informed there was a specific family seating order, and not to put a jinx on the games, I obediently took my assigned place.

I have often remarked that Trudy was not just my sister-in-law; she was my dearest friend. I was living in the area when Trudy's mother died. At the funeral service, Grandson Peter paid a beautiful tribute to his grand-mother in his letter, "Dear Grandma."

Brenda and Walt, Kellie and Kirk with Courtney, later Dave and Shellie with Natalie and Zach, all lived within a half-mile radius that made up a loving family commune. I added to the family mix. Due to proximity, my involvement with Brenda and her family was more intense. My sister was sensitive to my needs; illness or otherwise, she was there to provide whatever support was needed. I shared many evening meals with Brenda and Walt in their home. After my kitchen was installed and I was able to cook, I reciprocated in kind.

The phone call came on July 9, 2001, from Brenda with the devas-tating news that Walt had been diagnosed with acute leukemia. He was admitted to University Hospital in Cleveland. Brenda took her laptop, pallet, and whatever else was needed and stayed with her husband for the next two months. I only saw her when she made a fast trip home to do laundry. Other times I visited Walt in the hospital. It was September before he was released to come home. Walt was sixty-eight years old, and he held tenaciously on to life. His disease progressed, and in early November he was placed with hospice care. He died on November 14, and three days later on Shellie's birthday, a memorial service was held for him at the Chapel Methodist Church.

Brenda's girls, Kellie and Shellie, were equally as loving and considerate as was their mother. Kellie and Kirk lived close, and they were there to help on many an occasion. In a moment of distraction, I backed my Dodge Durango into the garage door, exposing the interior of my heated garage. It was winter, and I was concerned that the exposed plumbing in the garage would freeze. I called a garage door repair service and was told a repairman would be sent out the next day. Kirk drove by, saw what had happened, got his dad who lived nearby, and between the two of them they were able to make temporary repairs to the door. Another time Kirk came with a backhoe, dug a trench from my house to the lake cliff, and installed PVC pipe for a needed drain system.

I was living close by when Kellie took the tests for her associate nursing degree. When she and her mother left for Racine, Wisconsin, I sent several small gift packages with Kellie tagged with comments like, "Open this when you need encouragement," "Open this when you feel nervous," or "Open this when it is time to celebrate." My joy knew no bounds when Kellie telephoned on January 20 that she had passed all her exams.

Shellie and Dave lived in Aliquippa, Pennsylvania. From a distance, she was equally thoughtful of me. One Valentine's Day she sent me yellow roses, remembering from the time she lived in Columbus that Charlie always gave me roses on that day. It was in January of 2003 that I learned Shellie and Dave, with Natalie and Zachery, would be returning to the area. I was delighted. Now the family commune was complete.

Special-event days provided an opportunity for family members to get together. Kellie helped me prepare for some of the large family gatherings that took place at my house, mostly birthday celebrations and Thanksgiving dinners. The family always gathered to celebrate Christmas with Walt and Brenda. There is one Easter celebration that stands out in my mind. The Rosenbaum family came from Okemos, Michigan, for the Easter weekend. Brenda prepared decorated Easter eggs and hid them outside. On Easter

Sunday morning, Brenda announced the Easter egg hunt. Her grandchildren, Natalie and Zach, with my grandchildren, Allison and Allen, streaked out of the house with baskets in hand, oblivious that it was raining, and ran helter-skelter about searching for eggs and other prizes. When Brenda told the children all the hidden treasurers were found, this sodden group of small-fry returned inside and immediately started to devour the treats while playing with their other bounty.

Candice was the first of the Nelson family to come for a visit. Courtney came with me to the Cleveland Airport in July 1999 to meet Candice's flight. From the airport the three of us continued sixty miles west to meet Barb and Terry, Allen and Allison, at Cedar Point. It was hot as hades. After spending a short time with the family, Candice and I returned home. Barb, Terry, and entourage followed later. That afternoon we gathered on the rock beach below my cliff-side deck. Kirk had brought his Jet Ski. Brenda and Walt came with Kellie. A fire was built on the beach, hot dogs were roasted, and smores were made. Living at the edge of Lake Erie had advantages. A big one was relief from the heat.

Not to be outdone, Bruce Allan came the following month for his visit to check out Grandma's lakeside abode. Courtney and I met Bruce at the Cleveland Airport and again made the trip to Cedar Point. This time the temperature was bearable, and we enjoyed a full day of excitement as we rode the roller coasters and anything else that took our fancy. During his three-day visit, Bruce and I went to Kent to view places where his father grew up. Bruce wanted to visit the site of the May 4, 1970, shootings on the Kent State University Campus. As we walked the area and stopped to read the plaques describing the events, it was a solemn experience for my fifteen-year-old grandson.

The month of July 2001, my guest bedroom was booked solid. Candice came for a week's visit. Rich Gass with Kevin and Darren followed for a three-day visit. Then Royce and Jan Fincher were there for a two-day stay. Bruce and Linda came for Thanksgiving and stayed for nine days. I think the house on the lake served as the magnet that attracted family. It was wonderful, all of it, but exhausting, and I prided myself in wearing the hats of maid, cook, and entertainer. Not all visits went off without a hitch, but I enjoyed them all.

Involvement with my stepfamilies waxed and waned. I saw a lot of Charlie's daughter Barb and family. I recall a trip to Okemos when I missed my exit off of the interstate and had to call Barb for directions, delaying my estimated time of arrival. When I finally drove up to the intersection close to their house, there were Allison (age six) and Allen (age eight) patiently waiting on the corner to give loving hugs to their Gran Henri. My trips to Okemos were planned so that I could attend their hockey games. I was fascinated by the skating ability and stick-handling skills of these peewee players.

A telephone call that came on December 19, 1999, alarmed me. Barb had a grand mal seizure. A CAT scan and MRI revealed a baseball-sized tumor behind her right temple. Surgery was scheduled for January 5, 2000, and I was there with the children when Terry took Barb to the hospital. The surgery was successful, and it was a relief to the family to learn that tests showed no evidence of a malignancy.

As much as I wanted to help, it was difficult for me to be with the children. The permissive parenting of Barb and Terry made it difficult for me, especially with Allen. I shuffled them between scheduled hockey games, birthday parties, and visits to see their mother. One evening I agreed to play Monopoly with the children, and Allen set the game up on the floor. Allison told her brother not to do that as "Gran Henri can't sit on the floor." To which Allen snarled, "Tough for her." My response to Allen—a tongue-lashing that had no effect.

The days passed. Terry kept his schedule of activities; I was with the children. I had been there a week, paying careful attention to weather reports and learned a severe snowstorm was predicted. By then, Barb was well on her way to recovery. I telephoned Terry, left a message saying I was leaving for home to get ahead of the storm and he would need to get the children from school. Granted, I left a day early, requiring Terry to cancel scheduled plans, but I needed relief from the stresses of the previous week.

In May 2000, George and Rita came for a three-day visit. They enjoyed their stay in my lakeside home. They would get up early and brew the coffee. I would find them sitting on the deck, enjoying the quiet of the morning, the view, and their hot coffee. We drove into Ashtabula and visited the Marine Museum located on a bluff overlooking the harbor area. We toured the museum and met the curator, Dennis Hale. Dennis was the **sole** survivor of the crew of twenty-nine from the ore carrier *Daniel J. Morrell* that sank on November 29, 1966. He told us he was writing a book describing his ordeal. His book was published on January 1, 2010, *Shipwrecked: Reflections of the Sole Survivor: An Autobiography*. On a later visit to the museum, I purchased the book, and it is an unbelievable, fascinating read. Dennis died on September 2, 2015, at the age of seventy-five.

Not only did family come to visit me, I traveled to be with family. My trip in August, 1998, to San Jose to be with the Fincher family (Janet Dickie) for my grandson Royce III's wedding remains uppermost in my memory. An incident occurred that caused me to analyze my Gran Henri role, at least with the father of the groom, Royce II. The wedding took place on a perfect day in a natural outdoor setting under blue, cloud-laced skies. The bride's brother performed the ceremony, having obtained the needed credential via an internet church. Food was served. I visited with family members and guests I knew, introducing myself to many I didn't know. Came time to leave, I sought out the bride and groom to say goodbye. The bride was surrounded, and as I approached, she introduced me as Royce's grandmother. Father Royce was standing nearby, and I heard him mutter under his breath, "Sort of." Dumbfounded, I asked, "What do you mean 'sort of'? I've been his grandmother since he was born." Father Royce jokingly said, "We did let you in the family picture." Members of the extended family will say, "Royce will be Royce." But his cavalier attitude was hurtful.

I stayed for another three days. With the tension of the wedding over, the family relaxed, and the final days of my visit were enjoyable. Unfortunately, the feeling of being an outsider remained with me. The saying "Blood is thicker than water" definitely applied to me.

Years ago, I was sent a list of statements entitled "What Have You Learned in Life?" One of the statements read, "I've learned that no matter how good a friend is, they're going to hurt you every once in a while, and you must forgive them for that." The word family could readily be substituted for *friend*. For many years, I lived long distances away from my families. Whenever we were together, it was a special occasion, and the annoyances of daily living did not creep into the relationship. Conversely, the statement applied to me as well; they had to accept including me in their lives.

THE FIRST EIGHT MONTHS I LIVED IN MY HOUSE, I kept my nose to the grindstone. I made no attempt to contact friends or meet my neighbors—family members were exempt from my self-imposed isolation. My first attempt at being social was to reach out to my neighbors. The issue of the shared driveway on the east side of my lot was resolved with Mary Jo Lilley as we shared pleasant afternoons together sitting on my patio enjoying refreshments and conversation. My neighbor Joan DeLancy, to the west, had no issue with the lot survey that took part of her sidewalk that encroached on my property with the installation of the privacy fence. As the months passed, I met other neighbors in the immediate area of my house.

My first effort to reach out to a known acquaintance in Madison was an emotional disaster. Luanne Billington and I were friends when students at the KSU extension in Ashtabula. My sons and I were guests in her home. It was in April 1999 that I invited Luanne to join me for lunch. She accepted, and upon arrival presented me with a hostess gift. As we ate, she maintained a mien of icy reserve. Conversation was superficial. I was mystified. Within the week I received a formal thank-you note. Granted contact had waned over the years, but I hoped Luanne would introduce me to others in the community.

Two years later, Brenda and I were browsing the booths at the annual Unionville Community Garage Sale when we stopped by the Historical Society exhibit, and whom do I see but Luanne. I greeted her. Obviously embarrassed, she immediately said, "I'm surprised you even speak to me. I never contacted you after you invited me to your home." By then I had become keenly sensitized to the blue-blood mentality of Madison—they did not extend themselves to the newbies. Luanne was a blue blood; I was a newbie.

Dave and Chris Van Duseun, a couple I did not even know, reached out in a most friendly way to both Brenda and me. Chris was the niece of Helen Goodwin, a friend from the time I worked for the West Shore School District in Lemoyne, Pennsylvania. Helen knew I had moved to North Madison and directed her niece to be sure to contact me. We were their dinner guests at the Madison Country Club. It was through Chris I met others in the community, and with it came a positive attitude change.

Out-of-town friends who were overnight guests required more planning and more time. Clarabel McDonald lived in Kent, a friend made when I lived there in the 1960s. Now a widow, Clarabel and I had maintained close communication. No matter where I lived at the time, we visited one another every six months. Clarabel always insisted that the next visit be noted on our calendars before we parted. Each visit was carefully recorded by Clarabel in her daily log in much the same way that Trudy kept track of our monthly luncheon dates—the places we went, the restaurants where we ate that included our menu choices, even our comments related to likes and dislikes. She was ten years older than me, a person I held in the highest regard.

Having lived in the Columbus area for almost fifteen years, I had made several close friends. They were stunned when, within the year after

Charlie died, I sold my house. Fueled by curiosity, all came to see the house on the lake.

Luna Cummins came in September 1998, only two months after I took possession of the house. Walls were torn out, construction debris everywhere. One bathroom, along with a stove and refrigerator, worked. I had little more than a bed, but Luna came bringing her sleeping bag.

Jody Wallace and Bob Reece were my next visitors in November. Their Christmas gift for me that year was a twenty-four-inch bronze aluminum level—greatly appreciated and what every homeowner should have.

Finally, curiosity got the best of my spinster friend, Emily Schuh. In June of the following year, she and her gentleman friend, Gene, made a day trip to check out my new home. To meet Gene—a dignified, poised, articulate, handsome six-foot man with coarse facial features—was an occasion in itself. The many years I lived in Columbus, Gene was Emily's best kept secret; I had not met him.

Traffic on Interstate 71 flowed both north and south. In October 1998, I attended the beautiful black-and-white-themed wedding of Susan Gardner's son Mike Reeve, held at the Columbus Art Museum. I returned to Columbus in October 1999 for her son John's wedding reception.

In March 2001, I was again in Columbus, this time to attend a Celebration of Life memorial for Susan Fox, my former neighbor on Richards Road. Susan had fought a valiant battle after being diagnosed several years earlier with breast cancer. Weather in Ohio is fickle, and on the return drive home, I experienced a whiteout snowstorm that added hours of white-knuckle driving to my trip.

⁘⁘⁘⁘

NOW THAT I WAS SETTLED IN MY HOME, I explored activities available in the area. I loved to square dance and wanted to continue with lessons. Trudy and Lloyd no longer square danced, and Trudy had no problem with Lloyd being my partner (referred to as an "angel") for the lessons. Beverley, Lloyd's daughter-in-law, was the square dance caller. Bev called Modern Western Square Dance for two clubs—the Broken Wheels in Kirtland and the other in Austinburg. Lloyd was my angel for each. At the end of the lesson series, the student, still needing their angel partner, was tested to determine if the required skill level was achieved to be given their certificate. The Kirtland club was kind to its students, embarrassing no one, but the Austinburg club members were of a different ilk. Student and angel were required to blow on a party horn while riding a tricycle around the dance floor. (A new square dance call?) I thought it was great fun, but not my brother. Embarrassed, he endured and survived. After the frivolity of the "test," the dancing began. That evening I danced with my nephew Peter, with my great-nephew Adam, and with my brother-angel, who had regained his dignity.

The times I danced with my brother were fun—that is, all but one. We attended a Valentine dance where the caller was setting up squares for another "set" (several square dances lasting for about fifteen minutes). Lloyd and I were seated at the time, and Lloyd made no effort to move to secure our place in a square. I was anxious to dance and remarked to my brother, "Come on, let's get our place. I know how to sit, I want to dance." Lloyd focused his eyes on me, and if looks could freeze, I would have turned to ice. In his coldest—what has been termed by his children—"Schumann voice," he said, "Henri, you piss me off." Never before, that I could remember, had my brother spoken to me in that way, but then I never challenged him. At first, I was mystified and upset, but tears gave way to anger. I wanted to leave and let him find his own way home. But sanity prevailed, and I settled into a stony silence. (I later learned Lloyd was supersensitive to square dance protocol and was concerned we would take someone's place in a square where the presence of an uninvited couple was verboten.)

My involvement with Brenda was daily and more varied than with Lloyd and Trudy. Brenda and Walt took me with them to the Reliance retirees luncheon. I mention this because I had worked at Reliance in the 1950s. Reliance was the only place I was ever given the moniker Hank. Sure 'nuf, when I arrived at the luncheon, I heard, "Hi, Hank" from several people. Just the sound of the name gave me a feeling of belonging.

Brenda took me with her to a local grief-care group—an outreach of the Behm Funeral Home. These were grief-therapy sessions and beneficial to me, but the best part was that several of the women in the group decided to form a Red Hat Society (unofficial, and not connected to the national organization). Decked out in red hats and purple dresses/slack outfits, we enjoyed monthly luncheons at different restaurants in the area. One month we opted to have lunch at the nearby vocational school. As we entered the cafeteria, we ignored the stares and snickers of the students who must have thought they somehow missed Halloween.

I wanted to find a church affiliation and Brenda willingly came with me. There were no Presbyterian churches in the immediate area, so our first visit was to the Park Methodist Church in Madison. Neither of us were pleased with the pastor or the service. Our next visitation was to the Chapel

Methodist Church within two miles of our home. The pastor of this church had been there many years and was loved by his congregation. My challenge was to get past the overweight, hairy, disheveled person and focus on the spiritual message of the service. This was the church Brenda and I chose to join. Along with Brenda, I also joined the bell choir of the church. At first, I was given only one bell to ring, but later the director felt I could handle two bells. Brenda was much more talented in the area of music than I. She became the church pianist and organist. I liked the church, the spirituality, the friendly congregation, the opportunity for involvement, and the social contacts.

Now I had time to volunteer, and I kept in mind the criteria set when I retired in 1992—learn something new, time spent was of value to me and to the group. I opted to volunteer for hospice, took the required orientation classes, and volunteered one Saturday morning each month in the hospice library. It was a quiet place, and I benefitted by scanning through the many books related to coping with loss of a loved one.

Brenda and I contacted the Mentor Performing Arts Theater and inquired about opportunities to usher at theater performances. We were informed they were in need of substitute ushers. Pleased with the opportunity, we took part in the mandatory orientation sessions, purchased our red jackets, and waited for a call. My first call came, and I was assigned to be with a man who was a veteran usher. To use an old farm expression, I was as useful as tits on a boar. I stood at my post until the performance began, then I left never to return.

I wanted to resume piano lessons, and Brenda joined me. After some false starts to find a teacher, we settled on B. J. Green, a member of the Western Reserve Arts Association staff. The WRAA offices were located in a century-old, two-story brick building located off the public square in Madison, about six miles from my home.

I practiced piano one to two hours daily. When BJ had her annual student recital, I participated. I had a keyboard, and as my piano skills improved, I reached out and joined a music group. Following the first practice session, I realized I lacked the necessary chording skills. BJ put a fainthearted effort into helping me, but it was evident she did not want to bother with something I should have learned as a child.

My seminal moment came when I mastered the piece "Loneliness"—a composition by a friend of Charlie's family. The piece had a tranquilizing melody, and Candice wanted it played at her wedding. Performing for family versus performing for a group are totally different performance experiences. I realized that difference at BJ's student recital. A piece played flawlessly at home was botched when played before the music students and their parents. Slightly embarrassed at the recital, I would have been mortified if this happened at the wedding. It was Candice who suggested I record the piece, even finding a small recording studio in the area.

It was to that studio that I went one Saturday morning with my support person, Brenda. I was momentarily intimidated by the studio Steinway grand. But I sat down, adjusted the position of the bench, placed my hands on the keyboard, and to my satisfaction, played the piece flawlessly.

The ultimate self-improvement challenge came with a computer. Again, it was at Brenda's insistence that I was brought kicking and screaming into the computer age. She and Jim Funck, the all-purpose handyman who did so much during those first demolition and remodeling months I was in the house, installed the computer. Moreover, it was Brenda's patience, along with computer classes, that enabled me to gradually acquire basic computer skills.

Christmas 1998, the Nelson family had given me a Meade ETX telescope. Candice took an astronomy class at UNLV that sparked her father's interest in astronomy, and that expanded to include me in Ohio. I knew little about the moon, stars, and planets, and nothing about telescopes. I learned of the Cuyahoga Valley Astronomy club (CVAS) and joined. The observatory was less than twenty miles from my home, and I attended the monthly meetings. Suddenly, I became interested in looking at the night sky, and in order to do that, I had to stay up later than 10:00 p.m.—my usual bedtime. The deck was a good place to set up the telescope. The ambient light was minimal, and there was an open space to view the sky. I recall the thrill the first time I focused on the moon, not seeing a smiling face of a man up there, but rather a rugged lunar surface. Reaching further out into space, my elation knew no bounds when I focused on the rings of Saturn. I was hooked on astronomy.

On another occasion, I was up in the early morning hours to view a Leonid meteor shower—nature's fireworks show. The most memorable of my sky-watching experiences was the night my nocturnal neighbor telephoned me at 3:00 a.m. and urged me to rush outside to view the northern lights. As best I can describe it, I looked to the north and saw the sky as a celestial canvas painted with all shades of the rainbow. Unfortunately, my interest in astronomy waned when, a few years later, I moved to an area with a high percentage of cloud-covered skies.

I liked to be active. I tried line dancing, took a class in tai chi at a local church, joined the YMCA where I swam daily, participated in a yoga class, and signed up for a bicycle spinning class to build up my leg muscles for cycling. I played golf, signed up for the Lake County Metroparks publication, and joined a hiking group. With new-made friends, I canoed and kayaked, and in the winter, cross-country skied. I was physically fit and able to enjoy any and all of these activities.

There were events to attend and places to go. The Geneva Grape Festival was an annual fall event. One year Brenda and I volunteered at the souvenir booth. Later, watching the parade, I was fascinated by the precision marching of a cadre of young black men from Cleveland. The Cleveland Museum of Natural History and the Cleveland Art Museum were located on the east side of the city and access was relatively convenient.

There were many venues for theater performances—musicals at local high schools, the Andrews School for Girls in Willoughby where I enjoyed *Brigadoon*, the Ashtabula Arts Center where my former neighbor, Roz Moulder, starred in *Deathtrap*, the Rabbit Run Theater in North Madison where my favorite musical, *1776,* was performed. The Lakeland Community College offered special programs. I recall attending a two-hour, one-woman show—*Tea at Five*—the life of Katherine Hepburn performed by a local actress.

For most of the years I lived in the area, I purchased tickets for performances at Playhouse Square in Cleveland. In September 1999, I ordered lodge tickets for several of the opera series performances—Puccini's *La Boheme* and *Madam Butterfly*, Verdi's La *Traviata*, and Gilbert and Sullivan's comic opera *HMS Pinafore.* Trudy reluctantly agreed to come with me and was noncommittal as to liking or disliking the performances, but I did enjoy her company.

It was Trudy who had introduced me to the opera in 1950. She invited me to join her and a friend for a performance of Bizet's *Carmen* at a Cleveland theater. I remember this introduction to the opera at an impressionable age, and I have always felt indebted to Trudy for this cultural experience.

MOVING TO A NEW PLACE required establishing oneself in all areas of living; finding the right doctors presented a challenge. With the help of Brenda and Lloyd, I had no problem connecting with a dentist and an ophthalmologist. Finding a PCP was another matter, and it took me almost four years to find one I liked. The first three doctors (one female, two males) were a disappointment—the female was cold and aloof, the first of the male physicians was repeatedly at least an hour late or more for his appointments, and the other male doctor was unwilling to give attention to my restless leg condition. I finally connected with a PCP, a woman, whom I found both professionally competent and compassionate.

Christmas 2000, I experienced severe abdominal pain and nausea that lasted for a twenty-four-hour period. It was not until March 2001 that I was able to see a urologist who diagnosed my condition as an enlarged left kidney and scheduled me to be evaluated by a nephrologist in May. Before I could keep the appointment, the pain and nausea returned, and Brenda took me to the ER. My urologist was not available, but fortunately I was in a hospital connected with the Cleveland Clinic, and Dr. Steven Streem took my case. He diagnosed my condition as a urinary tract infection (UTI). The ureter that drained the left kidney had a kink in it. A minimally invasive procedure was scheduled for September 4, 2001, at the Cleveland Clinic to place a stent in the ureter to straighten out the kink. I was in the hospital overnight. Brenda and Kellie were with me. The stent was removed after several weeks, and Dr. Streem encouraged me by saying 90 percent of patients experiencing this procedure had no further complications.

Apparently, I fell in the 10 percent group because in October, 2002, the acute pain and nausea returned. On November 15, Dr. Streem performed ureteropelvic junction obstruction (UJO) surgery to correct the problem. This time my hospital stay was three days. Again, Brenda and Kellie were with me throughout the ordeal. Bruce and Linda came from Las Vegas and stayed for a week. Of all the body part repair/replacement surgeries I had, I can say without equivocation that this was the most painful.

In follow-up appointments with Dr. Streem, he assured me he was now 100 percent certain my problem was resolved. Tragically, Dr. Streem was diagnosed with brain cancer and died the following year at the age of fifty-nine. He was one of the finest, most compassionate surgeons I have ever known.

IN SPITE OF ALL THE ACTIVITY that swirled around my life, I missed male companionship. I attended a Reliance retiree luncheon and checked out if there were any available men that I knew. Seeing none, I scratched that contact off my list. I took part in several bicycle tours, and on a Michigan ride, I met Phil Kline. There were qualities that attracted me to him. He was tall, had a muscular cyclist physique, perhaps in his midfifties, and a writer. I attempted to stay in touch through e-mails. After three e-mail exchanges Phil answered my last questions but was too busy to continue with any further contact. That ended that.

I was drawn to another cyclist who rode in a local bicycle club. Al Olson was my height, had a bicyclist's muscular physique, nondescript looks, by livelihood a baker now retired, and had bicycled solo throughout the world. I was impressed and pleased by his friendly mannerisms. Being with Al was like being with my brother.

The humdinger that caught my eye was Ernie Whitney. Ernie rode with a Thursday night group of friends who cycled little and socialized a lot. Ernie was short, rather stocky, older than I, hair flecked with gray, and he seemed somewhat interested in me. When I learned his hobby was wood carving, I inquired if he had ever been to the Warther Museum in Dover, Ohio (a distance of about one-hundred miles to the south) where the intricate wood carvings of Ernest Warther were displayed. He enthusiastically accepted my invitation to visit the museum. The date was agreed upon, and two days before we were to leave, Ernie telephoned and asked if he could invite his friend Mary Lou to join us. What could I say but "Of course"? I chauffeured Ernie and Mary Lou, who sat comfortably in the back seat enjoying the scenery, as I drove them to the museum of this famous wood carver. After that, I would see Ernie at our Thursday night gatherings but kept a careful distance. I obviously had misread his intentions.

Brenda made an attempt to help. She arranged a dinner at her home inviting a neighborhood friend and her dad, whom Brenda knew was single. The dinner was a pleasant social event. Karl was a good conversationalist, but nothing further developed.

I even resorted to calling a 900-number listed in the lonely-hearts section of the *Cleveland Plain Dealer*. Jim returned my call and remarked that of all the responses, mine was the most pleasant voice. (Apparently, those elocution lessons taken in my youth had unforeseen benefits.) I met Jim for dinner at the Unionville Tavern. It only took a few minutes of conversation to realize this was a mistake.

It was in July 2000, with Brenda's encouragement, I attended the Jefferson High School annual alumni dinner for all JHS graduates.

Attendees were encouraged to sit with members of their graduating class. I found the class of 1947 table near the entrance door and sat down. My back was to the doorway. I noticed the person across the table from me look up and speak to someone. There must have been some indication by the person's demeanor that he was confused. When asked what graduating class, I heard a male voice respond "1947." He was invited to join us, taking the empty seat next to me.

His name was Randall Presley. I vaguely remembered him. As I recalled he was one of the unseen members in our class—did not stand out academically, athletically, or socially. As we chatted, I learned he was a carpenter by trade, now retired. This accounted for his rugged complexion, muscular arms, and calloused hands. He had two children, was divorced, and lived alone. As we parted, I slipped him my phone number and suggested he call so we could continue reminiscing about school days at JHS.

It was three weeks before Randy called and invited me to go with him to the area Medieval Fair. I accepted, found him to be a comfortable salt-of-the-earth person, and enjoyed the afternoon. We dated over the next months. I was comfortable with Randy, and I invited Brenda and Walt to join us one evening at my home for dinner. Later, both commented that they liked him, but then there was no reason not to like him. Randy was not an aggressive or argumentative person.

I continued to see Randy, even encouraged his friendship, though I came to realize he had enough medical problems with their side effects to fill one side of an eight-and-a-half-by-eleven-inch sheet of paper—congestive heart failure, pacemaker, prostate cancer, and painful knees. In spite of this, we did a lot together. One weekend in July 2001, we drove to the Cleveland lakefront and boarded the tall ships docked there. Ringway Tours, operating out of Ashtabula, offered trips to interesting places. We traveled to Akron for a buffet lunch at the Tangiers Restaurant followed by an Irish music show at Quaker Square. We took another of their bus tours to Pittsburgh, where we boarded the sternwheeler *Majestic* for a ride on the Monongahela River. Randy had heard of the Sauder Village Living History Farm & Museum located in northwestern Ohio. We spent three interesting days there and stayed in luxury quarters at the Sauder Inn. Randy fulfilled my need for a male companion. I enjoyed his company and accepted the limitations of the relationship.

In 2002, my grandson Bruce Allan was to graduate from the University of Las Vegas. With Bruce and Linda's permission, I invited Randy. I offered the choice of traveling by car or by plane. Never having been in the West, Randy opted for the road trip.

A route was planned that would take us over I-90 through the northern tier of states and, on our return, would travel through several of the southern states along Route 66. We left on May 31 and returned on June 29. Our priority was to visit national parks, as well as other places that piqued our interest along the way. We drove through parts of fifteen states and covered a distance of 6,247 miles.

In South Dakota we visited the Corn Palace in Mitchell. There was a heavy rain the day we drove through the Badlands. In Wall we stopped at Wall Drug and got an unheard-of five-cent cup of coffee. Mount Rushmore was concealed in fog the day of our arrival, but by the next morning, the fog had lifted, and we stood there looking up in wonderment at the faces of four great American presidents—George Washington, Thomas Jefferson, Theodore Roosevelt, and Abraham Lincoln. We left the park and continued west.

Devil's Tower, located in the Black Hills region of Wyoming, is a rock formation that rises 867 feet above the earth's surface and can be seen for many miles. Arriving at the tower, I walked around the base, and as I recall, it was a distance of about one mile. Randy opted to sit on a bench in the shade and wait. A visit to Yellowstone National Park was at the top of our national park must-see list. I had visited the park in previous years and was vaguely familiar with the area around Old Faithful. At best, Randy's physical condition allowed for a limited amount of physical exercise. Now in higher altitudes, the atmospheric conditions curtailed all exercise. I was able to find a place to park that gave us a vantage point to view the geyser. It was a compromise, but at least Randy caught the sight of Old Faithful as it blew.

Heading south into Utah, we drove through Bryce Canyon, Zion National Park, and found lodging for the night on the north rim of the Grand Canyon. Randy was having great difficulty breathing, and all sightseeing had to be done looking out the window of our van.

Ever since our route had taken us into higher altitudes in Wyoming and Utah, I feared for Randy. Each night before going to sleep, I made sure I had the exact location of our lodging in the event I must call 911. As we left the Grand Canyon and drove into Nevada, our first stop was the veterans' hospital near Nellis Air Force Base outside of Las Vegas. Randy was a veteran and received his medical care through a veterans' hospital near home, so he was immediately admitted as a patient at this VA hospital and

seen by a physician who diagnosed "altitude sickness." The doctor reassured
Randy that, now he was at lower elevation levels, his breathing difficulties
would be minimal. We left the hospital greatly relieved, for the remainder
of our trip did not include any mountainous areas.

We arrived at Bruce and Linda's home on June 11. Two days later
we attended Bruce Allan's graduation at the University of Las Vegas. Bruce
graduated with high honors, a proud moment for all of the family. During
the week we spent with family, we were treated to the Danny Gans show at
the Mirage, a cruise on Lake Meade that included a view of Hoover Dam
from the water, swimming, and picnicking.

We left Las Vegas on June 20, Father's Day, and connected with Route
66 in Seligman, Arizona. It was here we met Angel and Velma Delgadillo.
Angel had devoted a lifetime to collecting Route 66 memorabilia. He
claimed that his interest in promoting Route 66 not only saved his town
from extinction but served as the catalyst for tourism that brought new life
to towns along the Mother Road. In Oatman we visited the hotel where
Carol Lombard and Clark Gable stayed on their honeymoon. One wall in
the hotel dining room was covered in paper money—mostly one-dollar bills
signed, dated, and tacked to the wall. Not to be left out, we tacked up our
signed donation. Route 66 took us along rough, potholed, unpaved roads.
We did leave the route to take in the worthwhile sights of the Petrified
Forest and the Painted Desert, both national parks in Arizona.

Crossing into Texas, near the town of Groom, I spied a huge cross
off to the side of the road. Wanting a picture, I stopped, walked to the area
of the cross, and was about to take a picture when I was approached by a
man who started to lecture me on the sin of abortion and the value of life.
I had no desire to listen to his preaching or to be argumentative. I fled the
scene, sans picture, sans donation to the prominently placed donation box.
In Adrian, Randy spotted a sign reading "Midpoint on Route 66; from
Chicago to Los Angeles." Our last stop in Texas was in the town of Elk.
I noted a carousel in the town's central park. Randy and I walked over to
the carousel, and in conversation with the operator, I learned all the horses
were solid wood, created and carved by a California sculptor, Ed Hale. The
ride had recently been installed at the cost of $640,000 and the operator
was doing test runs. He invited Randy and me to climb onboard and select
our rides. Randy chose one of the benches. I mounted the most colorful
high-stepping horse I could find. As the calliope music began to play, the
carousel sprang to life and slowly started going around and around and
around, all the time picking up speed, and with each orbit of the carousel, I

reached in vain for the brass ring, all the time reliving in my mind the thrill of my childhood at the Ashtabula County Fair.

In Arcadia, Oklahoma, we stopped and toured a round barn built in 1898—first one I ever saw and have never seen one since. The man giving the tour described how the jigs were made to insure uniformity and accuracy in the curve of the lumber and how the rafters were secured to support a roof with no horizontal posts. In Claremore and Oologah near Tulsa, we visited the museum and birthplace of Will Rogers. Continuing our journey, we drove for miles on the Will Rogers Turnpike (I-44), stopping in Vinita to walk through the world's largest McDonald's that spanned the highway.

We left Route 66 at Saint Louis to visit the Gateway Arch. I stifled my feelings of claustrophobia as we rode the interior car up through the curve of the arch to enter the observation area at the top—a room seven feet, two inches by sixty-five feet by six feet, nine inches. My view from the height of 630 feet was limited to a small seven-by-twenty-seven-inch window. I stepped to the window, pressed my nose against the glass, and looked out to see the mighty Mississippi River and the park area below. Fortunately, there was little wind that day, and I felt only a slight movement of the arch. Tests showed deflection to be eighteen inches in 150 mile-per-hour winds.

Leaving St. Louis, we took a direct route home, stopping for one night in Cincinnati. The final day of our trip, our last stop was at the National Museum of the US Air Force located at Wright-Patterson Air Force Base outside of Dayton, Ohio. For me, the highlight of the museum visit was entering Air Force One, the plane used by several presidents that included Truman.

Once home, I reflected on our road trip, and realized how naive I was regarding Randy's physical condition, giving no thought to the effect of higher altitudes on his weakened heart. I gave thanks that a medical emergency was avoided and there were no vehicle mishaps on our month-long odyssey.

Randy kept in close communication with his cousin Earl, who lived in Ocala, Florida. Randy had family portraits, and he wanted Earl to have these. It was I who suggested not packaging and shipping them to Earl but rather that we take another road trip. I knew on the drive to Florida there would not be another elevation problem as there was on our trip to the West. I was willing to chance that no other medical issues would surface. Randy was overjoyed as he had not seen his cousin for a number of years.

We left on March 1, 2003, and returned on March 7, a fast-paced trip with no time for sightseeing. On the first night of the trip, I was the one who was sick. I must have eaten something that gave me food poisoning. We stopped for the night at a motel, and I became violently ill. I felt better the next morning and was determined not to abort our plans. We continued south, and Randy drove most of that day. Fortunately, my illness was short-lived.

Arriving in Ocala, we experienced no difficulty in finding Earl's home. He lived in a government housing project. When Randy asked Earl how he got along with his neighbors (whom we observed were all black) his response was, "Whoever moves in, I'll get along with 'em." I think he would, for Earl was a delightfully positive person—cheerful, with a sense of humor, talkative, overall a very likeable character.

We spent one night in Ocala. Randy stayed with his cousin; I chose to lodge in a nearby motel. The next morning, we said our goodbyes and headed north on I-75. Before leaving the state, we noted signs along the road directing travelers to the Stephen Foster Folk Culture Center State Park in White Springs. We exited the highway and made our one tourist stop of the trip. The gift shop held our interest as we listened and looked through familiar music composed by the American songwriter often referred to as the father of American music.

I noted the exertion of travel was taking its toll on Randy's weakened heart. We spent only one night in a motel on the return trip. If Randy needed a doctor or hospital care, I wanted to be home. I drove 650 miles that second day. With rest and proper nutrition, Randy recovered. I breathed a prayer of thanks that another medical emergency was avoided. Once home, I realized how foolhardy I was to even suggest the trip.

Looking back, I've attempted to analyze my relationship with Randy. I was lonely, and he provided companionship and was comfortable to be with. My diary entry of November 18, 2000, read, "Now that I've met Randy, I am not as restless." I met his family—son and his wife and their two children, his daughter and his sister, a couple who were his best friends. At first all seemed wary of me. It was the son who first realized his dad was much happier and fully accepted my efforts to interact with the family.

Randy's health was an issue. I assumed the responsibility for all of his medical appointments—doctors, trips to the Erie VA Medical Center, and one trip to the VA Pittsburgh Healthcare System that required an overnight stay. As Randy weakened, I bought a wheelchair. This gave us the flexibility to go more places.

When I first met Randy, he lived on the second floor of his house in Ashtabula. The first floor was filled with a collection of antiques and junk.

As his heart continued to weaken, he lost the ability to climb the stairs to the second floor. I helped clean out the first floor, painted walls, arranged furniture, put up drapes, and even washed the outside of the dirt-encrusted windows.

I was careful not to make any verbal commitments to Randy, but I knew in my heart, because of all I did for him, he took our relationship to be much more serious than I did. As events came to pass, I removed myself from Randy's life, and by so doing I know I deeply hurt him.

———————⊹⊹⊹⊹⊹⊹———————

I ENJOYED TRAVEL, and no sooner was I settled in the house than I joined my Columbus friend, Emily, on a weeklong sightseeing bus tour to Canada in September 1999. We visited the cities of Quebec, Montreal, Toronto, and Niagara Falls. As on all arranged tours, our tour guide related information about historical highlights and significant sights in each of the cities we visited. Adequate time was allowed for shopping and sightseeing. Our weeklong trip took Emily and me outside of the parameters of common interests and behaviors. Emily's shopping and dining interests were different than mine; she was less flexible with schedule changes. We parted barely speaking.

Naysayers predicted there would be catastrophic happenings with computers at the turn of the century. I was talking on the telephone with Bruce and Linda when the witching hour of midnight EST arrived, and it was a nonevent transition to January 1, 2000. Was I relieved? Yes, the hype of the media can cause one to feel a heightened degree of angst.

The Meade ETX telescope that the Nelson family had given me piqued my interest in astronomy. In January of 2000 I was in Las Vegas, borrowed a car from the family, and drove to King's Ranch located in central Arizona to take part in an Elderhostel offering. There were several classes open to participants, but my main interest was astronomy. As I recall the classes were very basic and held little interest for me, but on my return trip, I visited the Lowell Observatory, located in the northcentral part of the state near Flagstaff. Percival Lowell (1855–1916), a businessman, author, mathematician, and astronomer, founded the observatory that bears his name. While there I looked through the scope used by Clyde Tombaugh in 1930 (the year I was born) when he discovered the planet Pluto.

A New York City singer-songwriter of contemporary folk music has memorialized Pluto in a song, "Planet X," part of her thirteen-song album, *Shining My Flashlight on the Moon.* A few select lines from the song follow:

Percival Lowell died in 1916
His theory still only a theory
'til 1930, American Clyde Tombaugh
In his scientific query
Discovered Planet X, 3 point 7
Billion miles from the sun
A smallish ball of frozen rock
Methane and nitrogen...
It joined Mercury, Venus, Earth and Mars, Jupiter
Saturn, Uranus and Neptune...
Now we look at the sky
And wonder what new surprises
Await us in outer space.

In 2006 the definition of a planet changed, and so did the status of Pluto. Its classification is now a "dwarf planet."

In the year 2000, I turned seventy. Bruce and Linda invited me to join the family in April for a weeklong cruise. Linda made all the arrangements. I was to connect with the family onboard the ship docked in Miami, Florida. I got my first view of the *Voyager of the Seas* as I walked up the dock, but nothing prepared me for what loomed before my eyes. The ship was massive—literally a floating city. It carried a maximum of 3,100 passengers (double occupancy) with a crew of 1,180.

As I stood in line waiting my turn to board, I engaged in conversation with a lady standing behind me. She wanted to know if this was my first cruise but, not waiting for my answer, went on to say she had been on several cruises and loved it. Her next statement has remained with me to this day. "You will either love it or hate it." I was about to find out.

I arrived before other family members (Bruce, Linda, Candice, and Bruce Allan; Linda's sister's family—Gail, John, and Erin). Once checked in, I found the inside state room I would share with Candice. Entering the room, my first sensation was one of claustrophobia—there was no porthole. But I soon realized I would spend little time there, and I didn't need a porthole when showering, dressing, or sleeping. While waiting for the family, I took a cursory tour of the ship. The top deck was given over to physical activities that included a swimming pool. The Royal Promenade, replete with shops, consumed another deck; on one of the lower decks I found a large auditorium. Everywhere there were bars and cocktail lounges, game rooms, and street entertainers. I was overwhelmed. Seeing a small chapel, I stepped inside for a moment of quiet relaxation.

Places to dine ranged from casual buffet to elegant, themed dining rooms—Carmen, La Boheme, and Magic Flute. I was informed at check-in the Nelson family was assigned to the Carmen dining room. I stepped inside and noted the grandeur of the sweeping staircase connecting the dining areas; crystal chandeliers hung from the ceilings; tables were covered with linen tablecloths, highlighted with bright floral centerpieces. Seeing all this magnificence, I was glad I heeded the directive to bring appropriate dinner-dress attire.

During the cruise, the ship alternated three days at sea with three days anchored offshore at ports of call. Joining the family, I took advantage of all shore excursions. At Labadee, Hispaniola, I snorkeled to the point of exhaustion and delighted in the beauty of the underwater reefs and myriad colors and shapes of the tropical fish. When we were at Ocho Rios, Jamaica, our guides tethered us together with a rope for the six-hundred-foot climb over the rocks of Dunn's River Falls through ankle-deep cascading water. Later in the day, I thrilled to a parasailing adventure with Bruce.

On one of the onshore days, we arrived back early to the sixty-foot, multilevel, cabin-cruiser shuttle boat that would return us to the ship. Once onboard, I followed the family to the top deck where we planned to stretch out and sunbathe while we waited. Bruce and John were the first to take a daredevil jump over the side into the water twenty feet below. Not to be outdone, I stepped to the rail and took a leap into space. My feet and legs cut the water as my body submerged for what seemed to be an interminable length of time before returning to the surface. Instantly I faced the ire of my son, who thought I had either drowned or been permanently injured. I was fine, and in truth, the experience was far more exciting than the parasailing I had previously done with Bruce. The final day ashore was in Cozumel, Mexico, and our visit to the Mayan pyramid and temple ruins at Tulum consumed the day.

The days at sea were another matter. Candice busied herself roaming the ship with her brother and cousin. Bruce and Linda, Gail and John busied themselves doing whatever couples most enjoyed doing when on a cruise. On my own, I explored every nook and cranny open to the public on every deck of the ship. The bars and cocktail lounges held no interest for me. The shops along the Royal Promenade, filled with street entertainers, held my interest for a time. Afternoon theater entertainment helped to while away more hours. On the final day of the cruise, I had exhausted all points and places of interest, and in desperation, I joined a napkin-folding class.

I met the family for dinners in the elegant Carmen dining room. The cuisine and wines tempted my salivary glands to work overtime, and I, being one who seldom tasted a food I didn't like, disembarked the ship weighing more than when I embarked a week earlier.

Looking back on the cruise, I was grateful the family included me on their vacation, but it was my undoing that I could not fill my time with solo activities that gave me a feeling of contentment. I was lonesome; I missed my mate.

In the 1960s, through friends of Allan Dickie, I learned about the Passion Play performed in Oberammergau, Germany. The drama took place once every decade, and 2000 was the year. I was determined to go! When living in Columbus, Charlie and I used Slater Tours, and I was delighted to learn they offered a ten-day trip to Oberammergau and Northern Italy in July. Wanting a travel companion, I immediately thought of Trudy.

With the encouragement of her children and the approval of her husband, Trudy agreed to come with me. Our flight landed in Rome on July 5. From there we would travel north by bus stopping at Assisi, Florence, Pisa, Venice, and Oberammergau, ending in Munich on July 14.

We arose early the morning following our arrival and boarded the bus that would take us to Vatican City. Once there we met our Sistine Chapel guide, Tony. Apparently, our group had VIP tickets, as Tony directed us to stand at the end of the "short" queue, which to me was a misnomer, for I estimated the line to be several hundred feet long. As our line started to move, we walked past another line of people standing and waiting that appeared to have no end. It was then I realized we were given preferential treatment. Tony spoke perfect English as he articulated information about the history of, and the artworks in, the chapel. We entered a room, he paused, would speak, and immediately move on, requiring our group to move with him through the mass of humanity that crowded the rooms. For whatever reason, Tony did not carry a flag aloft that would better enable us to see him. I was terrified I would lose the group. I wanted to pause, to look up, to look around, to absorb the frescoes painted by Michelangelo, specifically the painting of *The Last Judgment* on the ceiling of one of the chapel rooms.

Leaving the chapel when the tour ended, I walked out into the sunshine and onto the plaza. Disappointment welled up from the pit of my stomach. I had walked through the Sistine Chapel, seen much, but absorbed little.

Our time in Rome passed quickly, and the next morning we were again on the bus headed to Florence, with a stop in Assisi—the birth and burial place of St. Francis. The Basilica of St Francis, built over the saint's grave, is a massive two-level church. The walls are covered with frescoes, giving a pictorial narration of the story of St. Francis and the life of Christ. Much of the work is credited to the painter Giotto (1267–1337) and his helpers. The day we were there the church was crowded with Polish pilgrims. Yet again, the opportunity to gaze in wonder at the frescoes was limited.

Sunday, we arrived in Florence, and my excitement was palpable, for here in the Academia Gallery stood Michelangelo's seventeen-foot statue of David. Years ago, I had read Irving Stone's book, *The Agony and the Ecstasy*, and Michelangelo was forever embedded in my mind as a great painter and sculptor. At the age of twenty-six, Michelangelo envisioned the figure of David in a neglected piece of marble referred to as *The Giant*. It took him two years to sculpt the statue. For the first time, I was not imprisoned by a mass of humanity. I stood and gazed up at the statue, and I felt a connection with the biblical story of the Israelite David who slew the Philistine Goliath. Before leaving the city, our group visited the tomb of Michelangelo in the church of Santa Croce. In my humble way, I stood there in reverence to pay homage to this man who gave so much beauty to the world.

That afternoon we arrived in Pisa. Located here is the famous *campanile* (freestanding) bell tower of the Pisa Cathedral. The construction of the tower began in 1173, and 199 years later, it was completed. The earth on one side of the tower was unstable and did not hold the tower's weight. Consequently, over the years, it developed a tilt. When completed in 1372, the tilt measured 5.5 degrees. In 1990 restoration began to stabilize the tower, and when completed in 2001, the tilt was corrected to 3.99 degrees. Knowing Lloyd's interest in construction, Trudy took numerous pictures of the restoration process. Visitors were not allowed inside, so I stood, looked, and regretted that I would not be able to enter and climb the 296 steps to the top for a panoramic view of the area.

From Pisa our travels took us to Venice, the city dubbed the Queen of the Adriatic. An unusual and romantic place. There ferryboats replace buses, sleek motorboats are used for taxis, a gondola is available to anyone desiring a leisurely float on the city's canals. Our introduction to the city was a motorboat ride on the palace-lined Grand Canal. Exiting the boat at St. Mark's Square, I stepped into several inches of tide water covering a large section of the plaza. There were pigeons everywhere—overhead and underfoot, leaving their droppings that would be washed out with the receding tides. A guide greeted our group, very knowledgeable, but again moved too quickly to allow time to take in the surrounding grandeur of St. Mark's Basilica, located on the square. Once inside, my eyes verified why this church was referred to as The Church of Gold. I was awestruck by the ground gold mosaics that appeared to radiate a brilliance from the ceilings and upper walls of the interior.

Having free time, Trudy and I entered the shop of a Venetian glass blower. It was fascinating to watch the artisan ply his skills as he formed a small vase from a molten glass bubble. We exited the studio and entered a shop where the wall shelves were filled with vases of all sizes and colors, including other miscellaneous glass pieces. Trudy was a window-shopper—not me. I selected ten small vases for self and family gifts. As we started to leave, I noticed a bluish glass cat displayed on a shelf—plump, with a sinister expression created by wide-angled eyebrows, and tiny nuggets for ears. At first glance I shuddered, thinking the artisan had encircled the cat with a reptile. The object was turquoise with blue circular strips that started at the base as a slender rope, swelling in size, tapering off as it draped over the cat's shoulder. Closer examination revealed it was the cat's tail—a most unusual cat. Ignoring the price tag, I beckoned the store clerk, Caesar, and obligingly handed him my credit card in payment for this additional purchase. My glass cat needed a name. It was Trudy who suggested I call the cat "Chaz," thinking of our friendly clerk. Today Chaz holds a place of honor among the other memorabilia from my travels.

Our gondola ride took place on the Palace River. It was a delightfully relaxing time as the gondolier poled along, relating stories about buildings and places that we passed. Before us was the white limestone Bridge of Sighs. A fully enclosed bridge spanning the river, with iron bars covering the small windows, the bridge connected a prison with interrogation rooms. I could only imagine the feeling of horror for those who walked across the bridge to be imprisoned. But this ominous feeling was soon dispelled as the gondolier related a love story. The bridge was made famous in the movie *A Little Romance*. Here, an American girl and a French boy kissed, declaring their eternal love for one another as their gondola passed under the bridge.

We left Italy the following morning, and our bus crossed over the narrow western "finger" of Austria, stopping briefly in Innsbruck before entering Germany. Our destination that day was Oberammergau, a picturesque town nestled in the valley of the Bavarian Alps. As soon as Trudy and I were settled in our cottage, we ventured into the town. I had learned of the Passion Play more than thirty years ago. Now, in the year 2000, I stood in the empty open-air theater and looked across the stage to the natural scenic backdrop of towering mountains and Alpine meadows. I cherished this moment, for tomorrow I would be one of the 4,700 "pilgrims" to view the sold-out performance.

The origin of the production is given in the English/German playbook (the play is performed in German) *Passionsspiele 2000 Oberammergau:*

> A play about life and death—promised in a time when every life was at stake—this is how the story about the Passion Play of Oberammergau begins. After months of suffering and death because of the plague, while the Thirty Years War was raging around them, the people of Oberammergau made a pledge to perform every ten years the 'Play of the Suffering, Death and Resurrection of Our Lord Jesus Christ.' At Pentecost, the year of 1634, they fulfilled their solemn pledge for the first time: They staged a play in their cemetery, over the freshly dug graves of their [sic] victims of the plague.

Trudy and I rose early to be at the theater and in our seats by 9:00 a.m. for the fortieth performance of the production that began with Jesus entering Jerusalem and ended with His resurrection. Forty percent of the town's population made up the cast—1,600 men and boys, 600 women and girls. Only people who lived in the town for at least twenty years were eligible to perform. The major players were approved by the town council, and it was expected that they would live pious personal lives.

The play lasted for six hours, with a welcomed three-hour lunch break. We walked to our assigned restaurant and afterward had time to browse in the local shops before taking our seats for the afternoon performance. I was thrilled to be there but will admit it was a test of my spiritual endurance.

The following morning, we boarded our bus, which would take us to Munich. En route, a stop was made at Linderhof Palace, one of King Ludwig's castles. The formal gardens and castle, built in the neo-French

Rococo style, were beautiful and ornate to the extreme. Settled in our room in Munich, Trudy and I left the hotel and walked to the plaza. A few years earlier, I had been there with my niece and nephew. Before my eyes, again the fairy-tale dramas of a wedding and dance of the coopers, accompanied by the bells of the Glockenspiel, played out in the plaza tower. I enjoyed the event more than the first time I saw it, as I knew what to expect.

The morning of July 14, we boarded our flight for home. During the hours on the plane, I reflected back on the tour. The lodgings provided us with large rooms and comfortable beds—the quaint Bavarian cottage in Oberammergau the best of all. Six-course dinners with complementary wines bordered on glutinous with rare exception. I belonged to the clean-plate club. The wide windows on the bus that took us from Rome to Munich allowed for comfortable viewing of the ever-changing scenery. In Italy there were acres of sunflowers, olive groves, cypress, and umbrella pine that clothed the fields and the hills. Travelling to Munich, there were dramatic vistas of the Apennine Mountains where some of the highest peaks were shrouded in clouds. Other than my spending spree in Florence and Venice, where I purchased a gold necklace and glass objects, shopping was not a priority. Traveling with Trudy was a joy, and my decades-long desire to attend the Passion Play was fulfilled.

Soon after I moved to North Madison, I had invited Courtney to come with me to see the French composer Georges Bizet's opera *The Pearl Fishers*, playing at a theater in Cleveland's Playhouse Square. Courtney enjoyed the performance. It gave me the idea to take her to New York City in 2002 as her high school graduation gift. I wanted to introduce her to some of the sights as Allan Dickie had done for me so many years ago. I specifically had in mind the Metropolitan Museum of Art.

As events unfolded, what was to be a twosome became a fivesome. The itinerary for the trip was different from what I would have planned had it been only Courtney and me, but I was happy to go along with the wishes of the group as it was a rare treat for the five of us to travel together. On October 10, Courtney, her mother Kellie, her grandmother Brenda, her Aunt Shellie, and I departed for a long weekend in the city. We stayed at the Hotel Edison, located on West Forty-Seventh Street in Manhattan.

Shellie was a fan of the popular Regis and Kelly morning show. It was top of her list to be part of the live audience, and to that end, she was able to secure three entry tickets. The five of us awakened early Friday morning and braved the heavy rain to take the subway north to the studio hoping, once there, we could obtain two additional tickets at check-in for Brenda and me—no luck. Unable to see the show, Brenda and I left the theater and managed to hail a cab in the heavy downpour. Wet through to our birthday suits, we returned to the hotel. By the time we were in our room and turned on the TV, we had missed seeing the faces of our family on the TV screen for their few-second appearance as the camera panned the audience.

On Sunday morning, we took part in two tours. On our first tour we attended a church service in Harlem. Our seats were in the balcony, and we rocked to the rhythm of the spirituals, all the while observing the swaying arms of the congregants below and hearing their shouts of "Amen!" and "Hallelujah!" that rose to the rafters. I was impressed by how fashionably the people were dressed, especially the festooned hats worn by the women. The second tour took us through Chinatown. This time the tour guide provided minimal information but maximum commercial tourist-trap exposure.

The Lion King, playing at the Minskoff Theater on Forty-Fifth Street, was perhaps the highlight of our NYC weekend. Nothing compares with sitting in a theater and being mesmerized by the music, costumes, and actors as they portray a story that transports one into a make-believe world.

We took a subway to Battery Park on the south end of Manhattan and boarded the ferry to Ellis Island. I felt only pride as I took my family to the place where the name of Ma and Pa Nelson was engraved on the American Immigrant Wall of Honor. Here is the only place in the United States where an individual can honor their family heritage at a national monument.

Before leaving the southern tip of Manhattan, we visited the site of the September 11, 2001, terrorists' attack. We stood behind the fence that encircled the gaping hole in the earth where the Twin Towers of the World Trade Center once stood. For myself, I felt an indescribable sadness, remembering.

While in the city we economized by purchasing our food in cafeterias or from street vendors. By and large, this was to our liking, except Brenda purchased what she termed "the world's worst bagel" from a food vendor on Ellis Island.

On Sunday, the fourth day after we arrived in the city, we checked out of the Hotel Edison. Shellie, emboldened with confidence, assured us she knew how we could take a bus to the airport, saving the taxi fare. She led the way as the five of us marched up Seventh Avenue, pulling our suitcases along, to the bus stop. We made all connections and arrived at the airport in adequate time to board our flight home. A memorable family adventure.

The Elderhostel astronomy classes that I attended at Kings Ranch in Arizona were interesting, and when I learned of a weeklong astronomy camp offered in May 2003 through Arizona State University, I signed on. The location was Mount Lemmon, just north of Tucson. My former Columbus neighbor, Myrtle Kelly, lived there near her son, Kenny, and his wife, June. I was delighted that my visit coincided with the family's celebration of Myrtle's 102nd birthday!

The morning following my arrival, I was at the rendezvous place to meet other camp participants. Eight of us climbed into the waiting van. For the most part, the drive to the 9,159-foot summit was over the paved Catalina Highway. In places the road was carved out of the side of the mountain. As we ascended, the views were both breathtaking and terrifying—there were sheer rock cliffs on the mountain side of the highway, with the view on the opposite side dropping off into space. At the top our van veered off onto a rough, unpaved road that led to the campsite.

The Mount Lemmon Observatory was formerly the site of a USAF radar base. The facilities were abandoned and given over to the United States Forest Service. The grounds, buildings, and telescopes that made up the Mount Lemmon Station Observatory were leased from the forest service by the University of Arizona.

I was assigned a room in one of the barracks buildings, requiring me to carry my luggage along a seemingly never-ending hallway. I noted most of the room's doors had a posted sign that read "Sleeping, do not disturb." What! In the middle of the day? How could I be so dense? Astronomers work at night and sleep during the day.

For the next six days I, too, became a night owl. I peered through the lens of a telescope at the moon, planets, stars, constellations, galaxies—on and on and on, my eyes blurry from looking and my mind reeling from information not understood. I kept the pace, saw much, but retained little. I vowed to spend more time studying my astronomy books when I returned home.

Camp ended, I said my goodbyes, and boarded the van for the drive down the mountain. Arrangements had been made for Candice to join me. I would rent a car, and we would drive back to Las Vegas. That night we were houseguests of the Kelly's, and only then did I realize I had overdone trekking over the rocky, uneven terrain on the mountain. My right artificial hip was very painful.

Kenny had mentioned the Biosphere that was located near Oracle, a few miles north of Tucson, and suggested it would be worth our time to stop on the way home. I had read about this place. The people who lived there were referred to as Biospherians and were sealed inside of a giant glass building that covered an area of 7,200,000 square feet.

Experiments of this self-sustaining community were conducted in two phases. The first group of eight lived inside for two years (1991–1993); the second group of seven were inside for seven months in 1994. The Biospherians grew and harvested their food and maintained their living space. When the 1994 group vacated the Biosphere, the facility was taken over in 1995 by Columbia University and maintained until 2003. Vacated once again, the facility, in a state of limbo, was almost replaced by a luxury housing development. Fortunately, in 2011 the University of Arizona acquired it to use for research and education.

In spite of my painful hip, I wanted to see it. My dear Candice was able to get me a wheelchair. Seated in the chair, with Candice pushing, we joined a tour group that took us through the interior—past rainforests, an ocean with a coral reef, wetlands, savannah grasslands, and a desert. At various levels there were stairs, no elevators. I managed to hobble up the steps, with Candice dragging the wheelchair behind. My granddaughter held out almost to the end before she told me, "Grandma, you're heavy. I'm getting tired." Somehow, she got me back to the car, returned the wheelchair, and headed the car north to Las Vegas.

I had spent seven exceedingly interesting days in Arizona and took part in two adventures: the astronomy planned workshop and the carpe-diem Biosphere experience.

‒‒‒‒‒‒ ·+++++· ‒‒‒‒‒‒

BICYCLING WAS MANNA THAT FED MY NEED for exercise. From the first week I lived in North Madison, I used my bicycle for errands. The terrain of Lake County was ideal for cycling, but one errand could have been my undoing. The Madison Post Office was located about six miles from my home. On a warm April day, I pocketed the letters to be mailed, made sure my helmet was secure and my hands protected with gloves, and took off on my bicycle. Within a half mile of the post office, on a side road, it happened.

In truth, I don't know what happened. My first memory was lying flat on my back in a vehicle looking up at a metal ceiling, a police officer huddled over me. I was in an ambulance, and I was being taken to the local hospital. X-rays of my shoulder and right hip and a CT scan of my head confirmed there were no broken bones or a concussion. I was badly bruised and released to go home even though the right side of my body revealed shades of purple, yellow, and other colors I referred to as "yuk."

Later I spoke with the officer who found me. He was patrolling in the area and apparently found me shortly after I had fallen. I was conscious, able to answer his questions, told him I swerved to miss a dog, and argued I didn't need to go to the hospital. I never recovered any memory of the accident. My doctor assured me not to be concerned, as with a head trauma of this type, memory blackout is common. Later, at a bike safety promotional event, I was awarded a "Saved by the Helmet" certificate from the Lake County General Health District.

When I lived in Columbus, bicycling served as a social conduit to meet others and form lasting friendships. My cycling accident did not squelch my desire to ride, and I took advantage of every opportunity to remain in touch with one special person, Jane Nickerson, whom I met through the Westerville Bicycle Club.

In 1998, Jane invited me to join her on our second Bon Ton Roulet tour in the Finger Lakes Region of New York State. The fully supported tour showcased the area's wine region. On July 26 we were in Auburn just north of Owasco Lake for the start of the ride. Over the next six days the tour route took us south and then west past the southern tips of Seneca and Keuka Lakes, to return north and east to Auburn.

The terrain challenged my limited biking strength. Granted there were stretches of flatland, but frequently I found myself laboriously pedaling up long hills (one so long and steep I thought my ears would pop before reaching the summit), to enjoy the effortless downhills.

As I rode, I marveled at the beauty of the lakes; the fields of corn, wheat, and oats; pastures where cows grazed and horses roamed; and the acres of vineyards. Wildflowers grew in abundance. Blue skies, with too few clouds, made the seventy-degree temperatures seem hotter. Each day we stopped at a different winery. I seldom indulged in wine tasting, as there was no way I would drink and ride.

One night our campground was at the southern tip of Seneca Lake. Watkins Glen gorge is located there, often referred to as the Eighth Wonder of the World. Several of us hiked in, and as I trudged along the narrow paths, climbed stairs, crossed connecting bridges, I marveled at the beauty of the rock formations, rushing streams, and picturesque waterfalls.

South of Keuka Lake in Bath, I took a bad spill. My approach angle to the railroad tracks was wrong, and as I started to cross, my front wheel slipped into the space between the rail and the pavement. Jane, riding with me, was horrified, thinking I must be seriously injured, but greatly relieved to find I was only badly bruised, not broken. My bicycle was not damaged; I got back on and continued to ride, but I hit my head so hard on the pavement it cracked my helmet. When the tour director learned of my accident, he loaned me a helmet until mine could be replaced. It is not safe to wear a damaged helmet. The 356 miles I rode on the tour challenged my endurance, but I persevered and survived yet another bicycle accident.

I willingly joined Jane the following year to take part in the 1999 Bon Ton Roulet. Along with tips about area wineries, we were provided information on famous people who had lived in the area. I took the opportunity to visit the homes of Frances Bellamy, a minister born in Mount Morris who wrote the US Pledge of Allegiance in 1892, and New York State Governor William Seward, who lived for a time in Auburn. Seward served as Secretary of State from 1861–1869 as a member of the Lincoln and Andrew Johnson cabinets.

Just as water seeks its own level, bicyclists seek others who ride with somewhat the same speed and stamina. Jane was a faster and stronger rider than I and teamed up with riders having comparable biking skills. Fortunately, I met Grant, a first-time rider with the BTR, and Bob, who came alone and was looking for riding partners. Grant signed on for the tour because he had heard the BTR had a reputation for serving gourmet food. On the second night out, a group of us were seated at a long cafeteria-style table in a self-imposed silence, chowing down food as only hungry cyclists can do. I heard Grant's voice cut through the silence. "I don't want you to think I'm complaining, but is this a gourmet meal?" Well, yes, by BTR standards, spaghetti and meatballs are gourmet food.

When I registered for the week's ride, there was information in our packet about a helmet-decorating contest. That could be a lot of fun, and I was interested. I had brought with me my purple T-shirt jazzed up with the message, "When I am an old woman I shall wear purple." Each day, as I rode along, I eyed roadside trash, selecting only colorful objects that would support the theme on my T-shirt—paper cup, artificial flowers, ribbons, but the *piece de resistance* was a red unused condom—I stress, **unused**!

The evening of the farewell dinner, I appeared with others vying for the prize. Each of us, in turn, stood before the assembled group wearing our decorated helmets and presented our skits. Those with musical talents sang songs, those with dramatic ability hammed it up reciting poetry or acting out a skit. I fell in the latter group. When my turn came, I sashayed in wearing my purple T-shirt and full-length floral latex leggings. The paraphernalia attached to my helmet bobbed, swayed, and rattled on my head as I dramatically recited the few lines I could remember from Jenny Joseph's poem "When I Am an Old Woman."

> *When I am an old woman I shall wear purple*
> *With a red hat which doesn't go, and doesn't suit me.*
> *And I shall spend my pension on brandy...*
> *and say we've no money for butter.*
> *...and learn to spit.*

At the conclusion of the competition, each of us stood before the group while the sound of the hoots, hollers, and applause was registered on the "scientifically reliable applause-o-meter." Wow! What a dramatic finish for my second Bon Ton Roulet. I won, and I was thrilled!

Jane moved from the area when her husband's work required him to relocate in Chicago. I visited her there, took my bicycle, and we spent several days riding the bike paths near her condo home. Jane and Steve moved back to Ohio a few years later and today live in Xenia. We continue to see one another at least once a year.

WANTING TO MEET OTHER CYCLISTS in the area, I became involved with four cycling groups. Lake Metroparks served as a rich resource for informational cycling brochures and also sponsored a monthly ride. Through Lake Metroparks, I learned about the Cleveland Touring Club. Several members of the Austinburg Square Dance Club rode bicycles together in the summer, and they invited me to join them. Through them I learned of the Ashtabula Cranks, sponsored by the Ashtabula YMCA. I was riding three nights a week on a regular basis, getting my exercise, meeting new people, and making new acquaintances. It just couldn't get any better than that.

Lake Metroparks provided recreational programs and activities for Lake County. I took part in their monthly bicycle rides. I recall one Sunday morning ride, the route took us through downtown Cleveland and into the Flats (low-lying area on the banks of the Cuyahoga River). There we stopped at a beer garden for lunch. As we entered the eatery, I overheard one in the group warn those within earshot that the place had a reputation for servers harassing the customers, making them the brunt of their jokes; forewarned was to be forearmed. I ordered a sandwich careful to avoid eye contact with the server. For some reason unknown to me, I became his target. My sandwich was served, and as I sat there trying to eat, he heckled, hassled, and hounded me. From out of nowhere he produced an oversized headdress made out of white butcher paper emblazoned in red marker with the words "WASHED UP PORN STAR" and plopped it firmly on my head. Embarrassing for me, hilarious to others.

It was through the Lake Metroparks Bike-O-Rama that I learned of the Cleveland Touring Cub. I joined the CTC, rode with them on Tuesday evenings, and took part in special-event rides. The one I remember best was the Emerald Necklace Tour through the network of parks that encircle Cleveland.

September 11, 2001, is a day I will never forget. That Tuesday morning, I was dressing to bicycle with my CTC buddies, who were to assemble at my house for the start of the ride, when the ringing of the telephone interrupted me. It was my sister. Her voice conveyed alarm as she said, "Henri, turn on your TV. New York City is under attack." Just at that same moment, the gals were at my door. I let them in and, too confused to give an explanation, rushed to the TV and turned it on. Six of us sat in shocked silence as we saw the first tower of the World Trade Center complex collapse. With little time to recover, we watched an airplane fly into the second tower. The buildings crumbled. Someone commented, "This is a hoax, a sci-fi movie." It was not a hoax; this act of terror was happening in real time. We did not ride our bicycles that day.

Through print or people contacts, I learned of many bicycle tours. When I read about the Dick Allen Lansing to MACkinaw (DALMAC) ride, I placed it at the top of my must-ride list. During the first years of our marriage, Sidney Nelson sailed for the Boland and Cornelius steamship line. Sid would speak of the self-unloading ore ships that plied the Straits of Mackinac to Escanaba, Michigan, for a load of taconite iron ore mined in the state Marquette Iron Range. In the late 1940s, a bridge did not span the strait to connect the lower with the upper peninsula. Sid would talk of the day when this would become a reality. The construction of the Mackinac Bridge was completed in 1957, and I was determined to ride over the five-mile span of this suspension bridge.

Dick Allen, a cyclist, was a member of the Michigan legislature and promoted legislation to build better roads throughout the state to accommodate bicycle riders. One of his colleagues challenged him that no one could ride a bicycle from Lansing to the Mackinac Bridge. Dick took up the gauntlet and, with family members and willing constituents, rode 215 miles over several days, proving it could be done.

In 1971 the DALMAC tour became a reality. It is a five-day camping tour starting at Michigan State University in East Lansing and ending in Mackinaw City or, for those willing riders, crossing the bridge onto the upper peninsula in St. Ignace. The annual 230-mile ride is scheduled over the Labor Day weekend and is limited to two thousand bicycle riders.

Ellen, an acquaintance I had made in the CTC, joined me for the 1999 tour. It was a surprise to me when Terry and Barb, Allen and Allison, who lived in Okemos a suburb of East Lansing, came to see us off. Barb had with her two T-shirts, each with a picture of a hockey player, and the printed words "This Grandma belongs to Allison" and "This Grandma belongs to Allen." Now how could a bicycling Gran Henri be made to feel more special than to have this loving send-off?

For convenience, Ellen and I wanted to provide our own sag-wagon service. To that end, we agreed to alternate days driving and cycling. This turned out to be fortuitous for me, but unlucky for Ellen. On the second day of the tour, a vehicle ran Ellen off the road. She sustained multiple bruises and an injured knee that made it too uncomfortable for her to continue riding, but not severe enough that she wanted to abort the tour.

As we headed north, Ellen enjoyed the scenery from the driver's seat in the Durango—rolling farmland, pine-covered hillsides, small lakes, and quaint small towns. My enjoyment of the scenery was minimized due to the extremes of weather—so hot I stopped by a creek to wade and cool off, so cold it snowed. The hills were rolling to steep, and strong headwinds challenged my stamina. I endured. It was a welcome sight each evening as I struggled into camp to see Ellen there ahead of me and our tents pitched on a prime campsite.

The fifth day of the tour, we were in Mackinaw City. The slight breeze and moderate temperature made it an ideal day for the bridge crossing—the bridge is closed to bicycle riders when winds are too strong. Each cyclist was required to have a ticket for the bridge crossing. At the appointed time (2:00 p.m.), I took my place in a long double-file line. Riders were admonished to stay with their riding partner and keep a close space with the bicycle ahead.

I'd like to report I looked about, gazed at the water below, at the circling birds above—but it was not to be. I kept my eyes glued to the bike wheel ahead of me. I was terrified I would crash. I made it without mishap, though, across to St. Ignace. Ellen was there with the Durango. I loaded my bicycle, and with Ellen driving, we headed south and home. I cycled 195 miles of the 230-mile route, which included my harrowing ride over the Mackinac Bridge.

I returned alone in 2000 to take part in my second DALMAC tour. Allan Dickie was from Michigan, and the route that year went through what I termed Dickie country. I rode by Higgins Lake and through the small town of Alma, past Alma College where Allan earned a bachelor's degree—two places frequently spoken of by him. That year, when the tour reached Mackinaw City, the winds were too strong and no bicycle riders were allowed on the bridge. Thankfully, I had fulfilled my bucket list dream the previous year.

It was either Ann, Mary, or Harriet with the CTC who learned about a Florida tour sponsored by Wandering Wheels. We were all interested, so the four of us signed on to the eleven-day tour scheduled for January 28 through February 7, 2001. The tour started in Cocoa Beach and followed Route 1 south for 350 miles, ending in Key West. Accommodation options for the thirty-six people who signed on were camping, motels, or sleeping on the "possum bus" (sleeper coach), which also served as our sag wagon. I opted to camp. Almost all meals were on our own, so no reason to complain if the food was not to one's liking.

For convenience I rented a bicycle supplied by the tour and started the ride with my friends but, along the way, made new acquaintances and rode with others during the duration of the ride. The moderate seventy-degree temperature made for pleasant cycling, but no one had warned me about the unrelenting southwest headwind. Every day was one of beauty. Blue skies dotted with fleecy clouds, landscapes of rustling pines, swaying palms, and fruit groves of oranges, flowers in abundance, and birds—cranes, seagulls, and egrets to name a few.

Camping held bizarre experiences. One night I was advised by a person in the know to be sure I didn't pitch my tent on a mound of red ants. Another night I listened to an animal (later learned to be a raccoon) unwrapping snack bars that I carelessly left outside of my tent. I spent one night in a church where I spread out my sleeping bag on the altar, then spent a sleepless night listening to a cacophonic chorus of snorers.

The route took us to the northern city limit of Miami. At that point my riding partner and I chose to ride the possum bus through the city. Once the bus was south of Miami, we reclaimed our bicycles and started pedaling. Our first overnight stay south of Miami was at a private home in Key Largo (the owner was a friend of the tour director). I pitched my tent on their deck. The day's ride had drained all my energy, and I was instantly lulled into a deep sleep by the gentle lapping waves against the dock.

Our hosts provided breakfast and invited us to swim, kayak, or enjoy an airboat ride through the everglades. I donned my bathing suit and jumped off the dock into the warm water. The homeowner came by with some lettuce leaves. He offered me a piece of lettuce, directed me to hold it in my mouth, remain still, and I would attract a manatee. I did as told and was delighted when the large mammal approached close enough to nibble on the lettuce. The owner, with camera ready, took my picture. I was elated!

Later, with several others in our group, I sat in the airboat and took a leisurely ride through the everglades into a stand of water-rooted mangrove trees. Here we stopped, and I accepted the dare to leave the boat and climb into a mangrove tree for another picture op. The night spent sleeping on the dock and the experiences that followed the next morning were high-lights of the trip that I've never forgotten.

Back on Route 1, my biking partner and I headed south. For the next 135 miles, a ribbon of highway connecting small coral islands by way of forty-two bridges (one seven miles long) would form the causeway to Key West. The temperature remained in the seventies, the winds swirled around us, and the previously experienced beauty of the tour was enhanced by the panoramic view of a shimmering sea and gulls gliding overhead in a cloud-less sky. Our last campsite was on a small island fifty miles north of Key West. That night I had an unobstructed view of the sunset. I watched the sun drop into the water and observed fingers of pink, orange, and purple shoot up into the darkening sky.

Lodging for the final night of our tour was in a Key West hotel. That evening I joined several others at Jimmy Buffett's MARGARITAVILLE C A F E. I had no previous awareness of this American icon—songwriter and performer of country, folk, and rock. Beer never tasted so good as I bounced and jived to the keyboard antics of Jimmy Buffett, the featured entertainer of the evening, sitting at his piano in his cafe named after his hit song "Margaritaville."

I used the free hours of the following day to walk through Old Town Key West and stopped at the home and museum of Ernest Hemingway where I learned it also served as the residence for his forty cats—to me, unimaginable. I toured the Winter White House of President Harry S. Truman. I am a registered Republican, but ever since reading David McCullough's book *Truman*, I hold only feelings of veneration for our thirty-third president, who had the office thrust upon him, who placed a sign prominently on his desk "The Buck Stops Here," and who had the steeled determination to give the order to drop the atom bombs that ended the war with Japan. As I exited the Winter White House through the gift shop, I noted a life-size cardboard replica of the president. I proudly stood beside it and had my picture taken.

Before boarding the possum bus that would take me to the Miami Airport for my flight home, I walked to the southernmost tip of the island. Here I posed beside a monument shaped like a large buoy with the words in red, black, and yellow painted on its side:

90 Miles to CUBA
SOUTHERNMOST
POINT
CONTINENTAL
U. S. A.
Key West, FL

I had finished another "like-wow" bicycle adventure and endured sun, headwinds, primitive camping, and cycled 245 of the 300-mile route.

In June 2002 Bruce and Linda celebrated twenty-five years of marriage. Their daughter Candice planned a surprise celebration to include, as guests, the judge who performed the ceremony and the eight members of the bridal party. Candice wanted me to be there, so never one to miss a family celebration, I made plans to attend. I was able to coordinate my Las Vegas visit with a six-day California Wine Country tour scheduled for June 16 through 21. The timing was perfect, as it enabled me to be in Las Vegas the following weekend for the party.

Bicycle Adventures, based in Redmond, Washington, advertised the wine country ride as a luxury tour—and luxury it was. We stayed in upscale bed-and-breakfast homes, all with swimming pools, dined in the finest restaurants, and had matchless sag-wagon service with gourmet lunches prepared by our guide. Five others, besides myself, were on the tour: an investment broker and his wife, a former airline stewardess; their daughter and her husband, both with careers in finance; and an emergency room doctor who was my riding partner throughout the tour. I found dinner table conversations to be provocatively interesting, covering topics related to world problems, finance, and even touching on politics.

The tour was described as over rolling hills, through idyllic groves of redwood trees, past cattle ranches, and across acres of vineyards. It was all true, but to the extreme. The rolling hills became too long and too steep for me, and I resorted to what is referred to as cross-training—I got off my bicycle and walked. Most of the ride was on paved roads, but when perched at the top of a steep hill, I found coasting down to be terrifying. I had to keep momentarily releasing my firm hold on the brake levers to prevent the brake pads from overheating and reducing the braking efficiency.

The weather was not idyllic for cycling. Temperatures were in the high eighties, creeping into the low nineties. At times there were strong headwinds. Each day we stopped at a different winery, but I seldom took part in the offered wine tastings. Common sense dictated it was not safe to drink and ride. At day's end, using my last reserve of energy, I managed to make it to our lodging for the night. Once there, after a refreshing swim in the pool, showered and dressed, I was ready to join the group for our late dinner. Even then my fatigue, the lateness of the hour, the wines accompanying a several-course dinner, made it a test of endurance to stay awake.

I enjoyed my week bicycling in California wine country and the camaraderie that developed within our small group. I am writing this in the fall of 2017. Tragically, the area through which I bicycled was destroyed by fires this past summer.

When I learned the New York Parks and Conservation Association sponsored an Erie Canal ride, I immediately placed it on my bicycle must-ride list. Personally, I had a vested interest in the Erie Canal. My mother told stories of her father Squair M. Shuart who, as a lad of ten to twelve years of age, drove a team of mules pulling the boats along the canal. Knowing this connection of my grandfather with the canal, I wanted not only to see it but to experience it.

The construction of the canal began in 1817 and at the time was ridiculed as "Clinton's Ditch," referring to the governor of the state of New York, DeWitt Clinton. The eastern terminus of the canal was at Albany on the Hudson River, followed the path used by the westward-moving Americans along the Mohawk River, and crossed the Appalachian Mountains with the western terminus in Buffalo on Lake Erie. The "ditch" was 363 miles long, forty feet wide, and four feet deep. A series of locks accommodated the 565-foot elevation rise. The vision of Governor Clinton and his "ditch," completed in 1825, advanced commerce and settlement and brought prosperity to the West.

The weeklong camping tour in 2002 provided sag-wagon service for equipment and suitcases. The ride began in Buffalo. Based on previous experience, I knew I would be left to my own devices to return to the point of origin. I wanted to ride the entire route, or as much as stamina allowed, of the 380-mile tour. With this in mind, I contacted three of my biking friends—two with CTC, and one whom I had met on previous tours. They agreed that if I provided the vehicle, the three of them would alternate days to ride and drive.

Friday, July 5, the four of us met in Buffalo and spent the first night in a motel room. We arrived a day early to take advantage of the pretour, fifty-two-mile Niagara Falls ride. We cleared customs at the Peace Bridge in Buffalo and cycled the bike path to a place where we had a full view of the three falls—Horseshoe Falls, the most powerful falls in North American, straddling the US-Canadian border; the American Falls; and Bridal Veil Falls, both within the United States. By any measure, Horseshoe Falls was the most dramatic, but the less turbulent American Falls were beautiful to behold as I watched the greenish-colored water (due to dissolved minerals) race and swirl below me. Inspired with the drama and by the beauty of what we had seen, the four of us retraced our route, quickly passed through customs, returned to our motel to relax, eat dinner, and a good night's sleep in preparation to begin our weeklong canal tour the following morning.

Sunday, July 8, the four of us were at the designated start place in Buffalo. My three cohorts decided among themselves who would drive and who would bike. For the duration of the tour, the temperature remained in the comfortable seventies. At times a gentle rain fell, but other than an occasional strong north wind, I biked comfortably along under blue skies, dotted with billowy clouds.

Road surfaces were another matter. One half of the route was on the canal towpath; the other half took us on secondary roads through small towns along the canal. Parts of the towpath were paved but required close attention to protruding tree roots and damage due to extreme weather conditions. The part not paved was a rough and muddy primitive trail— not conducive to my bicycle's narrow road tires. For any nature lover, knowledgeable about the flora and fauna of the area, the towpath was a treasure trove of flowers, trees, birds, and small animals. I was not of this ilk and kept my eyes glued to the path to avoid any hazards that might cause me to fall. In truth I was bored. I much preferred riding on the secondary roads. There was more to captivate my interest.

College campuses or community centers were selected for campsites. The first night, we set up camp on the grounds of a community college. Our personal sag-wagon driver had arrived well in advance of the tour herd. She reserved a camping area under a shade tree. I thought it idyllic, until I settled down to sleep. The tree was within thirty feet of a dorm. Dorm windows were open, and the music, laughter, and chatter brazenly cut through the night air. Earplugs didn't help. Sleep eluded me until the wee hours of the morning. Fortunately, there was no repeat of this problem at any of the other campgrounds during the tour.

The Erie Canal **was** the attraction, but suggestions were made as to places of interest within proximity of the canal. I visited the Women's Rights National Historical Park in Seneca Falls and learned that traffic on the canal was a means of spreading ideas for social and religious reform. A woman's right to vote was one progressive idea for social change that was first promoted in towns along the canal. The state of New York played a key role in the passing of the Nineteenth Amendment in 1920, ensuring universal suffrage to all women.

When we were in the area of Pittsford, I left the canal route and rode to the Terry Bicycle Corporate Headquarters. Georgianna Terry, a woman engineer and avid cyclist, designed and hand-built bicycles for women. I owned a Terry bicycle, and I was delighted to meet the person responsible for taking into account a woman's body proportions in the design of a bicycle frame.

The tour took us through the Old Erie Canal State Historic Park located between DeWitt and Rome. As I rode along the thirty-six-mile canal path that paralleled the original canal, I imagined my grandfather singing "The Erie Canal Song:"

> *I've got a mule, her name is Sal,*
> *Fifteen years on the Erie Canal*
> *She's a good ol' worker and a good ol' pal,*
> *Fifteen years on the Erie Canal...*

True, it is a canal folksong, but the earliest reference is 1905, and my grandfather was well past the age of the lad who walked along leading a mule team pulling a canal barge. Nevertheless, I enjoyed letting my imagination have free reign.

The ride ended in Albany. I rode 332 miles of the 360-mile route. I was glad I did it from a personal and historical perspective. I wouldn't do it again, as the canal path did not make for easy or (to me) interesting riding. It was the same o', same o' every day: sun/rain, hot/cold, flora/fauna, and those ever-present pesky bugs. But the experience, along with my imagination, served me well, and for a fleeting moment in time, I felt close to my maternal grandfather whom I never met.

Pursuant to previous bicycling adventures, Marion, my NYC biking buddy, invited me to join her in Amherst, Massachusetts, for the League of American Bicyclist's 2002 BikeFest ride. Ever ready to explore new places, I accepted. Not wanting to drive the distance of 550 miles alone, I invited Harriet, a member of the CTC, to join me. Harriet agreed and in so doing asked if she, in turn, could invite her biking friend Jane. In good faith, I could not rescind the invitation, so I agreed. That was a mistake.

We arrived at the University of Massachusetts on August 2, and it was hot! We registered for the ride, found our dormitory, crammed our stuff into the small elevator, and located our fourth-floor, sparsely furnished, suffocating rooms. I was exhausted, but still needed to take the Durango to my assigned parking lot blocks away. Finally, back at the room, I found Marion there, stretched out on the bed with a nearby fan blowing hot air across her body. I barely managed to be civil.

Ride routes over the next two days followed along the Connecticut River Valley, past lush farmland, and over gentle hills into the states of Vermont and New Hampshire. I admit I did not enjoy this bicycling adventure. Our dorm room was insufferably hot and the cafeteria food tasteless. I rode in torrential rains and blazing sun. There was a lack of cycling camaraderie among the four of us—Harriet and Jane paired off, leaving Marion, a stranger to them, and me to fend for ourselves.

The area is steeped in history, and the redeeming feature for me was my visit to the home of Emily Dickinson, a recluse who lived out her life in Amherst. Her fame came posthumously when her sister discovered her poetry and had it published. I bought a copy of her book, *Collected Poems of Emily Dickinson*. Here is my favorite poem in the book:

I'm nobody! Who are you?
Are you nobody, too?
Then there's a pair of us—don't tell!
They'd banish us, you know.
How dreary to be somebody!
How public, like a frog
To tell your name the livelong day
To an admiring bog!

Once home, I mentally looked back on the trip. I'd supplied the transportation, many times felt like a social fifth wheel, and drove 1,100 miles to bike two and a half days. Was I nuts?

While in Amherst, Marion shared an Elderhostel publication featuring a Canadian Bike/Theater. She was looking for a roommate and asked if I would be interested. I quickly skimmed through the information—a ten-day tour with biking during the day and six evening theater performances at stops in Toronto, Stratford, and Niagara-on-the-Lake. The tour would be fully supported with sag-wagon service. What was there not to like? Never able to say no to a promising adventure, I signed on.

This time I drove, took my own bicycle, and arranged to meet Marion in Toronto for the start of the tour. I arrived a day early, found the Metropolitan Hotel, and settled in for the night. The next morning, I awakened late, dressed, left the hotel, and walked to Canada's National Tower. Opened in 1976, the CN Tower is 1,815 feet high—an icon of the Toronto skyline. At the top of the building is a restaurant that rotates 360 degrees, providing diners a view of the city. The restaurant was almost empty when I arrived. The maître d' seated me by the window, and as the restaurant slowly rotated, I enjoyed my solitary lunch while observing the panoramic view of the city unfold below me.

Returning to the hotel, I met the tour leaders and tour participants. That evening we assembled at the Alexander Theater to see the play *Mamma Mia*. Our seats were the last row in the top balcony—cramped and hard. The music was loud. I was so uncomfortable I left at intermission and walked back to the hotel. The group was to leave for Niagara-on-the-Lake the following day. I was so discouraged from the first night's theater experience that I considered leaving the tour and returning home, but Marion and I shared a room. I didn't want to appear a quitter.

I had a mild case of poison ivy, and when Marion realized this, I was a pariah in our motel room. Adding to my misery was the fact that Marion was a TV surfer, never asked if I had a program preference, and monopolized the bathroom. None of this came to light when we shared the dorm room in Amherst. There was no TV, and the shared bathroom was down the hall.

The visit to Niagara-on-the-Lake was interesting. During the afternoon, I was on my own and signed up for the historic walking tour. The leader kept facts to a minimum and human-interest stories to the maximum. Niagara-on-the-Lake was a terminus point for slaves escaping from Southern states in the United States, and upon arrival in Canada, they were free.

There were five days remaining on the tour and several more theater performances. Bicycling was minimal, many times in city traffic, and when in rural areas, cycling was on gravel roads. Most days there was a strong headwind. The distance between cities was too great for biking, so we were transported in the sag-wagon van. Dinners were late, lengthy, and I OD'd on food. I did not enjoy the late theater performances that followed the late dinners. I was tired from the day's activities and drowsy from eating too much.

When I learned one of the tour leaders would be driving to Toronto, I used my poison ivy as an excuse, said goodbye to Marion, and returned to Toronto. We arrived back at the Metropolitan Hotel at ten thirty that night. I loaded my bicycle and suitcase into the Durango and drove out of the hotel garage at eleven o'clock, planning to get a motel room. Unfortunately, I was not able to find one. I drove all night and arrived in North Madison at five fifteen the following morning.

Once home, it was apparent to me I had given little thought before agreeing to join this latest cycling adventure. The idea of a combined bicycle/theater tour appealed to me. I failed to take into consideration the energy I would need to keep up with planned activities. I knew Marion only as a casual biking buddy whom I had met on previous tours. Sharing a hotel room with her was another matter. I'd made another bad decision. Would I ever learn?

***

I CONNECTED WITH TWO RIDING GROUPS in Ashtabula County. The Ashtabula Cranks, sponsored by the YMCA, held monthly night rides planned by a ride director. The other, an informal gathering of twelve to fifteen friends, met on Thursday evenings for a leisurely fifteen-mile ride.

Sandra and Arnold Brown were the dynamic couple that kept this group together. The emphasis was social. Riders rotated responsibility for planning the route and selecting the restaurant. I met, and made, several friends through these two groups. Two of those friends would dramatically impact my life—Al Olson and Rosemary Brenkus.

Al Olson was a retired baker. He packed his bicycle pannier bags and spent his retirement years cycling in countries throughout the world. Al and I became friends, and we enjoyed riding the byways of Ashtabula and Lake Counties. Al was interested in only a platonic relationship. In his words, "Romance only complicates one's life." I knew he had a lady friend for a theater companion. I knew he had a lady friend with whom he skied. I learned he had another lady friend with whom he traveled when not bicycling. I joined this harem of friends and became his lady biking friend.

An out-of-town adventure, shared with Al in October 1999, was the annual Hilly Hundred Weekend Bicycling tour, sponsored by the Central Indiana Bicycling Association. The tour could accommodate up to five thousand cyclists and most opted to camp, as did we. Registration was in the Bloomington High School where vendors displayed their wares, and high school classrooms were used for special-interest seminars. The school auditorium served as the venue for the awards night program. Riders were supplied route maps with clearly marked rest stops where the weary could relax and enjoy snacks, while being entertained by local music groups. Obviously, this was a big event, and there was an air of excitement that reverberated throughout the ride venues.

I had no idea what the words "Hilly Hundred" meant, but I soon found out. On Saturday I rode fifty very hilly miles that included one long hill with 8 to 10 percent grade the final hundred feet. I managed it without getting off of my bicycle because a sympathetic bystander observed me struggling, reached over, and provided the needed push that got me over the top! On Saturday I rode thirty miles and, to my relief, on a less hilly route.

I wanted the "Mature Woman Award" that would be presented at the Sunday night award ceremony. Sunday night came, and seated in the auditorium, I waited with bated breath, expecting to hear my name announced as the winner. Disappointment. A woman aged seventy-three won the award. I was a babe of seventy. It may sound like sour grapes, but I observed her on the route, and she walked some of the steepest hills. I rode them all. Life isn't always fair.

Still, it was a glorious weekend. The weather was perfect, the trees majestic in their colorful fall clothes. I cannot adequately describe my feelings during that weekend ride; it had to be experienced.

I listened to Al tell stories of his self-contained bicycle adventures, and I wanted to have this experience. My success in riding the Hilly Hundred emboldened me to ask Al if he would consider an overseas bicycle tour with me. Without hesitation he agreed, and we set a tentative date for late summer or early fall in 2000. I suggested Scotland and England, to which Al added Ireland as he had connections in Dublin.

The first thing Al told me was that my Terry road bike frame was not sturdy enough to accommodate the weight in my pannier bags. Taking his advice, I purchased a Giant bicycle with heavier frame and wider tires. Concerned that I would not have the needed strength and stamina to ride this heavier, fully loaded bicycle, I asked Al if we could do a several-day dry run.

In May 2000 we set out on a 150-mile, three-day, self-contained bike ride. I found Al to be a pleasant travel companion who paced himself to fit my riding style. As a test of my stamina and strength, the route selected had hills, different road surfaces, and at times Mother Nature added to the challenge with the bicyclist's nemesis—a headwind. I passed the test, not with flying colors, but enough confidence that I felt I was ready!

In preparation for our three-week cycling holiday in Ireland, Scotland, England, and the Isle of Man, Al boxed my bicycle for shipping while I packed my travel needs into four pannier bags. The smaller two would hang from the frame of the front wheel; the larger two would hang from the carrier behind the bicycle seat. The bags weighed in at a total of thirty-eight pounds. Al arranged for our flights from the Pittsburgh International Airport. By registering for a one-night stay at the Airport Plaza Motel, I was able to park my Durango there for the duration of our trip.

On September 11, 2000, I pulled the Durango up at the airport curbside check-in for US Air. The porter unloaded our two bicycle boxes and luggage, checking it through to Dublin. In Boston we transferred to Aer Lingus for the five-and-a-half-hour overseas flight. Flying east through five time zones, the plane touched down in Dublin on Tuesday morning at six o'clock.

Before leaving the Dublin airport, I exchanged dollars for punt—the name given to the Irish pound. The airport porter hailed a van taxi, large enough to transport bicycle boxes and luggage to Eagan's House, where Al had made advance reservations. The ride cost twenty punts—almost $30.00 as the exchange rate at the time was $1.43 = one punt.

Upon arrival, the host couple at Eagan's House gave us a warm welcome and provided a hearty breakfast which we quickly devoured. As soon as we got settled in our rooms, we unpacked and slept several hours to make up for sleep lost during our trans-Atlantic flight. That afternoon, Al unpacked our bicycles, suggesting we venture out for a quick ride about the area.

This ride was a first for me. I had never bicycled in a country where the rule of the road was left-hand traffic—the opposite of the United States which is right-hand traffic. At pedestrian crossings, large white letters alerted the walker to first "LOOK RIGHT," then "LOOK LEFT"—again the opposite of what we are taught from childhood in the United States. The wide left-side curb lane was painted with highly visible white letters reading "BUS AND BIKE LANES." In spite of the signage, in spite of the fact I rode with traffic, I felt I was riding in the "wrong" direction. On the straightaway I was okay, but it was the roundabout that utterly confused me. Fortunately, I was able to follow Al, and after a harrowing hour of cycling, I returned unscathed to the B&B.

The morning of September 12, following our arrival in Dublin, we cycled north toward Belfast, stopping overnight in the towns of Drogheda, Newry, and Downpatrick. In Downpatrick I came to the realization that I needed to lighten the weight in my pannier bags. Before leaving town, we rode to the post office, and I mailed five pounds of my excess stuff home—at the cost of twenty-three punts, or about $35.

The two-lane paved roads were narrow. When traffic was heavy, it became downright dangerous, as there was little room to maneuver. On occasion we turned off onto country lanes, only to find them rough, strewn with rocks and numerous potholes. We rode between hedgerows too thick for animals to penetrate. The serendipity of lane detours was coming upon blackberry and blueberry bushes laden with ripe fruit. Weary from riding, we would stop and eat our fill.

On the fourth day we reached Belfast. There we were to take a ferry to Scotland. Having no clue how to find the ferryboat dock, Al stopped an officer patrolling in a squad car and asked. The officer knew the ferry schedule, and he also knew we had a distance to ride. He directed us to follow him. With police escort, we wove our way through a maze of streets to the dock, just in time to make the ferry to Stranraer, Scotland. The Stena Line Ferry was a drinking, eating, gambling, shopping, floating village. The one-hour crossing was smooth, and Al and I spent the time at the stern of the deck, the only place passengers were allowed due to the speed of the vessel.

As I pedaled along on my loaded bicycle, I felt I became one with the road—the flatlands inviting, the steep and long hills challenging, and the scenery enveloping. I passed fields of vegetables, hay, and grain, pastures with grazing cows, all sectioned by either fieldstone walls or hedgerows. I noted the strategically placed stiles that enabled one to easily negotiate a wall that sectioned the fields. In Ireland I observed grazing sheep marked with colors red, green, and blue—markings that identified the owner.

Throughout our three-week tour, temperatures remained in the sixties to mid-seventies, very pleasant cycling weather—as long as it wasn't raining. Most days were sunny, but when it rained, it poured. When that happened, I would put on my Gore-Tex jacket and pants and place rain covers over my pannier bags. Above all, I was extremely careful riding on the wet pavement.

The route laid out by Al took us into Northern Ireland where we crossed the Irish Sea to Scotland, then south to England, again crossing the water to the Isle of Man, and back to Dublin. Our itinerary was flexible. When we entered a town, our first stop was the Tourist Information Centre where we secured B&B lodging for the night. In the initial planning of our trip, I was adamant that I wanted my own room. Al and I had a platonic relationship, and I was not about to subsidize his pocketbook. It did add to the cost for the trip. Almost all B&B rooms were double occupancy, and we each had to pay the double occupancy rate.

Throughout our tour, we stayed in fourteen different B&Bs. Room prices were £18 to £30 per night. Accommodations ranged from a simple room with bath down the hall, to luxury en-suite rooms. Everywhere we stayed, cleanliness was next to godliness. Several places served refreshments when we arrived. All provided a bountiful breakfast. Our hosts ran the gamut from homeowners renting out spare rooms to professional businesses.

I was taken by the cityscapes, the people, and the houses. City streets were free of debris, and street flower shops were common in city centers. Overall, the people looked healthy. There was little obesity. In the outlying areas, I was fascinated with the houses. Stone and brick were in common use, many houses painted white with the window and door trim painted in accent colors. Roofs were thatch or tile. Lace curtains hung at sparkling windows, and attached to the windowsills were flower boxes filled with a variety of colorful flowers—frequently roses and dahlias. Inside some of the iron-fenced yards, garments gently flapped in the breeze from clotheslines, providing a home-loving appeal to a domestic scene.

Traveling as Al and I did, we had many opportunities to converse with the people. The Irish, Scots, and English had interesting idioms in their speech. Parking lots are "car parks," and for anyone unfortunate enough to park illegally, their car is "clamped." Returning to your car, you "rejoin." Carryout is "takeaway." Ask directions, and they "show you." Talking is "jaw-whacking," and many things are referred to as "lovely." A sign next to a sheer cliff in Scotland read "Danger Area Subject to Landslip."

All of our B&B hosts were congenial. Some, more loquacious than others, shared information about themselves and were interested in our adventures. Along the way we stopped to talk with a number of people. We met Harry, who lived in Belfast during the 1960s and '70s. He told us how the family suppressed their identities in the midst of the warring factions between the Catholics and the Protestants.

When we were in Dumfries, Scotland, I needed to have the brake adjusted on my bicycle. We located a bicycle shop, entered, and found it so jammed with all types of biking paraphernalia that Al and I had difficulty finding adequate floor space to comfortably stand. The owner appeared fastidiously dressed—creased pants, jacket, white shirt and tie, wearing shiny black shoes. A shop coat protected his immaculate clothes. He quickly diagnosed the problem with my wheel brake. and while we stood by waiting, he repaired it. He had little to say, in dramatic contrast to the clutter of his shop.

In Gatehouse of Fleet, Scotland, we observed a woman in a museum shop making a kilt. She explained to us that the original wool kilts, used by the Scots, were a big wrap. The material measured five feet wide by twenty-nine feet long, defied the pesky midges, and when wet, the wool thread swelled, making the wrap almost waterproof. Originally kilts were worn draped over one shoulder and wrapped around the body. Later the utilitarian use for the kilt morphed into a stylish garment, known as a phi-libeg—or little wrap—made with pleats sewn into the back, covering only the lower portion of the man's body. Never did find out what a man wore under his kilt.

At one stop along our travels we apparently appeared flummoxed because a man strode up and offered his help. Al told him where we wanted to go. His verbal directions were not clear, and we voiced confusion, so he drew us a map. He was a bicyclist, and his parting comment was, "No matter what direction you ride, the wind will always be in your face." Difficult to believe, but to the cyclist, all too true.

On Grafton Street, the trendy center of Dublin, Al and I secured our bicycles and entered a coffee shop where we were told we could purchase computer access. It was a hangout for the college crowd. We bought thirty minutes of computer time, retrieved and sent e-mail messages, and left to "rejoin" our bicycles. As we approached our bikes, we were surprised to note several young men and woman standing about who seemed to be engaged in an inquisitive conversation. As we approached, one of the men pointed to my bicycle and asked, "Which one of you rides this one?" To which I responded, "Me." Another in the group gleefully shouted, "I win! I knew only a woman would ride a bicycle with drop handlebars." Really? I never got an explanation as to why drop handlebars were associated with the supposedly weaker sex.

Al and I ate to live, not lived to eat. All B&B breakfasts were basically the same—sausage and/or bacon, scrambled eggs, sweet breads, and always with fried tomatoes. Several of our host B&Bs provided afternoon tea or coffee with sweet breads, but never any evening meal. On one occasion the host family packed us a hearty lunch as they sent us off on our day's travels.

It was a rare occasion when we treated ourselves to dinner in a restaurant. We were in Stranraer, Scotland, and told we must visit the nearby seaside town of Portpatrick and dine in Campbell's Restaurant. We cycled into town, found the restaurant, and the moment we walked through the door, the ambiance beckoned us to enjoy a leisurely meal. That we did. I ordered salmon cakes with sesame seed, with a first course of tomato soup, and a dessert course of ambrosia. While we were enjoying dinner, the couple at an adjoining table introduced themselves. They knew we were bicyclists by our attire. He was a Scot, a bike racer, and had visited the United States in Los Angeles, Las Vegas, Miami, and New York. His dining partner was English. An interesting young couple. The detour was well worth the effort, for the conversation was stimulating and the cuisine was scrumptious.

Another tasty meal was enjoyed in the Methodist Church in Brampton, Scotland. Al and I attended a Sunday morning service. In spite of the fact that wearing our biking attire caused some raised eyebrows among members of the congregation, we were invited to the dining hall for their monthly dinner. We devoured a delicious home-cooked meal of roast pork, mashed potatoes, carrots, and peas with a fruit compote for dessert that would have equaled the cuisine of a restaurant but lacked the ambiance.

For the most part, at the end of a day's ride, we would stop at a local grocery and buy whatever food tempted our palates for our evening repast. We did this not to save money but as a way to relax in our rooms after a bone-weary day of riding.

Al and I arrived at a division of labor when it came to trip planning. Al laid out the general direction of our travels, keeping track of mileage and time so that we would be back in Dublin for our scheduled flight home. My task was to identify interesting places along the way. Our first adventure was a guided tour sitting on the upper deck of a double-decker bus in Dublin. The bus stopped by a statue of Molly Malone with her barrow, and our guide related the amazing story of a little girl who endeared herself to the people of the town. In the early nineteenth century, Molly lived with her fishmonger parents in the seedy waterfront neighborhood. From the time she was old enough to walk, they took Molly with them as they plied their wares throughout Dublin. To those impoverished people who saw her, she was a ray of sunshine that brought hope and gladness into their dingy lives. Her small, plaintive voice cried out, "Cockles and mussels alive, alive, oh." Molly was taken with a fever at age seventeen and died. Her tombstone epitaph epitomizes the love the town held for her:

> *Here Beneath This Cold Hard Stone*
> *Lies Lovely Lifeless Molly Malone.*
> *Cruelly Snatched From This Vale of Tears at*
> *The Tender Age of Seventeen Years.*
> *To See Her Was to Love Her.*

We stopped in Arbigland, Scotland, to visit the birthplace of John Paul Jones. Jones came to America at the beginning of the Revolutionary War and earned recognition as the Father of the American Navy. He is credited with uttering the famous words, "We have not yet begun to fight." His birthplace was a small, rectangular (possibly twenty-four-foot-by-eight-foot) stone cottage with a tile roof, an entrance door, and a single small window on each of the building's four sides. One entered the house into a room that served as the kitchen. The heat and cooking source was a large fireplace, with a brass bust of Jones on the mantel. A wooden table, several wooden chairs, utilitarian crockery, and brass cooking utensils completed the room's furnishings. An interior door gave access to the second room where an alcove bed filled one wall. A wooden rocking chair and cradle were the only furnishings. Difficult to imagine families existing in such spartan quarters, but realistically much better than others had at the time.

We planned to spend only one night in Dumfries and stopped by the information center to secure our B&B lodging. There I picked up a brochure highlighting places of interest in the city and was astonished to learn that Robert Burns lived there most of his adult life. All I knew about Burns was the song "Auld Lang Syne" that I sang each New Year's Eve at the stroke of midnight. I suggested to Al that we stay an extra day and visit the Robert Burns Information Center. He assured me we had the time.

At the center we learned of a day long self-directed walking tour that highlighted places of interest in the life of Robert Burns. Consulting the map we were given, the first stop of the tour was in the central park of the city. Here we paused by a reddish-brown sandstone pedestal at least eight feet high. Placed on top of the pedestal was a full-size, white marble statue of Burns seated with his dog at his feet.

There were numerous stops on the tour, and a few stand out in my memory: the tenement house where Burns first lived when he arrived in the city; the two-story family house with the red sandstone facade; and the Theatre Royal where Burns was a frequent patron. Weary from walking, we entered his favorite pub, Hole in the Wa. Al and I were enjoying scones and coffee when the owner came by and pointed out the "hole" in the wall where the pints were passed through to imbibing guests—a pragmatic reason that gave the pub its name.

The most impressive stop on our walk took place at the Globe Inn, a two-story stone building frequented by Burns and referred to as his HOWFF (meeting place with friends). The manager of the inn, an attractive brunette of medium height, guided us through the building. For our final stop, she took us into a room filled with memorabilia from Burns' life. Here, with a twinkle in her eye and a lilt to her voice, she directed me to sit in Burns' favorite chair and recite lines from one of his poems. I clearly recall her saying I would have to treat all patrons in the barroom to a pint should I fail to recite. Taken unawares, my mind froze. I sat there speechless. I felt like a child caught unprepared by my teacher. The blood rushed to my face, turning my cheeks scarlet from embarrassment. I was not a

Burns scholar, but I did manage to stutter out a few lines from his most famous poem (later turned to song) "Auld Lang Syne." My feeble effort was accepted; I received absolution. To this day, I wonder if anyone has ever been held to task.

Our final stop on the tour was the kirkyard at St. Michael's Parish Church (oldest church in Dumfries built of local red limestone). Here in a white marble mausoleum with a doom roof, Grecian pillars stand as sentinels on each side of the black-iron grill door. Robert Burns, his wife Jane, and five members of his family are entombed there. Born on January 25, 1759, died July 21, 1796, on the day a son was born. The Ploughman Poet was thirty-seven-and-a-half years old.

Due to my embarrassment in being unfamiliar with Burns' poetry, I purchased a copy of his poems in the gift shop of the HOWFF. Originally written in the Scots language, the poems have been translated into a light Scots dialect, yet I find even the translation difficult to read.

As a footnote, General Ulysses S. Grant was familiar with Burns' poetry. Ron Chernow, author of *Grant,* writes that after the battle of Fort Donelson in 1862 as "Grant watched a parade of bandaged warriors trudging by, one aide heard him softly recite verse from Robert Burns: 'Man's inhumanity to man / makes countless thousands mourn'."

That same day Al and I visited a significant building located in the historic area of Dumfries. We climbed a steep hill to a windmill tower used two centuries ago to grind the town's grain. Now the building housed the camera obscura. The mechanism for the camera was explained to us—a wooden turret, revolving on an iron ratchet, was secured at the apex of the building twelve feet above our heads. The turret held a mirror, tilted by means of a pulley rope, that reflected images onto a white plaster-topped table around which we stood. In a totally darkened room, this simple-yet-complex mechanism gave a panoramic view of Dumfries and the surrounding countryside. In the high-tech days of the twenty-first century, this mechanism seemed magical to me.

The morning of September 23, we left Dumfries. As we headed south toward Carlisle, we were intrigued by road signs that directed the traveler to the Devil's Porridge H.M. Factory in Eastriggs. There during World War I, 17,000 women and men lived near, and worked in, a factory that straddled the Scottish/English border to make a nitroglycerin paste that was kneaded into gun-cotton to form a cordite rope. The ammunition factory was credited with making a major contribution to the Allied victory. I found this to be quite interesting, as I knew my dad served in the army during World War I and spent time with a medical corps in France.

In Gretna Green, we stopped to watch a wedding. A newly married couple was being serenaded by a piper as they left the church. We learned this town had a reputation for being a wedding destination. In 1753, England passed an act that both parties to a marriage must be twenty-one, or parental consent was required. The act did not apply in Scotland; there a couple could marry at the age of sixteen without parental consent.

Young couples from England eloped to Greta Green, Scotland, to the blacksmith's shop—the focal point of the town. There a local magistrate would perform the marriage ceremony. The blacksmith's anvil, where metals were joined together with the heat of fire, became the symbol for eloping couples who were joined in marriage in the heat of the moment.

I was intrigued by this interesting tidbit of folklore but was oblivious to the historical significance of the area we were in. Our destination for the night was a B&B in Longtown. At breakfast the following morning, our host, also a bicyclist, recommended we ride to Hadrian's Wall. It was only a few miles distant. Al admitted he knew little about the Roman conquest of England and wasn't keen on the idea. I explained to him that I had walked on the Great Wall of China, and learning I was this close, I must see Hadrian's Wall. Al relented.

We backtracked ten miles to Brampton where we were able to secure lodging for the night in a B&B. To lighten my load, I removed the panniers from my bicycle and stored them in my room. We followed the road signage and began our climb to Hadrian's Wall. We cycled uphill for seven miles. The final three fourths of a mile presented us with a challenging 8 to 12 percent grade. Al's first comment when we crested the hill was, "I don't know why those Romans needed a wall at the top of a hill this steep."

Emperor Hadrian visited Britain in AD 122 and realized the Roman Empire should not expand further. He identified the northern border with a wall constructed with forts, turrets, and ditches that stretched for seventy-five miles from the east coast to the west coast.

My first view of Hadrian's Wall shocked me. The wall I was looking at stood no more than four feet high—no ditches, no forts, no turrets! I walked for a short distance along the top of the crumbling wall and stood there in speechless amazement as Al took my picture. Returning to our bikes, we headed down the hill to Brampton and our lodging for the night. Need I add that it was a fast descent?

On September 25 we again crossed the border into England and spent the night at a B&B in Penrith. The following day we cycled to Heysham where we boarded the ferry to the Isle of Man, a self-governing crown dependency in the Irish Sea. The crossing was in sharp contrast to what I'd experienced at the beginning of our trip when we sailed from Belfast to Stranraer, Scotland. The rough sea caused me to be seasick, and I barely made it to the ladies' room latrine before I barfed. Noting my distress, a kindly cabin attendant advised me to sit on the floor and brace myself against a wall. In this position, I would not feel the extremes of the rolling and tossing vessel. I followed her advice, with barf bags in hand, and sat down on the floor to wait out the remainder of the trip. As I sat there, I noted a woman rapidly approaching holding her hand over her mouth. I instinctively reached up and handed her one of my barf bags. She grabbed it, placed it to her mouth, and upchucked. Saved, and just in time! I would have been in her stream of "fire." Al was not affected by the rolling of the ship, and entertained himself chatting with others and watching videos, totally ignoring me. In my state of misery, I could have used some TLC.

The ferry docked at Douglas, the capital city of the island. This "Jewel of the Irish Sea," the Isle of Man measures fifty-two miles longitudinally and fourteen miles latitudinally. We secured lodging at a comfortable B&B in Douglas and prepared to make the most of our two-day stay.

We cycled the hills and flatlands of the island, enjoying the bucolic countryside. We rode past fields of harvested corn and grain and spied Manx cats, native to the island, known for their unique features of short tails (stumpy), no tails (rumpy), large elongated hind legs, and rounded heads. Farmers sheltered the cats, for they were skilled hunters and controlled the rodent population. We saw a herd of Loaghtan sheep, having dark-brown coats of wool with four (sometimes six) horns protruding from their heads. Cycling along the picturesque coast, seals were seen sunning on the rocks.

From a distance of several miles, a large, red wheel caught our attention. The Laxey Wheel was built in 1854 and used to pump water from a depth of several hundred feet to run the mine's steam powered pumps; coal was not available on the island. The pumps drained the water from the Laxey Mine where lead, copper, zinc, even silver were excavated.

The mine closed in 1929, but the wheel, seventy-two feet, six inches in diameter, continues to operate, providing water to the area. Al and I were fascinated, and the stair built by the side of the wheel invited us to ascend.

I counted ninety-two steps to the top. Standing on the small observation platform, I had an exhilarating panoramic view of the entire island. This experience was a highlight of my brief stay.

Ferry service to the island was limited; the summer service ended on the last day of September, and at all times was weather dependent. Knowing this, we scheduled our return to Dublin for September 27. We did not want to risk a cancellation of the last scheduled ferry which was to sail on the twenty-ninth. On the twenty-seventh we boarded the ferry to Dublin in a pouring rain. Fortunately, the crossing was smooth. The heavy rain continued as we disembarked at the city dock. Al and I were dressed in our yellow rain gear, aiding our safety, as we cycled amidst heavy traffic in search of the information center.

Eagan's House, where we stayed at the time of our arrival, was booked for the night. The clerk found us a room at the Portobello B&B. Adding to the misery of the heavy rain was darkness. Directions were inadequate, but after eight inquires, we arrived safely at our destination. It wasn't the ideal lodging. I was accustomed to having my own room. Here Al and I shared a room, but for me, any port in a storm. At least I had a dry bed for the night.

Back in Dublin, Al arranged to meet his Ashtabula contact, Darren Kortyka, who lived in the city. Darren had provided Al with information that helped him in planning our trip. We met Darren and his friend, Leah, on Sunday morning, and the four of us attended the service at St. Patrick's Church.

Before leaving the grounds of the church, Darren took us to the Chapter House and pointed out a rectangular hole cut in the Door of Reconciliation. I was about to learn a bit of Irish folklore. The year was 1492. Two prominent Irish families were locked in a feudal battle—the Butlers of Ormonde and the FitzGeralds of Kildare. Sir James Butler, with his followers, took refuge in the Chapter House of Saint Patrick's Cathedral. Gerald FitzGerald realized the futility of the feud, but peace overtures made to Sir James were spurned. Sir Gerald then devised a plan to show his sincerity. He ordered a hole cut in the door, thrust his arm through, and extended his outstretched hand. Realizing no harm was meant, Sir James grasped the extended hand, thus ending the feud. Hence the saying "to chance your arm"—to take the initiative.

On our final day in Dublin, we walked the hallowed grounds of Trinity College and entered the Old Trinity College Library where *The Book of Kells* was on display. Written in Latin and produced in the ninth century by the monks of Iona, this illuminated manuscript of the four gospels was truly an item of unparalleled beauty. I stood and gazed in reverent silence.

Fortunate for us, our host at Eagan's House was able to provide lodging for our last night in Dublin. Upon arrival, we were greeted with friendly hugs and words of thanks for our safe travels. We busied ourselves packing—Al dismantling our bicycles while I repaired the battered cardboard packing boxes. The following morning, luggage was loaded into the waiting van taxi, and we were off to the airport and our flight home.

By any measure, I experienced a one-of-a-kind bicycling adventure. I toured in parts of four countries—Ireland, Scotland, England, and the Isle of Man; cycled in traffic unfamiliar to me and mastered the roundabout; and managed hills and headwinds, along with the ever-changing weather. Our flexible schedule allowed us to take advantage of places and events that piqued our interest. During the three-week tour, I rode 550 accident-free miles. It was my friend Al Olson who made this adventure possible. Al died on August 4, 2016. Knowing him enriched my life, and I miss him.

———— ·+++++· ————

Rosemary Brenkus bicycled with the Ashtabula cranks. She always arrived for the Tuesday night rides dressed in fashionable cycling garb, blonde hair fastidiously coiffured, and makeup tastefully applied. I expected to see this tall, posture-perfect, slender woman stand by her bicycle posing for a photographer, and her picture would appear on the cover of *Bicycling* magazine.

Rosemary was not a model; she was one of us—but not really. No matter the heat, the wind, the rain, the distance, nothing seemed to faze her appearance. She didn't even sweat! Perhaps I exaggerate, but not by much. I admired this attractive woman who possessed so many of the attributes that I lacked. I gave little thought to my cycling clothes—I dressed for comfort. I referred to my hairstyle as wash and wear. My face was sans makeup, and I do sweat!

Rosemary and I both joined the Ashtabula Cranks the spring of 1999. She had a gentleman friend with whom she rode and I never felt comfortable approaching her. Our group held a monthly potluck social event. One particular month, I think it was July, I finished eating, glanced about, and noted Rosemary was sitting by herself at one of the picnic tables. Without hesitation I walked over, introduced myself, and asked if I might join her. Her response was warm and welcoming. I sat down across from her, and we conversed for a time.

That was the beginning of our friendship. She lived in Geneva about seven miles from my home in North Madison. Bicycling was our common interest, so we started to meet during the week and ride our bikes together. When fall came and the weather was not conducive for biking, we started meeting for lunch at area restaurants, settling on one in particular—the Anchor Inn, a bar and grill on Route 20 not too far from my home.

As we became better acquainted, we found we had many interests in common. Rosemary was widowed, as was I. She had grown children, as did I. She was retired from a career in education, as was I. We both had two siblings. But the kicker was, we both unashamedly admitted we liked men! Over the years, our chance acquaintance morphed into a lasting friendship.

The date was September 1, 2002. Rosemary and I made a luncheon date to meet at the Anchor Inn. I was about to leave when my phone rang. Rosemary had called to tell me she was in Mogadore, Ohio, with her brother Cordell and his family. There had been a car accident; she did not know when she would be home and provided no further details.

I saw very little of Rosemary that fall and into the winter of 2002. Rosemary and Cordell were very close, and he reached out to her during those grief-stricken weeks and months following the accident that took the life of his wife. Rosemary always spent the month of November in Florida. That year Cordell joined her; in January they took part in an Elderhostel program in California. Shortly after returning from California, Cordell had surgery. Rosemary stayed with him during his convalescence. His three children lived in the area, and they, as well, were loving, caring, and solicitous of their father.

Apparently, during the eight months Rosemary was with her brother, she picked up on his desire to get back into the dating scene—to meet other women, but with the blatant proviso, "She better like sex." That comment sparked an idea in Rosemary's head, and she thought "I know just the gal for you." But years passed before this bit of information was made known to me.

In spring of 2003 Rosemary was back home, and we resumed meeting for lunch at the Anchor Inn. On this particular day, seated at our favorite table by the window, sipping our favorite wine, chatting about our favorite subject—men—Rosemary abruptly stopped me in midsentence, looked me in the eye, and asked, "Would you like to meet my brother?"

TWENTY-ONE

AUTUMN LOVE

A difficult chapter to write, framed with facts and overflowing with emotion. Erich Segal's book *Love Story*, beautiful as it is, falls short in my mind in comparison to what I experienced.

I WAS BLESSED WITH THREE SUCCESSFUL MARRIAGES. Sidney Nelson and I married young. During the twelve years of our marriage, my desire to have a home and children (Bruce and Vernon) were fulfilled. Widowed at age twenty-nine (1960), I married my favorite professor, Allan Dickie, at age thirty-three. The twenty-three years of marriage to him were ones of intellectual and emotional growth. Widowed the second time at age fifty-six (1986), I married Charles Gass one and a half years later. I can best describe this marriage as a ten-year honeymoon—living, loving, retiring, and traveling. Regrettably, I was again widowed at age sixty-seven (1997).

When Charlie died, I had little hope in finding another mate, thinking I was too old. I felt sadness, better described as anger, when my dear friend Jody returned the duck pin I had given her years earlier. At the time, Jody was actively seeking a relationship. Wanting to support her in this endeavor, I gave her a silver pin—three little ducks waddling along in a row. On the enclosed card I wrote, "This may help you get your ducks in a row and find that special person." It worked. Jody met Bob, and marriage happened.

Rosemary knew my yearning for a companion and, while eating lunch that spring day in 2003, queried me, "Would you like to meet my brother?" Now a widow for five years, my answer was, "Yes." Little did I know the duck pin was about to work its magic once again.

———— ·+++++· ————

Cordell Richens Glaus was born to Charles and Mary on November 10, 1927. He was the eldest of three children—sisters Lilafay, born in 1929, and Rosemary, in 1930. Cordell was born with a sense of purpose that gave him a strong drive to achieve. At a young age he asked his father for money to buy fireworks. He wanted to celebrate the Fourth of July in style. It was the Depression. Money was scarce. There was no money to give, but his father gave his son something with far more substance—instilling in him the value of work. His dad sharpened the blades on the family rotary lawn mower and encouraged his son to use it and earn his own money. Over the years, Cordell mowed lawns, delivered newspapers, worked as a school custodian, tried his hand at teaching, and enrolled in the military, later benefitting from the GI Bill—jobs that set him on the road to financial independence.

Graduating from college, he became a registered architect, working for firms that provided him with the know-how to start up, with others, an engineering and architectural firm known as the GPD group. Retiring years later from the business, he was energized to take on another entrepreneurial challenge. He, with his two sons, built the Portage Hills Vineyards in 1987 and operated it for fifteen years, before again retiring in 2002, this time to enjoy a life of leisure and travel with his wife, Lois.

———— ·+++++· ————

That was not to be, for fate intervened. The evening of August 31, 2002, Cordell and Lois enjoyed an evening of dining with friends. Homeward-bound, a horrific two-car accident occurred at a dangerous intersection. Cordell was driving and the only survivor of the accident. Rosemary spent time providing comfort to her brother and his family, later becoming his traveling companion.

Cordell soon realized he needed more than a traveling companion; he wanted female companionship. Writing in his memoir, My Life in My Years, he said, "In one of my conversations with Rosemary I had confided to her that I was ready to seek out female companionship, and made the flippant comment that whomever it might be, 'She better like sex'. Physical compatibility is an important part of the marriage union."

On April 1, 2003, Rosemary had hip replacement surgery. Cordell came to be with her during the convalescence, and she took this opportunity to finesse a flawless request for me to meet her brother. Had Cordell suspected a tender trap was being set, he would have bolted.

Rosemary directed me to stop by on Tuesday, April 8. With heart pounding, feeling giddy, I climbed the front steps onto her porch, crossed to the door, and rang the bell. I expected to see my friend. To my surprise, the door was opened by a man about five feet eight inches in height, pudgy belly, with thinning white hair and pleasant facial features. The corners of his mouth turned upward in a smile as he greeted me, identifying himself as Rosemary's brother. He invited me to come in and informed me that Rosemary was busy with her physical therapist.

I was momentarily stunned but regained my composure enough to identify myself and stammer out my connection to Rosemary. I collapsed into the offered chair. For starters, our conversation was stilted and disconnected, but it didn't take long for us to settle on topics related to interests and activities. For the most part, I was pleased to play the role of the listener. An hour later, Rosemary put in her appearance.

ROSEMARY'S BROTHER WAS TRULY A RENAISSANCE MAN. By his own admission, he was born with traits of stubbornness, independence, and resolve, but also sentiment and nostalgia—not for things, but for people. A favorite picture of Cordell's was taken at the Harmon Photography Studio in Ashtabula the summer of 1929. Curly hair, chubby face, mischievous sparkle in his eyes, mouth formed into a self-satisfied expression revealing his upper teeth. But the viewer's eye focuses on his extended left arm, the palm of his hand turned outward, and you can almost hear his childish voice bragging, "See what I can do." In his memoir Cordell wrote, "I acted as though I was in charge and the picture does reveal that aspect of my character."

Cordell had no desire to be popular in high school. He took pleasure in not being counted among the popular kids, the "innies." He was an "outie"—his own person. (Terms used by Ralph Keyes in his book *Is There Life After High School?*). He took pride in wearing a white shirt and tie to school—a lot of work for his mother, but Cordell said she never complained.

His talents took him into creative areas of watercolor painting, writing, and music, both as a performer and as an enjoyer. Never one to stagnate, Cordell's avocational interests were varied—fly fishing, hunting, flying, and enology—developing land, and building the Portage Hills Vineyard. He traveled widely, visiting many of the states within the United States, and abroad in England, Russia, and China.

His character traits evidenced a plucky self-esteem, perfectionism, conscientiousness, honesty, openness to new experiences, and a steadfast work ethic. He admitted he could be obstinate, and to a degree, I admired this trait, if it didn't conflict with my bullheadedness!

When I queried Rosemary about why she thought I would suit her brother, she replied, "I knew you were strong enough to be your own person." Rosemary was right. Years ago, I took to heart the wisdom of the words of Kahlil Gibran in *The Prophet*, writing in "Love and Marriage":

> *Give your hearts, but not into each other's' keeping,*
> *For only the hand of LIFE can contain your hearts,*
> *Stand together, yet not too near together,*
> *For the pillars of the temple stand apart,*
> *And the oak and the cypress grow not in each other's*
> *shadow.*

⁘⁘⁘

IT WAS UNCANNY HOW OUR LIVES paralleled one another. Growing up, we lived seven miles apart—Cordell was a city kid; I was a corn-fed country kid. Due to district school lines, we attended different schools. Cordell lived within a mile of the Edgewood Schools. I attended a one-room schoolhouse for grades one and two. When districts were consolidated in 1937, I was enrolled in the Jefferson School District, a distance of twelve miles from my home.

As a youth, Cordell took piano lessons from Mrs. Hennigar, who lived on the east side near his home. He wrote in his memoir, "She was a sweet lady and a very good teacher." Under her tutelage Cordell learned to play the piano. Unfortunately, Mom placed me with Miss Davis, who also resided on the east side, but was a martinet. I quit.

We both attended the East Side Presbyterian Church, but at different times in our lives. Cordell was active with the youth group in the church.

I attended years later with my sons. We both became close to the pastor, Rev. Fred Vermeulen.

Every Saturday my dad delivered fresh eggs to the East Side Diner, located across from Edgewood High School. I was fourteen at the time, and Dad persuaded the owner to hire me as a dishwasher. I would work on Saturday while Dad took care of his egg customers. The summer between Cordell's junior and senior year, he had a job as a full-time janitor. On his lunch break, Cordell and his buddy would walk across Route 20 to the diner for their favorite lunch—a pint of ice cream and a cup of coffee. He adamantly claims that he noticed me standing over the large stainless steel sinks scrubbing pots and pans. Some years later, the romantic Cordell wrote of this and entitled it, "A 59 Year Old Story,"

> The boy was a 16-year-old with normal teen age hormones freely flowing through his body. Look at every pretty girl, and then dream that she is yours, that she can hardly wait to be with you. After all, you are a manly 16-year-old. She probably wishes you will say something to her.
>
> Then thunder strikes, a voice says "get to work" and I will protect you from those rowdy boys that come to this dinner to just eat ice cream and drink coffee and to eye and bother my working girls.
>
> But she is really pretty. She doesn't go to my school. Maybe someday I can meet her. Then poof, the dream is gone. You never even talk to her. Your life moves on. A world of experiences consumes you, and I'm sure that of the pretty girl also.
>
> Then by chance, 59 years later, do you see her again? Could it be that you have discovered that the pretty girl lived only seven miles away from you in 1944?
>
> You could have ridden your bicycle to see her. And now she has come home and lives close to you? Is this by chance? Is there a field of magic that works in our lives that now says "you deserve this-here it is-savor in it."

We learned that we enjoyed tent camping with our young families at Cook's Forest in Pennsylvania. At the time, money was scarce for both of us, and it was a place where a family could have an inexpensive vacation.

The Edgewood Cemetery is located a half mile from Cordell's home. His parents and other family members are interred there. In another part of the cemetery, Sidney is buried in the Nelson family lot.

Most of this information came to light during our first meeting.

———————————

As I LEFT THAT DAY, MY BRAIN REELED from learning how much Rosemary's brother and I had in common. Dare I hope to see him again? I expressed my desire to Rosemary, for she was the one who could make it happen. I knew she and Cordell had weekly Sunday morning conversations. Unbeknownst to me, during their talks, Cordell had expressed that he was equally impressed with me.

Days passed, and she seemed somewhat aloof when it came to any further talk of her brother. I was pleasantly surprised the day she called and gave me Cordell's e-mail address. Her cagey mind always working, she suggested a ruse—send him a message saying I would be visiting a friend in Kent and she would be coming with me. Could the three of us meet for lunch at the Pufferbelly? I composed the message as directed, signed it, "Sincerely, Henri (Henrietta Nelson)" and hit the Send button. His response was immediate, brief, and in the affirmative. A second meeting was in the works!

The days between the first meeting and the second passed at a glacial pace. Finally, the day arrived. The morning sun rose over Lake Erie with the promise of a perfect spring day. I rose early, ate breakfast, carefully selected what I would wear—a blue top that complemented my white hair worn with black pants that helped to slim my figure. Just as I was ready to leave, my phone rang. It was Rosemary. With a weak voice she told me she was too sick to travel. I was chapfallen, thinking I needed to cancel the luncheon date.

Rosemary assured me Cordell would be there—**go**! I had anticipated the one-and-a-half-hour drive to Kent would be filled with pleasant conversation. Instead it became, for me, a muddled mixture of mental anxiety, fueled by apprehension. I consoled myself that I had an exit plan if the meeting appeared to be a fiasco.

Butterflies fluttered in my stomach as I pulled into an empty diagonal parking place next to the Pufferbelly Restaurant. As I got out of my vehicle, a battered red pickup truck drove into the adjacent parking spot. It was Cordell. He wasn't surprised to see me alone. Rosemary had called him to say she was too ill to travel but persuaded him to keep the luncheon date. We walked into the restaurant together.

Seated in a booth across from one another, sipping wine, enjoying our lunch, we resumed conversation, as comfortable as two old friends. But we weren't two old friends; for my part, I wanted to learn as much as possible about Cordell and encouraged him to talk about himself. Three hours later we vacated the booth, returned to our vehicles, and shook hands with the expressed hope to see one another again. My heart sang as I headed north to my home. I knew Rosemary had connived for us to have lunch alone, just as she had arranged her physical therapy appointment to coincide with my first visit. For sure Rosemary, a.k.a. Cupid, was at work.

———————— ++++++ ————————

OUR PARTING WORDS "to see one another again" were easily spoken—a challenge to fulfill. We continued to communicate through sporadic e-mails. I was circumspect when it came to answering his messages. If it were three days between messages, difficult as it was, I waited an equivalent number of days to respond.

A month passed before I saw Cordell again. He sent a message alerting me he was driving up in his new Mercury Grand Marquis to see Rosemary on June 13 and invited me to have dinner with him that evening at the Unionville Tavern. I paid no mind that it was Friday the thirteenth. With a degree of coolness in my e-mail response, I replied I would be pleased to join him for dinner.

Friday turned out to be one of those perfect June days—moderate temperature, slight breeze, and a calm lake. I prepared wine and hors d'oeuvres for us to enjoy on the deck before dinner. As we sat there in what I thought was pleasant conversation, I must have made a comment that caused Cordell to bitingly remark, "I can't imagine you wanting to get married for the fourth time, in fact I can't imagine getting married the second time." I was shocked into silence, as Cordell continued, "I have no interest in your financial affairs, and I certainly don't care to share any of mine with you." That put me on high alert—no talk of marriage or of money.

The Unionville Tavern, a nineteenth-century stagecoach stop between Cleveland and Erie, was **the** place to dine in the Madison area. The low-ceilinged room, with windows on three sides, was a perfect setting for relaxed dining. The hostess seated us at a table by a window overlooking a formal garden.

The cuisine was outstanding and famous for its corn muffin swimming in maple syrup, served before the entrée. In spite of Cordell's earlier comment, conversation flowed easily. I recall we said little during the return drive to my home; my thoughts kept returning to the (almost) pleasant evening I had with this man. Cordell later told me he too enjoyed the silence and welcomed the fact that I was not one to blather.

I did not want the weekend to end. I knew Cordell was staying over until Sunday with Rosemary. Brenda had commented that the play, *Mornings at Seven*, playing at the local Rabbit Run Theater, was outstanding. Based on her recommendation, I called Rosemary the following morning and asked if she, her gentleman friend Bob, and Cordell would like to be my guests that evening at the theater. Rosemary returned my call an hour later, letting me know my invitation was accepted. My joy knew no bounds. She suggested we go out to eat prior to the performance. I was sensitive that Cordell and I were not a bona fide couple, and I certainly did not want him to assume I expected him to pick up the check. With this in mind, I suggested to Rosemary that she, Bob, and Cordell stop by my house prior to the performance. I explained that, with minimal effort, I could prepare a dinner using one of the casseroles I always had at the ready in my freezer. She agreed, and the four of us enjoyed a relaxed meal before leaving for the theater.

That evening, seated next to Cordell in the darkened theater, I placed my hand conveniently next to his, hoping he would take it. No luck. The play ended, and as we walked side by side back to the car, Cordell did take my hand and held it during the drive back to my house. I found his touch to be electrifying.

Afterward, seated around the table, the four of us enjoyed dessert and coffee while critiquing the performance. It was almost midnight when the three of them got up to leave. Rosemary and Bob immediately returned to the car, but Cordell held back. As we stood there, he commented how much he enjoyed the weekend but didn't know when we might get together again. His calendar was filled with various and sundry appointments through the end of July. On that disappointing note, I bid him good night.

I sensed a reluctance on Cordell's part to get together. It brought back memories of incidents that happened while dating both Allan Dickie and Charlie Gass. I wanted no part in another cat-and-mouse dating game. It was unfortunate our schedules were in conflict as I was open through June but had plans made for most of July. Unknowingly, it was my niece, Beverley Schumann, who moved our relationship out of neutral and into high gear.

On June 15 I received an e-mail from Bev with an attachment—"Dr. Phil's Compatibility Test." There were ten questions in the test, with each question having three to five answer choices. Each choice had a different numerical value. Add up the ten values for your total score. This would be used for comparison purposes. Test questions related to time of day you feel best, interaction with others in social situations, reaction to interruptions or amusements, posture and speed when walking, position when sitting or sleeping, favorite color, and dreams. I forwarded the test to Cordell and commented that if it piqued his interest, he could take it, and we could compare our scores. Within three days I received a request to forward my score to him. The scores revealed only a one-point difference.

How scientific was the test? I didn't care; I liked the result. Cordell must have thought the same, for I received word he would be driving up for a weekend visit with Rosemary on June 27. His message included an invitation for dinner, only this time he would bring the wine. An overwhelming happiness washed over me. I replied by saying I preferred dining at home and brazenly added, "Bring your toothbrush, we may get to talking, and who knows what the evening may hold for us."

I wanted the evening to be perfect. I set the table using a white linen tablecloth, candles, floral centerpiece, china, and sterling silver. At the appointed hour the doorbell rang. Squelching feelings of nervousness, I opened the door to greet Cordell, who stood there with a small ice chest in his hand. He took one step inside, dropped the ice chest, and gave me a crushing hug and a demanding kiss. Releasing me, he retrieved the ice chest and walked to the kitchen counter where he opened a bottle of wine. With a plate of hors d'oeuvres in my hand, followed by Cordell carrying two glasses of wine, we seated ourselves on the red recliner love seat. The wine was barely sipped, the hors d'oeuvres remained untouched. We hungered for one another—and fortuitously Cordell had brought his toothbrush.

OUR FRAGILE RELATIONSHIP MATURED into a bonding love. We realized we needed to reach out to our children and hopefully receive their blessing. Bruce and Linda were first to be aware that someone special had entered my life. In telephone calls to Las Vegas, the happiness in my voice was palpable. Soon the question was asked by my son, for I had had two May–

December marriages, "How old is Cordell?" Bruce was relieved to learn my newfound love was close to my age and in good health. Later, when asked, Cordell gave only a glowing report of my health to his daughter Diane.

Cordell's three children and spouses lived in the immediate area. I met Diane and Doug first. Diane paved the way for my acceptance by her two brothers. I met Kent and Janet at Cordell's Mogadore home for an informal cookout. Later I met Gary and Cheri. Cordell was relieved that his three children, and their spouses, accepted me. They realized their dad had met someone who could give him a renewed lease on life.

Cordell had six grandchildren, either living at home, or away at school. As the opportunity presented itself, I met them—three girls and three boys, all good-looking, industrious young people seeking their place in life. The last grandchild I met was Melissa, a petite blonde with an engaging smile and a vivacious personality. When Cordell introduced me, she acknowledged the introduction by quipping, "I'm so happy to meet you, and I want you to know Papa has saved the best for last—me." I was equally impressed by them all.

Cordell arranged one family event that wisely did not include me. Cordell and Lois were married on July 25, 1953. July 25, 2003, marked their golden wedding anniversary. A dinner with his children and grandchildren was planned for Sunday July 20. All family members were present, and Cordell paid tribute to Lois in a written testimonial entitled, "Lois, A Wife, Mother, Grandmother, and a Person of Dignity."

That evening, in an e-mail, Cordell shared his thoughts with me. "I believe the best part of the evening was when I asked Kent to give the blessing before we ate. He went through the normal thanks and blessings and then, to my surprise and appreciation he asked for blessings for 'Henri and Dad and their new life together.' That sure did make me feel good." This gave Cordell a sense of closure, and with renewed energy, he was ready to meet my children.

OUR ENGAGEMENT BECAME OFFICIAL the weekend of July 18. I drove to Mogadore to be with Cordell. It was early Saturday morning; neither of us could sleep. I got up, made coffee, and returned to the bedroom with a cup in each hand. We sat up in bed sipping the hot, black liquid, quite relaxed and just talking, when suddenly Cordell turned to me and said, "I could marry you. Do you want to marry me?"

His proposal was a total surprise. The scene was the same when, tongue-in-cheek two weeks earlier, I had said to him, "I could marry you." In response, all I got was a pregnant silence. Now he was **voicing his proposal to me**, repeating some of the same words I had previously said to him. I almost spilled the hot coffee on the bedclothes. It didn't take me long to regain my composure and with no hesitation answered, "**Yes**." For some time, I had mentally entertained the thought of being Mrs. Cordell Nelson-Glaus.

WE REFERRED TO IT AS OUR WESTERN HONEYMOON—leaving on July 23 and returning on August 4. The evening before we were to leave, seated on the red love seat, Cordell reached into his pocket and brought out a small box. He opened it and removed a ring. Gently taking my left hand, he placed the ring on my finger. I sat there looking at the white gold band, set with three sparkling diamonds. I was overcome with emotion and unable to speak. Cordell wanted me to be wearing my engagement ring when he met my children.

On Wednesday, July 23, our flight landed in Spokane, Washington. Cordell rented a Ford Taurus, and we drove to the home of Mary, my son's significant other. Vernon was there to greet us. Introductions were made, and we spent two days with Vern and Mary. Cordell summarized this meeting in his memoir: "At first Vern was skeptical of his mother getting married again. But it soon became evident to Vern that I was right for his mother and over time I was fully accepted by him."

Friday morning, we left Spokane, headed southwest, and drove along the beautiful Columbia River Gorge to Newport, Oregon. We stayed two nights at the Sylvia Beach Hotel, recommended to us by my Columbus friend, Susan Fisher. Rooms in this establishment were named after famous writers; ours was the Hemingway Room. We left Newport, and for the next six days enjoyed a leisurely, scenic drive along the ocean before heading inland to Las Vegas where Bruce and Linda lived.

We arrived at Bruce and Linda's home middle of the afternoon on Saturday, August 2. Cordell parked our rented car on the street. We had not alerted them to our arrival time, so no one was home. Unable to enter the house, we managed to open the gate to the fenced-in backyard, made ourselves comfortable in two of their poolside lounge chairs, and settled in to wait. As five o'clock approached, Cordell went to the car and returned with a bottle of Gewürztraminer wine and two glasses. An hour later we heard Bruce and Linda enter the house, but we remained quiet on the patio. Bruce was first to open the sliding glass doors, and when he saw us seated there sipping wine, the first words out of his mouth were, "What the hell?"

We spent two active and joyous days with Bruce and Linda. While there, they introduced Cordell to all facets of the family business and drove us through Red Rock Canyon. Bruce demonstrated flying his remote-control plane and took us on a cruise to see the waterside of Hoover Dam. The evening before we left, my grandchildren, Candice and Bruce Allan, with their significant others, joined us for a family dinner. By then, I knew that Cordell was accepted into the family fold. Bruce took us to the airport the morning of Monday, August 4, and Cordell recorded in his memoir: "It was with joy that Henri and I boarded a plane for home knowing we had passed the initial test with all of our children."

———————————————

WE WERE TOGETHER WITHOUT INTERRUPTION for twelve days—days filled with romance and adventure. During the many hours we spent in the car, we shared our life story; we shared hours of silence with the loving reassurance that comes with holding hands. Years later, Cordell recorded his thoughts: "Our Western Honeymoon was a beautiful time together. We came home different than when we left—our love for one another is much deeper and with a sensitive understanding we didn't possess before."

There were incidents which evidenced that our love shone through. People noticed and realized we had something special. The first took place in Spokane. Cordell and I were holding hands while walking along the sidewalk in a residential area. As we passed one house, we observed a family seated on their porch and heard a voice call out, "Are you two married? How long?" We stopped, answered their questions, chatted a bit, and as we walked away, we heard someone say, "You do look in love."

The second time occurred in Las Vegas. We were walking in Bruce and Linda's neighborhood. We passed by one house where a Japanese man was working in his yard. He greeted us, saying, "Walking is good exercise." We exchanged social niceties, and as we were about to go on our way, he asked, "Are you married?" Cordell answered, "No, but soon to be." The man's immediate response was, "That good, everyone needs someone to scratch their back."

A third occurrence was on the flight home, and because we were in a confined space, it was the most intensive. A flight attendant, "deadheading" from Orlando, was seated across the aisle from us. After watching us for some time. she finally spoke. "How long have you been married?" Cordell and I laughed, giving her our now-standard response: "We're on our honeymoon. We find we love one another so much, we are going to get married." That opened the way for some intensive questioning. How long have you known one another? Other marriages? Children? Date of wedding? Finally, her questions stopped, and without any prompting from us, she gave an account of her love life. She had been married and divorced three times, was now in a fourth relationship. The chemistry seemed right, but no desire to marry; she wanted to keep the romance alive. As she talked, feelings of sympathy centered on this unfortunate woman. Apparently, she did not understand what inner qualities were needed for two people to move from the romance of first love to form a relationship deep enough/strong enough to surmount the vicissitudes of life.

Now that we had met all of the children, our desire was focused on introducing our families to one another. Plans were made to have a beach party at my home in North Madison. My nephew, Kirk Peine, would supply his water toys—ski boat and Jet Ski. We'd have a cookout on the deck, enjoy the beauty of the day, and make this a pleasant opportunity for all to get acquainted. It happened, but not as planned.

Sunday, August 31, it rained. The temperature dropped, and the weather was miserable, negating all previously made plans. Twenty people crowded into my house. Gary later remarked, "Perhaps it was for the best. The weather forced all of us to be close and get to know each other better."

Over time we met one another's friends, but for immediacy there were special friends that we brought into our confidence and were comfortable sharing our wedding plans with them. For Cordell it was Al and Juanita Moutz and Bill and Ruth Frieden. The three couples lived in Mogadore, had known one another for decades, and had children about the same age.

After the tragic accident that took the life of Lois, Bill Frieden held a deep concern for Cordell and his future. He took on the role of matchmaker, entertaining in his home and ensuring that one widow was always part of the group. Fortunately for me, none caught Cordell's eye. When Cordell told Bill and Ruth of his engagement, Bill insisted that they meet me. I found them to be an interesting couple. Bill was quite outspoken and brash; Ruth a quieter, sensitive person, whom I immediately liked. Later, Cordell shared Ruth's assessment of me. "Ruth was wanting to tell you how much they enjoyed you—you have a 'great wit.' You have their stamp of approval, and since Ruth is the most respected woman in Mogadore, you are in, my dearest! In Mogadore, that means you have won the gold medal."

Like my children, my friends lived a distance away, so there was no immediate opportunity for Cordell to meet them. The ones with whom I was closest were my girlfriends who lived in the Columbus area. When I telephoned Jody to tell her the duck pin had worked its magic, she immediately remarked, "I knew it! I can hear the happiness in your voice."

My friend Randy, who lived in Ashtabula, presented me with a concern of a different type. He had fulfilled my need for companionship over the past four years. Now he was under hospice care. I shared with Cordell the place Randy had in my life and that I wanted to continue to support him as best I could. But Cordell insisted I tell him of my pending marriage and make a clean break. Realizing what I must do, I prayed to God that he would take Randy before I had to tell him and spare him the pain of knowing. God's plan is not man's plan, so I came to terms with the inevitable.

With Cordell's help, I composed a letter to Randy. The letter was secondary—an explanation. My conscious dictated that I meet with him face-to-face when I broke the news. I asked Randy's son Kevin to meet with me the evening of July 16. I shared with him my marriage plans. Kevin was not too surprised and commented that he understood my need to move on with my life. He asked that I stay in touch, but that did not happen.

The evening of July 17, I sat with Randy in his home when I told him. He was stunned and looked as if I had hit him with a baseball bat. I handed him the letter and left. The last time I saw Randy was on October 4, a week before my marriage. He asked me for my address. I evaded answering, knowing if Cordell saw any correspondence from him, he would be furious. I left him sitting in his chair. I am still able to visualize the haggard, forlorn, helpless, and hopeless look etched on his face. He died on January 19, 2005.

I felt emotionally vulnerable, fearful that something might happen to destroy our love. I shared this with Cordell, and he said, "Stick with me, for I can ward off evil spirits," and proceeded to tell me the legend of the Dream Catcher. According to the American Indian, the Dream Catcher is woven from natural sinew. The center of the weaving is open and covered with feathers. As one sleeps, evil and good spirits battle. Only the good spirits survive to escape the web. Cordell, being a good spirit, would escape and be my protector. Romantic as this explanation was, it provided me with a sense of surety.

———— ‡‡‡‡‡‡ ————

OUR E-MAILS WERE THE FOUNDATION that fostered our budding romance. In the space of six months, I had met Cordell, fallen in love, sold my home in North Madison, married for the fourth time, and moved to Green, Ohio. During those intervening months between our meeting and marriage, we exchanged nearly 250 e-mail messages. On August 29, Cordell commented, "I look back and read our early e-mails and reminisce on how our love has grown. It is a beautiful fast-moving love story."

Cordell took the time to record a sampling of our sign-offs and sent them to me the following day, reporting, "We came a long way in two short months."

May 13: Sincerely	June 29: My love
May 15: Thank you for pleasant hours	(the toothbrush happening)
June 16: Contact you later	June 30: All my love to you
June 19: Your Dream Catcher (Cordell)	July 9: Your life's traveling companion
June 19: Your Tantalizer (Henri)	July 15: My love forever
	July 19: Your loving wife

Our e-mail messages emboldened us to express our innermost thoughts. We both acknowledged it was understandable how people got carried away with this type of romance. One can be whatever one wants to be in cyberspace, but frequent telephone calls and time together combined to ground us, and our love deepened.

As I read, and reread, our e-mails, I acknowledge that Cordell was the romanticist. He expressed his love philosophically and creatively. I was more the pragmatist. I knew life experiences, combined with my present level of maturity, were contributing factors to my feelings for Cordell. In saying this, I do not mean to diminish the love my previous husbands had for me or I for them. I only gave thanks for this gift of love so beautifully expressed in an e-mail on September 26. "I expect to capture your love as no other man has done."

To us, it was a miracle. Could it possibly have been foreordained? Cordell wrote of this in "A 59 Year Old Story" shortly after we met in 2003. "Love Changes Everything" applied to us. It became our song, and it was sung at our wedding.

Love—love changes everything
Hands and faces earth and sky
Love—love changes everything
How you live and how you die
Love can make the summer fly
Or a night seem like a lifetime
Yes love—love changes everything
How I tremble at your name
Nothing in the world will ever be the same

Love—love changes everything
Days are longer words mean more
Love—love changes everything
Pain is deeper than before
Love will turn your world around
And that world will last forever
Yes love—love changes everything
Brings you glory brings you shame
Nothing in the world will ever be the same

Off into the world we go
Planning futures shaping years
Love bursts in and suddenly
All our wisdom disappears
Love makes fools of everyone
All the rules we make are broken
Yes love—love changes everything
Live or perish in its flame
Love will never let you be the same
Love will never let you be the same
Love changes everything
Hands and faces earth and sky.

⸺⸺ ·+++++· ⸺⸺

WE WERE GOING TO BE MARRIED, and a multitude of things required our
attention. Where would we live? I grew up in Ashtabula County and had
lived in Lake County for the past five years. My brother, sister, and their
families lived in the area. I belonged to three bicycle clubs and identified

myself with the community through church and volunteer work with Hospice. When I became engaged, it was a no-brainer that I would move to be with Cordell in the area where he had raised his family and established himself professionally. We agreed we would both sell our houses and buy a condo. We wanted to be free of home-maintenance responsibilities.

I contacted the Symthe Cramer real estate company and signed the papers on August 15. The asking price was $248,000. The following day, a "For Sale" sign was placed in my front yard. That evening I wrote in my diary, "The daybreak was perfect. I walked out to the deck with a cup of coffee in my hand. I think it was a blue heron that took off just as I approached; as I sat there, a flock of geese flew by. The lake was calm and I watched the ever-changing pallet of colors reflecting on the lake as the sun rose in the sky." I did not feel any remorse that I would be leaving this haven on the lake. My future held such promise.

The realtor was aggressive in promoting the sale of the house, and within six weeks I received an offer that was acceptable to me. On October 24, two weeks after our marriage, Cordell came with me to the realtor's office to sign the papers. Again, I bought high and sold low—I accepted $243,000.

Having moved so many times, I was efficient at packing. Cordell was helpful and commandeered his son Gary, and friend Dan, to help in the move. By the time the house sold, the small items were in storage and the large items were ready for a professional mover.

I spent several days with Cordell in the Portage/Summit County area looking at condos. After touring several properties, I wondered how I would adapt to condo living—smaller rooms, many without a basement, all crowded together. Wisely Cordell saved the best for last. Al and Juanita Moutz lived in a condo near the Ohio Prestwick Country Club in Green, ten miles south of Mogadore. On August 16 they had invited us to be dinner guests in their home. Following dinner, we toured their two-level, spacious residence with an open view of the third fairway of the Prestwick Country Club golf course. This condo was to my liking!

Al remarked there was a similar condo for sale, just up the street on the same side. The next day Cordell contacted the realtor, and that evening we toured a spacious, 3,400-square-foot condo. Originally priced over $400,000 and with no takers, the owners kept reducing the price. We offered $319,900, and it was accepted. On August 11 we signed the sale agreement. The closing date was October 5, with possession on October

9. It worked to our advantage. We would get possession before we were married.

The sale of Cordell's house in Mogadore did not move as smoothly as had mine. Someone close to Cordell expressed a desire to buy the family home. This relieved Cordell of finding a realtor, and as he said, we would not need to "sanitize the place for open house and inspections." A sale agreement was made.

We spent a good part of November in Florida, and after we returned in early December, Cordell received a message that the sale would not go through. We were not yet settled in our home and were faced with the necessity to sell Cordell's Mogadore house.

The first realtor Cordell used was a disaster. After the three-month contract expired, he contacted a second realtor, a very aggressive Mogadore woman who found a buyer for the house. All this cost us time and dollars, but it all worked out in the end.

———————

WE BOTH AGREED THAT OUR WEDDING would be uniquely ours. Cordell and Lois had a traditional church wedding. My weddings had run the gamut from eloping to standing in a church with only the minister and our attendants present to being married in the home of my son and his wife in Las Vegas surrounded by loving family members.

Cordell put our creative talents to work, and we planned our wedding with the enthusiasm of two lovestruck sixteen-year-olds. We chose not to have a honeymoon. I knew members of my family and stepfamilies, all from out of town, would be in attendance, and I wanted to enjoy their brief stay with us. Also, Cordell planned to keep a commitment made with Rosemary before he met me. They had reserved a condo in Seaside near Panama City, Florida, for three weeks in November. For these reasons involving our respective families, we felt it sensible not to take a honeymoon. Unfortunately, we were to find out what seemed sensible is not always best.

Top of the to-do list was to set the wedding date. Our first choice was October 4, Bruce's birthday. Cordell wanted both of his sons, Kent and Gary, to stand with him; for me, it would be Brenda and Rosemary, only to learn that Rosemary would be traveling in California and not home until October 3. Cupid had to be there; we moved the wedding date ahead to the following Saturday, October 11. This turned out to be fortuitous for all.

Weather the weekend of October 4 was abominable—cold, rain, and wind. Weather the weekend of October 11 was perfect—warm, sunshine, and a refreshing breeze. Once again, Cupid's arrow hit the bull's-eye.

Other items on our list were wedding invitations, choosing the location, securing a minister, and getting the marriage license. It was Diane who suggested the Viking Vineyards, an area winery conveniently located on Old Forge Road in Brimfield. We visited the bucolic setting and found it to our liking. I telephoned Reverend Fred Vermeulen, now retired from the Edgewood Presbyterian Church, to ask if he would perform the ceremony. To our disappointment, Fred declined, citing his wife's ill health. Cordell then contacted his former pastor at the Mogadore Methodist Church, the Reverend Karen Graham. During the wedding planning session with Karen, she stressed Cordell must have the license with him— no marriage license, no ceremony! Neither of us were procrastinators. On September 22 we walked into the Summit County Probate Court, filled out the necessary form, and walked out with our marriage license in hand.

About this time, we were able to secure lodging for our out-of-town guests at the Days Inn. It was conveniently located, with enough available rooms and moderately clean. Our first choice was one of the more upscale motels in the area. We found all were booked for that weekend due to a major event at Kent State University.

Using a picture Brenda had taken of us with Lake Erie in the background, Cordell designed our wedding invitations. They were mailed in late August. To anyone who asked, we passed the word that dress was informal. The groom wanted to be comfortable and refused to wear a tie at his own wedding.

In early September Rosemary, Brenda, and I went dress shopping. I found it to be an exhausting task. After numerous try-ons, we each, in turn, selected a dress that was given mutual approval. Mission accomplished, we were off to lunch, and the relaxation of wine, food, and a camaraderie that can only be shared with a significant happening.

It befuddles me to this day how it happened that I bought Cordell a Howard Miller grandfather clock—triple chimes, mirrored back, and interior adjustable curio display shelves. The gift I planned to buy was a mantel clock. Once in the clock store, he fell in love with the grandfather clock, and I was in love with him—that made it a *fait accompli*.

Our energy was boundless as we checked off all the items that needed to be done on our to-do list. Cordell, familiar with area resources, made appointments for us to meet with the musicians (pianist and soloist), florist, caterer, and photographer. We returned to the jewelry store where he purchased my engagement ring and selected our matching wedding bands.

Business matters required our attention prior to marriage. A joint checking account was established at the local bank. We needed to complete a prenuptial agreement, protecting assets for our children. Cordell made an appointment with an attorney friend who served as legal counsel for his GPD firm. I thought this quite convenient, as my attorney lived in Ashtabula. My thoughts of convenience were shattered when we received the bill for his professional services. I felt it was exorbitant. I suddenly came to the realization that I knew nothing about the business side of my soon-to-be husband. It did cause me concern, and I started to pay closer attention to expenditures and business contacts.

THE WEEK PRECEDING MY WEDDING, I experienced the emotional high of unmitigated joy, and the despondent feelings of sadness and despair. My granddaughter's husband telephoned me early Monday morning to say he would not be coming to my wedding as there were marital problems that appeared to be insurmountable. In a later conversation with Candice's parents, I was relieved to learn that she would be coming with them.

Although this news was very disturbing to me, it paled in comparison to the telephone call I received from my nephew, Peter Schumann, the afternoon of October 6. Peter told me his mother had died that morning at home. There were complications that had resulted from Trudy's recent knee replacement surgery. I knew both Lloyd and Trudy were looking forward to sharing my wedding day with me, having not attended any of my three previous marriages. Trudy was cremated, and a memorial service was held for family and a few invited guests at the home of Peter and Beverley. I made the painful decision not to attend but to remain in Mogadore with Cordell as we finalized preparations for our wedding on Saturday.

On Friday evening, October 10, our families gathered at the Mogadore house to socialize and enjoy finger foods washed down with beer and wine. Brenda came and, with gentle understanding, was able to persuade Lloyd to come with her. When they walked into the room, I rushed to embrace my brother, my eyes filling with tears and a prayer of thanks forming on my lips.

———————— ·|·++|·+·· ————————

CORDELL WROTE IN HIS AUTOBIOGRAPHY, "October 11, 2003 was the most beautiful day of that year. God must have known we were going to be married on that day."

Viking Vineyards was located five miles south of Kent. One entered the grounds of the winery off of Old Forge Road, drove along a half-mile narrow potholed, gravel lane with a swamp area to the left and a small lake to the right. The lake side of the lane was lined with elm, oak, and maple trees clothed in their resplendent fall colors. The end of the lane opened into a peaceful, bucolic setting. A grassy area surrounded the ranch-style winery/hospitality building that had red siding and white trim on the windows and doors. Vineyards enhanced the surrounding acreage. A patio furnished with tables and chairs overlooked the small lake. Several picnic tables were randomly placed in the grass areas. This simple, unpretentious setting was the idyllic place for our wedding.

The prewedding reception was set for 11:15 a.m. Cordell and I greeted our guests as they arrived. We posed for photographs with various family groupings and assembled friends for a group picture. As Cordell and I posed for our official wedding photo, two swans floated by on the lake. We named them Dream Catcher and Tantalizer.

Guests were summoned indoors, where accommodations were made to seat the seventy-five people. The ceremony began promptly at 12:00 p.m. with Melissa Smith singing "Music of the Night," accompanied by Dave Day at the keyboard. Previously, Rosemary had given Cordell a poem "True Love," written by Judith Viorst, saved out of a September/October 1999 publication of the *AARP Modern Maturity* magazine. Cordell rewrote the poem, personalizing it and changing the title to "Autumn Love." He introduced it by saying, "We are beginning a new life together at a time in our lives that we call our autumn love. Reading in turn, we wish to share these thoughts with you."

(H)   He enters a being of eternity.
(C)   She enters a being of eternity
(H)   And after great loneliness
        We who are left behind find each other.

From what we were
To a new companion to each.

(C)   Our children and grandchildren rejoice,
saying in many ways,
We wish only for your happiness.

(H)   We do not abandon our lost mates,
for we honor them.
We do not abandon our children
and grandchildren,
For they are a part of our being.

(C)   We who are left behind find each other,
The essence of our being
Renewed in a loving embrace.

(H)   And in our hearts,
We express gratitude for such gifts,
such intimacy, such love.

When we finished the reading of "Autumn Love," Missy sang our song, "Love Changes Everything," while Reverend Graham and the attendants stepped into place. Karen intoned the wedding vows; we repeated them, making our solemn pledge to one another. When it came time to exchange the rings, Brenda quietly took my left hand and soaped my ring finger so Cordell would have no problem slipping the ring over my arthritic knuckle. The last song that Missy sang was "Annie's Song," made famous by John Denver. The song held a significance for me because Bruce chose it to be sung at his wedding to Linda in 1978.

As the final strains of the music faded, Cordell stepped forward and changed the solemn mood that filled the room to one of frivolity. "You all must know of the huge risk I am about to take, for this is the first time ever that we have danced in public, for after this Henri may dump me. But I'll risk it. May I have this dance, my dearest wife?" Kicking off my uncomfortable shoes, I welcomed the embrace of my husband as we danced.

I asked Lloyd to give the blessing before the lunch was served. He said he would try, but if he became overcome with emotion, he wanted to have someone ready to take his place. That someone was Kent. Lloyd, however, was able to complete a beautiful blessing. I cannot fathom the emotional toll it took on my brother to be with me, and then to participate in my wedding, having just lost his beloved Trudy.

A buffet lunch was served, and when all guests were again seated, it was time for the toasts. In turn Candice, Kent, Bruce, and Brenda spoke. I have no recorded comments made by Candice or by Bruce. I only recall they were brief expressions of happiness for us.

Kent's toast, single-spaced, filled an eight-and-a-half-by-eleven-inch sheet of paper. He spoke to the tenderness of love and the meaning of marriage. In part it reads, "To find love once is a gift from God; to find love again is divine destiny. So, let us please raise our glasses and offer a toast of thanksgiving to Henri and my Dad: We thank you for sharing your obsession of love with each of us. Cheers!"

Brenda, as well, had written her toast. She spoke to both of us, commenting we had taken every opportunity available for growth in our professional and personal lives. She ended by saying, "A toast to the next volume in your library of life! May it be the best one yet!"

Now, it was our turn to give toasts. Cordell movingly spoke directly to Rosemary. "In all probability, we all would not be here today if it had not been for one person—that one person has been for as many years as I can remember my very best friend, and by coincidence, my sister. Yes, Rosemary, it is you who is responsible. You and I have been confidants since we were teenagers—sitting up many nights drinking coffee; as adults, wine was the preferred beverage, but always talking and sharing confidences. Now you have shared your best friend with me, who is now the second Mrs. Cordell Glaus."

My turn came, and my toast to Rosemary was, "It all started as bike riding buddies. We became friends enjoying lunches together… Recognizing that we had much in common, we became each other's confidant. As the years passed you got to know me—my interests, my activities, my desires, my dreams. At one of our luncheons, you asked me if I would like to meet your brother. I answered in the affirmative… Yes, you played **Cupid**, then **coach** to our budding romance, and today **sister-in-law.** Rosemary, I thank you, I love you. May we all raise our glasses to **Cupid** with a Swedish toast for good health—**skoal**."

Our wedding was unique, planned by us, and shared with loving family and close friends. As the guests departed, each family was given an envelope containing our "Autumn Love" poem. When we left the hospitality room, the sun had crossed its meridian in the sky, but still shone brightly, highlighting the colors of the leaves. The swans we had named Dream Keeper (Cordell) and Tantalizer (Henri) continued to glide lazily on the lake. For all who could take the time, we urged them to stop by the home of Mr. and Mrs. Cordell Glaus at 2173 Prestwick Dr. in Green. There the celebration continued.

By our request, Gary made a video of our wedding. We looked at it once—never again. We agreed, we looked old.

———— ++++++ ————

I WOULD BE REMISS to leave the reader with the impression that my path over those six months was strewn only with rose petals. There were thistles along the way—happenings that caused utter frustration and disharmony in our relationship. Soon after we returned from our Western Honeymoon, Cordell called to my attention that he did not like, or want, to be compared with my previous husbands. Apparently, while in Las Vegas, one family member commented he looked like Allan; another disagreed, saying he reminded her of Charlie. Cordell further remarked that I had called to his attention that his initials were the same as those of Charles Gass. Worse yet, I had mistakenly called him Charlie. In my defense, the name Cordell was unfamiliar to me, and in stressful situations, I had trouble with immediate recall of his name. However, over the coming years, Cordell developed a sense of humor related to my previous marriages. When my former daughter-in-law came to visit me in Green, Bobbie became somewhat flustered as she introduced her daughter Shanna to Cordell, calling him Charlie. With a twinkle in his eye and laughter in his voice, he quickly responded, "No, I am Cordell, number four."

Any mention of Randy Presley was verboten. Much as it pained me, after I met with Randy and told him I was to be married, I made no further mention of him. Randy was one person I hurt deeply; it became my cross to bear.

One night, in the motel room in Lake Tahoe, I was restless. Cordell was sleeping soundly. As the night hours crept slowly by, I felt I was a prisoner in the room. I promised him I would not go out alone at night, but I became increasingly agitated and awakened Cordell. He reluctantly agreed to get dressed and walk with me. As we left the motel room, I walked at a rapid pace, giving Cordell the "silent treatment." He exploded, "All right, walk alone." My behavior had forced a we-need-to-talk incident. He was right in his concern for my safety. I was not used to being controlled, and exercise and silence were my ways of coping. We had words so serious that I called off the engagement and returned his ring. Fortunately, we calmed down, and harmony was restored.

These incidents seem inconsequential as compared to what happened on the night of Sunday October 12. The Nelson family stayed on for another day after the wedding; they would be leaving Monday morning. All day Sunday, members of the extended families had been in and out of Cordell's Mogadore home. I was delighted that the Nelson family would spend their final evening with us. We were in the kitchen, seated around the table drinking wine and enjoying the frivolity that comes with family closeness. It went unnoticed by me that Cordell was becoming more and more agitated. It was late, and as the family made overtures to leave, I looked at Cordell and said, "I would like for us to join the family for breakfast in the morning." I was shocked by Cordell's curt response. "No, I have things to do." Still oblivious to his irritation, I tried to persuade him otherwise. He was adamant in his refusal.

I was devastated. As soon as they left, I needed to get outside for some fresh air and to walk. Cordell, not wanting me to be alone after dark, came with me. My coping behaviors were in high gear. I walked fast, and during the hour-long walk, not a word was exchanged between us. Returning to the house I showered, lay down on the bed, and covered my eyes with my arm. Cordell came in, grabbed my arm, and glared down at me. I could feel the heat of his anger. He accused me of giving him no choice in front of others. We both experienced a sleepless night. In the morning Cordell came with me to the motel. When we arrived, the family had eaten their breakfast and were packed ready to leave for the airport. What should have been a joyous goodbye, for me, was emotional and subdued.

THROUGHOUT THE TEN YEARS of my marriage to Cordell, I gradually peeled back layer upon layer of this remarkable man, gaining insight into his personality. I stood in awe of him, but I soon came to the realization that I needed to maintain my own independence and not be in his shadow.

Cordell was prescient in his awareness that such situations would disrupt the harmony in our marriage. He acknowledged we were both strong-willed people. In an e-mail dated July 15, 2003, he wrote, "I hope the overwhelming love we have for each other will help guide us through what we know will be other issues, I'm sure we will face as we prepare for an ever-lasting life together. Whatever these issues may be, and we know there will be many, let our love bond us together so that we may converse honestly and fully enjoy each other in body and spirit."

Years later, Cordell and I were able to talk about the incident with the Nelson family. He admitted he was ashamed of his behavior and the grief it caused me. Over the years, Cordell's love for the Nelsons only deepened.

Our mistake was remaining at home and not leaving on a **honeymoon**.

TWENTY-TWO

MARRIAGE TO CORDELL GLAUS MOVING TO GREEN (2003–2010)

T HE CITY OF GREEN, LOCATED IN THE SOUTHEASTERN CORNER of Summit County, midway between Akron and Canton, covers an area of 33.54 square miles. The 2010 census listed the population as 25,943. When I first moved to Green, I observed large farms within the city limits. Why? I was curious.

This area of gently rolling hills and rich farmland contained deposits of coal. Over the years after its founding in 1840, there was a gradual transition from agrarian and mining to business and manufacturing. With the change came population growth. By 1950 farmers were selling their land to residential housing developers. In 1991 Green Township was incorporated as the Village of Green; the following year it became the City of Green.

A small US Post Office building in Greensburg, a hamlet within the city, provided only post-office boxes for residents. Mail delivery within the city was given over to four US post offices—Akron, North Canton, Clinton, and Uniontown, located in contiguous Stark County. It took some explaining that we lived in Green, but our mailing address was Uniontown.

At the time we lived there, the resident population of the city was 95 percent white, 2 percent black, with 3 percent Native American, Asian, and mixed race. Major employers were Diebold, Harry London, Fed Ex, InfoCision, Green Local Schools, YMCA, Target, and the Akron-Canton Regional Airport. There was no Main Street. Most of the services and businesses were located on two parallel north–south arterials—Cleveland Avenue and Arlington Street.

The weather was not too different than what I experienced living in Ashtabula and Lake Counties—ninety-degree temperatures in the summer, single-digit temperatures in the winter. Sun, rain, and wind patterns were similar with one exception—the ever-present day and night cloudy skies. It was here I would make my home with Cordell for the foreseeable future.

OUR CONDO WAS LOCATED in the northeastern quadrant of the city, a densely populated area of town houses, apartment buildings, condo associations, and residential developments. To access our home off of Raber Road, we drove three fourths of a mile up Glen Eagles Parkway, past the Ohio Prestwick Country Club, past a multibuilding apartment complex, past the ten-unit Fairways I condos, to enter the Fairways II seventy-seven-unit condo neighborhood. Our address was 2173 Prestwick Drive, located on the third fairway of the golf course.

The street view of our condo was deceptive as to size. One first noticed a large attached double-car garage that protruded out about twenty feet from the front entrance, located to the left. Our two-level, three-bedroom, three-bath unit had 3,400 square feet of living space. Cordell and I both remarked it was the most luxurious home either one of us had ever owned.

We lived a few miles from the Akron-Canton Airport. Our location along a direct flight path onto the airport's runways was a plus for Cordell. When outside, every time a plane flew over, no matter what he was doing or with whom he was talking, Cordell stopped to watch. Being a small-plane pilot, he enjoyed observing the large planes as they gracefully descended toward the runway or, when taking off, their majestic rise above the billowy clouds, out of sight into the sky.

As soon as we took possession of the condo, Cordell measured all the rooms and drew a floor plan to scale. Previously, Cordell asked me to take measurements of all my large furniture pieces that would be moved. Templates were made, and we discussed furniture placement.

A week after our marriage the movers arrived. Cordell handed the men a drawing of the floor plan with noted furniture placement. As the items were brought in, I became aware that some of the furniture placements we thought would work wouldn't. Amidst all the chaos, I attempted to bring this to Cordell's attention, thinking it best to utilize the muscle of the men. My request fell on deaf ears. It was as it was, and that was it! Cordell could be stubborn as the proverbial mule.

ONE MONTH FOLLOWING OUR MARRIAGE, many boxes yet to be unpacked, Cordell and I left to spend three weeks with Rosemary in Florida. Cordell wrote in his memoir:

> Prior to marriage I had made arrangements with Rosemary to spend the month of November in a condo near where Lois and I had vacationed for many years. I kept that commitment and the three of us spent a relaxing three weeks at Seaside near Panama City Beach.

That was Cordell's take on our trip; mine was different.

There was much to be done at home. However, Cordell felt a strong obligation to keep his commitment with Rosemary, and I understood his sibling loyalty. We left on November 7, driving first to Valparaiso, Indiana, to attend my stepgrandson's bar mitzvah. From there we drove to Seaside Village, located near Destin on the Miracle Strip in northwestern Florida.

Rosemary was there to greet us. Our second-floor, two-bedroom condo was located on the waterfront. Seated on our deck, we could see for miles along the sparkling white-sand beaches and look out over the shimmering blue ocean. We swam in the private pool for Seaside guests, enjoyed the clear night skies, gazing at the stars and identifying some of the constellations—my all-time favorites Orion, the Gemini Twins, and Cassiopeia's Chair. We took long walks on the beach, bicycled, and dined in area restaurants enjoying our fill of fresh-caught fish. We spent evenings in the condo preparing meals in the efficiency kitchen, played cards, and read.

Weather patterns varied. There were days of pleasant temperatures and sunshine, and days with strong winds, rain, and high humidity. The worst were the winds out of the north that brought the small pesky, biting flies. We found the flies particularly aggravating when in the swimming pool.

Days passed. It wasn't all harmony among the three of us. We had brought Cupid on the honeymoon, and with it came a change in our relationship. Rosemary was the intermediary that brought us together. Now married, we no longer needed her as the go-between in our relationship. In fact, her presence created disharmony. We were a threesome, and if two of us went off together, the third was left out. Rosemary felt it most acutely. Cordell and I wanted to be alone. I tried scheduling a lunch with Rosemary as in the old days, but Cordell felt left out. Her presence affected our intimacy, to the point where Cordell found another condo we could rent for the duration of our stay. Even I could see the folly in this and advised against it, pointing out it would be devastating to Rosemary.

Cordell and I had made arrangements to spend Thanksgiving with my stepson George and wife Rita in Thibodaux, Louisiana. The family wanted to meet Cordell, and Rita planned an open house during our stay. We invited Rosemary to join us; she refused the invitation. We were gone for five days, and when we returned on November 29, Rosemary had left.

On November 30, the rental lease was up. We packed and left, headed the Dodge Durango north, and arrived home on December 2 to rooms filled with unpacked boxes—silent sentinels awaiting our return.

The circumstances that fractured the relationship Rosemary and I shared were devastating to me. I wrote and expressed my regrets. It took time, but Cupid eventually resumed her role as Cordell's sister and accepted me as her sister-in-law.

———— ·+++++·· ————

AS SOON AS THE BOXES WERE UNPACKED, I started to make plans for minor interior decorating in the condo. Fortunately, the "scalded milk" wall paint color used throughout was to our liking. But Cordell made it known he wanted to be involved in all interior decorating decisions. That was new to me, as all previous husbands had no interest and allowed me total freedom to decorate as I liked. It took time, but in the end, I developed a level of verbal skill in presenting ideas so that the end result would be to my liking.

The walls of the wide stairwell to the lower level were Cordell's place of choice to hang his favorite paintings. One walked down seven steps to a landing, turned abruptly left and down another seven steps to enter a large recreation room. Cordell placed an extension ladder on the landing and, while I held my breath and assisted, hung the first paintings near the ceiling, working his way down, filling the entire stairwell wall area with his paintings of lighthouses and nature scenes.

The foyer was the perfect place for the Howard Miller grandfather clock. The wall areas of the cavernous living room, with the cathedral ceiling, were used to display memorabilia from our travels. One area was given over to items from China. The focal point of this display was an impressionist painting of the Great Wall. In another area of the room, Cordell's harpsichord was placed next to a wall. Here he hung his cornet, bugle, and a balalaika brought from Russia. My rolltop desk was positioned on the "pony" wall, separating the living room from the stairwell and foyer. Here, Cordell's triptych three-season painting was displayed.

Pictures of ancestors and present-day family members were used to decorate walls throughout the condo. The kitchen and dining room were one long, open space. We purchased a screen divider and positioned it to make a visual barrier between the two rooms. I painted the bare side of the divider with a magnetic paint and, using magnetic frames, was able to showcase current snapshots. However, this presented a challenge. I had to keep the display up to date so that whenever family members or friends came to visit they could find at least one picture of themselves on the display board.

The lower level recreation room and bar area were not neglected. Here Cordell hung a large three-by-two-foot Don Drumm wooden sculpture. The bar area showcased his Portage Hills Winery awards—ribbons, medallions, and framed newspaper articles.

I moved often enough to know it was necessary to discard old furniture and buy new. Cordell had taken the room off of the entry foyer as his office—a showplace with sliding glass pocket doors, solid cherry cabinets lining two of the walls, and an expansive three-sectioned picture window on the fourth wall. Cordell had a bare-bones pine desk, hardly the right fit for this stately room. He needed a new desk, and he found one at a nearby furniture store. The two-pedestal solid-cherry executive desk, with a veneer top of birds'-eye finish, was the right fit.

We moved two households of furniture into the rooms of the condo. It took a few years, but I finally came to the realization that some of my furniture could go. My granddaughter Candice had recently moved into a new home and had the space to accommodate what I termed family heirloom pieces. In 2009 Bruce came to visit for the purpose of building large shipping crates to hold the furniture. He knew my fear that items might be stolen when using a commercial mover. (This happened in 1977 when Allan and I moved from Lemoyne, Pennsylvania, to Las Vegas, Nevada.)

The cherry dining room set, along with other pieces of furniture, filled three "big ass boxes," seven by four by four feet. My nephew, Kirk Peine, made arrangements for the boxes to be shipped with Landstar, the company with which he held a franchise. Two weeks after the date the crates were loaded on a truck, Bruce telephoned to say they had arrived, and when unpacked, all items were in pristine condition. That year Candice and Will hosted a family Christmas dinner. Bruce's comment warmed my heart. "When I walked into the dining room Mom, it felt like home on Vineland Avenue in Ashtabula."

With my dining room set gone, the sunroom, with windows on the north and east walls, provided a place with good light for Cordell to paint. He purchased a replica of a commodore's desk and positioned it on the north wall. This became his sanctuary for painting.

Within the first year, we identified needed interior as well as exterior changes. The condo faced west, and the brutal summer sun made the office unbearable. Condo rules prohibited installing an awning. Cordell read of a film applied over window glass that would reduce the heat gain from direct sunlight. A contractor who advertised this as his specialty was contacted. He applied the film over the glass of ten windows on the main floor. It gave only minimal relief from the intense summer heat.

Cordell and I planned to age gracefully in our new home, and to that end, we needed to remodel our three bathrooms. This required removing carpet, installing tile floors, ADA toilets, faucets with handles, and grab bars on the tub and in the showers. The large Jacuzzi remained the white elephant in the master bathroom. The tub was big, allowing the water to cool too rapidly to enjoy taking a bath. I literally crawled over the side and into the tub to clean it. I detested that Jacuzzi.

Originally, I took the room off of the recreation room for my office. We had many overnight guests and soon realized we needed another bedroom. Amidst the dust and dirt created with the remodeling of the lower-level bathroom, carpet was removed from an area in the recreation room and a laminate floor installed. This was to be my new office. I liked it. My former office was converted to a bedroom, providing our guests with total privacy.

A wall divided the dining room/kitchen area from the living room. A large, rectangular opening provided access between the rooms. Here Cordell's creativity came to the fore. He designed, and a contractor installed, an enclosure for the opening using four oak doors mounted on a sliding mechanism. Each door contained fifteen clear glass lights, thirteen by six and three quarter inches each. Cordell removed five of the lights from two of the doors and made sketches of scenes from our marriage at Viking Vineyards, our travels, our bicycling, and his interest in viticulture. He knew a craftsman skilled in glass etching and entrusted him to etch the designs onto the ten lights. The doors with the etched glass lights added an artistic touch to the wall enclosure.

We moved into the condo fall of 2003. The following spring, I noted the deck required attention. Thinking the maintenance would be relatively easy, I took a wire brush and, scraper in hand, prepared to clean away the chipped surface areas, only to find the wood had deteriorated. The deck needed to be replaced.

There was no stair connecting the deck to the lower brick patio. Realizing the deck needed to be replaced, Cordell designed a stair to connect the two levels. When installed, the spiral metal staircase took on the appearance of a black curling sculpture rising out of the patio.

Wanting to avoid future deck maintenance, we selected a Trex composite material. Again, condo rules gave us little choice in color, and we settled on a rustic red, not to our liking. We named it the "dog bite deck." The previous fall, while on one of our country-road bike rides, a dog ran out, passed Cordell by, and took a bite out of my left leg. Fortunate for me, the owner provided proof that the dog had all required shots. Unfortunate for me, the bite did not heal properly and required treatment by a wound specialist. Cordell kept meticulous records of all medical expenses. We hoped the owner's insurance would cover medical costs of about $2,000. When the insurance adjuster telephoned and asked if we would settle for $16,000, I had difficulty controlling myself not to blurt out, "That is too much!" I signed the check. It covered the cost of our new deck.

Living alongside a golf course presented its own challenges. Until the deck was replaced, we had always been fortunate to be far enough from the tee that erratic slices did not dent our aluminum siding or, worse yet, break one of the windows. Our enjoyment was in watching the golfers as they teed off, critiquing their shots as they moved up the fairway. Building code required deck rail height to be thirty-six inches. When seated, the top of the new deck rail obstructed our view. This became a major annoyance.

We took care of the problem by purchasing a metal pub table with chairs. Now when seated, we were above the rail and had a clear view of the fairway. We further enhanced the deck by installing a retractable awning that protected us from the sun and the rain.

An eight-foot-high wooden wall served as a privacy divider between our deck and our roofmate's deck. Cordell visualized hanging a Don Drumm, two-dimensional metal sculpture to beautify the dull brown wooden wall. I agreed and visualized that sculpture to be an iconic Don Drumm sunburst. At the studio, Cordell spied a sculpture of Icarus almost hidden from view in a far corner of the outdoor display area—the perfect choice.

Lawn care was the responsibility of the association; condo owners were responsible for the planting areas around their unit. The previous owners were guilty of gross neglect in this area. The first two years we lived there were spent cleaning out the overgrown Hosta and daylily vegetation. In its place we planted annuals—impatiens, petunias, marigolds, zinnias, poppies, and geraniums. The constant watering and weeding caused our enthusiasm to wane and soon gave over to using more mulch and planting fewer flowers.

A small garden beneath the condo's front window was filled with shrubs. We laid a stepping-stone walk to enhance the area. The concrete plant near us had a large display of decorative lawn items—large urns, bird baths, figurines, and small animals. Driving by one day, I saw a statue of the David. I had seen Michelangelo's famous statue in the Academia Gallery in Florence, Italy, and I wanted this replica for our garden. Cordell bought it for me. We were somewhat cheeky placing it in our shrub garden and planting colorful flowers and ivy at its feet. To anyone who had the audacity to make a snide comment our retort was, "At least his private parts are covered with a fig leaf."

Residents of the Fairways II Condos were primarily Caucasian and retired. Couples had raised their families, wearied of home maintenance responsibilities, and preferred spending winter months in a warmer climate. Cordell and I fit the profile of the first two statements, but not the third. We liked the cold weather.

We gradually became acquainted with our neighbors. Our roofmate was overly friendly, causing us to be cautious regarding any social involvement with her. The neighbors on the other side were of Italian descent. When Chuck learned that Cordell owned the Portage Hills Winery, he invited us over to sample his wine. Offered a glass of Dago Red, I accepted. The alcohol content had to be twice that of commercial wines. With Cordell's help, I staggered home.

We were frequent dinner guests of Al and Juanita Moutz, Cordell's friends whom I had previously met. Al and Juanita spent their winters in Clearwater, Florida, and in 2005 invited us to join them. We rented a four-pedal surrey bicycle, lost money at the dog races, swam, walked, talked, and ate, ate, ate—good friends, good times. The visit was delightful.

One couple who lived several condos to the south of us enjoyed playing board games—Rummikub and Dominoes were the favorites. We scheduled game afternoons with them on a biweekly basis. It didn't take us long to realize that the husband was arrogant, thoughtless, and a bore. His wife had been diagnosed with Parkinson's disease, and her husband's lack of patience made us very uncomfortable. It took a few months, but we did phase out our times together. The wife had remarked that, as a couple, they never spoke unkind words or argued. I understood why—she was the obedient half in the marriage.

Gwen and Pete purchased a condo across from us in 2008. Pete was a man's man, and Cordell was immediately drawn to him. Pete expressed an interest in learning how to make wine, and Cordell obligingly assumed the mentor role. It took time, but the men's friendship reached out to include the wives, and the four of us enjoyed social times together.

When we first met Chuck Schutte and Sue Kurtz, we wondered if they were married, having different surnames. We soon learned that Chuck and Sue were, indeed, married, and we shared a common link—the anniversary date of our wedding, October 11. We enjoyed their company, and for years we celebrated our mutual anniversary date together.

I availed myself of all opportunities to meet neighbors. There were social activities for the women—scheduled monthly luncheons and afternoons spent playing board games. At first, I felt out of place, having little in common, but as time passed, I gradually developed a feeling of belonging.

WE EACH SETTLED INTO OUR NEW LIFESTYLE. Knowingly, or unknowingly, we took to heart the advice of Kahlil Gibran writing in *The Prophet* on "Love and Marriage:" "Stand together, yet not too near together… For the oak and the cypress grow not in each other's shadow."

We did "stand together," for we had common interests, but to "grow not in each other's shadow" meant we must pursue our own interests. We both enjoyed reading. We subscribed to two newspapers—the *Akron Beacon Journal* and the *Cleveland Plain Dealer*. Our breakfasts were eaten in silence while we read articles, editorials, and the columns of favorite pundits George Will, David Brooks, William Safire, and Charles Krauthammer. *CPD* columnists Connie Schultz and Dick Feagler were particularly dear to us. Connie hailed from Ashtabula and was a voice for the underdog and underprivileged. In 2005 she was awarded the Pulitzer prize for Commentary. Dick Feagler's writings were honest and feisty. In one column he ridiculed the widespread promotion of Viagra writing, "All a man needs is a fifteen-second hug from the right woman."

As much as we enjoyed our togetherness in the silent reading of the morning papers, it was surpassed by our morning coffee enjoyed in our lower-level garden room. Here we took on the roles of reader/listener. I enjoyed reading out loud, and Cordell enjoyed listening. A collection of 365 short writings in a booklet, *Acts of Faith* authored by Iyanla Vanzant, provided a daily meditative reading that sparked self-examination and philosophical discussions.

Throughout his life, Cordell had read little poetry. My enjoyment of poetry was limited, but I introduced him to two of my favorite poets— Robert Frost and Emily Dickinson. Frost's poems were easy to read, and we identified with the agrarian simplicity evidenced in his poems.

Many evenings at home were given over to playing games. Cordell had brought his bumper-pool table from Mogadore. With Cordell's patient instruction, I acquired a minimal amount of skill in handling a cue stick. I lost more games than I won.

We spent hours seated at the game table playing Scrabble. Thinking back to my childhood, I rarely bested my brother in any game played. Rather than hang in there and learn, I gave up and was a poor loser. One night I lost to Cordell big time in a Scrabble game. Cordell opened and formed a word with his seven tiles, immediately earning fifty extra points. In follow-up draws, he had a gold mine of tiles—a blank, X, Q, U, and Z. He formed words and played them on spaces that gave double or triple points. I threw a major snit. Ridiculous! It was only a game! Later I apologized for my childish tantrum. The pleasure I got from the hours we spent together playing games far outweighed the fact that I usually lost.

We both realized we must remain physically active to minimize the effects of aging. We walked, and we bicycled. In our basement recreation room was a Concept 2 rowing machine, a stationary bicycle, and a treadmill. We used them all. Three mornings a week we would rise early, drive to the nearby YMCA, and were at the natatorium door when it was unlocked by the life guard at 6:00 a.m. This worked for a time, but we wearied of the antics of the early-morning swimmers who rushed in to take control of a lane. In truth, we realized, as retirees, we could swim anytime during the day. This didn't work for us; we gave up swimming.

We attended a variety of local events. The Akron soapbox derby held a fascination for me but not for Cordell. He had seen it in years past and remarked it wasn't very exciting. I insisted, and Cordell took me to Derby Downs. As I sat there watching the racers roll down the hill, I understood Cordell's lack of enthusiasm. We had no vested interest in any of the competitors, and to me it was as boring as watching grass grow or paint dry.

The Christmas season came, and with it extravagant light shows. In the local paper we read of the Penguin Park light exhibit in a neighborhood near us. One night we drove slowly past the two houses where the fully lit exhibit was displayed. Christmas music blared from the loudspeakers, Mr. and Mrs. Santa Claus, sleigh and reindeer, elves, and Disney characters filled two adjacent lawn areas. The main attraction was a roller coaster with penguins seated in the cars. The exhibit was short-lived—only two seasons. The neighbors got up a petition to have it closed down, citing too much traffic congestion in a residential area.

Cordell introduced me to First Night. It is a family friendly event that takes place in downtown Akron featuring the region's best in music, dance, theater, and the arts. Brenda joined us for many of these New Year's Eve celebrations.

Cordell and I both enjoyed movies. We discovered the Cleveland Cedar Lee Art Theater and for several years drove the fifty miles into Cleveland to see foreign films, independent films, and documentaries not available in regular theaters. The Regal Theater was located about five miles from our condo, close enough for us to ride our bicycles. There I saw my all-time favorite movie, *The Bucket List*, with Jack Nicholson and Morgan Freeman.

There were many venues for live theater, and we took advantage of several. Whenever my niece, Beverley Schumann, was in a production at the Ashtabula Art Center, we were there. The Carousel Dinner Theater was close to us. Cordell and I, with his children Kent and Janet, Diane and Doug, had season tickets to Sunday matinee performances. Sadly, the theater closed and with it the opportunity for family camaraderie.

Attending the Saturday night performances of the Cleveland Orchestra at Blossom Music Center was a highlight of our summers. Cordell and I would pack our small garden cart with a picnic supper, wine, self-inflating sleeping pads, and blankets. We were the first through the gate to claim a prime viewing spot on the lawn. As the sun sank in the west, and we heard the discordant sounds of the instruments being tuned up, we would lie back on our comfortable pads, cover ourselves with a blanket, gaze up at the stars, and let the melodic strains of the music envelope us. When the season ended, we were at a loss as to what to do come Saturday night.

One day I read in the *Akron Beacon Journal* a review by art critic Kerry Clawson of a performance at the Actors' Summit Theater in the nearby city of Hudson. She gave an outstanding review of the musical *Quilters,* based on diaries written by women pioneers. Cordell and I attended the show, and we were hooked. Actors' Summit Theater catered to the white-hair crowd. Historical narratives and musicals came to life on their stage. When the Hudson venue closed, and they replicated their intimate theater in the round on the sixth floor of the majestic Greystone Building, formerly the Masonic Temple in Akron, we were there.

I attended the play *Menopause*, at the Hannah Theater in Cleveland four times. I saw it for the first time in 2004, with Diane and Janet. I went again with several other women, Brenda among them. Each time I went, I came home laughing and relating to Cordell some of the antics of the show.

My enthusiasm piqued his interest. He wanted to see it and made it a theater party by inviting his three children and their spouses to join us. I was disappointed our seats were in the back of the theater, making it difficult to hear the dialogue and songs. During the performance the Glaus men were discombobulated, not understanding why the women roared with laughter. They couldn't relate to the innuendos of food cravings, hot flashes, memory loss, nocturnal sweats, and sexual predicaments. They were good sports but left totally mystified. Isn't that life? What man does understand the woman's torment of menopause?

We were members of the Akron Art Museum, but visits were infrequent. We were frequent visitors to the Columbus Art Museum only because my friend, Susan Gardner, was an art aficionado. The memory of seeing the Dwayne Hansen special exhibit of life-size stuffed human figures remains with me. Cordell and I were meandering in and out of the various exhibit rooms. I exited one of the rooms into the hallway and saw a man seated on a chair holding a camera, poised to take a picture. Not wanting to obstruct his line of vision, I stood there waiting and listening for the shutter click. I waited, and I waited, and suddenly the shutter click was in my brain. He wasn't real; he was one of the Hansen stuffed figures. The date might as well have been April 1, for Dwayne Hansen played the quintessential April Fool caper—he got me!

We both served on the condo board of directors. As soon as we were semisettled in our home, at the first opportunity, Cordell had his name placed on the ballot and was elected for a two-year term. (Board terms were set for two or three years to ensure continuity in board membership.) He was assigned the responsibility of condo maintenance. When his term was up, he opted to run again. This time, he encouraged me to place my name on the ballot. There were openings for two three-year terms. Cordell was elected by a wide margin; the other person elected resigned before taking office. By default, I filled the open seat. This time, Cordell was assigned the office of treasurer; I was assigned secretarial duties. The positions were equally demanding of one's time. I found board politics to be frustrating and infuriating—irate residents ever ready with the complaint, but never a compliment from the silent majority.

As board secretary I was in a position to appoint and oversee the committee responsible for planning and promoting condo socials. Our lower-level garden room and large patio area were an ideal venue for these. By all accounts they were a success, bringing residents together to imbibe, eat, renew old acquaintances, and make new ones.

When our terms were up, Cordell was encouraged to run again, but the president of the board discouraged me from placing my name on the ballot. It caused too much controversary for a husband-wife team to serve together on the board. My efforts to bring a modicum of organization to the office of secretary went unrecognized. I was cast aside, and it hurt.

We lived in Green for several years before making any effort to connect with a church. Our first attempt was to attend services at The Chapel, a nearby nondenominational church. We liked the pastor's messages, but we found the jazzy orchestral music that reverberated throughout the cavernous sanctuary jarring to our ears. When we learned of a monthly luncheon sponsored by the church, we became regular attendees. We enjoyed the lunch and found Pastor Paul's talks to be practical and applicable to daily living—"Don't Sweat the Small Stuff," "Watch Your Tongue," and "Watch Who You Associate With" are just a few examples. One message I'll never forget. Pastor Paul's wife joined him, and as a couple, they spoke on "Marriage and Family Responsibilities." Pastor Paul spoke first. His wife, a fashionably dressed slender middle-aged woman rose to speak. I paraphrase one of her comments: Wives, invest in your underwear and you invest in your marriage. Keep your role as his sex partner top of your priority list.

Cordell and I were not prudes, but we both agreed she should have been more delicate in presenting her thoughts. Whatever the reasons, the following year the Table Talk luncheons were canceled, and within a short span of time, there was a new senior pastor for the church.

After our disappointing experience with The Chapel, Cordell suggested we attend the Mogadore Methodist Church where he and Lois were active members for more than fifty years. The first Sunday we attended as a couple, Cordell felt warmly received. I missed having a church affiliation and, without hesitation, transferred my membership from the Madison Chapel Hill Church to the Mogadore Methodist Church.

———— ⁺⁺⁺⁺⁺ ————

It was through bicycling we met, and bicyclists we remained. The lower-level, three-season garden room with sliding-door access to the patio was the ideal storage place for our four bicycles. Cordell did not like riding the stoker seat of the tandem, and neither did I. I sold it to my Columbus friends, Jody and Bob. My Bike Friday—a collapsible bicycle that can be packed in its custom suitcase—presented a challenge to sell. When single, I purchased it with the idea of checking it as luggage when I traveled by plane. I advertised it in the newsletter of the Cleveland Bicycle Club. I had one inquiry from a woman who planned to bicycle with her husband in France. That was all I needed. She came to my home, test rode the bicycle, and bought it.

Cordell rode a heavy Giant bicycle, and I rode a Bike Friday. We both traded for ten-speed, aluminum-frame Trek road bikes. The four bicycles we had owned were now reduced to two.

The bike trails and streets of Summit and Portage Counties were ideal, scenic, low-traffic roads for cyclists. Cordell and I explored many of them. Riding the towpath trail in the Cuyahoga Valley National Park, we spotted several deer grazing by the side of the trail. We stopped, I took out our camera, handed it to Cordell, and he captured a picture of two deer in graceful flight, clearing the white fence bordering the bike trail.

It is a saying among bicyclists, "We ride to eat." Two of our favorite ride destinations were the Arabica Coffee Shop in Hartville for scones and coffee, and Lindsey's Restaurant in the Lakemore Shopping Mall where the chef made the best BLT of any restaurant in the area. On a ride to the

Arabica, we passed Sunflower Road, where tall blooming sunflowers had been planted around the signpost. When riding to Lindsey's, we passed a road with the signpost Henrietta Street—both scenes captured with a click of our digital camera.

Another saying among bicyclists, "If you don't have to stop and pee every hour, you are not drinking enough water." I had no problem with that, for no matter what the length of a ride, I carried two, sixteen-ounce water bottles. For Cordell, it was another matter. He drank very little water on our rides. One extremely hot afternoon, two miles from our home, Cordell stopped and falteringly toppled off of his bicycle. Alarmed, I rushed to his aid as he fell. I helped him stretch out under the shade of a tree, saturated two bandannas with water, placed one on his forehead, the other around his neck. He sipped water, rested, and recovered enough to bike home.

I had two bicycle happenings that could have meant disaster. One, when making a left-hand turn crossing a lane of traffic, I failed to note a car approaching from the rear. Fortunately, the driver was alert and swerved to miss me. Cordell was following, later telling me my life passed before his eyes in that moment. The other occurred when I rode up Glen Eagles Boulevard. I momentarily took my eyes off the broken pavement to glance at the azure blue sky. The front wheel of my bike slipped into a wide crack, thrusting my body forward and sending me crashing headfirst onto the concrete surface. Miraculously, I sustained no serious injury; my helmet saved my head, and no bones were broken.

My biking companion in Europe, Al Olson, had ridden Going-to-the-Sun Road in Montana's Glacier National Park. When I expressed an interest, but also my reservations about having the needed strength and stamina to achieve this arduous feat, Al assured me I could do it. The summer of 2003, I had registered for the ride with Backroads Tours. Plans dramatically changed when I met Cordell.

Now married and living in Green, my dream to bicycle Going-to-the-Sun Road remained with me. I persuaded Cordell we could do this together. While riding in 2004, we searched for challenging hills in our area. Not far distant on Mayfair Road was a half-mile hill with a 4 percent grade, which had a short 8 percent challenge near the top. The first time we drove the hill in our van, I remarked to Cordell, "There's a hill I want to ride." Cordell told me I was nuts. Now well into our training, he could ride the hill faster than I and be waiting for me at the top.

We were in Kalispell on August 5, 2005, and joined six other riders with Backroads Tours, all eager to conquer Going-to-the-Sun Road. The road was closed to vehicular traffic between the hours of 7:00 to 11:00 a.m. That gave us four hours to reach the summit. I set my bicycle odometer at zero. We started at an elevation of 2,984 feet with a 6 percent grade that increased sharply to 8 percent at Logan Pass. Cordell and I paced ourselves as we negotiated the many switchbacks. We knew muscles would tire, the atmospheric pressure would change, making our breathing more difficult. We stopped at every scenic overview. The vistas were majestic—sparkling waterfalls, acres of forest, mountain glacier peaks, and sculptured valleys. I persevered, and when I made the final turn, there was Logan Pass a few hundred feet ahead. Exhausted, arm and leg muscles burning, I kept repeating to myself, "One more pedal turn, one more pedal turn..." I crossed the Continental Divide at an elevation of 6,646 feet. I'd conquered the 21.5 miles of the climb.

Exhausted, I found a place to sit, drank water, sucked on oranges, and devoured a sandwich prepared by our tour guide. Once rested, I fell in line behind Cordell as we started the perilous ride down. We were warned not to continuously hold tight to our brake levers, but to occasionally let up during the descent. Brake pads could create a heat buildup on the rims resulting in a tire blowout. I found it a delicate balance between hold and release to control my speed, all the while feeling and hearing the wind whistling past my helmet. Need I add, I felt immense relief when I safely reached the bottom? I had successfully completed the most challenging ride of my bicycling experience.

<hr />

As Kahlil Gibran had written, "the oak and the cypress grow not in each other's shadow." Cordell did stand apart from me in pursuing his interests, and in so doing I benefitted from his creative talents.

He adapted a basement area where he could make wine. Cordell used six-gallon glass carboys for fermenting the juice. They were heavy, and when it was necessary to rack (siphon from one container to the next), he would ask for my help. When the wine was ready to bottle, I assisted. That was the extent of my involvement in enology. But I showed no hesitation when it came to drinking this fruit of the vine.

Being both a viticulturist and an enologist, Cordell knew and understood the vocabulary of body, crisp, finish, fruity, oaky, or tannic when discussing a wine. But in his vernacular, a wine was either dry or off-dry (semisweet); the wine had good legs (body) or it didn't; he either liked it or he didn't. I regret that I did not take the time to benefit from his knowledge and learn the art of winemaking.

Alcoholic beverages were verboten in my childhood home. In fact, I had a fear of alcohol, and it was not until married that I learned anything about alcoholic drinks. Sidney was a beer drinker; I didn't like the taste. Allan drank bourbon, and I developed a liking for Manhattan cocktails. Charlie enjoyed scotch, so I switched to scotch highballs. With Cordell, I associated wine with relaxation and enjoyed the evening hour when we sipped our favorite white or red wine. This I knew for certain: I would never drink to excess, as I liked the taste, not the effect.

Cordell would spend hours at his painting table in the sunroom. The romantic Cordell would paint a special Valentine for me each year. Brenda called it to my attention that we did not have any good pictures of our family's farmhouse. She planned to approach a local artist and ask him to render a painting for her. It was then the thought entered my mind that Cordell might consider doing this for the family.

I asked, and he agreed. During the process, he allowed me the rare privilege of looking at his preliminary sketches. In doing so, I requested he include the barn and the outhouse in the painting. To do this he needed better photographs, and with that purpose in mind, we drove to Ashtabula County, visited the farm on Maple Road, and took the needed pictures.

The painting was almost done. I noted the clothesline, the willow tree, our farm dog, Teddy, and the cow my dad pastured in the front yard to keep the grass from becoming a hayfield were missing. Cordell agreed to include all but the cow. His artistic sensitivity would not allow him to include this animal in the painting, believing it would destroy his work. My gentle persuasion compelled him to compromise. He would not place the cow in the front yard; he would paint it to the side of the house near the willow tree.

Cordell learned of a giclée process—a technology using a high-quality inkjet printer that reproduced an image so perfect, only a practiced eye could tell the difference between the original and a reproduction. We had giclée reproductions made of the farmhouse and distributed them to interested family members. The original hangs over the fireplace in our home.

Cordell painted scenes from our wedding—the Viking Vineyards hospitality party building, the lake with the swans Dream Catcher and Tantalizer, and the lakeside trees dressed in their fall red and golden colors.

Visits to Las Vegas were captured on Cordell's canvas—a painting of Bruce and Linda's home, the marinas on Lake Mead, and the Lake Mead

Wishing Well. The large outcrops of red sandstone nestled among gray and tan limestone were captured by Cordell in a series of six paintings, scenes from the Valley of Fire State Park north of Las Vegas.

Three original stained glass windows were found in the attic storage area of the Mogadore Methodist Church. Cordell's design talents were tapped by a church committee when he was asked to design a placement holder for the windows to be installed on a wall in the overflow room off of the sanctuary. He agreed but expressed great frustration during the process. Returning home one evening, after making a design presentation, he blurted out in exasperation, "I'd forgotten how much insipid talk, lack of focus could take place in committee work."

Cordell's talent for creative writing was evidenced in his short stories. Ma Nelson gave me a small brown suit worn by Sidney when he was three years old. Both of Sidney's boys, Vernon and Bruce, wore it. With the help of Bruce and Linda, we managed to get my grandson Bruce Allan, screaming and fighting, into the suit. Granted he wore it only long enough for father Bruce to take his picture. I had the suit framed and attempted to write the suit's story. Cordell read what I had written and asked if he could revise it. He rewrote my version and, in personifying the suit, enabled it to tell its own story in the vignette "The Little Brown Suit"—a remarkable, creative piece of writing.

In the winter of 2006, Cordell observed a bird perched on the railing of our deck, and he wrote about it in "A Message for Henrietta:"

> Thursday December 7, 2006 a wise owl sat on the deck railing of Henri's and Cordell's home in Green, Ohio.
>
> After a few moments of observation by Henri and Cordell, it flew away. Three hours later they looked onto the snow covered deck and observed three large bird feathers mounted vertically in a neat row in the snow. No track, human, bird, or animal was visible.
>
> Friday December 8, 2006, exactly 24 hours later, Henri and Cordell observed that the three feathers had disappeared.
>
> Again, there were no traces of tracks, human, bird, or animal.
>
> For believers of omens, it could be:

The spirit of Henri's three previous husbands rode on the feathers and visited Henri at her home with Cordell. They were accompanied by the wise owl, who said to Henri, "You have been very wise again, having chosen a fourth mate."

Shortly after we were married, I sold my Dodge Durango, and we purchased a Dodge Grand Caravan. About the same time Cordell sold his Mercury Grand Marquis, and we bought a red, convertible Chrysler PT Cruiser. We named our new vehicles Snazzy (convertible) and Smoothy (van) and installed vanity license plates. One day Cordell drove the van to a local shopping center, parked, and upon return to the vehicle noted a man giving it a good look-over. As Cordell approached, the inquisitive person asked how he liked it, to which Cordell replied, "I like it so much I named it Smoothy." The stranger's retort was quite clever. "Oh, I noticed your license plate, and I didn't know if that referred to the driver or the vehicle." Needless to say, it made a good story for my handsome white-haired husband to relate to his friends.

Cordell melded his talents and interests into our new lifestyle with ease. For me, the challenge was minimally successful. My resolve for independence weakened shortly after our marriage when I made the decision to change my surname to Glaus. Soon after Charlie died, I appeared before a magistrate in Columbus and had my name legally changed from Henrietta S. Dickie-Gass to Henrietta S. Nelson, vowing never to change it again. I should never have said **never**.

Prior to marriage, I discussed with Cordell my desire to keep the Nelson name. As I recall he readily agreed, making the comment, "It might be best to have only one Mrs. Cordell R. Glaus." Once married, I sensed confusion by family and friends. Were we Mr. and Mrs. Cordell Glaus? Cordell Glaus and Henrietta Nelson? Or some form of both? Another heartfelt talk with Cordell, and together we arrived at the decision there would be a second Mrs. Cordell R. Glaus. For the fourth time in my life, I went through the onerous name-change process, contacting government agencies, financial institutions, businesses, etc.—something in our culture a man is not required to do.

Cordell and I each brought our pianos. We envisioned playing duets. It never happened. I attempted to continue my enjoyment in playing the piano, but that didn't work either. I brought my telescope. The ever-present cloudy skies thwarted my interest. The telescope remained in the box. My lifestyle was changing and, with it, other demands placed on my time.

My first attempt to join a book club was at the local library. I attended their meeting, and other than a few slight nods, no other effort was made to welcome me. The discussion leader was absent. Any attempt made to discuss the current book soon dwindled into a casual conversation among friends. I never went back.

A group of women with the Akron Art Museum opted to formalize their book discussion group and opened it to interested persons. I joined and found the women to be friendly, knowledgeable, insightful, and articulate. I learned a lot about art. One book I thought would hold no interest for me, *Just My Type*, authored by Simon Garfield, was about fonts. This book was so engrossing it was difficult to put down.

I wanted to learn photography skills in relation to digital storage and printing. This was more my interest than Cordell's, but he registered both of us for a three-week Saturday morning Photoshop class at Stark State Junior College. The learning curve was steep. When the class ended, I was more confused than before. I called the instructor and asked if he could recommend someone willing to come to my home and provide one-on-one instruction. Much to my surprise, he stated a willingness to be my tutor. Through his patient teaching, I gained a basic understanding of how to set up files, save photos, and use basic Photoshop tools. To this day, I continue to be flummoxed with the complexity of it all.

Fortunately, I had basic sewing skills, and I used them when making window coverings, for upholstery projects, and baby quilts for Glaus great-grandchildren.

Cordell's interests took untold hours of his time. In truth, I was relieved to have the freedom to pursue my few interests apart from my husband.

———— ✦✦✦✦✦ ————

Family remained at the center of our lives. Cordell was supportive of me in both joyful and sorrowful events that involved my families. My stepson Darren Gass became a man in a bar mitzvah celebration, and we were there. My granddaughter Candice was married in Las Vegas, and we were there.

My stepson George Dickie telephoned to tell me he had been diagnosed with Parkinson's disease. Stepson Royce Fincher died unexpectedly in California. The last of the five Nelson siblings, Evelyn Nelson Brandenburg, also died in California. The urn containing her cremains was sent to Ashtabula for interment in the Nelson plot at Edgewood Cemetery. With Cordell's help, I arranged a service honoring my dear Nin. We kept relationships intact with visits to family members in California, Indiana, Michigan, Nevada, Pennsylvania, and Virginia. Through it all, Cordell was by my side.

Cordell's three children were equally accepting of me. I felt like a bride on display when we hosted a family dinner for his children on January 3, 2004. Cordell couldn't understand my nervousness. Entertaining his children and grandchildren was commonplace for him, but not for me.

Fifteen of us were seated around our two tables in the dining room/sunroom area. I served an apricot chicken casserole, rice, sautéed green beans, Waldorf salad, and key lime pie. Even though I sat down to eat, I couldn't taste the food. I was too nervous. It must have been okay, for the proof was in the eating and Cordell later complimented me on the tasty dinner. Later an older grandson told his Papa that he resented being placed at the kid's table.

Our home became the center for Glaus family dinners. I soon learned how to relax and willingly accepted help with planning, setup, food preparation, and best of all—the cleanup.

As best we could, we took advantage of all opportunities to be with his children—on special event days, weddings, child baptisms, graduations, and funerals. Each event, joyous or sorrowful, enriched our lives.

OVER THE YEARS I was fortunate to make lasting friendships. I took to heart the saying, "Make new friends, but don't forget the old. One is silver, the other is gold." I maintained a strong commitment to stay in touch with friends through cards, letters, telephone calls, and occasional visits. The following gives examples of some of my friends and ways in which I stayed in contact.

I met Clarabel McDonald in the 1960s, when I lived in Kent. No matter my address, we kept a rotating six-month visitation schedule. Through Clarabel, I met her friend, Charlene Barker, who lived within a half mile of me in a townhouse allotment off of Glen Eagles Boulevard. In her later years, Clarabel moved into the Stowe-Kent Retirement Center. Whenever I visited Clarabel, I would take Charlene with me. Charlene had no family, and she voiced the hope I would become her newfound friend. I couldn't, and I felt sad that I couldn't. But I knew time spent with Charlene apart from Cordell would not bode well with my new husband. I limited my involvement with her to visits with our mutual friend Clarabel.

Cordell enjoyed getting to know Sr. Frances Flannigan, whom I met in the 1970s when we were struggling PhD students at Kent State University. Sr. Frances retired and lived with the Sisters of the Humility of Mary near New Bedford, Pennsylvania. We visited her there on the 250-acre farm reconstituted by the order. Sr. Frances was diagnosed with Alzheimer's disease and died a few years later. I was informed of her death and given details of the mass to be held in her honor. I chose not to attend, thinking it best I remember her as she lived. I regret that decision. Had I attended the mass, it would have provided closure on the life of a dear friend.

Susan Gardner was my friend from the 1980s when we were neighbors on East Selby Boulevard in Worthington. Life had moved on for Susan, as it had for me, but we remained fast friends. When I married Cordell, Susan suggested we have a wine-and-cheese reception at her home in Westerville, providing my friends with the opportunity to meet my new husband. Cordell designed the invitation, and we mailed it to friends and acquaintances alike in the Columbus area. Almost all came, some out of curiosity. I know for certain all were impressed with husband number four.

Bill and Ruth Frieden were longtime friends of Cordell, but new friends for me. Bill invited us to their home one evening to play Racehorse Pinochle. I was not a card player and reluctant to join the game, but Bill insisted and took me as his partner. As the game progressed, it was obvious to Bill I wasn't fibbing. I didn't understand the rules, wasn't able to arrange and hold the copious number of cards in my hand. Worst of all, Cordell and Ruth were taking all tricks, infuriating Bill. Fortunately, the evening ended before our nascent friendship imploded.

————— ✦✦✦✦✦ —————

Travel was a stimulating part of our lives. On August 1, 2005, we left in our Dodge Caravan on a thirty-day, accident-free, 6,266-mile western road trip. A highlight of the trip was our bicycle ride in Glacier National Park. We attended a wedding in Spokane, drove south along the scenic coastal highway SR101, headed east to Las Vegas, and stayed several days with the Nelson family. Leaving LV, we drove to Tucson, Arizona, to visit my former Columbus neighbor, Myrtle Kelly—an active, attractive, feisty

103-year-old lady. We left Tucson with plans to stop in Houston, Texas, to visit a niece. From there to Thibodaux, Louisiana, for a short stay with my stepson, George Dickie, and wife Rita.

Mother Nature interrupted our plans. As we entered the state of Texas, we learned of the advancing Hurricane Katrina, aborted all plans, and headed northeast for home. We stayed ahead of the effects of the hurricane until Indianapolis, Indiana, where heavy rains caught up with us. Fatigued from the demands of the hazardous driving, we finally made it to Green. Once home, we uttered a prayer of thanks for a safe journey.

During the years we lived in Green, we were frequent travelers to the West. We made Las Vegas our base of operation, and from there would take sojourns to California to visit members of Allan Dickie's family.

Mother Nature again bedeviled us on our western trip in April 2010. Our reservation home was on a Northwest Airlines flight, transferring in Denver to Akron–Canton. We had taken this flight several times, enjoying the two-hour layover in Denver allowing us time to walk and browse the shops before settling in for the final leg of our journey.

The morning of our departure, Bruce drove us to the McCarran International Airport. Once inside, checked through security, and at our departing gate, we learned there was a two-hour delay of the flight into Denver. This gave us a feeling of great anxiety. Two hours was our cushion of layover time between flights. Once airborne and nearing Denver, the cabin attendant assured us the pilot had been in contact with the airport control tower and the Akron-Canton flight would be held. Arriving at the gate, we were given the courtesy of first to deplane. Cordell and I grabbed our carry-on luggage and rushed to the gate to get our connecting flight, only to find we had arrived five minutes after the fuselage door was closed—not to be reopened. The flight was not held. Disheartened, we stood there and watched as the plane was pushed away from the gate, slowly taxied to the runway, took off, and soared out of sight into the sky.

We placed our names on a stand-by list for the Akron–Canton flight later that night. That afternoon a winter storm came through, so severe the airport was closed. We queued up in line, got our names on another stand-by list, with the hope we would get seats on the flight scheduled for the next morning.

We resigned ourselves to the fact we would be spending the night in the airport. Seat arms could not be lifted to allow a person to stretch out. Cordell and I found a secluded spot, spread our coats on the floor, lay down, and managed to get a few minutes of fitful sleep—one of the longest, most uncomfortable nights in my memory.

Morning came, the storm passed, and the airport reopened. We were at the gate for the scheduled late morning flight to Akron. Our names were not called. Fatigued and hungry, we stood there and watched as another plane was pushed back from the gate and we were not onboard.

The next flight to Akron was scheduled for late that night—another line, another stand-by list, another promise. The third attempt was the charm. We were given assigned seats on the plane and contacted Diane with our 3:00 a.m. arrival time. She was there to greet two disheveled, exhausted, and very disgruntled travelers.

We spent thirty-six hours in the Denver airport, and the physical impact of this perilous adventure surfaced within a week. We both developed severe chest congestion, treated with antibiotics prescribed by our PCP. It could have been worse, but at the time it didn't seem so.

++++++

For as long as I can remember, birthday celebrations held as much excitement as Christmas celebrations. Only birthdays were special; it was my day not to be shared. When I married and had my own family, I continued the traditions set by Mom. Cordell recognized this, and the romantic side of his personality surfaced when he planned special celebrations for me.

In 2005 I was seventy-five. Cordell saw an ad in the *Cleveland Plain Dealer* for a Romantic Weekend at the Ritz Carleton. Unbeknownst to me, he made a reservation for an overnight stay the weekend preceding my April 7 birthday. When I first learned of this, I was shocked, for I could not imagine myself a guest at the toney Ritz Carleton.

We arrived, checked in, and were escorted to our room by a professionally solicitous bellhop. As I entered the room, the first thing I noticed was a large heart shape made of rose petals in the center of the bed. Champagne and chocolates were on the bedside table. I know I was blushing and wondering what this youthful bellhop must be thinking. I enjoyed the luxury of our stay at the Ritz Carleton—delicious cuisine and pampered at every turn.

Cordell, Bruce, and Linda, with the help of Candice, planned a seventy-fifth party that exceeded my wildest dreams. Cordell made arrangements for the celebratory luncheon to be held at the Ohio Prestwick Country

Club. Invitations were mailed, and seventy-six family members and friends came to share my special day.

The Nelson family prepared a PowerPoint presentation showing my life to be in a state of perpetual motion—pictures of my growing-up years, education, husbands, names, homes, families, jobs, and on and on and on. My son could not resist adding a cartoon of a coffee pot plunging down a set of stairs. Admittedly, throughout my life, the demands of daily living created an inner stress buildup. At times this erupted in physical form, revealing a part of my volatile personality that I preferred to keep hidden from public view. The PowerPoint presentation, including the "roast," was informative and entertaining. I think I laughed the loudest of anyone in the room.

Bruce presented me with a handcrafted heart-shaped box, unspeakably beautiful in design, crafted from purple heartwood, satin to the touch, and a soft, purple-reddish hue pleasing to the eye. The celebration ended with the arrival of "Elvis," who entertained the guests with his guitar, singing, gyrations, and biting commentary.

Later Candice presented me with a photograph album containing cards, messages, and memorabilia of the day. I spent the remainder of April writing thank-you notes to family and friends.

Cordell planned another unique event to celebrate my seventy-eighth birthday. When reading my father's Line-A-Day diary, I noted the addresses where he had lived while in Akron. Cordell mapped out a route taking us by these ten places. We saw houses in disrepair, houses well kept, vacant lots, and one place devoured by the I-76 highway.

Cordell parked the car in front of a well-kept house at 1270 Lexington Avenue. There stood the house where I was born. I got out and stood on the sidewalk, trying to envision myself in a baby carriage. Mom used to tell me of the neighbor girl, maybe eight or ten, who loved to take me for carriage rides. This was the one lasting memory I had of the time my parents lived in Akron. As the day ended, I was filled with thoughts of regret that I knew so little about my father's life.

Equally unique was my seventy-ninth birthday celebration. After seeing the movie *The Bucket List*, I remarked to Cordell that an item I had in my bucket was a ride in a hot-air balloon. Cordell seized the opportunity and contacted Heaven Bound Ascensions. Imagine my delight when I opened my birthday card and there were two tickets for a hot-air balloon ride.

Due to unfavorable weather, the flight date was rescheduled three times. On October 18, 2009, we drove to a field, twelve miles to the southeast of Kent in Stark County, our point of departure. The first thing I saw were six humungous deflated balloons spread out on the field of grass. After an hour-plus wait our balloon, now fully inflated, was ready for ascension. (By then I had already made one trip into the woods to pee, concerned that my bladder might not hold out for the duration of the flight.)

The basket held six passengers and the pilot. With the help of a stepstool, and a derriere push from Cordell, I climbed over the four-foot side and dropped into the basket. During the first minutes of the flight, there was little talking, only "the sounds of silence." The balloon, propelled by a gentle southeasterly breeze, floated lazily along at an altitude of 1,100 feet. I looked down and saw the deciduous trees clothed in their autumn colors of bright red and orange leaves—a heart-stirring sight.

We were aloft for an hour when our pilot located a field (private property) where he could maneuver the descending balloon to a safe landing. During the descent, we were instructed to hang on and prepare for body-jarring bumps when the basket connected with the ground. Once the basket landed, the deflating balloon continued to pull it along for fifty or more feet before coming to rest. We were warned; it was a rough landing!

A chase vehicle followed our route and drove onto the field. I was ready to get in the van and return posthaste to our point of departure, for as the balloon deflated, my bladder continued to inflate. Imagine my shock when I heard the pilot say there was work to be done. Once totally deflated, the six of us were directed to roll up the balloon and place it in the chase vehicle's trailer. There is a tradition in hot-air-ballooning—after a successful flight, you drink champagne. While the six of us stood there sipping the bubbly, the pilot recognized each in turn, handing out certificates and pins.

At last we were allowed take our seats in the van. The return ride was an interminable thirty minutes. Cordell managed to find a McDonald's before I peed my pants.

My advice to anyone thinking about taking a ride in a hot-air balloon is: (1) Bring a suitcase of patience with you; (2) be agile enough to climb into the basket; and (3) ration your liquid intake to ensure your bladder will hold out for the questionable duration of the flight.

My eightieth birthday was a double celebration—the first with my family in Las Vegas and the second arranged by my nieces and nephews in Madison.

Cordell and I spent a week in Las Vegas the middle of March 2008—days filled with excitement, joy, and sorrow. Bruce and Linda took us to the recently opened City Center Aria. Here Maya Lin's 87-foot, 3,700-pound sculpture of the *Silver River* (Colorado River) hangs suspended from steel cables above the registration desk. It is a radiantly graceful impressive sight. (Maya Lin designed the Vietnam Memorial.)

Granddaughter Candice and husband Will hosted a family dinner in their home. The dining room was appointed with festive lavender decorations and the table—carefully crafted by Bruce in Green—was set with flowers, linen, china, and silverware. All reminders of home on Vineland Avenue in Ashtabula. Tradition held, and the three-layer cake on the pedestal cake stand, adorned with lighted candles, was set before me while voices blended in singing "Happy Birthday."

I thought the evening was perfect, but Bruce made it more so. With a sheepish look on his face he brought forth an odd-shaped item wrapped in wrinkled paper. I dared not hope. I had asked Bruce years ago if he would make me a replica of my mom's little rocking chair, stolen when I moved from Lemoyne to Las Vegas. I tore the paper from the package, and there it was, a child's rocking chair—cherrywood, satin to the touch, caned seat, and handcrafted by my son!

Both joy and sorrow were companions during that visit. Bernie, the companion of Linda's mother, Betty, died the day after Cordell and I arrived. We attended Bernie's service and took part in the Jewish tradition of throwing dirt on the casket.

During the days of my visit, I felt like a queen and left before I was dethroned.

My second eightieth birthday celebration was held on Sunday, April 11, at the home of Kellie and Kirk Peine in Madison. My niece Jill was in charge of arrangements, and the cousins supplied the food.

When I arrived, a number of guests were there to greet me. But a surprise that held no equal took place when I entered the kitchen. There stood Bruce and Linda, with a self-satisfied look on their faces. Always the ones to pull off an "I gotcha," they gave no hint during the Las Vegas visit that they would be coming.

DURING THE SIX-MONTH ROMANTIC PROLOGUE to our marriage, we were fortunate that health issues did not rear their ugly heads.

In September 1994, I had read in *Modern Maturity* about a condition called restless leg syndrome (RLS), defined as a disorder characterized by an unpleasant tickling, twitching, or crawling sensation in leg muscles when sitting or lying down, relieved only by moving the legs. At last, I was able to put a name to the painful condition that plagued me.

Soon after marrying Cordell, the condition worsened. I joined the RLS Foundation, read widely, and learned about exercise and diet. Nothing helped. Cordell referred me to a chapter in Deepak Chopra's book *Quantum Healing*, telling about the effects of stress on the body. Granted, my marriage was a positive change in lifestyle, but nevertheless it caused stress.

In January 2005, I gave in and scheduled an appointment with my primary care physician (PCP), only to be seen by his physician assistant (PA). She listened and, with no further questions, diagnosed my condition as RLS and prescribed Sinemet. From the offset, the medication helped, but as time went on, the symptoms returned, and with each visit to the office, the PA increased my dosage. Over the following months, I came to the realization that something was wrong.

Unhappy with our PCP, whom we never saw, Cordell and I changed doctors. On my first office visit with Dr. DePerro, he referred me to a neurologist. Dr. Rafecas immediately recognized I was addicted to the drug Sinemet and placed me on a withdrawal schedule. During the withdrawal phase, the RLS symptoms returned with a vengeance, but I held out, and at a follow-up appointment, Dr. Rafecas commented, "You must have been mad as hell to get off of that drug so quickly." Yes, I was angry that, while under a doctor's care, this happened to me. But the offhand comment by Dr. Rafecas recognizing the hell I went through made it all worthwhile.

Dr. Rafecas placed me on a medication schedule of Ropinirole and Gabapentin. He put the fear of God in me not to increase the dosage—to take it only as prescribed or I would experience a repeat of the previous drug's addiction. I took the warning to heart, and at this writing ten years later, my RLS remains under control.

X-rays confirmed there was a problem with my right hip replacement done in 1988. The prothesis had loosened in the femur. The hip held out for the duration of the Going-to-the-Sun Road tour, but I knew revision surgery awaited me soon after we returned from our Western travels in August 2005.

Early in the morning of October 17, I was at Aultman Hospital in North Canton being prepped for a surgery that would take four hours.

Later Dr. Conlan reported to Cordell that the revision surgery was without complications. A twelve-inch prosthesis, held in place with steel bands and screws top and bottom, replaced the original. I spent four days in the hospital. From the hospital I was transferred to the Woodlawn Rehabilitation Center for another five days of intense PT before I was released to go home.

Cordell's twice-a-day visits were my lifeline while at Woodlawn. At lunchtime he always brought with him two thermoses filled with tomato soup. To this day, tomato soup remains a comfort food because of the memory of those special lunches with Cordell.

Although Dr. Conlan never said the femur in my leg was fractured during the surgery, I sense it was. For weeks I was restricted to sleeping on my back. I used a walker and was allowed no more than a toe touch to the floor with the right foot. For pain I was prescribed OxyContin and Percocet. One night I dreamed there was a green snake in my bed. I grabbed it, killed it, and threw it on the floor. I saw ants crawling on the ceiling and bugs creeping along cracks in the floor. I knew I needed to withdraw from the pain meds ASAP.

Weeks passed. I progressed from walker to cane. On January 20, 2006, three months after my surgery, I was set free by Dr. Conlan. Through it all, family and friends supported me. My husband was a loving caregiver. I wanted for nothing. He managed the household, took me on outings, and calmed me during moments of despair.

At the time of my 2005 right-hip revision, an X-ray of the left hip showed it was a candidate for replacement. Walking with Cordell in the fall of 2006, I felt an excruciating pain in my left groin area. Contact was made with Dr. Conlan, appointments followed, and the surgery was scheduled for early Monday morning, November 26.

Bruce and Linda arrived that year to spend Thanksgiving with us. They and Diane were with Cordell at the hospital to wait out my surgery. Less complicated than the right hip revision, I was back in my hospital room in record time, resting comfortably in a semiraised position in my bed. The effects of the drugs clouded my mind, but I do recall watching the four of them sitting there in silence, and I, ever the consummate hostess, said, "I don't know how I can entertain you." I've never been allowed to forget that *obiter dictum*.

This time my hospital stay was three days. Again, I experienced post-surgery woes—outpatient PT three days a week, sleepless nights, monotonous days, and drugs that played havoc with my system. Cordell once more assumed responsibility for my care and managing the home. My convalescence lasted five weeks. January 7, 2007, was a day for celebration. Cordell gathered all the orthopedic equipment and placed it in the garage attic.

With the arrival of spring, Cordell and I planted flowers in areas surrounding the condo. On Sunday morning, May 8, I went into the garage and loaded a dolly with supplies needed to finish a small planting area in the flower beds. As I moved the dolly I heard something fall off, turned to retrieve it, caught my left foot on one of the wheels, and fell, smashing my right knee on the concrete floor.

I screamed for Cordell. He took me to the Aultman Hospital ER. After several hours of bureaucratic frustration, I was admitted for surgery. The force of the fall broke the patella into four sections, crushing the lower left section into cornflake-sized pieces.

Dr. Conlan was out of town. His partner came to see me late Sunday afternoon and told me he'd been in surgery all day, admitting he was too tired to attempt putting my kneecap back together. He recommended another surgeon who could perform the surgery the following day. In truth, I was impressed with his forthrightness and honesty, realizing my accident wasn't a life-threatening situation.

Surgery went well. I was released on Tuesday wearing a straight-leg brace. Cordell retrieved the walker from the attic. I lugged that brace around for two weeks, even had to sleep with it. The third week I was allowed some flexion in the leg, discarded the walker, used a cane, and reported for outpatient physical therapy.

The muscles in my knee were weak. The doctor brought me to tears when he told me I'd probably need a second surgery. My grit and commitment to physical therapy, combined with the God-given ability of the body to heal itself, proved him wrong. At last, I was able to ride my bicycle and to drive.

The fall of 2007, I realized I needed to find a surgeon to repair a rectocele problem I'd been dealing with for many years. A telephone call to my PCP sent me to a gynecologist, who in turn referred me to an urogynecologist. Surgery was scheduled for December 14; the following day I was home. More PT, this time Kegel exercises—something many women know about, but few men.

I'd like to report that 2010 was free of health issues. It wasn't. On August 3, I joined Cordell and Kent for lunch. It was raining, and as the three of us entered the foyer of Grill 39 in Green, I slipped on the wet tile. Kent tried to save me, couldn't, and I fell, striking my head on the metal frame of a full-length window. I lay stretched out on the floor, bystanders gawking, when the EMT arrived.

I knew I cut my scalp when I fell, I could feel the blood in my hair, but I didn't think it was serious, so I kept repeating, "I'm all right, I won't go to the hospital." My plea was ignored, and at the behest of both Cordell and Kent, I found myself being placed on a gurney and loaded into the ambulance. My injury was not life-threatening. There were no sirens, traffic was heavy, so it was a slow ride to the hospital. I lay there strapped on the gurney looking up at the metal ceiling and thinking, "What bad karma got me into this mess?"

The ER physician examined my head, found the cut to be superficial, put a tube of antibiotic salve in my hand, and sent me home. Cordell took care of filing the insurance claim against the restaurant. Management denied any culpability in the accident and, as an example, noted a 102-year-old man entered the restaurant just ahead of me and had not fallen. I maintained negligence as the tile floor was wet and there was no protective carpet runner. The restaurant's insurance policy covered only my medical costs. This accident was not a cash-cow like the dog-bite incident.

Through all of my surgeries and convalescent care, Cordell never uttered one word of complaint. In fact, he remarked to me, "Be careful, don't become too dependent on me. I know you like your independence, but I like taking care of you."

Overall, Cordell's medical problems were ongoing and chronic, whereas mine were structural and fixable. Shortly after we were married, Cordell missed a bullet. We were walking on Glen Eagles Boulevard, and he tripped on a piece of the broken pavement, falling forward, and hitting his face full force on the concrete. He did not lose consciousness and was able to walk the short distance back to our condo. His fall resulted in a large goose egg on his right temple and shades of black, yellow, and blue encircled his eyes. We joked I might be accused of spousal battery.

Throughout his life, Cordell enjoyed sunshine and never protected his body with a hat, proper clothing, or sunscreen. Now all that sun required regular visits to Dr. Hawkins, a dermatologist.

Cordell's eyesight was of grave concern not only to him, but to me. Regular visits were scheduled with Dr. Woodruff, an ophthalmologist, who treated Cordell's eyes for glaucoma and virus infections. Over the years his vision weakened, and his driver's license was restricted to daylight-hours driving.

Ignored at home, but embarrassing when in public, was the chronic cough that started shortly after we were married. In the beginning, our PCP tried to relieve the condition. A swallowing test (commonly referred to as the cookie test) gave normal results.

Concerned that it might be lung congestion, an appointment was made with a pulmonologist who scheduled a bronchoscopy. The procedure revealed congestion in the lower right lobe of the lung; biopsy samples were negative. To cure what was thought to be a bacterial infection in the congested area, the doctor placed Cordell on a three-month rotation of powerful ABC antibiotics (Amoxicillin, Bactrim, Cipro). It didn't help.

Thinking the problem might be a sinus drip, Cordell was sent to an ENT specialist, who in turn prescribed a nasal inhaler and suggested the use of a Neti Pot (sinus saline irrigation). This treatment provided only temporary relief. The cough returned with a vengeance. Another thought it might be an acid reflux condition. We purchased an adjustable bed, allowing Cordell to sleep in a semiupright position. No help there either. Over the years the chronic cough stayed with him.

In 2008 Cordell complained of severe knee pain. An appointment with Dr. Conlan confirmed knee replacement surgery was necessary. Diane was with me the morning of January 6, 2009, for her dad's surgery. Knowing we had hours to wait, we went to the cafeteria to get our lunch. Diane ordered a large helping of mashed potatoes, commenting this was her comfort food. I ordered the same. To this day, I have tomato soup (hip-surgery memories) or mashed potatoes (knee-surgery memories) when I feel the need for comfort.

Cordell's surgery went well. He was released from the hospital in three days. Now I was the "care coach," lovingly and willingly performing all required tasks. While in bed, Cordell used a machine for passive flexion exercise of the knee. Once mobile, a physical therapist came to our home, forcing him to do the painful exercises necessary to stretch the knee muscles for full flexion. I had heard, but didn't believe, that PT for the knee was more painful than PT for the hip. Watching Cordell grimace, I became a believer. Cordell's determination to do the prescribed PT exercises paid off. He was released by Dr. Conlan in April. In May he was back on his bicycle.

From an early age, I had scheduled dental appointments every six months of my life. With that background of dental experience, I could sense a good dentist. My first venture to find a dentist in Green ended in disaster. The man was overly fawning, inappropriately touchy-feely, stout of figure, and middle-aged. One appointment and I did not go back.

A write-up in our local paper featuring a Dr. Lubinsky caught my eye. He had recently opened a dental office in Green. Cordell was interested in changing dentists, so he came with me when I scheduled an introductory appointment. We were favorably impressed by this young man. For me, he satisfactorily answered all questions related to my dental care—root canals, caps, implants, and dentures. Cordell saw himself in this young man—the need to break away from a group to establish his own practice in a competitive profession boded well for his self-confidence. We were never disappointed in our choice for a dentist.

As I look back on the health issues that faced us during those first years of our marriage, I marvel how we took it in stride. We supported one another, always with faith we would be restored to full health.

———— ·+++++·+ ————

CORDELL WAS THE FIRST to express his dissatisfaction with condo living. He voiced his thought in a very casual way when he asked me, "Wouldn't it be nice to own our own home, relieved of the imposed restrictions of condo living?" Perhaps he sensed my growing uneasiness. I often commented how I resented feeling like a criminal when I hung our clothes out to dry on our deck. At other times I expressed a desire to live in Kent. I would read in the paper of interesting events taking place at the university or in the downtown area and longed to be a part of them.

Selling our homes and buying a condo was the right decision at the time of our marriage, but now we realized condo living was not to our liking. There was too much sameness—in buildings, in the age-range of residents, and in socioeconomic status. Our involvement on the board of directors made us aware of the lackadaisical management of the association. When it came to policy decisions, a vocal negative few overpowered the silent majority.

Our condo home was perfect for us, and we wished we could place the building on a magic carpet and plop it down on a lot in Kent within walking distance of KSU. We had invested in customizing the condo to fit our needs, money that would not be recovered when sold.

Once we acknowledged our wish to sell and move to Kent, this passion took on a proverbial life of its own. The summer of 2007, we spent days driving and biking through residential areas in Kent near the university. There were homes for sale, realtors contacted, tours taken—nothing to our liking.

On a fall Sunday in October, we loaded our bicycles into the van and drove into Kent. Once there we parked the van, got on our bikes, and rode through the residential area of University Woods, an upscale neighborhood within a mile of the main campus. A "For Sale" sign on the lawn of a white two-story, colonial-style house on Oakwood Drive took our eye. We contacted the listing agent, Karen Claxton.

The following day we met Karen, toured the house, found the living space comparable to our condo, tastefully decorated, and very much to our liking. The asking price was $379,000; we offered $350,000. Within a day Karen called and said the owner would not budge from the asking price. The house had all the amenities we wanted, and the location was perfect. Determined to buy the house, we were willing to pay the asking price.

Another call was made to Karen, and we arranged to meet her for lunch on October 11. We met at a coffee shop, were seated, and before Cordell could speak, Karen informed us the owner had taken the house off the market that morning. We were devastated, causing us to back off from our desire to move to Kent.

Real estate agents are dogged individuals. A call came from Karen on February 12, 2008. She knew of a repossessed house on Frances Drive, recently placed on the market. The weather was abominable, but we hazarded the unfavorable road conditions and drove into Kent to meet Karen at the house. Utilities had been shut off, so the house tour was made using a flashlight. We saw enough of it to know it was right for us—a brick ranch with full, finished basement. The location was in University Heights, not controlled by a Homeowner's Association, and closer to the university.

The asking price was $253,900. Karen recommended we up our offer to $255,000 because she learned there were others interested in the property. She further recommended we submit a certified letter from our bank verifying available funds for a cash deal. We did as instructed and waited for what seemed to be an interminable amount of time, only to be informed on May 10 that the bank approved the sale of the house to another party.

We later learned that Karen didn't have the "juice," as they say in Las Vegas. The person who owned the real estate agency, for whom Karen worked, had done some sly maneuvering for a client who bought the house for his son. Karen was a pawn in this entire charade.

Disappointed that our second attempt to move to Kent failed, we again settled into condo living. However, Karen kept us in her "tickler" file and on July 21, 2010, called to tell us of another house for sale. Reluctantly, we agreed to meet her.

The two-story colonial-style house located at 432 Burr Oak Drive, on a dead-end street, was within two blocks of the main campus. We walked through the house and recognized that some remodeling and major redecorating needed to be done. On the whole, we liked it. The next day we telephoned Karen, letting her know we would pay the asking price of $154,900, contingent upon the house inspection report. Our offer was accepted and the house inspection scheduled. Based on the report's findings, noting needed major repairs, we made a second offer of $146,000. The owner accepted our revised offer. The third effort to buy a house in Kent was the charm!

We immediately contacted the Keller Williams Real Estate Agency. We knew condos were not a hot sale item in our area and priced it at $350,000, per the agent's recommendation, and signed the three-month contract. Suggestions were made as to what should be done for showcasing our home—simplify, simplify, simplify. We rearranged and discarded furniture, took down wall decorations, and patched and painted the visible nail holes. Open-house showings were a major disruption in our lives but had to be endured. Our first offer was a contingency contract, which we refused. When our time with Keller Williams expired, we did not renew.

We took a respite from the ardors of condo showings before contacting another realtor in November. We met with Teresa, an agent from Howard Hannah Realty. Realizing the cost in maintaining two properties—taxes, insurance, utilities, maintenance—we reduced the sale price to $289,900 and signed the obligatory three-month contract.

Teresa was an aggressive agent, which resulted in a number of showings. Several couples liked the condo but had their own homes to sell, and we were not interested in any contingency contracts.

In March of 2011, we were made an offer of $258,000. For us, it came close to an insult as we had significantly lowered the listing price from the original asking price. Cordell called to my attention what it cost each month to own the condo. Best to take the offer and be done with it. We signed the sale contract with Gar and Ellen Compton on March 11, 2011, divesting ourselves of what might become a white elephant.

The timing was perfect. Our Kent house was ready for occupancy. On April 4, Two Men and a Truck came with two trucks and four men. In the span of ten hours, they moved us out of 2173 Prestwick Drive and into our house at 432 Burr Oak Drive—in pouring rain.

--------·++++·--------

ONCE OUR VOWS WERE SPOKEN, the courtship romance segued into marriage reality. The transition was not always smooth, and there were **incidents**! Our children independent, career goals achieved, and financially secure, it was just us and we had to learn to live together in harmony.

Sex played a role in our relationship, and Cordell alluded to that when he wrote, "We are both heavily driven by our passion for sex. We are very much alike in this and partly why we are so attracted to one another." Now married, the demands of daily living weighed heavily on us, requiring a depth of understanding well beyond sexual attraction.

I married a talented, self-confident man and, concealed during the courtship, a controlling personality. A widow for six years and fiercely protective of my independence, it was evident I needed to change, or our marriage would fail. I couldn't change Cordell. That he'd have to do himself. I could only change myself, and to this end I realized that:

I was too **bossy**. A good example of this took place in the kitchen— my domain invaded by Cordell. If I made suggestions regarding his cooking, he sulked or, worse yet, became outright defensive. I learned, difficult as it was in all areas, to make suggestions only when asked.

I questioned his **expertise**. Here I would tread lightly, careful when choosing to speak and when best to remain silent.

I was **impatient**. In dealing with service personnel, Cordell's style was to clearly state what he wanted and wait. My style was to demand immediate results. The need to change went against my DNA. I was moderately successful—not totally.

I was **inconsiderate**. I would criticize, critique, or interrupt when I should have remained silent. I had a penchant for putting my mouth in gear, while my brain remained in neutral—a lifelong habit difficult to control.

I questioned **financial expenditures**. At first, I paid little heed to how our money was spent. The financial arrangement of our marriage was fifty-fifty, so I believed I had a right to question. When I did, I met an impregnable defensive wall. It took time, but I learned how to approach this volatile subject.

There were other incidents caused by stress, emotion, and insecure feelings. Through it all we persevered, and our salvation was in our ability to communicate honestly and openly. We never allowed misunderstandings to fester. We spent hours talking and probing the depths of one another's very being, trying to understand each other's point of view. As Cordell had said early on in our marriage, "We hold no secrets." He changed as much as I. We became true soul mates, and over the course of time, we both grew intellectually and matured emotionally. We took our marriage vows seriously and together looked forward to whatever lay around the next bend.

TWENTY-THREE

MARRIAGE TO CORDELL GLAUS RETURNING TO KENT (2010–2013)

T HE KENT WE RETURNED TO IN 2010 was far different from the city of eighteen thousand where I lived in the 1960s, and certainly not the quiet college town where Cordell attended school in the late 1950s. The population of the city now totaled twenty-eight thousand, and the KSU main campus enrollment counted twenty-two thousand undergraduate and eight thousand graduate students.

The Town-Gown division, often referred to by Allan Dickie, no longer existed. During the second half of her tenure, President Carol Cartwright (1991–2006) commissioned a study to be done by the College of Architecture and Environmental Design envisioning a blending of town and gown into a "Univer-City." The recommendations of the study impacted not only KSU, turning it from a commuter school into a residential campus, but is recognized as a catalyst in the revival of the downtown.

The original campus buildings along Hilltop Drive were refurbished. New buildings were constructed on university acreage to the south and east. Houses, mostly rental, on the west side of the university were purchased and either moved or torn down to make way for an esplanade, named for President Lester A. Lefton (2006–2014). This imposing brick walkway connected the city with the west campus.

Private and public funds were invested in the renewal of the downtown. Local businessman and entrepreneur Ron Burbick, beginning in 2005, bankrolled the Phoenix Project. He purchased a section along the south side of East Main Street, had it renovated, and expanded into what is now known as Acorn Alley. Later, with others, he purchased the vacant Franklin Hotel located on the southeast corner of Main and Depeyster Streets. The hotel was authentically restored and is listed on the US National Register of Historic Places.

Plans for a Portage County Municipal Court Kent Branch building, to be constructed further east on Main Street, were published in the local paper. The original design called for a corner entrance, although the building would be constructed in the middle of the block. Cordell, the architect, saw this as a design flaw. He wrote a letter to the editor stating his rationale for relocating the main entrance. The suggestion, along with others, was taken under advisement. The courthouse opened in 2014 with the main entrance doors located in the center front of the building.

About this time, four city blocks were razed in the southeast quadrant of the downtown. Anchor buildings constructed in this area were Ametek Technical & Industrial Products and Davey Tree Expert Company. Across Depeyster Street the KSU Hotel and Conference Center, the Portage Area Regional Transportation Authority (PARTA), with a 360-space parking deck, were built. A number of mixed-use buildings filled the remaining area, giving it a big-city feel—microapartments, restaurants, offices, businesses, and boutiques. This Univer-City is where Cordell and I chose to make our home.

JERRY WILAND, A WIDOWER forced by declining health to move into an assisted living residence, reluctantly agreed to sell the family home on Burr Oak Drive. This is the house that Cordell and I bought, and when word got out, a number of family members and friends came by. We welcomed all opportunities to provide tours of our recent real estate acquisition. Some walked through and remained noncommittal; others were candid in their comments.

In the Bible, the aged father Israel presented his favorite son, Joseph, with a "coat of many colors;" the parents of the six Wiland children gave no such gift to their offspring, instead allowing them the privilege of selecting the paint color for their bedrooms. Walls were painted bright orange, light lavender, fuchsia, bright blue, and olive green.

The parents were not to be left out of this colorful palette. The master bedroom was pink—pink walls, pink carpet, pink drapes, even a bathroom with pink fixtures, and beside the commode, pink toilet paper. Walking into this room, my friend Jody blurted out, "A Pepto-Bismol room!" The man of the house had close ties with Kent State University, and this gold-and-blue connection was evidenced in the living room: light-blue carpet, dark-blue walls, and gold drapes with sheer light-blue back panel.

There were four bathrooms in the house—one, previously mentioned, was pink; the other three had fixtures of yellow, blue, and white. The sunroom windows were stained with sap that dripped from the forest of backyard trees. The room smelled of mold. When Jane Nickerson toured the house, her feisty comment was, "This room has got to go," further adding, "I hope you two have a good vision for this place."

WE WERE FORTUNATE that Karen Dinehart, our real estate agent, was a classmate of Jay Tischendorf—one of the six Wiland children. Jay lived in the West, and on one of his visits to Kent, Karen made arrangements for the two of them to stop by 432 Burr Oak Drive. Their visit took place shortly after we purchased the house and before any changes were made. It was through Jay that we learned the provenance of the house—and much more. Cordell's amazement was indescribable when he realized he had met the grandson of a professor whom he held in high esteem.

When Cordell appeared on campus for his first day of classes in the late 1940s, green with naivete, as he entered the industrial arts building, he asked the first person he saw for directions to his classroom. Elbert W. Tischendorf, a kind, unassuming man, came to Cordell's aid, and a remarkable chemistry developed between professor and student. From that day on, Professor Tischendorf served in the unofficial capacity as Cordell's mentor during his undergraduate years at KSU.

The land on which our house was built was owned by Professor Tischendorf, head of the Industrial Arts Department at Kent State University. Professor Tischendorf's son, Alfred, also a professor, was involved in research work in Buenos Aires, Argentina. He fell ill while there and died. Jay's mother, Joyce, now a widow with two young children, met Jerry Wiland, a widower with three children. Jerry and Joyce married, and about this time, Elbert gifted the lot on Burr Oak Drive to his widowed daughter-in-law. Here in the 1960s, she and Jerry built a house for their family that totaled six children after a son was born to them. One might say the Wiland family was akin to the TV family of the Brady Bunch and their six children. Only for Jerry and Joyce, it was his three, her two, and their one—four boys and two girls.

During Jay's visit we walked through the rooms and were captivated by the stories he related about the family. The girls each had their own bedroom and use of the second-floor blue bathroom. The boys were consigned to the basement with the white utilitarian-tiled shower, bowl, and commode. They knew the consequences in store for them if dirty clothes or wet towels were left on the concrete floor, later to be discovered by either parent.

When we entered the bedroom with the bright-blue walls, red carpet, checkered red-and-blue drapes and white woodwork, a mobile was hanging from the ceiling. Jay expressed surprise and delight when he saw it and asked if he might have it. He explained the mobile held a special significance for his brother, and he wanted to send it to him. Without question, we were delighted to accommodate this request.

Other stories related to the small Pullman-style kitchen and the sunroom. I asked how their mother could possibly cook for a family of eight in the close space. The solution—no one was allowed in the kitchen when she was preparing a meal. The sunroom that Jane had so blatantly remarked "had to go" was a favorite place for the siblings to read or play board games

———— ·+++++· ————

THE CONDO HAD BEEN DECORATED TO OUR LIKING. In contrast, the Burr Oak house required an entire makeover. The years we lived in the condo, we had minor remodeling work done by THE RAY COMPANY. The work was to our satisfaction, so without hesitation, Cordell contacted the owner of the company, Randy Renninger. After preliminary talks, we made the decision to contract with them to remodel/redecorate our 2,400-square-foot house.

All windows and doors were replaced. The kitchen, laundry, and bathrooms were remodeled. The house electrical system was upgraded, a new furnace and air-conditioning installed, and the hot-water tank replaced. Every square inch of the 2,400-square-foot house received attention. Throughout the entire process, we often commented we never could have done this when we were first married. At best it would have driven us to divorce; at worst one of us might have committed a homicide.

We traveled near and far to businesses recommended by Randy in making our material selections. Most frustrating were the visits to plumbing and floor covering businesses—too many choices. Our visit to the Mont Granite warehouse was sheer delight. We commented that the colors and designs found in nature's granite equaled, or eclipsed, the paintings of the masters. We walked up and down aisle after aisle lined with four-by-eight-foot slabs of granite brought from mines throughout the world. We were awestruck by the natural beauty of the stone, finally selecting a slab of Yellow River granite mined in Brazil.

All walls and ceilings were covered with a coat of drywall plaster, then finished very smooth and lifeless. I carefully walked a fine line and got Cordell to agree to a knockdown texture that gave life to the foyer and powder room / bath walls. I visualized the knockdown texture on the fireplace wall in the family room, but Cordell wouldn't hear of it. I wisely took heed; there might be future decorating battles to be won.

Fortunately, our decorating tastes were similar, and we made material selections based on a palette of earth tones—rich colors of umber, ochre, and sienna. We preferred simplicity. Natural fiber Roman shades were hung at the windows. The bedroom carpet was "Tea Biscuit." The laminate floors in our offices and living/dining rooms had names like "Italian Walnut" and "Lodge Oak." We selected hickory cabinets for our kitchen/laundry, and off-white for the bathroom. All walls were painted "Steamed milk"—a color we never tired of the seven years we lived in the condo. But too much sameness can be monotonous. I lost in my attempt to have the knockdown texture on the family room fireplace wall, but I congratulated myself when, with the use of delicate persuasion, I was able to get Cordell to agree to have the wall painted an accent color—"Cinnamon Stick."

———————— ++++++ ————————

Ray Company employees, master carpenter, Mark, and his assistant, Jeff, worked full time and were responsible for all carpenter work. Chaos reigned when electricians, plumbers, drywall plasterers, painters, and employees from businesses were in and out of the house. To stay out of the workmen's path, Cordell and I busied ourselves outside. We raked up years of leaf accumulation in our forested backyard. We met with men from the Yarnell Tree Trimming Company to have the trees trimmed.

I was there the day the Yarnell workmen came. A fifty-foot-tall blue spruce grew just off the back deck of our house—shapely and resplendent when looking at it from the house side, but not so grand when looking at it from the back side. The bottom portion of the tree was barren of branches. A few trees in our backyard forest were marked to be cut down, but not the blue spruce. I was standing in the house watching the action of the tree-trimmers when I observed one of the workmen approach the blue spruce with chainsaw in hand positioned to cut down the tree. I ran out onto the rickety back deck and screamed at him not to touch the tree! To this day, the thought of this overzealous worker cutting down the blue spruce makes me shudder. The tree is home to birds and romping black squirrels. Following a heavy winter snowfall, the boughs are covered with a soft, white blanket of snow. To me, the blue spruce is the regal tree in our backyard forest.

When we weren't shopping for supplies or working outside, Cordell and I worked inside, careful to stay out of Mark's and Jeff's path. I cleaned cobwebs and dirt from the basement rafters, as well as layers of dust that covered the furnace ducts. Knowing the boys used the basement toilet/shower area, I was amused when I found hidden beer cans. (When I related this to Jay, he was disappointed I had not kept at least one of those cans.) Jeff was assigned to clean out the family room fireplace pit. His work was so slovenly I donned rubber gloves, crawled into the space, and scrubbed the soot of the ages off the firebrick myself.

Cordell spent hours drawing the remodeling plans for the kitchen/laundry and designing the tile layout patterns for the foyer, family room/kitchen, laundry, and bathroom floors. He purchased a push mower from Sears and was pleased with himself that he was able to mow our crab grass lawn. Sentimental person that I am, I brought rocks and stepping stones from the condo and placed them in our backyard. One year, Bruce and Linda had given me a hybrid hydrangea plant for Mother's Day. I brought it from the condo and replanted it next to our Kent house where it flourished.

In September 2010, the RAY COMPANY workers started at our Burr Oak Drive house and did not leave until April 2011. During those months, work did not progress on a smooth upward trajectory. There were material delays. Wrong materials were sent and had to be returned; other materials were unavailable. But the worst mistake made was by the Pella employee who mismeasured the size of the double-hung windows in the house. To avoid a long delay, we accepted the windows with the assurance Mark could rectify the mistake by installing a molding on the windowsill.

Work progressed in spite of the tool clutter that covered the floors, impeding mobility and wasting minutes spent finding the right tool for the task at hand. Jeff's lackadaisical work habits led both of us to the conclusion he was useless. He would walk around, hands in pockets, waiting for the next directive from Mark. Frequent trips were made to his truck where we observed him engaged in lengthy cell phone conversations. Cordell made several early-morning trips to the Kent house to find out if Jeff reported for work on time. Given, we had signed a contract with Randy for each phase of the operation, but it appeared to us that the job was set up to keep his men employed throughout the winter. Cordell made a list of our concerns, mostly related to Jeff's work habits, and presented them to Randy. He was incredulous. No one had ever complained about Jeff's work ethic before! Nothing changed.

Randy was not a hands-on contractor. He would stop by with materials, or to check on something, and then stay and talk and talk and talk, keeping his men from their work or us from our appointed tasks. One day a subcontractor stopped by to inform Randy there was an additional cost related to one of the jobs he was doing and needed to know how to proceed. I overheard Randy reply not to be concerned. He had charged enough to cover this type of contingency, so "go ahead with the job." This supported our conjecture that we were being overcharged from the get-go.

We were relieved when Mark and Jeff gathered up their tools on March 9, 2011, and vacated the premises. The house would be ready for our April 4 move-in date.

BEFORE THE HOUSE WAS READY FOR US TO MOVE IN, we took advantage of every opportunity to meet our neighbors, albeit my first encounter could have proved disastrous. Cordell and I were seated in the family room on the window seat facing the street. As we sat there talking, I noticed a man walking by with a dog on a leash. The dog stopped, sniffed about, wandered onto our crab-grass lawn, crouched, and pooped. Finished with nature's call, tail wagging, man and dog continued on their walk. I was incensed. I jumped up, grabbed a plastic bag, and rushed outside, summoning the man to stop. I had the presence of mind to pleasantly greet him and remarked I would pick up his dog's droppings this time but to please do so in the future. The man voiced bewilderment, commenting he didn't realize anyone lived in the house (as if that made a difference). I introduced myself as the new owner. He told me his name and remarked he lived two houses down on the same side of the street. I was mortified! He took no umbrage with my confronting him, and later whenever we saw one another, we would speak. Better yet, he and Cordell recognized they had common interests and became friends.

At first our neighbors across the street appeared to be aloof. One evening we observed the couple examining the plants in their street-side garden. Cordell and I took the opportunity to walk over and introduce ourselves. Rachel and Jim were very congenial, offered us a homegrown tomato, and over time we became friends. We enjoyed the antics of their creative five-year-old daughter, Lila. She would perform for us—songs learned and original plays. We watched her father run along beside her when she was learning to ride her two-wheel bicycle. She sold me make-believe ice cream but would not accept make-believe money.

Gradually other couples from the ten homes on our dead-end street stopped by to introduce themselves or to invite us over for wine, hors d'oeuvres, and get-acquainted conversation.

·+++++·

As soon as the house was finished, our furniture was moved in, and we were semisettled, Cordell and I planned two open-house events. The first open house, scheduled for August 9, was for the workers and businesses that supplied the materials. The second open house was to follow on August 14 for friends and condo acquaintances curious to know what prompted us to make this insane move. Then the unexpected happened.

The day was Wednesday, the date August 3, 2011. Cordell had been working outside moving heavy yard items. That evening he complained of sore muscles, but what alarmed me more was his shallow, painful breathing and fast pulse. I took him to the emergency room of Robinson Memorial Hospital in Ravenna. He was diagnosed with an infection in the right lower lobe of his lung and admitted to the hospital. On Friday, an unsuccessful attempt was made to drain fluid from the infected area.

Diane was with me on Saturday for the thoracic surgery. Immediately following the surgery, Cordell's heart stopped. He was revived, placed on chemical life support, intubated, and transferred to the Cardiac Care Unit (CCU). Diane and I were told by the anesthesiologist and surgeon not to expect him to live through the night. Miraculously he lived, sedated in a drug-induced sleep. Tubes protruded from every orifice of his body, and a respirator kept him alive. Cordell's worst nightmare was happening. He was being kept alive by machines. A compassionate hospital doctor informed me of the palliative care resource and a meeting was scheduled for Thursday with Dr. Deiter and his team. At that meeting, I was given information about hospice care.

Over the next several days, unsuccessful attempts were made to wean Cordell off of the respirator. Bruce arrived from Las Vegas and was with me on Thursday morning, August 11, when we walked into Cordell's room in the CCU. Cordell was sitting upright in bed with what looked to me like a feed bag—similar in appearance to those used to feed animals on our farm—attached and hanging from the lower half of his face. Somehow Cordell had managed to dislodge his breathing tube. It was evident the attending nurse was angry this happened on her watch and, without cause, was unprofessionally brusque with Bruce and me. What looked to me like a feed bag was an oxygen bag that replaced the breathing tube. Later, when Cordell was alert, he was asked by Dr. Deiter if he wanted to have the tube reinserted. His response was, "I've had enough."

The following day, Friday, Cordell was moved from the CCU to an ICU with a pressurized oxygen mask in place. Dr. Deiter and his team started the hospice discharge process. On Saturday morning, the medical equipment was delivered to our house. I met with the hospice nurse and was given information regarding Cordell's care. That afternoon I returned to the ICU, fully expecting my husband would be discharged. Instead, I was informed that Cordell's pulmonary physician, Dr. White, refused to sign the hospice release papers. An ICU nurse had noted a slight improvement in his condition. Dr. Deiter's team had been contacted, and that afternoon the medical supply company returned to our house and removed the equipment. A nightmare! And all done without any communication with me.

Over the next few days, I spent long hours by Cordell's bedside. He talked very little due to the pressurized oxygen mask that covered the lower half of his face. On Monday I left his bedside for a short time to get some lunch. While I was gone, Dr. Deiter and his assistant visited Cordell for the purpose of knowing his wishes. Apparently, Cordell told them, "Do whatever you have to do, I want to live." That afternoon, Cordell was transferred to a step-down unit.

The disconnect in communication only got worse for me. Dr. Deiter directed his assistant, Cathy Bissler, to schedule a family conference with Diane, Gary, and me for the next day. Monday evening the telephone rang. It was Cathy Bissler informing me of the Tuesday meeting to discuss a plan for Cordell's care. When I asked if Cordell would be present, I was told, "No." Dr. Deiter would inform him later of whatever decisions were made. When I hung up the phone, something snapped inside of me. I was alone. Bruce had returned home. I let out a primordial scream. I swore. I smashed a plastic tray on the kitchen counter. My anger polluted my very being.

I knew I needed help. I telephoned Brenda and asked her to come. She arrived that evening, and as we sat sipping wine and talking, I was able to begin to release the anger that consumed me.

With Brenda by my side, we arrived at the hospital late Tuesday morning for the scheduled meeting. We were sitting in a third floor waiting area when Dr. Dieter and his staff passed by. As we followed him down the hall, I passed Cordell's door and observed him sitting up in bed with a questioning look on his face. I walked into his room and told him about the meeting called by Dr. Deiter. Cordell became enraged. "Why the hell am I not a part of this?" I immediately left the room, found Dr. Dieter, and conveyed Cordell's anger.

Realizing my agitated state, Dr. Dieter summoned his hospital team to reassemble in Cordell's room. Diane and Gary entered with them. I was already seated in a chair at the foot of Cordell's bed. Brenda sat beside me.

Cordell spoke first, very articulate in stating his desire to live, to regain full physical function, and that he would do whatever was necessary to achieve this goal. When asked, I commented that Cordell was fully cognizant, able to make his own decisions, and my role would be to support those decisions. Diane spoke in terms of thankfulness, and Gary concurred.

Dr. Dieter informed Cordell of his options and advised him to clearly state his wishes in writing. He would remain in the step-down unit for a few more days before being transferred to Altercare in Brimfield for needed therapies. The meeting adjourned. Dr. Dieter and staff left without look or comment. I remained seated and, looking at Cordell, saw a need for love in his eyes, but I was unable to respond. Something had snapped inside of me. Finally, my husband broke the silence when he asked Brenda to give us some privacy.

Cordell motioned for me to move closer. When I did, he took my hand and asked me to listen while he talked—his words were a plea for love, for understanding. Something he said required a response, and with my response came an outpouring of all that had happened since his admittance to the hospital. He was shocked. With the telling, Cordell was able to understand my comment, "I need time to heal."

Sitting there holding Cordell's hand, relating the happenings of the past trauma-filled days, the ice I felt in my being melted away and was replaced by the love I had for this man. Together we cried, and the emotional healing began. In my mind, we were victims in this bureaucratic hospital charade. I was Cordell's wife, the one responsible for his care. Yet I was ignored when the decision was made to withdraw hospice support, and later, it seemed to me, I was no more than a postscript when informed that a meeting was called to determine his care. Is it any wonder I had an emotional meltdown?

--------++++++--------

ON FRIDAY, AUGUST 19, fifteen days after Cordell was admitted to the hospital, he was taken by ambulance to the Altercare Rehabilitation Center in nearby Brimfield. There he was given physical, speech (needed due to poor swallowing habits) and occupational therapies. Each day, therapy sessions were completed by early afternoon. For the remainder of the day, as well as weekends, Cordell was in a monotonous holding pattern. At first, I visited him twice daily, as he had done when I was hospitalized.

As Cordell gained strength, I requested permission to bring him home for the few hours between his last therapy session of the day and the evening medication schedule. Permission was given, and for both Cordell and me, it was our salvation. With portable oxygen tanks in tow, I brought him home where we could relax and enjoy dinner together before I took him back to Altercare.

I took comfort in helping Cordell with personal bedtime rituals. Before leaving, I would organize needed items on his bedside table. No matter how they were placed, he would methodically rearrange them. I found this frustrating until my niece Kellie, a nurse, commented that patients as infirm as Cordell tenaciously hang on to whatever they can control. For Cordell, this was arranging the items on his bedside table.

I had one unfortunate driving incident during the weeks Cordell was at Altercare. Returning home late one evening, fighting sleep all the way, I turned onto Burr Oak Drive and allowed myself to relax just enough that I dozed off. The van wheels jumped the curb, shocked me awake, and I slammed on the brakes just as I was about to collide with a sign that read "NO PARKING." I maneuvered the van back onto the street, drove the few hundred feet to our house, parked in the garage, and breathed a prayer of thanks that I was not injured.

On September 9, after twenty days at Altercare, Cordell came home. Physical, occupational, and speech therapies were continued along with a Home Health Services nurse. Cordell was committed to regaining his strength, and to that end, he set up an Excel spreadsheet and recorded his progress, later writing in his memoir, "If one has never been in this type of situation one has no idea what good medicine it is for the patient to know others care. I know what has happened to me will make me much more sensitive to others in the future."

During the weeks of Cordell's convalescence, family and friends remained in close communication—telephone calls, cards, visits, and some overnight guests. My former Columbus neighbor, now living in Spokane, was in the area and drove through a heavy rainstorm to visit Cordell and me. I know the visit was a disappointment to her because I was constantly distracted with phone calls and other matters related to his care.

The physical and emotional demands of the previous weeks took a toll on my health. Worst of all was not sleeping at night. For the first time in my life, I asked my PCP for a sleeping pill prescription. I found it interesting that, as he wrote out the scrip, he spoke of my request as situational insomnia, and that it was. As Cordell gained strength and resumed normal activities, I no longer needed sleeping pills.

As our lives resumed a degree of normalcy, another matter required our attention. We made a concentrated effort to update all of our legal papers, clearly defining our end-of-life decisions. In turn, we met with each of our children to be certain they understood our decisions. At last, a degree of normalcy returned in our lives.

++++++

Now living in Kent, I expressed an interest in finding a new church home. In December 2012, Cordell and I made our first church visitation. The United Church of Christ (UCC) was located only one mile from our house. The service was uninspiring and the sanctuary acoustics poor. One visit was enough; we didn't return.

Cordell was indecisive about leaving the Mogadore Methodist Church (MMC), but incidents that occurred in December and January confirmed it might be best if we sought out a new church home. Cordell's son, Kent, died on Thursday, December 20, 2012. The following Sunday we attended the MMC. Cordell wanted to make a verbal prayer request for Kent and his family. Unfortunately, it was youth Sunday, and that portion of the service was omitted. The Sunday after, on January 6, Cordell had flowers placed on the altar of the MMC in memory of Kent. We were there, and during the announcement portion of the service, the young minister made no mention of the flowers or Kent's passing. At the conclusion of his message, the pastor remained standing behind the lectern and proceeded to voice his New Year's resolutions. He ended with, "I'll be the best father ever," paying no recognition to his wife, who remained seated in the front pew of the sanctuary. What an ego trip. Cordell lost all interest in the MMC.

We resumed church visitation in Kent, this time attending the United Methodist Church of Kent (UMC of Kent), located across the street from the UCC. We entered the sanctuary and seated ourselves. Our first impressions were of the narrow, floor-to-ceiling, faceted, colored-glass windows in the sanctuary, the heavy wooden cross suspended from the ceiling at the front, and two large video screens encased in built-in ceiling mounts on each side of the altar, projecting images that supported the service. Add to that the organ music and the familiar hymns. Dr. Palmer's sermon, "I Believe," was based on the Apostle's Creed. We left feeling the friendliness of the congregation was genuine and later discussed Dr. Palmer's thought-provoking sermon. We had found our church home. Cordell agreed to transfer his MMC membership, and contact was made with Dr. Palmer. We signed up for the required membership orientation classes. On June 16, 2013, by transfer, we became members of the UMC of Kent.

————— ·+·+·+·+·+·· —————

THE CITY OF KENT AND THE SURROUNDING AREA were rich in resources that challenged, informed, and provided entertainment. Cordell was interested in the architecture of the city, both old and new construction. The police station, referred to as a citadel by James A. Michener in his book *Kent State: What Happened and Why*, was an outdated building in need of replacement. Hoping to convince voters of funds needed to replace the building, Michelle Lee, chief of police, directed tours of the outdated structure. On the tour, we walked through a maze of small rooms that served as offices, passed the jail cells, and entered a room identified as the communication center. What we observed was unbelievable—a mass of tangled wires covered the four walls.

Cordell exited the building, convinced it was a disaster waiting to happen. He wrote a letter to the editor, published in the local paper along with others, supporting the proposed sales-tax increase that would be on the November ballot. It failed. The citadel on the corner of Routes 43 and 59 would continue, for the foreseeable future, to house those who performed their duty in keeping the city free of crime.

There were year-round weekend festivals and activities—wine, art, music, Christmas with lights and Santa's arrival by train, and ice sculpting to name only a few. On Earth Day weekend we toured the Water Treatment

Plant and were admonished that if we purchased bottled water, we were wasting our money. The plant manager proudly proclaimed Kent to be one of five cities in the country to receive the Best Municipal Water 2011 award. On many Saturday mornings, Cordell and I would ride our bicycles to the Farmer's Market and stop by our neighbor, Rachel Wagner's, stand to purchase some mouthwatering Shmookies Cookies.

We frequently walked to the Kent Public Library, located slightly more than a mile from our home. On our return we'd stop by our favorite restaurant, the Pufferbelly, for lunch. I joined the library's Page to Screen book club where we would read a book, view the film, then meet and critique the connection between the two. One of the best book clubs I ever joined.

Kent Roosevelt High School hosted several community events. Each spring the Kent Area Chamber of Commerce sponsored an exhibit featuring area businesses. The school's theater and music classes produced exceptional performances. Their production of *Joseph and the Amazing Technicolor Dreamcoat* was outstanding. When I learned that a senior prom was held at the high school for area senior citizens, which piggybacked on the high school junior/senior prom, we were there. The orchestral music of the '40s and '50s reverberated so loud throughout the gymnasium conversation was impossible. The food was mediocre, but the hundred or so white-haired guests appeared to enjoy the event. We didn't and never returned.

We explored the city and the KSU campus, alone or together, on foot or on bicycles. On these jaunts we discovered a treasure of sculptures as part of the cooperative Downtown Redevelopment Project and the Ohio Arts Council. Located in the center of the newly constructed downtown plaza is the black *Squirrel with an Attitude.* In a park, next to the PARTA station, stands a statue honoring *Three Veterans.* The Wick Poetry Park is located on the esplanade that connects the city with the campus; in the park's center stands a twelve-foot bronze sculpture, *Seated Earth 2014.* Other sculptures are located on the picturesque grounds of the original KSU campus: *STARSPHERE 2010, Eye to Eye, Behind the Brain Plaza, The Witnesses.* We returned again and again to observe and to ponder the messages conveyed through these artistic works.

Other campus resources were available to us. The building and grounds surrounding Taylor Hall were transformed into a commemorative site recognizing the tragedy of the May 4, 1970, shootings. We visited the museum in Taylor Hall and left acknowledging that the tragedy had been sensitively communicated through the memorabilia and video displays.

Cordell and I enjoyed the twice-yearly Bowman Breakfast, another town/gown cooperative venture. The first breakfast we attended was in October 2012. The editor of the *Record Courier* spoke. His talk was interesting, but my enjoyment was winning a door prize. The large carry-all bag was stuffed with useful items. For me, the significant one was the book *Most Noble Enterprise: The Story of Kent State University, 1910—2010* by William H. Hildebrand. I read this captivating book aloud to Cordell during our morning coffee sessions.

Other areas of interest were the KSU/NASA Observatory, KSU Fashion Museum, and student art exhibits, but outranking all was our desire to audit university classes. Winter/spring semester 2012 we registered as senior guests for two classes—Comparative Religions and Morality in Medicine. The religions class was a disaster. Wanting to be as unobtrusive as possible, we sat in the last row in the stadium-style classroom. From that distance, the whiteboard used by the instructor was impossible to read. The teacher was of foreign descent and impossible to understand, and the class met at eight o'clock in the morning. It was a no-brainer to opt out.

Morality in Medicine proved more promising. The class met twice a week at five o'clock in the afternoon. The female professor introduced us, encouraged us to sit in the front row of the traditional classroom, and welcomed our participation. Her words belied her behavior. She had her lesson plan, and we sensed any comments by us that would steal precious minutes from her lecture would meet with unspoken disapproval. We both felt our lack of participation was a loss for the students. We could have initiated dialogue that would have taken the professor's lectures away from the pedantic and brought health-care issues into the world of reality.

There were activities in the surrounding area that interested us. I signed up for a folk dance class in Ravenna. The class was very different from the folk dancing I enjoyed while living in Columbus. The dances did not have an international flair. Participants swayed and stepped to jazzed-up country music. After two sessions, I dropped the class.

Each fall the nearby Sunbeau Valley Farm was the site of a hot-air balloon festival. The one time we went, Diane and Doug joined us. The day was pleasant with a feel of autumn in the air as we stood there watching the multicolored balloons gently rise into the sky and drift out of sight. As we left, I had the feeling of been-there-done-that and had no desire to return.

In May 2011, GPD, the architectural-engineering firm built by Cordell and four of his colleagues, held a fiftieth anniversary celebration for three hundred invited guests at the Cleveland Botanical Gardens. During the informal stand-on-your-feet / walk-about event, no recognition was given to the two living founders in attendance. As we were leaving, someone handed Cordell a large framed caricature drawing of the original five (Glaus, Pyle, Schomer, Burns, and DeHaven). I knew Cordell had prepared a short talk acknowledging his twenty-five years with the company that included comments giving recognition to the employee ownership's success over the next twenty-five years. Disappointed he was not asked to speak, Cordell kept his feelings to himself. I was verbal with my thoughts, wanting to support my husband and make him aware I was sensitive to his disappointment.

I shopped out of necessity, not for gratification. But when the Hartville Hardware opened in 2012 in the small town of Hartville, located thirteen miles to the south of us, I shared Cordell's enthusiasm to visit the store. The hardware is privately owned, fully stocked, with knowledgeable employees available to answer shoppers' questions—a rarity in today's world of big-box stores. In this two-story building, advertised to have 305,000 square feet under the roof, a 1,850 square foot Made-in-the-USA Idea House was built. Is it any wonder that the Hartville Hardware served two purposes in our lives—a destination to purchase hardware supplies and as a destination to entertain houseguests?

---------- ·+·+·+·+·+· ----------

FAMILY REMAINED CENTRAL TO US. Involvement with Cordell's family was casual and ongoing; with mine, it continued to be a major event. In July 2011, Bruce and Linda came for a weeklong visit. Bruce wanted to take a trip down memory lane and visit Nelson-Kennedy Ledges State Park, located twenty miles northeast of Kent. Ma Nelson was the first to take the family there. As children, this was where Bruce, with his brother Vernon, his Aunt Brenda, and cousin Karen, would explore the stone ledges while Ma prepared a mouthwatering meal of bacon and eggs over an open fire, supplemented with her homemade Swedish cinnamon rolls. We sat at a wobbly picnic table placed on the sloping hill near the entrance to the ledges, legs leveled with flat rocks underneath. These special times shared with family were never forgotten. With the passing of the years comes change. This time, Bruce served as chef using a Coleman gas stove, the sweet rolls were store bought, and food was prepared and eaten at a picnic table in a grassy area far removed from the previously precarious location at the base of the ledges.

When Lloyd, Jill and Garvin, Pete and Bev came to visit, Cordell and I took them not to an outdoor venue but to 101 Bottles of Beer on the Wall. There the beer drinkers in the family could choose from an unending flow of a variety of beers. Snacks were available rather than real food, and customers were encouraged to bring their own. Knowing this, I packed a picnic basket. We would get our beer, belly up to a bar-high table, and take out our lunch. We sat there eating and sipping, enjoying the time together, seasoning the conversation with laughter.

When Candice and Will came to visit, Chef Will wanted to prepare his specialty—flank steak with sausages. To do this right required a grill. Not having any, they bought me one. Brenda and her entourage were invited. It rained. The meal was prepared on the grill in the garage and eaten in the dining room. The succulence of the roast gave credit to Will's culinary talent, and the camaraderie enjoyed by the family made up for the inclement weather.

With an increase in family size came an increase in birthday, graduation, and wedding celebrations. Papa was there to celebrate the first birthday of his great-granddaughter, Grace. The following year, in November 2012, Kent, Gary and Diane planned a celebration for their dad's eighty-fifth birthday. The family event was at Gary's home. They presented him with a Don Drumm leaf motif plaque—most appropriate, given that our backyard was a forest.

In December of that same year, Cordell and I were in Las Vegas to be with grandson Bruce Allan, to celebrate with him the awarding of an Executive Master of Business Administration (EMBA) degree from UNLV. Earning the degree was impressive, but the ensuing event at the celebratory family party is what remains with me. Bruce A. called everyone together in the living room, stood before the gathering of about forty people, and thanked those who supported him on the arduous path to the EMBA. Then he invited his girlfriend, Rachel, to join him, assumed the bended-knee position, and proposed to her. The proposal was a total surprise to most of us, and an audible gasp filled the room as I, with others, strained to hear Rachel's answer. I know I held my breath in the two-second time lapse before her "yes" was heard—a joyous moment shared with family!

There were weddings. Cordell's granddaughter Danielle was married in June 2012. The day was hot, and a rainstorm threatened. The outdoor ceremony took place at picturesque Springfield Lake Park. The minister pronounced Randy and Danielle "man and wife" only moments before the rains came, sending guests scurrying for shelter. Contrast that to the wedding of my great-nephew, Adam Schumann, to Amanda Wight the following month. The weather was perfect. Their wedding took place amidst the natural beauty of trees and plants at the Holden Arboretum. Mother Nature is fickle—especially in Ohio.

Our families were not exempt from illness and death—the part of life's cycle that tests one's mettle. In May 2011 Kent told his dad he had been diagnosed with a critical kidney condition. This alarmed Cordell as he had no previous awareness of his son's medical problem. Most alarming was the telephone call from Diane in early December telling her dad that Kent had been diagnosed with inoperable lung cancer. Kent was given only months to live, but it wasn't months; it was days. On December 20 Diane again called, this time with the devastating news that Kent had died. The shock of Kent's death left Cordell stunned, for a time unable to speak of it. Family members, friends, and former students gathered for Kent's memorial service, held at St. Hilary Parish in Fairlawn, on Friday, December 28. Sadness enveloped the many who loved him.

My side of the family was not exempt from the big C (cancer). Bruce telephoned in November 2012 to tell me he had been diagnosed with prostate cancer. He followed up the surgery with radiation treatments. Much later, Bruce called, this time ecstatic, with the good news that the treatments had destroyed all trace of cancer cells in his body and commented, "I felt a death sentence had been lifted from me."

On May 15 of the following year, a call came from Rita telling me my stepson, George Dickie, had died. His battle with Parkinson's disease was ended. Within days, I was in Thibodaux, Louisiana, to attend his memorial service held at the Episcopalian Church. More than two hundred family, friends, and colleagues gathered to pay their last respects. This sad event took me to Thibodaux but also provided me with quality time spent with Rita, my stepdaughter Jan, and my stepgrandchildren Renee, Nancy, Scott, and Georgia.

WE REMAINED LOYAL to friends and acquaintances, and they to us. Shortly after our move to Kent, Terri Eberwine, self-appointed social secretary of the condo association, arranged a farewell party held at the Ohio Prestwick Country Club. Having served on the condo board of directors, a thankless job, Cordell and I were pleasantly surprised to find more than thirty residents in attendance, effusive with their praise of our contributions to the association and expressions of regret for our leaving. We were humbled by their comments.

We continued to celebrate our mutual wedding anniversary date with Sue Kurtz and Chuck Schutte. Cordell's wine-making protege, Pete Weber, and wife, Gwen, not content to drink only their wine, invited us to join them at area wineries.

We were all getting older, and sadly there was too much "draping of the black crepe" among our friends. Dave and Marcia Shanafelt were long-term friends of Cordell and Lois. In May 2011, we attended an eightieth birthday celebration at the Congress Lake Country Club for Dave. In December of that year we, with many others, were with him for the memorial service for Marcia, his wife of more than fifty years.

The Glaus, Frieden, and Moutz couples were inseparable. Neighbors in Mogadore, they worked, played, and raised their children together. In October 2011, Cordell and I invited the two couples to our Kent home for the grand tour, followed by dinner and levity in conversation that takes place only with longtime friends. In less than a year, Bill and Ruth Frieden moved into a residential-care facility. In September 2012, Bill died. Within six months, Ruth died—possibly of a broken heart. They were married more than sixty years.

Living in Kent, I was within six miles of Stowe-Glen Retirement Village where my friend Clarabel had lived for the past ten years. I'd like to say I made frequent visits to see her, but I didn't. I allowed life to get in the way. In July 2012, her grandson called and alerted me that Clarabel would like me to come for a visit. The next day I was at my friend's side. She was in bed, obviously very weak. Communication was limited. I sat holding her hand, and when I rose to leave, she opened her eyes and said, "Henrietta, come again." On August 15 her stepson called to tell me Clarabel had died peacefully in her sleep at two thirty that morning. Cordell and I, with her good friend Charlene, attended her memorial service at the Kent United Church of Christ. Clarabel was the loyal friend who insisted on keeping a rotating six-month visitation schedule.

Lu and Bob Lee were neighbors on Vineland Avenue in Ashtabula. Whenever I was in the area, I stopped to visit. After her husband Bob passed away, Lu continued to live in her home. Visits with Lu were delightful. In spite of her physical limitations, requiring almost round-the-clock care, she continued to be the perfect hostess. She would greet me with a joyous hello, arms extended in a welcoming hug, with wine and hors d'oeuvres made ready to be enjoyed while we talked. I didn't know it at the time, but on a day when the temperature was in the nineties and a soft breeze rustled the trees, it would be my last visit. When I arrived, I found Lu seated on their covered deck, made inviting by the placement of several urns of colorful flowers. She was looking out over their manicured lawn edged with daisies, hostas, bluebells, begonias, and lilies—to name only a few. Lu died on May 15, 2013. The following month Cordell and I attended her memorial service. Lu was my neighbor whom I had known for more than sixty years. She and Bob supported me and my boys in many ways after the death of Sidney in 1960. My feelings of loss went deep.

Susan Gardner's mother went to great effort to locate my telephone number so that she could call to let me know Susan was in St. Ann's Hospital in Columbus, intubated and on dialysis, not expected to live. Miraculously she lived, telling me later she subconsciously willed it so, knowing her widowed son needed her help in raising his two daughters. Susan spent many months in physical therapy. Thankfully, I was able to drive to Columbus to visit my dear friend during that time.

HEALTH ISSUES AGAIN RAISED THEIR UGLY HEAD, not for me but for Cordell. My health issues were minimal and patchable. I had cataracts removed from both eyes, and my ophthalmologist alerted me that I had the beginning of age-related macular degeneration (AMD), to be treated with vitamins and eyedrops. When I complained of severe neck problems, my PCP sent me for PT, and I later purchased a Saunders Cervical Traction device and used it as needed. A face condition was diagnosed by my dermatologist as rosacea; he advised me to stay out of the sun, wear a hat, and use sunscreen. I had concerns related to my right-hip implant. After looking at the X-rays, my surgeon assured me that it was as solid as the day he put it in but informed me I had arthritis and disc degeneration in my lower back, which I managed to keep under control with regular home exercises learned in previous PT sessions. A painful case of plantar fasciitis in my right foot was temporarily relieved with a cortisone shot, permanently relieved with custom insoles. I do not mean to seem blasé regarding my maladies, but at least for the time being, all were kept under control. Not so with Cordell.

Cordell appeared to be on a downward health spiral. His brush with death the summer of 2011 required a follow-up appointment in December with Dr. White—the hospital pulmonary specialist. At that appointment, Dr. White assured Cordell his lungs were clear and dismissed him with the comment to contact him only if needed. The following winter, a chronic cough developed, accompanied by a loss of appetite. A multitude of remedies were tried. A vaporizer placed by his bedside provided temporary relief. The thought came to Cordell that it might be the wine, and in March 2013, he discontinued imbibing. Acid reflux was suggested as a cause, and he started taking Pepcid. The cough continued. Apple cider vinegar was given as a possible cure, and for a short time it seemed to help. Maybe he was allergic to his bedding? I washed all bedding and changed his down pillow to foam rubber. Someone suggested shallow breathing might be the cause of his cough, so Cordell tried sleeping in a more upright position. His ENT doctor prescribed a nasal spray. Nothing worked. His cough worsened and wracked his weakening body.

Cordell's eyesight also weakened. His left eye had been his strong eye. Now he could read only the large E on the vision chart. The ophthalmologist attributed this loss of vision to heart stoppage after his surgery. In an effort to control the double vision that plagued him, Cordell was fitted with prism-lens glasses. This helped, especially his distance vision. He took advantage of any device that would help when reading—large print books and a Kindle tablet. Jody Wallace, my friend who lived in Columbus, was visually impaired. She suggested Cordell look into a closed-circuit television (CCTV) reader. An optometrist in the Akron area specialized in vision problems, and it was through him Cordell ordered the device. He used multiple eyedrops to control his failing vision, and I took over the twice daily task of administering them. There was no panacea.

Cordell's hearing failed. He was fitted with hearing aids by an audiologist, the best available at the time with settings touted to aid one-on-one conversations and minimize background noise. In social situations, the aids were useless. Cordell would sit there, isolated from the conversations that whirled about him. Hearing loss is referred to as the unseen handicap. I observed this with my husband.

Over the months, prescribed drugs played havoc with his system. He lost his appetite, and most of his nourishment came from the food supplement, Ensure. He lost energy; the smallest task exhausted him. On January 21, 2013, I was driving our van and heard a loud noise I identified as coming from the area surrounding the transmission. When I asked Cordell if he would like to call the garage, his angry outburst puzzled me. Later I commented that I was sorry my anxiety about the van caused him to become so upset. His response terrified me. "The van is the least of it. I've been coughing up bloody sputum all afternoon." The first appointment available with his pulmonologist was April 8. I have no explanation as to why we waited so long to see Dr. White only to learn, after he listened to Cordell's lungs, that his problem was probably due to heavy sinus drainage. A follow-up appointment on June 27 with our PCP gave Dr. Shanafelt grave concern. Tests were ordered, and while we waited for the results of the X-ray and CAT scan, we felt a heavy, black cloud was hanging over our heads.

The CAT scan revealed masses in the lower left lobe of Cordell's lung. The diagnosis, along with concerns for Cordell's erratic heartbeat, was reason enough for Dr. Shanafelt to have him admitted to the hospital on July 8 for further testing. Cordell insisted his flannel bed socks I had made for him be included with his toiletries for the overnight hospital stay. Those bed socks got more attention from the staff than Cordell's medical condition. In fact, if I were of a mind, I think I could have started a bed sock business right there. Cordell was released the following day and advised that the test results would be sent to his PCP. While we waited, that black cloud seemed larger and hung lower over our heads.

Sunday, July 14, Cordell planned to attend church but realized in his weakened state, he couldn't. That evening, I recorded in my diary, "For the first time Cordell commented that he is depressed over what is happening to him."

Monday morning, July 15, Dr. Shanafelt's nurse telephoned to tell us the results of the tests were back and the doctor could meet with us at four fifteen that afternoon. The minutes ticked away the hours. Arriving at the doctor's office, we were ushered into one of the examination rooms to wait. We sat there holding hands, each in our own bubble of silence.

After what seemed an eternity, Dr. Shanafelt entered and quietly engaged us in some superficial medical conversation before sharing the results of the tests. In clear, no-nonsense terms, looking straight at Cordell, he told him it was cancer. The primary site was the colon, but the cancer had metastasized into the lungs. We sat there in stunned silence. Cordell spoke first. "How long do I have?" Dr. Shanafelt replied, "Three to six months if you choose no medical intervention, possibly more if you do. Either way, I will abide by your decision." The following silence that filled the room suffocated me, and I shattered it when I looked at Cordell and spoke. "I think we need a drink. Let's go home."

That evening, Cordell first called his daughter, Diane, later his son, Gary. The following day he called Dr. Shanafelt's office and advised his nurse that he'd made the decision to be placed under hospice care.

ON JULY 17, 2013, THE HOSPICE EQUIPMENT was again delivered to our house—a bed with electrical controls, mattress, bedside table, commode, rollator, and oxygen with two supplemental tanks. The hospice social worker and nurse arrived. Innumerable forms were filled out, questions asked and answered. The palliative care medications they left helped Cordell's cough. That night he slept soundly.

The nurse made regularly scheduled visits, monitored Cordell's vital signs, his medications, answered our questions, and as needed, provided other information. When the uninvited guest is death, an angel of compassion arrives as well. Accepting the inevitable provided Cordell and me with time and tender moments shared. At the close of one very busy day, I opened a bottle of Cordell's Gewürztraminer wine. We sat there sipping our wine, conversing, allowing ourselves to feel the peace that engulfed us.

Cordell and I had started preliminary planning for his memorial service. He had already asked Doug Denton, the Minister of Pastoral Care, to speak at his funeral. The date was Friday August 23. I stopped by the church office to get needed information. The sun shone brightly that afternoon, and I took time to walk into the sanctuary to view the ceiling-to-floor windows. The angle of the sun was perfect to bring the colors of the four-inch, faceted glass pieces to life. The instant I saw the windows, I knew I must go home and return with Cordell, for this was a must-see moment. Arriving back at the church, I wheeled Cordell into the sanctuary. In the peaceful silence, we sat and gazed in wonder at the radiant rainbow colors illuminating the figures in the windows that conveyed the story of events in Jesus's life.

Cordell dedicated himself to finishing his memoir. Diane, and grandson Adam, helped him in the selection of family pictures to include in his book. As I observed Cordell at his task, I felt only happiness; his mind was occupied, if only for a short time, allowing him to forget the reality that consumed him. With his manuscript in hand, we went to Wordsmiths, a local printing shop, and Cordell selected the soft cover for his eight-and-a-half-by-eleven-inch book and placed an order for fifty copies. The owner of the shop recognized Cordell's weakened condition, marked "rush" on the order, and in one week, I received a telephone call alerting me that the books were ready.

Over the next few days, Cordell busied himself with composing short personal messages to family members and select friends to be written on the flyleaf of each book. Writing was difficult, so I served as his scribe, thankful that Cordell was able to sign his name. He took pleasure in personally delivering his books to those living in the area. The rest were mailed.

Our personal financial records were kept in an Excel program. I knew nothing about Excel, so Cordell attempted to teach me. He sat in front of his computer, looked at the Excel spreadsheet open on the screen, but said nothing. His body language communicated his frustration. Over the months, my heart ached as I observed this gifted man deal with the loss of hearing, vision, strength, and now it had invaded his brain.

Cordell's body continued to weaken. He required oxygen around the clock. The tubing connected to the concentrator was long enough that he could be moved to different places throughout the house. Morning hours were spent on the front porch, afternoons on the shaded back deck.

The idea of daily outings occurred to me. At 5:00 p.m. each day, I loaded Cordell's wheelchair into the van and drove to different venues about the city or in the surrounding area, where we would take an afternoon stroll. Pushing Cordell in the wheelchair, I walked the paths of the city parks. Our favorites were the paved Hike and Bike trail that paralleled the Cuyahoga River; the esplanade that connected the KSU campus with the downtown (grandson Dustin took Papa on this walk); and Fred Fuller Park where we enjoyed watching the antics, spiced with the gleeful sounds, of children at play. One evening we went to Mogadore. I drove past the family home and through the city park Cordell designed. Another time we explored the paths of Wingfoot Lake Park. There we rested at a site overlooking the lake and watched as the Goodyear blimp descended and, tethered by ropes, maneuvered into the hanger.

After the first month of hospice care, Cordell verbalized the stress he felt by having so many different nurses. Too many repetitive questions asked, and no chance to develop a patient/nurse rapport. When I queried the person in charge of scheduling, I was told Vickie, the nurse originally assigned to Cordell's care, requested a schedule change. Thankfully, we were able to resolve the problem by coordinating visits with the days Vickie worked.

It alarmed and frightened me that Cordell had hallucinations and at times became disoriented. One night in late August, I was awakened to find him sitting in his chair in the family room. He was greatly distraught. "Everything is wrong, black is red, green is black, where am I," and on and on and on. I managed to calm him by sitting there and holding his hand as he mercifully drifted back into sleep. On Vickie's next visit, I described the incidents to her. She explained the disease progression—colon cancer metastasizes to the lungs, to the lymph nodes, and ultimately, to the brain. The fact that Cordell remembered and could speak coherently about what happened was proof the medications were not the cause. The aggressive cancer caused Cordell's heart to work overtime. Vickie alerted me he could have a heart attack and die in his sleep, or he could live for days, for weeks, but not for months. Her counsel prepared me for the inevitable.

Through it all I did my best to keep Cordell comfortable. He experienced a fluid buildup in his body and with it the swelling in his feet and legs. Our nightly ritual included leg and foot massages. I applied lotion to keep his skin soft. For a time, Cordell refused to take Lasix. He had it in his mind that the Lasix pill would prolong the dying process, and he wanted none of that—**comfort only**. He wouldn't listen to Vickie, but when Brenda told him the medicine was prescribed only to remove excess fluid from the body, he started taking the pills, and the result was immediate.

———————

THROUGHOUT THE HEARTACHE OF CORDELL'S ILLNESS, family and close friends supported us every step of the way. As early as July 19, only two days after we learned of Cordell's cancer diagnosis, granddaughter Melissa and husband Ben planned to visit. Papa sent word not to come; he was too weak. That very day my granddaughter Candice, visiting her cousin in Madison, telephoned and said she would like to come the next morning and have breakfast with us. Cordell told me "no" as well. That evening I recorded in my diary:

> It would have helped if Cordell would have thanked me for understanding—he didn't. I can't say a word to a terminally ill man. I pray God gives me patience and strength for what lies ahead. Later that evening when I was massaging Cordell's feet and legs he did comment to his fast, insensitive response. I'm so thankful I kept any negative thoughts to myself.

Shortly after Diane became aware of her dad's cancer diagnosis, her sensitive, loving comment to me was, "I can't imagine how difficult this is for you." She cooked for us. She prepared a meal of baked chicken in wine sauce, feta cheese and spinach salad, brown rice, blueberry wheat muffins, and Boston cream pudding. The meal was so tasty Cordell called his daughter and told her how much he enjoyed the dinner. Granddaughter Danielle stopped to visit Papa and brought potato ham soup. Daughter-in-law Janet Glaus, with grandson Adam, came often and, with each visit, brought soup and on one occasion chocolate ice cream.

Members of my family came. Brenda and daughters, Pete and Bev with my brother, Lloyd, who was barely able to walk himself. Bruce and Linda telephoned and wanted to come for a five-day visit. When I told Cordell this, he responded, "I'll have to go to respite care while they are here." It broke my heart to call them back and tell them Cordell was too ill and not to come. As soon as I hung up the phone, I called Brenda and asked her to telephone Bruce and explain; I knew they were deeply hurt. Later she assured me they understood.

Dear Rosemary (Cupid) came. Later Cordell's sister Lilafay and husband, Ralph, who lived outside of Washington, DC, visited. During their visit, Cordell passed on to Lilafay the painting, dear to him, that their mother had painted of them when they were small children.

Such were the sentimental and sorrowful moments shared with loved ones over the final weeks of Cordell's life. By August 18, Cordell had become so weak he asked his children not to visit. Now it was the two of us, the hospice nurse, and the social worker. Cordell no longer slept in our second-floor bedroom but chose to sleep in the hospital bed placed in front of the floor-to-ceiling living room windows overlooking our forested backyard. I continued to sleep upstairs in the small guest bedroom. It concerned me that I would not hear Cordell if he needed my help. I bought a child monitoring system and set it up by our beds.

Cordell talked very little. It required too much energy. The evening of August 25 he said to me, "This must be very hard on you." My response, "Yes, it is but more so, my emotional suffering is for you having to endure this process of dying."

We continued to enjoy the 5:00 p.m. strolls. But the demands of Cordell's care, coupled with managing the home, were draining my energy. I reluctantly asked if Diane could come by to take him on his evening outings. Thankfully, Cordell agreed. On Monday, September 2, Diane loaded the wheelchair into the trunk of her car and took her dad to Wingfoot Lake. I was grateful for the hour respite it gave me. The outing with Diane was good for Cordell. When they returned, he seemed refreshed. Later that evening we were relaxing, enjoying wine, and weak as he was, he raised his glass in a toast and thanked me for all I'd done for him.

———————— ·+++++· ————————

IN THE EARLY MORNING HOURS OF SEPTEMBER 3, I heard sounds coming over the monitor by my bed. Awakened, I glanced at the clock, noting it was 3:30 a.m. I hurried downstairs and found Cordell not fully awake, but in bed fitfully thrashing about. I was able to calm him and sat there until I was certain he had drifted into a relaxed sleep. Later that morning, he insisted on his usual routine. I was amazed that, somehow, he had the strength to climb the stairs to the second-floor bathroom to take his shower.

Showered and dressed, Cordell returned to the family room. He was adamant that he would not take any of his medications. When Vickie arrived, she observed signs of nerve twitching and withdrawal. I explained to her Cordell's loss of appetite, confusion, hallucinations, and unwillingness to take medications. She gently explained these were the beginning signs of actively dying.

Before she left, Vickie persuaded Cordell to take his meds. As the drugs took effect, he became noticeably calmer. He asked me to help him get back into his bed, something never done before during the day. When Diane arrived at 5:00 p.m. for her dad's outing, Cordell was still in bed, sound asleep.

I needed fresh air and exercise. Diane was with her dad, so this was a good time for me to take a bicycle ride. As I was preparing to leave, I tripped on my untied shoelace and fell forward, hitting my forehead firmly on the tile floor. For a moment Diane was frantic—her terminally ill dad in bed, his wife had taken a bad fall. I managed to get up, checked myself for broken bones, and assured Diane I was okay. In truth, I was shaken, unsure of my balance. I aborted my plan to take a bike ride.

Diane poured us a glass of wine. We were sitting in the family room quietly talking when we noticed Cordell, with the aid of his walker, entering the small first-floor bathroom. We immediately went to help, and it took the strength of us both to get him back into his bed. Diane was in the process of making her dad as comfortable as possible when we realized something was happening. Guttural sounds came forth out of Cordell's mouth. One look and we knew he was dying! Grief-stricken, I sobbed and hugged him. Diane had the presence of mind to suggest we bring our wine glasses to his bedside. We stood there, on opposite sides of the bed, raised our glasses, expressed our love, gently poured a few drops of the fruit of the vine Cordell had enjoyed so much into his open mouth. With a kiss, I closed his lips, Diane his eyes. "Peace, my beloved husband, your travails on this earth are over." The time was 8:00 p.m.

———— ·++++·+ ————

My FIRST PHONE CALL WAS TO HOSPICE. The nurse on duty arrived within the hour and verified the time of death. Cordell's directive was to use the services of Hopkins Lawver Funeral Home in Akron. While Diane and I waited for them to arrive, we each spent a few private minutes with Cordell to say our goodbye. I knew Cordell wore his bed socks. In death I could not remove them.

Diane and I were quietly sitting in the family room when the men from Hopkins Lawver arrived, and there we stayed. Neither I, nor Diane, wanted to see Cordell placed in the black body bag and transported feet first out the front door. Diane would have stayed the night, but I encouraged her to return home and, in her time of grief, be with her husband, Doug. I needed to be alone, to allow my mind and body to feel, to absorb, and to remember all of the emotions I had felt this final day of my husband's life. That night, and many times since, I have thanked God that Diane was there the night her dad died.

The business arm of hospice is unemotional in its efficiency. In the morning, the medical supply company truck was in the driveway before 9:00 a.m. The men dismantled the bed and collected the equipment. Within thirty minutes, the truck pulled away. I was numb. It is crass to write, but from previous experience, I knew the drill. Telephone calls were made to family members. A person from Hopkins Lawver arrived, and I signed the cremation directive. Contact was made with the church and an appointment set to meet with Dr. Palmer and Reverend Denton. The date for the memorial service needed to be included in the obituary. On September 6, Cordell's obituary appeared in three newspapers—the *Record Courier*, the *Akron Beacon Journal*, and the *Ashtabula Star Beacon*. Gary selected family pictures and prepared a PowerPoint presentation to be shown on the sanctuary's large television screens prior to the memorial service, scheduled for September 14.

All progressed smoothly, until I received a frantic telephone call from Rosemary the evening of Friday, September 6. She understood the service was to be the next day and had so informed Lilafay and Ralph. They were here, staying at a motel in Kent. She asked me to call and inform them of the snafu. Rosemary had learned of the mistake only that evening when talking with her daughter. Later I recorded in my diary: "I think she believes I told her the wrong date. Can't go there don't know how the mix-up happened."

That evening, the feeling of loneliness enshrouded me, and I gave in to my grief—screamed, cried, asked WHY? Cordell and I, each having experienced the pain of loneliness that comes with losing one's mate, had often said, "We want to go out in a fiery crash together!" It didn't happen. Now I was left, for the fourth time, to cope with being a widow.

———————

A DAY OR TWO PRIOR TO THE SERVICE, Bruce and Linda arrived along with others. Angry about the date mix-up, Lilafay and Ralph did not return. On Saturday morning, family members assembled in the narthex of the church and mingled with friends and former colleagues of Cordell, who came to pay their respects and express sincerely spoken condolences. In the sanctuary, pictures of Cordell's life flashed on the video screens. Flowers banked the tripod stand at the base of the altar, on which a large portrait of Cordell was displayed. All the while the soft sounds of sacred music played by the organist filled the sanctuary.

Hymns "How Great Thou Art" and "In the Garden" held special meaning for Diane or me and were sung during the service. Carol Groh, who knew Cordell from his years of active involvement in the Mogadore Methodist Church, spoke of his many contributions. Members of the Glaus family declined to speak at the service. At my request, Bruce spoke and paid an eloquent tribute to Cordell for the powerful influence he had on his life during those few years he was privileged to know him. Dr. Palmer and Pastor Denton's messages included insightful anecdotes about Cordell, with an assurance of life in the hereafter as promised in the scriptures. In tribute to Cordell's military service, "Taps" was played as we left the sanctuary.

Arrangements were made for lunch to be served in the church dining hall. I took the opportunity to move from table to table and thank all for coming and sharing this moment with the family. Later, many gathered at 432 Burr Oak for a time of informal camaraderie. Fall was in the air. A gentle breeze rustled the leaves on the trees just beginning to reveal their fall colors—a day Cordell would have savored. That afternoon, a person from the funeral home stopped by with three receptacles containing Cordell's ashes—one for me, and two for Diane.

Bruce and Linda stayed on for a few days. They, with Diane, were with me on Sunday to attend the church service. On Monday Bruce, Linda, and I drove to Brenda's home in Madison. Our destination was the Edgewood Cemetery in Ashtabula. There I sprinkled a few of Cordell's ashes on the graves of his maternal grandparents, the Richens, on the graves of his paternal grandparents, and on his parent's graves. A few ashes remained. Those I sprinkled on the grave of Sidney, where my name is engraved on his marker.

Brenda brought with her a bottle of pinot noir bottled by Cordell. The wine was apportioned into each of four wine glasses, with the remainder poured onto the ground, soaking Cordell's ashes and flowing into the earth. Few words were spoken; we were overcome with sadness.

We returned to Brenda's home. Wanting to dispose of Cordell's large picture portrait, and not wanting to consign it to the recycle bin, I had brought it with me. Brenda had put a large metal container in her driveway. Cordell's portrait was placed on top of the tinder in the bottom of the container and lit. I stood there watching as the flickering flames became tongues of fire that consumed the twenty-by-twenty-four-inch poster-board facsimile of Cordell's torso. Before leaving, I collected the cooled ashes and poured them into the now-empty container that previously had held Cordell's cremains.

I was alone when I sprinkled the ashes under the blue spruce and made my farewell toast to my husband. I voiced the words of the last sentence Cordell wrote in his memoir. "I know this is one fish that has finally settled contentedly into its pond."

TWENTY-FOUR

BROTHERS

My original intent was to include both of my sons as I wrote about their lives throughout the chapters of this book. But midway through my memoir, I realized I could not do justice to Vern's story told piecemeal, apart from his brother, for during their adult years, their lives became intricately intertwined. My sons are very different, and the ebb and flow of the years evidences those differences and, along with it, their changing sibling roles. From a mother's standpoint, in the telling I will be revealing heights of joy and depths of despair.

VERNON WAS BORN ON APRIL 11, 1948. Four and a half years later, his brother, Bruce, was born on October 4, 1952. Both were difficult births. Barbara Ehrenreich in her book *Natural Causes* writes, "It was routine for obstetricians to fully anesthetize women in labor. Babies were born to unconscious women... Since the anesthetized or sedated woman could not adequately use her own muscles to push the baby out, forceps were likely to be deployed..."

Following thirty-six hours of unproductive labor, Vernon was a forceps delivery. When I awakened from the drug-induced sleep, an eight-pound, eleven-ounce baby was brought to me. At first glance, I thought I had given birth to a girl. The baby placed in my arms was angelic—delicate facial features without blemish, blue eyes, and a frizz of red hair.

Sidney was twenty and I was only four days past my eighteenth birthday when Vern was born. Being young parents, we made the decision to wait before having another child. Our goal was to be in a better position financially and living in our own home. When Bruce was born, I had a different doctor, but again, after many hours of unproductive labor, I was placed in a drug-induced sleep, and forceps were used to facilitate the birth. When my nine-pound, fourteen-ounce baby was placed in my arms, all I could see were two huge bumps on the top of his head and a smashed, battered nose, blue eyes, and a frizz of blond hair. The child in my arms looked like he had to fight to be born.

Not long after Bruce's birth, Sidney and I vowed not to have more children. We commented we each had a son. Vern's red hair and temperamental personality lent itself to the Schumann side of the family. Bruce, with his blond hair and contented personality (his laughter seemed to swell upward from his toes), was the spitting image of his father's baby pictures.

We were one of several young families living on Vineland Avenue, on the outskirts of Ashtabula. Ours was a basement home that we lived in while our house was being built over us. Sidney had quit his job on the Great Lakes freighters and was employed full-time with the Ziegler Furnace Company. The boys attended Ridgewood Elementary School near our house. I was taking classes at the recently opened Kent State University Center in Ashtabula. Life was good.

There were children of all ages on the street, and the boys had their special friends. For Vern there was only one—Bob Lee, his mischievous teenage buddy. The two of them would hang out by the railroad tracks near our house and jump a freight train and ride to Erie, Pennsylvania, sixty miles to the east, then catch a return train home, and I would be none the wiser. Nor was I ever aware when the boys would wait until we were asleep and push the Chevrolet Corvair past our bedroom window onto the street and drive off to Geneva-On-The-Lake for a risqué night at the burlesque. Bruce, more social than Vern, was friends with a number of children in the neighborhood.

Vern wanted to make some money, so he got a job delivering the *Ashtabula Star Beacon* afternoon paper, but he soon tired of the responsibility. When a paper carrier gave up their route, the policy of the paper required the carrier to find their replacement. Vern finagled his brother into taking his route. Bruce was in the fourth grade, and this was the job that launched him into the hard knocks of the world of work. Bruce stayed with the route until circumstances were such that he had to quit.

In 1960 our halcyon life changed—Sidney died. A few years later I married Allan Dickie, a professor at Kent State University and moved with my sons to Kent. Vern's universe underwent a dramatic change when he enrolled as a junior in Kent Roosevelt High School. He found himself in a hostile school setting with classmates already formed into cliques. Vern did not bring with him the talents of a star athlete, nor did he have a personality that ingratiated himself to others. He was a loner.

With this change came periods of silence, moodiness, and a personality that made Vern a social pariah. At the end-of-year senior assembly, the class last will and testament was read, and the entire student body heard the bequeath statement, "Vern Nelson wills his ability to have no friends at Roosevelt High School to…"

"Unspeakably cruel" are the only words I can use to describe this happening. Looking back, this probably was an accurate description of a traumatized teenager who lost both his father and grandfather the same year. His mother remarried, took him away from classmates he had known since kindergarten, and placed him in an unfamiliar setting his junior year to either sink or swim, and Vern sank. With hindsight, I realize this was a parenting mistake of the greatest magnitude. Had I asked, I think Vern could have lived with the Lees for his final two years at Edgewood High School. I didn't ask.

During his public school years, Bruce's personality was quite different from that of his brother. Bruce entered the sixth grade when we moved to Kent. Under the tutelage of a male teacher, Bruce flourished. He took part in many of the activities available to him. One of the first was school-crossing guard. Later he was a regular at the Kent Youth Center. He made friends through his interest in music and sports. Bruce was quite social, and when Allan and I were out of town one weekend, he took full advantage of the situation and hosted a raucous party at the house. Overall, Bruce was accepting, considerate, open to new challenges, and certainly never rebellious.

Sports and music were different for the brothers. Vern tried a brief stint on the football team but had no stomach for the rough-and-tumble sport. He attempted wrestling and found he lacked an aptitude for that as well, ending all further efforts to engage in sports.

Music interested Bruce, not Vern. When the boys were young, both took piano lessons. Bruce appeared to have an aptitude for music. Unfortunately, piano lessons stopped after their father died. Now living in Kent, Bruce took up the saxophone. This time it was his need for orthodontic care that nixed his playing the instrument. To fill the saxophone void, Bruce bought a guitar and joined a group of like-minded budding musicians. Now it was his dad that stymied his music interests.

Allan did not like the persona of the youthful musician—long hair and manner of dress.

At his dad's insistence, Bruce reluctantly set aside his interest in the guitar and applied himself to sports. After a bad start in basketball his junior year, which resulted in a falling out with one coach, he was selected and mentored by a different coach his senior year. As a result, Bruce received the Most Valuable Player Award (MVPA) at the spring sports banquet. He excelled at track and field. His long legs were a natural for the high hurdles, running 120 yards in 15.15 seconds, and he mastered the Fosbury Flop, clearing the bar set at close to six feet.

Both boys did well academically, although Vern was not selected for the National Honor Society. He met the academic requirements but fell short in the community and social involvement areas. Bruce had longer to adapt to the school and the community, which was to his advantage. His senior year, he was initiated into the National Honor Society. Vern graduated from Roosevelt High School in 1966; Bruce graduated in 1971.

Throughout their school years, the boys found jobs that interested them. For Vern it was cars. He worked after school and weekends in a small garage near our house. He came close to being fired when, after changing a car's oil, he failed to tighten the engine block drain cap. Fortunately, the owner discovered oil leakage before any permanent damage was done to the engine. Allan spoke with the garage owner, and it was his stepdad's intervention that saved Vern's job.

Bruce's interest was to make money. Now an experienced paperboy, his first job in Kent was delivering papers. the Cleveland *Plain Dealer*, a morning paper, required getting up at 4:00 a.m. The *Record Courier*, an afternoon paper, was delivered after school. Bruce braved extreme weather conditions to deliver the papers. I recall many a winter morning he'd return home shivering from the cold and crawl back in bed to get warm before leaving for school. What disgusted Bruce the most were people who refused to pay him in a timely manner. One customer was so disagreeable that Bruce stopped delivering his paper. When the customer voiced a complaint against Bruce, Allan came to his stepson's defense and supported Bruce's decision.

During his high school years, Bruce took on the job of caddying weekends at the local Twin Lakes Country Club, carrying double for eighteen holes, and on many occasions the caddy master required caddies to carry double for thirty-six holes. At the time, Bruce did not have access to a car, and his means of transportation was his feet, unless a passing motorist stopped and gave him a ride.

———————— ·+·+·+·+·+· ————————

AFTER GRADUATING FROM HIGH SCHOOL, Vern and Bruce took similar paths before settling on their careers. Vern's interest being cars, he applied for a co-op scholarship with the General Motors Institute in Flint, Michigan. His acceptance letter came in spring of his senior year. That fall he reported to the General Motors Institute to begin the academic part of the program, later traveling to the General Motors production plant in Lordstown, Ohio, for his on-site training.

Allan retired in 1966 and we moved to Fort Walton Beach, Florida. Before we moved, we bought Vern a new car so he would have dependable transportation between Flint, Kent, and Lordstown. We were shocked when after only two rotations, a call came from Vern telling us he'd quit the program. My son realized early on he never could be "organization man," as described in William H. Whyte's book *The Organization Man.* Distraught as I was over Vern's decision, it was years later before I came to the realization that my son lived by the ancient Greek maxim "Know thyself" and applied it in his choice of a career.

Vern wanted to transfer to Kent State University and pursue a liberal arts degree, but the Vietnam War was raging, Vern had a low draft number, and Allan would have no part of it. He was adamant when he insisted Vern enroll in the service and recommended the navy—the branch he served in during World War II. Vern accepted his fate and tried to enroll in the navy, only to learn the quota was filled. Vern then applied for, and was accepted by, the Air Force.

On January 3, 1967, Vern reported for basic training at Lackland Air Force Base near San Antonio, Texas. He completed his six weeks of basic training and received orders to report to the Air Training Command at Kessler Air Force Base near Biloxi, Mississippi. Here he engaged in a year-long computer-repair specialist program.

While at Kessler, Vern used his mechanical talents in a way that, had he been caught, would have had dire consequences. At the time, Vern owned a Volkswagen Beetle (Bug) that developed a faulty carburetor. Try as he might, Vern could not fix the problem. He observed an officer on the base who owned the same type of Bug—model and year. I'd like to think it was Vern's momentary lapse in judgment that compelled him to

devise a plan to switch carburetors. He practiced removing and reinstall-
ing the carburetor on his own Bug in the dark of night. When he felt
confident enough to pursue the dastardly deed, one pitch-black night he
flawlessly switched carburetors with the officer's Bug. The man never had
a clue as to why his car suddenly developed an engine problem. (I was
not told this by the perpetrator of the act; I learned of it years later from
Bruce.)

Vern successfully completed the year of intensive study at Kessler.
Before reporting for duty in February 1968, at Topsham Air Force Station
near Brunswick, Maine, Vern's attention was given over to a priority of the
heart. He left Biloxi and drove the 1,100 miles to Kent to see Bobbie, his
high school sweetheart, proposed, and on February 1, 1968, placed a ring
on her finger. Plans were made to be married the following September.

Vern was granted leave to come home, and on September 12, 1968,
I accompanied my son to the Court House in Ravenna. (Allan and I, not
liking Florida, had recently returned to Kent.) I signed the marriage application that enabled Vern and Bobbie to get their marriage license since
Vern, being twenty, wasn't of legal age. The law was changed on March 23,
1971, when Congress passed the Right to Vote XXVI amendment that gave
suffrage to eighteen-year-old US citizens.

Vern and Bobbie were married on September 14, 1968, at Faith
Lutheran Church in Kent. After a brief Niagara Falls honeymoon, they
returned to Kent, and Vern immediately underwent back surgery for a
slipped disk at the VA Hospital in Cleveland. When Vern was released to
travel, they packed their worldly possessions in a U-Haul trailer, hitched it
to the Bug, and left to begin their life together in Maine.

Vern's orders came in January 1970 to report to Malmstrom Air Force
Base in Great Falls, Montana. As she had done in Topsham, Bobbie was
able to gain employment as an X-ray technician in a Great Falls hospital.

As a teacher, my summers were open, and Allan and I took advantage,
visiting Vern and Bobbie in Maine, and later in Montana. On our last visit,
Bobbie was not her usual loving self; Vern was aloof. I sensed something
was awry with the marriage, and in the not-too-distant future, I learned my
gut level feeling was on the mark.

While at Malmstrom AFB, Vernon enrolled at the College of Great
Falls. During his service years, Vern was influenced by members of the
medical profession, acquiring an interest in medicine. Following up on
this interest, he pursued a premed course of study during his undergraduate years. He maintained a 4.0 average, received an $800 scholarship for

outstanding academic achievement, was president of the veterans' club, a member of the science club, and graduated summa cum laude with a bachelor's degree on May 13, 1972. During those service/college years, Bobbie continued to work, providing her husband with both emotional and financial support.

The University of Nevada Reno (UNR) added a School of Medical Sciences in 1971—a two-year medical curriculum that served as a feeder school to fill attrition openings in four-year university MD programs. Vern applied to UNR and was accepted for the September 1972 class. With an honorable discharge and college degree in hand, Vern and Bobbie again packed up a U-Haul trailer, hitched it to their car, and this time headed the 970 miles south to Reno, Nevada.

Rather than rent an apartment, Vern and Bobbie bought a trailer. Vern spent the summer getting settled in their new home in preparation for the arduous academic program he was about to undertake. A telephone call came on August 11 of that year. Vern was so distraught I could barely understand him. Something was wrong; he needed to come home. The following day I was at the Cleveland Airport to meet my son. I watched in disbelief as Vern walked out of the jetway. My handsome son plodded toward me, shoulders slouched, face contorted in grief. He managed to get out a few words, telling me he'd learned Bobbie had been unfaithful. He was leaving her. We drove to Kent in silence. Vern stayed with us for ten days.

During his stay, I had long conversations on the phone with Bobbie. She, too, was devastated. In my son's mind, he was the victim. In my mind, I wasn't so sure. Bobbie was a victim too. I knew that between Vern's military duties and his intense academic program, there was little time or attention given over to his wife. Unfortunately, Bobbie looked for companionship elsewhere.

Vern returned to Reno, moved out of their trailer, arranged to share an apartment with another first-year med student, and started classes in September. That fall, Allan, concerned that Vern's personal problems would derail his academic goal, took a flight to Reno to reassure himself Vern was okay.

During Christmas break I, too, visited Vern. I stayed in a motel close to Vern's apartment. The day he took me to see his abode, I was appalled. The place was a disaster—dirty dishes in the sink, bathroom unspeakably dirty, clothes everywhere, not an uncluttered inch on any flat surface. I later described it as a place the health department would condemn.

Once again Vern excelled academically and was awarded a $500 Teddy Bear Havas Motors Scholarship. Near the completion of the two-year program Vern applied to, and was accepted by, the University of Washington School of Medicine in Seattle.

With Vern's singular focus on his academic program, there was no reconciliation for him and Bobbie. On January 4, 1973, their divorce was final. Whatever caused Bobbie to stray destroyed their marriage. As Allan so wisely said, "If Vern had been more mature, he could have seen beyond the infidelity to realize he was as much at fault as Bobbie." I loved Bobbie, and at this writing, forty-five years later, we remain good friends.

Apparently, Vern needed companionship, as had I throughout my life. I knew little about his romantic flings, but about a year after his divorce, when he felt secure in his academic program, I received a letter from him telling me of two women to whom he was strongly attracted.

Jane Simonson was a medical student at UNR. I never met her, but while in the service, Bruce visited his brother in Reno. During that visit he met Jane. Bruce later described Jane to me as an attractive, kind, sensitive, and compassionate woman. Apparently, Bruce was spot-on in his assessment of Jane's personality. While stationed in the Philippines, she took the initiative to write to him. Jane's letters took on a significance that someone, whom he had met only once, cared.

Judith Poulsen was the second woman Vern mentioned in his letter. The daughter of a professional/businessman, part of a respected family well-known in the area, Judy was a comely, tall, slender, blue-eyed blonde. She worked in one of the offices of the medical school, was divorced, and maintained her own home where her daughter, about age five, lived with her. In his letter, Vern mentioned she was five years older than he.

Vern recounted the pros and cons of each woman. For Jane and he, there was the need to finish medical school and, once graduated, to be burdened with debt. For Judy, already independent in her own right, he would find himself on a faster track to financial security.

Vern never again wrote to me regarding matters of the heart. His letter arrived in late fall of 1975, informing me that he and Judith Poulsen were to be married on December 21. Perhaps the goal for financial security outweighed his attraction to Jane that carried with it the struggle to establish themselves professionally and financially.

Bruce was living in Las Vegas and that fall came to our new home in Red Lion for Christmas. Storage space was at a premium, and I wanted

Bruce and Vern to have their childhood memorabilia plus some of their father's tools. He and Allan loaded a U-Haul trailer, hitched it to Allan's Ford, and drove to Las Vegas. Allan, with trailer in tow, continued north to Reno and was there in time to attend Vern and Judy's wedding. Bruce opted not to attend, and I was unable to due to my job responsibilities with Red Lion Schools.

Vern married Judy while still a student at the University of Washington. He completed the requirements for his MD, and on June 5, 1976, he was awarded the investiture of doctoralhood. Judy, her father, Allan and I, with Bruce, were in attendance.

Vern accepted a position as emergency room (ER) physician for two hospitals in Spokane. Vern and Judy purchased a home in the city. Their daughter Darci Ann was born in July 1976. A second daughter, Kristen, was born in December 1977.

At some point during his first years as an ER doctor, Vern explored other residencies that would be more lucrative and give him more status in the profession. He was offered a residency in radiology. I think the hospital was located in Eastern Washington. If he were to pursue this residency, he realized there would be years of additional study with limited financial revenue and the necessity to relocate his family. For these reasons, he opted to stay on in his ER position at the two Spokane hospitals. At the time, the ER position did not require a residency. Following his decision to remain in Spokane, Vern became integrally involved in the development of hospital residency requirements, and by so doing gave status to ER physicians.

BRUCE GRADUATED FROM HIGH SCHOOL IN 1971. The Vietnam War continued, and the draft was still in force. College students were given a deferral, and at his stepfather's urging, Bruce enrolled at Kent State University and registered for a summer-session English class. Allan, thinking it to Bruce's advantage to have the full collegiate experience, required him to live on campus. He completed the English class and signed up for a full-load fall quarter. He now had seventeen quarter hours of college credit with a 3.0 GPA. At the end of the quarter, he announced he was dropping out of school to enlist in the Air Force.

We were living in Kent at the time. I was in graduate school, and at Allan's insistence, it was he who took Bruce on February 6, 1972, to the federal building in Cleveland. From there, with other enlistees, Bruce was transported to Lackland Air Force Base in Texas for six weeks of basic training.

Following basic training, Bruce was assigned to take a Mandarin Chinese language immersion course at Presidio Army Base near Monterey, California. Still rattled by the KSU academic experience, and not wanting to immerse himself in the study required of an intensive language program, Bruce managed to get reassigned to Munitions Specialist School at Lowry Air Force Base outside of Denver, Colorado. Completing his training at Lowry, then it was hurry-up-and-wait before he was sent to Nellis Air Force Base outside of Las Vegas, Nevada, in August 1972.

At Nellis, Bruce bought a vintage bread truck that gave him reliable transportation. How well I recall that truck. Allan and I visited him soon after his arrival at Nellis and Bruce met us at the airport with his bread truck. The truck was equipped with only a driver's seat. Allan stood, but I made the jarring ride to the base seated in the step-well entrance of the truck. Bruce made arrangements for us to stay in the base's guest quarters. Allan was delighted and paid no mind to the Spartan furnishings in the room. The rate appealed to his Scottish frugality—$2 per night.

During his time at Nellis AFB, Bruce volunteered for an overseas assignment and was sent to the Philippines. While there, a dark-haired, brown-eyed, buxom maiden made a play for my son that even included me. When Bruce came home on leave, he brought with him a gift from Morita—enough yardage of a rose-colored, delicately embroidered cotton sheen fabric that I had made into a fashionable floor-length gown. Fortunately, Bruce resisted Morita's advances and got away single. While in the Philippines, Bruce volunteered twice for temporary duty (TDY) in Taiwan—the first time for five months, the second time for two months. It wasn't that Bruce found the tropics so captivating; he knew the TDY assignments would reduce his total overseas time in the Philippines.

Returning stateside to Nellis Air Force Base, Bruce was honorably discharged in December 1975. I didn't know it at the time, but much later in life, Bruce told me that during his youthful years, he vowed to escape from the harsh winters of the Midwest. Me-thinks his decision must have been predicated on his 4:00 a.m. *Plain Dealer* newspaper route.

Like his brother, Bruce took college classes while in the military. He stayed on in Las Vegas and enrolled as a full-time student at the University of Nevada Las Vegas (UNLV), graduating in the spring of 1978, with an undergraduate degree in hospitality.

As fate would have it, while enrolled at UNLV, Bruce met the girl who would become his wife. Linda Gripentog, the third of four children, was soft-spoken, with an average build, a beautiful face and engaging smile, hazel eyes, and brown hair. On March 11, 1976, Bruce had a blind-meet (her word) in the student union with this captivating young woman. From the first time Bruce saw Linda, Roy Orbison's song, "Oh, Pretty Woman," became his song.

Linda's parents owned Las Vegas Boat Harbor located on Lake Mead, thirty miles slightly south and to the east of Las Vegas, as well as the Dry Dock Boat Sales on Boulder Highway in the city.

Well I remember the first time I met Linda. I went to Las Vegas for a professional meeting. My son, with Linda, met me at the airport—this time in a car, not the bread truck. On my previous visit to the city I had not seen the glitz and glimmer of the Strip, so Bruce opted to drive down Las Vegas Boulevard. When I went to get into the back seat of the car, Linda insisted I sit up front because I would have a much better unobstructed view. I recall thinking, "I like this young woman, she is sensitive to others." The years have never proven me wrong.

Bruce proposed to Linda New Year's Eve 1976. They were married by Nevada Supreme Court Justice Alfred Gunderson on June 24, 1977. (The day was hot, the thermometer registering 105 degrees in the shade. Both bride and groom, as well as the wedding party and guests, were saturated in sweat. The photographer and the camera were affected by the heat as well. No formal wedding group pictures were taken, only informal scenes at the reception.) The wedding took place in the pleasant backyard of Linda's parents' home. The couple stood under a wooden arch festooned with flowers. Allan Dickie, recovering from surgery, was not present; Jan came to Ohio to be with her dad so I could attend the wedding. Brenda was with me. Also, Bruce's Aunt Dorothy, as well as Jan's husband, Royce and their children, Renee and Royce II. Vern did not attend.

Bruce and Linda started their married life living in a house trailer parked on the lot behind the Dry Dock Boat Sales with Bruce's dog, Spooky, a small black mutt that liked to steal food off the kitchen counter. Bruce and Linda moved out of their trailer into their first small house in Las Vegas before Candice Lisanne was born in June 1980. Their third move was to a larger house before Bruce Allan's birth in June 1983. They lived there for the next twenty-eight years. Bruce, remembering the trauma of the number of times his life was disrupted by moving, vowed not to allow this to happen to his family.

Bruce's first job was working for his father-in-law, Bob Gripentog. But working for the family business was not to his liking, and he used his hospitality degree to get a position as assistant manager, later promoted to manager, of a Denny's Restaurant in the city. On one of Jan and Royce's visits, we stopped by the restaurant to say hello to Bruce. Entering the dining room, Bruce was nowhere to be seen, and inquiring as to his whereabouts, we were told he was in the kitchen, filling in for the chef. Royce, ever the prankster, directed the server to rush into the kitchen and summon Bruce, saying there was a food fight in the dining room.

The three of us, now seated in a booth, waited only a brief moment before Bruce exploded through the kitchen's swinging doors, surveyed the dining room, saw nothing, then spied Royce, who by now was exploding in laughter. Bruce failed to see the humor of the moment.

Bruce stayed with Denny's for two and a half years, realized it held no future for him, and took a job as the office and credit manager for Nevada Beverage. He stuck it out for five years before he acknowledged that, as well, was a dead-end job and quit. Thinking opportunities in money management might be more lucrative, he accepted a position with American Express IDS but found this to be the least appealing of any of his career moves. He quit after six months. Each time he quit one of his jobs, he would return to work for his father-in-law. The family business was that—a family business—and Bruce finally conceded it was best to be a part of it rather than an outlier. Once Bruce recognized and accepted this, the years passed, and he became the manager of the Marine Center—the service arm of the business.

———— ·++++·· ————

THE BROTHERS HAD PROFOUNDLY DIFFERENT avocational interests. Vernon's was cars, and in his off hours, he could be found working in his garage, first rebuilding Judy's Porsche, which he later sold. The man who bought it wrecked the car. Vern found this agonizing as he had put blood, sweat, and toil into rebuilding the Porsche. Later he purchased and rebuilt his own Porsche, vowing never to sell it.

Bruce inherited his father's love of woodworking. When he graduated from college, Allan and I gave him a Shopsmith, which he used until his woodworking talents outgrew the equipment. Over the course of the next thirty years, Bruce partially remodeled the three houses in which the family lived.

Today Bruce has a large dedicated shop area in one of the buildings at the Marine Center facility. His shop is complete with band and table saws, shaper, planer, and an extensive vacuum system. His pride and joy is his Powermatic Lathe. Bruce admits he is a woodworking fanatic and is a member of the local Wood Turners Association. For Cordell's eightieth birthday, Bruce made him a hollowed-out cherry wine bottle, referred to as a "wine holder," large enough for a standard-size bottle of wine. Cordell's engraved initials are on the wooden bottle. Admiring the craftsmanship of Bruce's work, Cordell looked him squarely in the eye and remarked, "You are an artist." With that compliment from Cordell, an artist in his own right, my son accepted he had finally arrived.

SADLY, I WAS ESTRANGED FROM VERNON FOR SIX YEARS, beginning shortly after Allan's birthday celebration in 1984 and not resolved until 1990. Two factors came into play that foretold of the disaster to come. Shortly after Vernon's marriage to Judith Poulsen, my brother, Lloyd, commented to me, "Henri, Vern married a woman in a social class above us, and that will be difficult for him to overcome."

My mother was a college graduate. Unfortunately, she repressed her education to fit in with the blue-color farm community where she grew up and lived. This was the social-economic milieu that made an imprint on Vern during his most impressionable years. In contrast, Vern married a woman who, by our standards, was raised in luxury. As previously noted, she was a member of a family well-known throughout the Reno, Nevada, area.

Vern earned an MD and married an attractive woman recognized on the society pages of the *Reno Evening Gazette*—heady stuff that required him to make major changes in his lifestyle. In doing so, Vern submerged his blue-color upbringing and, with it, pride in his blue-color family.

I, too, was a product of this environment. Consequently, I did not understand Judy, nor could she understand me. Looking back, we each had expectations of the other that were impossible to fulfill.

The first disastrous happening occurred in April 1976. I was not able to attend their wedding the previous December, but plans were made for me to go to Reno to meet my daughter-in-law and, while there, to celebrate both Vern's and my birthdays by going out for brunch together. Due to job responsibilities, there was not enough time for me to extend my travel to visit Bruce in Las Vegas. I asked Vern if I could invite Bruce to come to Reno. Vern gave his okay, never telling Judy.

Sunday morning, April 11 (Vernon's twenty-eighth birthday), we were together in Judy's home. The brothers started to argue over who would/ should get which items brought out in the U-Haul trailer the previous December. At the time, I failed to designate ownership. Excluding Judy, I secluded myself with my sons and attempted to resolve the issues. We talked for two to three hours. It was noon before we finally emerged from the room. Judy was waiting for us with her daughter Kim and informed us other plans needed to be made for lunch; the brunch reservation had been for 11:00 a.m.

To her credit, Judy made the best of it, and that afternoon, birthdays were celebrated. Judy gave me a beautiful Norman Rockwell plate, one of the Four Seasons collection. She sent three more individually wrapped gifts home with me—two for Allan and one for me. Returning home to Red Lion, Allan and I opened the three packages. I was elated. When I thanked Judy for the beautiful plates that completed the collection, she was devastated. Special days were important to her, and I had prematurely spoiled Allan's birthday and our Christmas gift surprise. My insensitive, impetuous actions totally destroyed Judy's efforts to make our first meeting a memorable one.

Granted, our relationship had a shaky start, but we all worked to improve familial relations. In 1980, Vern and Judy invited Allan and me to come to Spokane for Christmas and sent us two plane tickets. On December 19, I received an emotional phone call from Vern, informing us that Judy's father had died in his sleep. Vern asked that we cancel our trip. My heart ached for them, and especially Judy. Thinking of myself and my needs when a traumatic emotional event happened in my life, I had wanted the comfort of loved ones near me. Allan and I ignored Vern's request and arrived in Spokane as scheduled. Our visit was a blur of activity. When we left, I felt an emotional emptiness. I finally came to the realization that I should have listened to my son. My presence was tolerated, not needed.

The Christmas of 1980 proved to be insignificant compared to the snowblower incident of Christmas 1981. On Tuesday, December 15, the nitpicking that had occurred at school that day weighed me down. I was looking forward to a quiet, relaxed evening at home with Allan. That day a large box arrived from Vern and Judy; Allan was waiting for me to come home before opening it. Tired as I was, we opened the box to find a snowblower. I recorded in my diary, "I am so upset! I don't want a snow blower. They should have asked us if it were something we could use before they bought it. It's something else for me to put together and to maintain." Allan was not one to work with anything mechanical, and I knew the maintenance would fall to me.

Allan and I discussed the impracticality of the gift. It was I who telephoned and spoke to Vern. In my paltry attempt to explain why we couldn't use the gift, I exaggerated by citing the analogy of using the snowblower to clean out our long driveway would be like attempting to use a bucket to empty Lake Erie. Apparently, this time Vern related to Judy what I had said, for I learned years later it was this analogy that Judy resented the most.

Vern suggested I ask Bob and Lu Lee (Vern's surrogate family) if they could use the snowblower. They, in turn, refused for much the same reason that we gave. When I related this to Vern, he told me just to send the snowblower back, this time not telling Judy of his directive to me.

Vern and Judy did communicate with us during the following year, but at best it was a frigid relationship. I learned they were taking the girls to Disney World during spring break in 1982. Allan and I had not been to Disney World, and the opportunity to see the recently opened EPCOT center was appealing to us. We planned our trip to coincide with their visit. From the vantage point of a tourist, the visit went very well. But our primary reason for going was to attempt to mend the breach that occurred over the snowblower. That did not go well at all!

During the three days we were together, Vern and Judy avoided any opportunity to have a quiet conversation. I managed to get them to listen to my haphazard, often-interrupted apology made while standing in a food or ride line. Their reaction was expressed in anger. They told me I was "off base for being so truthful." With twenty-twenty hindsight, they were right.

Given that they would not accept my honest explanation, another incident occurred on the trip that revealed the futility of my efforts to heal the breach. On the day we arrived, before checking into our room in the Sheraton Lakeside Hotel, we stopped by their room. Four-year-old Kristen ran to me, gave me a big hug, and expressed her childish delight to see me. Her five-year-old sister, Darci, was more reserved.

As we were about to leave to check into our room, Kristen kept holding my hand and came with me. Once in our room, while unpacking my suitcase, this adorable redheaded little girl, the spitting image of my mother at that age, looked up at me and said, "You're not my real grandma, Mor Mor is" (a couple who were neighbors of Vern and Judy who, by design, had assumed the grandparent role). I couldn't believe what I was hearing. Later I tried to talk with Vern about Kristen's comment, and his response was, "I want my children to have a grandparent experience like I had growing up on the farm. You live too far away for that."

One year later, in March 1984, the relationship with my son and his family totally imploded. Jan planned a family reunion to celebrate Allan's eightieth birthday. A five-bedroom, three-and-a-half-bath beach house was rented in Santa Cruz, California. The house was large enough to accommodate the extended family with overflow lodging nearby. The guest list included the honoree, Allan, and me; George with Rita and children Nancy, Scott, and Georgia; Jan and Royce with children, Renee and Royce II; Vernon and Judy with children, Darci, Kristen, and Kim; Bruce and Linda with children, Candice and Bruce Allan. Other family members were Bob and Evelyn (Nin) Brandenburg, née Nelson, and Marby Hambright. Jan did a superb job organizing room assignments, area entertainment, and meal responsibilities, which included a Saturday catered dinner.

For the family it was a celebratory event honoring the patriarch. For me, personally, it had a devastating outcome. Vern carried with him an attitude of resentment that easily flamed into anger. Due to a freak storm in the Cleveland area, our flight was delayed, and we arrived a day late. Of their own volition, Vern and Judy took over the master bedroom Jan had reserved for Allan and me, choosing not to use the smaller room assigned to their family. When we arrived, Allan assessed the situation and insisted we have the room given over to us. This required Vern and Judy to transfer all their belongings to the room originally assigned to them. I knew that Vern's inevitable resentment did not bode well for me.

After the evening's catered dinner, all took part in a delightful few hours of conversation and hearty laughter. On Sunday afternoon the family again gathered and, with much hilarity, roasted Allan in verse and prose. To commemorate the celebration, a formal picture was taken on the grounds of Cabrillo College, located in nearby Aptos.

Perhaps it was an innocent suggestion on my part which was the final straw that lit the conflagration of resentment in my son and his wife. On Sunday evening, plans were made for Monday. Several of our group were leaving; Vern and Judy were staying on until Tuesday, as were Allan and I. They were in charge of Monday's evening meal. Noting the refrigerator was full to overflowing, I suggested we eat leftovers. Neither Vern nor Judy commented, but a frigid silence filled the room. Monday morning Vern, with his family, left, not to return until late evening, leaving us with Jan and Royce on our own for dinner.

On Tuesday morning I made the effort of a pleasant goodbye to my son and his family. By then even Kristen held back from my farewell hug. I felt a great sadness that issues with my son had tainted Allan's eightieth birthday celebration, but what followed was far worse than any loss I had previously experienced, and that included Sidney's death.

Allan and I returned home on March 6, and on March 14, a letter from Judy arrived in the mail. I eagerly opened it and started to read. The envelope contained four, single-spaced typewritten pages filled with venomous accusations and expressions of anger and frustration—unbelievable! Two days later, I received an audio tape from my son. My first thought was the tape contained an explanation related to the letter. I hurriedly and excitedly changed into my walking garb, grabbed my earphones and cassette player, and took off without telling Allan about the tape. As I walked, I listened to my son's voice. Hearing his words, I experienced an emotional shock far greater than when I read Judy's letter. My son's words were vindictive and accusatory as he expressed internal anger that had been building ever since he married Judy. He made no reference to Judy's letter; it seemed impossible to me he was unaware of its existence. In both of their communications, Vern and Judy spoke of my transgressions. To name a few: I was controlling, manipulative, miserly, insensitive, and most hurtful to me was the accusation that I was inattentive to Darci and Kristen. The tape and the letter created a holocaust that enveloped Allan, Bruce and Linda, Lloyd and Trudy, and, to a lesser degree, Jan and Royce, but not George, who refused to be a part of the fray.

During the following year, with Allan's heartfelt support, I made attempts through telephone calls and notes to Vern and Judy, hoping to resolve the issues. Vern refused to communicate with me but wrote letters and made telephone contacts with his stepdad. (From the get-go, Allan was Teflon, and no faults were attributed to him.) Supporting me, Allan was uncomfortable with the situation and, in March 1985, wrote to Vern and told him if he were unable to include his mother in his communications, to cease all contacts with him.

At this point, my brother, Lloyd, became involved. He made a thirty-minute video in which he spoke of insights gained over the years about his parents—Vern's grandparents. He talked about growing up on the farm. He recounted the tempestuous marriage of Mom and Dad. At the conclusion of the videotape, my brother acknowledged that he regretted his inability to converse with his mother and cautioned Vern not to go down that path.

Lloyd asked me to view the tape before he sent it to Vern, commenting that if I disapproved, he would not send it. I did give Lloyd the go-ahead, although I disagreed with some of the content. As I previously have written, my brother's perception of Mom was far different than mine.

In his videotape to Vern, my brother spoke to the power of imprinting that occurs in the first years of a child's life. My sister put it quite succinctly: "The sun rose and set in that boy." When I sought my brother's council regarding Vern's unwillingness to meet to discuss our problems, I commented to Lloyd, "Over the years, Vern has continued his behavior of manipulating and controlling." Lloyd agreed with me responding, "I had it right."

The videotape prompted an exchange of letters between Vern/Judy and his Uncle Lloyd. In his next interchange, Lloyd responded with a long typewritten letter sharing his philosophy regarding parenting and suggested a format for reconciliation between Vern and me. Vern refused to accept his uncle's suggestions. He stated unequivocally that only an apology from his mother would suffice.

Lloyd's communications with his nephew helped me to arrive at the realization that Vern had a far different perception of his mother than did Bruce. To Vern, I was a controlling, inflexible woman; to Bruce I was an understanding mother who managed to surmount the challenges life placed before me.

Bruce and Linda were privy to the information that Vern and Judy sent me, as well as my responses. Young as Linda was at the time, she was honing her skills of defusing confrontation and facilitating compromise. She took the time to write a thought-provoking letter to Judy and Vern, expressing her hope the issues could be resolved. She and Bruce wanted nothing more than to have a good relationship with their family. Linda's effort fell on deaf ears.

Up to this point, all overtures were either rejected or ignored by Vern and Judy. Unwilling to give up, I spent the first part of the summer of 1985 responding point by point to their accusations. When completed, the epistle filled thirty-four single-spaced, typewritten pages. Along the way, Allan was flummoxed as to why I was doing this, and my response was, "I find it emotionally therapeutic." Later, when all of my reasons and explanations were rejected, I had to accept the fact that Vern and Judy operated from a reality base far different than mine.

My response packet was mailed on July 18, 1985. A few days later, the telephone rang. Allan answered. Hearing a voice he thought to be Vern, he silently mouthed, "Vern is on the line." My heart raced as I picked up the extension phone receiver. I know my voice must have conveyed the excitement I felt as I said, "Hi, Vern." The voice on the other end dryly replied, "No, Mom, this is the son that is still speaking to you." Ever the jokester, Bruce's comment in that tense moment brought me to laughter.

Allan died on May 9, 1986. Vern did not attend his funeral. On August 11 of that year, I received a letter from Valley Memorial Hospital. The content of the letter informed me Dr. and Mrs. Vernon Nelson had given a generous monetary contribution to the construction of the educational wing of the hospital. I would like to think there is a plaque affixed to a wall someplace in the hospital complex honoring Allan—a fitting tribute to his influence in Vern's life.

Over the next several years, communication with the family was minimal. I received Mother's Day cards and, on occasion, a rare phone call. I heeded Bruce and Linda's advice and was resolute in contacting Darci and Kristen on special days that included their birthdays and Christmas. In 1988, I invited them to come to Ohio for a visit. Sadly, they declined. The girls were collateral damage in this family tragedy.

———— ✦✦✦✦✦ ————

NOT TOO LONG AFTER ALLAN'S DEATH, I met a man with whom I wished to share my life. On November 28, 1987, Charles Gass and I, surrounded by several family members, were married in the living room of Bruce and Linda's home in Las Vegas. Vern and Judy did not attend.

I brought with me to the marriage emotional baggage of an estranged relationship with my son and his family. Fortunately, it did not prevent Charlie and me from settling into a fulfilling life together in his house on Richards Road in Columbus.

Sunday, March 25, 1990, was a typical Ohio spring day. The clouds and bone-chilling temperature did not dampen our spirits for it was Charlie's seventy-seventh natal day. We finished our lunch and settled down to enjoy a relaxed afternoon at home. The phone rang, and I answered to hear a cheery voice on the other end of the line say, "Hi, Mom, this is Vern." Was it really Vern? Were my ears deceiving me? I knew it wasn't Bruce; he would never play that cruel of a joke on me. Vern set the tone of the conversation that was without emotion, just a general catch-up chat related to family. We talked for forty-five minutes, and as we were about to sign off, I said to my son, "I love you." His response, "I love you, Mom," brought me to tears as I softly replaced the receiver.

Throughout the previous six years, Vern and Bruce did keep up a modicum of communication, mostly at Bruce's behest. Not known to me at the time, Bruce quietly and patiently urged his brother to make amends with Mom. Years later, when I learned this, it brought me to the realization that the dynamic between the brothers was changing. No explanation was ever given by Vern as to why he called that March day. In my mind I know it was Bruce's influence that prompted Vern to pick up the phone and call me.

Nor did Vern ever make any reference to the events that led to the estrangement. That grieved me, for I knew no complete understanding could ever be reached without examining our past. I have in my file an article taken from the May 12, 1985, publication of *The New York Times*. I quote from that article, "The Secret of Redemption:"

> All of us, whether guilty or not, whether old or young, must accept the past... It is not a case of coming to terms with the past. That is not possible. It cannot be subsequently modified or undone. However, anyone who closes his eyes to the past is blind to the present.

Since that watershed day in March 1990, I consciously walked a narrow path, never making reference to the past, nor did I challenge my son's controlling behaviors. The price paid would be too high.

⊹⊹⊹⊹⊹

DURING THOSE YEARS when communication with Vern was almost nonexistent, he served as his own general contractor in the construction of an estate for his family in Spokane. One day, while browsing the *Spokesman Review* newspaper, Vern noted an acreage of undeveloped land for sale within the city limits. Following up on the ad, he visited the property, found it to his liking, and bought it. He hired an architect to draw up the plans for their house, modeling it after a home in old Spokane he and Judy had admired over the years. The acreage was divided into three lots, with the smaller lot serving as a common area for a tennis court and swimming pool. Charlie and I saw the home for the first time in the early 1990s. Vern had built his own private club, and on our first and subsequent visits, Charlie and I benefitted from all of the estate amenities.

I was not privy to any of the details regarding the actual construction of the house until later, but one anecdote stays with me. Serving as his own general contractor, Vern assumed the responsibility of acquiring all the needed construction permits. One of the officials, wielding the power of position, caused my son undue grief. Vern persevered, jumping through the required hoops to get the needed permit.

Within a few months following this incident, a man appeared in the ER, telling the nurse an object was lodged in his anal region. Dr. Nelson was summoned, and when Vern stepped behind the curtain, the two men simultaneously recognized one another. The man, flat on the table, spat out, "Don't say a word, just get the damned thing out." It was a sex toy. Oh, but karma is a bitch!

———— ᛁᛁᚦᚦᚦᛁᛁ ————

A TELEPHONE CALL FROM JUDY came on November 26, 1992. Vern was on duty in the hospital ER when he, the doctor, became the patient. While examining a patient, blood suddenly gushed from Vern's nose. An MRI revealed a tumor on the base of his olfactory nerve. He was admitted to the University of Washington Medical Center, the school where he earned his MD in 1976. His surgery was scheduled for February 6, 1993.

Based on the fragile relationship with my son's family, I shared my reluctance to be in Spokane at the time of the surgery with Bobbie. It was she who strongly advised me to be there, referring back to Vern's disappointment when I failed to attend his college graduation in Great Falls, Montana. I took her advice. Judy was in Seattle with Vern. I stayed in Spokane with Darci and Kristen.

Vern was diagnosed with a rare cancer—asthesioneurolblastoma, only a few hundred known cases in the world. Over the next thirteen years, Vern underwent fourteen surgeries. He experienced a medical nightmare of infections, radiation, tube feeding, and epileptic seizures that kept him from driving for months at a time. During those first years of his medical odyssey, Vern survived near-death experiences of sepsis and dehydration, but he held fast to his optimism that he would be cured.

Vern's illness impacted the lives of his family both emotionally and financially. He was informed on April 17, 1994, that his ER position with the hospitals was being terminated. This news devastated him, realizing he never would practice medicine again. They sold their large house and bought a smaller one. In all of this, there was one saving grace. A doctor who mentored Vern in the first years of his practice had advised him to obtain a disability insurance policy to protect himself and his family in the event of any catastrophic happening. This Vern wisely did.

My son's optimism was critically tested one day when he was home alone with workmen hired to do some house remodeling. Judy was away with the girls. In early afternoon, Vern was on the back deck of their house when he had a grand mal seizure. The men in the house failed to hear his calls for help and left at the end of their workday. Vern lay on the deck, the hot sun beating down on him. Evening came; his calls became weaker and weaker. About 9:00 p.m., a neighbor, whose lot was contiguous with theirs, opened her bedroom window and heard his weakened voice calling for help. Vern later related hearing a voice say, "I heard you, help will be coming," and thought it the voice of an angel. The emergency squad arrived. Vern was severely dehydrated and his body temperature a critical 103 degrees. Given proper medical attention, Vern lived.

Early on in his brother's illness, Bruce asked me if I thought it would be okay for him to take his family to Spokane for a weekend visit. My concern was for Judy, and I advised against it. Wisely, Bruce ignored my advice. This marked one of the few times the brothers' families were together.

Vern coped with his illness and kept idleness at bay by involving himself with different groups and activities. At the hospital, he chatted with patients in the radiation treatment waiting room. Vern spoke of a special fondness for one elderly lady, and when he realized this was her final treatment, he congratulated her. The woman's response distressed Vern. "I'll miss coming. I have no family, few living friends, and I live alone. I looked forward to these weekly visits, and I'm sad they are ending."

One year, Vern served on a cancer fund-raising committee and was recognized for bringing in the most dollars. I recall that his appeal letter to his family aided him in achieving that recognition. Vern volunteered with Habitat for Humanity, and his expertise in all areas of the building trades were an asset, but he didn't stay long with Habitat. As with GM years ago, he could not accept the protocols of the bureaucracy. He refused to accept why design changes could not be made to fit the needs of prospective owners since people were required to invest hours of their time in the construction of what would be their house.

Vern tried delivering Meals on Wheels. He would deliver a meal, and many times the person would want him to stay and visit. His delivery schedule did not allow time for visiting, and their loneliness left him shaken.

Vern enjoyed skiing. He knew he had the requisite skills to be a member of a rescue ski patrol and volunteered at a local ski resort. New recruits were required to pass a skiing skills test. Unknown to Vern, a nurse from the hospital where he had worked was a member of the testing team, and she didn't like Dr. Nelson. Vern did not pass the test. Did he lack the required skiing skills? Was it his medical history? The actual reason was never given. Another devastating blow, as Vern loved to ski.

⧫⧫⧫⧫

Bruce's major medical issues were curable, given the caveat that all surgeries carry life-threatening risks. In 2010 he was diagnosed with prostate cancer. After attempts to connect with a urologist in Las Vegas, Bruce took the advice of his primary care physician (PCP) and arrangements were made for surgery at the City of Hope Hospital in Pasadena, California—leaders in robotic surgery. Knowing the seriousness of his brother's cancer, Bruce, when asked about his bout with cancer, would facetiously respond, saying, "Mine is only 'cancer light.'"

Not long after his prostate surgery, Bruce again went under the surgeon's knife. Two main lifestyle factors contributed to his need for knee-replacement surgery. Bruce has never been one to shy away from manual labor. When questioned about some of the jobs he had done, applying his wry sense of humor, Bruce answers, "I've been a beast of burden on too many jobs in my life." That, combined with his love to play basketball, took its toll on Bruce's knee joints. In 2015 he underwent knee-replacement surgery at a hospital in Las Vegas. The right knee caused him the greatest discomfort, so he opted to have that knee done in the spring. The annual insurance deductible was a contributing factor to having his left-knee surgery in the fall.

Other than the abovementioned surgeries, and a couple of mishaps working with tools in his shop, Bruce enjoys good health. For that I am thankful for him, for his family, and for myself. As he will say, "I have now outlived my father and my brother, so I am the last man standing in the room," adding, "Well, not really. I have a son and grandson in the Nelson lineup."

⧫⧫⧫⧫

When communication with Vern resumed in 1990, the fragile relationship with him and his family held. When in their home, I felt a tension that made me very uncomfortable. There were many long telephone conversations listening to Judy vent about their marriage.

In April 1996, I learned they were seeing a marriage counselor. On rare occasions, I heard comments from each that their situation was improving and there was hope for the marriage. Overall, I remained fully cognizant that I was skating on the proverbial thin ice and to be careful. One time I did reflect on a thought shared with me and was harshly reprimanded by my son for reference to his personal life. From both came the message, "It is all right if I say it, but don't you dare even hint at our marital problems."

Over the years, I observed that when Vern was in a state of medical emergency, Judy was loving and supportive. As Vern improved, Judy returned to venting about her husband. In November 1999, Vern made his first visit to a divorce attorney. In January 2000, divorce papers were served on Judy, and the resentment that had lain dormant for years erupted. For a time, the girls sided with their mother—devastating to their father.

Vern moved out and secured a room in the house of one of his buddies. The arrangement was short-lived when Ron learned Vern believed in the evolution of man and ordered Vern out posthaste. Ron was a staunch fundamentalist who believed in the biblical creation. He could not have a heathen living under his roof. Vern was homeless. After numerous attempts to find a place to live, he finally settled into a first-floor apartment located in a building in Brown's Addition (an upbeat area in Spokane) overlooking a picturesque park. A property settlement was arrived at, and the divorce was finalized in 2000. In fairness to Judy, I believe in the very early years of her marriage to Vern, she tried. I felt deep sadness for the family.

On one of Vern's first visits home after his divorce, he made the comment, "You know, Mom, too many men give more thought to buying a car than they do to choosing and keeping a wife." Now twice divorced, I felt he was referring to himself.

My relationship with my grandchildren was as different as the relationship with their fathers. Each of my sons had two children. Two girls born to Vern and Judy—Darci Ann and Kristen Ann. A daughter and a son born to Bruce and Linda—Candice Lisanne and Bruce Allan.

As the bloodline grandmother of Darci and Kristen, I involved myself as much as time and distance allowed. Over the years I visited Spokane, and reciprocal visits were made to visit me. In the interim, telephone and snail mail were means of communication. One thing I could not change were the two thousand miles between us. For this reason, Vern and Judy promoted the couple next-door as surrogate grandparents. Darci and Kristen lovingly referred to them as Mor Mor and Grandad. Although I was accused of being jealous of this relationship, nothing was further from the truth. Vern wanted his girls to have a grandparent experience like he had, and in my son's mind, distance precluded that relationship with me. I remained the elusive Gran Henri.

An incident in March 2003, involving Darci and Kristen, remains clear in my mind. Alone and living in North Madison, I invited Brenda to join me on a visit to Spokane. Vern had been divorced for several years and was now romantically involved with a businesswoman who owned a mansion in Brown's Addition.

When Mary learned Brenda and I were coming to Spokane, she invited us to stay with her. We reluctantly accepted. Soon after our arrival, Mary planned an afternoon tea and invited Darci and Kristen. Vern came, as did Darci's gentleman friend, Andy. Vern arrived first. Brenda and I were seated with him in the library when Darci, Andy, and Kristen arrived. Introductions were made. We sat sipping tea. Brenda and I put forth an effort to talk with the girls only to receive the briefest of responses. In turn, Darci and Kristen maintained an animated conversation to the exclusion of others. Later, Brenda and I commented we felt like we had been covered with vanishing powder.

My dream that this visit would be the catalyst for a new beginning did not materialize. When the girls were married—Darci to Andy Hastings and Kristen to Nick Lobdell—I was not included on the guest list. When Darci's daughters were born, Rowan in 2009, and Tatum in 2012, their mother sent me birth announcements and pictures. The same with Kristen, whose daughter, Reagan, was born in 2011 and son, Finn, in 2013.

As I write this, the vanishing powder incident happened fifteen years ago. I have not seen my granddaughters since, nor have I met my great-grandchildren. I keep communication open through snail mail cards for special days and e-mail. Darci responds through e-mail and includes pictures of the girls. For this I am grateful. Kristen's communications are occasional but joyously welcomed.

Looking back, I realize Vern and Judy had unrealistic grandparent expectations that I was unable to meet. As a result, Darci and Kristen were denied opportunities to get to know me, their paternal grandmother. During those years of family estrangement, irreparable damage was done. Much later, Vern acknowledged he was a major player in the family breakdown.

My stepdaughter, Jan Fincher, suggested the moniker Gran Henri at the time Renee was born. I liked it, giving no thought to when my sons might have children. When Vern's daughters were born, it was only natural for Vern and Judy to refer to me as Gran Henri. When Bruce and Linda's children were born, I was Grandma. Did the moniker Gran Henri versus Grandma make a difference as to how Vern's children perceived me? I think not; they saw me through the eyes of their parents.

In contrast, Bruce had a solid marriage and a wife steeped in family values. Candice and Bruce Allan always knew I was their Grandma. I know Bruce and Linda, from the get-go, referred to me as Grandma and that attests to the strong filial bond held by Linda. I have come to recognize this as a part of the Gripentog DNA. Candice and Bruce Allan have grandparents, great-grandparents, and surrogate grandparents of all stripes, but there never has been any doubt in the children's minds that I am their Grandma.

The two thousand miles between us never hampered the development of a close bond with my younger son's children. I was there during their growing-up years, for their high school and college graduations, and an honored guest at their weddings. When Candice's twins, Alexandra Lynn and Sydney Jean, were born on February 6, 2014, I traveled to Las Vegas to meet the babies when they were three months old. I had my picture taken holding them, sitting in the same rocking chair where I held their mother when she was a baby. Bruce Allan's first child, Grace Jane, was born on November 6, 2015, followed by a son, Luke Jordan, born on February 17, 2017. I met both of these great-grandchildren when they were only a few months old.

———— ++++++ ————

PLANES FLY IN BOTH DIRECTIONS, and I took advantage, visiting Spokane or Las Vegas, but also welcomed visits from my sons and their families. After Vern's diagnosis of cancer, the loss of his profession, and his divorce, I saw him more often. He made at least one, sometimes two, visits to Ohio each year. By Vern's very nature, he was inquisitive, enjoyed a variety of entertainment venues, and felt he earned his keep by being Mr. Fix-It.

On each visit, our days were a flurry of activity revolving around events, dining out, movies, and home-repair projects. The year AmeriFlora, an international horticultural exhibition, was in Columbus, Vern enjoyed visiting the site and taking in the music, food, and international pavilions. On one occasion, mother and son were kids again when, together, we rode the merry-go-round. I'd given Vern a copy of Steven Newman's book *The Worldwalker*. Vern was captivated reading about Steve's adventures, and on one visit he drove to the author's home near Cincinnati just to meet the man and shake his hand. For Vern, this meeting launched a lifelong friendship, and in turn, their friendship enriched my life as well.

In 1998, on Vern's first visit to my home in North Madison, the contractor had just started with the house makeover. That first morning, Vern walked out of his makeshift bedroom, greeted me in the kitchen, and asked, "Tell me, Mom, just what did you like about this house?" Obviously, my answer was, "Location, location, location."

One time, Vern rode his motorcycle from Spokane to North Madison. He was determined to visit Cedar Point Amusement Park, 110 miles to the west, and spend the day riding roller coasters. He invited Brenda to join him. She had no choice but to ride "bitch" on the back seat of the motorcycle. This gave Walt grave concern, and he remarked, "I can't believe I am allowing my wife to ride a motorcycle with her nephew, diagnosed with brain cancer and subject to seizures."

Vern and Brenda left early in the morning, not to return until near midnight. That day, working in the yard, I was stung by a bee and broke out in hives. I had no idea what caused my intense itching and found the only thing that gave me a modicum of relief was a cold shower. I was still up when Vern walked in the house. He took one look at me, learned of the bee sting, rushed to the drugstore for Benadryl, and gave me a megadose, remarking, "Anyone else would have been in the ER." That is one of the rare times I benefitted from my son's medical knowledge.

On another visit, Vern was with me for two weeks. The first week was pure pleasure. We enjoyed one another's company, but that changed the second week when his lady friend arrived. My son wanted something special to give her when they first met at the airport. For that purpose, I gave him an exquisitely delicate bud vase, purchased in Greece. On our way to the airport, we stopped at a floral shop, and he bought a yellow rose. We arrived at the airport, I parked in the garage, and as we were walking to the gate, Vern tripped. As he fell, he kept a straight arm, fingers holding tight to the vase, as his body gyrated around, landing him outstretched on his back on the concrete. The vase, holding water and flower, remained intact.

Vern's excitement to spend the week with the woman he loved was dampened by the emotional and financial baggage that Mary brought with her. She spent hours on the phone or on the computer, giving attention to her business or the needs of a neurotic daughter. That left her with little uninterrupted time for Vern. The cheerful, pleasant days I shared with my son the first week became days filled with melancholy the second week. My heart ached for him, albeit I could do little to help. Sadly, I felt only relief when I took them to the airport for their return flight to Spokane.

For the times we were together, I was cognizant of Vern's mercurial personality. He could be pleasant and accommodating. Without explanation, he could become disagreeable and stubborn. Thinking back, he was that way as a child, and it carried over into his adult years, but without question, his medical issues exacerbated the problem.

Due to the demands of the family business, it was difficult for Bruce and Linda to get away. For that reason, over many years I made semiannual visits to Las Vegas. I had a closeness with Bruce's family that I never felt with Vern's family.

In 1997 we were all together in Las Vegas when Bruce and Linda hosted the Schumann Huddle. Charlie had recently died and I traveled alone to Las Vegas for the event. Vern rode his Harley Davidson from Spokane to join the family. The weekend was filled with festivities—amusement rides at the casinos, a Siegfried and Roy show at the Mirage, relaxed times around the pool and hot tub at Bruce and Linda's home, and a Saturday cruise on Lake Mead with boat and water toys providing fun for all.

No matter the occasion, the number of visits, or the length of the visits, Bruce and Linda welcomed me with open arms, extending the welcome, "Mi casa es su casa." It pleased me when they requested that I cook and bake; cabbage rolls and Ma Nelson's rye bread were favorites.

DIFFERENT AS THE BROTHERS WERE in their careers, in their avocational interests, and in their choice of a mate, there was one thing they both wholeheartedly agreed on, and that was owning a Harley Davidson motorcycle. In late 1994, Vern made an unannounced visit to his brother. Late one night, beers in hand, relaxing poolside and just talking, the brothers hatched the plan to buy motorcycles and tour the country. Bruce first suggested it, and Vern enthusiastically took up with Bruce's voiced dream.

The brothers agreed upon Harley Davidson bikes—the Ultra Classic "big-baggers."

Bruce was first to order a bike. Inundated with boating business demands that required six-day work weeks, he asked his bother to order the Harley for him from a shop in Spokane. This Vern willingly did, and in early 1995, the bike was delivered. To inform Bruce his dream machine had arrived, Vern sat on the bike, called his brother on the phone, revved up the motor, and tantalized him by the throaty sound of the Harley booming in his ear.

Vern had the Harley broken in and ready for their first road trip when he rode the bike to Seattle to meet Bruce and Linda at a Bayliner Boat Convention. (Bruce gave Vern recognition, as well as their company some additional prestige, by introducing his brother as the company's Dr. Nelson.) By then Vern was the experienced rider and assigned his brother to the bitch seat when he headed the bike south along scenic Highway 1, leaving Washington, through Oregon, and as far as southern California before heading east to Las Vegas. But two more years passed before the brothers were positioned to fulfill their dream. During those years, Vern had another surgery and seizures that prohibited his driving until he was six months seizure-free. Finally, in 1997, the brothers were able to take off on their first road trip, each riding their own Harley Davidson.

Over the next six years, Bruce managed to take time away from the business for several limited road trips and two major ones. Bruce realized what his brother was facing, and on all their road trips, Vern controlled and Bruce followed.

The first of the big trips was referred to by bikers as the Big Hole Tour that took in Meteor Crater and the Grand Canyon in Arizona. The second of their major road trips was to Sturgis, South Dakota, in August 1998. The brothers planned to stay for a good part of the ten-day rally, but the revelry of five hundred thousand bikers drinking, loud music, and lack of sleep shortened their stay. They left the third day.

Vern's physical and mental capabilities were being destroyed by the cancer that had invaded his body. Bruce recognized his brother's weakening condition was compromising his ability to control his bike. He was a liability to himself and to others. With a depth of sadness, Bruce voiced his concern and advised his brother to give up riding. Reluctantly, Vern heeded the advice, and their last road trip together was in Vern's 2001 Inferno Red

PT Cruiser. Bruce went to Spokane, and together the brothers drove south to Las Vegas.

++++++

AFTER VERN'S ACRIMONIOUS DIVORCE, his eviction from the home of Ron, temporary overnights with his daughters, and unsatisfactory apartment living, he finally settled into an apartment overlooking a picturesque park in Brown's Addition—a culturally diverse neighborhood reflected in the architecture and businesses of the area. Cabin Coffee, a rustic espresso establishment, opened there in 2001 about the same time Vern moved into his apartment located only two blocks away. Cabin Coffee became Vern's hangout. He would stop by several times a day to sip coffee and engage in repartee and/or board games with other patrons. The co-owner, Rebecca Mac, acknowledged that Vern was very helpful as her volunteer handyman, with the requisite skills to repair anything that needed fixing.

At Cabin Coffee, Vern met Mary, who owned and operated a Victorian Mansion in Browne's Addition. The mansion, famous as an upscale bed-and-breakfast, was located on authentically Victorian landscaped grounds with a picturesque wedding venue, as well as a secret garden for children's parties.

I first met Mary on a visit in 2001. She stands about five feet six inches, has dark hair and eyes, an engaging smile and sparkling-white, even teeth, and a curvaceous figure. Mary exudes energy and happiness. My heart sang with joy when I realized my son had met a woman whom he loved, but over the few years they were together, I observed there were times that Mary was a source of distress to Vern. This occurred when her business affairs and/or her daughters took priority in her life. Granted, those times were few and short. Overall, she gave Vern a depth of compassion and understanding that saw him through some of the darkest days of his illness.

Mary kept Bruce and me apprised of Vern's medical condition and, to a lesser degree, his financial matters. I knew nothing of his finances, only that he managed his own money. Looking back, I am not certain whether Mary's motives were altruistic, selfish, or a combination of both when she alerted Bruce that Vern's daughters were able to access his checking account and were draining his finances.

At Mary's urging, Bruce became involved and met with Vern's attorney. As a result of that meeting, Vern was persuaded to give Bruce his durable power of attorney for property with the authority to dispose of his personal possessions upon his death. The personal property oversight given to Bruce created a firestorm with Darci and Kristen at the time of their father's death.

———— ·⁺⁺⁺⁺·⁺ ————

DURING THE LAST YEAR OF VERN'S LIFE, I traveled monthly to Spokane, accompanied by Cordell, whom I had married in 2003. We stayed at a nearby motel. Bruce and Linda joined us in Spokane for Mother's Day in May 2004. The five of us were seated around the table in Vern's apartment. I was handed a small box tied with a blue ribbon. Excitedly, I untied the ribbon and removed the lid from the box to find a silver, heart-shaped locket. The locket contained miniatures of my boys.

Vern was rapidly losing his ability to communicate, and visits became more challenging. Before each visit, I searched for topics that might be of interest to him. I didn't know it at the time, but what would be my last visit with my son was especially fulfilling. I brought with me a book I had written many years ago for a college freshman English class. *Rugged Weekend* told of camping experiences Sidney and I had with the boys at Cook's Forest in Pennsylvania, not too distant from our home in Ashtabula. I sat with Vern, took out the book, and started to read even though my son appeared to be sleeping. I had read for a few minutes when I noted the story now held my son's interest. Vern became alert, he laughed, his body language communicated he was reliving those delightful days of his childhood when we camped, hiked the trails, swung on the tree grapevines, attempted to trap a chipmunk, attended Sunday morning church service seated on a log, and roasted marshmallows over a campfire. A moment in time shared by mother and son.

———— ·⁺⁺⁺⁺·⁺ ————

DOUG CLARK, A COLUMNIST FOR THE *SPOKESMAN REVIEW* became aware of Vern's health issues and gave him the moniker "Energizer Bunny." Doug's first column about Vern appeared in May 2001: "MAN HAS SURVIVED THROUGH SEVEN SURGERIES, SEVERAL CLOSE CALLS." On January 24, 2002, the second column appeared—"BRAIN CANCER CAN'T KEEP HIM FROM FAST LANE." I was not aware of this recognition until the third column appeared on June 12, 2003. That morning my telephone rang, and when I answered, I heard Vern's voice. He said he wanted to read me an article that appeared in their morning paper. I quote from my diary:

> What an incredibly beautiful morning this has been. I received a telephone call from my son in Spokane. A writer for the city newspaper did a special article on Vern. With great difficulty Vern attempted to read it to me before he had to pass it over to his lady friend Mary, who finished reading it. The article was written with insight and sensitivity to his medical condition of the past 10 years. I will admit it made me cry.

Doug's final article appeared on November 8, 2004. "Cancer Finally Claims Upbeat, Courageous Doc." In that article, Doug recounted his last visit with Vern, asking the question, "It's frustrating for you, isn't it?" Vern lowered his head and expelled a breathy "Yeah." Doug's final sentence in his column was, "Rest in peace, champ. The fight's over."

The final weeks of Vern's life were under hospice care. He died at home on November 6. His daughters, Darci and Kristen, were with him, as was Mary.

﹢﹢﹢﹢﹢﹢

As soon as Bruce was notified of his brother's death, he realized it fell to him to immediately designate to whom Vern's personal items should go. Prior to his death, Vern was aware both Darci and Kristen wanted to own the yellow Porsche. He couldn't give it to one, excluding the other. Even Mary voiced her interest in owning it. Vern knew that when he died, all of his financial resources were to be divided between Judy, Darci, and Kristen. Yet he wanted to acknowledge Mary's loving faithfulness during those final years of his life. Anything given to Mary must come from his personal possessions.

Not saying so by words spoken, but rather by inference, Vern let his brother know that it would be okay to resolve the conundrum with his daughters and give the Porsche to Mary. To that end, Bruce gave her not only the Porsche but added the 2001 Inferno Red PT Cruiser and the Harley Davidson motorcycle—referred to as the Big Three. When doing so, Bruce verbally requested of Mary that when the day came that she no longer had use for the Porsche, to give it to the girls. (Years later, Bruce learned Mary negated her promise and sold the Porsche. The disposition of the vehicle had plagued Bruce for years, and when he learned it was sold, he felt a sense of closure to a difficult situation handed off to him by his brother.)

When Kristen learned what her uncle had done, "Hell hath no fury like that of a woman scorned." Kristen's anger set the stage for an agonizing time for Bruce and Linda, Cordell and me, as well as Vern's stepbrother, George Dickie, when, later that month, we gathered in Spokane to attend Vern's memorial service.

THE SERVICE WAS PLANNED by Vern's daughters and held in one of the ballrooms at the Davenport Grand Hotel in downtown Spokane. Doug Clark was the MC and the main speaker. Bruce and I were originally scheduled to speak. The girls, in their state of grief and frustration fueled by anger, removed us from the program.

Darci and Kristen, with their mother, sat together in the front row. Given what had happened, we knew it was best to remain as inconspicuous as possible and seated ourselves in the back of the ballroom. The memorial was well attended. There were medical staff from area hospitals, friends from Brown's Addition, former neighbors, friends, colleagues, as well as those connected with Darci and Kristen. Mary maintained a polite distance as she was one of the speakers.

The service ended, and refreshments were served. Several neighbors and friends I had met over the years were in attendance and graciously reintroduced themselves and expressed their heartfelt condolences. Prior to the service, I made the effort to speak to my granddaughters, but during the reception, there was no effort made by them to have any further communication.

Darci made arrangements with the funeral home for Bruce and me to each have a small urn containing some of Vern's ashes. For her thoughtfulness, I remain eternally grateful.

RETURNING TO OHIO, the desire to have a memorial service for Vern in Ashtabula, his home for the first sixteen years of his life, consumed me. But where? The holiday season was rapidly approaching, and the area was limited in the number and size of available venues. Vern's surrogate parents, Bob and Lu Lee, came to my rescue and offered the use of their home. (It is important to note that even with the Lees, Vern's volatile personality had erupted, and he accused Bob and Lu in a vitriolic telephone call of being disloyal to him and his family and ceased all communication with them. When Bruce learned of this, he called Bob and Lu, asking them to understand Vern's verbal cruelty was evidence of the cancer's effect on the frontal lobe of his brain—ofttimes referred to as the social filter. Once understanding this, all was forgiven.)

Cordell designed the invitation. On the front of the card was a picture of Vern with Bruce, the brothers poised on their Harley Davidson bikes, ready to take off on one of their "Hog" road trips. The picture was captioned "Riding Life's Blue Highways." Vern was taken by the vagabond lifestyle of author William Least Heat Moon as told in his book *Blue Highways: A Journey into America.*

I selected pictures that told the story of Vern's life. Cordell mounted them on several large poster boards displayed on tripod stands throughout the house. On Sunday, December 5, 2004, there must have been upward of two dozen family members, neighbors, classmates, and friends of Vern who gathered to remember. Almost everyone spoke to Vern's influence in their lives.

My brother Lloyd reflected on his role in his nephew's life, anchoring his comments in the Bible.

Kellie, Vern's cousin, read a descriptive account of how much her new shoes pinched her toes when she was a junior bridesmaid in Vern and Bobbie's wedding.

Cordell spoke of Vern's attitudinal change, from resentment to one of love, that occurred during the few months they knew one another. Cordell described how torturous it was for Vern, on what was our last visit, to rise from his chair to give him a hug and whisper, "I love you."

Rogene Swift told how Vern was "an answer to my prayer," relating how she sat at her restaurant table in nearby Pierpont and prayed for a skilled craftsman to come and help her with needed repairs. (Vern told me, when he learned this, "I never thought of myself as an answer to prayer, but you know I do like helping people.")

Last to speak were members of Vern's surrogate family, Bob Lee Sr. and son Bob. Both father and son choked with emotion as they told their stories; they had lost a member of their family too.

The memorial service planned by Vern's daughters evidenced the professional life of Dr. Nelson. The memorial service in Ashtabula evidenced the blue-collar life of Vern Nelson. Both services were honest representations of my son's life.

IN APRIL 2005, BRUCE AND LINDA, WITH CORDELL, planned a seventy-fifth birthday party for me near our home in Green. The day following the celebration, Cordell and I, Bruce and Linda with Mary, drove to the Gageville Cemetery near the Schumann/Shuart farm. It was here, at Brenda's urging, I had a headstone for Vern placed on the family plot, with a military plaque installed on the back side of his headstone.

Brenda and Lloyd, Bob and Lu Lee joined us at the cemetery. The sun shone brightly on Vern's headstone, illuminating his name, the years of his life, his military service, the caduceus, and a motorcycle. I had with me the small urn containing Vern's ashes and, speaking a few words, sprinkled them on the graves of his paternal grandparents, his maternal great-grandmother's, and his own grave.

We left Gageville and continued to the Edgewood Cemetery located just to the east of the Ashtabula city limits. Bruce had his urn with him, containing his brother's ashes. We visited the Nelson plot. After brief, heartfelt comments, Bruce gently emptied his brother's ashes onto the ground behind their father's headstone. Brenda had brought a bottle of wine, supplied us with glasses, and we joined in a toast to father and son, deeply loved, both taken from us too soon.

DOUG CLARK REFERRED TO VERN in the first of his columns as the Energizer Bunny (EB). Vern's illness took its emotional toll on his brother. In dealing with his pain, Bruce purchased Energizer Bunnies, large and small. The small ones he passed out to family and friends. The large one he gave to me, and it now has its place on a shelf in my home.

Sitting next to the EB is a white, soft, cuddly teddy bear angel with feathered wings and a satin garment adorned with a golden cord—a gift from Cordell's son and his wife, Kent and Janet. From Diane and Doug, daughter and husband, is a Danbury quartz clock inscribed "IN MEMORY OF VERN NELSON 4-11-48—11-6-04."

Although I had been married to their father for only one year, Kent and Janet, along with Diane and Doug, never having met Vern, came to be with me at the Ashtabula Memorial service and spoke briefly to my loss.

Myself, I believe Vern is with his father who, sometime during the years following his cancer diagnosis, came to him in a dream saying not to be afraid. Now, together, they are cavorting with the angels.

⁺⁺✦✦✦⁺⁺

IN MAY 1995 Charlie and I were on a bicycle holiday in Greece. Prior to our leaving, Vern gave me a small package, admonishing me not to open it until Mother's Day. On the appointed day, I opened the package to find a pink envelope containing my Mother's Day card. Tucked inside of the card were two sheets of green paper. The following verse was printed in Vern's hand:

I Wonder

My childhood seems so long ago
By all accounts it was good
I miss my father and wish I remembered better
But I've had a family that helped fill the void

My young adult life also seems distant
I worked hard for my career
I wish I would have worked as hard on my family
The blinders it takes to get certain carrots can be costly

I enjoyed my young family immensely
I also enjoyed my work
My work is now gone and I accept that
My family is here, I love you all

My health has been such an issue
Three and one half years
I can only believe it will improve
How else can I view this

Our relationship has seen its days
Life is so short
I thank you for all that you have done
I believe you and I will only improve

I wonder
What is around the next corner
I'm not afraid
I love you so very much
Thank you for always being there.
                                    Love, Vern

THE PARABLE OF THE PRODIGAL SON told in Luke 15:11–32 could be told of my sons.

My prodigal son was the older, not the younger, although Vern had no inheritance to squander, nor did he return home destitute. By my standard, he lived in luxury. More valuable than money is time, and Vern squandered six years of our lives when contact with him was almost nonexistent. A mother's love is deep and forgiving, and without hesitation, I rejoiced when he "returned to the fold."

In contrast to Vern is my younger son, Bruce, who throughout his entire life has been unwavering in his love, his acceptance of my decisions, never judgmental, never blaming, and always constructive when I would seek his advice related to critical family issues.

One time the brothers got into a friendly banter as to who was the favorite son. This elicited the remark from Vern, "I am Mom's favorite, I have a step up over you on the ladder." To which Bruce replied, "I don't think so. I'm already standing on an extension ladder."

All levity aside, did I love one son more than the other? I think not. In my heart they stand side by side. For the first half of Vern's life, I might metaphorically say he stood on the extension ladder and was the controlling brother. In the last decades of Vern's life, the positions of the brothers switched. Now Bruce stood stalwart on the extension ladder and served to support his brother. Those days of childhood are gone, so poignantly revealed in the "Worm Story." The boys were going fishing, and I overheard Vern say to Bruce, "I'll find the worms, you pick them up."

————————

I COULD NOT HAVE WRITTEN THIS CHAPTER without the council of Bruce. He edited it, corrected misinformation, and suggested a number of additions that enriched and provided a better balance in my telling the story of the brothers. Whenever I challenged Bruce, his response was, "Mom, it is what I say it is," adding, "I really did love that guy."

TWENTY-FIVE

SCHUMANN SIBLINGS

L LOYD, TWO YEARS OLDER THAN I, was born on June 22, 1928. I have written often of my brother in this memoir. But I feel it is important that I speak of him again. He was the eldest of we three siblings. Living in a farm community of mostly boys, Lloyd looked out for me to be sure I wasn't the brunt of their taunts and pranks.

Life on the farm was not all work. When my brother was old enough to drive, he would take me square dancing on Saturday nights. (Years later we were again square-dancing partners when, due to physical limitations, his wife no longer cared to square dance and I, a widow, lived in the area.)

When I married Sidney, there was an instant filial chemistry between the two men. Lloyd gained a brother. In those first frugal years of my marriage, Lloyd, skilled in all aspects of the building trades, saved Sidney and me unknown dollars in home-construction costs.

Lloyd was devastated when Sidney died. Immediately, he and Trudy assumed a caring role for me and my sons. We spent Sunday afternoons at their home where I, and sometimes my boys, would help Lloyd with refinishing the Lyman boat he had stored in his garage. Later we joined in the family camaraderie, feasting on foot-long hot dogs roasted over a wood-burning fire in the living room fireplace.

As adults, both Lloyd and I learned to play golf, hacking our way around local golf courses, caring little for our scores, enjoying nature and each other's company. Much as my brother would have liked, I made only a feeble attempt to learn the game of Bridge. We did not play cards as children, so I never developed what one refers to as having a card sense.

If asked, I was hard-pressed to name the four suits of a deck. Lloyd had learned the game while in the navy.

When I married Allan Dickie and lived in Kent, my brother's three children, David, Peter, and Jill, would spend time with us each summer. My niece and nephews were very competitive, and their Uncle Allan had a lot of fun setting up tournaments in croquet, shuffleboard, and Ping-Pong. For me, not having a daughter, my joy was taking Jill shopping for school outfits. That is, until she became a teenager and nothing could please her. I can say with certainty that my brother's children enriched my life in many ways, and continue to do so to this day.

The call came on March 16, 2014, that Lloyd had had a minor stroke and was in the veterans' hospital in Erie, Pennsylvania. I visited him there the following day. He never returned to his home, but was first transferred to the Ashtabula County Medical Center in Ashtabula, Ohio, and a short time later to the Austinburg Nursing and Rehabilitation Center in nearby Austinburg.

Prior to the stroke, over a period of months, Lloyd had been weakening and became less able to care for himself. Placing their dad in a care facility was not by choice; it was by necessity. Shortly after his admittance to the Austinburg facility, I visited my brother. I made this diary entry on April 12, 2014:

> I entered the common area and glancing around I saw my brother seated alone at a table, listlessly turning the pages of a magazine. He is looking down, I walk over kiss him on his forehead and greet him with "Hello Brother Dear." He is pleased to see me. We talk, he doesn't complain, no negative comments. Before I leave, I return with him to his room. It is private. Family pictures decorate the walls. It is furnished with a bed, lounge chair, bookcase, bedside table, and a small refrigerator. I know it is Lloyd's choice that the window's drapes are closed, allowing only an eerie light to penetrate the room.

Eight weeks after being admitted to the rehab facility, Lloyd developed pneumonia. His directive was "no medical intervention." He died peacefully on June 3, 2014, surrounded by his three children, their spouses, and his five grandchildren. I had been with him the previous day, and as I left his bedside, few words were needed, for Lloyd and I felt the enduring love formed in the early years of our childhood.

My brother was cremated, his ashes mingled with those of his beloved wife of over fifty years who had passed away on October 6, 2003. Lloyd's private graveside service was attended by family and a few invited guests. A military honor guard fired their rifles in a three-gun salute, taps were played conveying the sadness felt by all. Now this stalwart man was with his maker and once again united with his wife.

During those years on the farm when my brother was my protector and best friend, I felt something missing. I yearned for a sister. Boys just didn't understand girls, and good as my brother was to me, that included him. For that reason alone, I kept pestering my mom and dad for a sister. Finally, in the fall of 1941, at the age of eleven…

———— ++++++ ————

"HENRIETTA, I AM GOING TO HAVE A BABY." I was busy at my daily task in the sink room just off the kitchen, washing the breakfast dishes, when I heard those words. I turned to look. Mom was seated at the round table in the kitchen sipping a cup of hot tea. Incredulous, I walked the few feet into the kitchen to ask, "Mom what did you just say to me?" She repeated, "Henrietta, I am going to have a baby."

The year was 1941. I was eleven years old, in the seventh grade, and little did I know how babies came to be. For some time, I had begged Mom for a baby sister. I never knew if my constant nagging was the persuasive factor in my parents' decision to have a baby, or the reality that in a few years, Lloyd and I would graduate from high school and probably leave home. In truth, the reason was probably the latter, not the former—the spoken whim of a preteen.

At the time, a woman's pregnant condition was referred to as "confinement," rarely to be seen in public. I had always enjoyed being with Mom when we would go into Ashtabula to do the weekly shopping, but when her pregnancy became noticeable, I was embarrassed.

My parents had made previous arrangements for me to stay in Ashtabula with my girlfriend from the United Brethren Church when the time came for Mom to give birth. One evening, soon after Dad came home from work, and with no forewarning, he took me into Ashtabula to the home of the Sitterly family. I never questioned why, for I welcomed any chance to be with my friend Shirley. I later learned that Granma and Lloyd were restricted to their respective bedrooms upstairs. Mom gave birth in the downstairs bedroom with Dr. Mills and Dad in attendance. Many years later, my brother reluctantly shared his feelings when he told me that, hearing Mom's cries, he prayed relentlessly for her relief.

I'd been with Shirley for three days when dad came to get me. I didn't want to leave, but Dad insisted, telling me a surprise waited at home. As soon as Dad stopped the car behind our house, I jumped out, entered through the back door, and raced through the sink room into the kitchen, in search of my surprise. Finding nothing, I heard Mom call. I rushed into the living room, looked in my parents' bedroom, and there was Mom, lying in bed, holding a baby in her arms. She beckoned me. "Henrietta, come meet your baby sister."

BRENDA LOUISE SCHUMANN was born on July 22, 1942. She was beautiful—delicate features, tiny hands and feet, with a trace of red hair covering her head. Mom enjoyed listening to the radio "soaps." One of her favorite programs had a lead character named Brenda. For that reason alone, Mom persuaded Dad that their baby girl should be given this name. Lloyd and I never knew what prompted the choice of our names. Truth be told, my brother never understood why he was named Lloyd and I was Henrietta, commenting that, if the father's name was used, usually it was given to the oldest son. Ergo, he should have been named Henry. Brenda has reminded me that the name Henrietta Nagel was on Dad's birth certificate, and she surmises I was named after a family friend. Anyway, I wish I hadn't been given the name. I didn't like it. In children's books, Henrietta was a chicken, maybe a duck, sometimes a ghost, and ofttimes a witch. Decades later I purchased a small, round customized helmet mirror from a bicycle vendor. Painted on the reverse side of the mirror was the picture of a woman, seated on a bicycle, having an oversize derriere and captioned with (what else?) the name Henrietta.

Not sure of the reason, but after birth, the doctor required the mother to remain in bed for ten days. Dad worked full time in town, and Lloyd's help was needed for care of the animals and other farm chores. That left Granma and me to do the daily household tasks of cooking, cleaning, washing, and caring for Brenda when she wasn't in the bed with Mom. Granma must have done most of the work, for I don't remember being much help, but I do recall one incident. I'd finished sweeping the living room floor and had the dirt in a neat pile, ready to pick up with the dustpan. I heard Granma open the door and greet the doctor. Before he entered the living room, on his way to the bedroom, I quickly swept the pile of dirt under the rug, where it remained until spring cleaning.

Brenda was a high-maintenance baby. She cried constantly, leaving Mom exhausted. When weather permitted, Dad started up the tractor, took Brenda for a ride, and when she was asleep, returned to the house and handed her off to Mom, who gently placed the sleeping baby in her crib. I helped as well. I recall sitting by Brenda's crib, gently moving it back and forth, lulling her to sleep. The months passed, and the family survived to celebrate Brenda's first birthday.

Second and third birthdays followed, and my sister became the inquisitive toddler. Brenda's first colicky year was a forewarning of how difficult she would be to entertain. She could be very mischievous and bedeviled Granma by taking her cane and running off with it.

I think it was the Christmas of 1945 that I got the special gift I begged for. I'd noticed a Persian cat on a shelf in the mezzanine-floor gift shop of Carlisle's Department Store in Ashtabula. The cat had tiny ears, blue beads for eyes, long, silky, white hair, and best of all, a hidden pocket in its belly where small treasures could be secreted away. I fell in love with that cat, and months prior to Christmas, I made it known to Mom what I hoped to find under the tree Christmas morning. I realized, due to cost, it would be my only gift. It didn't matter; I would be fulfilled. Imagine my unspeakable joy when I opened the newspaper-wrapped box (Mom didn't waste money on store-bought paper) Christmas morning to find my Persian cat inside.

Christmas vacation ended, and I returned to school, secure in the knowledge that I had placed my cat in the middle of my second-floor-bedroom bed, safely out of Brenda's reach. That afternoon, I came home from school to find Brenda sitting in the middle of the living-room floor, contentedly playing with my cat. I begged Mom not to let her have it; she would ruin it. My pleas fell on deaf ears. The cat entertained my little sister, and Mom was able to get some work done. Brenda was allowed to destroy my beautiful white Persian cat with the long, silken fur! I think I was angrier with my mom than I was with my sister.

This story was told so many times that it put a guilt trip on Brenda. Brenda told me she had no memory of doing this dastardly deed, but years later, she gave me a gift—a facsimile stuffed Persian cat. As a teenager, I blamed Brenda for what she did. Later, when I had children of my own, I came to the realization that the responsibility lay with Mom, for in many things Brenda was neither disciplined nor denied.

Another incident happened only two days before Christmas when she was five years old. Usually Lloyd and I would venture across the road to the Fischer woodlot, select, cut down, and bring home a pine tree to be set up in our living room to be decorated on Christmas Eve in readiness for Santa's arrival. Lloyd had graduated from high school and was in the navy. I was sixteen at the time and asked Mom and Dad if I could get the tree. As always, my parents had too much to do and not enough time to do it, so they willingly agreed. As I prepared to leave the house, Mom asked me to take Brenda. I had no choice but to comply.

Leaving the house, I grasped Brenda's hand, and together we crossed the road and entered the woods. With my charge in tow, the going was slow as we trudged through the deep snow. I didn't immediately see a tree to my liking, and I wanted to search further. I took Brenda to an open area among the trees and admonished her to stay put and not move until I returned.

Off I went and soon found the almost-perfect tree. As I proceeded to cut it down, it started to snow, covering my tracks. I lost my directional bearing, and dragging the cut tree, I started back to where I thought I had left Brenda. As I plodded through the snow, I kept calling out again and again, "Brenda, where are you?" The only answers that came were the song of the birds and the keening of the wind through the trees. I panicked, realizing I had lost Brenda. I dropped the cut tree and somehow managed to find the road and make my way back to the house.

Mom and Dad were in the kitchen when I breathlessly burst through the door and cried out, "I lost Brenda among the trees!" My parents hurriedly donned their coats, and together we reentered the woods. I led them to where I thought I had left my sister. Dad directed us to spread out in our search. It wasn't long before I heard him call out, "I found her." Brenda had remained obedient to my charge and not moved. While searching for Brenda, Dad found the cut tree too.

Daylight was rapidly fading into dusk as the four of us wearily trudged through the deep snow and returned to the warmth of the house. This time Mom held Brenda's hand, and Dad pulled the tree. No words were spoken, but I know each of us in our own way gave thanks that Brenda was safe. I wasn't disciplined for my careless act, but for me it will always be a Christmas remembered. Years later, Brenda told me she heard my cries, saw me wandering among the trees, and answered.

But I never heard her. The sound of her childish voice was carried away by the wind.

---------------- ++++++ ----------------

In August 1947, I married Sidney Nelson. Brenda remembered Sid as "tall, big, but not fat, not skinny either." In the eyes of a five-year-old, he was a gentle blond giant who would roughhouse, joke, tease, and many times amuse her by speaking with a Swedish accent. My little sister fell in love with my husband.

Shortly after our marriage, Sidney took a job in the engine room of the *Adam E. Cornelius,* a freighter owned by the Boland and Cornelius Company. The ship was someplace on the Great Lakes in April 1948, when Sid received a ship-to-shore call from his sister Dorothy informing him he was a father. He had a son. Fortunately, Sid was able to arrange to come home for a few days. As it was when Mother gave birth to Brenda, doctors continued to require a woman to remain in bed for ten days following the birth.

I was living on the farm at the time. Overjoyed that Sidney was able to come to see me and to meet his son, I wanted to be home when he arrived. The doctor grudgingly signed the paper for my hospital release, with the explicit order that I be taken home in an ambulance. Mom was at the hospital with Brenda when the attendants wheeled my gurney into the ambulance. The nurse handed the baby to Mom, who in turn placed him on my five-year-old sister's lap, waiting excitedly in the car. As the ambulance pulled away from the hospital, Mom followed with Brenda holding her six-day-old nephew on her small lap—no seat belts, no car seats.

Now Brenda had a playmate. She would push Vernon in his baby buggy up and down the gravel road in front of our house. As Vernon grew, the two of them were constant companions. One of their favorite mischievous activities was to go to the Concord grape arbor and, while eating their fill of grapes, spit them at one another leaving blotches of dark purple grape juice on faces and clothing.

One Thanksgiving in the early 1950s was especially memorable for Brenda and Vernon. Sidney and I no longer lived on the farm. We had our own home in Ashtabula. Plans were made that we, with Lloyd and family, would have Thanksgiving dinner at the farm. Vernon was already there to "help" his grandma, but more so to play with Brenda. Thanksgiving Day, a lake-effect storm dropped a foot of snow that the wind formed into huge drifts. Lloyd attempted to maneuver the car through the shifting snow. We got within a mile and a half of the farm before he turned back. The roads were becoming impassable. Once home and safe, I telephoned Mom to let her know we could not get through. Her disappointment was palpable, as Mom had prepared the traditional full-course Thanksgiving meal.

Mom's disappointment was not shared by Brenda and Vernon though. There was an overabundance of food—a drumstick apiece, stuffing, mashed potatoes and gravy, sweet potato balls rolled in nuts with a melted marshmallow center, and seconds on the pumpkin pie. Aunt and nephew (more like brother and sister), bellies bloated from overeating, enjoyed their Thanksgiving feast in kid fashion, happy they did not have to share.

When the four of us lived in our basement home on Vineland Avenue, Brenda attended Jefferson Elementary School. She was having so many problems with her sixth-grade teacher that Mom asked me if Brenda could come to live with us and attend Edgewood Schools.

Sidney was an easygoing Swede, and there was a special bond between the two, so he voiced no objection. To offset the cost of my sister's keep, Mom offered to give us a supply of meat from their freezer. I knew this would significantly reduce the amount we spent on groceries. We were saving to build our house, and I pinched every penny until the Indian hollered. Admittedly, it was a major factor in my agreeing to the arrangement.

The fall of 1953, Mom withdrew Brenda from Jefferson Schools, and I enrolled her at Edgewood Elementary School in the sixth grade. Brenda's legal residency and my role as her pseudo guardian were not questioned.

Living arrangements were tight in our basement home—kitchen/dining area, living room, large bedroom, small bathroom with shower, and laundry/furnace area. Five of us shared the bedroom. Sid and I slept in the double bed, Bruce (age one) slept in his crib, Vernon (age five) slept in the bottom bunk bed, with Brenda assigned to the top bunk. There was no privacy.

Ours was a busy household. Sidney worked for Ziegler Heating, Vernon was in the first grade, and Bruce stayed with a friend of the family the hours I worked a part-time job at the Reliance Electric Credit Union. The time Brenda lived with us, for the most part, remains a blur. But negative incidents, like the squeaky wheel, are what get the attention and are remembered.

Brenda seemed to like school and made friends. I would attend Wednesday evening prayer meetings at the Church of God while Sid stayed home with the boys. While I was gone, Brenda acquired the habit of long telephone conversations with her friends, ignoring home tasks. This angered me, and one Wednesday, as I was about to leave, I unplugged the telephone and took it with me, denying her the pleasure of long chats with newfound friends.

Brenda enjoyed spending time with Sid and willingly helped him when asked. Sid was attempting to lay tile on the uneven basement concrete floor. Asphalt tile, when cold, is not malleable. Sid found that by heating each tile with a blowtorch, it would shape and adhere to the floor—a labor-intensive task. He asked Brenda to help, which she willingly did, hour after hour after hour. One night my sister awakened us from a sound sleep. Alarmed, I turned on the light, looked up at Brenda in the top bunk, and saw her right arm extended straight up, moving back and forth as she kept repeating, "Sid, I got this one too hot."

Little did I realize my sister, at the age of eleven, possessed the resolve of an adult. One day Brenda, as a ploy, rode her bike to school. Instead of going to school, she continued to the Greyhound Bus Station located next to Carlisle's Department Store on Main Street in Ashtabula. She purchased a round-trip ticket to Cleveland. The bus left at 8:00 a.m. and conveniently returned at 3:30 p.m.

I knew nothing of this at the time and learned of it years later when I read Brenda's account of the escapade in her daughter Kellie Dennis-Gibson Peine's book *Heirloom Memories: Our Family Story*:

> It was a marvelous day! It was a little scary, but it was so much fun! I went into each of the department stores. I went to May Company, Higbee's, Halle's, and Stirling Linder Davis. It was totally amazing and I was just in awe of all the people and the sights. As I recall, I had enough money that I bought some material for a blouse and a piano music book. I got back to the bus terminal in plenty of time to catch the bus back to Ashtabula and wonder of wonders, my bike was right where I had left it… I got back to Henri's and told her school went very well. I think I must have forged a note to cover my absence from school, as I know a note would have been necessary. No one was ever the wiser.

Looking back, it would have been better had I known. It might have deterred a later happening near the end of her sixth-grade year. An incident occurred when Brenda's word was believed over mine that resulted in my estrangement with Mom. Although Brenda was the cause of the problem, she was also the solution. During the summer she telephoned to say how sorry she was and asked if I would call and talk to Mom. Surprised by the mature outreach taken by my sister, I called Mom. In doing so, family harmony was restored and the incident never spoken of again. Brenda returned to live with us for her seventh-grade year. But living with us was not the ideal school solution. She completed the seventh grade and returned home to be with Mom and Dad.

Mom applied for Brenda's admittance to the Andrews School for Girls in Willoughby. Whatever the reason, she was not accepted. To compensate Brenda for being rejected and to make life on the farm more exciting, Brenda got a horse. She had wanted one for years. Looking through the local paper, Brenda saw a for-sale ad for a pinto horse. The ad was placed by Dr. Miller, a psychologist, who lived with his daughter Joanie on Gageville Road, one mile to the north of our farm. Dad bought the horse for Brenda. She and Joanie became horse-riding friends, exploring wide-ranging areas in the county during the summers of their high school years.

As far as I knew, Brenda did very well at Jefferson High School. She made friends, excelled academically, took part in high school plays and musicals, and her senior year, she was initiated into the National Honor Society.

As fate would have it, our marriages held too many similarities. At seventeen years of age, I married Sidney Nelson. We eloped to Covington, Kentucky. Two sons were born of the union—Vernon in 1948 and Bruce in 1952. At the age of thirty-one, Sidney died of a heart attack. We were married for eleven and a half years. At seventeen years of age, Brenda married Paul Dennis. They eloped to Winchester, Virginia. Two girls were born of the union—Kellie in 1960 and Shellie in 1964. At the age of thirty, Paul died of a massive stroke at the base of his brain. They were married for nine and a half years.

At thirty-three years of age, I married Allan Dickie. We were married in the East Side Presbyterian Church in Ashtabula; Brenda was my matron of honor. At the age of eighty-two, Allan died of a ruptured aorta. We were married for twenty-three years. At twenty-eight years of age, Brenda married Theren Gibson (Gibby). They were married at her home in North Kingsville; I was her matron of honor. At the age of forty-nine, Gibby died of lung cancer. They were married for seven and a half years.

At fifty-seven years of age, I married Charlie Gass. We were married in Las Vegas at the home of Bruce and Linda. Brenda was not able to attend, but several extended-family members were with us. At the age of eighty-four Charlie died from heart surgery complications. We were married almost ten years. At forty-three years of age, Brenda married Walter Spadaro. They were married in the North Kingsville Presbyterian Church. At the age of sixty-eight, Walt died of cancer. They were married just shy of sixteen years. Brenda has no plans to marry again. At the age of seventy-six, she has been a widow for seventeen years. She has lived in Ashtabula or Lake Counties in Ohio her entire life.

At seventy-three years of age, I married Cordell Glaus. We were married at the Viking Vineyards near Kent, Ohio. Brenda was my matron of honor. At the age of eighty-five, Cordell died of cancer. We were married for almost ten years. I have no plans to marry again either. At the age of eighty-eight, I have been a widow for five years. In contrast to Brenda, my life has been an ever-changing scene, having lived in four states—Florida, Nevada, Ohio, and Pennsylvania.

Due to life's vicissitudes, our contact would wax and wane over the years. But whenever needed, we were there for one another.

In 1970, when Paul died, I lived in Kent. Kellie and Shellie were young at the time. I took a few days off from my teaching to be with them and hoped I could be of some help. Brenda was away from the house on an errand, and I took it upon myself to clean out the refrigerator, only to have the minister and his wife stop by to find the kitchen in total disarray. Many family and friends came to the calling hours or attended the funeral. I stayed several days with my sister, and during that time, if nothing else, I gave her my loving support.

Las Vegas was my place of residence when the telephone call came on September 13, 1978, that Gibby had died. The afternoon of September 14, my flight landed at the Cleveland Hopkins Airport, and my nephew Peter met me and took me to Brenda's home in North Kingsville. Calling hours were that evening at the Richmond Ross funeral home in Ashtabula. Brenda was in total control of her emotions and provided comfort to family members and friends who came to pay their respects. Her stoic emotional state did not surprise me as I knew she had given in to her grief when she learned of Gibby's diagnosis. The memorial service was the following day. Afterward many gathered at her home, and later that evening, Brenda and I sat up late into the night—sisters just talking.

Before my return flight to Las Vegas, Brenda treated us to dinner at the Samurai Restaurant in Beachwood. Seated at a horseshoe-shaped table with a center grill, I was fascinated as I watched the chef prepare our dinner. I later dubbed him The Fastest Knife in Town.

On September 22, eight days after my arrival, Brenda stood with me at the airport departure gate. I noted in my diary, "No long goodbye. A quick hug, words not spoken. We felt, and we knew." My flight was called; Brenda placed a gift in my hand to be opened once the plane was in the air. The small box held a gold wishbone pin with an inset diamond. It remains one of my priceless treasures. I wore it as "something old" when I married Cordell Glaus.

At the time of Walt's death, I lived only a few houses down from Brenda's home on Lakeshore Boulevard in Madison, Ohio. Walt had been diagnosed with a rare blood cancer, and Brenda stayed with him in his hospital room 24/7 for four months. Finally, the time came that he was placed with hospice care. I sensed how difficult this was for my sister. Her daughters, now adults and both nurses, were with their mother. Kellie lived in the immediate area; Shellie came from Pittsburgh. My best support was to remain in the background. Any offer to help would bring a "no thanks," although I knew she was exhausted.

I understood on the intellectual level, but on the emotional level, I missed my sister. The evening of November 13, 2001, I stopped by for a brief visit. I sensed Brenda did not want to have any conversation and asked me to sit with Walt while she took a shower. I readily agreed. This small request meant a lot, for I had done so little. When Brenda again entered the room, I was surprised when she asked if I planned to spend the night. I sensed her tenseness. Thinking she preferred to be alone, I immediately said goodbye and walked back to my house. At the time I did not know that Walt's son and family were on their way from Omaha, Nebraska, driving through the night, hoping to get there in time for Jeff to say goodbye to his dad. They arrived in time; Walt died the following afternoon.

The deaths of both Sidney and Allan were sudden, and family were with me after the fact. For Charlie it was different. I lived in Columbus.

Charlie was in the hospital, and when death was imminent, I called Brenda. She and her daughter Kellie were with me when he died.

Cordell and I lived in Kent when he was diagnosed with terminal cancer and opted for no treatment, requesting placement with hospice. For three months, Brenda's telephone calls and frequent visits served as a rock that sustained me during those devastating emotional times.

BRENDA COMMENTED THAT A FAMILY TREE was inadequate to document our families; it would take a bramble bush. Most important, our multiple families remained a priority in our lives.

Brenda, her daughters, and granddaughter, lived within a mile of one another in North Madison. I would often comment to Brenda that she had her own commune. Shortly after graduating from high school, my sons enlisted in the United States Air Force. At the time their four-year enlistments were up, they were serving on Air Force bases in the West. Both were enrolled in college, met and married local girls, and settled down to raise their families. Our visits were always major events.

Suffice it to say, relationships with our stepfamilies were different. Brenda's two marriages added ten stepchildren. Several of her stepchildren lived in the area, and Brenda was one that gave priority to her husband's children over her own. But after becoming a widow for the last time, she felt the freedom to fully enjoy her own daughters.

My three marriages added seven stepchildren. Contact with my stepfamilies was less frequent. All but Cordell's children lived out of state, and visits were major happenings. I never felt pressured to give priority to them over my own children.

Brenda assumed the responsibility to decorate family graves with flowers and flags each Memorial Day, not by default because she lived in the area, but by commitment. Mom, Dad, and Granma are interred in the Gageville Cemetery located in Sheffield Township, two miles from the farm. Brenda's husband Paul Dennis is buried in Oakdale Cemetery in Jefferson; Theren Gibson in Greenlawn Memorial Gardens in North Kingsville; Walter Spadaro in Fairview Memorial Cemetery in Madison. My husband Sidney Nelson is interred at the Nelson family plot in the Edgewood Cemetery on the east side of Ashtabula. Graves of my other husbands are out of the area. For Brenda, caring for the family grave sites is a labor of love coupled with respect for our mother who made it her priority.

Brenda spent the winter of 2007 collecting, scanning, printing, and organizing genealogical information about the family. The repetition of the procedure became downright boring; she took little time for physical exercise, and food became her motivation. When completed, the work filled eight thick binders. Brenda laughingly laments that she gained ten pounds during the four months she devoted to the task. The binders contain a gold mine of information for interested future generations. I used it when writing the beginning chapters of this book.

I credit Brenda with the painting of the farmhouse. While collecting memorabilia to include in the binders, she commented that it would be nice to have an actual painting, for any pictures she had of the farmhouse were very poor. Cordell's avocation was painting, and I asked him if he would take on the task. It took him the better part of a year to complete the painting. The original hangs above the fireplace in my home. But with the digital technology of giclée reproduction, Brenda, Bruce, and several other family members have copies that are difficult to discern from the original.

———— ++++++ ————

BRENDA IS AN INTELLIGENT, DETERMINED PERSON. Our brother recognized her potential many years ago when he commented, "In Brenda we have a very strong personality. She seems to be capable of anything she sets her mind to."

Growing up on the farm, Brenda learned cooking, food preservation, basic sewing skills and crocheting from Mom. At that time, housework was not her forte. I recall cleaning her bedroom and finding dried orange peels under her bed. As payback for the times she messed up my room and wrote on my mirror with lipstick, I placed the dried peels under the bottom sheet when I made up the bed. Surprise!

Brenda's piano skills were far greater than mine. In high school, and later during her adult years, she was the accompanist for various musical performers and choirs. When I lived in North Madison, I agreed to play a duet arrangement of "Chopsticks" with her as part of the entertainment at a church luncheon. We practiced and I felt confident until I sat next to her on the piano bench. For whatever reason, I couldn't get the correct keyboard secondo finger placement, and it turned into a minor comedy act with two false starts before the rhythmical sounds of "Chopsticks" filled the room. After that, I was content to be Brenda's page turner whenever she accompanied a choir.

For two summers prior to Brenda's senior year in high school, Mom enrolled her for courses in typing, shorthand, bookkeeping, and office machines at the Ashtabula Business College. She was good enough that she worked as a volunteer secretary for the elementary principal her senior year in high school. Much to my surprise, I later learned Brenda possessed sales skills that she used to her advantage during high school selling magazine subscriptions over the telephone.

As soon as Brenda turned sixteen and passed her driving test, Mom and Dad sent her into Cleveland to take an aptitude test at Fenn College, now Cleveland State University. Test results confirmed Brenda could be anything she wanted to be. What she wanted to be was a veterinarian. But our parents nixed that idea, and she settled for nursing, accepted into the program at Huron Road Hospital School of Nursing through Fenn College.

Brenda had been dating Paul Dennis; her plans changed when she realized she was pregnant. They were married the spring of her senior year. Tragically, Dad never accepted the marriage and shunned his daughter. At the time, I lived in Ashtabula with my family, and I was unaware of the drama that took place that spring of 1960. I attended the high school graduation ceremony with Mom and Dad. I sat next to Dad and noted his hands were clenched into fists that he never relaxed during the entire ceremony.

Brenda graduated, and with a baby on the way, she and Paul lived at the farm. They needed money, and Brenda went to work for the Carlisle Allen Department Store in Ashtabula. Her first position was secretary to Ted Carlisle. Brenda took a leave of absence when she gave birth to Kellie, then later returned to work as a part-time sales associate in the store.

As soon as possible, Brenda revisited her goal to become a nurse and managed the superhuman feat of juggling marriage, motherhood, and school. In 1958, at the age of sixteen, she had been accepted for the nursing program at Fenn College, but withdrew when she married Paul. In 1961 she reenrolled in the program and, for three years, made the daily commute of sixty miles from the farm into Cleveland to earn her associate degree in applied science in June 1964.

Over the ensuing years, Brenda held different positions in the health field. In 1968 she was hired by Reliance Electric and Engineering Company at their Ashtabula plant to fill the position of industrial nurse (IN). During her years as IN, she set up a program for Total Accident Prevention that was so effective the need for a plant dispensary staffed by a nurse was phased out and replaced with certified first aide employees. She had effectively worked herself out of a job.

For the optimist, one door does not close but another opens. This was true for Brenda. The announcement was made in 1990 that the Ashtabula Reliance Electric plant would begin to downsize in preparation for the plant's closing in a few years. The management job for plant human resources manager was advertised. Brenda, knowing she possessed the needed qualifications and skills, applied for and was awarded the position. She stayed in this post until the Ashtabula plant closed in 1999, enabling her to earn full retirement.

Over the years, Brenda not only adapted to career changes, she adapted to different husbands and acquired new skill sets. Paul died, and she married Gibby. They started the Gibson Refrigeration service and repaired travel trailer refrigerators. They also ran the Torchlight business where they bred, raised, and sold Arabian and Morgan horses. Brenda continued to live in North Kingsville after Gibby died, worked full time, and successfully managed the businesses.

Her home in North Kingsville was set on a two-acre plot of land, and to maintain it, Brenda became adept at using the tractor and other farm implements. I'm not certain how she did it, but my sister "treed" the tractor. She was working along the tree line at the back of her property with the tractor's large front bucket in the raised position. Her attention must have been diverted, for she ran the tractor into a large oak tree that stood in her path. The tractor's powerful back wheels propelled it, with raised bucket, about ten feet up the tree trunk. Brenda had the presence of mind to turn the key to shut off the engine and climbed down from the precarious angle. When in trouble, call your brother, and Brenda did just that. Lloyd came, assessed the situation, and managed to safely back the tractor off of the tree. Now it makes a good story, but it could have been so different. Brenda could have been seriously injured, or killed.

Brenda's talents included unusual decorating tastes. Allan and I planned to spend Christmas 1979 in Las Vegas with Bruce and family. I made no plans to decorate the house for Christmas—not even a tree. The night before we were to leave, there was a knock on our door. Allan opened it, to be greeted by a young man holding a silver tree decorated with old socks (holes in the toes), tin cans, lids, broken light bulbs, and worse yet, rotten oranges and bananas. Our delivery boy greeted us with, "Hey, is this where the Scrooge lives that doesn't want a Christmas tree?" The rotten fruit was garbage and treated as such; all that remains of that gussied-up tree are the holey socks, saved in my cedar chest. The tree was compliments of Brenda.

When she married Walter Spadaro, his children lived in the Madison area, twenty-five miles distant, and at Walt's insistence, weekend visits became commonplace. Tiring of the weekend trips, Brenda's solution was to move to the area. It took two years to find the right house, but it happened. Walt was visiting his daughter on Lakeshore Boulevard. Standing in her yard looking up the street, he noted a realtor placing a sign in front of one of the cottages. He saw, he acted, and that very day signed a purchase agreement to buy the cottage with an unobstructed view of the lake. With the aid of a contractor/carpenter, the vacation cottage was transformed into a beautiful home.

Walt, then retired, needed another project to fill his days. They purchased a cottage contiguous to their property, and Walt proceeded to remodel the interior. He died before the work was completed. Brenda hired the contractor who remodeled their Lakeshore house and with saw, drill, and hammer in hand worked with him to complete what Walt had started. She decorated the interior, giving it the whimsical look of an oversized dollhouse. In 2006 she advertised the cottage with Vacation Rentals by Owner (VRBO) and marketed it as a vacationer's dream bungalow. At the time of this writing, Brenda has successfully promoted the cottage for the past twelve years.

Thinking it wise to pay down the mortgage on her properties in 2008, Brenda enrolled in a sixteen-week refresher course through Cleveland State that, upon successful completion, enabled her to regain her knowledge and nursing skills. The course required a clinical experience, which was done at University Hospitals in Cleveland. Brenda's final evaluation was outstanding, and at the age of sixty-eight, she was hired as a floor nurse by the hospital. Again, the daily commute. This time it was only twenty-five miles from North Madison into Cleveland. The paychecks were good, but the demands of floor nursing, managing the vacation rental, and keeping up her own home wore her down. Wisely, she resigned her position after not quite two years.

It took me years to accept that my sister is a task-driven person. No dust settled around her, nor would grass ever grow underfoot. She exchanged the paycheck earned in the world of work to be home, and with it came the flexibility to do only what she chose to do. She continued to manage her vacation dream cottage. Five years as church pianist for the Chapel Methodist Church was enough, and when asked to return, Brenda finally dredged up the word no, which for years lay dormant in her vocabulary. Instead, she used her secretarial and human-relations skills to serve as board secretary for the Lake Breeze Park Association and the Madison Historical Society. She also agreed to serve on the board of the Friends of Madison Library and assumed responsibility for the memberships. Brenda remains in touch with her 1960 graduating class and assumed the task of planning monthly luncheons and class reunions.

My sister inherited Mom's love of quilting. Early on she gave me basic instruction in hand quilting, even supplying me with several quilt kits over the years. Brenda started as a hand quilter, but in 2010 she took part in several workshops sponsored by the Lake Farmpark Quilt Show. She learned machine quilting techniques from experts. Brenda will often say, "You can't pay me enough to make a quilt, but I will lovingly give one to those special people in my life." Brenda's "happy place" is her sewing room. Her sewing machine is placed in front of the window that gives her an unobstructed view of Lake Erie.

+++++++

LIVING ALONE WHEN I HAD MAJOR SURGERY was the decisive factor that prompted my decision to move near my sister in North Madison. Charlie died in the spring of 1997, and the following January, I had surgery. Thinking myself strong enough to manage with the help of friends, I found I wasn't as strong as I thought. Alone and in a weakened condition, there were times I was terrified. Brenda came and was with me for two days. During her stay, I must have expressed how comforting it would be to live near family.

Over the coming months, the idea of selling my Columbus home and moving to North Madison percolated in my brain. I made it known to Brenda and Walt that I would like to move to the area, adding the caveats that any house I purchased must have an unobstructed lake view with a list price under $200,000.

My telephone rang on a Saturday morning in June 1998. I heard Brenda and Walt's excited voices on the other end of the wire telling me they had found the perfect house. Price was right, built on the lakeside, and one quarter of a mile to the east of their home on Lakeshore Boulevard. The house was not listed with a realtor; they learned of the sale through word of mouth. I drove up the next day and, with Walt and Brenda, made a quick tour of the house. It was everything I wanted. I came, I looked, and I signed a purchase agreement with the owners, all on the same day.

There were many positive aspects that came with living near my family. Brenda brought me kicking and screaming into the world of computers and patiently answered my myriad questions. My sister-in-law, Trudy, suggested we Schumann women get together for monthly lunches. I had a serious medical condition that required surgery. Brenda and her daughter, Kellie, were with me all the way—I was not alone. Brenda and I resumed piano lessons, taking them with the same teacher. That was when we joined the Chapel Methodist Church.

There was nary a day went by that we didn't see one another. Reflecting on that time, I know I assumed too much as the older sister, forgetting that my kid sister was a grown woman with a husband and family of her own. It took time before I came to the realization that moving into Brenda's commune created some dissonance. She and her daughters, now adults, were very close. There were times of conflict when I was unable to "get with the program," as Kellie once remarked. But as far as Brenda and my nieces were concerned, they were my family, and during the years I lived there, I attempted to live by the words in a song made famous by Bing Crosby: "You've got to accentuate the positive, and eliminate the negative."

In May of 2003, my biking buddy, Rosemary Brenkus, a.k.a. Cupid, introduced me to her brother Cordell Glaus. We married in October of that year. I sold my home on Lakeshore Boulevard and moved to Green, and later to Kent. Both cities are located more than fifty miles from North Madison. Living so close to Brenda taught me a valuable lesson. We are both very independent women, and with miles between us, I feel closer to my sister than when we lived on the same street.

EARLY ON, BRENDA AND I WERE SO INVOLVED with raising our families and working we had no time, and little money, for travel. In October of 2002, while living in Madison, Brenda, Shellie, Kellie, her daughter, Courtney, and I visited New York City. Shellie's love affair with Regis and Kelly's talk show trumped my suggestion to visit the Metropolitan Art Museum. But seeing the Broadway performance of *The Lion King* was a choice agreed upon by all. The enjoyment of being with my sister and my nieces outweighed my disappointments. After my marriage to Cordell, I lived in Green. Brenda, now widowed, joined us on several occasions for the First Night event in Akron.

On our first First Night adventure in 2005, we endured the cold to see the midnight fireworks show. In successive years, common sense prevailed, and we would venture downtown early, take in several venues, return home, turn on the TV, and toast in the New Year while sipping Gewürztraminer wine and watching the spectacle of the ball drop at Times Square.

Brenda and I made a road trip that stands apart from any other travel experiences we had. Over the years, Brenda had mentioned visiting Hustler, Wisconsin, with Dad when she was fourteen years old. She spoke of the cemetery where our paternal grandparents were buried, the rock wall where Dad carved his initials, and the family farm. Each telling piqued my interest, and I wanted to visit the place of our dad's childhood home.

Brenda's days were filled with responsibilities caring for her dog, Ozzie, and cat, Sammy, community involvement, and her vacation rental property; but somehow, in July 2017, she arranged to be away. She offered to use her vehicle for the trip—a 2011 Dodge Ram. Knowing I had a restless leg condition (RLS) and I needed to stand and walk about every hour, Brenda planned for us to be gone the better part of a week. Allowing two days to drive the six hundred miles to our destination, another two days to return home, while spending two days in the area. Miraculously, we managed the trip in three days. Brenda's willingness to stop every one to two hours, combined with the comfort of her truck, allowed us to make it to our destination the first day. The second day we spent in the Hustler area. The third day we returned home.

The visit to Hustler was all I hoped it would be. We walked the streets of the small town where Dad grew up. We think we identified the family homestead, now a large dairy operation. We visited the cemetery, and stood at the Schumann monument that marks the plots where family members are buried. Brenda was disappointed she was not able to locate the rock wall where Dad, when a young boy, carved his initials.

Knowing we would be confined for many hours in the vehicle, we planned to entertain ourselves listening to audio tapes. The tapes were never used. As the odometer clicked off the miles, we talked and we talked and we talked. And during those hours of conversation, I gained a new understanding of my sister.

Growing up, she felt like an only child. Lloyd and I had left home. For Lloyd it was enlisting in the navy; for me it was marriage and moving into Ashtabula. Brenda's childhood years were spent in solitary play—with her dolls, playing in the woods and along the creek, reading, and sewing or crocheting. Mom was her "playmate," and she played games with Brenda when she wasn't burdened with household and farm chores. Brenda felt Mom and Dad were overwhelmed by her antics, as she was a kid with lots of energy, and they seemed very old and tired.

My sister expressed feelings that bordered on envy. In an earlier chapter, I wrote about the good times Lloyd and I had playing with the neighbor kids. When Brenda read this, she wrote the following comment: "I admit I'm jealous of the interaction you had with the neighbors. For me, I was not allowed to play with the VanSlyke girls or Viola Fischer next door. I remember a very lonely childhood to which I adapted maybe too much so."

We talked about our parents. Brenda acknowledged that Dad deferred to Mom when it came to discipline issues. In Mom's eyes, Brenda was perfect and could do no wrong, referring to the conflict with her sixth-grade teacher. As an adult, my sister realized Mom thwarted her maturing when Mom asked, and I agreed, to let Brenda live with me and attend Edgewood Schools. It would have been much better if Mom had approached the problem head-on and learned the reason behind Brenda's conflict with her teacher.

We both acknowledged that Dad provided little overt direction in influencing our choices in careers, dating, and marriage. Here, Mom sent us mixed signals. She encouraged us to do our best in school, for there was always room on top. Yet she, with Dad's overt or covert permission, allowed us to date at a very young age, and with it came the unspoken message of marriage, rather than advancing our education.

To this day, we both sincerely believe our parents did the best they possibly could for us. The financial devastation of the Depression changed the direction of their lives and possibly influenced how we were raised. We never questioned their love.

———— ⋅+⋅+⋅ ————

In April 1982, I received an exceptionally beautiful birthday card from Brenda. The card was a "keeper," and I had an idea, not original with me, as a way of using it. Back when I was living in Lemoyne, Pennsylvania, I had stopped by the home of an acquaintance. While there, the doorbell rang, and the mailman had a special delivery letter requiring a signature. The lady signed, closed the door, and carefully placed the envelope on a table, commenting that today was her husband's birthday and the letter was a birthday card from his uncle. But it wasn't just any birthday card. The men had exchanged the same card for more than twenty-five years. A few years back, they felt the card was so valuable they feared its getting lost in the mail and henceforth agreed to register it before mailing.

The words written on the face of the birthday card I received from Brenda that April in 1982 were "A Sister is someone Special." Recalling the birthday card incident while living in Lemoyne, I suggested to Brenda we make this our annual birthday card, adding a short message each year. Brenda was receptive to the idea. It took only a few years before there was little space left on our revolving birthday card for even a signature. At the time, I was living in Columbus, and my husband, Charlie Gass, knew a Hungarian bookbinder. I took the card to him, and he bound it into a beautiful, green, leather-covered book with the title *Sister to Sister* embossed in gold leaf on the cover. Now, thirty-six years later, even the pages of this book are almost filled.

At some point along the way, Brenda came up with the idea that if we wanted to send more detailed messages, we would have to place the pages in binders. This we did, filling one large binder and well on our way to filling a second. Recently, as I skimmed through the pages, one difference became obvious—our writing styles. Brenda's entries were factual happenings about her life, the lives of her family, and of her friends. My style embellished the factual with descriptive and emotional passages. Unknowingly, Brenda is writing her memoir year by year on her pages placed in the binder. Not so for me—four years ago I started to cut back on what I write to place in the binder. Instead, I am writing my memoir that will be self-published in book form.

⋅⋅⋕⋕⋕⋅⋅

EASTER WEEKEND 1990, Brenda and Walt visited Charlie and me in Columbus. Sunday morning the four of us attended church. As we were leaving the church, Brenda and I stopped in the restroom. We stood in line waiting for an empty stall when a black lady emerged from one, looked us up and down, and asked, "Are you twins?" Our taste in clothes is comparable, and on this day, Brenda and I wore suits very similar in style and color. Being the older, I was flattered as my sister was a very attractive woman. As soon as the woman was out of earshot, Brenda looked at me and spit out, "Payback is hell!"

This age thing with Brenda has a history. As a little girl, Brenda attracted a lot of attention. She had fair skin and delicate features, but her crowning glory was her red hair that Mom fashioned into thick French braids. From the time she was four years old, Mom would have me take

Brenda with me into town when I did the Saturday shopping. I was a mature-looking sixteen-year-old. Too many times to recall, I was asked by strangers, "My, what a beautiful child. Is this your little girl?"

The first time the twin-question was put to us, I paid little heed. But over the years, others made the same observation. In 1999, while living in North Madison, Brenda and I attended one of her granddaughter's basketball games. We sat side by side on the bleacher. A little girl, perhaps ten years old, seated just below us, turned around, looked up, and out of the mouth of this innocent child came the question, "Are you twins?" I loved it. Apparently, I was aging very well.

I thought the question had ran its gamut when, in 2017, I sent a Christmas card to an elderly friend. The card was a picture of Brenda and me taken the previous summer when we were in Whistler. My friend was delighted to hear from me and responded with a note commenting, "What a nice picture of you and your daughter." The question had come full circle—but not quite!

August 2018, Brenda and I attended a performance of *Hamilton* at Playhouse Square in Cleveland. As we were leaving the theater, anticipating the forty-mile drive home, we stopped by the handicap bathroom. The door was locked; we stood waiting. When the door opened, Brenda stepped forward to help the woman using a walker to exit the room. As she shuffled through the door, she first looked at Brenda, nodding her thanks, then glanced at me. Almost as if on cue came the question, "Are you twins?" Unbelievable! Brenda muttered "No," but I added, "Yes." Confused the woman then asked, "Well, who is older?" Regrettably I answered, "I am by twelve years!" I realized much later I had missed my chance to add some levity to this recurring question. I should have responded, "Yes, by twelve minutes."

---------------- ++++++ ----------------

BRENDA WAS THE BABY SISTER I BEGGED FOR, and in those early years she was the little sister I tolerated. I never thought of myself as the older sister who spewed out sage advice—that is, until I read Brenda's answer to a question put to her by her daughter: "Person who had the most positive influence on your life?"

Brenda's answer to Kellie's question was included in her 2010 book, *Heirloom Memories: Our Family Story:*

I guess I would have to say, my sister, Henri. During the two years I lived with her when I was 11 and 12, I was somewhat of a troubled "preteen"-Not very many people liked me. I was in her kitchen when I was complaining of this situation. She turned to me and said: "Brenda if no one likes you, then you have to do something about it." This resulted in an insight that I have passed on to others.

In 2018, a birthday message from Brenda read in part, "In many ways we are different." Our lives have taken different paths, and following those paths, we have become who we are today—two uniquely different persons, both in personality and in interests. For me the joy of having a sister far outweighs any dissonance, spoken or unspoken, that from time to time weighed heavily on us.

From the bottom of my heart, I say, "Thanks, Mom and Dad, for giving me a sister."

TWENTY-SIX

ALONE AGAIN

I N AN AUGUST 25, 2003, E-MAIL, Cordell, the romantic, wrote these words:

> Our wedding invitation will say "a new beginning together." This is what we are doing—a new life... Let us live it to the fullest. We will make our mark on the world. That is our destiny, for our love for each other is that strong... We will write our book in the surroundings of our new home telling the story of "December Love," telling the world how to enjoy real and deep love at the most beautiful time in our lives... but with knowledge, wisdom, and experience unsurpassed... I constantly vision us at 85, 95, and on... Our marriage will continue to grow and reward us.

Now fifteen years later, I asked myself, "Just what did we accomplish during those ten years of our marriage?" What we accomplished was that two strong-willed, obstinate people changed enough that we experienced a harmonious and fulfilling marital relationship. Our book never written, the essence of our marriage died with Cordell.

One evening, near the end of Cordell's life, we sat sipping a glass of Gewürztraminer wine. A feeling of peace engulfed us. I put the question to my husband, "How can I possibly cope after you are gone?" His response, "You are strong, you will do all right."

Difficult as it was at the time to accept his factual, unemotional response, it proved to be a beacon of light through those first dark days, weeks, and months I was alone. With Cordell's passing, the activity that filled my days abruptly stopped. My daily schedule changed from being a full-time caregiver to days with no commitments. There was much to do, but I lacked the desire to do it. The dinner hour was the most difficult time. Many days, I had to get out of the house; I took a walk, a bicycle ride, or ran errands.

The first task I set for myself was to write notes of appreciation and thanks to all who had expressed their condolences in one way or another. That done, I next turned to business items related to house management and personal finances. I was advised by our bank to close out the joint checking account with Cordell and open a new account with my son, Bruce, as cosigner. Seemed a good idea, until I faced the stark reality that when the joint account was canceled, all auto-deduct payments were voided. When I attempted to correct the mistake, I faced a bureaucratic nightmare that accounts in Cordell's name only must be registered to my name before any changes could be made. A daunting task, especially in my fragile emotional state. But I had no choice, and I did it.

My grief consumed me, and I knew I needed to reach out to others. I learned about the Grief Care Place (GCP), offering programs and social activities for those who had lost a loved one. Eating alone was depressing, and through the GCP, I was put in touch with groups that dined together. I tried them all—breakfast, lunch, and dinner. Because the dinner hour was the most difficult, I settled on two groups that met in the evening—the I Hate to Cook group met weekly, and the Widows group met monthly.

One Friday evening there were perhaps eighteen of us gathered around several tables in the restaurant, laughing and having a good time. I noted a couple seated nearby inquisitively watching. As they got up to leave, the lady came over and inquired about our group. One of the members spoke up, "This is the I Hate to Cook group, I hope you never have reason to join us. We are all widows."

I stayed with the two dining groups that first year. But I found the programs and monthly breakfasts offered through hospice more to my liking. I developed a casual friendship with two of the ladies and, on occasion, joined them for lunch.

Cordell died on September 3, and before the year ended, there were several special events that were difficult to ignore. October 11 was our tenth wedding anniversary, and I dined with Sue and Chuck, the couple with whom Cordell and I shared the same wedding date. November 11 was Cordell's eighty-sixth birthday, and I invited his children and spouses to join me for dinner at the Pufferbelly Restaurant in Kent. November 28 was Thanksgiving; breaking with tradition, I traveled to Columbus and enjoyed Thanksgiving dinner with my former neighbor on East Selby Boulevard, Susan Gardner, and her mother.

Christmas was the most challenging. I spent Christmas Eve with an aged friend who had no family in the area. Christmas morning, I received a FaceTime call from my grandson, Bruce Allan, and his wife, Rachel. This was my first FaceTime experience, and I brought some humor to the connection when Bruce A. said to me, "Grandma, get your finger off of the camera lens. We can't see you." Later, I delivered flowers from church to shut-ins. The joy of the recipients made my heart sing.

In the afternoon I drove to Geneva to spend the night with Lloyd. My brother told me not to bring any food, he had a stash of prepared survival dinners, and I was to choose and prepare one for our Christmas meal. I selected a concoction of pasta and chicken sauce that proved to be quite tasty. Lloyd and I spent the evening talking, for we were two lost souls without our mates, and we connected in the loneliness that consumed us. I stayed the night and returned home the next morning with a feeling of relief that 2013 would soon end, and a new year awaited me.

Being alone, I kept in constant motion, and it took a toll on me both mentally and physically. I became forgetful, unable to concentrate, slept poorly, and experienced stomach upsets that verged on chronic. I slowed my pace and kept only the church and hospice activities.

I took steps to ensure my safety. Bruce was concerned that I lived alone. Reluctantly, I agreed to get a Lifeline connected to my telephone and wore the alert button on a black cord about my neck. Unfamiliar with the area outside of Kent, I purchased an iPhone and learned how to use the GPS app. Later I bought a Jeep Cherokee with a backup camera and more bells and whistles than I knew what to do with. In fact, I often commented that the car was smarter than me.

⸻ ✦✦✦ ⸻

I SOON CAME TO THE REALIZATION that 432 Burr Oak Drive, the home Cordell and I created to our liking, required constant attention. I needed a handyman. A friend recommended Chet-4-Hire. Chet was a masterful jack-of-all-trades. He agreed to do a concrete wall repair project on the back of the house and scheduled it at a time when I was in Las Vegas. I neglected to tell my neighbor, Rachel, that Chet would be working at the house and gave no thought to the one living directly behind me. Little did I realize how observant she was in the attention given to what was going on in the neighborhood. Looking out the back window of her house, she observed a man working near my basement patio door and called the police to report a break-in. Not one, but three, police cars responded to the call. Had I informed Rachel that Chet would be working at the house, she could have defused the situation. Confronted by the officers, Chet provided sufficient proof as to who he was and why he was there. When I returned home and learned what had happened, I called Chet and profusely apologized for the unfortunate incident. He took it in good stride, quipping, "It was okay, but one officer would have been sufficient, not three!"

Rick Bennett was the general contractor we had hired to remodel our sunroom. Both Cordell and I were pleased with his work, and when I realized there was excessive moisture in the house attic, I contracted with Rick to replace the wooden soffit boards with vinyl sections that allowed for a flow of air to dissipate the moisture. Rick did other jobs for me, but when it came to moving my workbench in the garage and installing a deadbolt in the house basement door, he apparently found the jobs too picayune and therefore was too busy. I had not connected with Chet at this time, and it was my nephew, Pete, and his wife, Bev, who came to my rescue.

Change was my constant companion. The owner of our lawn care company was having personal and financial difficulties, causing his service to be unreliable. Difficult as it was, I changed to a different company. They provided better service, especially in the winter when I needed not only my driveway plowed but the sidewalks shoveled as well.

When we purchased the house, a selling point was the natural look and feel of the forested backyard. One spring day I was walking about among the trees, picking up fallen branches, paying careful attention to where I stepped as I traversed the rough ground. Stopping for a moment, I glanced up and blinked, thinking my eyes played a trick on me. Within three feet of where I stood, a fawn lay next to the foundation of the house. I thought the animal dead until I detected a gentle rise and fall in the lung area of its body. I quietly left, returning an hour later with my camera. The fawn, eyes now open, had changed its position. When I approached to take its picture, there was no movement; the fawn remained statue-still. Now my concern was not a dead fawn but an abandoned and hungry one. I returned to the house, came back with a saucer of milk, and placed it close to the fawn's mouth. That evening while eating my supper, I glanced up and saw a deer walking across my front yard followed by a wobbly legged fawn. I rushed to the back of the house. All my previous anxieties related to a dead, hungry, or abandoned fawn vanished. The only evidence to show that the fawn was ever there were the empty saucer and a slight indentation in the ground's foliage. As much as I disliked deer, for they ate many of my flowers, I was relieved to know the fawn would be safe and warm; the weather forecast was for a stormy, cold night.

The soil on the lot was clay and rocks—very difficult to cultivate. The only flowers I had were in pots or in baskets hanging from a heavy iron tripod placed by the front door. One Saturday in October, I was cleaning out the pots and reusable baskets in preparation for winter storage. When I dumped the earth from the last hanging basket, I was startled to see a mouse fall out with four newborn pinkies, eyes still tightly closed, attached to the doe's teats. In the blink of an eye, the doe got up and ran toward a rock pile with the four pinkies still hanging on, never to be seen by me again. What a picture, and I didn't have my camera! Such were the delights of nature on my city estate.

The backyard sloped, and the ground was rough. In truth, I feared falling when walking over the rough terrain. For that reason alone, I contacted Rick Bennett about a brick walk that would connect the house sidewalk with the shed. Rick, in turn, put me in touch with his stone mason, Jim Warman. Jim possessed design talents and was a master stone mason, with an eye to spot potential problems. The lower-level concrete patio and brick retaining wall were cracked and, to protect the house foundation, needed to be replaced. Jim drew up a design for a large, oval walkway connecting the upper-level house sidewalk, the lower-level patio, and the shed. Having this done would correct the problems of slope, rough terrain, cracked patio, and retaining wall. The project was well over my budget, but I understood the gravity of the situation and signed the contract.

Jim and his men started work in the fall of 2014, finishing in the spring of 2015. When finished, the walkway was not only functional, it was beautiful. The crowning features were the plantings and the installation of a split rail fence that provided stability as I walked up/down the grades of the oval. I sent pictures to Bruce with the comment it looked like a park, and I knew Cordell would have approved, and we jokingly said it should be named for him. A few weeks later, UPS delivered a large, heavy, unwieldly box. Bruce had crafted a two-by-three-foot oak sign, with letters routed out and highlighted with black paint forming the words "The Cordell R. Glaus Memorial Park." Included in the box was an arrow-shaped sign with the words "Deer Crossing," but it would take much more than a sign to keep those dastardly deer from devouring my plants. I invited the Glaus family for a cookout. We gathered in front of the sign, now secured to a tree, raised our wine glasses in a toast, and dedicated the park to Cordell. A friend took our picture to capture the moment.

When storms hit the area, trees were at the mercy of the strong winds. For that reason, I was proactive, rather than reactive, when it came to tree care. Not so for two neighbors who lived directly below me. A large double-trunk oak tree grew on their lot line. During a summer storm, a strong west wind took down one of the large trunks of this tree, and it fell onto my property, just missing the shed. Rot had weakened the base of the tree. The part that fell onto my property was eighteen to twenty-four inches in diameter and forty feet in length. When I learned the law clearly stated that a property owner was responsible for whatever was on their land, my first thought was, "T'ain't fair!" If I wanted it moved, it was my responsibility. For $750, my lawn-care company sawed it up and hauled it away. Given the law was not fair, my neighbors were. They reimbursed me for the cost of removal.

———————— ✦✦✦✦✦ ————————

CORDELL AND I HAD LIVED ON BURR OAK DRIVE long enough to have a speaking acquaintance with all the neighbors, and a friendship with one. Jim and Rachel lived across the street and frequently invited me to join them for evening meals. But it was an incident with Jim Cooney, the neighbor whom I met when his dog pooped on our yard, that brought laughter and a smile to my face. One afternoon, I was out in the front yard when Jim came slowly walking by and stopped to visit. Knowing Jim tired easily, I invited him to sit on the porch and rest a bit before returning home. We sat there chatting, when Jim noticed his wife, Sondra, walking briskly along in front of the house with their leashed terrier dog. As she passed, Jim called out to her. No answer. Thinking she didn't hear, he called again. Still no answer. But Jim's third call elicited a response, and without even a momentary halt, Sondra's voice reflected her annoyance as she muttered, "I was expecting you home fifteen minutes ago." There was an unspoken message in that reply, and Jim got it, for he abruptly stood and said, "I best be going, Sondra worries about me when I am gone too long." Justified or not, I, too, got a red alert: "Don't get too friendly with my husband."

Not all encounters were with my immediate neighbors. One time I noticed a group of young men with a video camera gathered on the devil's strip in front of the house. Curious, I walked out to join them. They rode BMX bikes and explained the camera was set up to record their stunt riding feats. The sidewalk ended at the top of the steps that led down to the school. Next to the steps was a railing constructed of two-inch steel pipe, the top rail installed three feet above the ground's surface. The stunt riding feat was for the BMX rider to gain enough speed to jump over the rail and land upright on the other side. I stood there and watched as rider after rider attempted the stunt only to land on the far side of the rail sprawled on the ground. For the umpteenth time Alex, a member of the group, got on his bike. He allowed about seventy-five feet to gain enough speed, then, at the top of the first step, jerked his bike handles up, flew over the rail, landing upright on the other side, and rode his BMX to the base of the hill. Elated, he pumped the air; his buddies cheered. They had been trying for over an hour to get a video of at least one successful jump, and I brought the luck that made it happen. There were five fellows in the group, and they lived in the area but traveled throughout the country in search of challenging steps, rails, bannisters, whatever would show off their riding skills. They made videos and posted them on their With Any Luck website, hoping one day to gain national recognition. To think this happened in my front yard. I never saw them again. They could have been an apparition, except they were there during daylight hours.

KENT AND THE SURROUNDING AREA offered many events, and that first year I took full advantage. I learned of the Kent Community Timebank—an organization where people shared their skills. This appealed to me, for I knew I would be needing help. I enrolled in the orientation class and became a member. As I perused the information related to skill sharing, I was hard put to come up with any skills I could share, so I never gave it a try and withdrew from the organization.

An event sponsored by the Chamber of Commerce to promote businesses in the city was the Valentine's Day Chocolate Walk. I invited Janet Glaus to join me. We registered, paid our fee, and with map in hand, started out. The day was bitter cold with snow on the ground. Twenty businesses were listed. Janet and I would enter a store, claim our complimentary chocolate treat, browse for a few minutes, leave, and move on to the next. It was fun, but not so much fun that I'd do it again.

Another downtown event took place in August and was more to my liking. The Budweiser Clydesdales came to town. The sidewalks along the posted route were packed with people, many families with small children. Unfortunately, where I chose to stand, my view was obstructed by the mass of humanity that surrounded me. As the red, white, and gold Budweiser beer wagon lumbered by, I got only a brief top-half glimpse of the driver who held the reins, guiding the three teams of Clydesdales that pulled the wagon. I wasn't disappointed. Just being there and experiencing the contagious excitement of the crowd was worth the effort.

Kent State University (KSU) offered a variety of activities and events that interested me. There were a number of guest speakers, but the one I wanted to see was Ken Burns—America's storyteller. I watched two of his series on PBS—*The Civil War* and *Prohibition*. I anticipated he would speak on the thought process in identifying a topic, the required research, and creative methods used in producing a series. For the most part his talk was a factual summary of different series he had produced. I left with a feeling of disappointment. But at least I had seen Ken Burns in the flesh.

In October 2014, when the groundbreaking ceremony for the Center for Architecture and Environmental Design (CAED) took place, I was one of several hundred in attendance. As I stood in line waiting my turn to sign in, I noted an attractive slight-of-build young woman with light-brown skin and dark hair ahead of me. She signed the name Christian Ford on the kiosk computer. That was the name of the young woman granted the first Joseph Morbito Study Abroad Fund scholarship set up by Cordell. I couldn't believe my good fortune.

This casual meeting with Christian led to luncheons and Sunday evening meals at my home. She graduated from KSU in 2016, and in June 2017, I was a guest at her wedding. The ceremony was to take place at the Columbus Conservatory. I drove to Columbus and stayed with Susan, who accompanied me to the wedding. June 14 was one of the hottest days of the summer, with a heat index over a hundred degrees. We arrived at the conservatory in adequate time for the one-o'clock ceremony, to learn the venue was an outdoor patio with no shade. Susan had no tolerance for heat and opted to remain inside the air-conditioned building. I stayed with Susan, but from where we were seated inside, we could not observe the patio, so I made frequent trips to find out if the ceremony was about to begin.

Each time I looked, a few more guests were seated, some using umbrellas to shield themselves from the blazing sun. On my one-thirty surveillance mission, I noted two couples standing inside the building near the patio entrance door. I overheard one of the men remark, "I thought the wedding invitation said one o'clock." To which the second man replied, "The kids put that on the invitation, hoping everyone would be seated by one thirty." The hands on the clock showed just passed 1:30 and still no sign of the wedding party. I reported back to Susan, and we left. Nor did we attend the reception. With the mind-set of the bride and groom, no telling what time it would have started.

Later I learned that certain cultures consider a suggested time as socially acceptable—guests arrive prepared to wait. I never asked Christian her race or her ethnicity. But this incident caused me to recall that anytime I invited her to my home, she always arrived late.

✦✦✦✦✦

MY FAMILIES WERE THERE FOR ME, and I needed them. I needed them for emotional support, for social support, and on occasion, for help with home-owner tasks. Cordell's daughter, Diane, lived in the area and was lovingly attentive, inviting me to share many meals with the family. On the third anniversary date of Cordell's death, Diane and I invited members of the Glaus family to join us at the Pufferbelly Restaurant. It was on this occasion that grandson Dustin introduced us to his friend, Katie Kaptain, who soon after became his fiancé. They were married on May 18, 2018, at the Aerial Party Center in Cleveland—a beautiful marble and granite structure. The ceremony was lovely, but the acoustics were terrible, with the sounds of the music and voices of eighty-plus guests bouncing off of the room's hard surfaces, making conversation impossible. Even though I did not stay for the reception, I am glad I went.

A Glaus family member I missed seeing was Cupid—Cordell's sister, Rosemary. Due to Rosemary's failing health, we no longer scheduled any luncheon engagements. One day I received a telephone call from her daughter, Barbara, informing me her mother had fallen, broken her hip, and was now a resident in a nursing home in the area where my sister Brenda lived. Barbara remarked her mother would like to see me. Knowing this, I made the effort to visit Cupid, and with each visit I left with a feeling of profound sadness. The bond that once held us so close was weakened by age, illness, and the death of her brother.

Contact with the Las Vegas Nelsons was ongoing. The weekend of October 25–27, 2013, I joined the family for the celebration of my grandson Bruce Allan's wedding to Rachel Robertson. The outdoor ceremony was held on the manicured grounds of a Marriott Hotel. The reception followed inside. I hoped to have at least one dance with my son and possibly a short spin around the floor with my grandson. Not to be. Guests were seated, food was served buffet-style, all the while the orchestra played ear-splitting music. I caught only passing glimpses of my son and the groom. Disappointed there would be no dancing for me and table conversation was impossible, I left early and returned to my room.

There were other events planned for the weekend. Sunday, Candice and Will hosted a brunch for family and close friends at their home. On Monday, Bruce and Linda took me and my stepdaughter, Jan Fincher, to see the family cabin located sixty miles to the west of Las Vegas in Trout Canyon on Mount Charleston. The solitude of the area was balm for my tired body. I sat on the cabin deck, gazed up at the deep-blue cloudless sky, visually inspected the wind-bent juniper trees and the spreading, bushy pinion pines. This paradise provided the perfect setting to rest and reflect before boarding my flight home the next day.

The following year another family event took me to Las Vegas. Bruce called me on February 6, 2014, with the blissful news that he and Linda were grandparents. Twins Alexandra Lynn, six pounds, eight ounces, and Sydney Jean, six pounds, one ounce, were born that morning. On April 3, when my flight arrived in Las Vegas, I exited the airport concourse and experienced a snafu of my own making. I took the wrong tram; my luggage went one way, and I went the other. It took time, but Bruce managed to retrieve my suitcase and drive to the area of the airport where he found me standing on the curb waiting to be rescued.

The frustration of the airport debacle behind me, it was all on the upswing for the remainder of my visit. Candice and Will went to an extreme to make my visit memorable. I met Alexandra (Alex) and Sydney (Syd), and held them on my lap, sitting in the same rocking chair where I'd held their mother when she was ten months old and had my picture taken. I spent the day with the family, pushing the babies in their strollers along the trail in Sunset Park, and enjoyed a relaxed lunch seated on the patio of their home. Will was the chef. The following day the newlyweds, Bruce Allan and Rachel, treated us to dinner at their home.

Sunday was the day set aside to celebrate my birthday. The Egg-Nazi Bruce, famous for his breakfasts, baked the traditional three-layer cake, decorated by Linda, and placed on the pedestal cake stand. Pictures were taken of the four generations present—babies Alex and Syd, parents Candice and Will, grandparents Bruce and Linda, and great-grandparents Betty and Henri. All I could think was how blessed these little girls are to be a part of this large, loving family.

The five days I was in Las Vegas passed swiftly. I'd met my great-grand-daughters and celebrated my eighty-fourth birthday with my loving family. It was a tearful goodbye the morning of April 8 when Bruce drove me to the airport for my flight home. I felt so loved, and I keenly felt the many miles that separated us.

All members of the Nelson family came to Kent for Thanksgiving 2014. Bruce and Linda, Candice, Will and the twins arrived on Sunday, November 23. The adults were tired and the ten-month-old girls were totally off their schedules, causing chaos to reign. On Monday the Egg-Nazi and Linda took over the kitchen and assumed all responsibility for preparing the Thanksgiving feast. My job was to stay out of the way. Other family members arrived and set to work doing whatever, wherever their help was needed. Those not staying at the house took up residency in rooms at the KSU Hotel. Beer was consumed by the case, work got done, and I continued to stay out of the way.

Thanksgiving Day arrived. Furniture was removed from the living room to accommodate the placement of tables and chairs, where twenty-eight family members and guests were seated. Appetites were whetted by the food aromas that wafted through the house. Once all were seated, pandemonium settled into quiet conversation as dish after dish was passed—succulent oven browned turkey, smoked ham, cranberry salad, sweet and mashed potatoes, vegetable casseroles, pumpkin pie, and other tempting desserts.

Friday everyone went their own way, selecting something of interest in the area. For some it was a visit to the Hartville Hardware, for others a trip into Amish country and a stop at the Warther Museum. Saturday was a hyped-up day when the clan gathered in front of the TV in the rec room basement for The Ohio State University-*ichigan (alumnae Jill Schumann's editing comment) game and enthusiastically cheered OSU to a 42–28 win. A fitting climax to an unforgettable Schumann Huddle Thanksgiving. Sunday came, family parted, and my life settled into the mundane.

Sunday evening, I purged the house of empty beer bottles that filled four trash cans, placing the overflow in black trash bags. I managed to get all cans and bags toted to the curb for the scheduled Monday morning pickup. I noted the four trash cans and the pile of neatly stacked trash bags, thinking the scene a good picture-op, but I was too tired to get my camera. I walked back into the house, collapsed in my comfortable glider chair, and luxuriated in the silence knowing "a good time was had by all."

On May 7, 2015, son Bruce called and told me to check my iPad; an important message was on its way. I did as told, accessed the message, watched and listened to a music video of the country song "Raise Them Up," sung by Keith Urban and Eric Church:

> So, you meet someone
> The only one.
> You take her by the hand
> Make a stand
> Buy some land
> Make some love
> And then babies come.

The word babies was synched with the picture of an ultrasound—Bruce Allan and Rachel had creatively announced their first pregnancy. The baby was born on November 6. My first introduction to my great-granddaughter, Grace Jane Nelson, was via a FaceTime call. Several months later, I was in Las Vegas for another memorable rocking chair picture.

When Bruce A. and Rachel shared the news of their second pregnancy, I was reluctant to commit myself to another Las Vegas trip. Jill offered to travel with me, and that was too good an offer to decline. On February 17, 2017, Luke Jordan Nelson was born. In April Jill and I arrived in Las Vegas to meet Luke Jordan and to celebrate my eighty-seventh birthday.

Bruce alone, or Bruce and Linda together, continued to make annual trips to Kent. Bruce and Linda's most recent visit was in January 2018. Snow, ice, and single-digit temperatures closed area schools, but main roads were salted and remained passable. The three of us planned to visit Brenda, who was recovering from hip replacement surgery. Driving north to Madison, we stopped in Garrettsville for breakfast. Leaving the restaurant, Bruce slipped on a sloped section of an icy sidewalk, falling backward and smashing his head against the concrete pavement. Momentarily stunned, he made the wise decision to abort plans and return home. Bruce said he was okay, refused medical treatment, returned to Las Vegas, and at the behest of his PCP, submitted to a CAT scan, confirming there was no residual brain damage from the fall. The incident did elicit a no-nonsense comment from my son. "Mom, that is the last time you'll get me to Ohio in the winter."

Communication with Allan Dickie's children and their families, all living out of state, was through e-mail, snail mail, or telephone calls. With the children of Charlie Gass, it was different. Rich's sons, Kevin and Brendan, attended Earlham College in Richmond, Indiana, and I was there for their graduation ceremonies. Rich made an annual summer visit, and if one of the boys was home, they would come with their father. Kevin always requested French toast for breakfast—not just two, not just four, but multiple slices, reminding me that young men have hollow legs. I was pleased to do it. Rich, a man of few words, would say as he bid me goodbye, "I enjoyed my visit."

I made a special effort to visit Barb and Terry in Okemos, Michigan, in September 2014. Granddaughter Allison was a senior at Michigan State University in East Lansing. She was a member of the university's band drum line, and I had never watched the band perform. The Saturday I was there was a clear, crisp fall day. The football game was dullsville, but I enjoyed the band's halftime show. When Allison was growing up, it was impossible to have too many pictures with her Gran Henri, but as a young adult, she became a martyr to picture taking.

Barb retired and moved to be with her family in Colorado. In June 2018, she returned to visit friends in Michigan, rented a car, and came to spend a weekend with me in Kent. Her visit was a delight, made more so by her help in selecting flowers for my front yard plant stand.

––––––––––– ++++++ –––––––––––

EQUALLY IMPORTANT was my need to remain in touch with friends from years past. Due to the vicissitudes of my life, I moved frequently. I had left Ashtabula decades ago, but an annual summer get-together has been a priority with Phyllis Ulshafer (the Ulshafers bought my Vineland Avenue house in 1962) and with Roz Moulder, my neighbor on the hill when I lived on Ridgewood Avenue in the 1980s.

Several people whom Cordell and I met while living in the Fairways II condo development continued to be important in my life. Cordell and Pete Weber became good friends when Cordell helped Pete in his initial wine-making endeavor. The friendship did not end with Cordell's death, for Pete and Gwen continued to schedule luncheon dates with me. During one of our luncheons, I lamented to Pete that I had shared the last bottle of Cordell's Gewürztraminer wine with friends. At my request, Pete made, bottled, and delivered two cases of the wine to my house.

I remained in close communication with Charlene, the friend I met through Clarabel McDonald. Charlene's health became very fragile. Whenever possible, I would take her to a movie, followed by dinner. One movie was *Gone Girl* starring Ben Affleck and Rosamunde Pike. I had no idea that I was exposing her to two hours of sex, violence, infidelity, and murder. As we were leaving the theater, Charlene, a nonagenarian with a wry sense of humor, quipped, "Well, guess I am never too old to learn a few things."

I have referred to Sue and Chuck often—the couple with whom we shared a common wedding anniversary date. Sue and Chuck married in 1970, Cordell and I in 2003. When we first celebrated together, we were four. When Cordell died, we were three. Then Chuck died, and we became two. In 2016, Sue and I were dining at the Bistro Restaurant in Green. The Bistro acknowledged birthdays and anniversaries with a complimentary bottle of wine. We ordered, our dinners were served, but we were missing the wine. I mentioned the oversight. "Where is the wine? We are celebrating our anniversary." No sooner had our server turned to leave than Sue quietly remarked, "She thinks we are a couple." I was mortified, never realizing my comment implied we were lesbians. When the girl returned with the wine, I felt an explanation was in order. The young woman expressed relief, saying she didn't know what to make of these two strange women sitting in her booth. So much for the proclaimed liberal attitudes of the twenty-first century.

While living in Madison, I rode with the Cleveland Bicycle Club and became friends with several of the women. In September 2014, four of the gals accepted my invitation to come to Kent. The day they came, the weather was pleasant with a temperature in the mideighties—an ideal day for bicycling, except we didn't plan to ride. Rather than drive to the restaurant, I suggested we walk along the new esplanade to our downtown destination. All were in agreement, and we started off chattering like magpies. Entering the esplanade, we passed the Wick Poetry Center house. Suddenly, one of the gals in our group veered off and walked into the garden area on the grounds. In the center stood an eight-foot bronze statue—a workman was making final adjustments to the installation. Jane inquired what this gargantuan thing was, and the man responded by pointing to a seat at the base of the statue, commenting anyone who sat there with another would remain friends for life. The four gals coupled up, sat, and pictures were taken. I was the fifth person in the group and sat solo for my picture. We left and ambled on to the Laziza Restaurant. Once seated at our table, I glanced up and noticed the lady from KSU that Cordell and I had dealt with when we set up our endowments. Ignoring the fact that she had a dining companion, I took the liberty of walking over to say hello. Mindy was gracious and introduced me to Robert Wick, sculptor of the bronze statue and philanthropist who established the Wick Poetry Center. Now that was a serendipity for the day!

I lived in the Columbus area for eighteen years—long enough to make lasting friendships. In 1984, when Allan and I moved to Worthington, our next-door neighbor was Susan Gardner. Over the years, we shared common life experiences. For me, the death of Allan, meeting Charlie Gass, marrying, and moving a short distance away in Columbus. For Susan, the death of her daughter, a divorce, and moving to the contiguous city of Westerville. Susan had a near-death experience, but miraculously recovered. We formed a close bond, and whenever I am in the area, I am her houseguest. Susan makes me feel so welcome I refer to her house as my second home.

When I married Charles Gass, I moved to Richards Road in Columbus. Marguerite and Stewart Weibel were our neighbors. They enjoyed entertaining, and we were frequent dinner guests in their home. By profession, Marguerite was a librarian—also an author in her own right. I enjoyed being with her, for there was something about her soft-spoken words that enhanced my self-esteem. Now she is retired and living with her husband in Seattle. Whenever she returns to the Columbus area, we manage to meet. Our time together is too short; I yearn for that time when we were next-door neighbors.

While working at the state department, I made several good friends. Jody Wallace and I joined the department the same year, now both retired. For a couple of years, we scheduled a girls' time together, meeting for an overnight at The Inn at Honey Run in Amish country—a halfway-point between Kent and Columbus. Jody is considerably younger than I and continues to be a very active person. Now, with the passing of the years, I am less active, and we have fewer common interests. We continue to communicate through telephone calls, e-mail messages, and annual visits, either here in Kent or when I am in her area. Our lasting friendship remains intact, but our lives have taken different paths.

Luna Zollinger Cummins and I worked together. When Charlie died, she and her husband, Jim, provided needed emotional support. When I moved to Mentor, before boxes were unpacked, Luna came to visit bringing her sleeping bag. She and Jim were guests at my wedding to Cordell Glaus, and they came for his memorial service. Now retired, health issues plague them. Recently, plans for a European cruise were canceled when Jim had triple bypass surgery. For these dear friends, I am unable to provide physical support. My emotional support is from a distance, and that makes me sad.

Another colleague, Emily Schuh, is retired and lives in the town of Granville west of Columbus. I count her as one of my most enigmatic friends. Emily is the daughter of a Lutheran minister, a career woman, never married, a lover of antiques, and in total command of all situations. We have intermittent communication—birthday greetings, a rare telephone call, and we see one another only when I am in the Columbus area. I enjoy those visits with Emily. She is a good listener and knows a lot about me as I am an open communicator. I know little about Emily as she relates only factual information. In spite of our differences, we became and remain friends.

My biking buddy Jane Nickerson is a light in my life. We met by chance when I responded to an ad she placed in the Westerville Bicycle newsletter wanting a person to share her motel room for the Great Ohio Bicycle Adventure (GOBA) ride. She has a twinkle in her eye and laughter in her voice. Jane has the sensitivity to know when and how to be a supportive person in times of joy and in times of sadness. She was there for me those first traumatic months after Charlie died. She and husband, Steve, were at my wedding to Cordell, and when he died, they came to his service. Bicycling is what brought us together; understanding is what deepened our friendship.

In a previous chapter, I mentioned June Grove, my secretary in the 1970s, when I was elementary supervisor for Red Lion Area Schools in Pennsylvania. June was the one who purged me of my PhD philosophical mind-set and brought me into the reality of the real world of education. Her common-sense approach to life grounded me then, and over the years our professional connection has morphed into a friendship. June no longer calls me Dr. Dickie. Now I am only Henri.

———————— ++++++ ————————

AS IMPORTANT AS FAMILY AND FRIENDS WERE, I needed the spiritual and social support of the church. My first year alone I took part in several church activities, but one request blindsided me. Within two weeks after

Cordell's memorial service, I was approached by a church member asking if I would donate his clothes to the upcoming Trash and Treasure sale. Realizing the request bordered on insensitive, she explained there was always an oversupply of donated women's clothing, but few items of men's clothing. I thought about it and could see the advantages for me as well as for the church. At some point it would need to be done, perhaps sooner was better than later. I forced myself to go through Cordell's dresser and closet, keeping only a few of his clothing items that held a sentimental attachment. To my surprise, I found donating his clothes to the church was emotionally fulfilling.

One Sunday, a guest speaker referred to the United Methodist Church of Kent as a "smooth operating machine." Volunteers were the ones who greased the gears of the operation, and I had no problem becoming a part of that machine. I joined a Sunday greeter team; I stood at the entrance to the sanctuary and greeted people as they arrived. I signed up as a social hour hostess whose responsibility was to provide snacks and beverages following the main Sunday morning service. I checked Sunday sign-in rosters for visitors and wrote short welcoming messages. For a short time, I helped to serve lunch on Tuesday to Rotary Club members. Last, but far from least, I delivered altar flowers to shut-ins and received joyful smiles in return. Of all the tasks I performed, this was the most fulfilling.

Both Cordell and I were impressed with Dr. Palmer's knowledge of the Bible and his ability to relate biblical teachings to daily living. When it was announced he would be teaching the Disciple 1 class the fall of 2013, we were the first to place our names on the sign-up sheet. Cordell died, but I was there the evening of September 24 for the first class. The thirty-four-week, two-hour course was a speed-read through the Bible. I stayed with the class for two months but found the required reading to be overwhelming. I opted out. In December I received a telephone call from one of the class members urging me to return. In truth I missed the people; given Melody's gentle persuasion, I went back. Cordell's and my original intent, so to speak, when joining the class was to sit at the feet of the master and learn from him. But Dr. Palmer's teaching method encouraged class participation. This allowed for some class members to monopolize class time, and I learned little at the feet of the master. I think I know what Cordell's reaction would have been: he would have dropped out and not returned.

Each spring the church sponsored an adult retreat. Participants stayed at a motel located in Amish country about forty miles to the south of Kent.

I attended for two years. The weekend was given over to Bible study but allowed for unstructured time to explore the surrounding area.

One evening we were dinner guests in the Amish home of the Miller family, who owned a large dairy farm. I knew the Amish do not subscribe to modern conveniences, but I don't know how they reconciled their beliefs to allow for a Delco-Light Farm Electric Plant that provided electricity for lights, milking equipment, and house appliances. The men used the milking machines to milk their large herd of cows. The women had electrical conveniences in their kitchen that aided them in the preparation of food for large gatherings—our group numbered twenty. The meal was savory—mounded platters of crisp fried chicken, bowls of fluffy mashed potatoes, seasoned vegetable dishes, crusty loaves of bread, crisp garden salads, and luscious fruit pies with flakey crusts. At the conclusion of the meal, the patriarch of the family spoke, providing us with an insight into Amish family and community beliefs. We came with our appetites, left satiated with food, and a smattering of knowledge about the Amish.

-------- ++++++ --------

DR. SHANAFELT WAS THE RIGHT DOCTOR FOR CORDELL, but not for me. After Cordell's death, I continued to schedule my required semiannual appointments, but during those short visits, I sensed a lack of communication with Dr. Shanafelt. A frightening thing happened at three thirty the morning of October 22, 2016, that confirmed my need to look for another PCP.

Awakened by a cramp in my right leg, I slid out of bed and carefully put weight on my right foot. The moment I stepped down, I heard a loud crack/pop and felt excruciating pain and was unable to move. Using my Lifeline alert button, I was taken by ambulance to the ER at University Hospitals Portage Medical Center (UHPMC). The Lifeline protocol was in place, and Diane was notified. She arrived shortly after I was checked in by the nurse, seen by the doctor, and found me waiting to be taken for an X-ray. The X-ray revealed no fracture. Following the orders of the doctor, the nurse placed an air brace on my right foot/ankle, gave me a scrip for pain meds, and told me to follow up with my PCP. Still flat on my back in the bed, I signed the release paper. But when I attempted to move from the bed into a wheelchair, then from the wheelchair into Diane's car, the indescribable pain returned. Neither Diane nor I questioned the ER diagnosis, and Diane took me home.

Brenda came and stayed. Over the next two days the pain subsided, and when I saw Dr. Shanafelt, he ordered an X-ray of my right calf, apparently saw nothing, and failed to report back to me. I had an appointment that week with my podiatrist to have my toenails clipped. He took one look at my foot and diagnosed my problem as a ruptured anterior tibia tendon and ordered an MRI scan that confirmed his visual diagnosis. Dr. Scott wrote two scrips—the first for PT exercises to strengthen the two remaining anterior tendons and the second for a leg brace to control my dropped foot. I contacted Acorn Stairlift and had stairlifts installed to the second floor and to the rec room in the basement. In spite of my conscientious effort with the exercises and wearing the leg brace, my enjoyment of walking was greatly compromised.

Dr. Shanafelt's failure to provide me with the needed medical follow-up confirmed my desire to change my PCP. But who? I knew many doctors were reluctant to accept Medicare patients. I had heard the name of Dr. Richard Banozic with UHPMC mentioned by two different people, Diane being one. I called his office and was able to get an appointment. Dr. Banozic is a rare breed in today's world—he listens, he advises, he acts, and he follows through. As I write this, I have been with him for two years. I have nothing but praise for his professional care.

⸻ ✛✛✛✛✛ ⸻

ONE MAN HELD AN IMPORTANT PLACE IN MY LIFE during the years following Cordell's death. Byron H. McCandless (Mac) was born in Florence, Colorado, on June 30, 1924, to Charles and Ella McCandless. He graduated from the local high school in 1942. World War II was raging, and within months, Mac enlisted in the US Army. When the war ended in 1945, he was mustered out of the service, returned home, attended Colorado A & M College (now Colorado State University), graduated in 1948 with a bachelor's degree in mathematics, and immediately enrolled for an advanced degree at Indiana University, where he was awarded his PhD in February 1953.

After graduation, Mac held positions in mathematics departments of Rutgers University in New Brunswick, New Jersey, and Western Washington State College (now Western Washington University) in Bellingham, Washington, before coming to Kent, Ohio, in 1966 as a full professor in the mathematics department at KSU—a position he held for twenty-five years, retiring in 1991.

While a student at Indiana University, he met and married Joan Ellington, a music major. Two children were born to their union—Susan and Bruce. Mac's wife of sixty-four years died in December 2013.

Cordell and I had recently joined the UMC of Kent and took advantage of the opportunity to socialize with others during the coffee hour following the Sunday morning service. We became acquainted with Mac and Joan the spring of 2013. Other than casual and polite conversation that took place around the table, any opportunity to get to know the couple better was interrupted by illness. For Mac, Joan's illness required placing her in a nursing home. Cordell was diagnosed with terminal cancer, and I assumed the responsibility for his care.

During the last half of 2013, my church attendance was sporadic. It was not until the first Sunday of January 2014 that I saw Mac again. I spoke to him as he was leaving the church and inquired if he and Joan would be attending the coffee hour. I was shocked when he told me Joan died on December 26. I felt a knife pierce my heart, as I had compassion for anyone who lost their mate.

Months passed before I attended the after-church social time and found myself seated at the same table where previously Cordell and I sat with Mac and Joan. Now there was only Mac and me. Within a short time, a comfortable acquaintanceship developed between us. Often, I walked to church, and the Sunday of June 22, Mac offered to drive me home. During the short drive, Mac casually commented he would be turning ninety on June 30. Birthdays were important to me, especially a birthday as significant as ninety. I asked him how he planned to celebrate and was surprised to learn he had no plans, commenting his children lived in Georgia. Right there before I exited the car, I invited him for a grilled steak dinner. Seconds passed. I waited. Finally, Mac responded, saying he would be pleased to accept my invitation.

At the appointed time on June 30, the doorbell rang, and I ushered Mac through the house to the back deck. We enjoyed a glass of pinot noir wine while I grilled the veggies. Not an expert in the art of grilling, I asked Mac to grill the steaks. I didn't want to be held accountable if they were not grilled to perfection. Entrée eaten, I brought out the traditional three-layer cake, and as I recall, little was eaten. The evening was casual, perhaps somewhat strained as we barely knew one another. Later, reflecting back on the evening, I was glad I made the effort. In my mind, everyone deserves recognition on their natal day, especially one as significant as the ninetieth.

Our first real date followed on July 22 when Mac reciprocated by inviting me to O'Charley's at Chapel Hill—a restaurant famous for their steaks. Returning home, Mac and I enjoyed coffee and dessert served on the back deck. Time came to part, and I accompanied him to the front door to say good night. But just as he was about to leave, he planted a quick kiss on my lips. I was surprised; Mac was so quiet, almost to the point of shyness, that his kiss startled me. I wanted male companionship, and with my advances, I wondered what I might have initiated.

We both were involved with hospice support groups. One of the groups met for monthly breakfasts, and we started attending this event together. Our friendship moved rapidly from casual to romantic. The first time Mac invited me to his house for dinner was on Tuesday, August 19. We enjoyed a glass of wine and hors d'oeuvres in his living room, soft music playing on the stereo. When it came time to make the final dinner preparations, Mac insisted I remain in the living room. When all was ready, he beckoned me to join him in the dining room. I was impressed! The presentation was beautiful—the table set with Noritake china, crystal goblets, and silver tableware. The entrée was baked crab cakes served with potato pancakes, corn, and salad, ending with coffee and a dessert. Not only was the dinner tasty, it was romantic.

Our evenings together became routine at either his house or mine—wine and hors d'oeuvres before dinner, snuggling together on the sofa following dinner while listening to soft music playing on the stereo. I soon learned how knowledgeable Mac was in the field of composers and their music, one time, much to my chagrin, correcting my pronunciation of Mozart (I gave his name the verboten long *o* sound). Mac introduced me to Jackie Evancho (b. 4-9-2000) singing *Ombra mai fu*—roughly translated "There is no shade like that of the Plain Tree." We both enjoyed Scottish music—our favorite the bagpipes playing of "Nearer my God to Thee" and "Amazing Grace." We never tired of listening to the Mormon Tabernacle Choir, or the piano playing of Floyd Cramer.

One evening in October, months after we had committed ourselves to be best friends forever (BFF), Mac asked me to play the music from Brigadoon, citing the song "There But For You Go I." He told me the words spoke his true feelings of my place in his life. Mac was not one to openly express his feelings, and I was profoundly touched by his words. But at the same time, words so sincerely spoken gave me cause for concern.

To me, Mac was a loving friend. Was I being selfish not to make a total commitment to him? I had been honest in telling Mac from the get-go that writing my memoir took priority in my life.

There were many activities we did together. We enjoyed dining at home or in restaurants. Our favorite restaurant was Applebee's in Kent. On several occasions, Mac took me to Arnie's West Branch Steak House on route 59 east of Ravenna. The redneck ambiance was pleasant, and the food delicious. We enjoyed the theater—Actor's Summit in Greystone Hall in downtown Akron; Porthouse Theater on the Blossom Music Center grounds; performances at the E Turner Stump Theater; and Cartwright Hall on the KSU campus. One time we drove into Cleveland to Playhouse Square to see *The Book of Mormon*, highly recommended by several, including my son. Our seats were in the balcony. Mac was squeezed into a narrow seat with limited leg room. I took the aisle seat to accommodate my restless leg condition. The music was loud, female voices shrill, and the best we could say for this highly touted musical was the terrific choreography. We left at intermission. KSU sporting events were more to our liking. On rare occasions I received a guest pass to the president's loge where Mac and I enjoyed complimentary food and drink while watching a football or a basketball game.

Over time Mac met my family, first here in Ohio, and later he made two trips with me to Las Vegas. Bruce was accepting of Mac and in awe of his ability to solve the Rubik's Cube puzzle. For Mac's ninety-third birthday, Bruce made him a wooden six-by-six-by-six-inch wooden replica of the cube. I first met Mac's children, Susan and Bruce, the summer of 2015 when they came to Kent to visit their father.

My stepdaughter, Diane, and husband, Doug, lived in the area and included Mac in many family events. Diane loved animals, particularly cats. Mac invited her to his home to meet Georgie, so named because Georgie was a rescue kitten given to Mac and Joan seventeen years ago by his daughter, Susan, who lived in Georgia. When Georgie died, Diane was the one who was able to provide Mac with the greatest comfort.

Soon after I met Mac at age ninety, he told me he had been diagnosed with myasthenia gravis—a chronic condition that caused double vision and, in time, could affect his muscle strength. For the first two years, we were able to do many things together. Beginning in 2016, incidents related to muscle weakness gave Mac cause for concern. Walking became more difficult. To compensate he started to use a cane and got a handicap sticker, allowing him to park close to business entrances. He hired a lady to clean his house. What surprised me the most was his announcement on March 28, 2017, that he would no longer drive. Apparently, over the past year, he had mishaps involving property damage, no personal injuries but enough that he realized it was best to give up driving.

This was a turning point in our relationship. I assumed a more active role in his life. I became his Uber driver—brought him to my home, took him for groceries, haircuts, medical appointments, and to church. Georgie died six months after Mac stopped driving. He commented one time how alone he felt. But I was obsessed to maintain my daily writing schedule, all the while managing my own home. Knowing he spent hours alone in his house, I did not increase the time we spent together. My heart ached for him, and I felt I was being selfish. But for the first time in my life, I put my own needs ahead of another.

Mac's health went into a downward spiral in 2018 when, on a Friday evening in the middle of April, he slipped on the slick floor of his garage while getting into my Jeep. Within two weeks of this happening, both of his shoulders became very painful, restricting his arm movements to where he was unable to prepare his own meals. It took a month to get an appointment with an orthopedic surgeon. In the interim, Mac called Susan on May 6 and told her she needed to come. She arrived the following Tuesday.

After Susan's arrival, I faded into the background. I knew Mac and his daughter spent many hours discussing the best solution for his care—domestic help, assisted living in the area, or relocating to Ellijay, Georgia, where he would be closer to his children.

I didn't see much of Mac during the time Susan was with him. We did keep up with our five-o'clock afternoon phone calls, and in one of those calls he informed me he would be moving to Ellijay. I invited him to come over for one last dinner together. His response was disappointing to me when he replied, "Not sure I'll have the time or energy. I think we will be leaving on Sunday."

The following morning the phone rang. It was Mac, and he was alone. Susan was out on errands, and he asked if I would care to come over. He sensed the abruptness of our phone conversation the previous evening had left too much unsaid. I immediately drove over to see him. We spent two hours reminiscing and speaking of our love for one another. We acknowledged our loving friendship had some "moments," but placing it in perspective brought a smile to our faces and a degree of levity to the seriousness of this last time we might be together.

Susan returned, I chatted for a bit, got up, and walked over to the chair where Mac was seated. Unable to speak, I bent over and gave him a farewell kiss, my eyes filled to overflowing with tears. The following morning, Sunday, May 27, Susan and her father left for Ellijay.

Susan later related that leaving was an emotional time for both. Her text message read, "He will never see his beloved home again. As we backed out of the garage the sun peeked through the clouds and a beam of sunlight shined on the address over the garage door, and Mac said 'the sun is shining on eighteen eighty.'"

I missed Mac's physical presence. I missed our snuggling on the couch while listening to music or watching movies. I missed my dining and theater companion. I missed sitting beside him in church and surreptitiously slipping my hand into his as Dr. Palmer stepped into the pulpit to deliver the weekly message. I missed being his Uber driver. We remained in touch through our evening telephone calls, and never once did this intelligent, resolute, yet gentle and sensitive person ever complain.

Mac is now a resident in Cameron Hall of Ellijay, located within ten miles of his daughter's home. All his physical needs are provided for, and he is near his children.

For me, it was another loss. But I am a survivor, and it gives me heart to know my son Bruce recognized this. For Mother's Day 2018, he sent me the following verse:

> *She is beautiful, but you really can't comprehend it until you understand that she is the result of the pieces that she refused to let life take from her.*
> *Alexis Allgood*

EPILOGUE

———— ✦✦✦✦✦ ————

T HROUGHOUT MY LIFE I have listened, learned, and adapted. Change has been my constant companion. Sidney and I were two kids starting a life together. When he died, I married a man many years older than I, who provided me with the opportunity for further educational advancement. When he died, I married Charlie and experienced honeymoon years filled with dance and travel. Accepting the probability that marrying again was nil, then came the miracle of my fourth marriage that embodied the attributes of the first three—shared values, strong work ethic, intellectual curiosity, love of travel, and creativity.

My life took me to different areas of the United States and with that came an awareness of the different cultures within our great country—Cajun Louisiana, liberal California, the Northwestern love of the outdoors, and finally returning to my roots of Midwestern conservatism. As I wrote about my life, I became my own best therapist. I noted patterns of change in my behavior toward others. Most evident was my willingness to accept others from different races, backgrounds, religions, and cultures.

Career options were limited for women of my day—nurse, teacher, or secretary. Those fortunate enough to attend college, for the most part, went to get their Mrs. degree. In the farm culture where I grew up, girls got married. With that goal in mind, during my high school years I filled my hope chest with linens and other small items needed by the homemaker. I did all of this in anticipation of marriage, a home, and children—although it didn't happen in that order.

In George R. Martin's *A Clash of Kings,* Queen Cersei's brother Tyrion Lannister remarks, "Truly sister, you were born to be a widow." As life would have it, not by choice, that was my fate as well, being widowed four times. Each time, I picked myself up and moved on with my life while instinctively taking the advice of Sheryl Sandberg, COO of Facebook:

"Picking the right partner...is the single most important career decision that a woman makes."

My family recognized the quality of my husbands, for my daughter-in-law Linda paid me the highest compliment. On December 23, 2007, I made this diary entry: "Linda told me how much I had enriched their lives with my four husbands."

During the years married to Allan Dickie, he provided the financial support, educational know-how, and encouragement that gave me the confidence to attain a Ph.D. With the degree came the opportunity for central office positions in public schools. Allan was retired—we were empty-nesters—ergo I was not limited geographically regarding job choice. Consequently, I embarked on a peripatetic twenty years of moving from one educational position to another—North to South, South to North, East to West, West to East.

The unspoken question, that elephant in the room, "Why so many job changes?" There were a variety of reasons—inadequate teaching resources, unrealistic job demands, conflict with superiors, inability to balance work with marriage, and last, but far from least, the issue of financial security. I returned to Ohio and found employment, making me eligible to consolidate my out-of-state-years in the State Teachers Retirement System of Ohio.

Every place I lived, I made friends but I kept moving away from them. As a result, I have made a herculean effort to stay in touch. For those of my generation, and the Baby Boomers that followed, remaining in touch was relatively easy—telephone, snail mail and the emergence of email. But I found the zeitgeist of Gen X and Millennials, to be a challenge. For many, their land-line telephones were replaced with smart phones they do not answer. Email became outdated, smart phones used, not for talking but for texting and FaceTime. Again, I adapted. I purchased a smart phone and learned how to text; even managed the miracle of FaceTime calls. Here a confession is necessary: the first time my grandson called me on FaceTime, I answered the call only to hear him say, "Grandma take your finger off of the camera lens so I can see you." At my age, trying to keep up with technology is a daunting task, but I must admit that FaceTime conversations with my Gen Z great-grandchildren are experiences of pure joy.

Writing my memoir has been intellectually and emotionally demanding. The easy part was relating information—get the facts right and the words flow. The emotional happenings in my life were difficult to write about. The psychiatrist M. Scott Peck writes that as people grow older, they become more genuine; they choose not to waste time being inauthentic. That shoe fit and I wore it as I wrote. When my editor found some of my written thoughts to be unkind or prejudicial, she gently brought me back to a rational equilibrium where I could be honest without being vindictive.

Somewhere along my writing journey, I came to the realization that my background was not a disadvantage to be overcome, but contained a richness of family, friends, influences, and experiences to be drawn on. That, coupled with my faith, has sustained me in the direst of times.

Recently I spoke with my niece, Jill, regarding a question about an endowment fund I had set up with KSU. Jill put the question to me, "Aunt Henri, what do you want your legacy to be?" The question aided me in resolving the endowment issue, but her words lingered in my mind. Just what did I want my legacy to be? My response—I want my progeny to realize that I lived, loved, and above all else, gave family and friends a priority in my life.

My Family

A simplified family tree, identifying major players in my story.

Paternal Grandparents
Squair Shuart m. Eda Dale Shuart
    Daughter: Rhoda Dale

Parents
Henry and Rhoda Dale Schumann (known as Dale)
    Children: Lloyd m. Gertrude (Trudy) McCarty
                Children: David m. Susy Shaffer
                          Peter m. Beverley Cork
                          Jill m. Garvin Rumberger
          Henrietta (see below)
          Brenda m. Paul Dennis
              Children: Kellie m. Kirk Peine
                       Shellie m. Dave Byrne
              m. Theren Gibson
              m. Walter Spadaro

Families of Henrietta
Henrietta m. Sidney Nelson (1947-1960)
        Children: Vernon m. Roberta Steffee
                     m. Judith Poulsen
                        Children: Darci m. Andy Hastings
                               Kristen m. Nick Lobdell
                Bruce m. Linda Gripentog
                      Children: Candice m. William Hayes II
                             Bruce Allan m. Rachel Robertson

        m. Allan Dickie (1963-1986)
                Children: George m. Rita Herbert Boyer
                      Janet m. Royce Fincher

        m. Charles Gass (1987-1997)
                Children: Richard m. Marcy Cohn
                      Barbara m. Terry Louis Rosenbaum

        m. Cordell Glaus (2003-2013)
                Children: Kent m. Janet Hudson
                      Gary m. Cheri Deschaine
                      Diane m. Donald Davies
                            m. Douglas Rice

ACKNOWLEDGEMENTS

M y thanks to the staff members at Christian Faith Publishing, Inc. for turning my manuscript into the finished product of a book. To all, your patience, sensitivity, and kindness has not gone unnoticed.

For statistical and general information, I have relied on the following: the free encyclopedia Wikipedia; the 1966 and 1971 *Theodore Roosevelt High School Rough Riders* yearbooks; and an Art Walk pamphlet produced by Kent State University.

Professionals, specific to their areas of expertise, willing to share their knowledge and their time, aided me in the development of my life story. June Grove, secretary in the Office of the Elementary Supervisor for the Red Lion School District, reviewed information related to Red Lion Schools. Jay Wuebbold, staff member for the Supreme Court of Ohio, provided me with pamphlets, answered my questions, and critiqued what I wrote about the Ohio State Office Building. Members of the Kent Free Library research staff answered my questions about the city of Kent. To each of you, my sincerest appreciation.

Special recognition must be given to Creative Portraits by Rapid Photo studio in Geneva, Ohio. Graphic design specialist Alexis Blasko is to be recognized for her expertise in the many steps required in making the photo images that are part of this book.

My Christmas card list contains 125 addresses, evidence of my bramble-bush family and many friends. Over the years our lives have commingled and theirs are part of my story. Some have helped in the preparation and writing of my memoir; you are mentioned by name. Others—family, friends, acquaintances—not mentioned here, nevertheless hold a significant place in my life. To one and all, my heartfelt gratitude.

I viewed a videotape dated April 1986, made when I interviewed Ruby Tyrrell and Alva Shuart, two grandchildren of Squair Shuart. Several of their stories became a part of my memoir. Ruby and Alva are deceased; I express my thanks to their families.

My siblings, Lloyd and Brenda, proved to be a repository of information. In preparation to write my memoir, I compiled a list of questions to ask my brother—questions about our grandparents, our parents, and our life on the farm. Sadly, Lloyd died before I finished this book, and with his passing many questions remain unanswered.

My sister spent one winter compiling the Schumann/Shuart genealogy. In the beginning chapters of my memoir, I relied heavily on information found in these volumes. As I continued to write about my life, many questions surfaced that required answers. I would contact Brenda. She patiently listened, answered, or researched to provide me with the requested information. My gratitude to her is deeply felt, difficult to express in words.

Nieces and nephews made contributions that enriched my story. Peter's suggestion that I share my manuscript chapter by chapter provided me with instant feedback and corrections. Beverly sent me information, that added a richness to key parts of the manuscript. Jill, my most critical reader, pointed out and corrected oversights. Kellie shared interesting and enlightening stories about her mother. Karin helped me fill in information gaps related to the Nelson family. To one and all, I am grateful.

There are two women whom I want to recognize: Mindy R. Aleman in the Center for Gift and Estate Planning at Kent State University, and Dr. Catherine Wing, Associate Professor, Department of English at KSU. Through them, Marybeth Cieplinski, former graduate student and instructor at KSU, came into my life. and has served as my in-house editor from the very beginning.

A close friend, Byron McCandless, Emeritus Professor of Mathematics at KSU, volunteered to edit my work. Reluctantly, I agreed. Byron (Mac) did the final "official" edit for all the chapters. Marybeth and I soon recognized that Mac had the ability to spot an incorrect word usage and/or misspelling two chapters in advance. For his editing talents, my sincere thanks.

Previous recognition has been given to Marybeth, but I choose to again acknowledge her in closing. Marybeth has served as my editor and stayed with me throughout the almost five years it has taken to write this memoir. She stands apart from all others. I truly believe that without her expertise in the idiosyncrasies of computers, her editing skills, and above all else her patience and understanding, this tome might still be floating on a cloud of unfulfilled dreams.